The Great Sea Serpent

The Great Sea Serpent

A.C. OUDEMANS
INTRODUCTION BY LOREN COLEMAN

NEW YORK

The Great Sea Serpent
Cover © 2007 Cosimo, Inc.
Introduction © 2007 by Loren Coleman

For information, address:

Cosimo, P.O. Box 416
Old Chelsea Station
New York, NY 10113-0416

or visit our website at:
www.cosimobooks.com

The Great Sea Serpent was originally published in 1892.

Cover design by www.kerndesign.net

ISBN: 978-1-60206-012-8

LOREN COLEMAN PRESENTS

LOREN COLEMAN has been investigating cryptozoological evidence and folklore since the Abominable Snowmen caught his interest nearly five decades ago. He is author of numerous popular books on cryptozoology, including *Mysterious America*, *Bigfoot!: The True Story of Apes in America*, and *Mothman and Other Curious Encounters*, and he regularly appears on radio and television programs—including National Public Radio, Coast to Coast AM, History Channel, Travel Channel, NBC, and other media—as an expert on strange creatures and inexplicable phenomena.

Today, as one of the world's leading living cryptozoologists, Coleman travels extensively to continue his fieldwork and lectures, and writes his daily blog at the Internet's most popular cryptozoology news site, Cryptomundo.com. He is the director of the International Cryptozoology Museum in Portland, Maine.

www.lorencoleman.com

COSIMO CLASSICS offers distinctive titles by the great authors and thinkers who have inspired, informed and engaged readers throughout the ages. For more Cosimo Classics titles, please visit cosimobooks.com.

Contents

Preface.
9

I. Literature on the Subject
11

II. Attempts to Discredit the Sea-Serpent. Cheats and Hoaxes.
23

III. Would-be Sea-Serpents.
58

IV. The Various Accounts and Reports Concerning Observations of Sea-Serpents, Chronologically Arranged and Thoroughly Discussed; and Criticisms on the Papers Written about the Subject.
89

V. The Various Explanations Hitherto Given.
287

VI. Conclusions.
362

This Volume is
Dedicated to
Owners of Ships
and Yachts,
Sea Captains
and Zoologists

"It is always unsafe to deny positively any phenomena that may be wholly or in part inexplicable; and hence I am content to believe that one day the question will be satisfactorily solved."

—A. G. Melville.

The Great Sea Serpent
ANTONIE CORNELIS OUDEMANS

Someone needed to collect and analyze the overwhelming number of the world's sea serpent sightings, and the job would fall to a Dutch zoologist named Antoon Cornelis Oudemans (1858–1943). In 1892, Oudemans wrote the first book completely devoted to a single cryptozoological subject, *The Great Sea Serpent*.

Between 1889 and 1892, Oudemans, who was the director of the Royal Zoological and Botanical Gardens at The Hague, collected all the reports of sea serpents that had been published until that time. After arranging them chronologically, he then went about eliminating the hoaxes and weeding out the obvious misidentification of known animals. This left Oudemans with 162 reports on which he would base his conclusions, though he would add another 25 to the appendix of his book, *The Great Sea Serpent*, just before its publication.

This book has had a wide readership for decades. The volume still influences thoughts and theories about the great unknowns in the oceans. Oudemans proposed in *The Great Sea Serpent*, then later rejected the idea, that these sea serpents might be ancient whales or zeuglodons, but formalized the remarkable notion of explaining sitings as glimpses a giant long-necked seal that he dubbed *Megophias megophias*. Nevertheless, his contemporaries and most subsequent theorists on the subject would largely ignore his idea about giant seals as the "true" sea serpent; the book still has an impact, for here is a scientist seriously investigating these reports.

Oudemans later wrote about the Loch Ness Monster, where his long-necked–seal concept found a more responsive audience. Today, cryptozoologists have enshrined Oudemans as one of the founding grandfathers of the new science.

—Loren Coleman

Preface

In all ages meteoric stones have fallen on the earth. Many of them were found by persons who were in search of them; they preserved them, and thus collections were made in private rarity cabinets and in natural history cabinets. Many learned persons believed in meteoric stones, but many others were sceptical, and their attacks were so violent, and their mockery about stones that fell from the atmosphere, or were thrown by the men in the Moon to the inhabitants of the Earth, so sharp as to shake the belief of many a collector, and the happy possessor, fearing the mockery of the so called learned men, concealed his treasures, or threw them away on the dust-hill, or in a ditch.

But at last there appeared a firm believer in aerolites, named Chladni, who took the trouble to collect all accounts concerning observations of meteoric stones from the ancient times up to the nineteenth century. He showed 1. The immense number of facts. 2. The strikingly concurrent testimony in all the accounts independent of one another.

In the year 1829 he published his work "Ueber Feuermeteore" (i. e. on Meteoric Stones) in Vienna, and from that moment the eyes of unbelievers were opened. Meteoric stones were again found, and were proved to be quite different from terrestrial stones. From that moment the belief in the existence of meteoric stones was fixed for ever.

The author of the present Volume has been at the pains to collect all accounts concerning observations of Sea-Serpents. His work has the same purpose as Chladni's had in 1829. It is his sincere hope that it may meet with the same success.

A. C. O. Jzn.

The Hague,
February 1st, 1891.

1 Literature on the Subject.

An asterisk (*), placed before the works, mentioned in the list, signifies that the author has had no opportunity to consult them.

1555.—**Olaus Magnus**. Historia de gentibus septentrionalibus, earumque diversis statibus, conditionibus, etc., etc. Romae, 1555, p. 771.

*1556.—**Olaus Magnus**. Historia de gentibus septentrionalibus, etc., etc., (Editio nec Romae nec Basileae).

1560.—**Gesner**. Nomenclator aquatilium animantium (=Historia animalium liber IV), Tiguri, 1560, p. 93, 94.

1567.—**Olaus Magnus**. Historia de gentium septentrionalium variis conditionibus statibusve, etc., etc., Basileae, 1567, p. 799.

*1608.—**Edward Topsell**. The history of serpents, or the second booke of living creatures. With wood couts in-fol. London, 1608, (315 pag.).

1640.—**Aldrovandus**. Serpentum et draconum historiae libri duo. Bononiae, 1640, p. 58, 59, 296.

1653.—**Jonston**. Historiae naturalis de piscibus et cetis libri V, et de serpentibus et draconibus libri II. Francofurti, 1653.

1657.—**Jonston**. Historiae naturalis de piscibus et cetis libri V, et de serpentibus et draconibus libri II, Amstelodami, 1657.

1660.—**Jonston**. Naeukeurige beschrijving van de natuur der vissen en der slangen en draken. Amsterdam, 1660. Deel II en IV.

*1665.—**Jonston**. Historiae naturalis de piscibus et cetis libri V, et de serpentibus et draconibus libri II, Amstelodami, 1665.

1667.—**Milton**. Paradise Lost. I, 192—208.

1668.—**Charleton**. Onomasticon zoicon. Londini, 1668. p. 34.

*1670.—**Berndsen**. Danmarks og Norges fruchtbare Herlighed, 1670?

1674.—**Adam Olearius**. Gottorfische Kunstkammer. Schleswig, 1674.

*1690.—**Ramus**. Norges Beskrivelse, 1690?

1718.—**Jonston**. Theatrum universale omnium animalium, Amstelaedami. Edidit Ruysch. 1718.

*1722.—**Jean Baptiste Labat**. Nouveau Voyage aux Isles de l'Amérique, contenant l'histoire naturelle de ces pays, etc. 6 Vols. Paris, Giffard, 1722. 12°.

1724.—**Jean Baptiste Labat**. Nouveau Voyage aux Isles de l'Amérique, contenant l'histoire naturelle de ces pays, etc. 6 Vols. La Haye, 1724.

1725.—**Père Labat**. Nieuwe reizen naar de franse eilanden van Amerika: In 't Nederlandsch in 't ligt gebracht door **W. C. Dijks**. Amsterdam, 1725, Vol. IV. P. I. p. 43. — Vol. IV. P. II. p. 105.
*1730.—**P. Dass**. Beskrivelse over Nordland. 1730?
*1740.—**Hans Egede**. (A Full and Particular Relation of his Voyage to Greenland, as a Missionary, in the year 1734, printed in Danish at) Kjoebenhavn, 1740.
*1740.—**Hans Egede**. Ausführliche und Wahrhafte Nachricht vom Anfange und Fortgange der Groenländischen Mission, etc. Hamburg, 1740. 4°.
1741.—**Paul Egede**. Continuation af Relationerne betreffende den Groenlanske Mission, Tilstand og Beskaffenhed, Kjoebenhavn, 1741.
*1741.—**Paul Egede**. Fortgesetzte Relationen die Groenländische Mission betreffend; Kopenhagen, 1741.
1741.—**Hans Egede**. Det gamle Groenlands nye Perlustration. Kjoebenhavn,1741.
1742.—**Hans Egede**. Des alten Groenlands neue Perlustration. Copenhagen,1742.
*1742.—**Paul Egede**. Journal of the mission to Greenland, 2d. Vol. London, 1742. (The first Vol. by **Hans Egede**, and the third Vol. by **Niels Egede** do not contain anything about the subject.)
*1742.—**Labat**. Nouveau Voyage aux Isles françaises de l'Amérique, VII, p. 341. Paris, 1742.
1742.—**Charles Owen**. An Essay towards a Natural History of Serpents. London, John Gray, 1742.
*1743?—**Paul Egede**. Efterretninger om Grönland. Kjöbenhavn, 1743? p.45-46.
*1745.—**Hans Egede**. A description of Greenland. London. 1745.
1746.—**Hans Egede**. Beschrijving van Oud Groenland, Delft, 1746.
*1753.—**Eric Pontoppidan**. Det förste Forsög paa Norges natuarlige Historie. Kjoebenhavn, 2d. Vol. 1753.
1754.—**Erich Pontoppidan**. Versuch einer natuerlichen Historie von Norwegen, 2d. Vol. Cap. VIII. § 1, 6, 7, 8, 9, 10. Kopenhagen, 1754.
1755.—**Eric Pontoppidan**. The Natural History of Norway. London, 1755.
*1760.—**Hans Egede**. New Natural History of Greenland. 1760.?
1763.—**Hans Egede**. Description et Histoire Naturelle de Groenland. Copenhague et Genève, 1763.
1763.—**Hans Egede**. Beschreibung und Naturgeschichte von Groenland. Berlin, 1763.
*1764.—**Jonston**. Theatrum universale omnium animalium. Heilbron, 1764.
*1765.—**Knud Leems**. Beskrivelse over Finmarkens Lapper, 1765.
*1767.—**Canutus Leemius**. De Lapponibus Finmarchiae eorumque lingua, vita et religione historia, c. notis **J. E. Gruneri**. (Text in Latin and Danish.) 2 Vols. 4°. with 100 figgs.
*1768.—**Jonston**. Historia naturalis de piscibus et cetis, et de serpentibus et draconibus. Rouan, 1768.

*1771.—**Knud Leems**. Nachrichten von den Lappen in Finmarken, ihrer Sprache, Sitten, u. s. w. Aus dem Dän. übers. v. **J. J. Volckmann**. Leipzig, 1771. 8°

*1789.—**Paul Egede**. (Intelligences from Greenland, in the original Danisch language). Kjoebenhavn, 1789.

*1790.—**Paul Egede**. Nachrichten von Groenland aus einem Tagebuch geführt von 1721—1788. Kopenhagen, 1790.

*1805.—**Peter Ascanius**. Icones rerum naturalium, ou figures enluminées d'histoire naturelle du Nord. Cah. V. Copenhague 1805. (In the first four Cahiers the author does not touch the subject).

1808, Nov.—*The Philosophical Magazine.* Vol. 32, p. 190.

1809, Jan.—*The Philosophical Magazine.* Vol. 33, p. 90.

1809, March.—*The Philosophical Magazine.* Vol. 33, p. 251.

1809, May—*The Philosophical Magazine.* Vol. 33, p. 411.

1809, July.—**E. Home**. An anatomical account of the Squalus Maximus, which, etc. — *Philosophical Transactions of the Royal Society at London*, 1809. Vol. 98, p. 206-220.

1811, March.—**Dr. Barclay**. Remarks on some parts of the animal that was cast ashore on the Island of Stronsa, September 1808.— *Memoirs of the Wernerian Natural History Society*, Vol. I.

1817, Aug. 20.—Extract from a letter from **S. G. Perkins**, Esq. dated Boston, Aug. 20, 1817, to **E. Everett**, in Paris.—(This extract, a manuscript, preserved in the Library of the Royal University of Göttingen, has never before been printed.)

*1817, Oct. 15.—*The Columbian* (newspaper).

*1817, Oct. 22 or 23.—(A New York newspaper).

1817, Nov. 13.—Letter from **Edward Everett** in Paris to the "Obermedicinalrath und Ritter" **Blumenbach** in Göttingen.—(This letter preserved in the Library of the Royal University of Göttingen, has never before appeared in print).

1817, Dec.—Report of a Committee of the Linnaean Society of New England relative to a large marine animal, supposed to be a sea-serpent, seen near Cape Ann, Massachusetts, in August, 1817. 8°. Boston, 1817, with two plates, 52 pg.

*1817.—*Transactions of the Linnaean Society of New England.* Boston, 1817.

1818, April.—**H. M. Ducrotay de Blainville**. Sur un nouveau genre de Serpent, *Scoliophis*, et le Serpent de mer vu en Amérique en 1817.—*Journal de Physique, de Chimie et d'Histoire Naturelle.* Vol. 86. Paris, 1818.

1818, June.—Sur le serpent nommé *Scoliophis.*—Extrait d'une lettre de **M. A. Lesueur** au Redacteur (**Mr. H. M. Ducrotay de Blainville**). *Journal de Physique, de Chimie et d'Histoire Naturelle.* Vol. 86. Paris 1818.

1818.—**Hoffmann** and **Oken**. Thier von Stronsa. **Oken's** *Isis*, II, 1818, p. 2096

1818.—**W. D. Peck**. Some Observations on the Sea-Serpent.—*Memoirs of the American Academy of Arts and Sciences.* Vol. IV. Part 1. Cambridge 1818.

1818.—American Sea Serpent.—*The Journal of Science and the Arts.*—Edited at the *Royal Institution of Great Britaine.* Vol. IV. London, 1818, p. 378.
1818.—American Sea-Serpent.—*The Quarterly Journal of Science, Literature and the Arts.* R. Inst. Vol. VI. London, 1818, p. 163.
1818.—Wieder eine ungeheure Meerschlange an America.—**Oken's** *Isis*, 1818, p. 2100.
*1818, June 9.—*Commercial Advertiser*, Boston.
1818, Aug. 21.—(Boston Newspaper). A paragraph from this newspaper is preserved in the library of the Royal University of Göttingen.
1818, Sept. 11.—Letter from **Mr. Andrews Norton** to **Mr. George Bancroft**, at that time a resident at Göttingen.—The letter is preserved in the library of the Royal University of Göttingen, and has never before appeared in print.
*1818.—W.... On the history of the Great Sea-Serpent.—**Blackwood's** *Magazine*, III. p. 33-42.
1819, Jan. — American Sea-Serpent.—*The Philosophical Magazine,* Vol. LIII, p.71.
1819.—**W. D. Peck**. Some observations on the Sea Serpent.—*The Quarterly Journal of Literature, Science and the Arts.* R. Inst. Vol. VIII. London, 1819, p. 68.
1819.—*Scoliophis.* Eine neue Schlangen-Sippe.—**Oken's** *Isis*, 1819, p. 113.
1819.—Meerschlange in Amerika. **Lesueur** aus Amerika an **Blainville.**—**Oken's** *Isis*, 1819. p. 263.
1819.—Ueber die Meerschlange an Amerika. Von **T. Say** aus Philadelphia an **Leach** in London. — **Oken's** *Isis*, 1819, p. 653.
1819.—Einige Bemerkungen über die Meerschlange von Amerika, von **W. D. Peck**, Prof. d. N. G. in Amerika.—**Oken's** *Isis*, 1819, p. 1123.
*1819, Aug. 19.—*Boston Daily Advertiser.*
*1819.—*Boston Centinel.*
1819.—Amerikanische Meerschlange.—**Oken's** *Isis*, 1819. p. 1754.
1819. Nov.—**C. S. Rafinesque Schmaltz**. Dissertation on Water-Snakes, Sea-Snakes and Sea-Serpents.—*Philosophical Magazine* Vol. LIV.
1820, May.—**Prof. Jacob Bigelow**. Documents and Remarks respecting the Sea-Serpent.—**Silliman's** *American Journal of Science and Arts.* Vol. II, p. 147-154. Boston (1819) 1820.
1820.—De beruchte Zeeslang op de kusten van Noord-Amerika.— *Vaderlandsche letteroefeningen voor* 1820, Tweede Stuk, Mengelwerk, Amsterdam 1820.
1821.—On the American Sea-Serpent.—*The Philosophical Magazine and Journal*, Vol. 57, 1821, p. 356-359.
1821.—**Walter Scott**. The Pirate, Vol. I, Chp. II.
1821.—**Otto von Kotzebue**. Entdeckungs-Reise in die Süd-See und nach der Behrings-Strasse zur Erforschung einer nordöstlichen Durchfahrt. Unternommen in den Jahren 1815, 1816, 1817 und 1818. Weimar, 1821, Zweiter Band, p. 108.

*1821.—**Otto von Kotsebue**. Voyage of discovery into the South-Sea and Behring's Straits, London, 1822.
1821.—Sea-Serpent.—*The Philosophical Magazine and Journal*, Vol. 58, p.454.
1821.—Analysis of one of the Vertebrae of the Orkney Animal.—*The Edinburgh Philosophical Journal*. Vol. V, p. 227.
1822. Jan.—**Froriep's** *Notizen aus dem Gebiete der Natur- und Heilkunde*, I, n°. 19, p. 294.
1822.—**Dr. Hibbert**. Description of the Shetland-Islands. London, 1822, p. 565
1822.—**Otto von Kotsebue**. Ontdekkingsreis in de Zuid-Zee en naar de Behrings straat in de jaren 1815, 1816, 1817 en 1818, tweede deel p. 277. Amsterdam, 1822.
*1822, June, 15.—*New-York...* (newspaper).
1822, Aug.—Die sogenannte Seeschlange.—**Froriep's** *Notizen aus dem Gebiete der Natur- und Heilbunde*, III, n°. 48, p. 53.
1823, Febr.—**Froriep's** *Notizen aus dem Gebiete der Natur- und Heilkunde*, IV, n°. 68, p. 24.
1823.—**A. de Capell Brooke**. Travels through Sweden, Norway and Finmark in the Summer of 1820. London 1823.
1823. June.—Nachrichten über die grosse Seeschlange.—**Froriep's** *Notizen aus dem Gebiete der Natur- und Heilkunde*, IV, n°. 84, p. 273.
*1824.—*Newbury port...* (newspaper).
1824.—**Froriep's** *Notizen aus dem Gebiete der Natur- und Heilkunde*, VIII, n°. 168, p. 218.
*1826. June 21.—*New York Advertiser*.
1826. Oct.—Sea-Serpent.—*The American Journal of Science and Arts*, conducted by **Benjamin Silliman**, Vol. XI.
1827.—**Dr. Hooker**. Additional testimony respecting the Sea-Serpent of the American Seas.—*The Edinburgh Journal of Science*, Vol. VI, 1827, p. 126.
1827, April.—**Dr. Hooker**. Fernere Zeugnisse über die Seeschlange in den Amerikanischen Meere.—**Froriep's** *Notizen aus dem Gebiete der Natur- und Heilkunde*, XVIII, n°. 256, p. 49.
1827, June.—Sea Serpent.—*The American Journal of Science and Arts*, conducted by **Benjamin Silliman**, Vol. XII, June, 1827, New Haven.
*1827, Aug.—Norwegische Handelszeitung zu Christiania.
*1827, Sept. 5.—Norwegische Handelszeitung zu Christiania.
*1827, Sept. 15.—Norwegische Handelszeitung zu Christiania.
1828, Jan.—**Froriep's** *Notizen aus dem Gebiete der Natur- und Heilkunde*, XIX, n°. 409, p. 193.
*1828.—**John Fleming**. A history of British Animals, etc., Edinburgh, 1828.
1829.—**Sam. L. Mitchill**. The history of Sea Serpentism.—**Silliman's** *American Journal of Science and Arts*, 1829.
1830, April, May.—*Chronicle*.
1830, June.—**Froriep's** *Notizen aus dem Gebiete der Natur- und Heilkunde*, XXVII, n°. 589, p. 265.

1832, Nov.—**Froriep's** *Notizen aus dem Gebiete der Natur- und Heilkunde*, XXXV, n° 756, p. 122.
*1834.—**Bakewell**. Introduction to Geology. Chap. XVI, p. 312; with a note of **Prof. Silliman**.
1834, June.—**Froriep's** *Notizen aus dem Gebiete der Natur- und Heilkunde*, XL, n° 879, p. 328.
*1834.—**C. S. Rafinesque Schmaltz**.—Abhandlung über Wasser-Schlangen, etc.—**Oken's** *Isis*, 1834. Extract from *Phil. Mag.* 1819.
1835, July.—A sea-serpent.—**Silliman's** *American Journal of Science and Arts*, Vol. 28, New Haven, July, 1835.
1835, Aug.—**Froriep's** *Notizen aus dem Gebiete der Natur- und Heilkunde*, XLV, n° 980. p. 186.
1837.—**H. Schlegel**. Essai sur la physionomie des Serpens, Amsterdam, 1837.
*1837, Sept.—The *"Adis"* of Drontheim, (newspaper).
1837, Oct.—**Froriep's** *Neue Notizen aus dem Gebiete der Natur- und Heilkunde*, IV, n° 67, p. 7.
1839.—**Dr. R. Hamilton**. Amphibious Carnivora, Group III, (Vol. XXV of **Jardine's** *Naturalist's Library*).
*1839.—*The Athenaeum*, London, 1839, p. 902.
*1839.—*Boston Mercantile*.
*1839.—*Kennebek Journal*.
1839, Oct.—**Froriep's** *Neue Notizen aus dem Gebiete der Natur- und Heilkunde*, XII, n° 248, p. 88.
*1840.—*Boston Daily Advertiser*.
*1840, Sept. 15.—*Journal du Havre*.
1841.—**H. Rathke**. Ueber die Seeschlange der Norweger.—*Archiv für Naturgeschichte 7er Jahrgang*, I, 1841, p. 278.
*1843.—*Christiansund Posten*.
1843, Nov.—**Froriep's** *Neue Notizen aus dem Gebiete der Natur- und Heilkunde*, XXVIII, n° 606, p. 184.
*1844.—**H. Schlegel**. Essay on the physionomy of Serpents, Edinburgh, 1844.
*1845.—*Cincinnati Gazette*.
1845, Nov.—*Proceedings of the Boston Society of Natural History*, Vol. II, p. 65.
1845, Dec.—*Proceedings of the Boston Society of Natural History*, Vol. II, p. 73.
1846, Jan.—*Proceedings of the Boston Society of Natural History*, Vol. II, p. 94.
1846, Febr.—**Froriep's** *Neue Notizen aus dem Gebiete der Natur- und Heilkunde*, XXXVII, n° 801, p. 134.
1847.—**Dr. R. Hamilton**. Amphibious Carnivora, Group III, (Vol. XXV, of **Jardine's** *Naturalist's Library*).
1847.—The Great Sea-Serpent.—*The Zoologist*, London, 1847, p. 1604-1608.
*1847.—*The Zoologist*, London, 1847, n° LIV, wrapper.
1847.—The Sea-Serpent.—*The Zoologist*, London, 1847, p. 1714-1716.

1847.—**Charles Cogswell**. A plea for the North Atlantic Sea-Serpent.— *The Zoologist*, London, 1847, p. 1841-1846.

1847.—The Sea-Serpent.—*The Zoologist*, London, 1847, p. 1911.

1847, July.—Ueber die Seeschlange.—**Froriep's** *Notizen aus dem Gebiete der Natur- und Heilkunde*, Dritter Reihe, III, 54, p. 148.

1847, Oct.—*The Zoologist*, London, 1847, Preface.

1848.—The Great Sea-Serpent.—*The Zoologist*, London, 1848, p. 2028.

1848, June.—**Froriep's** *Notizen aus dem Gebiete der Natur- und Heilkunde*, Dritter Reihe, VI, 131, p. 328.

1848.—The Great Sea-Serpent.—*The Zoologist*, London, 1848, p. 2192-2193.

*1848, Oct. 9.—*The Times*.

*1848, Oct. 13.—*The Times*.

*1848, Oct. 21.—*The Literary Gazette*.

*1848, Oct. 21.—*The Globe*.

*1848, Oct. 23.—*The Times*.

1848, Oct. 28.—The Great Sea-Serpent.—*The Illustrated London News*.

*1848, Nov. 2.—*The Times*.

*1848, Nov. 4.—*The Times*.

1848, Nov. 4.—The fossil Sea-Serpent.—*The Illustrated London News*.

*1848, Nov. 11.—**Prof. Richard Owen.**—The Great Sea-Serpent.—*The Times*.

1848, Nov. 15?—Note on the subject "Dodo" of **Mssrs. Strickland** and **Melville**.—*Annals and Magazine of Natural History*, 2d. Series, Vol. II, p. 444.

1848, Nov. 15?—**Prof. Richard Owen**. The Great Sea-Serpent.—*Annals and Magazine of Natural History*, 2d. Series, Vol. II, p. 458.

*1848, Nov. 21.—*The Times*.

1848, Nov. 23.—**Prof. Richard Owen**. The Great Sea-Serpent.—**Galignani's** *Messenger*.

*1848, Nov. 25.—*Boston Daily Advertiser*.

1848, Nov. 25.—The Great Sea-Serpent.—*The Illustrated London News*.

1848, Nov. 27.—The Great Sea-Serpent.—*The Zoologist*, London, 1848, p. 2306-2324.

1848, Nov. 27.—*The Zoologist*, London, 1848, Preface.

1848, Dec.—**Prof. Richard Owen**. Ueber die Seeschlange. **Froriep's** *Notizen a. d. Gebiete der Natur- und Heilkunde*, Dritter Reihe, VIII, n° 169, p. 231.

*1848.—*Transactions of the Linnaean Society of New England*, Boston, 1848.

*1848, Dec. 30.—*Bombay Bi-monthly Times*.

*1849.—Life and Letters of Campbell, 1849?

*1849. Jan.—*Westminster Review*.

*1849, Jan.—*Bombay Bi-monthly Times*.

*1849, March?—*Boston Atlas*.

*1849.—*Montrose Standard*.

1849.—Enormous undescribed animal.—*The Zoologist*, London, 1849, p. 2356

1849.—Inquiries respecting the Bones of a large Marine Animal, cast ashore on the Island of Stronsa, 1808—*The Zoologist*, London, 1849, p.2358-2363.
1849, Apr. 14.—The Great Sea-Serpent.—*The Illustrated London News*.
1849.—The Sea-Serpent?— *The Zoologist*, London, 1849, p. 2395-2398.
1849.—A strange Marine Animal.—*The Zoologist*, London, 1849, p. 2433.
1849, May, 19.—The Sea-Serpent.—*The Illustrated London News*.
*1849, July, 9.—*The Sun*.
1849, July.—Ueber die Grosse Seeschlange.—**Froriep's** *Notizen aus dem Gebiete der Natur- und Heilkunde*, Dritter Reihe, X, n° 205, p. 97.
1849.—The Great Sea-Serpent.—*The Zoologist*, London 1849, p. 2458-2460.
1849.—The Great Sea-Serpent.—*The Zoologist*, London, 1849, p. 2541.
1849.—*The Zoologist*, London, 1849.—Preface.
1850, Jan. 12.—The Sea-Serpent.—*The Illustrated London News*.
1850, Jan. 19.—The Great Sea-Serpent. *The Illustrated London News*.
*1850.—Romance of the Sea-Serpent or Ichthyosaurus. Also a collection of the ancient and modern authorities, with letters from distinguished merchants and men of science. Cambridge, U. S. 1850, 12°, 172 pages.
*1850.—*Christian Mercury* (U. S. newspaper).
*1850.—*Charlestown Courier*.
1850, April 20.—The Great Sea-Serpent.—*The Illustrated London News*.
1850.—The Great Sea-Serpent again.—*The Zoologist*, London, 1850, p. 2803.
*1850, Sept. 2.—*Cork Constitution*.
*1850, Sept. 7.—*Cork Constitution*.
1850, Sept. 7.—The Sea-Serpent again!—*The Illustrated London News*.
*1850, Sept. 11.—*Cork Reporter*.
1850, Sept. 14.—The Sea-Serpent.—*The Illustrated London News*.
1850.—The Great Sea-Serpent.—*The Zoologist*, London, 1850, p. 2925-2928.
1850, Dec.—*Proceedings of the Boston Society of Natural History*. Vol. III, p. 328.
1851.—**Rev. Alfr. Chrl. Smith**. Notes on Observations in Natural History during a Tour in Norway.—*The Zoologist*, London, 1851, p. 3228.
1851, Oct.—**Froriep's** *Tagsberichte über die Fortschritte der Natur- und Heilkunde, Abth. Zoologie und Palaeontologie*, n° 395.
*1852, Febr.—*New York Tribune*.
1852, Febr.—**Galignani's** *Messenger*.
*1852, Febr.—*Philadelphia Bulletin*
*1852, Mrch, 10.—*The Times*.
1852, Mrch, 13.—The Great Sea-Serpent caught at last.—*The Illustrated London News*.

Literature 19

1852, Mrch.—**Froriep's** *Tagsberichte über die Fortschritte der Natur- und Heilkunde, Abth. Zoologie und Palaeontologie*, p. 486.
1852, Mrch.—**Froriep's** *Tagsberichte über die Fortschritte der Natur- und Heilkunde, Abth. Zoologie und Palaeontologie*, p. 491.
1852, Apr.—Reported Capture of the Sea-Serpent.—*The Zoologist*, London, p. 3426-3429.
*1852, Nov. 17.—*The Times*.
1853, Jan.—The Great Sea-Serpent.—*The Zoologist*, London, 1853, p. 3756.
1854, June?—**Dr. T. S. Traill**. On the supposed Sea-Snake, cast on shore in the Orkneys in 1808, and the animal seen from H. M. S. "Daedalus" in 1848.—*Proceedings of the Royal Society at Edinburgh*, III, n° 44, p. 208.
1855, Febr. 17.—The Sea-Serpent Once More.—*The Illustrated London News*.
*1855, Aug. 13.—*Buffalo Daily Reporter*.
1855, Sept. 15.—The Great Serpent.—*The Illustrated London News*.
*1855, Oct. 1.—*The Times*.
1855. The Great American Snake Caught. *The Zoologist*, London, 1855, p. 4896.
1856, May, 3.—Another Sea-Serpent.—*The Illustrated London News*.
1856, Oct. 4.—The Sea-Serpent again. *The Illustrated London News*.
1856.—The Great Sea-Serpent. *The Zoologist*, London, 1856, p. 4948.
1856.—The Sea-Snake Story a fiction. *The Zoologist*, London, 1856, p. 4998.
*1857, Febr. and March.—*Cape Argus*.
*1857, March. 14.—*Cape Argus*
1857, June 13.—The Great Sea-Serpent.—*The Illustrated London News*.
*1858, Febr. 5.—*The Times*.
*1858, Febr. 13.—*The Times*.
*1858, Febr. 16.—*The Times*.
*1858, Febr. 23.—*The Times*.
1858, Febr.—*Revue Brittannique*, n° 2, p. 496.
1858, March. 20.—Another Sea-Serpent.—*The Illustrated London News*.
*1858, July or Aug.—*Java Bode*.
*1858, Oct. 6.—*Amsterdamsche Courant*.
1858.—Another Peep at the Sea-Serpent.—*The Zoologist*, London, 1858, p. 5989.
1858.—The Sea-Serpent.—*The Zoologist*, London, 1858, p. 6015-6018.
1859.—Another Sea-Serpent.—*The Zoologist*, London, 1859, p. 6492.
1860.—**Dr. R. Hamilton**, Amphibious Carnivora, Group III, (Vol. XXV of **Jardine's** *Naturalist's Library*.)
1860.—**P. H. Gosse**. The Romance of Natural History, Vol. I, Lond., Nisbet, 1860.
1860.—A Sea-Serpent in the Bermudas.—*The Zoologist*, London, 1860, p. 6934.

1860.—The Great Sea-Serpent.—*The Zoologist*, London, 1860, p. 6985-6993.
1860.—The Sea-Serpent.—*The Zoologist*, London, 1860, p. 7051-7052.
1860.—On the Probable Origin of Some Sea-Serpents.—*The Zoologist*, London, 1860, p. 7237.
1860.—Captain **Tailor's** Sea-Serpent.—*The Zoologist*, London, 1860, p. 7978.
1860, Sept.—*Skibbereen Eagle*.
1860, Sept.—*Cork Constitution*.
1861.—A Sea-Serpent.—*The Zoologist*, London, 1861, p. 7354.
*1862.—**Grattan's** *Civilized America*, p. 39.
1862.—The Sea-Serpent.—*The Zoologist*, London, 1862, p. 7850—7852
1863.—The Great Sea-Serpent.—*The Zoologist*, London, 1863, p. 8727.
1863, June 13.—The Great Sea-Serpent.—*The Illustrated London News*.
*1870, April 9.—**F. Buckland**, The Sea-Snake Again.—*Land and Water*.
1872, June 13.—*Nature*, Vol. VI.
1872, Aug. 1.—*Nature*, Vol. VI.
1872, Aug. 17.—Sea-Serpent, lately seen near Galveston. *The Graphic*.
*1872, Sept. 7.—*Land and Water*.
1872, Sept. 12.—*Nature*, Vol. VI.
1873, May.—Appearance of an Animal, believed to be that which is called the Norwegian Sea-Serpent.—*The Zoologist*, London, 1873, p. 3517-3522.
*1873, Nov.—*The Scotsman*.
*18,73, Nov. 20.—*The Times*.
1873, Dec.—The supposed Sea-Serpent.—*The Zoologist*, London, 1873, p. 3804.
1875, Nov. 20.—The Great Sea-Serpent.—*The Illustrated London News*.
1875, Dec. 4.—*Illustrirte Zeitung*.
1876, June 29.—The Sea-Serpents of the seventeenth Century.—*The Graphic*.
*1876, June.—*The Scotsman*.
*1876, June.—*The Courant*.
*1876, Dec.?—*London and China Telegraph*.
*1876, Dec.—*Good Words*.
*1877.—**J. Adams**. Account of a supposed Sea-Serpent seen off Nepean Island. *Proceedings Lit. Philosophical Society of Liverpool*, n° XXXI, p. LXVIII.
*1877, Jan. 6.—**J. K. Webster**.—The Sea-Monster.—*Advertiser and Ladies' Journal*.
*1877, Jan. 10, sqq.—(Newspapers of Liverpool).
1877, Jan. 13.—*Illustrated London News*, p. 35, 3d column.
*1877, Jan. 15.—**R. A. Proctor**. Strange Sea-Monsters.—*The Echo*.
1877, Jan. 27.—The Sea-Serpent.—*The Graphic*.
1877, Febr. 3.—Zur Geschichte der Seeschlange.—*Illustrirte Zeitung*.

*1877, Mrch.—**R. A. Proctor**. Strange Sea-Creatures.—*The Gentlemen's Magazine.*
*1877, June 13?—*Portsmouth Times and Naval Gazette.*
*1877, June 14.—*The Times.*
1877, June 16.—*The Graphic*, p. 563, 34. column.
1877, June 30.—The Sea-Serpent. — *The Graphic.*
*1877, Sept. 4.—*Manchester Courier.*
*1877, Sept. 8.—**F. Buckland**. Occurrence of a Sea-Serpent.—*Land and Water.*
*1877, Sept. 15.—**F. Cornish**, Reply to **Buckland**.—*Land and Water.*
*1878.—*Wochenblatt für das Christliche Volk.*
*1878, May 24.—**F. Buckland**. Supposed Sea-Snake caught in Australia.—*Land and Water.*
1878, Sept. 5.—The Sea-Serpent explained.—*Nature*, Vol. XVIII.
1878, Sept. 6.—*The Scotsman.*
1878, Sept. 12.—The Sea-Serpent explained.—*Nature*, Vol. XVIII.
1878, Sept. 19.—The Sea-Serpent explained.—*Nature*, Vol. XVIII.
1879.—**Andrew Wilson**. Leisure Time Studies; chiefly biological; a Series of Essays and Lectures. With Numerous Illustrations, London, Chatto and Windus, 1879.
1879, Jan. 30.—(Critic of **Mr. Wilson's** Leisure Time Studies).—Nature, Vol. XIX.
1879, April 19.—*The Graphic.*
1879, July 19.—*The Graphic.*
1879, July 24.—The Sea-Serpent.—*Nature*, Vol. XX.
*1879, Sept. 24.—*The Times.*
1880.—**A. Günther**. The Study of Fishes, p. 521. Edinburgh, 1880.
1880, Nov. 18.—**Searles V. Wood**, Jun. Order Zeuglodontia.—*Nature*, Vol. XXIII.
1881, Febr. 10.—**Searles V. Wood**. Zeuglodontia.—*Nature*, Vol. XXIII.
*1881, Sept. 8.—*Madras Mail.*
1881, Oct. 8.—*Le Monde Illustré.*
1881, Oct. 13.—*Nature*, Vol. XXIV.
1881, Nov. 12.—**A. C. Oudemans**, Jzn. Iets over fabelachtige verhalen en over het vermoedelijk bestaan van de groote Zeeslang.—*Album der Natuur*, 1882, p. 13-26. (The issue appeared already Nov. 12, 1881).
*1881, Nov. 15?—*Cape Argus.*
1881, Nov. 17.—*De Zuia-Afrikaan.*
1881, Nov. 26.—*Nieuws van den Dag.*
1882, Jan.—**P. Harting**. Een Zeeslang.—*Album der Natuur*, 1882, p. 66.
*1882.—**Catherine C. Hopley**. Curiosities and Wonders of Serpent-Life. London, 1882, 8° p. 247-267.
*1882, May 22.—Giant cuttlefishes.—*Scotsman.*
*1882, June.—The Sea-Serpent at Shetland.—*Glasgow Herald.*
*1882, June.—*Newcastle Chronicle.*
1882.—Die Neueste Seeschlange.—*Illustrirte Zeitung*, p. 2035.
*1882, July, 1.—A Stradling.—*Land and Water.*

1882.—**G. Verschuur**. Eene reis rondom de wereld in vierhonderd en tachtig dagen. Haarlem, 1882.
1883.—**Henry Lee**. Sea Monsters Unmasked.—London, Clowes & Son, 1883.
1883, Jan. 25.—The Sea-Serpent.—*Nature*, Vol. XXVII.
1883, Febr. 1.—The Sea-Serpent.—*Nature*, Vol. XXVII.
1883, Febr. 8.—The Sea-Serpent.—*Nature*, Vol. XXVII.
1883, Febr. 15.—The Sea-Serpent.—*Nature*, Vol. XXVII.
1883, Oct. 9.—The Inevitable Sea-Serpent.—*The Graphic* p. 387.
*1883, Nov. 4.—**Chambers'** *Journal*, p. 748.
*1884, Sept 14.—*Inverness Courier*.
1884, Nov.—**C. Honigh**. Reisschetsen uit Noorwegen.—*De Gids*, p. 300.
*1885, July, 29-Sept. 6.—**W. Reid**. History of Sea-Serpents.—**John O'Groat** *Journal*.
*1885, Sept. 1—The Sea-Serpent again.—*Scotsman*
1885, Sept. 10.—*Nature*, Vol. XXXII.
*1886, Sept. 15.—The Sea-Serpent again.—*Evening Dispatch*, Edinburgh.
1886, Sept. 25.—*The Graphic*.
1886.—**W. E. Hoyle**. Sea-Serpent.—*Encyclopaedia Brittanica* Ed. 9.
1886.—**W. E. Hoyle**. Contribution to a Bibliography of the Sea-Serpent (read 21st. April, 1886).—*Proceedings of the Royal Physical Society of Edinburgh*. 1886.
*1889, May 21.—*De Grondwet*, n° 38.—(Journal, edited in Holland, Michigan, U. S. A.)
1889, June 6.—*Haagsche Courant*.
1889, Dec. 7?—**John Ashton**. Curious Creatures in Zoology.—With 130 Illustrations throughout the text. London, John C. Nimmo (1890) p. 268 - 278.
1890, July 12. — *De Amsterdammer*, Weekblad voor Nederland.

and probably:

*17—?—**Mongitore**. Remarkable Objects of Sicily.
*18—?—**Leguat**. Travels to Rodrigues Island.
*1888.—**A. Nicholson**. Snakes, Marsupials and Birds.

Should any reader know of any other contribution to the literature of the sea serpent, he is earnestly requested by the author of this work to inform him about it.

2 Attempts to discredit the Sea-Serpent. Cheats and Hoaxes.

Home from their first voyage, sailor-lads, as Mr. Gosse says, are commonly eagerly beset for wonders. And what tales do they palm upon their credulous listeners? If they do not draw on their own invention, they tell the old stories they have heard when on fine evenings they were together with the old tars talking and chatting on the fore-deck. Of the latter many have no other origin than the imagination of a sailor's brain; they are merely hoaxes; others again are exaggerated and garbled reports of what they have seen with their own eyes, or of what their comrades or their captain saw! There are the tales of the Unicorn, of the White Whale, that terrible "Moby Dick" of the Polar Regions, there are the fables of the Mermaids and Mermen, there are the exaggerations of the Kraken and the Sea-Serpent!

Except the last, all the other animals that gave rise to the terrible tales are known to Zoologists, and by their enlightenment even to the sailors themselves. This probably explains sufficiently why our sailors do not report any more encounters with Mermaids, or with the Kraken. They know now that they saw, or harpooned, manatees, or dugongs, and gigantic squids, or calamaries.

But suddenly the newspapers spread the rumour of a Sea-Serpent having been seen by Captain So and So, of the Royal Navy, and by the master, several midshipmen, and some men of the crew! The news is printed in hundreds of newspapers, and passes from mouth to mouth, in short, it becomes the topic of the day! A schooner, or a brig runs into a harbour, say that of Liverpool, and the Captain, and the crew are immediately asked if they have seen the sea-serpent. Unaware of the existence of such an animal they of course answer in the negative! But soon convinced by the affidavits printed in the newspapers, they swear that when on their next voyage they meet with it, they will bring it home! But on the next voyage, though they are constantly on the watch, the sea-serpent does not appear, and the time for returning home arrives. One of the sailors, perhaps even the captain hits upon an idea, a splendid one! Though he did not meet with the serpent, yet he has seen it with his own eyes! but the beast swam so rapidly that he could not pursue it! So in a moment he is resolved on hoaxing the gullible!

It is clear that the unbeliever must have had a great pleasure in inventing the hoax upon the subject, and in playing some splendid tricks on the believers!

Some of these hoaxes are admirably set up, and I will begin by telling my readers some of them, which I met with in the various works I had the opportunity to consult.

The earliest hoax or exaggerated report is that, published for the first time in the *Report* of 1817. There we find in a letter from the Rev. Mr. William Jenks the following:

"He" (Mr. Staples of Prospect) "told me also that about 1780, as a schooner was lying at a mouth of the river, or in the bay, one of these enormous creatures leaped over it between the masts—that the men ran into the hold for fright, and that the weight of the serpent sunk the vessel 'one streak' or plank. The schooner was of about eighteen tons."

Now follows the hoax of a Joseph Woodward, who had reason to be satisfied, for his tale appeared in many newspapers at Boston, New York, etc. It runs as follows:

"Another sea-serpent, different to the one first seen near Cape Anne, is said to have been seen, and the following declaration has been drawn up and attested in proper form."

"I, the undersigned, Joseph Woodward, captain of the Adamant schooner of Hingham, being on my route from Penobscot to Hingham, steering W. N. W., and being about 10 leagues from the coast, perceived last Sunday, at two P. M. something on the surface of the water, which seemed to me to be of the size of a large boat. Supposing that it might be part of the wreck of a ship, I approached it; but when I was within a few fathoms of it, it appeared, to my great surprise, and that of my whole crew, that it was a monstrous serpent. When I approached nearer, it coiled itself up, instantly uncoiling itself again, and withdrew with extreme rapidity. On my approaching again, it coiled itself a second time, and placed itself at the distance of 60 feet at most from the bow of the ship."

"I had one of my guns loaded with a cannon ball and musket bullets. I fired it at the head of the monster; my crew and myself distinctly heard the *ball* and bullets strike against his body, from which they rebounded, as if they had struck against a rock. The serpent shook his head and tail in an extraordinary manner, and advanced towards the ship with open jaws. I had caused the cannon to be reloaded, and pointed it at his throat; but he had come so near, that all the crew were seized with terror, and we thought only of getting out of his way. He almost touched the vessel; and had not I tacked as I did, he would certainly have come on board. He dived; but in a moment we saw him appear again, with his head on one side of the vessel, and his tail on the other, as if he was going to lift us up and upset us. However, we did not feel any shock. He remained five hours near us, only going backward and forward."

"The fears with which he at first inspired us having subsided, we were able to examine him attentively. I estimate that his length is at least twice that of my schooner, that is to say, 130 feet; his head is full 12 or 14; the diameter of the body below the neck is not less than six feet; the size of the head is in proportion to that of his body. He is of a blackish colour; his ear-holes (ouies), are about 12 feet from the extremity of his head. In short, the whole has a terrible look."

"When he coils himself up, he places his tail in such a manner, that it aids him in darting forward with great force: he moves in all directions with the greatest facility and astonishing rapidity."

"(Signed)"
"Joseph Woodward."
"Hingham, May 12, 1818."

"This declaration is attested by Peter Holmes and John Mayo, who made affidavit of the truth of it before a justice of peace."

This hoax was reprinted in the *Quarterly Journal of Science, Literature and the Arts of the Royal Institute at London*, Vol. VI, 1818, and was apparently believed in by the sender. Mr. Oken also inserted the tale of Woodward in his *Isis*, of 1818, p. 2100.—Thirty years afterwards Mr. Edward Newman, the editor of *The Zoologist*, published it in his journal of 1848, p. 2028, without, however, mentioning the source from which he copied it! Why did not he do so? Apparently because he felt ashamed of giving such an old story, and because he was aware of the fact, that the whole account was wonderful, and contained many impossibilities!

Astonishing enough, Mr. Froriep translated this piece from the *Zoologist*, and incerted it in his journal (*Notizen*, Third Series, Vol. VI, n°. 131, p. 328), and ends this article with the following remark:[1]

"This communication tallies with those about the sea-serpent, published in our 3d. volume p. 148, which are also taken from the *Zoologist*. Some German newspapers have then amused themselves with our communications, as with a newspaper-hoax. We, however, shall go on to gather whatever from time to time will still come to us to solve an apparently fabulous matter in Zoology."

The story, however, roused the indignation of Mr. W. W. Cooper, of Worcester (see *The Zoologist*, 1848, p. 2192). I will let him speak himself:

"I have waited anxiously to see whether any more competent person than myself would offer any observation upon the statement of Captain Woodward, published in the March number of the Zoologist, relating to the Great 'Sea-serpent'. As no one has done so, I beg to offer you the following: In a note which you added in this statement, you say, 'The foregoing statement was formally signed and sworn to at Hingham, by captain Woodward, on the 12th of May'. What 12th of May? You should have told your readers. Now, evidence given upon oath is generally considered as conclusive, except where the party swearing is known to be unworthy of credit, or the evidence given is not consistent with itself. Of Captain Woodward I know nothing; I never heard of him till I read the 'Zoologist' for last March. It is, therefore, upon the latter ground that I venture to attack his statement, and I do so because in a disputed question it is necessary to throw aside all evidence that will not stand the stricktest scrutiny. Captain Woodward tells us nothing of his where-abouts, except that he was sailing from Penobscot to Hingham, steering W. N. W., nor of the date when he says he saw the serpent, except that it was on 'Sunday last at 2. p. m.' This is not sufficiently accurate. But these are trifling points. The most extraordinary part of the statement will appear from this: Captain Woodward says, the beast moved with *extreme*, or, as he afterwards expressed himself, *astonishing* rapidity; that when he fired at the monster it was sixty feet at the most from the bow of the ship, which appears to have been the nearest part of the vessel to the animal; but after he fired the beast advanced towards his ship; that he had caused his cannon to be reloaded and pointed at its

---

1) The translations are done as literally as possible.

throat,—of course while it was advancing towards his vessel,—but before he could fire his crew were seized with terror; that he tacked and got out of its way. So here we have an animal sixty feet from the ship, moving with astonishing rapidity *towards the ship*, which it appears was also moving *towards the animal*, and yet allowing time to load a cannon, point it at its throat, and afterwards to tack to get out of its way. Truly a most accommodating serpent! But again, the animal remained five hours near the ship, allowing itself to be minutely examined, but yet no further attempt to kill the beast! And what is almost equally strange, though even the position of the ear-holes is mentioned,—such minute observation does Capt. Woodward seem to have made,—yet no description is given of any scales, or anything else, to account for what is before stated, that Capt. Woodward and his crew 'distinctly heard the ball and bullets strike against his body, from which they rebounded as though they had struck against a rock'. It is much to be regretted that these inconsistencies did not strike you before you made public the statement in question; it is also to be regretted that no one better able than myself to point them out has undertaken to do so. But it is highly desirable, in the present state of our ignorance upon this subject, that none but the most inexceptionable evidence should be received. Let us have 'the truth, the whole truth, and nothing but the truth.' I need hardly add, that in these observations I am actuated by no unfriendly feeling towards Captain Woodward: my desire is to get at the truth of the matter; and I should hail with delight the day when one of these monsters of the deep, whatever they may be (for some animal with which we are unacquainted has, I firmly believe, been seen), is brought to our shores and lodged in one of our museums, to be at once the wonder and admiration of naturalists.—W. W. Cooper; Claines, Worcester, June 2, 1848."

Here ends the history of this hoax, utterly smashed!

Mr. Edward Newman has never answered to this attack!

In 1818, when again notice was given of the presence of a sea-serpent in the neighbourhood of Boston, a reward of 5000 dollars was offered to the whalers for securing it, and bringing it home dead or alive. I will insert here the whole history of these attempts, for they finished with a trick.

In the copy of the *Report of the Committee* of 1817, which I have borrowed from the Library of the Royal University of Göttingen, there is a paragraph from a newspaper of August, 21, 1818, the head or title of which is wanting; it runs as follows:

"Boston, Aug. 21."

"Transmitted by our N. Y. Correspondents.

"Capt. Rich, who went from here a few days since, in pursuit of the Sea-serpent, writes the concern as follows:

"*Squam River, Aug. 20th. 12 o'clock.*—After several unsuccessful attempts, we have at length fastened to this strange thing called the Sea-Serpent. We struck him fairly but the harpoon soon drew out. He has not been seen since, and I fear the wound he received will make him more cautious how he approaches these shores. Since my last, yesterday, we have been constantly in pursuit of him; by day he always keeps a proper distance from us, to prevent our striking oars. But a few hours since, I thought we were sure of him, for I hove the harpoon into him as fairly as ever a whale was struck; took from us about 20 fathoms of warp before we could wind the boat, with as much swiftness as a whale. We had but a short ride when we were all loose from him to our sore disappointment."

"Rich'd. Rich".

"Gloucester, Aug. 20.—As I thought it would be interesting to you to hear from Capt. Rich, and as he is at some distance, I will give you some particulars of his cruise. On Monday last, he sailed from this in a large whale boat, and two smaller ones well manned. My brother commanded one of the boats. Yesterday they met the Serpent of Squam, and chased him about seven hours, when they closed with him. He passed directly under the bows of Capt. Rich's boat; he immediately threw the harpoon, which pierced him about two feet; he drew the boat a considerable distance but went with such a velocity that he broke that part of the boat through which the rope passed and drew out the harpoon. I hope they will have another opportunity before they give up the chase."

"He has *no* scales on him, and no bunches on his back, but his skin is smooth, and looks similar to an eel. In the attack, Capt. Rich had one of his hands wounded. These particulars I have in a letter from my brother".

"Saml. Dexter".

After the perusal of this work my readers will know why I am disposed to believe that the animal struck by Captain Rich was really a Sea-Serpent. As far as I can judge, after having read all that I have found about the sea-serpent, this is the only time that the animal was struck with a harpoon. Balls have often been fired at it, but it has never been killed yet. In the same copy of the *Report of the Committee* of 1817, there was a letter from Mr. Andrews Norton to Mr. George Bancroft, at that time a resident at Göttingen. I give here an extract from this letter concerning the matter in question.

"Last Friday morning upon going to breakfast at Dr. Ware's, I found there the papers of the day, in which was announced the most interesting fact, that the Sea-Serpent had been taken by the expedition fitted out for that purpose. In the Daily Advertiser in particular nearly a column was filled with the circumstances of his capture, and of the manner in which the information had been received, viz. from a person whose name was given, and who had come express from Gloucester, the evening before, to bring the news. He was said to be 120 feet long, and the Board of Health had sent down two boats to stop him in the Harbour. After talking about it all breakfast time, I immediately went to Reed's stable, got a horse and chaise, put a news-paper in my pocket, rode to Professor Peck's, showed him the paper, and offered to carry him into Boston, and to procure a boat to go out with him into the Harbour, that he might examine it. He was not well, and said at first that he could not go; but gradually grew warm upon the subject, and concluded at last that it would never do for him not to see it. When I had fairly got him into the chaise, his spirits rose with the exertion he had made, with the thoughts of the memoir and letters which he should write, and with the triumph which he anticipated over the Linnaean Society and their 'diseased black snake', as he contemptuously called it (meaning the small serpent, killed near the shore at Gloucester); for he pledged himself that we should find that the sea-serpent had no bunches on his back. I too anticipated with great satisfaction the honorable mention of me, which his gratitude would induce him to make in his memoir upon the subject, and expected confidently to float down to posterity behind Mr. Peck, upon this enormous animal. We entered Boston, and rode immediately to the end of Central Wharf to the store of a Mr. Rich, who had fitted out the expedition. The first person we saw was Judge Davis, whose countenance foreboded evil. His first words were to inform us that we had come in to be disappointed, for that the serpent was not taken! (I am not in the habit of using notes of admiration, but the present occasion seems to require one). The sailors, however, armed, as he said, that they had taken some most extraordinary fish of very large size, which he was going to see. I had little appetite left for seeing extraordinary fishes, but went to accompany Mr. Peck. We proceeded a wharf to the South End, and making our way through a croud, obtained admission into the dark lower room of a store where we found a considerable number of other gentlemen waiting. After some delay the fish was dragged in from the small vessel in which it had been brought, wrapped in sail. As soon as it was uncovered and fairly exposed to view, it was pronounced by all who knew any thing on the subject to be nothing but a Thunny, or Horse Mackerel, of a common size.—We had been gradually prepared for the disappointment, so that the shock was not so great as you might suppose. The report in the morning's paper had arisen from a *mystification* performed upon the person who brought it to Boston, by the crew of the vessel engaged in the expedition. The sailors who dragged in the fish were part of this crew; and instead of their being tossed over the wharf into the water, by way of punishment for their imposition, and to teach them better morals, as they infallibly would have been by any mob out of Boston, there was actually a collection made to reward them for their trouble in taking the fish and bringing it to exhibit. This fact, I think, deserves to be recorded for the honor of Boston, and particularly of us gentlemen present.—I have only to add that if you should learn that any one of the German literati is writing a volume upon Sea-Serpents, I beg you will assure him, that we do not consider the circumstance, connected with the deception just mentioned, as affecting the evidence before obtained for their real existence.—In the Messenger of this week which I will send by the next opportunity you will find one or two notices of this affair p. 756 and p. 758."

I have had no opportunity to consult the above mentioned passage from this *Messenger*. I think most of my readers know a tunny (*Thynnus thynnus* (Linn.)). For those, however, who don't, I give here a figure of it.

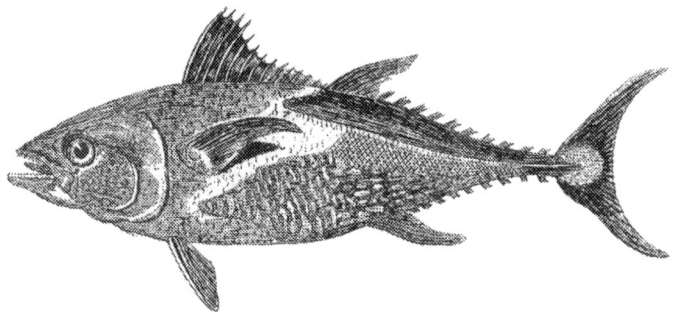

FIG. 1.–*THYNNUS THYNNUS* (LINN.).

In the *Philosophical Magazine*, Vol. LIII, p. 71, of January 1819, we read:
"T. Say, Esq., of Philadelphia, in a letter received from him by Dr. Leach, announces that a Captain Rich had fitted out an expedition purposely to take this leviathan, of which so much has been said in the newspapers and even in some scientific journals. He succeeded in 'fastening his harpoon in what was acknowledged by all the crew to be the veritable Sea-serpent (and which several of them had previously seen and made oath to): but when drawn from the water, and full within the sphere of their vision, it proved that this serpent, which fear had loomed to the gigantic length of 100 feet, was no other than a harmless Tunny (*Scombrus Thynnus*) nine or ten feet long!"

We see that Mr. Norton and Prof. Peck immediately recognized the whole story as a Yankee-trick, but that Prof. T. Say was the dupe of it!

From a letter from Prof. Jacob Bigelow to Prof. Benjamin Silliman (*Am. Journ. Sc. Arts, Vol.* II, Boston, 1820) I conclude that Prof. Say's letter was printed in Thomson's *Annals* for Jan. 1819. If anybody can tell me the exact title of Thomson's *Annals*, he will oblige me, indeed. I have had no opportunity to consult it. A part of this letter was translated into German, and inserted in Oken's *Isis* of 1819, p. 653. I will try to translate this part into English again:

"I regret that many scientific journals in Europe have in good earnest treated of the absurd story of the Great Sea-Serpent, which is nothing but a result of defective observation connected with an extravagant degree of fear. You will already know, that Capt. Rich has thrown light upon the subject; out of his own means he fitted out a ship to catch this Leviathan. He succeeded...." (etc., the rest of the letter runs like the part from the *Philosophical Magazine*, quoted above).

Mr. Rafinesque Schmaltz, however, says, (see *Phil. Mag.* Vol. LIV, 1819):
"The *Pelamis megophias*, or Great Sea-Snake, appears to have left the shores of Massachusetts, and to have baffled the attempts to catch it, probably because those attempts were conducted with very little judgment. But a smaller snake, or fish, nine feet long, and a strange shark, have been taken, of which the papers give no description: let us hope that they will be described by the naturalists at Boston".

And Prof. Jacob Bigelow, of Boston (Silliman's *Am. Journ. Sc. Arts*, Vol. II, Boston, 1820):
"In the following year" (1818) "Capt. Rich of Boston, went on an expedition fitted out for the purpose of taking the Sea-Serpent, and after a fruitless cruise of some weeks, brought into port a fish of the species commonly known to mariners and fishermen by the name of Tunny, Albicore or Horse Mackerel, the *Scomber Thynnus* of Linnaeus, and which fish he asserted to be the same as that denominated Sea-Serpent. This disappointment of public curiosity was attended at the time by a disbelief on the part of many, of the existence of a distinct marine animal of the serpent-kind, or of the dimensions and shape represented by the witnesses of Gloucester and elsewhere."

"It is hoped that the unsuccessful termination of Capt. Rich's cruise will not deter others from improving any future opportunities which may occur for solving what may now perhaps be considered the most interesting problem in the science of Natural History."

This was written in 1820, and the problem is not quite solved yet!

The trick of Capt. Rich is also mentioned in the paper of Mr. Mitchill, spoken of further on.

Again Colonel T. H. Perkins relates in the *Boston Daily Advertiser* of November 25, 1848, the trick of Capt. Rich as follows (copied from the *Zoologist* of 1849, p. 2361).

"As it happened, a circumstance took place which did not do much credit to the actors in it, but which served to fortify the unbelief of our southern brethern. Believing that the possession of the sea-serpent would be a fortune to those who should have him in their power, many boats were fitted out from Cape Ann and other places in the neighbourhood of his haunts, armed with harpoons and other implements, and manned with persons used to the whale fishery, in hopes of getting near enough to him to fasten their harpoons in his side. Among others a Captain Rich (not Benjamin Rich), of Boston, took command of a party, which was fitted out at some expense, and went into the bay, where they cruised along shore two or three days without seeing the serpent. With a view, however, to keep the joke from themselves, they determined to throw or attempt to throw it upon others, though at the *expense of truth!* They spread a report that they had caught the serpent, or what had been taken for one, and that he was to be seen at a place mentioned in the advertisement."

"Thousands were flocking to see this wonder, when it was found to be no other than a large horse macquerel, which (though a great natural curiosity, weighing sometimes 600 or 700 pounds) very much disappointed those, who had been induced to visit it. Those who had declared their disbelief of the existence of the Sea serpent amongst ourselves were delighted to find their opinions were confirmed, and gave themselves great credit for their judgment and discrimination. The report spread from Boston to New Orleans, that what had been thought by some persons to be a seaserpent had proved to be a horse macquerel, and even those who had been believers now supposed that those who had reported that they had seen the serpent had either misrepresented or had been themselves deceived. As no report of the snake having been seen after the capture of the macquerel was made, during that year, Captain Rich had the laugh with him, until circumstances, which have transpired since, have borne rather against him. Thus much for the transactions of the past years."

The Lake Erie Serpent.—In Mr. Rafinesque's *Dissertation on Sea-Snakes*, we read (See *Phil. Mag.* Vol. LIV, 1819):

"It appears that our large lakes have huge serpents or fishes, as well as the sea. On the 3d. of July, 1817, one was seen in Lake Erie, three miles from land, by the crew of a schooner, which was 35 or 40 feet long, and one foot in diameter; its colour was a dark mahogany, nearly black. This account is very imperfect, and does not even notice if it had scales; therefore it must remain doubtful whether it was a snake or a fish. I am inclined to believe it was a fish, until otherwise convinced: it might be a gigantic species of eel, or a species of the above genus *Octipos*. Until seen again, and better described, it may be recorded under the name of *Anguilla gigas* or Gigantic Eel."

And in the *Additions* to this dissertation:

"The Water-Snake of Lake Erie has been seen again, and described to be of a copper colour, with bright eyes, and 60 feet long. It is added, that at a short distance balls had no effect on him: but it is omitted to mention whether it was owing to have hard scales (in which case it might be a real snake of the genus *Enhydris* or *Pelamis*), or to the indexterity of the marksman."

Every one feels that Mr. Rafinesque was the dupe of a hoax, and that he was so, indeed, will be seen from Mr. Mitchell's dissertation (see below) in which more hoaxes are to be found.

Unbelievers not only invented tales to play a trick to believers, but when scientific men, they even read papers before learned assemblies, with a view of ridiculing the matter. I believe there has been no greater attempt to throw discredit on the sea-serpent, than that of Mr. Samuel L. Mitchill. I am obliged to communicate to my readers his whole paper, even at the risk of wearying them. It was published in Silliman's *Am. Journ. Sc. Arts*, 1829, and runs as follows:
"The History of Sea-Serpentism, extracted from Samuel L. Mitchill's Summary of the progress of Natural Science within our United States, for a few years past; read before the New York Lyceum, at a succession of sittings during October, 1828.—N°. 35.—The Sea-Serpent. (Communicated for this Journal)."
"This subject, the author observed, would scarcely be worthy of notice, before this learned and respectable assembly, if it had not happened, that during several years, it, or something so imagined and so called, had frequently been presented for public consideration; and that paragraphs and statements in the newspapers and journals, do yet, from time to time, attract the attention of their readers."
"This alleged monster of the deep first haunted the coast of Massachusets, and frightened more particularly the neighbourhood of Gloucester with his presence. Observations were made, and evidence was collected to a large amount. These were so considerable and imposing, that the Linnean Society of New England published a book on the subject, with the figure of the enormous reptile under the name of *Scoliophis*. As the fishermen and naturalists could not catch him and bring him ashore for inspection, it was concluded to fortify the story by oaths. Accordingly, affidavits were made to great extent, containing the particulars of what the several deponents believed they had seen, and, as far as swearing went, such solemn declarations presented a strong case. Their operation however upon my mind was, that there was nothing better to show than those statements upon paper, which were, in no sense of the words, proofs of the fact, but merely expressions of the opinions formed by the deposing witnesses of what they had observed in the water. I who was a believer in the first instance, was gradually sworn into scepticism, which finally ended in incredulity."
"About this stage of the panic, General David Humphreys did me the honor of a visit, and requested me to listen while he read a manuscript. To this I instantly consented. I discovered that my distinguished friend had visited Massachusetts for the express purpose of collecting all the testimony he could find concerning the sea-serpent. He was highly delighted with his success; and had reduced his researches into the form of letters addressed to Sir Joseph Banks, then President of the London Royal Society. He evidently intended to take the lead of the Linnean Society, and to acquire the honor and glory of making the wonderful intelligence known first to the sçavans of Europe. He did not vouchsafe, even to name me in the communication. After a very pleasant interview, during which I found that he positively considered himself right in the investigation, and I determined on my part to enter into no discussion about it, he requested me to receive the writing, and engage some bookseller to cause it to be put to press without delay. The reason

for this was, that he was obliged to return forthwith to New-Haven. I made a contract in his behalf, and directed the proofsheets to be sent to him there. I had a lucky escape from an association with the extraordinary creature."

"Afterwards, a mutilated specimen of a snake, killed on the land, somewhere thereabout, was brought to me preserved in alcoholic spirit. This had been exhibited as the spawn or young of the Great Scoliophis. The head, which contains the strong *ophiological* characters, had been crushed and destroyed. But, as far as I could judge, from the formation of the belly and tail, it had been a native of the land, (apparently a *coluber*,) and had, of course, no pretention to claim kindred with its pretended parent of the ocean."

"I was the better enabled, I thought, to form a more correct opinion, relative to the matter, by reason of my possessing in my museum, at the time, four true sea-serpents, which my navigating friends had brought me from the Gulf of Mexico, and the Chinese Sea."

"The history of Sea Serpentism is a very memorable part of the sayings and doings in this enlightened age and country. For the benefit of the present generation, and of posterity, it ought to be written. In proceeding to pen a short sketch of it, I must premise, that I am one of the last persons in existence who would presume to put a limit to creative power. I admit that the allmighty being could make a water-snake as easily as a fish; and that such an animal might be as big as a *Kraken*, as easily as the diminutive size of the *Stickleback*. Yet, on reviewing these legends of the times, there is found such a propensity towards the strange and the marvellous, that the men of the present day show a credulity very much resembling that of the remote ages, when the terraqueous globe was peopled with gorgons, mermaids, chimeras, hydras, dragons, and all the monsters of fabulous zoology."

"(a). The first tale I remember to have considered seriously relative to it was this: it had been determined, they said, to put a steam boat in operation at Boston to coast along shore and to convey passengers. It was foreseen that such a vessel would traverse the currents and pass among the islands with an ease and a speed unknown to boats moved by oars and sails; and of course, much of the business of transporting passengers would be taken away from the small craft heretofore employed. The large boat would thus destroy the small ones, or, as was expressed by another word, devour them. Under these forebodings, the steam-vessel made a trip, with favourable auspices. Some wag, the account proceeds, wrote for one of the gazettes, an allegorical description of a sea-serpent, that had been descried off Nahant and Gloucester, and had probably come there to consume all the small fish in the place. The narrative, given with such grave diction and imposing seriousness, was received by many as an actual and literal occurrence, and credited accordingly."

"(b). Long Island Sound put in a claim for a sea-serpent. On this fiction I am well satisfied of the particulars that follow. An active young fellow who had become weary of ploughing the land, bought a little sloop of about fifteen tons, which I remember to have seen; and resolved to try his luck in ploughing the waves. He named his vessel the *Sea-Serpent*. She was mostly employed in carrying country produce to the New-York market and in bringing manure back, with the advantage of passengers when any offered. This boat was on her way from Mamaroneck harbor or thereabout toward the city, and was met by a sloop from that place, a short distance from City-Island. The captain of the latter, on arriving at home, was eagerly interrogated by a quidnunc for news; and being a man of some humor and fancy, told his neighbor, the querist, he had just seen the sea-serpent. He then described how (alluding to the barrels on deck) he had seen the bunches on his back; how high the head (meaning the bowsprit) was out of water; how the black and white colours (meaning the painted waist) were variegated; how he saw the lashing of the tail (meaning the motion of the boom in jibing as she was going along before a fair easterly wind); that this sea-serpent was proceeding with a speed equalling at least from five to six knots an hour, which made all white before him (meaning the foam at the bows). The good man took the joke in real earnest, went away and told it to a sensible acquaintance. This latter wrote a formal and solemn account of it; which, travelling an extensive round in the sheets of intelligence, was finally embodied in the aforesaid book, where it is registered as a part of the evidence."

"(c). It was about this period of these transactions that I received from Boston an ichthyological production, enclosed in a letter, respectfully written, and with postage paid, submitting to me whether that article was not a piece of a sea-serpent's hide? It had been found on the shore of the region which the alarming visitor frequented; and was supposed to have been separated from his body by one of the musket balls which had been fired at him and washed ashore. To this serious communication I returned for answer that it was simply a portion of skin with closely adhering scales, belonging to the bony scaled pike (*Esox osseus*), an inhabitant of the Atlantic Ocean."

"(d). So much curiosity and excitement were now raised about the sea-serpent, that he was a prominent topic of conversation. The feeling was more intense, inasmuch as it was confidently declared he had been frequently observed near boats and vessels. It was at length concluded to fit an expedition, expressly for the purpose of catching him, with a select crew, under the command of Captain Rich. Day after day he cruised over tracts where the sea-serpent had, according to information, been observed, without discovering anything like him. At length, a creature was descried, which some of the men on board said they had seen before, and that it was the sea-serpent. The captain pursued the game a considerable time longer, with much vigilance and patience, until it was at a distance near enough to be harpooned. He was taken on board, and found to be a fish of the Mackerel family. I saw the preparation of it in the Greenwood Museum, and satisfied myself that it was an individual of a well known species called *Tunny* in the Mediterranean, and *Albicore* in the Atlantic sea."

"After the capture of the fish, the persons who, when they saw him in the water, declared positively that he was the sea-serpent, now changed their minds, and swore he was not."

"At length the man of successful exertion arrived with his prize; and unexpectedly and unfortunately drew upon him the displeasure of his employers for attempting to impose upon them a *Horse-Mackerel* (as they call it) for a *Sea-Serpent!* He told me the story himself."

"(e). In this fervor of opinion, it was supposed for a time that a sea-serpent existed in Lake Ontario. A coasting navigator, somewhere between Kingston and York, had several times during his trips observed among the islands and rocks something that appeared to be a long animal with vertical flexures of the back, resembling lumps or humps of variegated black and white hues. He told some of his acquaintances what peculiar appearances had presented themselves to his view; and that he intended the next opportunity to take a more close and correct survey. He did so, shortly after, when the whole phenomenon ascended into the air! It turned out to be a speckled mother duck, with a numerous brood of young ones. They swam in a line, with the parent bird at the head. And as they rose and descended on the undulations, gave an appearance so like that ascribed to the sea-serpent, that the captain, though a wary man, would have solemnly declared, until he was undeceived, his belief in the existence of a sea-serpent there!"

"(f). Lake Erie brought forward pretensions too for a sea-serpent. One of the coasting vessels, navigated by three men, as she was steering eastward from Detroit, discovered something afloat on the hither side of the islands called 'The Sisters', which, when she arrived at the place of her destination on the southern shore, was reported by the men at the tavern and the printing office, to be the very creature. Mr. Printer wrote a paragraph on the subject, and inserted it in his paper, in which it travelled far and wide. It may be relied on that this alleged inhabitant of that inland sea, has been reduced to genus and species, by a distinguished naturalist, and registered very orderly in zoology. Now let us find what the production really turned out to be. The sheriff of the county, a sensible man, heard of the marvel, and conceiving that he knew as much about the lake as any person whatever, went on board full of curiosity, to make inquiry about it. He found but one of the people on board, whom he interrogated closely concerning the wonderful sight, with which he and his associates had entertained the neighbourhood. The sailor was soon implicated in contradictions. The querist, aware of the fellow's confusion, asked him if he was not ashamed to propagate such falsehoods? He then said, if the sheriff would not be affronted, he would relate the whole story just as it was. At the place aforesaid, they passed a dry tree afloat; and concluding that the butt or root would do for a head, some knots on the trunk for knobs or bunches, and the top for a tail, they would have a little pastime by telling a story of a sea-serpent, which they thought their lake was as much entitled to as any other water. The whole three had agreed to tell the same tale and support it!"

"(g). When the skin, &c. of the huge basking shark, that had straggled from the Northern Ocean and had been killed in Raritan Bay (*Squalus Maximus*), was exhibited in New York City, the inhabitants were openly and earnestly invited by notice in words at length displayed in front of the house, to enter and behold the sea-serpent. The conceit took very well!"

"Now, after all these mistakes, deceptions and wilful perversions on the subject, every person of consideration may admit that the gambols of porpoises, the slow motions of basking sharks, and the yet different appearances of balaenopterous whales, all of which have fins on their backs, may have given rise to those parts of the narrations, not already herein commented upon."

Professor Silliman, the editor of the journal, could not help saying in a note:

"We give place to the *scepticism* of the learned author, although not ourselves *sceptical* on this subject. We do not see how such evidence as that presented by Dr. Bigelow Vol. II p. 147 of this Journal—particularly in the statements of Capt. Little of the Boston Frigate, and of Marshall Prince and family, and of Mr. Cabot, can be set aside—although we have no doubt that there have been on this subject both error and imposition; and we are far from believing that every thing that has been called a sea-serpent has really been such."

Now in the whole dissertation there is not one single *proof* of the non-existence of the sea-serpent. Mr. Mitchill gathered some *hoaxes*, which no doubt greatly amused his audience, but his statements are sadly wanting in correctness. He says, that the sea-serpent *first* haunted the coast of Massachusetts, while if he in October 1828, had taken the trouble to look up the literature on the subject, he would have found that the sea-serpent had already appeared on the coasts of Norway, in the Northern Atlantic, in Davis' Straits, in the Northern Pacific near Behring's Isle, and all along the Eastern coasts of the United States. The Linnaean Society, he further asserts "published a book on the subject, with the figure of the enormous reptile under the name of *Scoliophis*". This is also untrue, for the Society only figured an individual of a sick and ill-formed *Coluber constrictor*, the so-called Black Snake, having only the length of about one yard. The "mutilated specimen of a snake" which was brought to him in alcoholic spirit, was the same figured by the Linnaean Society; and where Mr. Mitchill says that he is convinced that the snake was a common native of the land, "apparently a *Coluber*", he expresses an opinion which the Society already printed in their little book. Consequently he cannot claim priority in this matter. And finally, where he says that the story of the active young fellow with his sloop, called "the sea-serpent" is published in the aforesaid book of the Linnaean Society, he has told his audience and his readers what is commonly called "a falsehood", for in the whole book there is not one "formal and solemn account" in which there is question of "white and black colours" which "were variegated", of a "tail" which "lashed" the water, and of a motion of "six knots an hour, which made all white before him".

I may safely express here my opinion that the whole paper of Mr. Mitchill is an unscientific, deceptive dissertation, unworthy of notice, and that the way in which he ridiculed the endeavours of the Committee was unfair.

Another hoax which appeared in some American newspapers I have found, translated into German, in Froriep's *Notizen*, of 1830, June, Vol. XXVII, n°. 589, p. 265:

"Again a story about the sea-serpent will be found in American newspapers. Capt. Deland with the schooner *Eagle* ran into Charleston on the 27th. of March" (1830) "from Turtle River, and with his crew is willing to confirm by oath the truth of the following declaration: On the 23d. of March, at 11 o'clock A.M., at about a mile from Simons Bay, we perceived at the distance of about 300 yards a large body, resembling an alligator, which sometimes moved with the vessel, sometimes lay motionless on the surface. Capt. Deland, who perceived that he approached the animal, loaded a musket with a ball, and steered so, that he approached it within 20 or 25 yards at a moment that it lay quite still and apparently careless. Capt. Deland aimed with great sagacity at the hindpart of the head, the only part that was just visible, and the ball evidently struck. At this moment the monster, to the great terror of the crew, came directly up to the vessel, and in passing dealt her two or three heavy blows with its tail, of which the first struck the stem, and caused a shaking, felt by every-one on board. The Captain, as soon as he perceived the animal approach, jumped upon the load of cotton which lay on deck, and the whole crew, the mate not excepted, only thought of their safety. They all had opportunity to see their enemy and agree that its length was about 70 feet. The body was as thick as or thicker than a sixty-gallon keg, of a grey colour, eel-shaped, without visible fins and apparently covered with scales, the back full of joints or bunches, the head and beak resembled an alligator's, the former 10 feet long, and as big as a hogshead. A smaller individual was observed at a great distance (!), which, however, disappeared at the shot, afterwards, however, both were seen again together, when they passed the North-Breaker where they disappeared.— Captain D. says, that four years ago he saw a similar creature at some distance off Doboy and had fired four times at it; without, however, causing such a visit as in the present case. He believes, that this terrible undescribed animal has strength enough to damage a vessel of the size of the *Eagle*, if not to destroy it, and feels happy to have got rid of it in this way. He further asserts that he has certainly not erred with regard to the shape of the sea-monster, and that it was different from whales and other inhabitants of the deep, which he has ever witnessed" (*Chronicle*).

Though the description of the form might lead to the belief that what is reported to have been seen was a real sea-serpent, yet I consider the whole account as a story, because it is not the habit of the sea-serpent to attack a ship after having been struck by a ball, but to plunge down and to disappear.

Again the sea-serpent was said to have appeared in Lake Ontario. In Froriep's *Notizen* of August 1835, Vol. 45, n°. 980, p. 186, we read:

"The Colossal Sea-Serpent is again reported in the American newspapers. Now it is even told that it has been seen in Lake Ontario, 78 feet long, as thick as a large flour-barrel, and of a blue colour spotted with brown. If this is not an illusion, the sea-serpent at last ought to have been explained or will be so very soon".

It seems that Mr. Froriep really believes, that if this report is not the result of an optical illusion, it is trustworthy, and that the appearance of the Sea-Serpent in Lake Ontario does not belong to the impossibilities! Every one will agree with me, that the report can only be the result of an illusion, or that it is a hoax.

In 1845 Dr. Albert C. Koch "exhibited a large skeleton of a fossil animal, under the name of *Hydrarchos Sillimanni* in Broadway, New York, purporting to be that of an extinct marine serpent. These remains consisted of a head and vertebral column, measuring in all 114 feet, of a few ribs attached to the thoracic portion of the latter, and of parts of supposed paddles" (see *Proc. Boston Soc. Of Nat. Hist.* Nov. 1845, Vol. II, p. 65). I show here to my readers the figure of this skeleton, which I have found in the *Wochenblatt für das Christliche Volk* of 1878. The description of this skeleton in full particulars is given by Prof. Wyman in the above mentioned American Journal. I will not trouble my readers with it, but only mention that Prof. Wyman in the same paper proved that "these remains never belonged to one and the same individual, and that the anatomical characters of the teeth indicate that they are not those of a reptile, but of a warm blooded mammal". And he comes to the conclusion that the greater part of the bones belonged to the genus *Basilosaurus* of Harlan, 1824, an animal allied to the seals. The same genus is called *Zeuglodon* by Prof. Richard Owen in 1839, *Dorudon* by Prof. Gibbes in 1845, and *Saurocetus* by Prof. Agassiz.

In the same *Proceedings*, of Dec. 1845, Vol. II, p. 73, Prof. H. D. Rogers too states, that according to the form and structure of some loose bones, the skeleton must be of at least two individuals of *Basilosaurus*.

Cheats and Hoaxes

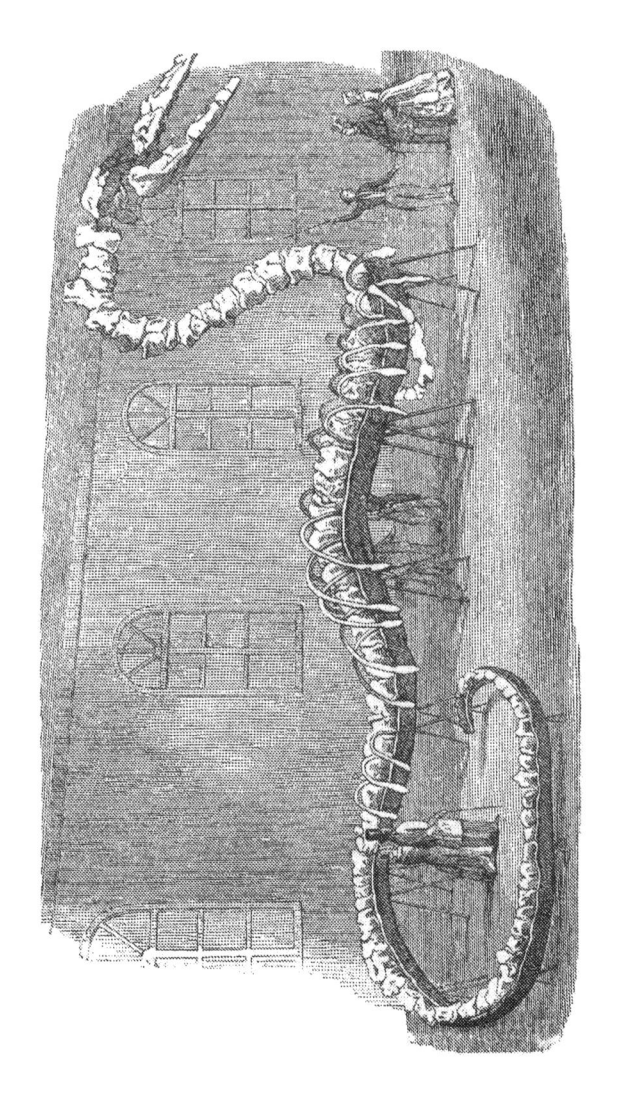

FIG. 2.—*HYDRARCHOS SILLIMANNI*, KOCH.

In the same periodical (of Jan. 1846, Vol. II, p. 94) we read that Dr. Koch also told the public that the bones had been found together, in a position which proved that they belonged to one individual, and that the vertebrae formed an integral series, arranged in the order in which they were lying when discovered. That this assertion too was a mere fabrication, is not only shown by Prof. Wyman, as we have seen above, but also in a letter by Dr. Lister, who stated that Dr. Koch had dug up the bones in *different* places in Alabama.

A little notice on this imposture was written by the New York correspondent in the *Cincinnati Gazette* which, translated into German, appeared in Froriep's *Neue Notizen* of Febr. 1846, Vol. 37, n° 801, p. 134.

In the *Illustrated London News* of Oct. 28, 1848, we read that Prof. Silliman attested: "that the spinal column belongs to the same individual, that the skeleton differs, most essentially, from any existing or fossil serpent, although it may countenance the popular (and I believe well founded) impression of the existence in our modern seas of huge animals, to which the name of Sea-Serpent had been attached".

These words were undoubtedly taken from another newspaper or journal, but I can hardly believe that Prof. Silliman had a share in this imposture.

In the *Illustrated London News* of Nov. 4, 1848, the Editor published a letter directed to him by the well-known Geologist and Palaeontologist Mantell:

"Sir,—Will you allow me to correct a statement that appeared in the last Number of your interesting publication? The fossil mentioned at the conclusion of the admirable notice of the so-called Sea-Serpent, as having been exhibited in America under the name of *Hydrarchos Sillimannii*, was constructed by the exhibitor Koch, from bones collected in various parts of Alabama, and which belonged to several individual skeletons of an extinct marine cetacean, termed *Basilosaurus* by the American naturalists, and better known in this country by that of *Zeuglodon*, a term signifying *yoked teeth*. Mr. Koch is the person who, a few years ago, had a fine collection of fossil bones of elephants and mastodons, out of which he made up an enormous skeleton, and exhibited it in the Egyptian Hall, Piccadilly, under the name of *Missourium*. This collection was purchased by the trustees of the British Museum, and from it were selected the bones which now constitute the matchless skeleton of a Mastodon in our National Gallery of Organic Remains".

"Not content with the interest which the fossils which he collected in various parts of the United States really possess, Mr. Koch, with the view of exciting the curiosity of the ignorant multitude, strung together all the vertebrae he could obtain of the *Basilosaurus*, and arranged them in a serpentine form; manufactured a skull and claws, and exhibited the monster as a fossil Sea-Serpent, under the name above mentioned—*Hydrarchos*. But the trick was immediately exposed by the American naturalists, and the true nature of the fossil bones pointed out.

"Bones of the *Basilosaurus* have been found in many parts of Alabama and South Carolina, in green sand belonging to a very ancient (Eocene) tertiary formation. Hundreds of vertebrae, bones of the extremities, portions of the cranium, and of the jaws with teeth, have from time to time been collected. Remains of species of the same genus have also been found near Bordeaux and in Malta".

"Professor Owen has shown that the original animal was a marine cetacean, holding an intermediate place between the Cachelots and the herbivorous species. It must have attained a length equal to that of the largest living whales; for a series of vertebrae was observed *in situ*, that extended in a line 65 feet. An interesting Memoir on the *Basilosaurus* by Dr. Gibbes, of Columbia, was published in the Journal of the Academy of Natural Sciences of Philadelphia, Vol. I, 2d. Series, 1847; and a Memoir on the remains of the same animal, by Prof. Owen appeared in the 'Transactions of the Geological Society of London', Vol. VI; a brief notice of which is inserted in my 'Medals of Creation' p. 826, under the name of *Zeuglodon cetoides*".

"Gideon Algernon Mantell".

"19, Chestersquare, Pimlico, Oct. 31. 1848".

In the *Proc. Bost. Soc. Nat. Hist.* (Vol. III, p. 328, Dec. 1850) we read:
"This animal" (the *Basilosaurus*) "was supposed by Dr. Koch to be a reptile, a marine serpent, but Dr. Wyman has exposed the fallacy of this opinion, and shown that it was a warm blooded mammal".

I do not think this to be the true view of the matter. I firmly believe that Dr. Koch knew very well what he did, and that he was in every way an impostor who cheated the credulous people of their money. The honour of the discovery that the *Basilosaurus* is a warm blooded mammal is due to Prof. Owen. Dr. Wyman has only recognized that the bones were of the *Basilosaurus*.

The further history of the large skeleton exhibited in New York is related to us in that same Journal:

"Koch's sea-serpent was carried to Dresden, where it was described by Carus, who figured it and even restored the cranium, of which then only a portion had been found. Carus restored the cranium of a reptile, but this was a mere fiction of his imagination; for an entire cranium has since been found, proving beyond a doubt that the Zeuglodon was not a reptile but a cetacean; the teeth being inserted by double roots into double alveoli is positive evidence that it was a warmblooded mammal. Müller has also carefully studied this specimen, and pronounces it unquestionably a cetacean."

The reader will further on see mention made of a report, generally known as that of the *Daedalus*. It appeared in the newspapers of October, 1848. As soon as it was published, the following letter was addressed to the Editor of the *Globe*. It first appeared in the number of 21. Oct., 1848, of that journal, next in the *Times* of 23d. Oct. and in the *Illustrated London News* of 28 Oct. It runs as follows:

"Mary Ann, of Glasgow, Glasgow, October 19".

"I have just reached this port, on a voyage from Malta and Lisbon, and my attention having been called to a report relative to an animal seen by the master and crew of Her Majesty's ship Daedalus, I take the liberty of communicating the following circumstance:—

"When clearing out of the port of Lisbon, on the 30th of September last, we spoke the American brig Daphne, of Boston, Mark Trelawney master. He signalled for us to heave to, which we did; and standing close round her counter, lay-to while the mate boarded us with the jolly boat, and handed a packet of letters to be despatched per first steamer for Boston on our arrival in England. The mate told me that when in lat. 4° 11' S., long. 10° 15' E., wind dead north, upon the 20th of September, a most extraordinary animal had been seen: from his description it had the appearance of a huge serpent or snake, with a dragon's head. Immediately upon its being seen, one of the deck guns was brought to bear upon it, which having been charged with spike-nails, and whatever other pieces of iron could be got at the moment, was discharged at the animal, then only distant about forty yards from the ship; it immediately reared its head in the air, and plunged violently with its body, showing evidently that the charge had taken effect. The Daphne was to leeward at the time, but was put about on the starboard tack and stood towards the brute, which was seen foaming and lashing the water at a fearful rate: upon the brig nearing, however, it disappeared, and, though evidently wounded, made rapidly off at the rate of 15 or 16 knots an hour, as was judged from its appearing several times upon the surface. The Daphne pursued for some time, but the night coming on the master was obliged to put about and continue his voyage".

"From the description given by the mate, the brute must have been nearly 100 feet long, and his account of it agrees in every respect with that lately forwarded to the admiralty by the captain of the Daedalus. The packet of letters to Boston, I have no doubt, contains the full particulars, which, I suppose, will be made public".

"There are letters from captain Trelawney to a friend in Liverpool, which will probably contain some further particulars, and I have written to get a copy for the purpose of getting the full account. James Henderson, Master, Broomielaw, Berth, n° 4".

The same story was inserted in the *Zoologist* of 27 Nov. 1848, and Mr. Newman the Editor who half a year before had fallen into the snare laid by the so-called captain Woodward, and who was taken to task by Mr. Cooper, grown more careful, now added:

"Doubtless the sagacious production of some selfstyled philosophical naturalist, who is pledged to one of the hypothetical modes of explaining away the existence of a sea-serpent, and who hopes by a hoax of this kind to throw discredit on Captain M'Quhae's statement".

Now, I think, Mr. Newman was on the right track!

In the *Illustrated London News* for 1850, April 20, Supplement, we read:

"The following we extract from the *Christian* (United States) *Mercury*.—The following letter from a gentleman of Beaufort gives exciting news of what may, by this time, be the 'seat of war'. The old fellow has got into close quarter, and if he does not make a sudden and fortunate dash, has nothing better than offering himself as an oblation on the altar of science:—Beaufort, March 15, 1850. The report of Captain Bankenship and passengers has been verified by many other witnesses. This formidable sea-monster has been seen again to day, we understand, in our waters. When discovered by those on board the steamer, his 'eminence' was in Port Royal Sound, a distance of seven or eight miles from this town. Since that time he has been lazily making his way up Broad River, and was seen by a gentleman, we understand, to-day in White Branch River, an arm of the Broad, he is reported to be making his way higher up still, when, perhaps, he may be captured. He is described as being from 120 to 150 feet in length, and of proportionate bulk; has the head of a serpent, which he carries, when in motion, five or six feet out of the water, about ten feet from his head is a hump, resembling a huge hogshead, and as far as he could be seen, out of the water a succession of humps was observed. He was pursued for several miles along the bank of the river, at times the party in pursuit coming very near to him. He was shot at with a rifle and shot gun, which had the effect of making him timid, and caused him to sink below the surface of the water when nearly approached. We understand that a party from this place has been made up to capture him, if possible. The plan is to man two large flats with a cannon to each, one going below where he is represented to be, and the other above, and then approach each other, and, when he is discovered, to fire into him. In this way he may be taken if, peradventure, he does not take them first. The Whale Branch is not more than 100 yards wide, and there is every probability of an animated conflict with this king of the waters within his own dominions; and I suppose it is admitted that the battle must be waged upon his own terms. The 'Charlestown Courier' has a letter from Beaufort, of the same date, and of a similar tenor to which is appended the following:—Information has just reached us that the said sea-serpent is ashore at the mouth of Skull Creek. If so, the prize is certain, and Beaufort immortalized."

Mr. Newman inserted this tale in his *Zoologist* of 1850, p. 2803, however, not without the following introduction:

"Ever since Prof. Owen attempted to confound this leviathan with the seals, on which he probably feeds, taking in whole shoals of them at a mouthful, and draining of the water with his *seaserpentbone* apparatus in the manner of a whale filling his stomach with medusae and shrimps: ever since the promulgation of this humilating hypothesis, the great sea-serpent has felt himself snubbled and has doggedly kept in deep water, pertinatiously resolved, no doubt, to withhold himself in future from the incredulous malevolence of men. But he has relented: the recurrence of St. Valentine has warmed his heart: he has once more risen to the surface, and has wisely concluded to shun the disparaging Britishers, and to select, as of yore, for the scene of his auto-exhibition, the shores of a nation, at once the smartest and most credulous on earth. The papers of the United States are fraught with intelligence respecting him; cannon have been discharged, and reports say that he is actually ashore. My first extract is from a religious newspaper, entitled the 'Christian Mercury.'"

The reader will afterwards get acquainted with Prof. Owen's suggestions; it is not now the right moment to enter into them; I will only observe that Mr. Newman also wrote the following last word:

"The London papers have repeated all this, intermixed with a perfect flood of wit: the shafts of which are directed against believers and unbelievers, in a very pleasing and impartial manner. Is it still a hoax, or a Brachioptilon Hamiltoni?—Edward Newman, London, April 20, 1850."

I must confess that I too am much inclined to believe, that all that has above been mentioned is a mere hoax, though the description of the animal agrees with that of the Sea-serpent. It is striking that the arm of the Broad-River is first called White-River, and a few lines afterwards Whale-River.—As to the *Brachioptilon Hamiltoni*, it is a kind of shark.

Again in the *Illustrated London News* for 1850, Sept. 7, appeared a hoax in the following terms:

"The *Cork Constitution* publishes the following circumstantial letter: Courtmasherry, Aug. 29.—Sir,—The following particulars, the accuracy of which need not to be questioned, will, I doubt not, interest many of your readers:—The different fishing establishments on the shore of this extensive bay, extending from the Old Head of Kinsale to the Seven Heads, have been within the last few days abundantly supplied with fish of every description, and the greatest activity prevails to profit by the bounty which has been thus sent to us literally in shoals. It has been noticed too, that some description of fish, haak for instance, has been captured further within the limits of the inner harbour than was ever known before. In fact, as I heard it observed, the fish was literally leaping ashore. These novel appearances, however, it was my lot to see fully accounted for yesterday (August 28). At about 1 o'clock A. M. when sailing in my yacht, with a slight breeze off shore, about two miles to the south of the beacon erected to the Barrel rocks, one of the party of four gentlemen on board (M. B. Of Bandon) drew attention towards the structure, with the interrogatory of: 'Do you see anything queer about the Barrels?' In an instant the attention of all on board was rivetted on an object which at first struck me as like the upheaved thick end of a large mast, but which, as it made out plainer, proved to be the head of some huge fish or monster. On bearing down towards the object we could distinctly see, with the naked eye, what I can best describe as an enormous serpent without mane or fur or any like appendage. The portion of the body above water, and which appeared to be rubbing or scratching itself against the beacon, was fully thirty feet long, and in diameter I should say about a fathom. With the aid of a glass it was observed that the eyes were of immense size, about nine inches across the ball, and the upper part of the back appeared covered with a furrowed shell-like substance. We were now within rifle shot of the animal, and, although some on board exhibited pardonable nervousness at the suggestion, it was resolved to fire a ball at the under portion of the body whenever the creature's unwieldy evolutions would expose its vulnerable part. The instant the piece was discharged the monster rose as if impelled by a painful impulse to a height which may appear incredible, say at least thirty fathoms, and culminating with the most rapid motion dived or dashed itself under water with a splash that almost stopped our breath with amazement. In a few moments all disturbance of the water subsided, and the strange visitor evidently pursued his course to seaward. On coming up to the beacon we were gratified to find adhering to the supports numerous connecting scaly masses, such as one would think to be rubbed from a creature 'coating' or changing its old skin for a new one. These interesting objects can be seen at the Horse Rock Coast Guard station, and will repay a visit. These particulars I have narrated in the clearest manner I am able, and if others, in other boats, who had not so good an opportunity of seeing the entire appearance of the animal as those in my boat had, should send you a more readable account of it, I pledge myself none will more strictly adhere to the real facts. I am, Sir, your very obedient servant, 'Roger W. Travers'", in the *Cork Constitution*, Sept. 2.

And in the number of September 14 of the same year, we read:

"The mysterious stranger has been again seen by Mr. Travers and his enterprising yachtsmen. They have brought four rifles to bear upon his left eye which, it seems, he most merrily winked at his pursuers. He would have laughed in his sleeve at the pleasant conceit, but we learn that he had just put off his coat. He, however, wished them a polite good morning, and descended to unknown depths".

"On Saturday last (August 31), the weather having the appearance of being settled fine, I put out to sea, determined, as far as the capabilities of my little craft would permit, to go any length in finding out the position of the stranger, hoping, by keeping a constant look out in every direction, to discover him. Nor was I disappointed, the animal, lured no doubt by the dense masses of fish now off the coast, having remained within a comparatively short distance of the land. At about 11 o'clock A. M., when off Dunwordy-head, one of my crew on the look out sang out: 'The sea-serpent on starboard bow' and on looking in the direction indicated, I had the pleasure of at once recognizing the same monster that I had before seen, and greatly do I regret, indeed, that you or some person conversant with natural history were not on board with me. We drew as close as I thought consistent with safety, and had ample proof of the creature being piscivorous, he being at the time engaged in bolting a great number of large haak or congereels. I had now for the first time a view of his tail, which entirely differs from the usual form of that extremity in most descriptions of fish, being furnished with no fin, but somewhat resembling a huge elephant's trunk or proboscis, the end long drawn out and curling and twisting in a very remarkable manner. I really feel afraid to hazard expressing in figures what I judge to be the dimensions of the animal, but I do believe that if it were stretched straight from head to tail it would be rather over than under thirty fathoms long, and of that length I am satisfied fully half is seven feet in diameter. The mouth is a most capacious organ, and opens something like that of an alligator. The small size of the gills, for I could discern nothing like the blowing holes of a whale, rather surprised me. The nose, I think, is formed of a soft flesh-like substance, not bony; and from the broken condition of the external coat of scales I am satisfied, as before observed, that the beast is now in its 'coating' state. After a little time it appeared evident that he had fallen asleep, as we could perceive him rapidly drifting on shore at the east side of Dunworly-head; and I once more, although I now feel with more rashness than discretion, resolved to try the effect of firearms in capturing him. Four rifles were prepared, brought simultaneously to bear on the animal's head, and, giving the word myself, and directing all to aim for the eye turned towards us, bang went the pieces in a volley, the shots taking evident effect. His first movement was to shake his head and wink the wounded eye in a rapid manner, and then, as if to cool the painful wound, he suddenly dived, since when I have not had the slightest trace of him either by my own observation or through others". *Cork Constitution*, Sept. 7.

"The *Cork Constitution*, referring to the foregoing says:— Since the above letter was received, the following information on the same subject came to hand. Monday last a party of gentlemen belonging to this city were enjoying a sailing excursion in the Antelope yacht, belonging to Mr. Wheeler, along the coast from Glandore to Kinsale. Passing the Old Head of Kinsale, the day unusually fine, they observed an extraordinary commotion in the sea, apparent to every one on board. The bay at Kinsale was at the time filled with fish. In a few moments they perceived a large serpent-like fish on the surface, that could not be less than 120 feet in length. In shape it resembled a long funnel of an immense steamer. Unfortunately they were not sufficiently near the monster to give a description, of the head and body. After lying on the surface for a few minutes, it suddenly dashed ahead with a velocity, as far as could be seen for a distance of two miles, of at least sixty miles an hour. It then disappeared. It was believed that the sea-serpent must have been in pursuit of the shoals of fish that thronged the bay. It is a singular circumstance that, notwithstanding the unusual quantity of fish that was observable, the Kinsale hookers were most unsuccessful, as it was stated they did not obtain a single take during the evening. The gentlemen who have witnessed the visit of the monster, and whose statement is detailed above, may be relied on as above all suspicion.—*Cork Constitution* Sept. 7.—

The *Zoologist* of course could not overlook such statements. In the year 1850 this journal inserted the three reports (see p. 2925):

"The Great Sea-Serpent has again appeared with immense *éclât* in the newspapers. Most respectable witnesses are called to speak a word in his favour, as will be seen by the following extracts from the daily press. It should, however, be premised that a number of brief and analogous paragraphs had previously located him 'at Howth', 'off Wexford', and 'off Cork'; so that he made the grand demonstration at Kinsale, he appeared to be taking a coasting trip round the shores of old Ireland."

Here follow the above mentioned three hoaxes, of Courtmasherry, August 29, August 31, and September 2. Further we read in the *Zoologist*:

"'A few friends accompanied me on a boating excursion this day (*Sept.* 9) whose names are William Silk, John Hunt, George Williams, Henry Seymour, and Edward Barry, and, being off the Souverein-Islands, our attention was directed by one of the party to an extraordinary appearance ahead of the boat; immediately all eyes were turned to see what it was, when, to our astonishment and fright, the above monster of the deep was bearing down to us; we were at once thrown into an awful fright, and thought it best to retreat for the shore; on our landing, Mr. W. Silk, who was armed with a double barrelled gun, discharged both barrels at the monster, but without effect. I need not describe his appearance, as you are aware of it before, but from inquiries from various boatmen I am told he has been off the harbour the last three days.'—John Good, of Kinsale." in *Cork Reporter*, Sept. 11.

Mr. Newman, the Editor of the *Zoologist*, adds:

"The next account states that a party encountered the monster in Ballycotton Bay, fired into him, and made him disgorge a shoal of fishes, some of which fell into the boat, and being handled, gave the crew the most terrific electric shocks; where upon the naturalist of the party immediately concluded, and I think, with great judgment, that the sea-serpent is neither more nor less than the electric eel (*Gymnotus electricus*)."

"The last account published in London, on this day (September 24), reports his capture and death at Youghal, in the county of Cork, together with full admeasurements, and the names of the parties concerned in the galant archievement."

"There was something that struck me as unsatisfactory about several parts of this highly exciting narrative. One o'clock in the morning, and without the assistance of a moon, was rather a strange time to make such exact observations. Again, about the scales; why not sent some to London or Dublin?—why keep them at the light-house? And again, the bearing of Kinsale bay did not quite correspond with my remembrance of the place: so I epistolized the chief actors, and particularly entreated Mr. Travers to send me a handful of scales, and a more detailed account: alas! there was no response. After a while I bethought myself of a friend in London who corresponds with the accountant of the Principal Bank at Bandon. To this gentleman my friend, with prompt kindness, applied, and I have now the pleasure of laying his most explicit answer before the readers of the 'Zoologist'."

"Dear Sir, I reply to your note relative to the Sea-Serpent, there is not one word of truth in the statements put forward in the newspapers: there is no such person

as Roger W. Travers, but there is a person named James W. Travers, to whom I believe it has been done to annoy (and indeed with great effect). Mr. Thomson's family has been staying in the neighbourhood, but do not hear a word of it except what is to be seen in the papers about it. Dear Sir, yours truly, H. O. 'Callaghan."
—Bandon, Sep. 18, 1850.

"Any comment on this would be superfluous.—Edward Newman."

The trouble Mr. Newman gave himself to get possession of the scales, and to know whether the reports were true or not, is the best proof that he was caught in the snare!

The Sea-Serpent caught at last! (See *The New York Tribune* for 1852, February, Galignani's *Messenger* for 1852, Februari, *The Illustrated London News* for 1852, March, 13, *The Times* for 1852, March 10, *The Zoologist* for 1852 p. 3426-3429, *Spenerishe Zeitung* for 1852, March).

"Ship Monongahela, at Sea, Feb. 6.—A small vessel has just been reported from my mast-head, and as she is apparently bound into some of the northern parts, I intend to speak her, purposely to acquaint, through your widely diffused journal, the people of the United States, of the fact of the existence and capture of the sea-serpent—a monster deemed fabulous by many—but the truth of whose existence is for ever settled, and, I trust I shall be excused in saying, by Yankee intrepidity. On the morning of January 18, when in lat. 13 deg. 10 min. south, and long. 131 deg. 50 min. west, the man on the look out, seated on the foretopmast cross-trees, sang out: 'White Water' and in reply to my 'Where away?' said 'Two points on the lee bow'. Supposing it to be made by sperm whales, and being very anxious to obtain oil, I ordered my ship to be kept off, and immediately went aloft with my spyglass. I will observe that for several days we had been struggling along with very light and baffling winds, but at daylight of the morning of the 13th. the wind had drawn to the south-south-west, become steady, and threatened to blow a gale. I was aloft nearly half an hour before I observed anything like 'white water' and then I presumed it to be made by a 'school', or rather schoal of porpoises; but wishing to be certain, I ordered the mate, as it was seven bells, to turn up all hands, square in the yards, and send out the port studding sails. It being my breakfast hour I urged the man to keep both eyes open, and came down; but before I reached the deck my attention was called to the sudden and vehement cry of Onnetu Vanjau, a Marquesan Islander, 'Oh! look! look! Me see!—too much—too much!' All eyes were instantly directed to the savage to ascertain where he was looking, and then all eyes turned to the lee quarter. I had just time to see 'black skin' when it disappeared. The native was excited, and in reply to my question said: 'No whale—too much—too big—too long. Me no see all same dat fellar—me fraid'. Not being able to tell which way the animal or fish was bound, I luffed and came aback, ordering the lines into the boat and the crews to 'stand by'. The horizon was scanned in every direction for nearly an hour, when giving up all hopes I braced forward and went below. The native continued to look with eagerness, pushed on by the observations of the crew, who asserted that he had seen nothing, but he proved the truth of his sight in a few minutes by uttering another cry, and with more vehemence than the first. I rushed on deck, and the first look, not a mile to leeward, rested on the strangest creature I had ever seen in the ocean. It was apparently still, but 'shobbing' up and down, as we say of sperm whales. I knew it was not a whale. The head I could not see, but the body had a motion like the waving of a rope when shaken and held in the hand. Every eye in the ship regarded it attentively, and not a word was spoken or sound uttered. In a few minutes the whole length of the body rose and lay on the water; it was of an enormous length. Presently the extremity or tail moved or vibrated, agitating the water, and then the head rose entirely above the water, and moved sideways slowly, as if the monster was in agony or suffocating. 'It is a sea-serpent' I exclaimed; 'stand by the boats'. There was a hesitancy, and the mate said, 'of what use is there lowering for him? We only lose time, and gain nothing besides.' I abruptly checked him, and ordered all hand to be called aft. When they had mustered I told them I wished to 'try' that fellow. I urged them with all the eloquence I possessed, telling them there were but few who believed in the existence of a sea-serpent, and that a wish had been expressed that a whale ship might fall in with one of them—that if we did not attack him, and should tell of seeing him when we got home, we should be laughed at and derided—and the very first question would be: 'Why didn't you try him?' I told them our courage was at stake—our manhood, and even the credit of the whole American whalefishery, and concluded by appealing to their cupidity—holding out that we might possibly get him into some southern port. 'I do not order one of you to go in the boats', I said 'but who will volunteer?' Let me say to their credit, every American in the ship stepped out at once, followed by all but one native and two Englishmen. I ordered the boat-steerers and officers to examine and see that everything in and about the boats was in perfect order. I had already jumped into my boat w hen the serpent began to move very rapidly, and it was necessary to stand after him. The wind was piping up strongly, but as we gained I continued to carry all sail, hoping to be able to lower before the gale rendered it impossible. The serpent worked to windward, which compelled me to haul on the wind, and soon after I carried away my fore topgallant mast; this was most unlucky for us, and, what was still worse, we lost sight of the monster. We repaired damages with all possible despatch, and still kept on the wind, hoping to see his snakeship. In less than an hour we saw him again, but some way to windward; soon ascertaining that he partly turned, and was headed baft for beam, I put the ship about on the other tack. The wind had increased so much, that I was obliged to put a single reef in the fore and mizen topsails. The serpent disappeared for a few minutes again, but when he rose he was a mile ahead of the ship, and going slowly to leeward, having made a complete circuit. I frankly admit my hopes were feeble of ever really capturing him, and the gale made me hesitate about lowering; but the time arrived, the serpent was still, and we nearly half a mile to windward. I came to with the head yards aback to have a better control of all the ship, and told the ship-keeper to keep close to us, and by no means to lose sight of us for an instant. We lowered, myself taking the lead, and in a few strokes—the wind and sea carrying us to leeward—I told the boat-steerer, James Wittemore, of Vermont, to 'stand up'. With calm and cool intrepidity he laid hold of his iron (harpoon), and, when I beckoned with a movement of my hand, quick as thought both of his weapons were buried to the socket in the repulsive body before us. I shouted 'stern, but there was no visible motion of his snakeship. I shifted ends with the boatsteerer, and cleared away a lance as quickly as possible, beckoning them to pull up, that I might get a lance, when a movement of the body was visible, and the head and tail of the monster rushed as it were to 'touch the wound'. The frightfulness of the head as it approached to boat, filled the crew with terror, and three of them jumped over board. I instinctively held out my lance, and its sharp point entered the eye. I was knocked over and felt adeep churning off the water around me. I rose to the surface and caught a glimpse of the writhing body, and was again struck and carried down. I partly lost my consciousness under water but recovered it, when I rose again in the bloody foam, the snake had disappeared, and I shouted, 'pick up the line'. The third mate Mr. Benson, caught a bight at my line near the end, and bent on his, which in an instant began to be taken out rapidly. The mate picked me up as soon as I rose to the surface, and in a few minutes all were picked up—one was severely bruised and another insensible, but he recovered and both are now well. The snake had taken my line, the third mate's, and was taking the second mate's, when I ordered the mate to bend on and give his line to the ship. The snake was sounding, and I cautioned the officers not to hold on too hard, for fear of drawing the irons. At first the line went out rapidly, but decreased gradually, nevertheless I was obliged to get up a spareline out of the fore hold and bend on. For fear that the ship would by its weight on the line draw the irons, I put on several drags and gave the line to the mate, when it became stationary. There were now out four boats' lines, 225 fathoms in a boat, and two-thirds of another line, 100 fathoms more—in all 1,000 fathoms, six feet in a fathom, 6,000 feet—better than one mile and an eighth, an enormous depth, and the pressure at that distance is inconceivable. It was now blowing furiously, and I scarcely dared to carry sail enough to keep the ship up, the boat was in peril, and I was obliged to take the line to the ship again, and run the risk of the irons drawing. I made the end of the line fast and took in all sail but enough to keep her steady, and waited in alarm the snake's rising, the parting of the line, or the irons drawing. At 4 p.m. the wind began to shift, which favoured us a little; at 5 p.m. it, to our great joy, began to abate. At 8 p.m. a sudden lull; line taut. The night was beautiful, sky clear, wind scarcely abreath and sea rapidly falling, no eye was closed in the ship—we were speculating on our prey. It was evident he was on the bottom. He stayed down a long time; but on reflection I considered that was his *forte*—that he was at home there. At 4 a.m. of the 14th., 16 hours after he went down, the line began to slack, I had it taken to the windlass, when we got nearly two lines "hand over hand", then there came a strain again. This strain continuing, I told every body to bear a hand and get breakfast, and just before we were through, the cook cried out, 'Here he is'. In no time all were on deck, and sure enough he had risen; but all that was visible was a bunch, apparently the bight of the snake, where he had been fastened to. I lowered three boats, and we lanced the body repeatedly without eliciting any sign of life. While we were at work he gradually rose to the surface, and around him floated what I took to be pieces of his lungs which we cut with our lances. To make our work sure we continued to lance, eagerly seeking for his life, when he drew himself up and we pulled away, and then witnessed the terrific dying struggles of the monster. None of the crew who witnessed that terrible scene will ever forget it; the evolutions of the body were rapid as lightning, seeming like the revolving of a thousand enormous black wheels. The tail and head would occasionally appear in the surging bloody foam, and a sound was heard, so dead, unearthy, and expressive of acute agony, that a shrill of horror ran through our veins. The convulsive efforts lasted 10 or 15 minutes, when they suddenly stopped, the head was partially raised—it fell—the body partly turned, and lay still. I took off my hat, and nine terrific cheers broke simultaneously from our throats. Our prey was dead. Luckily he floated buoyantly, and we took him alongside, and while doing so he turned over, lying belly up. Every eye beamed with joy as we looked at him over the rail, and the crew again cheered vociferously, and I joined them. We now held a consultation as to what we should do, and I had requested all hands to offer their opinions. After a short talk, all of us felt convinced that it would be impossible to get him into port, and then we concluded to try and save his skin, head, and bones, if possible. In the first place I requested a Scotchman, who could draw tolerably, to take a sketch of him as he lay, and the mate to measure him. It was now quite calm, and we could work to advantage. As I am preparing a minute description of the serpent, I will merely give you a few general points. It was a male; the length 103 feet 7 inches; 19 feet 1 inch around the neck; 24 feet 6 inches around the shoulders; and the largest part of the body, which appeared somewhat distended, 49 feet 4 inches. The head was long and flat, with ridges; the bones of the lower jaw are seperate; the tongue had its end like the head of a heart. The tail ran nearly to a point, on the end of which was a flat firm cartilage. The back was black, turning brown on the sides; then yellow, and on the centre of the belly a narrow white streak two-thirds of its length; there were also scattered over the body dark spots. On examining the skin we found, to our surprise, that the body was covered with blubber, like that of a whale, but it was only four inches thick. The oil was clear as water, and burnt nearly as fast as spirits of turpentine. We cut the snake up, but found great difficulty, and had to 'flense' him, the body would not roll, and the blubber was so very elastic, that when stretched 20 feet by the blocks, it would, when cut off, shrink to 5 or 6 feet. We took in the head, a frightful object, and are endeavouring to preserve it with salt. We have saved all the bones, which the men are not done clearing yet. In cutting open the serpent we found pieces of squid and a large blackfish, the flesh of which dropped from the bones. One of the serpent's lungs was three feet longer than the other. I should have observed that there were 94 teeth in the jaws, very sharp, all pointing backward and as large as one's thumb at the gum, but deeply and firmly set. We found it had two spoutholes or spiracles, so it must breathe like a whale; it also had four swimming paws, or imitations of paws, for they were like hard, loose flesh. The joints of the back were loose, and it seemed as if, when it was swimming that it moved two ribs and a joint at a time, almost like feet. The muscular movement of the serpent after it was dead made the body look as if it were encircled by longitudinal ridges. We were nearly three days in getting the bones in, but they are now nearly clean, and are very porous and dark coloured. The heart I was enabled to preserve in liquor, and one of the eyes, but the head, notwithstanding it is cool, begins to emit an offensive odour; but I am so near the coast now that I shall hold on to it as it is; unless it is likely to breed a distemper. Every man in the ship participates in my anxiety. 2 p.m. I have just spoken the vessel; she proves to be the brig Gipsy, Captain Sturges, eight days from Ponce, P. R., with oranges and merchandise, bound to Bridgeport. He has kindly offered to put these sheets in the post office when he arrives. As soon as I get in I shall be enabled to furnish you a more detailed account.—I am, Sir, your obedient servant, Charles Seabury, Master, Whale-ship Monongahela, of New Bedford."

Mr. Newman, the Editor of the *Zoologist*, adds:

"Very well like a hoax, but well drawn up."

Mr. Robert Froriep, the Editor of the *Tagsberichte über die Fortschritte der Natur- und Heilkunde*, (Abtheilung Zoologie und Palaeontologie n°. 486, 1852, March), says:

"The picturesque description of the adventure is lively and reads pleasantly, yet it makes the impression, as if the whole is one of the stories, so often occurring in American newspapers. Nothing can be concluded with any certainty from the description of the animal of 104 feet length and 16 feet thickness, with two spoutholes and a skin like that of whales. The intrepid captor of the monster says that he has preserved the bones, the skin, the skull with its flesh adhering to it, an eye and the heart, and as he must come back ashore, a naturalist will at last have opportunity to examine and determine these remains, and we shall learn then, whether the fable of the Sea-Serpent is founded, and what the Sea-Serpent may probably be. As soon as possible we will mention more accurate reports."

Some time afterwards Mr. Robert Froriep wrote, (same journal n°. 491):

"As it was supposed, we learn from a communication of the *Philadelphia Bulletin* that the story of the capture of the Sea-Serpent is a fiction. The crew that was said by the *New York Tribune* to have met with the ship of Captain Seabury in the open sea and to have taken home the report, has declared, that it has nowhere met with a ship *Monongahela*, Captain Seabury."

Another reported capture of a sea-serpent was published in the *Buffalo Daily Republic*, of the 13th. of August, 1855, partly inserted in the *Illustrated London News* of the 15th. of September, of that year, and *in toto* in the *Zoologist* of that year, p. 4896, and in the *Times* of October, 1, 1855:

"The 'Buffalo Daily Republic' of the 13th. of August, announces the capture of the great American water-snake on that day in the Silver Lake, near Perry Village, New York. On Sunday, the 12th. the snake came to the surface, displaying 30 feet length of his body. On Monday morning all were on the alert. At nine o'clock the snake appeared between the whaleman's boat and the shore: he lay quiescent on the surface, and the whaleman's boat moved slowly towards him, Mr. Smith, of Covington, pointing his patent harpoon. On reaching within ten feet of the snake, the iron whistled in the air, and he darted off towards the upperpart of the lake, almost dragging the boat under water by his movement. Line was given him, and in half an hour his strength seemed much exhausted. The whaleman then went ashore and gradually hauled the line in. When within fifty feet of the shore, the snake showed renewed life, and with one dart nearly carried off the whole line; but he was dragged slowly ashore amid excitement unexampled in the district. Four or five ladies fainted on seeing the snake, who, although ashore, lashed his body into tremendous folds, and then straightened himself out in agony with a noise that made the earth tremble. The harpoon had penetrated a thick muscular part, eight feet from his head. He is 59 feet 8 inches in length, and has a most disgusting look. A slime a quarter of an inch thick covers his body, and if removed is instantly replaced by exudation. The body is variable in size. The head is the size of a full grown calf. Within eight feet from the head the neck gradually swells to the thickness of a foot in diameter; it then tapers down, and again gradually swells to a diameter of two feet in the centre, giving about six feet girth; it then tapers off towards the tail, and ends in a fin, which can expand in fan-shape three feet across, or close in a sheath. Double rows of fins are alternately placed along the belly. The head is most singular. The eyes are large, staring and terrific, with a transparent membrane attached to the lids, protecting the eye without impeding the vision. No gills appear. The mouth is like that of the fish called a sucker; it can stretch so as to swallow a body a foot and a half in diameter: there are no teeth; a bony substance, extending in two parallel lines, covers the upper and lower part of the head. The sides and back are dusky brown; the belly is dirty white. Although sinuous like a snake, there are hard knot-like substances along the back. The harpoon is still in him. He lies in the water, confined with ropes, which keep his body in a curve, so that he cannot get away. He can use his head and tail, with which he stirs the water all around. When he rears his head (which he generally keeps under water) he presents a fearful aspect. In expanding his mouth he exhibits a blood-red cavity, horribly to look at, and the air rushes forth with a heavy short puff."

The well known Mr. Spencer F. Baird, the late zealous Secretary of the *Smithsonian Institution*, Washington, U. S. on reading this in the *Zoologist*, sent to the Editor the following letter (*Zoologist*, 1856, p. 4998):

"In the November number of the 'Zoologist' (Zool. 4896) I notice an extract from an American paper, respecting the capture of the 'Great American Snake'. You have probably since learned that the account is an unmitigated hoax, manufactured by a newspaper-editor, while on a summer vacation, for the purpose of furnishing material for his editorial correspondence.—Spencer F. Baird, Smithsonian Institution Washington, U. S. December 28, 1855."

The following splendid trick is of Captain Taylor, who is even called "a respectable and trustworthy gentleman", nay, who, when the truth of it was inquired into, even "confirmed the statement"!

In the *Zoologist* of 1860, p. 6985, we read:

"The following extract from the log of the 'British Banner', which arrived at Liverpool on Sunday, 18 March, last, appeared in the Liverpool Daily Post of March 20. "On the 25th. April in lat. 12° 7' east, and longitude 93° 52' south, felt a strong sensation as if the ship were trembling. Sent second mate to see what was up; the latter called out to me to go up the fore rigging and look over the bows. I did so, and saw an enormous serpent shaking the bowsprit with his mouth. There was about thirty feet of the serpent out of the water, and I could see in the water abaft of our stern; must have been at least three hundred feet long; was about the circumference of a very wide crinoline petticoat, with black back, shaggy mane, horn on his forehead, and large glaring eyes, placed rather near the nose, and jaws about eight feet long; he did not observe me, and continued to shake the bowsprit and to throw the sea alongside into a foam, until the former came clear away of the ship. The serpent was powerful enough, although the ship was carrying all sail, and going at about six knots at the time, he attacked us, to stop her way completely. When the bowsprit with the jibboom sails and rigging went by the board, the monster swallowed the foretopmast staysail and flying jib, with the greatest apparent ease; he also snapped the thickest of the rigging asunder like thread. He sheered off a little after this, and returned apparently to scratch himself against the side of the ship, making a most extraordinary noise, resembling that on board a steamer when the boilers are blowing off. A whale breached within a mile of the ship at this time, and the serpent darted off after it like a hash of lightning, striking the vessel with his tail, and staving in all the starboard quarter gally. Saw no more of it, but caught a young one in the afternoon, and brought it on to Melbourne.—*William Taylor, Master, 'British Banner'*."

"[The British Banner arrived here on Sunday, and is now in the Albert Dock. Captain Taylor declares that the above statement is perfectly correct.—*Editor Daily Post.*]"

Mr. Edward Newman, the Editor of the *Zoologist*, adds hereto:

"It is impossible for any story to read more like a hoax than this, but I had ready means of procuring, through a friend at Lloyd's, the information that there is such a ship as the 'British Banner', that she is commanded by Mr. William Taylor, a respectable and trustworthy gentleman, and that she did arrive at Liverpool on Sunday, 18 March, last past, and is now in the Albert Dock. Armed with this information I wrote to Capt. Taylor, who has replied in the most courteous manner; he confirms the above statement, adding that he sent it to the Daily Post himself, and adding also that the young one reported to have been caught was presented to the Museum at Melbourne, were it was thoroughly inspected and pronounced to be a veritable sea-serpent."—

It is not quite clear whether Mr. Newman was a second time the dupe of a trick, or not, but I think he really was!

Mr. George Guyon, Ventnor, Isle of Wight, on the contrary, wrote the following poem (see *Zoologist*, p. 7051, 1860):

"I've a story to tell—I don't say that it 's true—
But just as I heard it I tell it to you.
A ship there was sailing upon the blue sea
With her canvas all set, when the captain, said he
'I feel that the vessel is all of a tremble,
A sort of sea earthquake it seems to resemble;
Send forward the mate to see what is the matter.'
When lo! what he saw would have made your teeth shatter,
An enormous big snake rising out of the sea,
Some three hundred feet long it might possibly be,
And in bulk it might equal a 'wide crinoline'
(At least seven yards round that description must mean).
With jaws eight feet long, and with eyes fiercely glaring,
A horn and a mane; he looked horribly daring,
While the bowsprit he shook in his terrible mouth.
'T was in Latitude east and in Longitude south,
This is somewhat obscure, but I think on the whole
It occurred th' other side of the Antarctic pole,
The ship making six knots—leaving foam in her wake,
Yet she stopped at the touch of this wonderful snake;
And the Jibboom and bowsprit were snapped like a straw;
But his strength was outdone by his marvellous maw;
For he swallowed the stay-sail and also the jib,
Like a boy gulping oysters—they went down to glib.
With his stay to his stomac he turned him about,
And gave with his tail such a vigorous flout,
That some timbers to atoms were crushed by the blow,
And what more might have happened we none of us know,
When an object appeared for the which he set sail,
And both object and story were much like a whale."

Afterwards, (*Zoologist*, p. 7278, of the same year) we find the following about the young sea-serpent of Captain Taylor:

"Captain Taylor's Sea-Serpent.—A friend, who has the opportunity of communicating with Melbourne on the subject of the young sea-serpent which Captain Taylor says (Zool. 6985) he presented to the Museum at Melbourne, has ascertained through Mr. Coates, of that town, that Captain Taylor is so far correct, that he did at the time specified present a specimen of *Pelamys bicolor* to the Museum in question, and Professor M'Coy exhibited the same to Mr. Coates. Of course there is no rational ground for concluding that this small sea snake is the young of any such gigantic creature as Captain Taylor has described.—*Edward Newman*."

But of a *great* Sea-Serpent of Captain Taylor we don't find any more statements!

We have read the various hoaxes which appeared in the *Cork Constitution* of 1850; the *Skibbereen Eagle* too is not averse to publishing a similar hoax (See Zoologist, 1861, p. 7354):

"As Samuel Townsend, Esq., J. P., of Whitehall, was sailing in Whitehall Harbour, he saw, following his wake, what appeared to him (from the many descriptions he had read of the monster) to be a sea-serpent about twenty five or thirty feet in length; and being in a small boat he endeavoured to keep as respectful a distance as possible. There was, however, another boat in the harbour at the time, in which was Mr. Samuel Hingston, his brother, Mr. John Hingston (of Trinity College, Dublin), and a party of ladies. These parties also saw the huge monster; and upon raising its neck about six feet above the surface the females became greatly alarmed, when Mr. John Hingston, who is a remarkably good shot, fired at it, upon which it immediately disappeared. Mr. Townsend informed us the serpent presented a beautiful appearance, having large, brilliant scales of a yellow hue, and is of opinion it was struck by the shot fired by Mr. Hingston. It was likewise distinctly seen from the windows of Whitehall-House. Mr. Robert Atkins told us he saw it the day before of Barlogue."—

The following hoax is not inferior to any of the foregoing (Nature, of 13th. of June 1872):

"Mr. J. Cobbin of Durban, forwards to the *Natal Colonist* the following account of a 'sea-serpent' seen by him:—'During my last passage from London, I saw no less than three sea-serpents, but an account of the last will suffice. On 30th. December last, on board the *Silvery Wave*, in lat. about 35' 0" S., and long. 33' 30" E., at 6.20 P.M. solar time, an enormous sea-serpent passing nearly across our bows compelled the alteration of our course. He was at least one thousand yards long, of which about one third appeared on the surface of the water at every stroke of his enormous fan-shaped tail, with which he propelled himself, raising it high above the waves, and arching his back like a landsnake or a caterpillar. In shape and proportion he much resembled the cobra, being marked by the same knotty and swollen protuberance at the back of the head on the neck. The latter was the thickest part of the serpent. His head was like a bull's in shape, his eyes large and glowing, his ears had circular tips and were level with his eyes, and his head was surrounded by a horny crest, which he erected and depressed at pleasure. He swam with great rapidity and lashed the sea into a foam, like breakers dashing over jagged rocks. The sun shone brightly upon him; and with a good glass I saw his overlapping scales open and shut with every arch of his sinuous back coloured like the rainbow.'"

I don't know whether the following, taken from the *Graphic*, is a true hoax, or an optical illusion, but I think it is a hoax. There we read in the number of August, 17th., 1872:

"Concerning this much discussed animal, whose existence mariners from the earliest times have firmly asserted, and landsmen as obstinately persisted in doubting, we have received the following from Mr. Walthew, a well-known ship-owner and merchant in Liverpool:—'Report of Captain A. Hassel, of barque *St. Olaf*, from Newport to Galveston, Texas.—Two days before arrival at Galveston, and about 4.30 P. M. on May 13, weather calm, smooth sea, lat. 26° 52', long. 91° 20', I saw a shoal of sharks passing the ship. Five or six came under the vessel's stern, but before we could get out a line they went off with the rest. About two minutes after, one of the men sang out that he saw something on the weather bow, like a cask on its end. Presently another one called out that he saw something rising out of the water like a tall man. On a nearer approach we saw it was an immense serpent, with its head out of the water, about 200 ft. from the vessel. He lay still on the surface of the water, lifting his head up, and moving the body in a serpentine manner. Could not see all of it; but what we could see, from the after part of the head, was about 70 ft. long and of the same thickness all the way, excepting about the head and neck, which were smaller, and the former flat, like the head of a serpent. It had four fins on its back, and the body of a yellow greenish colour, with brown spots all over the upper part and underneath white. The whole crew were looking at it for fully ten minutes before it moved away. It was about six feet in diameter. One of the mates has drawn a slight sketch of the serpent, which will give some notion of its appearance.—A. Hassel, master of Norwegian barque St. Olaf.—Witness to signature, J. Fredk. Walthew.'"—

The accompanying engravings are also published, and I give facsimiles of them in Fig. 3 and 4.—I think that Captain Hassell after having seen the shoal of sharks, two minutes afterwards saw four of these individuals swimming perfectly in a line, the foremost occasionally lifting its head above the surface, and the backs with the backfin of each animal being visible. The distance between the first and the last being about seventy feet, the whole row looked like a huge serpent, and gave thus rise to the story, which, as I have already said above, may be a hoax, or a true statement of what they saw. Evidently one of the mates first drew the sketch exactly as he saw the four sharks, but afterwards, answering his own question: "how would the serpent look, if floating on the surface?" sketched the second figure, where a boa or python with four fins is represented floating on the water like a cork, or better like the skin of such an animal puffed up!

54 The Great Sea-Serpent

FIG. 3 AND 4.–WOULD BE SEA-SERPENT SEEN NEAR GALVESTON.

A splendid hoax was again communicated by a correspondent of the *Monde Illustré* to the Editor, and published in the number of October, 8, 1881, of that journal.

"On board the steamer *The Don*, of the Royal Mail Steam Packet Company.— Captain Robert Woolward."
    "Sunday, August 14, 1881".
"To the Editor."
"I commence my letter by asking you a correspondent's diploma of the journal *Le Monde Illustré* for my friend Mr. E. de Contreras y Alcantara, an inhabitant of Ponce, Isle of Porto Rico, Spanish colony."
"I owe to Mr. de Contreras the subjoined sketch, the exactness of which is guaranteed by the seven signatures of the eye witnesses, who are:
    "Mr. E. de Contreras y Alcantara, of Ponce, Isle of Porto Rico,
    "Mr. Carlo Lopez Aldana, of Lima, Peru,
    "Mr. Henrique Roman, of Cartagena, Columbia,
    "Mr. A. E. Ximenes de San José, of Costa Rica,
    "Mr. Maurice Renard, of Paris,
    "Mr. C. Renard, of Paris, your correspondent.
"The appearance lasted for ten minutes, in full moonlight. As I made the sketch, my son noted down his observations, Mr. Contreras too; we compared and exchanged our several observations, these gentlemen at the little window of the smoking-saloon, and I just above, resting upon the port-hole and supported by a rope."
"The monster seemed to measure about forty or fifty meters, from the head to the tail, as far as the numerous coils made an approximative estimation possible. The body from the dorsal ridge to the midst of the belly seemed to be covered by several ranges of scales, or a rough skin like that of sharks, but forming overlapping layers of scales. The back is very darkish and gradually growing lighter towards the belly, where it is a dirty grey. The entire body is marked with alternating transversal stripes, darkish green, chesnut coloured, and grey; the tail seems to taper in a point, like that of eels. I preserve for the end the description of the head, which we have properly examined, and which is very remarkable. This head is not oval, and rather pointed, as in most of the snakes; it forms at its cranium a great mass with rough and irregular outlines. From the occiput it is provided with a hard and movable crest, with very sharp points; this crest may be lowered on the neck so as to become invisible. The upper jaw projects, as is shown in the sketch, the end is doubled up, and a dark hollow, like a nostril is visible there; the lower jaw, more pointed, shows below hollow and convex outlines, like sacs, doubtless for the act of swallowing. The teeth are sharp, enormous, and white. From the throat, attached to a kind of cushion, projects a hard tongue, pointed, provided with suckers, and glittering like steel, and phosphorescing as the sea occasionally does; the eye is round, very glittering, very movable, and seems to be able to look backward, so rapid and '*bien combinées*' are the animal's evolutions; the orbit is bordered by a ring of lighter colour and seems to be overarched by an eye-brow provided with hairs or bristles."
"The face, from the snout to the neck presents a lateral oblique line, grey in colour, on both sides of which three other similar lines run towards it."
"The movement of the animal in the water, seems to produce no sound at all, but undulating waves and a very slight ripple."

"It caused a stench enough to make one ill; this smell, which hung about us for more than half an hour, was like that of a fermentation by heat on a large scale of the house of Lesage, the great gatherers of Asnières, mingled with that of a dozen of charcoal-black works of Billancourt."

"To neutralize it, all the shops of several of our best perfumers would be wanted."

"The monster seems to be old, judging partly from its dimensions, and partly from its colour and the roughness of its integument."

"This is not the first time that similar animals are observed.

"The first time it was seen in 1847 by the Portuguese ship *Ville de Lissabonne*, captain Juan Alphonso Zarco y Capeda."

"This date coincides with the buffooneries of the *Charivari* on the *Constitutionel*, and with the first disease of the potatoes."

"In 1864, the second of *The Don* observed a similar animal near the coast of Japan; he tattooed it on his arm."

"I end this series of reports by assuring you that the monster was seen on wednesday evening, August 10, 1881, by the undersigned, at a quarter to ten P. M. in

    latitude 29° 60'

    longitude 42° 40'

reckoning the degrees, according to the log-book on board, from the meridian of Greenwich."

"C. Renard."

"(Here follow the seven signatures above-mentioned)."

The Editor of the *Monde Illustré* adds:

"We leave to the author of this letter and of the subjoined sketch all the responsibility of an assertion which seems to us, least to say, strange, and the details of which we communicate to our readers with due reserve."

Let us now pass on to reports of would-be sea-serpents.

Cheats and Hoaxes

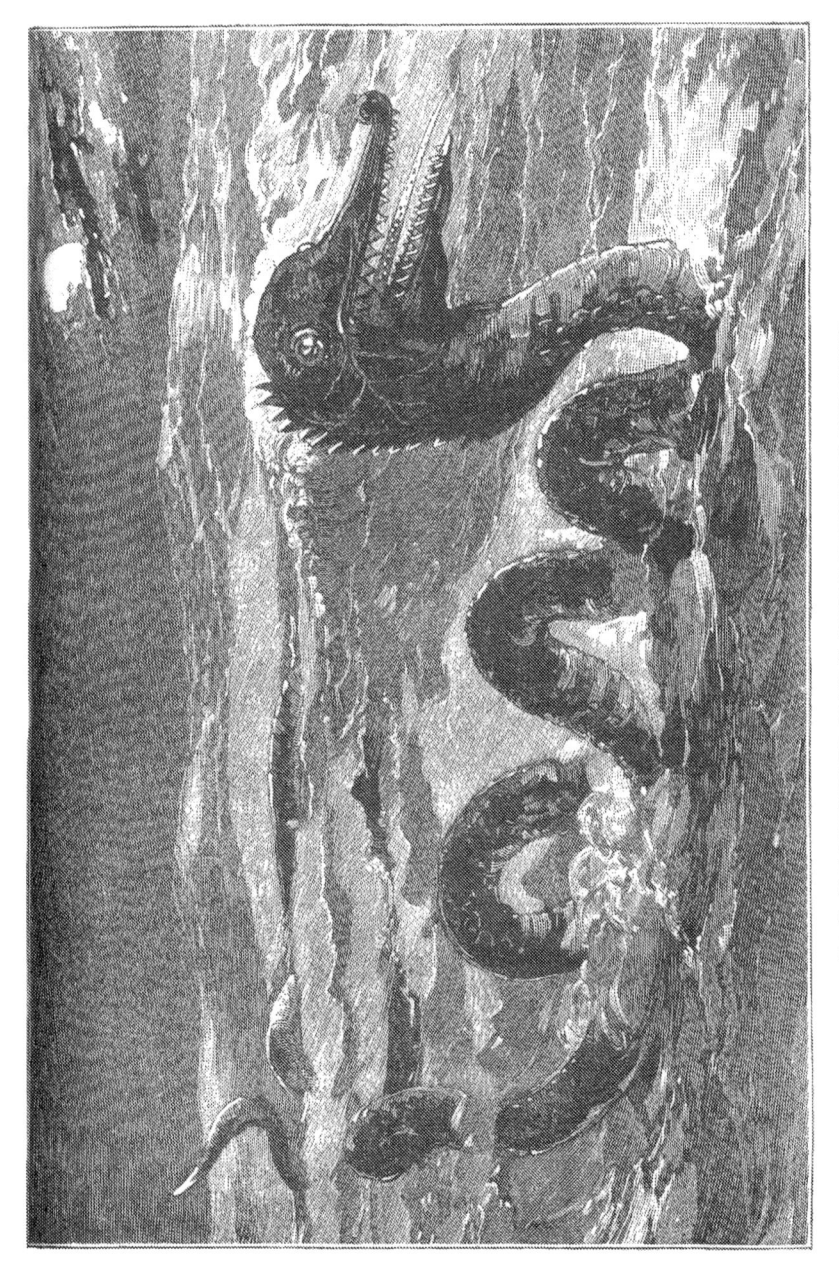

FIG. 5.—THE SEA-MONSTER, AS MR. C. RENARD SUPPOSED TO HAVE SEEN IT.

3   Would-be Sea-Serpents.

It is by no means astonishing that in the vast waters of the ocean several objects, totally different from the animal generally known as the Great Sea-Serpent, gave rise to tales of that Great Unknown, such as wrecks, gigantic sea-weeds, or even animal beings. So we meet with an account dated:

1720.—(See Pontoppidan.) "Thorlack Thorlacksen has told me that in 1720 a Sea-Serpent had been shut up a whole week in a little inlet, in which it came with high tide through a narrow entrance of seven or eight fathoms deep, and that eight days afterwards, when it had left the inlet, a skin of a snake or serpent was found. One end of the skin had sunk into the water of the inlet, so that its length could not be made out, as the inlet was several fathoms deep, and the skin partly lay there. The other end of this skin was washed on the shore by the current, where everybody could see it; apparently, however, it could not be used, for it consisted of a soft slimy mass. Thorlacksen was a native of the harbour of Kobbervueg."

It may be that a real sea-serpent remained a week in the inlet. The Norwegian fishermen know the sea-serpent too well to make mistakes. Another animal would not have been called a sea-serpent, and a short description of it would have been given. But the skin wrongly attributed to the sea-serpent, was certainly nothing else but a putrified long arm or tentacle of a gigantic calamary. The description "soft and slimy mass" proves this sufficiently. The great calamary died in the fjord, or inlet, and its long dead arm was floated ashore by the current, while the body sank. Such great calamaries, the true Krakens, have been measured, and found to have a body of 30 feet in length with long tentacles of 58 feet (see Lee, *Sea Monsters Unmasked*, London, 1883). I give here a figure of the largest ever found. (See our Fig. 6.)

1808.—*The Animal of Stronsa.*—Perhaps no stranded animal, even the so-called sea-monks of the seventeenth and the eighteenth century caused such an excitement among the learned as "the animal of Stronsa".

The oldest report of it is certainly a letter from Mr. Campbell, in which only the following lines refer to it:

"A snake (my friend Telford received a drawing of it) has been found thrown on the Orkney Isles, a sea-snake with a mane like a horse, 4 feet thick and 55 feet long, this is seriously true. Malcolm Laing, the historian saw it, and sent a drawing of it to my friend."

The letter was first printed in the work entitled: "*Life and Letters of Campbell*", and afterwards the above quoted lines were reprinted in the *Zoologist* for 1849, p. 2395.

In the *Proceedings of the Meeting of the Wernerian Natural History Society* on the 19th. Of November, 1808, printed in the *Philosophical Magazine*, Vol. 32, p. 190, we read:

Would-be Sea-Serpents 59

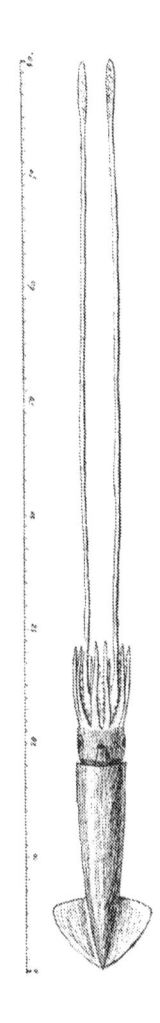

FIG. 6.—THE LARGEST CALAMARY EVER FOUND, WITH A SCALE OF 80 FEET.

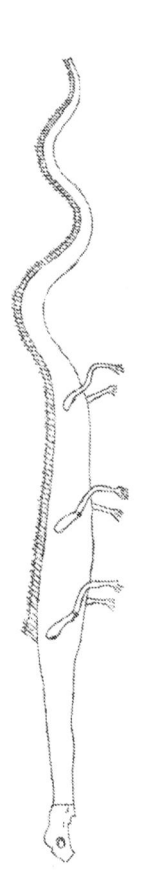

FIG. 7.—THE ANIMAL OF STRONSA.

"At this meeting Mr. P. Neill read an account of a great Sea-Snake, lately cast ashore in Orkney. This curious animal, it appears, was stranded in Rothiesholm Bay, in the Island of Stronsa. Malcolm Laing, Esq., M. P. being in Orkney at the time, communicated the circumstance to his brother, Gilbert Laing Esq., advocate at Edinburgh, on whose property the animal had been cast. Through this authentic channel Mr. Neill received his information. The body measured fifty five feet in length, and the circumference of the thickest part might be equal to the girth of an Orkney pony. The head was not larger than that of a seal, and was furnished with two blow holes. From the back a number of filaments (resembling in tecture the fishing-tackle known by the name of silk-worm gut) hung down like a mane. On each side of the body were three large fins, shaped like paws, and jointed. The body was unluckily knocked to pieces by a tempest; but the fragments have been collected by Mr. Laing, and are to be transmitted to the Museum at Edinburgh. Mr. Neill concluded with remarking, that no doubt could be entertained that this was the kind of animal described by Ramus, Egede, and Pontoppidan, but which scientific and systematic naturalists had hitherto rejected as spurious and ideal."

In the meeting of the same Society on the 14th. of January, 1809, (see *Phil. Mag.* Vol. 33. p. 90.),

"Dr. John Barclay communicated some highly curious observations which he had made on the caudal vertebrae of the Great Sea-Snake, (formerly mentioned) which exhibit in their structure some beautiful provisions of Nature, not hitherto observed in the vertebrae of any other animal."

"And Mr. Patric Neill read an ample and interesting account of this new animal, collected from different sources, especially letters of undoubted authority, which he had received from the Orkneys. He stated, however, that owing to the tempestuous season, the head, fin, sternum, and dorsal vertebrae, promised some weeks ago to the University Museum at Edinburgh, had not yet arrived; but that he had received a note from Gilbert Meason, esq., (the gentleman on whose estate in Stronsa the sea-snake was cast,) intimating that they might be expected by the earliest arrivals from Orkney. In the mean time, he submitted to the Society the first sketch of a generic character. The name proposed for this new genus was *Halsydrus*, (from Üöö the sea, and ýäñïö a water snake); and as it evidently appeared to be the Soe-Ormen described above half a century ago, by Pontoppidan, in his Natural History of Norway, it was suggested that its specific name should be *H. Pontoppidani*."

Mr. Malcolm Laing and Dr. Grant, living on Stronsa, were requested to take down the affidavits of the eye-witnesses, and at the meeting of the Wernerian Society on the 11th. of February, 1809, (see *Phil. Mag.* Vol. 33. p. 251),

"the Secretary (Mr. P. Neill) laid before the Society copies of those affidavits made before the justices of peace at Kirkwall in Orkney, by several persons who saw and examined the carcass of the great sea snake (*Halsydrus Pontoppidani*) cast ashore in Stronsa in October last; with remarks illustrative of the meaning of some passages in these affidavits."

The above-mentioned communication of Dr. John Barclay was printed in 1811 in the first Volume of the *Memoirs of the Wernerian Society*, and contains a detailed description of some vertebrae of the animal. The figures of these vertebrae are splendid, also those of the dried and shrivelled skull and a portion of one of the pectoral fins, with the cartilages that connect it with the body. As well the descriptions as the figures betray at a glance the shark nature of the animal. We will not trouble our readers with them, and we will also omit the figures, except one; it is a drawing made after the description of one of the eye-witnesses. (See our Fig 7).

The Paper of Mr. Barclay was entitled: *Remarks on some parts of the animal that was cast ashore on the island of Stronsa, Sept.* 1808. The above-mentioned affidavits were also printed in 1811, in the first Volume of the *Memoirs of the Wernerian Natural History Society*, and run as follows:

"At Kirkwall, Nov. 10. 1808.

"In presence of Dr. Robert Groat, Physician in Kirkwall, and Malcolm Laing, Esq. M. P. Two of his Majesty's Justices of the Peace of the County of Orkney.

"Compeared Thomas Fotheringhame, house-carpenter in Kirkwall; who solemnly declared, That being in Stronsa during the gales of wind in October last; he went to see the strange fish that was driven ashore in Rothiesholm Bay: That he measured his length with a foot-rule, which was exactly fifty-five feet, from the junction of the head and neck, where there was the appearance of an ear, to the tail: That the length of the neck, from the ear to the shoulder, was ten feet three inches, as nearly as he recollects. And being shewn a drawing of the animal, he declared, That the neck appeared to him to be too long. That the fins or arms, or, as they were called on the island, the *wings* of the animal, were jointed to the body nearer the ridge of the back than they appear in the drawing: That the toes were less spread out, and tapering more to a point, unless when purposely lifted up; but were not webbed unless the space of an inch and a half in breadth, where they joined each other; and the length seemed to be about eight inches: That he measured one of the wings next the head, which was four feet and a half in length, and in shape, from the first joint to the extremity, it resembled a goose-wing without the feathers: That the hollow between the snout and the upper part of the skull, appeared to him not to be quite so deep as represented in the drawing: That in every other respect the drawing appears to be so exact, that if the fish had not been mentioned, it would have brought it to his recollection: That from the ridge of the back to the belly, the body appeared to be four feet in depth, and the circumference rather oval than round; but that he did not measure either: That the mane or bristles of the back extended from the shoulder to within two feet and a half of the tail, and were of a shining appearance when wet; but shrunk up, and turned yellow, when dried: That the mane was thin, about two inches and a half in breadth towards the shoulder, and two inches in breadth at the tail: That the skin seemed to be elastic when compressed, and of a greyish colour, without any scales: it was rough to the feeling, on drawing the hand over it, towards the head; but was smooth as velvet when the hand was drawn towards the tail: That the extremity of the tail was about two inches in thickness, and somewhat rounded; and as he saw no part of the bones, he cannot say whether any part of the tail had been broken off or not: That the eyes appeared to be no larger than those of a seal: That there were two spout holes on each side of the neck, about an inch and a fourth in diameter, and at the same distance from the head as appears in the drawing: That he lifted up the snout, and examined the throat, which was too narrow to admit his hand: That a part of the bones of the lower jaw, resembling those of a dog, were remaining at that time, with some appearance of teeth, which were soft, and could be bent by the strength of the hand: That he observed no nipples, or organs of generation; the belly having been burst open by the violence of the sea: That the stomach was about the size of a ten gallon cask; and the bowls about the bulk of those of a cow: That the bristles of the back which had been pulled off through curiosity, were luminous in the dark, while they continued wet. And all this he declares to be truth, &c.

"(Signed)"
"Thomas Fotheringhame."

"Kirkwall, Nov. 19, 1808."
"Compeared John Peace, tenant in Dounatoun in Rothiesholm; and being interrogated, solemnly declares, That on the 26th. day of September last, he went a fishing off the east part of Rothiesholm-head, when he perceived as he imagined, a dead whale, on some sunk rocks, about a quarter of a mile from the Head: That his attention was first directed to it by the sea-fowl screaming and flocking about it; and on approach of it, in his boat, he found the middle part of it above the surface of the water: That he then observed it to be different from a whale, particularly in having fins or arms, one of which he raised with his boat-hook above the surface of the water: That this was one of the arms next the head, which was larger and broader than the others nearer the tail; and at that time the fin or arm was edged all around, from the body to the extremity of the toes, with a row of bristles about ten inches long, some of which he pulled off, and examined in the boat: That about ten days afterwards, a gale of south east wind came on, and the surge drove the fish ashore on Rothiesholm-Head: That he measured it by fathoms, and found it about fifty-four or fifty-five feet in length: That he observed the six arms, or wings as they are called on the island; but perceived no part of the bristles then round the edges of the fins or arms, and supposes, that being in a putrid state, they had been beaten off by the sea, or washed away: That a small part of the belly was broken up when he saw it then, from which the stomach, as he now supposes it to have been, had fallen out: That the stomach, which he took at first for the penis, from the one end of it being joined to the body; but on seeing it after it was opened, he concluded it to have been the stomach, as it resembled the second stomach of a cow: That he did not measure the circumference of the animal, but it appeared to be of the thickness of a middle sized horse round the girth, of twelve or thirteen hands high. And being shewn a drawing of the animal, and desired to point out the resemblance or difference, he declared, That the Joint of the foremost leg was broader than represented in the drawing, being more rounded from the body to the toes, and narrower at the upper end than at its junction with the toes: That the limb itself was larger than the hinder ones, and the uppermost joint or shoulder was altogether attached to the body: That in all other respects the drawing appears to him to be an exact resemblance of the fish, as it lay on the beach: That the mane came no further than the shoulder, and extended to the tail, part of which appeared to have been broken off: That the length of the neck, the situation of the spout-holes, and of the eye, the shape of the snout, the position and distance of the limbs from each other, appear to him to be exactly preserved in the drawing: That the lower jaw was awanting when he saw it: That the fish was of a greyish colour: That he observed no nipples or organs of generation, unless as above mentioned: That the part of the belly which was burst open, and from which the stomach had fallen out, was between the two limbs that are situated in the middle of the animal. And all this he solemnly declares to be truth. And declares he cannot write."

"*Eodem die*"

"Compeared Mr. George Sherar, tacksman of Rothiesholm in the island of Stronsa; who being interrogated, solemnly declared, That on the 20th. of October, being in Rothiesholm-head he saw the crew of John Peace's boat examining something on the water, which he took to he a dead whale: That about ten days afterwards, a gale of east wind having taken place he went to see if the whale was driven ashore, and found it in a creek, lying on its back, about a foot under water; and from the view which he had of its figure, length and limbs, his curiosity induced him to return a day or two after the gale had abated, when he found it thrown upon the beach, a little below high water mark, and lying on its belly, as represented in the drawing: That he returned next morning, with a foot-rule, purposely to measure it, and found it to be exactly fifty-five feet in length, from the hole in the top of the skull (which he has brought to town with him), to the extremity of the tail: That the length of the neck was exactly fifteen feet, from the same hole to the beginning of the mane: That he measured also the circumference of the animal as accurately as he could, which was about ten feet, more or less; and the whole body, where the limbs were attached to it, was about the same circumference: That the lower jaw or mouth was awanting; but there were some substances or bones of the jaw remaining; when he first examined it, which are now away: That it had two holes on each side of the neck, besides the one on the back of the skull: That the mane or bristles were about fourteen inches in length each, of a silvery colour, and particularly luminous in the dark, before they were dried: That the upper part of the limbs, which answers to the shoulder-blade, was joined to the body like the shoulder-blade of a cow, forming a part of the side: That a part of the tail was awanting, being incidentally broken off at the extremity; where the last joint of it was bare, was an inch and a half in breadth: That the bones were of a gristly nature, like those of a halibut, the back-bone excepted, which was the only solid one in the body: That the tail was quite flexible, turning in every direction, as he lifted it; and he supposes the neck to have been equally so, from its appearance at the time: That he has brought in, to deliver to Mr. Laing, the skull, two joints of one of the largest limbs, next the head, with different parts of the backbone, besides the bones that were formerly sent in: That there were either five or six toes upon each paw, about nine inches long, and of a soft substance: That the toes were separate from each other, and not webbed, as far as he could observe; and that the paw was about half a foot each way, in length and in breadth: That a few days thereafter, a gale of wind came on, and drove it to another part of the shore, where it was broken to pieces by the surge, and when Mr. Petrie came out to take a drawing of it, no part of the body remained entire: That he endeavoured to convey an idea of the animal to Mr. Petrie, by drawing the figure of it as accurately as he could, with chalk, on the table, exactly as it lay on the shore, after which Mr. Petrie made six or seven different sketches or plans of the fish, before he could bring it to correspond, in each minute particular, with the strong idea which he retains of its appearance: That he was the more attentive to its shape, dimensions and figure, in order to be able to give an accurate account of it to any travellers that might come to Rothiesholm, and that he is ready to make oath that the drawing is an exact resemblance of the fish, as it appeared when he measured it; and corresponds in all particulars with the idea which he entertains of the figure, dimensions, and proportions of the fish: That the substance of the body appeared like coarse, ill coloured beef, interlarded with fat or tallow, without the least resemblance or affinity to fish; but when put into a lamp, and the lamp placed on the fire, it neither flamed nor melted, but burned away like a gristly substance: That he perceived no teeth in the upper jaw; the lower jaw and tongue being awanting, and the palate also away: That the aperture of the throat appeared to be so wide, that he might have put his foot down through it: That the joints of the limbs were not united by a ball and socket but were lapped over each other, and united by some means which he does not comprehend That there were two canals, one above and another below the backbone, large enough to admit one's finger, and extending from the vertebrae of the neck, to the extremity of the tail, containing two ligaments, which he supposed, enabled the animal to raise itself up, or to bend its body in a spiral form: That a tract of strong easterly wind had prevailed, before the body was discovered upon the shore, and that he saw the body on two or three different occasions, after he had measured it, and before it went to pieces. And all this he declares to be truth, &c."

"(Signed)" "Geo. Sherar."

"Compeared Mr. William Folsatter, tacksman of Whitehall, in the island of Stronsa; who being interrogated, solemnly declared, That having heard that it was a dead whale that had come on shore in Rothiesholm-head, he did not see the body till about the 28th. day of October, when it had gone to pieces: That he saw about nine or ten feet of the back-bone, and some bones of the paws, and what was supposed to be the stomach which last he had the curiosity to open; that it was about four feet long, and as thick as a firkin, but flatter: That the membranes that formed the divisions, extended quite across the supposed stomach, and were about three sixteenth of an inch in thickness, and at the same distance from each other, and of the same substance, with the stomach itself: That the section of the stomach, after it was opened, had the appearance of a weaver's reed: That he opened about a fourth part of the supposed stomach which contained nothing but a reddish substance, like blood and water, and emitted a fetid smell: That he was very doubtful at the time whether it was really the stomach or not; but that each end of it had the appearance of terminating in a gut. And all this he solemnly declares to be the truth, &c.

"(Signed)" "Wm. Folsetter."

"The said Mr. George Sherar being again interrogated, declares, That he examined the supposed stomach, after it had been opened by Mr. Folsitter, and that he laid it open to the farther end: That there was something like a gut at the end which he opened, about two inches long, with a small aperture: That the stomach had the same appearance from end to end, and contained nothing but a substance like blood and water: That the large bone of which a drawing was taken, was considered as the collar-bone; and that it was situated with the broad and thick part downwards and the open part towards the vertebrae of the back: That he observed no appearance of fins about the neck or breast, or other parts of the body, except the six paws already described. And all this he solemnly declares to be truth, &c."

"(Signed)" "Geo. Sherar."

One of the ablest ichthyologists of those days, Mr. Everard Home examined the "sea-snake", and recognized it for a Basking shark. Immediately after his paper in the *Philosophical Transactions of the Royal Society of London*, Vol. 98, entitled "*An anatomical account of the Squalus maximus (of Linnaeus), which,* &c.," especially of an individual of thirty feet six inches, "entangled in the herring nets, belonging to the fishermen of Hastings, 13 Nov. 1808", Mr. Home goes further:

"I cannot close the present paper without mentioning, that nearly the same period, two other Squali of large dimensions were thrown upon our coast. The probable cause of this event, is the season being uncommonly boisterous and tempestuous. On the 3d. Of January, 1808, a fish was thrown ashore at Penrhyn, in Cornwall. On hearing of it from a person on the spot, I sent down a drawing of the subject of this paper to compare with it, and the fish proves to be of the same species, and a male, measuring thirty-one feet in length."

"The other was thrown ashore on the 7th. of October, 1808, at Rothiesholm, an estate of Gilbert Meason, Esq. in Stronsay, one of the Orkney isles. It had been seen lying on some sunken rocks, eleven days before, was in a half putrid state, and the sea fowls were in great numbers feeding upon it. Those who saw it, reported that the skin was rough in one direction, and smooth like satin in the other. At the time of its being examined, the skin and a great many other parts of the fish were wanting."

"Mr. Meason, with a zeal for science which does him infinite credit, upon hearing the strange accounts which were given of this sea-monster, got his brother, Malcolm Laing, Esq. and Dr. Grant, an eminent physician (both justices of the peace), to take depositions on the spot, from those persons who had seen the fish, that its real appearance might be ascertained. This examination, however, did not take place till six weeks after the fish was thrown ashore."

"These depositions were sent to Sir Joseph Banks, who put them into my hands. (The depositions are very long, and exceedingly minute; they are preserved in the Board-book of the Royal Society). I also received, a short time after, from my friend Mr. Laing, in consequence of a request I made for that purpose, that part of the skull, which contained the brain, the upper jaw having been separated from it, a considerable number of the vertebrae of the back united together by their natural attachments, a portion of one of the pectoral fins, with the cartilages that unite it to the spine, and a long and short cartilage forming the support of one of the gills. On comparing these different parts, with those of the Squalus maximus, they were found to agree, not only in their form, but also in their dimensions. This led to the opinion of the fish being a Squalus, a very different one from what was formed by those who saw it in the mutilated state in which it was thrown ashore, and who called it a *sea-snake*. In the different depositions, several parts are accurately described, such as the valvular intestine, which was taken for the stomach, and the bristles of the mane, which are described as ligamentous fibres, one of them is in my possession, and is of the same kind with the fibres forming the margin of the fins of the squalus maximus. The drawing that was made from memory, and which I have annexed, will enable me in a few words to point out how much, in some things, those who saw the fish adhered to truth, and in others allowed their imagination to supply deficiencies, for one of them declared, with confidence, that the drawing was so exact a representation of what he had seen, 'that he fancied he saw the beast lying before him, at a distance on the beach.'

"The drawing is correct in the representation of the head, and anterior part of the fish, from which the skin, the upper and lower jaw, the gills, and gullet, had been separated by putrifaction; and when we consider that the liver and the other viscera were all destroyed, except the valvular intestine, which was taken away by the observers, the size of the body that remained would be nearly in proportion with the drawing. The legs are tolerably exact representations of the holders in the male Squalus maximus, described in a former part of this paper, and therefore are not imaginary, only that four have been added which did not exist. This is satisfactorily determined by the pectoral fin, which is preserved, having no resemblance to them. The mane, they said, was composed of ligamentous fibres, one of which was sent to London; this corresponds, in its appearance, with the fibres that form the termination of the fins and tail of the Squalus maximus, such an appearance therefore was seen, but could only be met with in the place of the two dorsal fins, instead of being continued along the back, as in the drawing. The contortions towards the tail are such, as the invertebral joints could not admit of, they are therefore imaginary."

"It is said, two different persons measured the fish; one by fathoms, the other by a foot-rule, and that it was fifty-five feet long. Their accuracy is at least doubtful, as the parts that are preserved correspond with those of a fish about thirty feet long, and it is rendered still more so, as the person who gives the length in fathoms, says, he saw at that time the six legs, the two foremost being larger than the hinder ones, and the lower joint more rounded from the body to the toes. The pectoral fin, which is preserved, proves this declaration to be incorrect: the person who measured the fish with a foot-rule, declares the length, from the hole in the head to the beginning of the mane, to be exactly fifteen feet, which is probably correct since a Squalus of about thirty-six feet long would measure, from the forepart of the skull to the dorsal fin, about fifteen feet; but the other measurement must be questionable."

"It is deserving of remark, that there is no one structure represented in this drawing, which was not actually seen. The skeleton of the holders corresponds with the legs in the drawing, the margin of the dorsal fin in a putrid state with the mane; so that the only errors are in the contortions towards the tail, the length of the fish and the number of the holders, which were mistaken for legs. (This mistake of the holders of the male shark for legs, has been frequently made. There is a drawing in Sir Joseph Bank's library, sent from Ireland, in which the fish is represented walking like a duck, with broad webbed feet. The skin of a male Squalus maximus was exhibited in London, some years ago, distended by means of hoops, and the holders were shown as its legs, on which it occasionally walked). And when we recollect that the drawing was made from memory six weeks after the fish had been seen by those, who describe it, during which interval it had been their principal subject of conversation, we may conclude that so extraordinary an object, as the mutilated fish must appear, when believed to be a perfect one, would, in their different discourses, have every part exaggerated, and it is only remarkable that the depositions kept so close to the truth as they have done."

"It is of importance to science; that it should be ascertained, that this fish is not a new animal unlike any of the ordinary productions of nature, and we are indebted to the zeal and liberality of Mr. Meason and Mr. Laing, who have collected a sufficient body of evidence. to enable me to determine that point, and prove it to be a Squalus, and the orifices behind the eye, which communicate with the mouth met with in the skull, renders it very probable, that it is a Squalus maximus."

"This opinion is further confirmed by the Squalus maximus, known by the name of the basking shark, being frequently seen upon the coast of Scotland."

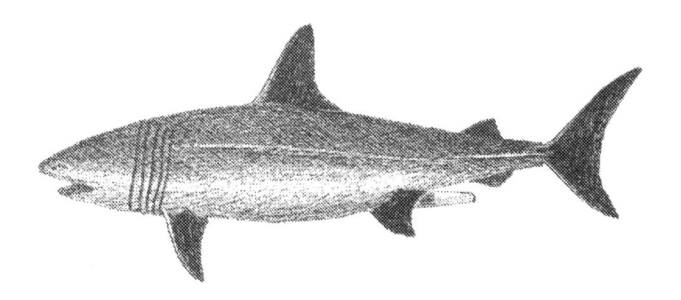

FIG. 8.–*SQUALUS MAXIMUS*, LINNÉ.

The only remark I have to make is: Mr. Home will never have believed that the animal of Stronsa really measured 56 feet, and so made himself guilty of throwing discredit on the accurate measuring of the eye-witnesses.

I present here to my readers the figure of a *Squalus maximus*, or Basking-shark, thus enabling them to make this animal's acquaintance, if they don't know it yet.

Of course Mr. Barclay rejected Mr. Home's supposition, and wrote a paper against it, printed in the first volume of the above mentioned *Memoirs*, running as follows:

"Since reading the first paper of Mr. Home, where he treats of the vertebrae of the Squalus maximus, I have seen another, entitled 'An anatomical account of the Squalus maximus'. In this last paper, he seems to be convinced, that the animal of Stronsa is a Squalus maximus. The scale on which he draws his figure of the squalus, is a scale of half an inch to a foot."

"Measuring by this scale, the head of his squalus is five feet and a half, from the joint of the upper jaw to the gills. The dried and shrivelled head of the animal of Stronsa, measures only twelve inches from the first vertebra to the farthest part that remains of the jaw."

"The diameter of the head of the squalus maximus, from right to left, at the angle of the mouth, was, according to Mr. Home, five feet. The broadest part of the head of the animal of Stronsa is, in its present state, only seven inches."

"The diameter of the larger vertebrae, near the head, in the squalus, was, according to Mr. Home, seven inches. The first cervical vertebra in the animal of Stronsa, is still adhering to the head, and is only two inches in diameter."

"Yet some of the vertebrae of this animal, which are still preserved, are six inches and a half in diameter; and the first vertebrae which I saw, were from four to five and a half inches across."

"The smallness of the cervical vertebrae, in the animal of Stronsa, confirms the account of those who saw it, that the animal had a neck. But the Squalus maximus, if Mr. Home's figure be accurate, had nothing resembling a neck. And, indeed, Artedi observes, that 'omnes pisces qui pulmonibus destituuntur, collo quoque carent: Ergo soli pisces cetacei collum habent.' The presence of a neck, therefore, as peculiar to cetaceous fishes, confirms likewise the account of the spiracula or ear-holes, ascribed to this animal of Stronsa."

"The length of Mr. Home's squalus was thirty feet six inches. The length of the animal of Stronsa, by actual measurement was fifty five feet, or, exclusive of the head, fifty four; and yet a part of the tail was supposed to be wanting. The circumference of the animal of Stronsa was, by actual measurement, about ten feet, meant, I suppose, at the thickest part. If the animal had been cylindrical at that part, the diameter from the dorsal to the sternal aspect must have been about three feet four inches. The diameter of the squalus at the thickest part, measuring from the dorsal to the sternal aspect, is nearly six feet; its circumference, had it been cylindrical nearly eighteen feet."

"The animal of Stronsa had a mane, extending from the shoulder to near the caudal extremity (i. e. about thirty nine feet), after deducting the length of the head and neck, which, when together were sixteen feet. I have still a specimen of that mane, which I got from Mr. Urquhart; and all the specimens which were brought here, confirm the accounts that were sent of it from the Orkneys. The bristles of that mane are not like the radii of a fin, nor, although they were, has the squalus a fin extending from the shoulder to the tail."

"A drawing, which was sent to me by our very active and obliging Secretary, Mr. Neill, was executed, I am told, from the original, by Mr. Urquhart; and its accuracy is confirmed by the dried specimen now before us. It represents the sternum and two parts corresponding two scapulae, and those organs which are named *paws*. Mr. Home says, that these organs resemble the pectoral fins of his squalus. But the length of the pectoral fins, measuring along the upper margin, is four feet, the length of the paw cannot be determined, as part of it is wanting; the part that remains, measures seventeen inches."

"The breadth of the fin, measuring across the radii, is three feet and seven inches; while the greatest breadth of the paw in its dried state, is only five inches and three quarters."

"Those parts which in form resemble the scapulae and exhibit articular surfaces at each extremity, were probably ribs."

"Mr. Home concludes by observing, that 'it is of importance to science, that it should be ascertained, that this fish is not a new animal, unlike any of the ordinary productions of nature.' Of what importance it is to science to admit no new genera or species into our catalogues of natural history, I cannot conceive. But it is certainly of much importance to science, that the naturalist should be cautious not to determine the species of an animal upon vague evidence. Now what evidence had Mr. Home that this animal was a squalus, and even to suppose that it was a squalus maximus?"

I may be allowed to make the following remark: Mr. Barclay does not seem to make any difference between "a head" of a Squalus and "a skull." It is true that the "head" of a *Squalus maximus* of thirty feet and a half measures five feet and a half, but its "skull" has only a length of ten inches. It is true that the diameter of the "head" of such a shark measures from right to left about five feet, but its "skull" would have only a few inches in breadth. It is true that the diameter of the larger vertebrae near the head of such an individual may be about seven inches, but what is indicated by Mr. Barclay in the head of his "animal of Stronsa" to be the "first cervical vertrebra", is (don't laugh!) the cartilaginous nose tip with its two contorted cartilaginous appendages!—No wonder that the animal of Stronsa had "a neck", for all the parts between the skull and the pectoral fins, except the vertebral column and some adherent flesh, were washed away, whilst the basking shark of Mr. Home had no neck, because it was entire.—Curious, indeed, is the naive passage in which Artedi quoted!

In the comparison of Mr. Home's basking shark and his own stranded animal, Mr. Barclay also wholly overlooks, when he states the dimensions, that they were those of the entirely putrified remains of an animal, and not of an undamaged being.

Dr. Barclay seems to entirely reject Mr. Home's idea that the "mane" had never extended over the whole back, but what was seen were only fibres of the putrified backfins, in the two places of the foremost and the hindmost backfin, and that the rest of the "mane" only existed in the imagination of the witnesses.

In comparing the dimensions of the pectoral fins and the paws, Mr. Barclay again forgets that he has only before him a totally mutilated specimen.

An extract from the "*Remarks*" of Dr. Barclay was given by Dr. Hoffmann in Oken's Isis, II, 1818, p. 2096, where amongst others he says:

"The paper is full of obscurities, which originate as well in the differences of the reports of uneducated eye-witnesses, as in the slubbering and inaccurate mode of describing of the writer himself;"

but Mr. Hoffmann himself is not free from inaccuracies! In none of Dr. Barclay's papers mention is made of a "membranaceous comb extended over bony rays, which was running from the shoulders to the end of the tail, over the back." He has evidently translated this (if we may use this expression) from the figure (see our fig. 7). But this figure was made for print by Mr. Syme, after a drawing made on one of the islands from the description given there, and Mr. Syme has changed the "mane" (long loose hairs hanging down) into a true backfin of an eel, which he figured exactly as he was accustomed to do. Every one will be convinced of the truth of my assertion, if he will give himself the trouble to compare the figures of eels and muraenas, made by the same Mr. Syme in the same volume, with the engraving of the "animal of Stronsa."

Immediately after this paper Mr. Oken, the editor of the *Isis*, wrote another one, in which he begins by saying that the imperfect description of the animal does not allow to prove any relationship with other animals. Further he comes to the conclusion, that, as no animal with a bony skeleton has six feet, it must have been a cartilaginous fish, a male one, of which the two pterygopodia (a pair of additional paring-organs, the so-called "claspers" or "holders") were regarded as the third pair of feet, whilst the ventral and pectoral fins were the other pairs. "It is, however, no shark," he goes on, and adduced 7 proofs for this theory; "it is, neither a cetacean," and for this opinion he gives 4 different reasons. And yet he has the boldness to conclude: "The animal consequently is more related to the sharks, and as it is not a true shark, it must be a *Chimaera*"; but the reasons given to prove this are of course still more forced and irrelevant. I will add here that he also says: "finally individuals of Chimaera of 30 feet in length, have already been caught", a manifest untruth, for the largest ever measured were of three feet and a half!—For those readers who never saw a *Chimaera*, or sea-cat, or a figure of it, I have delineated the *Chimaera monstrosa* in our fig. 9.

In the *Edinb. Philos. Journ.* Vol. V, 1821, an analysis is published of one of the vertebrae of the Orkney-Animal. The analysis was made by Dr. John Davy, and communicated "a considerable time ago" by Dr. Leach to the Wernerian Society. To trouble my readers with this analysis would be superfluous.

Dr. Hibbert in his *Description of the Shetland Islands*, 1822, really believes that:

"The existence of the sea-snake,—a monster of fifty-five feet long, is placed beyond a doubt, by the animal that was thrown on shore in Orkney, the vertebrae of which are to be seen in the Edinburgh Museum."

Dr. Hamilton too, in his *Amphibious Carnivora*, 1839, is of the same opinion: "We turn first" he says "to an account of an animal which apparently belonged to this class" (viz. the class of sea-serpents), "which was stranded in the Island of Stronsa, one of the Orkneys, in the year 1808", and he goes on giving some details of the stranded animal, taken from the *Memoirs of the Wernerian Society*. Later on we learn from him that:

"Dr. Fleming" in his *History of British Animals*, 1828, (this work I have not been able to consult), "in his notice of this animal, suggests that these members were probably the remains of pectoral, ventral and caudal fins."

Mr. Rathke in the *Archiv für Naturgeschichte* of 1841, after having published some accounts, collected by him in Norway about the sea-serpent, and after having declared that he himself is a firm believer in it, goes on:

"To which group of known animals, however, this being belongs, cannot be asserted with any degree of certainty. The supposition, however, is at hand, that it is closely related to that animal, which in 1816" (read 1808) "stranded in Stronsa, one of the Orkneys, and of which several pieces of the skeleton are said to be preserved in the Museum of the University of Edinburgh, and in the Museum of the Royal College of Surgeons. I have read a note about it in the London Journal the *Athenaeum*, 1839, p. 902, which note is taken from the work: *The Naturalist's Library, Amphibious Carnivora, including the Walrus and Seals, also of the Herbivorous Cetacea*. By B. Hamilton, M. D. (Edinburgh, Lizars). An ample description of

FIG. 9.–*CHIMAERA MONSTROSA*, LINN.

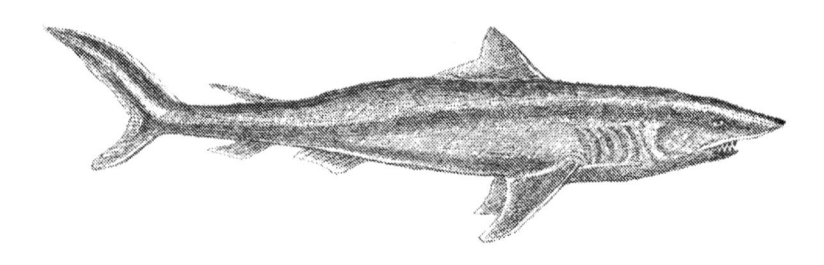

FIG. 10.–*LAMNA CORNUBICA* (LINN.).

the saved rests of the animal is said to have been written by Dr. Barclay in the first Volume of the *Memoirs of the Wernerian Society*. I had, however, not the means of consulting this dissertation. According to the above-mentioned note or extract the creature stranded in Stronsa measured 56 feet and had (on its thickest part?) a circumference of 12 feet. The head was small and one foot long, the neck slender and 16 feet long. The organs of motion are said to have consisted of three pairs of fins: one pair of which is believed to have been properly a caudal fin. The foremost pair of fins measured 4 feet; these were the longest, and their tops looked like toes, partly, however, webbed together. From the shoulders a kind of bristly mane extended to near the extremity of the tail. The skin was smooth, without scales and of a grey colour. The eye was as large as a seal's. The throat was too narrow to admit the hand."

"Judging from these truly incomplete statements, viz. that the head was relatively very small, the neck very long and slender, and the extremeties were like fins, one may suppose that the animal stranded in Stronsa resembled a *Plesiosaurus*; and that consequently it belonged to the *Amphibia*, viz. to the Saurians."

Prof. Dr. W. F. Erichson, the well known Editor of the *Archiv für Naturgeschichte*, expressed his opinion about the animal of Stronsa, immediately after the appearance of Mr. Rathke's dissertation. After having given full details of Mr. Barclay's paper, and an ample description of the saved parts, he says "All these parts belong undoubtedly to a shark," and:

"Everard Home already declared the animal to be a shark, and in spite of all that Dr. Barclay asserts to the contrary, it will be so for ever, only it may not have been a *Selache maxima*, but a *Lamna cornubica*, which also reaches a considerable length. So the animal of Stronsa has no relation at all with the sea-serpent of the Norwegians."

I have only to observe that I am surprised that Mr. Erichson could arrive at this conclusion, as the *Lamna cornubica*, or porbeagle has never attained a length above 18 feet.—Our fig. 10 represents a porbeagle.

It is astonishing, yet it is true, that Mr. Newman, the Editor of the *Zoologist*, after all that had been written about the animal of Stronsa, was not yet convinced of its being a shark. In his journal of 1849, p. 2358, he asked the following

"Inquiries respecting the bones of a large marine animal cast ashore on the Island of Stronsa in 1808."

"In the 'Memoirs of the Wernerian Natural History Society' (vol. I. p. 418) is a paper by Dr. Barclay, on a large animal cast ashore on the island of Stronsa. In illustration of his paper, the Doctor figures the head with a vertebra attached, four other vertebrae and a sternum with a paddle "and two parts corresponding two scapulae" attached. He speaks of the originals of these figures as specimens then before the audience he was addressing.

He gives seven inches as the diameter of the head, and two inches as the diameter of the cervical vertebra then still attached to the head. The total length of the animal is given as fifty-five feet, and this from actual admeasurement. It is now positively asserted that the animal in question was a shark; but the utter impossibility of a shark fifty-five feet in length having a head only seven inches in diameter, and cervical vertebrae only two inches in diameter, is so manifest that further inquiry seems desirable; and I shall esteem it a great kindness if any naturalist who may possess the means of doing so will reply to the following questions:—

"1. How were the bones by Dr. Barclay obtained?
"2. What is the evidence that they belonged to one animal?
"3. Where are these bones preserved?
"4. What is their present state?
"5. Has the skull ever been denuded of skin, muscle, etc.?
"6. Has it ever been examined by a competent comparative anatomist? and if so, what opinion has he pronounced on it?

"Surely there are naturalists in Edinburgh who can answer the questions at once. It seems very irrational to speculate on the genus, order or class, to which a recent animal belongs, while the head and sternum of the creature are still in existence."—

The following "Reply" to these questions was given, printed in the *Zoologist* for 1849, p. 2396:

"*Reply to Mr. Newman's Inquiries respecting the Bones of the Stronsa Animal.*— Seeing your queries regarding the bones of an animal cast on shore at Stronsa, described by Dr. Barclay in the 'Memoirs of the Wernerian Society',—after some little trouble I have been able to answer most of these questions."

"1. How were the bones described by Dr. Barclay obtained?—It will be seen in the 'Wernerian Memoirs' (Vol. I. p. 438), that George Sherar, one of those who saw the animal, mentions that he brought away, to deliver to Mr. Laing (the Scotch historian), the skull, two joints of one of the largest limbs next the head, with different parts of the back-bone, besides the bones that were formerly sent in. Mr. Laing, I suppose, forwarded them to Dr. Barclay."

"2. What is the evidence that they belonged to one animal?—The answer to this is simply that the aforesaid George Sherar took them from the same animal."

"3. Where are these bones preserved? 4. What is their present state?—Three of the vertebrae are in the Museum of the Royal College of Surgeons, Edinburgh, in a dried state, and are 6 inches in diameter; and four in the University Natural History Museum, preserved in spirits, and are still articulated to each other, whereas the other three are separate."

"5. Has the skull ever been denuded of skin, muscle, &c.?—6. Has it ever been examined by a competent comparative anatomist? if so, what opinion has he pronounced on it?—This is answered by the annoying fact that the skull has not been preserved."

"On inquiring of Professor Goodsir with regard to the vertebrae, he tells me he has examined them, and that they are undoubtedly those of a Shark (*Squalus maximus*), as are the skull, sternum and scapulae, figured in the 'Wernerian Memoirs', p. 418."

"We would naturally suppose that the affidavit of those who saw this extraordinary animal would be of some avail; but on closer inspection even these will be found to have little weight in the argument. In the first place it is infortunate that no well-educated person saw it: they were all ignorant, illiterate men, who most likely knew nothing further of a shark than that it was an animal with a huge mouth, capable of discussing so many seamen at a bite, and whose teeth are peculiarly adapted for amputating limbs. In the next place we find these witnesses agreeing in one most absurd particular, viz., in the animal having six legs: on this point it is needless to expatiate; every one knowing anything of comparative anatomy must see at once the impossibility of such a structure: moreover, even granting its possibility, it is at once cancelled by Mr. Urquhart's figure of the sternum and scapulae with an ordinary fin thereto attached (Wern. Mem. Vol. I. p. 418); the third pair of appendages Dr. Fleming in his 'British Animals', supposes were claspers. In the last place we may notice one striking contradiction in the evidences: Thomas Fotheringhame seems to have been astonished at such a large animal having such a narrow throat,—so narrow indeed that it would not admit his hand; while George Sherar would have had no difficulty in putting his foot down it: and as there is nothing to prove that Thomas Fotheringhame's hand was larger than George Sherar's foot, we are led to the conclusion that one or other must have made a mistake in his calculation."

"We might further suggest the improbability of any animal sixty feet long having a head only seven inches in diameter, and we might even suspect the carpenter's footrule of showing a decided taste for the marvellous; but we must now conclude with this single remark, that if the Stronsa Animal was not a shark it was certainly not the great sea-serpent, which, if it does exist, will most likely be allied to the Plesiosauri of by-gone days, and to which the animal seen by the Rev. Mr. Maclean, Eigg-Island (Wern. Mem. I. p. 442), seems to have borne a strong resemblance.— Jas. C. Howden; Musselburgh, February, 1849."

As to the animal seen by Mr. Maclean, see our report n°. 31, in the following chapter.

One would think that the question about the "animal of Stronsa" was now set at rest. Not at all! Dr. Thomas Stewart Traill wrote a paper about it, published in the *Proceedings of the Royal Society of Edinburgh*, Vol. III, n°. 44, 1854, June, comparing it with the animal seen by the Captain, officers and crew of H. M. S. *Daedalus* (see our report n°. 118 in the next chapter). The part of his dissertation, respecting the "animal of Stronsa" runs as follows:

"The discussions which arose about four years ago on the animal reported to have been seen on 6th. August 1848, by Captain M'Quhae, the officers and crew of H. M. S. Daedalus, in the Southern Atlantic, between the Cape of Good Hope and St. Helena, about 300 miles off the African shore, recalled my attention to the materials I had collected respecting the vast animal cast ashore on Stronsey, one of the Orkneys, in 1808."

"I was not there at the time, but copies of the depositions made by those who had seen and measured it were transmitted to me by order of Malcolm Laing Esq., the historian of Scotland, on whose property it was stranded; and I obtained other notes from several individuals resident in Okney."

"The evidence of the most intelligent persons who had seen and measured the animal was carefully collected, and copies of it were transmitted by Mr. Laing to Sir Joseph Bankes, and other naturalists. Soon afterwards Mr. Laing sent, through his brother, the late Gilbert Laing Meason, to the Museum of our University the skull and several vertebrae. The cartilaginous omoplates, to which a portion of the pectoral fin, or *wing*, as it was termed by the natives, were afterwards sent to Edinburgh, where I saw and examined them."

"Two of the vertebrae were transmitted to me with portions of what was termed the *mane* of the animal, which I now exhibit."

"The dead animal was first observed by some fishermen lying on a sunken rock, about a quarter of a mile from Rothiesholm-Head; but in a few days a violent gale from the S. E. cast it on shore in a creek near the headland, where it remained for some time tolerably entire; and it was subsequently broken up by the fury of the waves. Before it was thus broken into several pieces it was examined, and measured by several intelligent inhabitants of the Island; and their testimony collected as above stated was forwarded to London, Edinburgh, etc. The declarations were, however, accompanied by a very absurd drawing of the animal, which was thus produced. Many days elapsed ere the tempestuous weather allowed any communication with other Islands; and when the storm abated, a young man was sent from Kirkwall by Mr. Laing, to collect what information he could on the subject. But by this time the body of the animal was completely broken up. This lad, who was no draughtsman, and ignorant of Natural History, endeavoured, from the descriptions of those who had seen the animal most entire, to delineate with chalk on a table a figure of the animal. The rude figure so produced was transferred by pencil to paper, and copies of it were handed about as real representations of the animal."

"That it had a general resemblance to the animal was admitted by those who had seen it; but from the accounts I afterwards obtained, it would appear that the *jointed legs*, which the lad had attached to it, are creations of his own imagination."

"The appendages, which gave rise to this strange representation, were never called *legs* by those who saw the animal, but were denominated by them *wings* or *fins* or swimming paws. 'That nearest the head was broader than the rest, about four-and-a-half feet in length, and was edged all round with bristles or fibres, about ten inches long'. The 'lower jaw was wanting when it was cast ashore, but there remained cartilaginous teeth in portions of the jaws'. Before it was discovered putrefaction had commenced, especially in the *fins*. The animal had a long and slender neck, on which there were two spiracles on each side."

"The *wings* would seem to have been the remains of fins, altered by incipient decomposition. The six may perhaps be remains of pectoral, abdominal, and anal fins, and perhaps they may have been placed, like those of some of the shark family, farther from the centre of the abdomen than in ordinary fishes. Indeed one of the witnesses states that 'the wings of the animal were jointed to the body nearer the ridge of the back than they appear in the drawing'."

"The portion of the anterior fin or *wing*, which was attached to the omoplates, consisted of cartilaginous rays; and when such a structure of fin is partially separated by commencing decomposition, the rays might easily, to the eyes of the uninitiated in natural science, seen like toes or fingers."

"Even the great Cuvier admits this resemblance when describing the fins of fishes:"—

"Des rayons plus ou moins nombreux soutenant de nageoires membraneuses representent grossièrement les doigts, des mains, et des pieds."

"As much of the value of the descriptions of the Orkney animal rests on the character and credibility of the individuals who saw it most entire, I may be permitted to state that I personally knew the three principal witnesses, Thomas Fotheringhame, George Sherar, and William Folsetter, to be men of excellent character, and of remarkable intelligence. They were not *ignorant fishermen*, as the witnesses were represented to be; but two of them were of the better sort of farmers in that part of Orkney; and the first and the last of them were also very ingenious mechanics, much accustomed to the use of the *footrule*, the instrument employed in measuring the animal."

"They were men of such honour, intelligence, and probity, that I can have no doubt of the correctness of any statement they made of their impressions of what they had so carefully observed."

"It was, therefore, not without surprise, that some months after these accounts were sent to London, I read a paper by Mr. Home (afterwards Sir Everard), in which he recklessly sets aside the evidence of the persons who saw and measured the animal in its most entire condition, as to its dimensions of length and thickness; and maintains that it was nothing but a Basking shark (Selache maximum!), which he supposes the love of the marvellous had magnified so enormously in the eyes of those whom he is pleased to call *'ignorant fishermen'*. Unfortunately for Home's hypothesis, the Basking shark was probably far more familiar to those men than to himself; for it is often captured among the Orkney Islands; and its length and proportional thickness are so totally different from the animal in question, that the two could scarcely be confounded, by the most 'ignorant fishermen' who had ever seen them."

"These witnesses assert that the Stronsey animal (though a portion towards the tail was broken off when they took its dimensions) measured no less than fifty five feet in length; whereas that of the largest Basking shark of which we possess any accurate account scarcely exceeds thirty six feet."

"The circumference of the two animals is no less widely different. My notes states the circumference at the thickest part of the body of the Orkney animal to be about ten feet, when it tapered much towards the head and the tail; whereas the circumference of a large Basking shark, where thickest, is not less than twenty feet. Besides, the shark-like figure of the latter could scarcely be confounded with the eel-like form of the Stronsey animal."

"(The diameter of the animal is a little differently stated by different witnesses. But as we are told that its contour was more oval than round, we can easily explain the discrepancy. One witness, who had not measured it, speaks of it as equalling a middle sized horse in thickness. On measuring four horses of from thirteen to fourteen hands in height, I found their greatest circumference to be from seventy-one to seventy-three inches, (or from five feet eleven inches to six feet one inch), or an average of six feet, that is less than the thickest part of our animal, but seemingly near that of its average dimensions.)"

"The *mane* as it is termed, may perhaps be the remains of a decomposed fin; but the fibres do not seem to be the rays of a fin; and the animal seen from the Daedalus is stated to have had a mane, floating about like sea-weed; and a similar appendage has generally been noticed in some less distinct accounts of a supposed sea-serpent."

"Supposing this to be a dorsal fin, it extended from the anterior *wings*, or pectoral fins, towards the tail for thirty seven feet, and differs from the dorsal fin of any species of shark. If the *mane* consisted of detached fibres extending for thirty seven feet on the back, it is analogous to no appendage of any known marine animal. That its rays or fibres are very peculiar, will appear from the specimen now exhibited. These round fibres are fourteen inches in length; and in the dried state, have a yellow colour and transparency, equal to that of isinglass."

"The vertebrae, which have been preserved in spirit in our Museum, have been exceedingly well described by Dr. Barclay, in the Wernerian Transactions, Vol. I; and undoubtedly, in their want of processes and cartilaginous structure, have much resemblance to those of chondropterygious fishes. One of the vertebrae adherent to the cranium, measured only two inches across; while that of the Basking-shark, in the same situation, is about seven inches in diameter. Dr. Barclay's paper is accompanied by an engraving of the omoplates, and upper portion of the pectoral fin, which are accurately given, from a drawing made from the recent remains, by the late Mr. John T. Urquhart, an accomplished draughtsman, and able naturalist. I know the representation to be correct, for I saw and handled the specimen. The substance of this part was a firm, but flexible cartilage, and seemed to have been placed in the muscles; just as Cuvier describes the omoplates of sharks to be: Leur omoplates sont suspendues dans le chair, en arrière des Branchies, sans articuler ni au crâne ni à l'espive. The Orkney animal seems to have had *two circular* spiracles on each side of its neck, about 1 1/4 inch in diameter; whereas the Basking shark has *five linear* spiracles on each side, a foot or more in length."

"The cranium, which I also very carefully examined, was far too small for that of a Basking shark of even one-fourth the usual length of that species. It measured in its dried state no more than twelve inches in length, and its greatest diameter was only seven inches. A Basking shark of thirty-six feet long would have had a head of at least five feet in length; and the diameter of the cranium at the angles of the mouth, would have measured probably five feet. These proportions positively show, that the Orkney animal could not possibly be confounded by intelligent men, accustomed to see the Basking shark, with that fish. There was a hole on the top of the cranium, something similar to the blow-hole of the cetaceans; but its lateral spiracles and cartilaginous bones forbid us to refer it to the order of cetacea".

"Every thing proves the Orkney animal to have been a chondropterygious *fish*, different from any described by naturalists; but it has no pretensions to the denomination of *Sea Serpent* or *Sea Snake*, although its general form, and probably its mode of progression in the Ocean, may give it some resemblance to the order of *Serpentes*. Certainly, it cannot be confounded with any known shark; nor does it belong to the family of Squalidae".

I am obliged to point out some discrepancies in Mr. Traill's paper. First he asserts that in a few days the dead animal was cast on shore by a violent gale "where it remained for sometime tolerably entire". This is not true, for the dead animal was already in a very putrified and damaged state, when it floated on the surface of the sea, for the pectoral fin was already putrified and the fibres had become loose.

Again: the teeth of the animal were not called "cartilaginous", but they were described as "soft, and" that "they could be bent by the strength of the hand".

Mr. Traill further says that "they would seem to have been the remains of fins, altered by incipient decomposition. The six may be remains of pectoral, abdominal and anal fins". Now there is no fish known to Zoologists, that has *two* anal fins. The anal fin is therefore called an *unpaired* fin!

In comparing the dimensions of the animal of Stronsa with those of Home's Basking-shark, the writer, like Dr. Barclay, permanently believes that the animal was "in its most entire condition"! Further he asserts that the "length of the largest Basking shark of which we possess any accurate account, scarcely exceeds thirty six feet". Consulting Prof. H. Schlegel's *De visschen van Nederland*, I read, however:

"The largest individual ever observed on the coasts of England, had a length of 36 feet. On the coasts of Norway, individuals are usually observed much larger than the boats fitted out for this capture, which are of about 40 feet. According to earlier intelligences, transmitted by trustworthy witnesses to the Bishop Gunner, sometimes individuals of more than 70, and even of more than 100 feet in length were captured on the coasts of Norway".

In considering the "mane" he also overlooks the fact that the two dorsal fins and the caudal fin were entirely decomposed, so that their fibres had become quite loose. According to the so called "first cervical vertebra" he made the same mistake as Dr. Barclay!

The two "circular spiracles on each side of the neck" have of course no relation at all with the five linear true gill-splits (not "spiracles" as Mr. Traill says) of the Basking-shark. These "two spiracles on each side of the neck" were in no case "spiracles". They may have been decomposed stems of the vascular system in the flesh near the skull of the animal.

Dr. Traill, no more than Dr. Barclay, seemed to have known the difference between the "head" of a shark and its "skull" or "cranium"!

The "hole on the top of the cranium" which is also figured in the engraving representing the skull in the *Memoirs of the Wernerian Society* is evidently the result of putrification and of an external injury.

I need not tell my readers what I think about "the animal of Stronsa". They may more than once have observed that I agree with Mr. Everard Home's opinion in all particulars, except in the so-called exaggerated dimensions. I firmly believe that the carcass of the animal measured fifty-five feet from the head to the end of the tail, and as a piece of tail seems to have been broken off, the vertebral column may even have been one of sixty feet. The dried and shrivelled skull measured twelve inches "from the first cervical vertebra to the farthest part that remains of the jaw". But as I have pointed out that this "first cervical vertebra" was in reality the cartilaginous nose tip with its two contorted cartilaginous appendages, and as this nose tip must have measured (see the drawing of the skull in the *Memoirs of the Wernerian Society*, Vol. I) two inches. the whole skull measured fourteen inches. But the skull was dried and shrivelled, consequently we may safely admit that it measured in its perfect state about twenty inches. Consequently I conclude that: the largest Basking-shark that ever stranded on the coasts of Great Britain measured upwards of sixty feet, viz. the so-called "Animal of Stronsa". The putrified body of it was floated ashore, and the putrification had continued so far that the almost black covering of the two backfins and the tail-fin were not only washed away by the waves, but that their yellow fibres had become loose. The eye-witnesses evidently reasoned that these fibres must have been present all along the back between these three parts, now far remote one from another, but were washed away, and they therefore concluded that the animal had "a mane, extending from the shoulders" (the part of the back at the level of the pectoral fins) "to the tail", i. e. to the end of the tail. Or, according to another witness it extended "to within two feet and a half of the tail"; which may be explained in two ways, viz., either he meant that the mane extended to within two feet and a half beyond the level of the last pair of paws (the claspers), consequently the level where the tail begins, and here is the exact place of the hindmost back-fin, or he meant that the mane did not quite extend to the point of the tail, from which we in our turn may conclude that the last two feet and a half of the tail had already been wholly cleared from the fibres of the putrified tail-fin.

Moreover putrification on one side, and the beating of the waves on the other side, had already removed the animal's enormous jaws, gills, with adherent muscles and cartilages, and all the entrails, except the valvular intestine. On persons who never saw such a mutilated specimen of a shark, the animal *must* have made the impression of being a sea-snake!

As to the sketch, made by Mr. Petrie after the descriptions of one of the witnesses, and with regard to the "mane" somewhat altered by Mr. Syme, it will appear at a glance that besides the ridiculous legs, the head (read skull) of it is drawn too large. The carrion was 56 feet long and the drawing only 74 lines, consequently the length of one foot is represented by a space of 1.3 line. A skull of 14 inches should therefore be in this drawing only 1.5 line long, and not 6 lines. Last not least, the "mane" is not delineated on only three different places, as it really was, but from the "shoulders" to the end of the tail, according to the wrong conclusions of those "most intelligent eye-witnesses"! This terrible "mane" was evidently the *only* cause of all this trouble, and of the whole puzzle!

1816.—*Phil. Mag.*, LIV, 1819).—The third sea-serpent described by Mr. Rafinesque (for he believes there are several species), is called by him:

"3. *The Scarlet Sea-Serpent*. This was observed in the Atlantic Ocean, by the captain and crew of an American vessel from New York, while reposing and coiled up, near the surface of the water; in the summer of 1816. It is very likely that it was a fish, and perhaps might belong to the same genus with the foregoing; I shall refer it thereto, with doubt, and name it *Octipos? coccineas*. Entirely of a bright crimson; head acute. Nothing further descriptive was added in the gazettes where the account was given, except that its length was supposed to be about 40 feet."

I am convinced that this "sea-serpent" was a great calamary. As the greatest ever found, measured from the tip of the tail to the tips of the extended shorter arms about 30 feet (a calamary reposing or swimming in the sea always has its long tentacular arms coiled up), the length of 40 feet probably is exaggerated. I give here a figure of a large calamary, swimming on the surface of the water (taken from Mr. Henry Lee's *Sea-Monsters Unmasked*, 1883, corrected, however, as to its proportions), and now my readers most probably will agree with me that such an animal has been seen. The hillocks of the short arms make the appearance of a long undulating body. The body of such an animal is quite scarlet or crimson, and the tail (the so-called head) is acute.

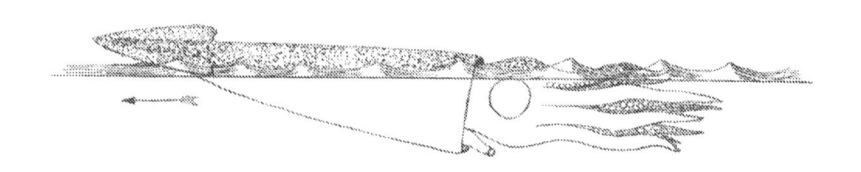

Fig. 11.–A large calamary, swimming on the surface of the sea.

1822, June.—In Froriep's *Notizen* of 1822, III, we read:

"Some time ago the American newspapers were filled with the reports of a seaserpent which showed itself in the neighbourhood. Also more than a year ago an animal was caught, supposed to be such a one, which, however, was recognized as a large tunny. It appears by the New-York newspaper of June 15th., that such an animal taken for a great sea-serpent has been caught in a bay near MiddletonPoint. This monster measured thirty feet and has a circumference of 18 feet. It had already been seen for some days, floating like a huge trunk. Some persons had fired at it with guns, but without any result. Having got into shallow water it could not regain the high sea, was killed with harpoons, towed aland and flayed. The liver alone produced three barrels of train-oil. It took six men two hours to drag the skin, which will be stuffed, to a distance of about 200 yards off. None of the old whalemen and seamen who saw the animal, knew it. There were no guts (?) and there was no heart (??). In the beak six rows of small sharp teeth were counted and the throat was wide enough for a tall man to pass. The skin was lead coloured and could be used as a stone for sharpening knives (apparently an unusual large shark?)"

About the tunny I allow myself to refer the reader to our fig. 1.—We immediately agree with Mr. Froriep that this animal was a large shark. Evidently it was dead, "floating some days like a huge trunk". The reason that no whaleman recognized the animal, that neither guts nor heart was found, is of course to be found in the fact that the animal was putrified, irrecognizable, and had already lost its guts and some other entrails. Evidently it was a basking-shark, *Squalus maximus* (See our fig. 8). The length of 30 feet and girth of 18 feet is normal in this species. Norwegian fishermen harpoon it to procure the train-oil from the liver. The teeth are comparatively small and conical, the skin is lead coloured and can really be used as a whet-stone.—

1849.—In the *Zoologist* of 1849, p. 2335, we read:

"*A young sea-serpent.*—On Friday, while some fishermen belonging to Usan were at the out-sea fishing, they drew up what appeared to them a young seaserpent, and lost no time in bringing the young monster to the secretary of our Museum. The animal, whatever it may be called, is still alive, and we have just been favoured with a sight of it; but whether it really be a young sea-serpent or not, we shall leave those who are better acquainted with Zoology than we are to determine. Be it what it may, it is a living creature, more than 20 feet in length, less than an inch in circumference, and of a dark brown chocolate colour. When at rest its body is round; but when it is handled it contracts upon itself, and assumes a flattish form. When not disturbed its motions are slow; but when taken out of the water and extended, it contracts like what a long cord of caoutchouc would do, and folds itself up in spiral form, and soon begins to secrete a whitish mucous from the skin, which cements the folds together, as for the purpose of binding the creature into the least possible dimensions."—"*Montrose Standard.*"—

"[This creature was probably a specimen of *Gordius marinus*. I am obliged for the extract.—E. Newman.]"

Mr. Newman suggesting this worm to be a *Gordius marinus* evidently did not mean the *Gordius marinus* of Linné, but that of Montagu. The former is a little worm of about one half of an inch in length, living parasitically in the entrails of some fishes, especially in herrings, whilst the latter is identical to *Lineus longissimus* of Sowerby, belonging to the family of *Lineidae*, to the order of *Nemertini*, to the class of *Platyelminthes* or Flat-Worms. Of this species individuals of thirty to forty-five feet in length have occasionally been dredged.

Having the means of consulting the splendid work of the British Nemerteans of Mr. Mc. Intosh, I am able to show my readers in fig 12 this *Lineus longissimus*, on a reduced scale.

1849, March 26.—Another would be sea-serpent; (Zoologist p. 2433 for 1849):

"*A strange marine animal*, of great size and strength, was captured on the 26th. of March off Cullercoats, near Newcastle. By the enclosed handbill, which has been forwarded to me, it appears to be quite unknown to the neighbouring *savants*. The honest fishermen who drew the struggling monster to land are not, however, overscrupulous about the name, provided it be attractive enough to extract from the pockets of 'ladies and gentlemen 6*d*.; working people 3*d*. each': they therefore boldly announce him as 'the great sea-serpent caught at last'. My correspondent very judiciously observes, that whatever the animal may be, it adds another to the many evidences constantly occurring that there *are* more things in heaven and earth, than are dreamt of by the most experienced practical observers. Some thirty five years since, the distinguished anatomist Dr. Barclay, was fain to reproach his contemporaries with the folly of affecting to suppose that they knew every thing. What additions have five and thirty years not given to Science! As the animal in question must be at least a local visitor, may we not hope, that some resident naturalist will favour us with a notice of it?"

"The great Sea-Serpent caught at last, by fourteen fishermen, off Cullercoats, on Monday last, March 26, 1849. This most wonderful monster of the deep was discovered by a crew of fishermen, about six miles from the land, who, after a severe struggle, succeeded in capturing this, the most wonderful production of the mighty deep. This monster has been visited by numbers of the gentry and scientific men of Newcastle, and all declare that nothing hitherto discovered in Natural History affords any resemblance to this. As an object of scientific inquiry, this 'great unknown' must prove a subject of peculiar interest. Many surmises as to its habits, native shores, etc., have already been made, but nothing is really known. The general opinion expressed by those that are best able to judge, is, that this is the great sea-serpent, which hitherto has only been believed to have a fabulous existence, but which recent voyagers declare they have seen. Now exhibiting, at the shop, 57, Grey Street, opposite the High Bridge. Admission: ladies and gentlemen 6*d*., Working people 3*d*. each."

In the *Illustrated London News* of May 19, 1849, we find the following account of this capture:

"The Sea-Serpent.—We observe in the Newcastle papers that a strange and hitherto unknown fish, nearly 13 feet in length, and possessing many of the characteristics which the captain of the *Daedalus* enumerated in his description of the great Sea-Snake, has really been caught off the Northumbriam coast, by the Cullercoats' fishermen, and has been exhibited in Newcastle, where it has created the greatest sensation. The members of the National History Society of that town

FIG. 12.—*LINEUS LONGISSIMUS*, SOW.

have duly reported upon it, and expressed their opinion, that it is a young specimen of the genus *Gymnetrus*, only four of which species, and those very rare, are known to ichthyologists, and described by Cuvier and others as inhabiting the Indian, Mediterranean and White Seas. The present specimen has become the property of a Newcaste merchant, who has presented it to the museum of that town; and we understand that, in accordance with a very general wish of most of our distinguished naturalists, it is now exhibiting in the metropolis."

As we read in the *Zoologist* for 1849, p. 2460-2462, Mr. Albany Hancock and Dr. Embleton now declared it to be a probably new species of the genus of ribandfish (*Gymnetrus*).

Fig. 13 shows the readers a kind of riband-fish, the *Gymnetrus gladius* of Cuvier and Valenciennes, taken from the *Règne Animal*. This fish is of a silvery colour, except the fins and the peculiar articulated head-ornaments, which are crimson. Its length is about ten feet, its home the Mediterranean. The *Gymnetrus Banksii* or *Regalecus Banksii* of Cuvier, closely allied to it, measures about twenty feet, sometimes more, and is, though rarely, hitherto caught only near the British shores. The fish in question therefore most probably belonged to this species.

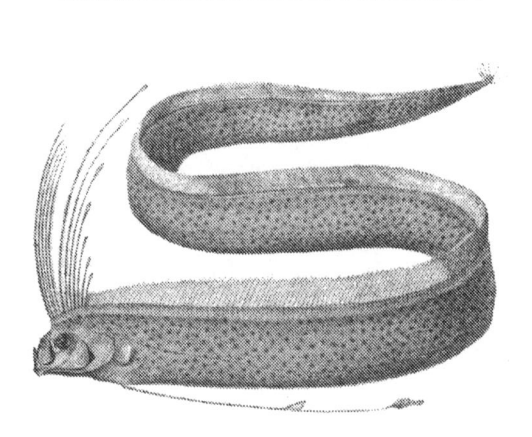

FIG. 13.–*GYMNETRUS GLADIUS*, CUV. VAL.

1852, Aug. 28. — Mr. Alfred Newton, of Elveden Hall, forwarded the following report to the Editor of the *Zoologist* (see this journal for 1853, p. 3756).

"I have lately received the following account from my brother, Capt. Steele, 9th. Lancers, who on his way out to India in the Barham, saw the sea-serpent. Thinking it might be interesting to you, as corroborating the account of the Daedalus, I have taken the liberty of sending you the extract from my brother's letter:—'On the 28th. of August, in long. 40°E., lat. 37° 16'S., about half-past two, we had all gone down below to get ready for dinner, when the first mate called us on deck to see a most extraordinary sight. About five hundred yards from the ship there was the head and neck of an enormous snake; we saw about sixteen or twenty feet out of the water, and he *spouted* a long way from his head; down his back he had a crest like a cock's comb, and was going very slowly through the water, but left a wake of about fifty or sixty feet, as if dragging a long body after him. The captain put the ship off her course to run down to him, but as we approached him, he went down. His colour was green, with light spots. *He was seen by every one on board.*' My brother is no naturalist, and I think this is the first time the monster has ever been seen to spout."

"I am told by a gentleman whose brother was on board the ship (the Barham) referred in the following extract from 'The Times' newspaper of November 17, 1852, that the occurrence there related took place between 35° and 40° S. lat. and 40° and 45°E. long., being about 650 miles due south of Madagascar. I understand that the particulars of the event as there stated closely agree with those furnished to my informant, and further, which is perhaps the most interesting part of the whole circumstance, that the animal was observed to 'blow' or 'spout' in the same manner that a whale does."

"*Extract from an Officer's letter written between the Cape and Madras.* You will be surprised to hear that we have actually seen the great sea-serpent, about which there has been so much discussion. Information was given by a sailor to the captain, just as we were going to dinner. I was in my cabin at the time, and from the noise and excitement, I thought the ship was on fire. I rushed on deck, and on looking over the side of the vessel I saw a most wonderful sight, which I shall recollect as long as I live. His head appeared to be about sixteen feet above the water, and he kept moving it up and down, sometimes showing his enormous neck, which was surmounted with a huge crest in the shape of a saw. It was surrounded by hundreds of birds, and we at first thought it was a dead whale. He left a track in the water like the wake of a boat, and from what we could see of the head and part of his body, we were led to think he must be about sixty feet in length, but he might be more. The captain kept the vessel away to get nearer to him, and when we were within a hundred yards he slowly sank into the depths of the sea. While we were at dinner he was seen again, and a midshipman took a sketch of him, of which I will send you a copy."—*The Times*.

Mr. Gosse, in his *Romance of Natural History*, 1st Series, p. 311, says of these rapports:

"The descriptions, however, show great discrepancy with that of the creature, seen from the *Daedalus*" (see report n°. 118 in the next chapter) "and cannot be considered confirmatory of the former account, otherwise than as proving that immense unrecognized creatures of elongate form roam the ocean."

"Mr. Alfred Newton, of Elveden Hall, an excellent and well-known naturalist, adds the guarantee of his personal acquaintance with one of the recipients of the above letters."

"I note this, because discredit has been undeservedly cast on the phenomena observed, by foolish fabulous stories having been published under fictitious names, for the purpose of hoaxing."

"If it were not for the spouting—which is not mentioned by one observer, and may possibly have been an illusion,—I should be inclined to think that this may have been one of the scabbard fishes, specimens of which inhabit the ocean of immense size. They carry a high serrated dorsal fin, and swim with the head out of the water."

By inserting these reports in the present chapter, I already show my readers, that I agree with Mr. Gosse, that this animal cannot have been a sea-serpent.

I confess that I am unable to give a decisive answer to the question as to what kind of animal it really was. *Apparently* the most plausible explanation is that given by Mr. Gosse, viz., that it was a riband or scabbard fish. The dorsal fin which in these kind of fishes begins at the occiput, is red or crimson coloured, and serrated, so that it may have given rise to the expressions of "a crest like a cock's comb", and "a huge crest in the shape of a saw". But riband fishes are deep-sea fishes. When floating on the surface they are dying or already dead. They never "swim with their head above the surface"! Moreover the green colour does not agree with the common silvery hue of these animals. A riband fish is delineated in fig. 13.

But wonderful it may seem that after having uttered this opinion, a few pages further on Mr. Gosse uses this report amongst others to fix the class of living creatures to which the sea-serpent belongs. And what is the conclusion he arrives at?—that it belongs to the group of *Plesiosauri*, or at least is related to it!

1858, July 9.—*Another Sea-Serpent.*—(*Zoologist*, 1859, p. 6492.)—"The Amsterdamsche Courant of October 6, 1858, inserts the following letter from Captain L. Bijl, of the Dutch bark 'Hendrik Ido Ambacht', to the 'Jorn-Bode':— 'Sailing in the South Atlantic, in 27° 27' N. Lat., and 14° 51' E. long., we perceived on July the 9th., between twelve and one o'clock in the afternoon, a dangerous sea monster, which during nine days constantly kept alongside of us to 37° 50' S. lat., and 42° 9' E. long. This animal was about 90 feet long. and 25 to 30 feet broad, and, most of the time, it struck the ship with such a force as to make it vibrate. The monster blew much water, which spread an unpleasant stench over the deck. The captain, fearing lest the animal might disable the rudder, did his utmost to get rid of his fearful antagonist, but without success. After it had received more than a hundred musket-balls, a harpoon and a long iron bar, blood was seen to flow from various wounds, so that at last from loss of strength, the monster could swim behind our vessel no longer, and we were delivered of it. By its violent blows against the copper the animal's skin had been damaged in several places.'— J. H. van Lennep, Zeist.") [1]

As to the animal, seen from the *Hendrik Ido Ambacht*, I think it must have been a sick spermwhale, which was out of temper; why else should it have been so angry that it followed the bark nine days, cuffing it "most of the time"? Moreover the nature of spermwhales is well enough known as angry and war-like.

1860?—In the *Zoologist* for this year we read p. 6934:

"*A sea-serpent in the Bermudas.*—I beg to send you the following account of a strange sea-monster captured on these shores, the animal being, in fact, no less

---

[1] *Jorn Bode* is most probably a misprint for *Java-Bode*. Zeist is the well-known charming village, east of Utrecht, the fourth town of the Netherlands.

than the great sea-serpent which was described as having been seen by Captain M'Quhae, of H. M. S. 'Daedalus', a few years since. Two gentlemen named Trimingham were walking along the shore of Hungary Bay, in Hamilton Island, on Sunday last, about eleven o'clock, when they were attracted by a loud rushing noise in the water, and, on reaching the spot, they found a huge sea-monster, which had thrown itself on the low rocks, and was dying from exhaustion in its efforts to regain the water. They attacked it with large forks which were lying near at hand for gathering in sea-weed, and unfortunately mauled it much, but secured it. The reptile was sixteen feet seven inches in length, tapering from head to tail like a snake, the body being a flattish oval shape, the greatest depth at about a third of its length from the head, being eleven inches. The colour was bright and silvery; the skin destitute of scales but rough and warty; the head in shape not unlike that of a bull-dog, but it is destitute of teeth; the eyes were large, flat, and extremely brilliant, it had small pectoral fins, and minute ventral fins, and large gills. There were a series of fins running along the back, composed of short, slender rays, united by a transparent membrane, at the interval of something less than an inch from each other. The creature had no bone, but a cartilage running through the body. Across the body at certain intervals were bands, where the skin was of a more flexible nature, evidently intended for the creature's locomotion, screw like, through the water. But its most remarkable feature was a series of eight long thin spines of a bright red colour springing from the top of the head and following each other at an interval of about an inch; the longest was in the centre: it is now in the possession of Colonel Munro, the acting Governor of the Colony; and I had the opportunity of examining it very closely. It is two feet seven inches long, about three eighth of an inch in circumference at the base, and gradually tapering, but flattened at the extreme end, like the blade of an oar. The shell of these spines is hard, and, on examination by a powerful glass, appeared to be double, some red colouring matter being between the shells; the outside, which to the touch and natural eye was smooth, being rough and much similar to the small claws or feelers of the lobster or crayfish. The centre was a wide pith, like an ordinary quill. The three foremost of these spines were connected for about half their length by a greasy filament; the rest being unconnected; the serpent had the power of elevating or depressing the crest at pleasure. The serpent was carefully examined by several medical and scientific gentlemen; the head, dorsal spine, and greater part of the crest are in the possession of J. M. Jones Esq., an eminent naturalist, who will, doubtless, send home a more learned description of this 'wonder of the deep'. I regret that the immediate departure of the mail for England prevents my preparing you any more careful drawing of this great 'sea-serpent' than that I enclose."

Mr. Newman, the Editor of the *Zoologist*, adds hereto the following note:

"Written by Captain Hawtaigne, of Her Majesty's 39 Foot. I place implicit reliance on the narrative, except as to the animal being identical with that seen by Capt. M'Quhae, of which I think there is no evidence. Mr. J. M. Jones is an old subscriber to the *Zoologist*, and a most intelligent; but the query occurs to me, "Is not *this* sea-serpent a ribband fish?"—

Yes, *this* sea-serpent was a ribband fish. And the "eminent naturalist", Mr. J. M. Jones, soon afterwards described this species for the *Zoologist*, p. 6986. Here we read that the Editor, Mr. Edward Newman has "received the following particulars of this most interesting capture from an old and valued correspondent of the

Zoologist. It must be read in connection with a previous note on the same animal in the April number of the *Zoologist.* (Zool. p. 6934)".

Now follows the description of the animal, by Mr. J. Mathew Jones, with which we will not trouble our readers, only referring them to our fig. 15 of a ribband fish, closely allied to the specimen, captured in the Bermudas.

Mr. Jones adds comparisons of this fish with the great sea-serpent seen by Captain M.'Quhae (see report n°. 118), and concludes that part of the reports concerning the great sea-serpent originated from the appearance of ribband fishes. His views of the matter, however, will be treated of in our chapter on the various explanations.

Immediately after this article Mr. Newman wrote another, in which he shows that this fish is a *new species*, giving it the name *Regalecus Jonesii*, Newman. How far Mr. Newman was right in doing so, I am unable to decide. He gives a full description of his new species, and adds that he is not competent to express an opinion upon the similarity of *Regalecus Jonesii* to Capt. M.'Quhae's sea-serpent.

1878.—The *Scotsman* of September 6th. of this year has inserted in its columns the following account.

"A Baby Sea-Serpent.—From Van Diemen's Land comes news of the capture of a queer fish. It is fourteen feet long, fifteen inches deep from the neck to the belly, tapering two inches to the tail, and eight inches in diameter in the thickest place. There are no scales, but the skin is like polished silver, with eighteen dark lines and rows of spots running from the head to the tail each side. There is a mane on the neck twenty inches long, and continues from the head to the tail; small head, no teeth, protrusive mouth, capable of being extended four inches like a sucker; eyes flat, about the size of a half crown, and like silver, with black pupils. There are two feelers under the chin, thirty-two inches long. The fish was alive when captured."

Mr. Andrew Wilson who communicated this capture in *Nature* of the 12th. of September, 1878, Vol. XVIII, thinks that this account "seems explicable only on the tape fish theory." I think he might have written "is explicable only on the tape fish theory", or in short: "this was evidently a tape fish." A tape fish is identical to a ribband fish. Though these fishes are deep-sea fishes, some species evidently don't live at great depth, and are occasionally cast ashore after a storm, as had also happened, in 1860, on the Bermudas (see hereabove).

1879, December 23. — (G. Verschuur, *Eene reis rondom de wereld in 480 dagen*, p. 51.)

On the 21st. of December, 1879, Mr. Verschuur on board the *Granada*, left Mazatlan, a harbour on the western coast of Mexico, for San Francisco. Probably on the 23d. the *Granada* passed Cape San Lucas at 23° N. lat. Mr. Verschuur says:

"Past Cape San Lucas, one afternoon, as I am gazing at the ocean surface, I see a long neck rising out of the water very close to the ship. I beckon some other passengers who are on deck, and after a few minutes the object in question appears a second time. It is the neck of a snake, one would say, and we estimate the length of the visible part of the animal at about a meter. The thickness is about that of the upper-arm of a full-grown man and the head ends in a point, and is as large as a child's head".

"We call the whole crew, and the captain as well as some officers run to. But the animal does not appear again. Nevertheless five of us had seen the animal distinctly, so that a violent altercation arose, when one of the officers said we evidently were mistaken, because the sea-serpent did not exist."

"Nobody of us, it is true, could affirm that it was a sea-serpent. We could only firmly maintain that what we had seen, agreed in all respects with the shape of a serpent."

"The second officer, who joined in the conversation, declared to have observed in 1871 near the coast of Australia, a sea-serpent which was several meters in length, and when this statement too was called in question, the quarrel got warmer and warmer, and, as it generally happens in such cases, every one kept his own opinion, and the world did not get any the wiser for it."

"Does the sea-serpent exist, or does he not? This is a problem which has been answered more than once in the most affirmative manner, and also in a negative sense. I have heard the question disputed on more than one voyage."

In order to obtain more particulars about the animal, I wrote to Mr. Verschuur Oct. 26th., 1889, directing to him the following questions:

"Did the features of the 'snake' make on you the impression to be those of a mammal, like those of a seal or sea-lion, though the pointed head more resembled that of a snake?"

"Or had the head, though being much larger, more the shape of that of an eel?"

"Were there just behind the head a pair of fins, as eels have?"

"Why did the visible part make on you the impression to be a 'neck'. You speak of a 'neck' of a snake. Was the diameter near the head smaller than that just above the water, as if the animal was still thicker under water?"

"Or did you observe the contrary?"

"Was the 'snake' perfectly round, or was it provided on its back with a fin, as in eels?"

"What colour had your snake, and had the belly and the back the same colour?"

"Did you observe any eyes, nostrils, ears, ear holes, gills, whiskers, or any other appendages?"

"These are all questions which a zoologist wants to have answered in order to determine somewhat, what animal may have been seen by you."

Mr. Verschuur had the courtesy to send me an early answer Oct. 30th., 1889. The part of this letter referring to my questions runs as follows:

"I greatly regret to say that my answers will not help you much. The distance at which I saw this strange animal was too great, and the appearance too short, to observe anything of the particulars stated by you."

"The part which we saw rise out of the sea had, if my memory does not deceive me, the thickness of a full-grown upper-arm, and the length of from 1 to 1 1/2 meter."

"The head seemed to be round, and of the common shape of a snake's head, i. e. having nearly the tapering shape of the 'cobra' or of the rattlesnake."

"Of scales, eyes, fins, etc., I could observe nothing, during this short appearance. The colour seemed to me to be a greyish one."

"I regret not being able to give you more details than those written by me in my book of travels."

I think this animal was of the eel-tribe, the dimensions were too small even to admit the supposition that it was a spawn of the sea-serpent.

We observe that many so-called great sea-serpents are to be explained by reference to *known* animals. There are, however, a great many sea-serpents which don't answer to the description of any *known* being at all, unless we venture upon a suggestion which is either wrong, forced, or premature, and which can be accepted only with a smile or a shrug of the shoulders.

Some sea-serpent explainers are in the habit of explaining *one single* sea-serpent, say by reference to a row of porpoises, and then try to account for others by this suggestion, the upshot of which is that the explainer does no longer see his way clear of the difficulties which beset him, and driven to his wits' end, cuts the Gordian knot, leaving a great many sea-serpents unexplained.

Others, like Mr. Gosse, Mr. Andrew Wilson, and Mr. Henry Lee, were prepossessed with opinions which made of every sea serpent a *Plesiosaurus*, an extraordinarily developed *Hydrophis*, or a large Calamary (*Architeuthis*).

But none of them hit on the plan to put all the accounts, tales, and reports of this great unknown animal side by side, to point out the statements which are immediately recognizable as strange, or explicable by reference to some known animal, and finally to decide which of the known animals may have been bold enough to present itself as a deceitful serpentine creature, or, if the result is negative and leads to the conclusion that the sea-serpent does not belong to any known species of animal, to decide, what kind of animal does exist, though *unknown* to zoologists! And to this inquiry we pass now.

4

The Various accounts and reports concerning observations of Sea-Serpents, chronologically arranged and thoroughly discussed; and criticisms of the papers written about the subject.

An account of the appearance of a Sea-Serpent, published in *Nature* of Nov. 18, 1880, induced me to make a study of that subject. A few months afterwards I wrote a little paper for the *Album der Natuur*, a Dutch periodical, designed to bring the latest progress and problems of Science in a very popular manner under the eyes of non-scientific readers.

In that paper I discussed the probability of the existence of an animal which was unknown to zoologists, but which nevertheless existed, and gave rise to all the narratives of the Great Sea-Serpent.

In January, 1889, I happened to come across a paper on the same subject by Mr. Henry Lee. In this work "*Sea Monsters Unmasked*" the sea-serpent is explained in several manners, as having been a row of porpoises following one another, as some gigantic sea-weed, as huge calamaries, and though hesitatingly as any still unknown animal belonging to a genus of reptiles, the representatives of which are only known in the fossil state.

Having given another explanation in my above-mentioned paper, and seeing that Mr. Lee did not mention my supposition, I am now so bold as to repeat my attempt at explaining the Sea-Serpent in another manner; I have chosen the English language as being known to all zoologists and to all navigators.

The Sea-Serpents and other serpents of extraordinary dimensions, quoted by Aristoteles (*History of Animals*, Book 8, chapt. 28), Plinius (*Naturalis Historiae*, Lib. 4, cap. 23, Lib. 8, cap. 14), Valerius Maximus (*de Factis Dictisque Memorabilibus*, Lib. 1, cap. 8, 1st. century), Florus (Lib. 2), Seneca (litt. 82), Silvius Italicus (Lib. 6), Aurus Gellius (Lib. 6, cap. 3), Orosius, Zonares, Diodorus Siculus, Voleterranus (*Commentariorum Urbanorum* libri 38, book 12), Petr. Martyr (Decad. 1, lib. 10), Bakius (*Posidonii Vita et Reliquiae*, p. 115), Aelianus, Vergilius, etc., were most probably nothing but pythons.

The various kinds of *Serpens marinus* alluded to by Aristoteles and Plinius, and afterwards described and figured by many other authors, evidently belong to the sea-eels, e. g. those of *Père* Jean Baptiste Labat in 1722, or were doubtless real sea-snakes, which reach no greater length than about twelve feet.

For these reasons we will pass all the descriptions of these different animals, and review only reports of no earlier date than the year 1500 A. D.

Having examined all the descriptions and figures of the Great Sea-Serpent published from 1500 A. D. up to this day, we come to the conclusion, as we have already stated above, that some of the so-called sea-serpents were fishes of slender form, others were cuttles of extraordinary dimensions (*Cephalopoda Decapoda Chondrophora*). In all these cases it is not impossible, and sometimes not difficult for a zoologist, who is familiar with these creatures and their habits, to explain those observations, but the greater part of the accounts of Great Sea-Serpents do *not* agree with the well-known shape of sea-weeds and cuttles, *nor* with the habits of porpoises. Mr. Lee tries a few times to identify the Sea-Serpent with these kinds of animals, but all who saw the sea-serpent moving with vertical undulations, and figured it thus, knew the habits of those animals, and some of them testified, that it could not have been porpoises, which they knew well enough to be sure of it. I will add here that porpoises move irregularly and have dorsal fins, which must of course be visible whenever they appear on the surface, whilst in none of the accounts mentioning the sea-serpent moving in vertical undulations, there is any question of dorsal fins visible on the coils of the sea-serpent.

But let us now pass to the accounts that have come within our reach, and peruse them in order of their date.

1.—1522.—(See Olaus Magnus, *Historia de gentibus*, etc.) "There is also another serpent of an astonishing size in an island called Moos, in the diocese of Hammer: which portends a change in the Kingdom of Norway, as a comet does in the whole world, as it was seen, anno 1522, raising itself high above the surface of the water and circling like a spire. Seen from afar this serpent was estimated by conjecture to be fifty cubits long; this event was followed by the banishment of King Christiernus and by a great persecution of the Bishops; and it also showed the destruction of the country, as Isidorus tells us of the birds of Diomedes."

In the original Latin we read *atque in modum sphaerae convolvens* (and wrinkling like a ball), but as this has no sense, I am convinced that we have to do with a misprint, and that the author evidently wrote *atque in modum spirae convolvens*, which I have translated above "and circling like a spire". This evidently signifies that the observer saw the animal swimming with vertical undulations, parts of which were visible above the surface of the water.

Further we must direct our attention to the statement that the animal raised itself high above the surface of the water.

Finally that it was estimated to be fifty cubits long, i. e. about seventy-five feet.

Olaus Magnus, the Archbishop of Upsala wrote in 1555 as follows:

"They who, either to trade, or to fish, sail along the shores of Norway, relate with concurring evidence a truly admirable story, namely that a very large serpent of a length of upwards of 200 feet, and 20 feet in diameter lives in rocks and holes near the shore of Bergen; it comes out of its caverns only on summernights and in fine weather to devour calves, lambs and hogs, or goes into the sea to eat cuttles, lobsters and all kinds of sea-crabs. It has a row of hairs of two feet in length, hanging from the neck, sharp scales of a dark colour, and brilliant flaming eyes. It attacks boats, and snatches away the men, by raising itself high out of the water, and devours them: and commonly this does not happen without a terrible event in the Kingdom, without a change being at hand, either that the princes will die or will be banished, or that a war will soon break out."

This narrative tells us that the sea-serpent frequents the shores of Norway, that it appears mostly in summer, that it has large dimensions, and a considerable thickness. It has a row of hairs hanging down from its neck, its colour is dark, its eyes are brilliant and flaming. It only appears in fine weather.

We consider its devouring hogs, lambs and calves, and its appearance on summernights on land to take its prey to be a fable. The eating of squids, cuttles, crabs and lobsters may be a fiction, or it may have been truly witnessed, the animal chewing them with its head above water, as seals and sea-lions do. The story of snatching away a man from the ships is evidently confounded with another tale, as it is not mentioned anywhere else with regard to the sea-serpent. It evidently refers to gigantic calamaries which occasionally attack boats and snatch away one of the crew. (See Lee, *Sea Monsters Unmasked*, I, *The Kraken*.). Its being covered with scales must be fictitious too, for they who saw a sea-serpent at a short distance, are unanimous in stating that it had no scales but a smooth skin.

On the same page of the text, Olaus Magnus has figured a sea-serpent in the act of swallowing a man from a boat, which has just anchored on a rock, wherein the serpent has its hole. I give a facsimile of that figure in Fig. 14.—Mr. Henry Lee who mostly sees calamaries and no other animals in the tales and figures representing the Great Sea-Serpent, tells us that: "the presumed body of the serpent was one of the arms of the squid, and the two rows of suckers thereto belonging are indicated in the illustration by the medial line traversing its whole length (intended to represent a dorsal fin) and the double row of transverse septa, one on each side of it".—As to the snatching away a man of the crew, I quite agree with Mr. Lee, as already said above, but as to the figure of the serpent itself, I am strongly convinced that Olaus Magnus or his draughtsman had no other intention than to delineate a large snake, and they gave it the large scales, mentioned in the text, but the scales are badly drawn. They further gave it a medial row of scales, as all snakes have such a medial row.

Fig. 14.–The sea-serpent as represented by Olaus Magnus.

FIG. 15.—THE SEA-SERPENT ILLUSTRATING THE TEXT OF GESNER.

Gesner in his *Nomenclator aquafilium animantium*, 1560, gives two figures of the sea-serpent of which I give facsimiles in Fig. 15 and 16.—Gesner says that there is a large map of Scandinavia in Olaus Magnus' work, and on this map our fig. 15 is drawn in the Baltic Sea, and our fig. 16 in the Atlantic Ocean. In the original edition of 1555 there is but a small map of Scandinavia, which shows only the heads of several animals in the sea. I therefore conclude that there still exists another edition of Magnus' work which I don't know. Returning to our figures we immediately observe that the drawer has delineated large *snakes*, the one without scales, and swimming with *vertical* undulations, the other with large scales, and that he did not intend to represent a dorsal fin by the medial line, but only a medial row of scales, unequal to the lateral. On the head three transversal rows of protuberances are visible, which evidently serve to represent the long hairs hanging down from the neck of the animal.

Of the sea-serpent Gesner tells us:

"In the Baltic or Swedish Ocean are found certain yellow sea-serpents of thirty or forty feet in length, which, when not provoked, do not harm any one. Of these sea-serpents Olaus Magnus gives the following figure in his Map of Scandinavia".—(See our fig. 15).

"On the same Map there is another sea-serpent, a hundred or two hundred feet long (as says the text, or three hundred, as states the number added to the figure), which sometimes appears near Norway in fine weather, and is dangerous to Seamen, as it snatches away men from the ships. Mariners tell that it incloses ships, as large as our trading vessels, made on our rivers and lakes, by laying itself round them in a circle, and that the ship then is turned upside down. It sometimes makes such large coils above the water, that a ship can go through one of them. I give the figure as it is on the Map."—(See our fig. 16.)

Here we meet with three other characteristics of the sea-serpent: it is harmless when not provoked, it encircles ships and turns them upside down, and its coils are so gigantic that a ship can go through one of them. The first characteristic is a real one: the sea serpent is perfectly harmless, if not provoked. We observe this in almost every account. The other two are of course extraordinary exaggerations of its dimensions.

The two figures of Gesner copied on a reduced scale, with an extract of his text, appeared in the *Graphic* of January 29, 1876.

FIG. 16.—THE SECOND SEA-SERPENT ILLUSTRATING THE SAME WORK.

94   The Great Sea-Serpent

The text in the edition of Olaus Magnus' work printed at Basle in 1567 is the same as that of the first edition printed in 1555 at Rome, but the figure between the text differs, and is doubtless a combination of our figg. 14 and 16, in miniature; see our fig. 17.

On the map of Scandinavia subjoined to the work also occurs a figure of the sea-serpent, which we have copied in our fig. 18.—This figure does not claim our attention; it represents an eel or a snake, it has no scales.—Not so fig. 17: it distinctly shows dorsal scales and ventral plates, just as snakes have. This seems to me a confirmation of my opinion that in all these figures the drawers had no other intention than to delineate a large snake, without any notion of the arms of a calamary. As to the seizing of a man, we believe that a large calamary was the robber, whose deed is wrongly attributed to the sea-serpent. Last not least, it distinctly shows the long hairs, hanging down from its neck, a true mane, and several credible persons declare to have seen them.

Aldrovandus, 1640, believes that the sea-serpent of the Baltic or Swedish Ocean is the same as that of the Norwegian Ocean. I believe he is right. Moreover he repeats the texts of Olaus Magnus and Gesner. His figures are enlargements of the figures on the Map of Scandinavia, which accompanies the edition of Olaus Magnus' work, unknown to me, and mentioned above. He only omits the water, the ship

FIG. 17.—THE SEA-SERPENT AS REPRESENTED IN THE BASLE EDITION OF OLAUS MAGNUS' WORK.

FIG. 18.—THE SEA-SERPENT, ILLUSTRATING THE MAP OF SCANDINAVIA IN THE BASLE EDITION OF OLAUS MAGNUS' WORK.

and the man in its mouth. Of his figures I don't give copies, because they are exact enlargements of our fig. 15 and 16.—

2.—1640?—(See Adam Olearius, *Gottorfische Kunstkammer*, Ed. I, 1650, Ed. II, 1674) "and that this is true has not long ago been confirmed by a Swedish nobleman at Gottorf, who declared to have heard from the Burgomaster of Malmoi, a trustworthy man, that, whilst standing on a hill on the Norwegian coast, he saw in the calm water a large serpent, which seen from afar, had the thickness of a wine barrel, and 25 windings. These serpents are said to appear on the surface of the water only in calm weather and at certain times."

Here again we have the statement, that in the Norwegian sea, and most probably in the Sound between Sweden and Danmark, a large animal was seen, looking like a huge serpent, and the confirmation that it comes to the surface of the water only in calm weather and at certain times. I beg the reader to fix his attention on those apparently insignificant statements, as it will be seen that they are given several times independant of one another.

Jonston in his *Historia Naturalis*, and his *Theatrum universale omnium animalium* of which several editions appeared in 1653, 1657, 1660, 1665, 1718 (edited by Ruysch, quoted by Prof. W. D. Peck in Mem. Amer. Acad. 1818, Vol. IV), 1764 and 1768, repeats the tales of Olaus Magnus, and the figures of Gesner and Aldrovandus.—

Milton in his *Paradise Lost*, printed in 1667, comparing Satan with huge monsters, also mentions the sea-serpent of the Norwegians, calling it Leviathan (Book I, verse 192- 208):
"Thus Satan, talking to his nearest mate,
With head up-lift above the wave, and eyes
That sparkling blaz'd; his other parts besides
Prone on the flood, extended long and large,
Lay floating many a rood, in bulk as huge
As whom the fables name of monstrous size
Titanian, or Earth-born, that war'd on Jove,
Briareus, or Typhon, whom the den
By ancient Tarsus held; or that sea-beast
Leviathan, which God of all his works
Created hugest that swim th' ocean stream:
Him, haply slumb'ring on the Norway foam,
The pilot of some small night founder'd skiff
Deeming some island, off, as seamen tell,
With fixed anchor in his scaly rind,
Moors by his side under the lee, while night;
Invests the sea, and wished morn delays."

We observe that he mixes here also another story of a large sea-monster on which sea-men, believing it some island, will anchor, a story told about the Kraken and about the sperm-whales.

Charleton in 1668 quotes only Aldrovandus and Olaus Magnus, giving neither description nor figures.

3.—1687.—(Ramus, *Norges Beskrivelse*, quoted by Pontoppidan).
"In the year 1687 a Great Sea-Serpent was seen several times by several persons in the Damsfjord, and once by eleven persons together. The weather was calm, but as soon as the sun set and the wind began to blow, it left the fjord, and like one who runs out a coil of rope can know the length thereof, so one could see how long it was, before it had wound off all its coils, and stretched itself at full length."

In this account we read again that the animal is seen in calm weather and that it shows coils or windings. For the first time the fact is mentioned that it can stretch itself, evidently in a straight line. Further on we shall read this several times.

4.—1720.—(Pontoppidan, *Det förste Forsög paa Norges naturlige Historie*).
"Thorlack Thorlacksen has told me that in 1720 a sea-serpent had been shut up a whole week in a little inlet, into which it came by high tide through a narrow entrance of seven or eight fathoms deep, and that eight days afterwards, when it had left the inlet, a skin of a snake or serpent was found. One end of the skin had entirely sunk into the water of the inlet, and no one could guess how long it was, the inlet in which the skin partly lay, being several fathoms deep. The other end of this skin was washed ashore by the current, where everybody could see it; apparently it could not be used, for it consisted of a soft, slimy mass. Thorlacksen was a native of the harbour of Kobbervueg".

It is evident that a true sea-serpent visited the little fjord daily during that week, most probably in its pursuit of fish, for the sea-serpent is sufficiently known to the Norwegians, and if it had been an animal different from the common Norwegian sea-serpent, I am sure that it would not have been called a sea-serpent. It is also stated that the animal left the inlet. But the skin found afterwards was certainly nothing else but a putrified long arm or tentacle of a great calamary. The soft slimy nature of the skin sufficiently proves my hypothesis. The great calamary died in the fjord or inlet, and its long dead arm was washed ashore by the current while the body sunk.

5.—1734, July 6.—The earliest account of Hans Egede's encounter with the sea-serpent we find in his work published in Danish at Kopenhagen in 1740,

Various Accounts 97

entitled: "*A Full and Particular Relation of his voyage to Greenland, as a Missionary, on the year* 1734".

I have not had the opportunity of consulting this work, but the passage about the sea-serpent runs most probably as follows:

"Anno 1734, July. On the 6th. appeared a very terrible sea-animal, which raised itself so high above the water, that its head reached above our main-top. It had a long sharp snout, and blew like a whale, had broad, large flappers, and the body was, as it were, covered with a hard skin, and it was very wrinkled and uneven on its skin; moreover on the lower part it was formed like a snake, and when it went under water again, it cast itself backwards and in so doing it raised its tail above the water, a whole ship-length from its body. That evening we had very bad weather."

In the same year there appeared a German edition of this work, entitled *Ausführliche and Wahrhafte Nachricht vom Anfange und Fortgange der Groenländischen Mission*, etc., Hamburg, 1740, 4°, which I have not been able to consult either.

I don't know whether there is an English or a French edition. In the *Illustrated London News* of Oct. 28, 1848, the writer of the article *Evidences of the former appearance of the Sea-Serpent* translated the passage from a Danish copy of Egede's *Full and Particular Relation* in the British Museum. Evidently he was not very well up in the Danish language, for his translation is partly incorrect. I am convinced that in the original text Egede does not mention the exact locality where he saw the animal. The translator tells us that it was off the south coast of Greenland, which of course is incorrect, as Greenland has no south coast. Of "sea-animal" he makes "sea-monster", for "above our main-top" he has "on a level with our main-top", for "it blew like a whale" he has "it blew water almost like a whale", for "its body was as it were covered with a hard skin" he has "its body was covered with shell-fish, or scales", and some parts are not translated at all.

In 1738 Hans Egede wrote a *Journal of his mission*, in which he did not mention the meeting, but his son Paul Egede in the continuation of this Journal, entitled *Continuation af Relationerne betreffende den Groenlandske Mission*, Kjoebenhavn, 1741, gives a full account of it, which we have translated above word for word.

I have not had the means of consulting the German translation of this work, entitled *Fortgesetzte Relationen die Groenländische Mission betreffend*, Kopenhagen, 1741, so I cannot say anything about the text or figures, but the translation which I found in the German edition of Pontoppidan's *Natural History of Norway* is correct. Not so the English translation entitled *Journal of the Mission to Greenland*, 2d. Vol. There we find, according to Mr. Lee who quotes the passage in his *Sea-Monsters Unmasked*, first *sea-monster* instead of *sea-animal*, further, that *it spouted water like a whale*, instead of *it blew like a whale*. There is a great difference between these two expressions. A whale does not spout water as is generally believed and figured. Further, that the body seemed to be covered *with scales*, instead of *with a hard skin or crust*, for the Danish *skiell* or *skiaell* is singular, and not plural. Finally, that the tail above the water was a whole ship-length from the *head* instead of from the *body*, for the Danish *Kroppen* signifies "the body". Of course I cannot say anything of the figures in this edition.

In the original Danish work of Paul Egede there is a map of a part of the coast of Greenland and of the Davis' Straits, called Baals Rivier, on which is situated the Danish Colony, the Good Hope (Gothaab). As it was generally done in those

FIG. 19.—THE SEA-SERPENT, AS SEEN BY HANS EGEDE, DRAWN BY BING.

days, Mr. Bing, a brother-missionary of Egede's, drew on his map not only the animal but also the vessel in the sea. I give here a facsimile of the figure of the animal, without the ship. We distinctly see that the animal has rather a serpentlike form with a large head, showing formidable teeth, an eye with a heavy eye-brow, and a nostril; two flappers on the fore-part of the body, the uneven skin, and a tail ending in a point.

On the same map there is also another figure, showing the animal's tail, after it had plunged back into the water. The tail is again figured terminating in a point.

We shall do well to observe the fact that the figure is an accurate illustration of the text with regard to the animal blowing like a

FIG. 20.—THE SAME INDIVIDUAL PLUNGING BACK INTO THE WATER.

whale; the breath which the animal exhales immediately after having been under water a long time, is condensed in the cold air and forms little curling clouds.

In the original Danish work of Hans Egede, entitled *A Full and Particular Relation*, etc., of which we have spoken above, there is also a figure. Though I have not had the opportunity to consult this work, I am thoroughly convinced, that the map of Baals Rivier with the two figures of the animal are quite the same, true facsimiles. The above mentioned translator drew this figure on a reduced scale for his article in the *Illustrated London News*, and as his text is incorrect, his figure is so too, for he changed the rough skin into scales, according to his own translation. (See our fig. 21.)

Afterwards Mr. Lee in his *Sea-Monsters Unmasked* made use of the figure of the *Illustrated London News* and so gave his readers again an altered figure. For history's sake I show here a true facsimile of the figure as it appeared in the *Illustrated London News*, Oct. 28, 1848, and in Mr. Lee's *Sea Monsters Unmasked*, London, 1883. A reduced copy of it also appeared in the *Illustrirte Zeitung* of February 3, 1877.

In the Danish work of Hans Egede *Det gamle Groenlands nye Perlustration* we read: "that it was seen at 64° lat. before the colony". "Its body was as thick as the ship and three or four times longer". Moreover the description of the animal is the same as in Paul Egede's Continuation of the Journal.

In the German edition of this work, entitled *Des alten Groenlands neue Perlustration*, Copenhagen, 1742, we read: "that it was seen before the Danish Colony, the Good Hope, that it had two broad flappers on the fore-part of the body".

FIG. 21.–THE DRAWING OF BING, AS REPRINTED AND ALTERED IN THE ILLUSTRATED LONDON NEWS OF 1848.

In the Dutch edition, entitled: *Beschrijving van Oud Groenland*, Delft, 1746, the translator did not allow himself so many liberties as the English and the German translators did, but was more correct in his expressions.

In the French edition, entitled *Description et histoire naturelle du Groenland*, Copenhagen et Genève, 1763, the translator allowed himself the liberty to tell his readers that "when the animal, which was covered *with scales*, plunged back into the water, it did so with *the belly turned upwards!*"

In the same year appeared a second German edition (translated from the French) entitled *Beschreibung und Naturgeschichte von Groenland*, Berlin, 1763, in which we even read that the animal *lay upon the water with its belly turned upwards* when it plunged back into the water!

In many respects the figure of Mr. Bing and Egede's text complete each other.

Let us now have a look at both the text and the figures. We may do this most safely, being convinced of the truth of Egede's words and Bing's figure. Egede "was a truthful, pious, and single-minded man, possessing considerable powers of observation, and a genuine love of natural history; his statements are modest, accurate, and free from exaggeration. His illustrations bear the unmistakable signs of fidelity." (Lee, *Sea-Monsters Unmasked*, p. 65.)

From what has been said of the animal, seen by Egede, we gather that it appeared on the 6th. of July, 1734, in fine weather before the Danish Colony the Good Hope, Davis Straits, Greenland; (Egede says: "the following evening we had very bad weather", so we may conclude that:) the weather was fine, when the animal was seen; it had a considerable length, say a hundred feet, and was much thicker than a snake of those dimensions would be, say some eight feet; it raised its head, its neck and the fore-part of its trunk high above the surface of the water, it had a long, sharp snout, it blew like a whale (the breath of an animal as large as a whale must of course have been distinctly visible in those cold regions; I also wish to fix the reader's attention on the figure where the animal is not spouting a stream of water, but where its breath is condensed by the cold, and forms little curling clouds of vapour). It had broad and large flappers. Egede does not say: it had broad flappers on the forepart of the trunk; as Egede does not state that the figure, made by Mr. Bing aboard his ship, directly after the appearance of the animal, is not truthful, we must consider it as being correct; so the animal had two large and broad flappers on the fore-part of the trunk. The body *seemed* to be covered with a hard skin. For truth's sake Egede wrote *seemed*, which is well done; for a hard skin or crust would not have been *wrinkled* when the animal bends its body. Like all known air-breathing sea-animals of those dimensions the animal must of course have had under its skin a relatively thick layer of bacon, and I myself have often seen that the skin of sea-lions and seals wrinkled, when the animal bent its body in such a manner as the Sea-Serpent of Egede did. And we shall afterwards repeatedly see that the sea-serpent has no scales but a smooth skin, as seals have. And if the animal could have scales, they would be very large ones, considering its colossal dimensions, in which case it must have been easy to see the scales from a distance, though they were wet with the water; but I can hardly believe that one can say of an animal, seen at some distance and quite wet and shining with the water, whether it has a crust or a soft skin. The latter has been the case, for the animal showed wrinkles when bending its body. Its lower part was formed like that of a snake, by which Egede evidently means to say that it was perfectly round and tapered to the end of the tail, and that he *did not see* any appendages (which does not exclude their presence, for the middle part of the body remained invisible, hidden by the water). The creature plunged *backwards* into the water. It evidently has a considerable flexibility, as is also shown in the figure. Consequently it cannot have been a snake, which has no dorso-ventral flexibility, nor a gigantic calamary, as Mr. Lee thinks, which has no flexibility at all! It had a very flexible, long tail, almost one half of the length of its body, which was distinctly seen by Egede and figured by Mr. Bing. The tail of the animal, being of a considerable length, tapered in a point, and had no caudal fins, neither horizontal nor vertical ones. The figure shows an eye with a heavy eye-brow, a nostril, and teeth; the flappers have external visible fingers, as sea-lions have; those of porpoises and dolphins are without them. Afterwards we shall more than once have occasion to observe that the sea-serpents's head is drawn by Bing too large, and the neck too short.

Mr. Lee says in his frequently quoted work *Sea-Monsters Unmasked*, "The sea-monster seen by Egede was of an entirely different kind" (viz. from those mentioned by Magnus and Pontoppidan). I am of the opinion that if Mr. Lee had written: The sea-monster seen by Egede was the same, but seen in an entirely different position, condition and direction, he would have been nearer the truth; for careful inquiry has shown me that the sea-serpents of Magnus and Pontoppidan are the same as those which still appear in the Norwegian seas, and those have all the characters of Egede's animal. Moreover we saw that the animal, mentioned in our accounts 1, 2, 3 and 4, and according to the descriptions of Magnus and Gesner had the following characteristics: 1. It raises itself out of the water to a considerable height. 2. It swims with vertical undulations. 3. It has an enormous length, probably upwards of a hundred feet. 4. It is much thicker than a snake of the same length would be. 5. It has a row of hairs hanging down from its neck. 6. Its colour is dark. 7. Its eyes are brilliant and flaming. 8. Its food consists of squids, cuttles, crabs and lobsters. 9. It is harmless, if not provoked. 10. It appears in fine weather. 11. It can stretch itself in a straight line.—Of these facts the 1st., 3d.,

FIG. 22.—BING'S DRAWING AS COPIED BY PONTOPPIDAN.

4th., and 10th. are stated by Egede; he could not mention the 2d., 8th., and 11th., because he did not see the animal swimming or eating. Most probably he could not see the 5th., because he did not see the animal on its back, but as the figure shows, somewhat on its belly and somewhat from aside; moreover there are individuals without a mane. Egede says nothing of its colour, its eyes, its harmlessness. Its colour was evidently a dark brown one, the common colour of large sea-animals, else he would have called it brilliant white, or green, or red. The eyes are figured by Bing, though not described by Egede, but in Pontoppidan's work we read in a note to Chapt. VIII, § 7, that Mr. Bing mentioned to his brother-in-law, Parson Sylow, at Hougs in the parish of Bergen, that the eyes seemed to be reddish and like a burning fire. So its harmlessness is the only fact we cannot derive with certainty from Egede's account.

Pontoppidan relating Egede's observation of the monster gives a copy of Mr. Bing's figure, but as often occurred in those days, it is not copied with great accuracy, and Bing's drawing has been altered by Pontoppidan so as to give quite another figure. (Our fig. 22 is a facsimile of that of the German edition.) Mr. Bing was right in figuring the vaporous breath of the animal, and Pontoppidan changes it wrongly into a waterspout of more than 100 feet long! Pontoppidan is convinced, when seeing Bing's figure, that there are several species of sea-serpents, all belonging to the same genus. I do not wish to discuss this point.

Still more exaggerated is the figure of Jardine's *Naturalist's Library*, or rather that which Dr. R. Hamilton presents to his readers. He makes of it a serpentine dragon which has also the power of spouting a splendid set of water some twenty feet high, a water-mass equalling nearly half the volume of the animal's body!

In his *Essay towards a Natural History of Serpents*, 1742, Mr. Owen repeats only (p. 14, and p. 143) the tales and reports of Olaus Magnus and Gesner.

FIG. 23.–BING'S DRAWING AS ALTERED IN DR. HAMILTON'S WORK.

6.—1743?—(Pontoppidan, Chapt. VIII, § 7).—"It is said that a few years ago a sea-serpent stranded on the cliffs near Amund in Nordfjord, perhaps with high water, and died there and the carrion also caused a dreadful smell."

7.—1744?—(Pontoppidan, Chapt. VIII, § 7).—"It is also told that a sea-serpent stranded near the Isle of Karmen and that the stranding of sea-serpents took place in more localities."

There is nothing strange in the stranding of sea-serpents. Unluckily the fear of the Norwegian people of sea-serpents is great enough to keep them far away from them, even from their carrions, and so these accounts don't mention anything as a result of closer investigation.

8.—1745?—(Pontoppidan, Chapt. VIII, § 1, note).—"A fisherman relates to me that, on Sundsland, two miles from Bergen, he once saw a long, large and strange animal so close to his boat, that the water, brought in motion by the animal, dashed against it, but immediately it disappeared again under water. The head resembled that of a seal, its skin was also as woolly, but the body was as thick and as long as a yacht of fifty tons, and the tail, which seemed to be about thirty-five feet long, tapered towards the end which was as pointed as a boat-hook."

Though Pontoppidan did not seem to believe that this animal was his sea-serpent, I am convinced that such was indeed the case, because the whole description is exactly that of the animal. It is remarkable that all the persons who saw the sea-serpent so close to their boat, as this fisherman did, agree in giving it a smooth skin; now seals when wet have also a smooth skin, and our fisherman was near enough to the animal to detect the real nature of such a skin, viz. that it is *hairy*, or as he expresses himself *woolly*. We shall afterwards more than once meet with statements in which the head is compared with that of a seal. The head, though resembling that of a seal, was of course much larger. The body was as thick and as long as a yacht of fifty tons, say about forty feet, and the tail was about thirty-five feet in length, and tapered to its pointed end, like the animal of Egede and those of the former writers Magnus, Olearius and Ramus, who compared the body with that of a snake. As the fisherman mentions the length of the tail, it is evident that he could see the beginning of it, so that it may be supposed that there was a difference in thickness between the body and the tail.

9.—1746, August.—(Pontoppidan, *Det förste Forsög*, etc.).—Pontoppidan relates: "Last winter I happened to meet the Royal Commander and Pilot-general at Bergen, Mr. Lorenz von Ferry, and we spoke about this subject. He told me that for a long time he had doubted the existence of the sea-serpent, but that at last his experiences in 1746 had convinced him. And though I could not say anything of importance against it, he ordered to my satisfaction and that of others, two seamen, who were with him in his boat, and had seen the animal and its blood which coloured the water red after a shot of von Ferry at it, to appear before the public court of justice at Bergen. What those men confirmed on oath may be found in the following instrument which I received in original, and which I therefore think valuable enough to communicate in extenso:"

"Albert Christian Dass, His Royal Majesty's Stadtholder at Bergen, Hans Christian Gartner, His Royal Majesty's Councillor of Justice and Commerce, at the same time Secretary of the town, together with Jan Clies, Ole Simenson, Ole Brinchmand, Joergen Koenig for Conrad von Lange, Matthias Gram for Elias Petrus Tuchsen, Claus Natler for Didrich Haslop, Jochem Foegh for Henrich Hiort, and Joergen Wiers for Hans Christian Byszing, sworn citizens and additional deniers there, declare, that on February the 22th., 1751, the Procurator Johann Reutz appeared before the public court of justice at Bergen, and presented a paper he had received that day, and bearing the date of the day before, from the honourable Captain and Pilot-general Lorenz von Ferry. And as the services of the appearer are requested in it, to supply him a judicial hearing of witnesses, concerning the event mentioned in the same paper, so the appearer, being there for that purpose, pointed out two men living in this town, named Niels Petersen Kopper and Niels Nielsen Anglewigen, begging that these men might be admitted to a declaration on oath, that all has happened in particulars so as is mentioned in the paper, which he begged to be registered in said instrument. The above mentioned paper was read to the witnesses and runs as follows:

"Mr. Johann Reutz."
"Sir,"
"In the latter end of August, in the year 1746, as I was on a voyage, on my return from Trundheim, on a very calm and hot day, having a mind to put in at Molde, it happened that when we had arrived with my yacht within a mile of the aforesaid Molde, being at a place called Jule-Naess, as I was reading in a book, I heard a kind of murmuring voice from amongst the men at the oars, who were eight in number, and observed that the man at the helm kept off from the land. Upon this I inquired what was the matter, and was informed that there was a sea-serpent before us. I then ordered the man at the helm to keep the land again, and to come up with this creature of which I had heard so many stories. Though the fellows were under some apprehension, they were obliged to obey my orders. In the meantime the sea-snake passed by us, and we were obliged to tack the vessel about in order to get nearer to it. As the snake swam faster than we could row, I took my gun which was loaded with small shot, and fired at it; on this he immediately plunged under water. We rowed to the place where it sank down (which in the calm might be easily observed) and lay upon our oars, thinking it would come up again to the surface; however it did not. Where the snake plunged down, the water appeared thick and red; perhaps the small shot might have wounded it, the distance being very little. The head of this sea-serpent, which it held more than two feet above the surface of the water, resembled that of a horse. It was of a greyish colour, and the mouth was quite black, and very large. It had black eyes, and a long white mane, which hung down from the neck to the surface of the water. Besides the head and neck, we saw seven or eight folds, or coils, of this snake, which were very thick, and as far as we could guess there was a fathom's distance between each fold. I related this affair in a certain company, where there was a person of distinction present, who desired that I would communicate to him an authentic detail of all that happened; and for this reason two of my sailors who

were present at the same time and place where I saw this monster, namely, Niels Petersen Kopper, and Niels Nielsen Anglewigen, will appear in court, to declare on oath the truth of every particular herein set forth; and I desire the favour of an attested copy of the said descriptions."
"I remain, Sir, your obliged servant,"
"L. von Ferry."
"Bergen, 21st. February 1751.

"After this the above-named witnesses gave their corporal oaths, and, with their finger held up according to law, testified and declared the aforesaid letter or declaration, and every particular set forth therein to be strictly true. A copy of the said attestation was made out for the said Procurator Reutz, and granted by the Recorder. That this was transacted in our court of justice we confirm with our hand and seals."
"Actum Bergis, Anno, Die et Loco ut supra."

"A. C. Dass."	"H. C. Gartner.
"J. Clies."	"O. Simensen.
"O. Brinchmand"	"J. Koenig.
"M. Gram."	"C. Natler.
"J. Foegh."	"J. Wiers.

As to Mr. von Ferry's declaration that the head of the sea-serpent resembled that of a horse, we cannot give another explanation than that it evidently was held at nearly right angles with the neck, that the nostrils were wide opened and large, and that the mane on the animal's neck altogether must have led him to think so. The statement that the colour of the head was greyish, apparently contradictory to what had as yet been said about the animal's colour, viz., that it is a dark brown one, may be explained, I think, as follows: the sea-serpent has a skin as woolly as seals and sea-lions have; it had swum a long time with its head two feet above the water, and the weather being very hot, its skin was dried up, and had got a colour quite different from that when being wet. When wet the common seal has a greenish or brownish black colour, but when dry a greyish yellow one, with a somewhat dark greenish hue; and the spots become less visible. So we see that sea-lions are dark brown when wet, but when lying on the stone border of their basin in our Zoological Gardens they very soon become dry in the sunbeams and show a greyish yellow colour. But returning to Mr. von Ferry's sea-serpent, the mouth, however, was black and very large. The eyes were black, the mane long and white (being dry) hanging down to the surface of the water. The coils, seven or eight in number, were very thick and the distance between them was a fathom. The colour of the coils is not mentioned; we may suppose that they were dark brown.

Prof. W. D. Peck (*Mem. Amer. Acad. Arts. Sc.* IV, I, 1818) calls this account a rational and credible one. "The figure which he" (Pontoppidan) "gives seems to have been made from the description of Capt. de Ferry, the officer above alluded to. In this figure, the head and jugular region are raised out of the water; a little below the head is a mane which seems to be inserted all round the back of the neck. The appearance of this mane was most probably an optical deception, and was nothing more than the water displayed by the neck in the progress of the animal through it, returning to its level. It had probably no mane. But of the existence of the animal, the testimony presented by the Rev. Bishop is sufficiently conclusive."

Prof. Peck seems not to have read Pontoppidan so accurately as might be expected from him, for the figure in Pontoppidan's work has quite another origin, as we shall see below. Prof. Peck would not have written his supposition of the mane, if one of the eye-witnesses of the animal near Cape Ann (see below, 1817), had seen a mane. Moreover Pontoppidan asserts that nearly all agree in representing the animal with a mane, and we shall read of several declarations further on.

As to the colour of the coils, Mr. Lee seems to be at one with me for in his frequently quoted work *Sea Monsters Unmasked* he says: "The supposed coils of the serpent's body present exactly the appearance of eight porpoises following each other in line", and: "I believe that in every case so far cited from Pontoppidan, as well as that given by Olaus Magnus, the supposed coils or protuberances of the serpent's body were only so many porpoises swimming in line, in accordance with their habit before mentioned." If Captain von Ferry had described the coils of his serpent as being white or red, Mr. Lee certainly would not have supposed that they were eight porpoises.

Further Mr. Lee remarks: "If an upraised head, like that of a horse, was preceding them, it was either unconnected with them, or it certainly was not that of a snake; for no serpent could throw its body into those vertical undulations."

Very well, but if Mr. Lee wishes to explain the coils by porpoises, he ought to account for the head which preceded them; this he silently passes by, only saying it was not that of a snake. A fine explanation indeed!

10.—1747?—(Pontoppidan, Chapt. VIII, § 7).—"Governor Benstrup is said to have had some years ago a similar meeting with the sea-serpent" (to Mr. von Ferry's) "and he has figured it. I should like to possess this figure to show it to my readers. I, however, show here another one sent to me by Parson Hans Stroem, which he himself has copied from the original."

The figure shows a head with a mane, and six coils of the body. The nostril is indicated, the mouth has no teeth, the eye is large.

It is remarkable that Mr. Lee tells us: "The figure of the sea-serpent given by Pontoppidan was drawn, he tells us, under the inspection of a clergyman, Mr. Hans Stroem, from descriptions given of it by two of his neighbours, Messrs. Reutz and Tuchsen, of Herroe; and was declared to agree in every particular with that seen by Captain de Ferry, and another subsequent observed by Governor Benstrup."

Not only does not the first part of this statement tally with the words of Pontoppidan, but also the second part is discrepant, for the learned Bishop goes on saying "This figure agrees with the descriptions given by two of his neighbours Messrs. Reutz and Tuchsen."

Mr. von Ferry is not mentioned at all on this occasion by Pontoppidan!

Mr. Benstrup's figure has also been copied by Mr. R. Hamilton in the volume of *Phocidae* (seals) of Jardine's *Naturalist's Library*, but it has been greatly exaggerated. It seems that Dr. R. Hamilton thought it to be the same animal as that seen by Egede, for he figures both animals with the same head and features. Of the figure of Benstrup too he makes a serpentine dragon, swimming with corkscrew motions! O horror!

Various Accounts 107

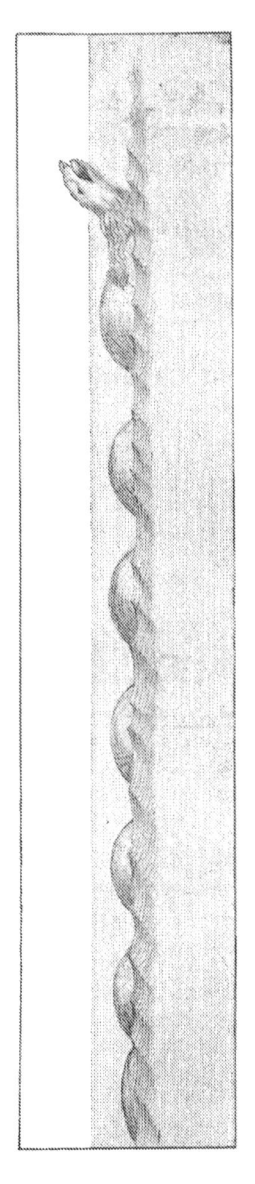

FIG. 24.—THE SEA-SERPENT AS SEEN BY GOVERNOR BENSTRUP.

FIG. 25.—BENSTRUP'S DRAWING AS ALTERED IN DR. HAMILTON'S WORK.

11.—1748?—Mr. Reutz of Herroe declared to Pontoppidan that the drawing of Parson Hans Stroem agreed even in particulars with what he saw of the serpent several times when he went in his boat to church.

12.—1749?—Also Mr. Tuchsen of Herroe made the same declaration. He too saw the animal several times when he went to church in his boat. Pontoppidan adds: "and then I do not even mention many other persons of the same high rank and trustworthiness. The same Mr. Tuchsen is the only one who told me that he distinctly saw the difference in thickness between the trunk and the tail of the animal, viz., the trunk is not gradually growing smaller where the tail begins, but becomes smaller at once and very distinctly. The body is as thick as a barrel of two hogsheads. The tail is tapering towards its end, which is very pointed."

This account is remarkable for the reason that it mentions the fact that the beginning of the tail is distinctly visible. So we must infer from it that the animal had thighs, and consequently had also hind-limbs. And knowing that the fore-limbs which Egede saw, are flappers, the hind-limbs too must be flappers; consequently the animal has four flappers.

13.—1750?—Pontoppidan, telling what he has learned from the north-sailors says:

"One of these north-sailors tells that he was once so close to the serpent, that he might have touched its smooth skin."

Here is stated by a person who saw the sea-serpent close to his boat, that the skin is smooth, a statement apparently contradictory to that of the fisherman (n°. 8), who declared it as woolly as a seal-skin. The fact is that the one has distinctly recognized the hairy nature of the skin, whilst the other did not discern it.

14.—1751?—(Pontoppidan, Chapt. VIII, § 1, note). "An incertain rumour tells me, that some peasants of Sundmöer have lately captured in their nets a serpent of eighteen feet with four paws under its belly; which they brought ashore. Thus it resembled a crocodile. The peasants in their terror fled from their nets, and by doing so they gave an opportunity to the serpent to do the same."

Though the Bishop does not call this animal a sea-serpent, I am sure it was one. In the Norwegian and Danish languages an Orm is a serpent, viz., a long slender animal with a rather small head and a pointed tail; and as it was captured in nets in the sea, it is certain, that this animal, which Pontoppidan compares with a crocodile, having a slender and round body like a snake and four paws (or flappers) is the same as the animal afterwards seen by Captain Hope (n° 119) and compared by him with an alligator. The dimensions not surpassing twenty feet, the animal must have been very young.

Now let us see what Pontoppidan himself says of the sea-serpent, after having heard hundreds of eye-witnesses:

"The sea-serpent, serpens marinus, by some people also called Aale Tust, is the second wonderful and frightful sea-monster which ought to be studied by him who looks with delight on the great deeds of the Lord, and which is considered as the greatest wonder next to the Kraken, which will be described hereafter. Before describing its habit and shape, I feel again obliged to prove the real existence of the serpent, as I did before with the mermen."

The first kind of wonderful and frightful sea-monsters were the mermen and mermaids. At present, we know with certainty what were and are the mermen and mermaids of ancient days and our own time. All zoologists are convinced they were nothing else but sea-cows or manatees (*Thrichechus manatus* L. and *Thrichechus senegalensis* Desm.) or dugongs (*Dugungus dugung* Gmel.). Mr. Lee believes that the occurrences of mermen and mermaids in the northern seas and even in the waters round Great-Britain and Ireland "afford some slight hope that the remarkable rytina (*Rytina borealis* Gmel.) may not have become extinct in 1768, as has been supposed, but that it may still exist somewhat further south than it was met with by its original describer, Steller." Some of the mermen of Pontoppidan were nothing else but Bladdernosed seals (*Cystophora cristata* (Erxl) Nilss) as I already proved in my little paper in the *Album der Natuur* of 1882, and I see that Mr. Lee comes to the same conclusion (*Sea Fables Explained*, London, 1883).

We also know with certainty that the Kraken of the Norwegian tales and the gigantic Octopus of Denys de Montfort really exist, and that they are nothing else but gigantic calamaries and cuttles (*Cephalopoda*).

But we don't know with certainty what the Great-Sea-Serpent really is. That it exists, has already been stated by the highest scientific persons, so no doubt need any longer be felt as to that fact.

"If it were not the wise and careful arrangement of the Creator, that this sea-animal perpetually lives in the depths of the sea, except in July and August, its pairing-time, during which it appears, when the sea is quite calm, but dives as soon as the wind ruffles the surface of the water; if this arrangement, I say, were not thus made for man's safety, the existence of the sea-serpent would want fewer proofs, than even in Norway, thanks to God! is the case, the shores of which are the only ones of Europe, frequented by this monster."

Here again it is stated that the sea-serpent is only seen in July and August (and Pontoppidan believes that these two months are the pairing-time of the animal), that it only appears in calm weather, and dives under water as soon as the wind rises. The writer believes that the animal frequents only the shores of Norway. According to an account of Olaus Magnus, it seems, however, that the sea-serpent was also seen in the Baltic Ocean, and we know now for certain that the animal which Egede saw in Davis' Straits at 64° N. lat., was also our Sea-Serpent. Evidently our Bishop did not hit on the idea that the Sea-Serpent could be a migratory animal.

"Like all who are enemies to credulousness I too doubted of the existence of the sea-serpent, when at last my doubt was dispelled by incontestable proofs. Amongst our ablest navigators and fishermen of this country there are many hundreds who prove the existence of the sea-serpent as eye-witnesses, and they agree pretty well in their descriptions, though there are many others who declare that they know the sea-serpent only from the tales of their neighbours. I, however, in my inquiry hardly" met with a person who, when born in the Northern provinces, did not answer immediately with the greatest certainty and assurance. Nay, some so-called north-sailors, who are here (in Bergen) every year for commercial interests, even consider it as a shame to be earnestly questioned on that subject. They consider this question as superfluous as that one, whether there exists a cod-fish or an eel."

We see hereby that in Norway the belief in the existence of the sea-serpent was as firm as possible amongst the sea-faring people.

"Though no one bas ever been able to measure this animal, many witnesses agree in telling that the serpent must be as long as a cable, viz., 100 fathoms or 300 ells, whilst it lay on the surface of the water, so that only here and there behind the head, which is held upwards, some parts of the back were visible, which were also held upwards, whilst the serpent bent; and from afar one would have believed that he saw some tuns or hogsheads, which floated in a line, so that there was a space between each of them."

Though the length of a cable or six hundred feet given to the sea-serpent is exaggerated, it may be more than 100 feet, why not? For there are other sea-animals, such as the whale, which measures more than 88 feet, and the fin-fish (*Balaenoptera loops*) which sometimes attains a length of about 105 feet.

It has been stated to Pontoppidan by most of the eye-witnesses that the animal shows by its vertical undulations several coils above the water, and that these coils resembled from afar tuns or hogsheads floating in a line. It is very remarkable that these facts are repeatedly stated by witnesses who are independent of one another, even by persons who never heard of a sea-serpent.

"The head of all these animals has rather a high and broad forehead; some, however, have a sharp snout, others a quadrangular beak as cows and horses have, with large nostrils, and on the sides there are a few stiff hairs, or bristles, as other animals have with a good nose. And that the sea-serpent has a good nose, is proved by its flying away at the smell of castoreum, which the people who go out in summer to fish on the great bank, will never forget to take with them."

The various ways of describing the head may be owed to this that different persons saw the head in different positions, that some of them saw it for such a short moment that it was impossible to say with certainty what form it had. It is not always explicable why one describes the head of an animal in one way and another in quite another. As to me I see in the head of a seal that of an otter, others distinctly see a man's or a cat's head in it, and the people in the service of the Zoological Gardens in the Hague exclaim "why, I can very well understand why that animal is called a sea-dog; it has a dog's head, to be sure!" The fact is that we don't know with any certainty the form of the sea-serpent's head, but *most probably* it resembles that of a sea-lion, which has also a head with a broad and flattened forehead, rather pointed, seen from one side, and blunt, seen in front. Here mention is also made of the large nostrils and the bristles on the lips of the animal.

"The eyes are, as one says, large and blue, they are rather like a pair of pewter plates."

The eyes again are described differently. We have already heard them described as being black, red as fire, and now they are blue, viz. the ordinary blue, called tin-colour, that is a bluish-grey or a greyish-blue; so a grey rabit is also called a blue rabit; and grey fowls are called blue-fowls; there is rather a lilac tint to be observed in it. I cannot explain those differences otherwise than in the following way: when an observer sees the eyes in an oblique direction, he will always see this grey colour; when more in the axis of the eye, the colour is a bright dark black- one, and when occasionally seen thus that the "tapetum lucidum" of the eye reflects the day-light, it is, as if the eyes were sparkling like fire.

"The serpent's colour is dark brown over the whole body, but thereby spotted, and with light streaks, or maculated with distinctly visible light spots, like a turtle or a lackered table, except in the region of mouth and eyes where it is rather dark, so that it resembles those horses which we call moorish-heads or black-faces."

We shall repeatedly have occasion to observe that these statements are correct. All eye-witnesses agree in this point.

"That this animal spouts like a whale through its nostrils, as Mr. Egede saw, has never been seen here by anybody."

It is remarkable that though Egede has nowhere asserted that his animal was a sea-serpent, our learned Bishop seems to have recognized it as such at once, believing, however, it to be another species of the same genus. We have already stated that Egede did not see the animal spouting water, but he only saw the warm breath of the animal condensed in the cold air, just as Bing, his brother missionary, figured it, and just as it is mentioned by accurate observers of whales. It is very easy to understand that Egede saw it, for the animal had apparently been under water for a long time; it suddenly appeared with so much violence, that a considerable part of its body was elevated above the surface of the sea, whilst, by a violent blow, the breath, hitherto held in, was pushed into the air. In this way parts of mucus of the inner surface of the nostrils and the little quantity of water adhering to the valves of the nose, must have been driven away at the same time, and the whole effect has been very accurately described by Egede and figured by Bing, but has afterwards been exaggerated and altered by Pontoppidan (see our fig. 22), and also in our century by Dr. R. Hamilton (see our fig. 23).

"But many agree in telling that when it swims rapidly through the water, it propels before it the water with such a violence that it murmurs like a small mill brook."

This peculiarity has been repeatedly confirmed by the most trustworthy eye-witnesses as we will observe more than once afterwards.

"Also the common sea-serpents of our shore differ from those of the Greenland-coasts, seen by Egede, in having no rough and hard skin, but a smooth one like a mirror, except on the neck, on which it has a mane, resembling sea-weed."

Remarkable again is the statement of its smooth skin, remarkable too is the declaration of the sea-serpent having a mane, and most remarkable the resemblance of this mane to sea-weed, an observation made by several eye-witnesses independant of each other. It is surprising that Pontoppidan silently passes over the difference between his two kinds of sea-serpents: that the Greenland one has two flappers on the fore-part of its trunk.

"As they cast their skin like common snakes, some people pretend, that a few years ago, a table-cloth has been made of such a slough found in the harbour of Kobbervueg. This made me so curious, that I wrote to one of the inhabitants of that harbour, to inquire after it, and as the proverb says, to get a strap of the skin. However, there was nothing of that skin, at least at that time. And a man of that harbour, who came to Bergen, told me he knew nothing at all about it."

As to the renewing of the skin, we see that the Bishop was taken in! But we must respect him that he did not rest before he knew the truth or the untruth of the fact, and that he also mentions his inquiry. Though the Bishop may have been deceived, his endeavours to find out the truth enhance his trustworthiness.

"That the flesh of these animals is soft, has been stated by some who tell of a small, and probably young sea-serpent which was taken unexpectedly on board a ship. It instantly died, and nobody dared to touch it, till the crew was forced at last to cast it over board, owing to the intolerable smell arising from the soft and tough slime, in which it was dissolved by the action of the air. But this animal cannot have been a sea-serpent, for, as will be remembered, it is only seen in the calmest weather and sinks into the deep at the least motion in the air."

We agree with the Bishop, though for other reasons than he.

After having related the two strandings of a sea-serpent (n° 6, 7), Pontoppidan goes on:

"I would that in such cases some one had inquired whether this serpent had a strong backbone, which seems to be necessary to keep together the mass of such a gigantic animal. The sharks, however, which are also cartilaginous fishes without bones, have such a backbone, but it is very subtile and even in the largest sharks only ten ells long. The sea-serpent, like sharks, eels and whales also seems to be a viviparous, not an oviparous fish, and most probably it seeks the other sex in the above mentioned season. It is said, that when this animal is ruttish, it looks after ships and boats, which it probably takes for something else. If this be true, as seamen say, those are wrong who think that the sea-serpent is not born in the sea, but on land, and lives in forests and among mountains, till it can no longer hide its body in it; it is said that it then seeks some river, and floats out to the sea, as some people pretend to have seen."

There is but one single reason why we think the sea-serpent is a viviparous being, viz. its hairy skin. It is certain that an animal with long hairs on its neck, has also hairs on its whole body, which has also been stated once already (n°. 8), and hairy animals are viviparous (except the *Monotrymata*). Most probably Pontoppidan called the sea-serpent viviparous for the same reason, otherwise I cannot find a single fact that would have led him to this conclusion. Its seeking the other sex cannot be a reason, for all animals do so in the warm season. I think that it looked after ships because it is a curious animal, knowing no fear of strange things or persons. It is evidently a fable that it brings forth young ones on the shore, probably originating in the fact that the sea-serpent has sometimes been seen in fjords, even in small ones, or probably originating in the fact that also seals creep ashore in the critical moment, whelp there and return with their young ones to the sea as soon as possible.

"The question which troubles us most is the following: Is this animal dangerous to men, and how are they to defend themselves against this monster? Arendt Berndsen (*Danmarks og Norges frugtbare Herlighed* p. 308) answers the first question in the affirmative, and tells us that the sea-serpent, as well as the spermwhale, even often runs down men and ships. That such things happened in this region, I never heard of with certainty; but the north-sailors tell that it had occasionally happened that the sea serpent raised itself and threw itself straight across a boat, nay across a large yacht of several hundred tons, and had dragged it to the depths. One of these north-sailors tells that he was once so close to the serpent, that he might have touched its smooth skin; he mentions at the same time that this serpent sometimes snatches a man from a boat, with its head raised upward and gives the others of the crew an opportunity to escape. Whether these reports are to be believed or not, I don't know, because it is uncertain whether these serpents live on prey."

We see the Bishop weighing and considering whatever he heard, and not accepting everything for truth. We think that Pontoppidan is right in giving no credit to the narrative that the sea-serpents made themselves guilty of sinking ships and eating men. It is mentioned already twice, that the sea-serpent raised itself high above the surface of the water; yet the flappers are not mentioned; so we may conclude that these are situated far from the head, or, what is the same, that the animal has a very long neck.

Pontoppidan further tells us that the sea-serpent sometimes encloses ships by laying itself round them in a circle, that the fishermen then row over its body there where a coil is visible, for when they reach the coil, it sinks, while on the contrary the invisible parts rise. Further, that the serpent swims with an incredible velocity, and that the fishermen who are much afraid of it, when seeing that it follows them, throw any object, for instance a scoop, at it, when the animal generally plunges into the deep. But most fishermen are in the habit of taking castoreum with them, for the serpent cannot bear the smell of it. And still further on he tries to explain the considerable length of the animal some witnesses speak of; the Bishop namely believes that two or more individuals followed each other, for they are only seen in rutting-time. And in his tenth paragraph, trying to answer the question, why those large serpents only frequent the northern seas, he says:

"To this question I answer that the Creator of all beings disposes of the dwellings of His different creatures in different places by His wise intentions, which are not to be known to us. Why won't the reindeer thrive anywhere but in the high and cold mountains? Why do the whales frequent only the north pole? Why are India and Egypt almost the only countries, where men have to fear crocodiles? No doubt because it pleases the wise Creator."

Here Pontoppidan takes leave of the Sea-Serpent, and begins to treat of the large snakes mentioned by Plinius and other ancient authors, and we too will take leave of our honest and trustworthy Bishop, who has so often been laughed at for what he relates in his chapter on monsters. And yet two of his monsters, the mermaids and the Kraken, are unmasked, why cannot his third be accounted for?!

Now let us again collect all the facts which are not impossible from a zoologist's point of view.

We have before us an animal of the following imperfect description:

The whole *length* of this animal far surpasses one hundred feet, and the smallest individual ever seen measured eighteen feet. The greatest *thickness* or diameter seems to be in the foremost third of its whole length, and in large individuals surpasses ten or even fifteen feet. Its *head* is small in reference to the body, its *neck* is long and slender, round as the body of a snake or eel; the thick *trunk* too is round: The *tail* is also round, thinner than the body and gradually grows thinner to its end, which is pointed. The animal has four *flappers*. The foremost are probably found about one fourth of the length, the hindmost probably in the middle of the whole length. The *skin* of the animal is hairy or woolly as a seal-skin; when wet it is smooth and glittering as a mirror. A long *mane* hangs down from the neck, and that mane is sometimes described as resembling sea-weed; when dry, the mane is whitish, or pale. The *head* is described as resembling that of a seal, or that of a horse. It tapers to the nose of the animal, so that some witnesses declare it has a sharp snout, others, however, that its end is like that of a cow's, or a horse's head, it has a broad and high, but flattened *forehead*. The *nostrils* are large, but as they are not always seen, it is evident that the animal can close them like a seal; on the *lips* some stiff hairs or bristles are planted. The *colour of the head*, when wet, is dark brown, when dry, however, greyish, except round the mouth and the eyes, where it is almost black. The *mouth* is large and provided with *teeth*. The *eyes* are large, sometimes described as being bluish and dull, sometimes black, glittering and brilliant, and sometimes reddish as a burning fire. We have already tried to explain these different statements. Its *eye-brows* are distinctly visible. Of the *neck* no particulars are observed except that it is long, round, and bears a mane, I should say like that of the Antarctic Sea-lions (*Otaria jubata*) but much more developed. Its *fore-flappers* are broad and large, and have probably an indented hind-edge, for Mr. Bing drew externally visible fingers. Of its *hind-flappers* nothing is mentioned. There is a visible *difference in thickness between the trunk and the* very long *tail* of the animal: the body is not gradually growing smaller where the tail begins, but becomes small at once, and very distinctly. Here the animal's hind-flappers must be placed. The *colour* of the body is said to be a dark brown, spotted and with light streaks, or marked with distinctly visible light spots. It has an astonishing flexibility in the neck as well as in the trunk and in the tail. It can bend its body sideways and backwards, and undulate it up and down like a rope. When the animal bends till it is U- or horse-shoe shaped, the skin obtains many folds or wrinkles. The *mode of swimming* is mostly by vertical undulations, which are partly visible above the surface of the water; the end of the tail is always hidden under water when the animal swims. From afar the visible parts of the coils are said to resemble tuns, buoys, wine-barrels or hogsheads. The coils are either very large, and then 7 or 8 of them are visible, and a distance of a fathom is between each two coils, or they are very small, and then it is said that twenty-five of them are visible. This is only to be explained by the degree of speed with which the animal undulates its body. For the same reason it also swims more or less swiftly; it may also swim with its body in a straight line, using in this case of course its flappers; this, however, happens very seldom; when swimming rapidly it propels the water before it with such a violence, that it boils and splashes up, with foam and a distinctly audible rushing. When swimming, the animal holds its head two feet above the surface of the water. Sometimes it raises its neck and head to a considerable height. Once the condensed breath of the animal was visible, and it was said to blow like a whale. It is only seen in summer and in fine weather. It is harmless when not provoked, it is curious and stupid. It feeds probably on cuttles, lobsters and crabs, (certainly however on fish.).

Now we will go on with the perusal of the accounts concerning the animal and we shall observe that in general the accounts or rather the descriptions of the eye-witnesses repeat, and sometimes even in particulars, what we have gathered from the 14 above mentioned accounts and from what Pontoppidan has taught us. I first invite the reader to follow me to the eastern coasts of the United States, next to the Northern Pacific, on the western coasts of Scotland, then again to the United States, and finally to Norway. In all these places, nay in every part of the world we shall meet with the animal which we shall find to be a true cosmopolitan, though the Atlantic seems to be its proper place of residence.

15.—1751.—In a letter from Capt. George Little to the Rev. Alden Bradford, printed in the second volume of Silliman's *American Journal of Science and Arts*, we read:
"A monster of the above description was seen in the same place, by Joseph Kent, of Marshfield, 1751. Kent said he was longer and larger than the main boom of his sloop, which was 85 tons. He had a fair opportunity of viewing him, as he saw it within ten or twelve yards of his sloop."
In the "above description" the sea-serpent is described as having the appearance of a large black snake, from 45 to 50 feet long, with a head of nearly the size of that of a man, which he carried four or five feet above the water, and with the greatest diameter of 15 inches. The individual which was seen by Joseph Kent was evidently larger; by "the same place" is meant Round Pond in Broad Bay and near Muscongus Island.

Knud Leems, as we learn in A. de Capell Brooke's, *Travels through Norway*, a northern divine, wrote his *Beskrivelse over Finmarkens Lappen*, 1765, in which he mentions, p. 332, the sea-serpent in the following terms:
"The Finmark Sea also produces the hydra or sea-serpent, a huge monster, forty 'passus' long, with a head resembling in size that of large sea-fishes, in shape that of a snake. This beast has a neck with a mane like a horse's, a grey back and a whitish belly. In the dog days, when the sea is free from wind, the sea-serpent will come to the surface, bend itself in several coils, of which some are partly visible above the water, whilst others remain hidden under it. The seamen greatly fear this monster, and they do not trust themselves on the sea, when the animal is on the surface."
The length of forty "passus", i. e. 200 feet, the large head, resembling that of a snake, the mane, the grey back, the habit of the animal to swim with vertical undulations, are all characters known to us. We have here a new one, viz. that the belly is whitish, which we shall frequently meet hereafter. It is, however, not the belly that is meant here, but the animal's throat. The animal's neck being cylindrical, and its flappers constantly hidden under water, the observers thinking that the animal is eel-shaped, always call its throat "the belly". We may safely suppose that the whole throat and the breast were seen, though not described, by Hans Egede, but that even he did not see the true belly.

16.—1770?—In a letter from Mr. Mc. Lean to the Rev. Alden Bradford written in Aug. 1803, and published in Silliman's *American Journal of Science and Arts* (Vol. II) we read:

"One of the same kind was seen above thirty years ago, by the deceased Capt. Paul Reed, of Boothbay."

17.—1777 or 1778.—(*Mem. Amer. Acad. Arts Sc.* Vol. IV, Part I).
"The next notice is from Capt. Eleazar Crabtree, who saw it in the same (Penobscot) Bay about the year 1785; he estimated its length at sixty feet, and its diameter he thought equal to that of a barrel, which is about twenty two inches."

A testimony on oath was forwarded by Capt. Crabtree to the American Academy of Arts and Sciences, "but this was lost or mislaid."—Fortunately, however, the notice was afterwards found back, and, as Prof. Bigelow (see Silliman's *Am. Journ. Sc. Arts* Vol. II) says, "is now in the hands of the corresponding Secretary of the Academy," Mr. John Q. Adams, "where it may be seen."

Mr. A. Bradford anxious to have all the information he could get, did not rest satisfied till he had a testimony of Capt. Crabtree. Capt. Crabtree, however, at that time an old man did not write this testimony himself, but had it written by another in his presence and signed it as a correct statement. It is published in the above mentioned Journal, Vol. II, and runs as follows:

"Capt. Crabtree, now of Portland, (late of Fox Islands, in the Bay of Penobscot), declares, that in the year 1777 or 1778, upon information of a neighbour, that a large serpent was in the water, near the shore, just below his house, and having often been told by individuals that they had before seen a similar sea-monster in that quarter, and doubting of the correctness of their reports, was induced to go down to the water to satisfy his own mind—that he saw a large animal, in the form of a snake, lying almost motionless in the sea, about thirty rods from the bank where he stood—that his head was about four feet above water—that, from the appearance of the animal, he was 100 feet in length—that he did not go off to the animal through fear of the consequences, and that he judged him to be about three feet diameter; he also says, that before that time, many people, living on those islands, on whose reports he could depend, had declared to him that they had seen such an animal—and that more than one had been seen by several persons together."

"Signed"   "Eleazar Crabtree."

We have again the statement that the sea-serpent held its head four feet above the surface of the water; its length was estimated at 100 feet, its diameter three feet; it was evidently this slenderness which led Capt. Crabtree to compare the sea-serpent with a snake. The undulations are not mentioned, consequently most probably it lay stretched out.

18.—1779.—(*Mem. Amer. Acad. Arts Sc.* Vol. IV. P. 1).
"It appears by papers sent to the Academy in the year 1810, that this serpent was first seen in Penobscot Bay about the year 1779, by Mr. Stephan Tuckey: he compared it to an unwrought spar (meaning probably one of spruce), which the scaly surface and dark colour of the animal would very much resemble; he thought it fifty or sixty feet in length."

It is evident that Mr. Stephan Tuckey only compared it with an unwrought spar, and estimated the length of the visible part to be fifty or sixty feet. Now Mr. W. D. Peck adds: "which the scaly surface and the dark colour of the animal would very much resemble". I, however, take it that the animal swam with its body in a straight line, elevating its back but very little above the surface of the water, yet showing a length of fifty to sixty feet, and so the back of the neck and trunk quite covered with a mane resembling sea-weed, and the dark colour of the animal must have led Mr. Stephan Tuckey to the comparison with an unwrought spar.

19.—1780, May.—"Captain George Little" who saw the animal, wrote "a letter" containing his observation to the American Academy of Arts and Sciences, "but this letter is lost or mislaid" (*Mem. Amer. Acad. Arts Sc.* Vol. IV, P. I.). When we consult Silliman's *Am. Journ. of Sc. and Arts* (Vol. II, 1820), we observe that Mr. Alden Bradford collected for truth s sake some affidavits of eye-witnesses; he had learned that Capt. George Little was an eye-witness, he asked him for an affidavit, which he received and forwarded to the corresponding Secretary of the Academy; after some trouble the letter was found back and published. It runs as follows:

"Marshfield, March, 13th., 1804."
"Sir",
"In answer to yours of 30th. of January last, I observe, that in May, 1780, I was lying in Round Pond, in Broad Bay, in a public armed ship. At sunrise, I discovered a large Serpent, or monster, coming down the Bay, on the surface of the water. The cutter was manned and armed. I went myself in the boat, and proceeded after the serpent. When within a hundred feet, the mariners were ordered to fire on him, but before they could make ready, the Serpent dove. He was not less than from 45 to 50 feet in length; the largest diameter of his body, I should judge, 15 inches; his head nearly of the size of that of a man, which he carried four or five feet above the water. He wore every appearance of a common black snake. When he dove he came up near Muscongus Island—we pursued him, but never came up within a quarter of a mile of him again."
"I have the honor to be sir,
"Your friend and humble servant
"Geo. Little."

It is evident that the animal moved away from the Captain, who thus saw only its occiput. As the head is thought to have nearly the size of that of a man, and the whole length to be 45 to 50 feet, it is evident that either the head is estimated too small, or the length too great; moreover it is clear that the captain saw nearly the whole length; this sometimes occurs; generally, however, only the foremost part is visible. Again it is mentioned that the sea-serpent held its head four feet above the surface of the water, and that the colour was black.

A letter from Mr. A. Mc. Lean to the Rev. Alden Bradford, printed in the same pages, contains a passage, running as follows:
"Another was seen in Muscongus Bay in time of the American war, two miles from the place where I lived then."
I consider this passage as relative to Capt. George Little's observation.

20.—1781?—In the same letter the above mentioned lines are followed by the words:
"and another soon afterwards off Meduncook".

21.—1782?—In a letter from the Rev. Mr. William Jenks, of Bath, to the Hon. Judge Davis, of Boston, dated September 7, 1818, and published in the *Report* of 1817, we read:
"Mr. Cummings observes, that the British saw him in their expedition to Bagaduse" ..... "The British supposed the length of that which they saw to be three hundred feet, but this Mr. Cummings imagines to be an exaggeration."
I think Mr. Cummings is right in this supposition.

22.—1783?—In the same letter we read:
"People also of Mount Desert have seen the monster."

23.—1784?—In the same letter we find:
"June 28th., 1809. Mr. Cummings observes that a Mr. Crocket saw two of them together about twenty years since" ..... "One of those seen by Mr. Crocket was smaller than that seen by Mr. Cummings, and their motion in the sea appeared to be a perpendicular winding, and not horizontal."
This appearance is also mentioned in the *Mem. Am. Acad. Arts Sc.* (IV, I, 1818) where we read about the inhabitants of Fox and Long Islands:
"and one of them, a Mr. Crocket, had seen two of them together about the year 1787."
And in Silliman's *Am. Journ. Sc. Arts* (Vol. II, 1820) we read in a letter from Mr. Abraham Cummings to the Rev. Alden Bradford, written Jan., 1804:
"About twenty years since, two of those serpents, they say, were seen by one Mr. Crocket, who then lived upon Ash Point."
The fact that there were two animals together only claims our attention, which is of course not wonderful, as they may have been a male and a female, or a mother and a young one. One of the two must have been quite small, as it is reported: "One of those was smaller than that seen by Mr. Cummings"; consequently the other was as large as or even larger than that seen by Mr. Cummings, ergo the difference in size of these two must have been considerable. The occurrence of two together is reported only a very few times. Evidently these animals lead solitary lives.
We see that the dates differ, but we will take the date of 1784, relying upon the words of Mr. Cumming's letter of 1804: "about twenty years since".

24.—1785?—In the same letter it says:
"Sept. 10, 1811. Have heard to day further testimony respecting the Sea-Serpent of the Penobscot. A Mr. Staples, of Prospect, of whom I inquired as I passed, was told by a Mr. Miller, of one of the Islands in the bay, that he had seen it; and 'it was as big as a sloop's boom, and about sixty or seventy feet long'."

25.—1786, August 1.—(*Zoologist*, 1847, p. 1911).—
"Having seen much notice taken in the *Zoologist* of the question of the great sea-serpent, allow me to subjoin an extract from the log-book of a very near relative, dated August 1st., 1786, on board the ship '*General Coole*', in lat. 42° 44' N., and long. 23° 10' W.—"

"A very large snake passed the ship; it appeared to be 16 or 18 feet in length, and 3 or 4 feet in circumference, the back of a light ash-colour and the belly thereof yellow."

"According to the log the ship was becalmed at the time. You may rely on the correctness of this, and any one desiring of satisfy himself may see the original log."

"S. H. Saxby; Bouchurch, Isle of Wight. September, 8, 1847."

Of course only the length is given of the visible part, else it would be impossible that an animal of 16 feet in length and 3 or 4 feet in circumference made the impression of being a serpent or snake; the whole trunk and tail must have been hidden under water. As the colour of the animal's back is noted as a light ash-colour, I suppose that the animal having swam a long time in the sun without diving under water, the skin had become dry and showed the ash-colour; the colour of the belly (read throat) is stated to be yellow. This statement already mentioned above we shall see repeated more than once.

26.—1787?—In the letter from the Rev. Mr. William Jenks, dated, Bath, September 17, 1817, to the Hon. Judge Davis of Boston, and printed in the *Report* of 1817, we read:

"Aug. 23, 1809.—Mr. Charles Shaw (then of Bath, now an attorney in Boston,) informed me, that a Capt. Lillis, with whom he had sailed, observed cursorily in conversation, that he had seen off the coast a very singular fish; it appeared, said he, more like a snake than a fish, and was about forty feet long. It held its head erect, had no mane, and looked like an ordinary serpent. He asked Mr. Shaw if he had ever seen, or read, or heard of such an animal."

27.—1794?—In the same letter from the Rev. Mr. Jenks, printed in the *Report* of 1817, we find:

"Mr. Cummings observes that the inhabitants of Fox and Long Islands have seen such an animal"......

"When he was seen by the inhabitants of Fox and Long Islands two persons were together at both times."

It is clear that the year 1794 must be fixed as the date for one of the two times, for in the letter from Mr. Cummings to the Rev. Alden Bradford, written in Jan., 1804, and printed in the second volume of Silliman's *American Journal of Science and Arts*, (1820), we find the following, passage:

"A few years before, perhaps ten years since, two of those large serpents were seen by two other persons on that Island" (Fox Island) "as their neighbours informed me."

Again two individuals were seen together.

28.—1799?—And the date of the second time, that the animal was seen, must be the year 1799, for in the same letter from Mr. Cummings (1804), it says:

"Two young men of Fox Island, intelligent and credible, saw an animal of this kind about five years since, as they then informed me. They told me, that the serpent which they saw was about sixty feet long, and appeared to have an ascending and descending motion."

29.—1802 July.—In the letter from the Rev. Mr. William Jenks, of Bath, to the Hon. Judge Davis, of Boston, dated September 17, 1817, and published in the *Report* of 1817, we read:

"June 28th. 1809. The Rev. Mr. Abraham Cummings who has been much employed in Missions in the District of Maine, and navigated his own boat among the islands, &c. in the discharge of his duty, informs me, in conversation, which was immediately written from his lips, that in Penobscot bay has been occasionally seen within these thirty years, a sea-serpent, supposed to be about sixty feet in length, and of the size of a sloop's mast. Rev. Mr. Cummings saw him, in company with his wife and daughter, and a young lady of Belfast, Martha Spring; and judged he was about three times the length of his boat, which is twenty three feet. When he was seen this time he appeared not to notice the boat, though he was distant, as nearly as could be ascertained, but about fifteen rods." ..... "A gentleman of intelligence (Rev. Alden Bradford of Wiscasset, now Secretary of the Commonwealth) inquired of Mr. Cummings whether the appearance might not be produced by a number of porpoises following each other in a train; but Mr. Cummings asserts, that the animal held its head out of water about five feet till he got out to sea; for when seen he was going out of the bay, and Mr. Cummings was ascending it. The colour was a bluish green about the head and neck, but the water rippled so much over his body, that it was not possible to determine its tint. The shape of the head was that of a common snake, flattened, and about the size of a pail. He was seen approaching, passing, and departing. Till this, Mr. Cummings was as incredulous in respect to its existence, as many of his neighbours. The weather was calm, and it was the month of August, in which month, Mr. Cummings remarks, that, as far as he had heard, the serpent makes his appearance on the coast."

"I am inclined to suppose that Mr. Cummings' account is that, which in one of the public papers was lately alluded to, as having been communicated to the American Academy of Arts and Sciences, but mislaid."

In the *Mem. Am. Acad. Arts and Sc.* Vol. IV. Part 1, 1818, we read also:

"A letter from this gentleman" (Mr. Cummings) "was forwarded to the Academy about the year 1806, giving a particular account of the animal, as he saw it at a small distance; but this letter is lost or mislaid."
Fortunately this letter was only mislaid, and found back in the hands of the corresponding Secretary, the Hon. John Q. Adams, and printed in Silliman's *American Journal of Science and Arts* (Vol. II, 1820). The letter runs as follows:

"Sullivan, Aug. 17th. 1803."
"My Dear Sir,"
"With peculiar pleasure I comply with your request, though the urgency of my affairs must excuse my brevity. It was sometime in July 1802 that we saw this extraordinary sea monster, on our passage to Belfast, between Cape Rosoi and Long Island. His first appearance was near Long Island. I then supposed it to be a large shoal of fish with a seal at one end of it, but wondered that the seal should rise out of water so much higher than usual; but, as he drew nearer to our boat, we soon discovered that this whole appearance was but one animal in the form of a serpent. I immediately perceived that his mode of swimming was exactly such as had been described to me by some of the people of Fox Islands, who had seen an animal of this kind before, which must confirm the veracity of their report. For this creature had not the horizontal but an ascending and descending serpentine motion. This renders it highly probable that he never moves on land to any considerable distance and that the water is his proper element. His head was rather larger than that of a horse, but formed like that of a serpent. His body we judged was more than sixty feet in length. His head and as much of his body as we could discover was all of a blue colour except a black circle round his eye. His motion was at first but moderate, but when he left us and proceeded towards the ocean, he moved with the greatest rapidity. This monster is the sixth of the kind, if our information be correct, which has been seen in this bay within the term of eighteen years. Mrs. Cummings, my daughter and Mss. Martha Spring were with me in the boat all that time, and can attest to the above description."
"I continue yours in christian affection
"Abraham Cummings.
"Rev. Alexander Mc. Lean.

Mr. Mc. Lean forwarded this letter to the Rev. Alden Bradford who says of it:

"The account was liable to some objections, and not so particular as might be wished. I therefore wrote Mr. Cummings, and in reply, received a statement more in detail,"
which runs as follows:

"Sullivan, Jan. 18th. 1804."
"Rev. and Dear Sir,"
"I can recollect nothing material which could render my description of that animal more convincing. I am not sure that this motion was ascending and descending; all we can say is, *it appeared so to us* (for he was seen not only by me, but by three other persons). His real motion might be horizontal. Perhaps his nearest distance from us was ten rods. The sea was then very smooth, and very little wind, but still there was such a constant rippling of the water over his body,

that I could not distinctly observe the magnitude or colour of any part but his head and neck. The degree of his rapidity I cannot explain. But certain I am that he had a serpent's head, of a colour as blue as possible, and a black ring round his eye. The head was three feet in circumference *at least*. Who ever saw fifty or sixty porpoises moving after each other in a right line, and in such a manner that those who formed the rear were no larger than haddock or mackerel, and none but the foremost shewed his head? Who ever saw a serpent's head upon a porpoise or whale? We saw him swim as far as from Long Island to the Cape before he disappeared. His head and neck all the time out of water. Now who ever saw a porpoise swim so great a distance without immerging at all? This is the best information which you can obtain from
"Your Friend and Servant"
"Abraham Cummings."
"Rev. Alden Bradford."
"P. S. The head and neck of the animal were of the same colour."

The first apparently inexplicable fact is that Mr. Cummings declares the colour of the head and neck first "blue", then "as blue as possible," and a few years afterwards "a bluish green." But I think that we must not rely too much upon this definition of the colour, for, as we observe in daily life, different persons will give different names to a dark colour; some will call a nearly black colour "blue" while another does not see any blue in it at all; consequently we may safely suppose that the colour was the common dark brown, nearly black one, and that Mr. Cummings called such a colour "as blue as possible" or "a bluish green." Yet it is probable that the colour of sea-serpents may sometimes vary as in our common seals.

It is a fact that claims our close attention that the first impression the animal made upon him was "to be a large shoal of fish" (read "porpoises") "with a head of a seal at one end of it, but wondered that the seal should rise out of water so much higher than usual". Here we have an almost faithful picture of the common appearance of the animal, which reminds us of Mr. Benstrup's figure (fig. 24). But as the serpent drew nearer to Mr. Cummings' boat, the resemblance diminished, because the serpent has not such thick upper lips as our common seal, so that the snout is rather sharp, and the forehead being moreover flat, the resemblance is also that of a snake's head! The mode of swimming was up and down, and Mr. Cummings in his second letter says "it appeared so to us, his real motion might be horizontal". Mr. Cummings expresses himself cautiously; and to explain his hesitation I think it is here the right place to mention a singular property of the sea-serpent. It is observed in 1818 that some witnesses distinctly saw the animal moving up and down and progressing very rapidly, and that some others of them declared that they distinctly saw the animal with many bunches on its back, that it moved through the water, apparently not by undulating up and down, but they were astonished that the sea-serpent moved. The sea-serpent further has the property of keeping his bunches when lying quite still. Consequently it may show itself in the following ways: 1. Lying perfectly still with the body in a straight line. 2. Lying perfectly still, but with many folds or bunches on its back. 3. Swimming with its body in a straight line, using its flappers. 4. Swimming with bunches on its back, propelling itself by its flappers, not by vertical undulations. 5. Swimming with vertical undulations, and not with its flappers. 6. Swimming with vertical undulations and with its flappers.

I repeat here the words of Mr. Cummings: "Who ever saw fifty or sixty porpoises moving after each other in a right line, and in such a manner that those who formed the rear were no larger than haddock or macquerel, and none but the foremost shewed his head? Who ever saw a serpent's head upon a porpoise or whale? Now who ever saw a porpoise swim so great a distance without immerging at all?" And we may add: Who ever saw porpoises without backfins? (The white whale, *Beluga leucas* has no back fin, but it is of a white colour, while the sea-serpent is almost black.)

I think it is here the right place to observe that the very different dimensions given to sea-serpents can be explained in two ways: 1. The animals may have been more or less visible above the surface of the water, and the hind part hidden under water is not always estimated in proportion to the visible fore-part. 2. The observers have not always seen the same individual, but of course young ones, middle-aged and old individuals, males and females.

I will insert here a letter from the Rev. Alden Bradford to the Hon. John Q. Adams, to show my readers how the former troubled himself about the question.

"Wiscasset, May 22, 1804."

"To the Honorable John Q. Adams, *corresponding Secretary of the American Academy of Arts and Sciences.*

"As one object of the Academy is to notice and preserve discoveries in *Natural History*, I am induced to communicate to the society the following account of a *Sea-Serpent*, which I have lately collected."

"It will probably be within the recollection of some persons conversant with Navigation, that in the course of a few years past, there have been vague reports of an animal of this description having been seen in or near Penobscot Bay. But little credit, however, was attached to the story, and no particular authentic account has yet been given to the public on the subject."

"A few months ago I happened to hear related the story of one, which was seen in the Bay of Penobscot in 1802. And for my own satisfaction, I have been inquisitive to the truth of the account, and to the general evidence of the existence of such an animal. The first correct information I received was from the perusal of a letter to Rev. Alexander Mc Lean, from Rev. Mr. Cummings of Sullivan; which is enclosed, and marked A. and some remarks were added by Mr. Mc. Lean at my request. The account was liable to some objections, and not so particular as might be wished. I therefore wrote Mr. Cummings, and in reply, received a statement more in detail, which accompanies this, and is marked B."

"I was afterwards informed, that George Little Esq. late commander of the Boston frigate, saw a sea-monster similar to the one described by Mr. *Cummings*, in the time of the revolutionary war with Great-Britain; and as I was anxious for all the information that was to be had, I wrote him on the subject, and he forwarded the enclosed (marked C.) in answer to my letter. I have also the testimony of a Capt. *Crabtree* of Portland, an intelligent man, which is direct and positive. This is also enclosed and marked D. It was written in his presence and received his signature, as a correct statement."

"All this evidence, I think, cannot fail to establish the fact *that a large sea-serpent has been seen in and near the Bay of Penobscot.* The existence of such a

monster can no longer be reasonnably disputed. But whether he constantly resides in that vicinity, or whether he coasts further south or north, during a part of the year, more particular information is necessary to ascertain. Nor is it known on what species of fish he subsists. By this communication I have it in view only to furnish evidence of the actual existence of the animal. It will probably operate in favour of further information, and lead to a particular history of this hitherto undescribed Serpent.
"I am with great esteem
"Your humble servant
"A. Bradford."

The four letters above mentioned and marked *A, B, C,* and *D,* are already inserted in their right places. I refer my readers to n°. 29, where the letters marked *A* and *B* are copied, to n°. 19, where that marked *C* is inserted, and to n°. 17, where the letter marked *D* will be found back.

30.—1805? Mr. Rafinesque Schmaltz (*Phil. Mag.* LIV, 1819) in his *Additions* to his dissertation, says:

"4. Mr. W. Lee has brought to notice another Sea-Snake, seen by him many years ago near Cape Breton and Newfoundland, which was over 200 feet long, with the back of a dark green: it stood in the water in flexuous hillocks, and went through it with impetuous noise. This appears to be the largest on record and might well be called *Pelamis monstrosus*; but if there are other species of equal size, it must be called then *Pelamis chloronotis,* or Green-back Pelamis."

The length of 200 feet is estimated more than once, though in many instances probably exaggerated. The definition of the colour to be a dark green one, we have already explained above, discussing the report of Mr. Cummings. The flexuous hillocks are of course nothing else but the vertical undulations, the impetuous noise is caused by the fore-flappers as will be stated afterwards. Of Mr. Rafinesque's determination I will say nothing, because it is a false one and a proof of his credulity.

31.—1808, June.—At a meeting of the Wernerian Natural History Society on the 13th. of May, 1809 (*Phil. Mag.*, Vol. 33, p. 411) "the Secretary read a letter from the Rev. Mr. Maclean of Small Isles, mentioning the appearance of a vast Sea-Snake, between 70 and 80 feet long, among the Hebrides, in June, 1808."

This letter is printed in the first Volume of the *Memoirs of the Wernerian Natural History Society*, (1811) and runs as follows:

"To the Secretary of the Wernerian Natural History Society."
"Eigg Island, 24th April 1809."
"Sir"
"Your letter of the first instant I received, and would have written in answer thereto sooner, had I not thought it desirable to examine others relative to the animal of which you wish me to give a particular account."

"According to my best recollection, I saw it in June 1808 not on the coast of Eigg, but on that of Coll. Rowing along that coast, I observed, at about the distance of half a mile, an object to windward, which gradually excited astonishment. At first view it appeared like a small rock. Knowing there was no rock in that situation, I fixed my eyes on it close. Then I saw it elevated considerably above the level of the sea, and after a slow movement, distinctly perceived one of its eyes. Alarmed at the unusual appearance and magnitude of the animal. I steered so as to be at no great distance from the shore. When nearly in a line betwixt it and the shore, the monster directing its head (which still continued above water) towards us, plunged violently under water. Certain that he was in chace of us, we plied hard to get ashore. Just as we leaped out on a rock, taking a station as high as we conveniently could, we saw it coming rapidly under water towards the stern of our boat. When within a few yards of the boat, finding the water shallow, it raised its monstrous head above water, and by a winding course get, with apparent difficulty clear of the creek, where our boat lay, and where the monster seemed in danger of being imbayed. It continued to move off, with its head above water, and with the wind for about half a mile, before we lost sight of it.—Its head was rather broad, of a form somewhat oval. Its neck somewhat smaller. Its shoulders, if I can so term them, considerably broader, and thence it tapered towards the tail, which last it kept pretty low in the water, so that a view of it could not be taken so distinctly as I wished. It had no fin that I could perceive, and seemed to me to move progressively by undulation up and down. Its length I believed to be from 70 to 80 feet; when nearest to me, it did not raise its head wholly above water, so that the neck being under water, I could perceive no shining filaments thereon, if it had any. Its progressive motion under water I took to be rapid, from the shortness of the time it took to come up to the boat. When the head was above water, its motion was not near so quick; and when the head was most elevated it appeared evidently to take a view of distant objets.

"I remain, Sir, &c.
"Donald Maclean."

To understand well what Mr. Maclean meant with "shining filaments" which he did *not* see, I must return to the "Animal of Stronsa", the putrified body of a large basking shark. My readers will remember that the putrified dorsal fins of that shark resembled bristles, which were transparent, and gave light in the dark (p. 61). Evidently the Secretary of the Wernerian Society writing to Mr. Maclean, asked him to give a full description of the animal seen by him near "the coast of Eigg", and whether he saw on its back "shining filaments" or not. Of course Mr. Maclean did not see them!

For the first time it is mentioned by an eye-witness that the shoulders were visible. Mr. Maclean adds: "if I can so term them". This is very remarkable, for we may safely take it for granted, that he, like all other persons, believed to see a sea-snake, or serpentine animal, and yet, though he could not know, that it has flappers, and probably would not have believed it, when it was told him, he has distinctly seen that the animal at once became much broader behind its long neck.

The animal plunged violently under water. When Mr. Maclean had reached his safe position he saw the animal swimming rapidly under water towards his boat. We must suppose that it swam so near the surface, though under water and invisible, that the surface rippled, and a wake was formed by the motion of the animal. The animal coming in shallow water, turned immediately and swam away. Once it did not raise its head quite above water, so that the neck was under water. When the head was most elevated, it appeared evidently to take a view of distant objects. These five habits as yet new to us, will be observed and reported several times afterwards. The other statements of Mr. Maclean are all mere repetitions of so often mentioned peculiarities.

32.—1808 June.—In the same letter we read:
"About the time I saw it, it was seen about the Isle of Canna. The crew of thirteen fishing boats, I am told, were so much terrified at its appearance, that they in a body fled from it to the nearest creek for safety. On the passage from Rum to Canna the crew of one boat saw it coming towards them, with the wind, and its head high above water. One of the crew pronounced its head as large as a little boat, and each of its eyes as large as a plate. The men were much terrified, but the monster offered them no molestation.—From those who saw it, I could get no interesting particulars additional to those above mentioned."

The dimensions given to the head and eye may be exaggerated. It is remarkable that the animal is so often coming in the neighbourhood of a boat, and is yet perfectly harmless. This confirms my supposition expressed above that the animal is sometimes very inquisitive. Pontoppidan would say "it thought to see the other sex, for it was pairing time!"

The whole letter from Mr. Maclean to the Secretary of the Wernerian Society is reprinted in Dr. Hamilton's *Amphibious Carnivora* (a volume of Jardine's *Naturalist's Library*), 1839, without any remark or explanation.

33.—1810?—Sir Walter Scott in the Notes to *The Pirate* says, according to Mr. Ashton (*Curious Creatures in Zoology*, 1889):
"The author knew a mariner, of some reputation in his class, vouch for having seen the celebrated Sea-Serpent. It appeared as far as could be guessed, to be about a hundred feet long, with the wild mane and fiery eyes which old writers ascribe to the monster."

I am convinced that the adjectives "wild" and "fiery" and the phrase "which old writers ascribe to the monster" are no additions made by the mariner, who simply may have told that the sea-serpent seen by him was about a hundred feet long, had a mane like a horse, or resembling sea-weed, and had red eyes. Unluckily neither the date, nor the locality is mentioned. The date cannot be far back from 1820; so I have chosen 1810, but of the locality of course nothing can be guessed.

34, 35.—1815, June 20 and 21.—In the *Report of a Committee*, of 1817, we read that this Committee wrote a letter to Mr. Samuel Davis, of Plymouth, requesting him to examine upon oath some respectable men of that place, with regard to the appearance of the animal in 1815. This letter runs as follows:

"Boston, September 1, 1817.
"Sir",
"At a meeting of the Linnaean Society of the 18th. ult., the subscribers there appointed a Committee for the purpose of collecting any evidence which may exist respecting a remarkable animal, denominated a *Sea Serpent*, reported to have been recently seen in and near the Harbour of Gloucester. The Committee have procured evidence from Gloucester, which they are preparing to report to the Society, and this evidence is of such a character, that they have thought it expedient to extend their inquiry to other reported appearances of a similar nature on our coasts. An appearance of this sort is mentioned as having been noticed by some persons at Plymouth two or three years since. We would ask your assistance in procuring the evidence on this subject."

"Your connection with the Society seems to authorize the request for your assistance in having the evidence on this subject, which may exist at Plymouth, properly taken and transmitted; but separately from any such claim, we know your habitual readiness to aid in any investigation in natural science. This subject is now of general interest among us, and will probably be so abroad. Any cooperation which you may wish from magistrates and intelligent gentlemen at Plymouth, we doubt not will be readily afforded you. We shall suspend our final report to the Society, until your communication shall be received."

"Yours respectfully and
"with esteem
    "John Davis   "Jacob Bigelow — Committee.   "Francis C. Gray

The answer was as follows:

"Plymouth, Oct. 2, 1817."
"Gentlemen."
"Inclosed is the deposition duly authenticated of Capt. E. Finney of this town, descriptive of an unusual animal, which was seen by him in the outer harbour of Plymouth, in June 1815. Capt. Finney lives a few miles from town, and is much engaged in business, which must apologize for the delay that has followed, since the receipt of your letter of the first of September. His deposition is impartial and unbiassed—and agrees uniformly with his first declarations in 1815—besides he has not read, whatever he may have heard, of the Cape Ann descriptions; he has been from his youth accustomed to a seafaring life—in the fishing employ, and in foreign voyages—has frequently seen whales, and almost every species of fish."

"The drawing on the other page (made by me) I have shewn to Capt. Finney, who says it illustrates his conceptions on the subject exactly. All your questions were asked him, and when his replies are negative, such as gills, breathing holes, &c. &c. it must not be inferred that such things were not displayed—but only that he did not see them, &c. Certain house carpenters, who were at work on a building near the spot, also saw it; as well as many others—these persons dwell with emphasis on the long and distant *wake* made in the water by the passage of the fish.—As to the point of time, it must have been from known data between the 18th. and 25th. of June. And I would remark, that this is exactly the season when the first setting in of mackerel occurs in our bay."

"Yours respectfully"
    "S. Davis."

And the deposition of Captain Finney as follows:

"I, Elkanah Finney of Plymouth, in the county of Plymouth, Mariner, testify and say: That about the twentieth of June, A. D. 1815, being at work near my house, which is situated near the sea-shore in Plymouth, at a place called Warren's cove, where the beach joins the main land; my son, a boy, came from the shore and informed me of an unusual appearance on the surface of the sea in the cove. I paid little attention to his story at first; but as he persisted in saying that he had seen something very remarkable, I looked towards the cove, where I saw something which appeared to the naked eye to be a drift sea-weed. I then viewed it through a perspective glass, and was in a moment satisfied that it was some aquatic animal, with the form, motion, and appearance of which I had hitherto been unacquainted. It was about a quarter of a mile from the shore, and was moving with great rapidity to the northward. It then appeared to be about thirty feet in length; the animal went about half a mile to the northward; then turned about, and while turning, displayed a greater length than I had before seen; I supposed at least a hundred feet. It then came towards me, in a southerly direction, very rapidly, until he was in a line with me, when he stopped, and lay entirely still on the surface of the water. I then had a good view of him through my glass, at the distance of a quarter of a mile. His appearance in this situation was like a string of buoys. I saw perhaps thirty or forty of these protuberances or bunches, which were about the size of a barrel. The head appeared to be about six or eight feet long, and where it was connected with the body was a little larger than the body. His head tapered off to the size of a horse's head. I could not discern any mouth. But what I supposed to be his under jaw had a white stripe extending the whole length of the head, just above the water. While he lay in this situation, he appeared to be about a hundred or a hundred and twenty feet long. The body appeared to be of a uniform size. I saw no part of the animal which I supposed to be a tail. I therefore thought he did not discover to me his whole length. His colour was a deep brown or black. I could not discover any eyes, mane, gills, or breathing holes. I did not see any fins or legs. The animal did not utter any sound, and it did not appear to notice any thing. It remained still and motionless for five minutes or more. The wind was light with a clear sky, and the water quite smooth. He then moved to the southward; but not with so rapid a motion as I had observed before. He was soon out of my sight. The next morning I rose very early to discover him. There was a fresh breeze from the south, which subsided about eight o'clock. It then became quite calm, when I again saw the animal about a mile to the northward of my house, down the beach. He did not display so great a length as the night before, perhaps not more than twenty or thirty feet. He often disappeared, and was gone five or ten minutes under water. I thought he was diving or fishing for his food. He remained in nearly the same situation, and thus employed for two hours. I then saw him moving off, in a northeast direction, towards the light house. I could not determine whether its motion was up and down, or to the right and left. His quickest motion was very rapid; I should suppose at the rate of fifteen or twenty miles an hour. Mackerel, manhaden, herring, and other bait fish abound in the cove where the animal was seen."

"Elkanah Finney."

"*Plymouth* ss. October 2, 1817. The above named Elkanah Finney appeared and made oath to the truth of the foregoing statement, by him subscribed, before me
    Nathaniel M. Davis, Jus Peace."

In vain have I tried to get a look at the above mentioned "first declarations in 1815".

Though the Committee now possessed the long wished-for drawing of the Sea-Serpent, it did not publish it, nor did-it state why it did not. The "questions" of which Mr. Davis writes will be presented to our readers hereafter. We see that the animal may remain quite still on the surface of the water, keeping, however, its coils, or joints, or bunches. It was a large individual. Its head seemed to be from 6 to 8 feet, its whole length far above one hundred and twenty feet. "Its head was a little larger than the body", we must of course read: "Its head was a little broader than the neck". It had a white stripe extending over the whole length of the head, just above the water, in the place where the underjaw must have been. We may look upon all the statements of Capt. Finney, as to the animal's colour, dimensions, motions, &c. as quite correct: he was a man too well acquainted with the different sea-animals, to be mistaken in any observation. Moreover, all his statements will soon and successively be repeated over and over again, till there remains not a shadow of doubt of their truth, which, in my opinion, is now already the case.

36.—1816?—In the "*Voyages*" of the well known Otto von Kotzebue, which appeared in Weimar in 1821, translated into English, in London, 1821, and into Dutch, in Amsterdam, 1822, we read that on the Isle of Unalaska, one of Aleutes, he had made the acquaintance of a Mr. Kriukof, living there since 1795, and being Agent of the American Company. Von Kotzebue writes:

"Mr. Kriukof's description of a sea animal which pursued him at Behring's Island, where he had gone for the purpose of hunting, is very remarkable. Several Aleutians affirm they have often seen this animal. It is of the shape of the Red serpent, and immensely long; the head resembles that of the sea-lion, and two disproportionately large eyes give it a frightful appearance. 'It was very fortunate for us' said Kriakof, 'that we were so near land, or else the monster would have swallowed us: it stretched its head far above the water, looked about for prey, and vanished. The head soon appeared again, and that considerably nearer: we rowed with all our might, and were very happy to have reached the shore before the serpent. The sea-lions were so terrified at the sight, that some rushed into the water, and others hid themselves on the shore. The sea often throws up pieces of flesh which, according to opinion, is that of this serpent, which no animal, not even the raven, will touch. Some Aleutians, who had once tasted some of it, suddenly died'."

This passage was told by Mr. Kriukof to von Kotzebue in Aug. 1817. So we have taken 1816 as the year of the appearance, though it may have happened earlier. When Mr. von Kotzebue wrote his book in 1820, he had already heard of the Sea-Serpent, which appeared in 1817 in the Harbour of Gloucester, Mass., and so he adds:

"If a sea-serpent really has been seen on the coast of North America, it may have been one of this frightful species."

What now are the most interesting parts of this notice? First of all that the Sea-Serpent is a common visitor of the Northern South-Sea, for the Aleutians affirmed that they often saw it. But the description of the head claims our close attention. We already said that the animal must have a hairy skin, for it has a mane, and those persons who saw it very closely confirm this. The head has already been twice described as resembling that of a seal, and afterwards we shall meet again with such a description; generally, however, it is said to resemble that of a snake, or a serpent, and sometimes to be sharp. What head combines these characters? I say the head of a sea-lion. It resembles more or less that of a seal, and seen from aside, more or less that of a snake, is rather pointed, because a sea-lion has not such formidable upper lips as seals have, and rather blunt. Why has nobody given this description? I say, because nobody among the eye-witnesses ever saw a sea-lion, neither the Norwegian, nor the many eye-witnesses of Massachusetts, nor even afterwards the other witnesses. The only one who could make this comparison was Mr. Kriukof, and the Aleutians, who live surrounded by these animals. The sea-lion's head is rather blunt, rather pointed, rather long, and flattened on the forehead, has also some whiskers, which are also attributed to sea-serpents by eye-witnesses in Norway, according to Pontoppidan, and afterwards again by a person who saw it at a few yards' distance from him.

Moreover Kriukof's comparison with the Red Snake a species evidently known to him, the disproportionate large eyes, the habit of the animal to stretch its long neck far above the surface of the water, apparently to look about for prey, to follow a boat at some distance, it being supposed to be inquisitive, though harmless, are all statements we have already met with or will meet with afterwards. It seems that sea-lions too often become the prey of the sea-serpent, otherwise these creatures would not have been so afraid of it.

As to the pieces of flesh, I am convinced that they are not of a sea-serpent, but either of sea-lions, of porpoises, or of another smaller kind of whales, which are the rests of a meal of our friend. They are washed ashore in a putrified state, and their not being to the taste of the ravens is probably a story, which, like the report of the death of the Aleutians who had tasted of it, must without doubt be considered as a mere fable. This report is reprinted in the *Philosophical Magazine and Journal*, Vol. LVIII, 1821.

"In the month of August, 1817," we read in the *Report of a Committee*, &c. printed Dec. 1817, Boston, by Cummings and Hillard,

"In the month of August, 1817, it was currently reported on various authorities, that an animal of very singular appearance had been recently and repeatedly seen in the harbour of Gloucester, Cape Ann, about thirty miles distant from Boston. It was said to resemble a serpent in its general form and motions, to be of immense size, and to move with wonderful rapidity; to appear on the surface of the water only in calm and bright weather; and to seem jointed, or like a number of buoys or casks following each other in a line."

"In consequence of these reports, at a meeting of the Linnaean Society of New England, holden at Boston on the 18th. day of August, the Hon. John Davis, Jacob Bigelow, M. D. and Francis C. Gray, Esq. were appointed a Committee to collect evidence with regard to the existence and appearance of any such animal. The following report made by that Committee is now published by order of the Society."

"Linnaean Society of New England."

Various Accounts

"The Committee appointed on the 18th. of August last to collect evidence with regard to the existence and appearance of a Sea-Serpent, said to have been recently seen in the harbour of Gloucester, now lay before the Society the following facts and documents."

"On the 19th. of August your Committee wrote to the Hon. Lonson Nash of Gloucester, requesting him to examine upon oath some of the inhabitants of that town with regard to the appearance of this animal, to make the examination as early as possible, to request the persons examined not to communicate to each other the substance of their respective statements, until they were all committed to writing; to have these statements signed and certified in due form, and sent to us. Our letter also contained certain rules with regard to the mode of conducting this examination, and questions to be put to the persons examined."

"In answer to it we received from Mr. Nash a letter, dated 28th. August, enclosing eight depositions, duly certified, which on the 1st. September were read before the Society as were also three depositions taken in Boston, on the 30th. August and 1st. September. You directed as to return your thanks to Mr. Nash for his readiness in complying with our request, to continue the investigation of the subject committed to us, in such manner as we should deem expedient, and to lay before you a formal report of the whole evidence that should he procured. In compliance with your directions, the chairman of the Committee wrote again to Mr. Nash on the 2d. September, and received from him an answer, dated 9th. September. We also wrote to Mr. Samuel Davis of Plymouth on the 1st. September, requesting him to examine upon oath some respectable men of that place, with regard to the appearance of an animal said to have been seen there in the year 1815, and to resemble the one lately seen near Gloucester; this letter contained the same rules and questions as were sent to Mr. Nash. In answer to this application, a letter from that gentleman was received on the 4th. October, enclosing the deposition of Capt. E. Finney. Your Committee have also received a communication from the Rev. William Jenks of Bath relative to the subject. All these documents are now laid before you in the following order."

"1. The rules and questions of your Committee.
"2. The letter from Mr. Nash of 28th August, enclosing the eight following depositions.
"3. The deposition of Amos Story.
"4. That of Salomon Allen.
"5. That of Eppes Ellery.
"6. That of William H. Foster.
"7. That of Matthew Gaffney.
"8. That of James Mansfield.
"9. That of John Johnston.
"10. That of William B. Pearson.
"11. The deposition of Sewall Toppan
"12. That of Robert Bragg taken at Boston.
"13. That of William Somerby
"14. The letter from our Chairman to Mr. Nash.
"15. The answer of Mr. Nash.
"16. Our letter to Mr. S. Davis of Plymouth.
"17. His answer, containing

"18. The deposition of Elkanah Finney.
"19. The letter from the Rev. William Jenks to your Committee.
"20. Is an account of a serpent said to have been frequently seen in the North Sea, extracted from the history of Norway, written by the Right Rev. Erich Pontoppidan, bishop of Bergen, in the year 1751.

I.

"Boston, Aug. 19, 1817.
"The Committee appointed by the Linnaean Society, at their meeting on the 18th. inst. for the purpose of collecting any evidence which may exist respecting a remarkable animal, denominated a *Sea Serpent*, reported to have recently been seen in and near the harbour of *Cape Ann*, have concluded on the following method of proceeding in the execution of their commission."

"I. The examination to be confined to persons professing actually to have seen the animal in question.

"II. Such persons to be examined as may be met with by either of the Committee, or by Hon. Lonson Nash of Gloucester, who is to be requested by a letter addressed to him from the Committee to undertake this service."

"III. All testimony on the subject to be taken in writing, and after being deliberately read to the person testifying, to be signed by him, and sworn before a magistrate. The examinations to be separate, and the matter testified by any witness not to be communicated until the whole evidence be taken."

"IV. The persons testifying to be requested first to relate their recollections on the subject, which being taken down, the following questions to be proposed, if not rendered unnecessary by the statement given."

"Questions."

"1. When did you first see this animal?"
"2. How often and how long at a time?"
"3. At what times of the day?"
"4. At what distance?"
"5. How near the shore?"
"6. What was its general appearance?"
"7. Was it in motion or at rest?"
"8. How fast did it move, and in what direction?"
"9. What parts of it were above the water and how high?"
"10. Did it appear jointed or only serpentine?"
"11. If serpentine, were its sinuosities vertical or horizontal?"
"12. How many distinct portions were out of water at one time?"
"13. What were its colour, length and thickness?"
"14. Did it appear smooth or rough?"
"15. What were the size and shape of its head, and had the head ears, horns, or other appendages?"
"16. Describe its eyes and mouth."
"17. Had it gills or breathing holes, and where?"
"18. Had it fins or legs, and where?"
"19. Had it a mane or hairs, and where?"
"20. How did its tail terminate?"

"21. Did it utter any sound?"
"22. Did it appear to pursue, avoid or notice any thing?"
"23. Did you see more than one?"
"24. How many persons saw it?"
"25. State any other remarkable fact."

II.

"Gloucester, August 28, 1817."
"John Davis,
"Jacob Bigelow, and Esq'rs.
"Francis C. Gray
"Gentlemen,
"I have received your favour of the 19th. inst. In that communication you request my assistance, in collecting evidence relative to a strange marine animal, that has appeared in the harbour in this place; and I have most cheerfully complied with your request. The subject is calculated to excite much interest, at home and abroad."

"The deponents were interrogated separately, no one knowing what the others had testified, and though they differ in some few particulars, still, for the most part, they agree."

"I am confident, from my own observation, that Mr. Allen is mistaken, as to the motion of the animal. His motion is vertical. I saw him, on the 14th. instant, for nearly half an hour. I should judge he was two hundred and fifty yards from me, when the nearest. I saw him twice with a glass for a short time, and at other times, with the naked eye. At that distance, I could not take in the two extremities of the animal that were visible, at one view, with a glass. His manner of turning is well described in Messrs. Pearson's and Gaffney's descriptions. The persons who have deposed before me, are men of fair and unblemished characters. The interrogatories that you sent to me were all put to the witnesses; but generally, I have omitted inserting them in the depositions, when the witnesses declared their inability to answer them."

"I think Mr. Allen is likewise mistaken, as to the distinct portions of the animal that were visible, at one time. I saw, at no time, more than eight distinct portions; though more may have been visible; still, I cannot believe that *fifty* distinct portions were seen, at one time. I believe the animal to be straight, and that, the apparent bunches were caused by his vertical motion."

"I have questioned Daniel Gaffney, who was in the boat with his brother Matthew, when he fired at the animal, and Daniel's answers corroborate Matthew's testimony."

"Respectfully, gentlemen,
"Your most ob't
"Lonson Nash."

We observe that the Linnaean Society has exerted all its energies in the matter and has acted with the greatest accuracy. In our historical treatice we, however, have not followed the above order, but arranged the depositions chronologically.

37.—1817, August 6?—In a letter from Mr. S. G. Perkins, dated Boston, Aug. 20, 1817, to Mr. E. Everett in Paris, preserved in the Library of the Royal University of Göttingen, and which we shall hereafter present to our readers *in toto*, we read:

"About a fortnight since, two women, who live near the entrance of the Harbour of Cape Ann, reported that they saw a Sea-Monster come into the Harbour, that it had the appearance of a Snake, was of great length, &c."

37.—1817, August, 10.—(See the *Report* of 1817).

"I, Amos Story of Gloucester, in the County of Essex, mariner, depose and say, that on the tenth day of August A. D. 1817, I saw a strange marine animal, that I believe to be a serpent, at the southward and eastward of Ten Pound Island, in the harbour in said Gloucester. It was between the hours of twelve and one o'clock when I first saw him, and he continued in sight for an hour and half. I was setting on the shore, and was about twenty rods from him when he was the nearest to me. His head appeared shaped much like the head of a sea turtle, and he carried his head from ten to twelve inches above the surface of the water. His head at that distance appeared larger than the head of any dog that I ever saw. From the back part of his head to the next part of him that was visible, I should judge to be three or four feet. He moved very rapidly through the water, I should say a mile in two, or at most, in three minutes. I saw no bunches on his back. On this day, I did not see more than ten or twelve feet of his body."

Though Mr. Story compares the animal's head with that of a sea-turtle, probably because he saw it in such a direction that it seemed short and thick; his statement that it carried its head a foot above the water, and that it was larger than that of any dog at a distance of twenty rods,—the head may even have been of about two feet—, that its motion was rapid, are all mere repetitions of facts well known to us. He did not see bunches on its back, the animal consequently swam with its body in a straight line, a habit we have also already met with. Just behind the head a part of the neck of about four feet was hidden under water, and then twelve feet of the animal's body were visible again.

39, 40, 41.—1817, August 12, 13, 14.—(See the *Report*, printed in 1817).

"I, Solomon Allen 3d. of Gloucester, in the County of Essex, shipmaster, depose and say; that I have seen a strange marine animal, that I believe to be a sea-serpent, in the harbour in said Gloucester. I should judge him to be between eighty and ninety feet in length, and about the size of a halfbarrel, apparently having joints from his head to his tail. I was about one hundred and fifty yards from him, when I judged him to be of the size of a half barrel. His head formed something like the head of the rattle snake, but nearly as large as the head of a horse. When he moved on the surface of the water, his motion was slow, at times playing about in circles, and sometimes moving nearly straight forward. When he disappeared, he sunk apparently directly down, and would next appear at two hundred yards from where he disappeared, in two minutes. His colour was a dark brown, and I did not discover any spots upon him."

"*Question.* When did you first see this animal?"
"*Answer.* I saw him on the twelfth, thirteenth, and fourteenth of August, A. D. 1817."
"*Q.* How often, and how long at a time?"
"*A.* I was in a boat on the twelfth inst. and was around him several times, within one hundred and fifty yards of him. On the thirteenth inst. I saw him nearly all the day, from the shore. I was on the beech, nearly on a level with him, and most of the time he was from one hundred and fifty to three hundred yards from me. On the fourteenth, I saw him but once, and had not so good a view of him."
"*Q.* What parts of it were above the surface if the water, and how high?"
"*A.* Its joints or bunches, appeared about eight or ten inches above the surface of the water"
"*Q.* Did it bend its body up and down in moving, or to the right and left?"
"*A.* He moved to the right and left."
"*Q.* How many distinct portions of it were out of the water, at one time?"
"*A.* I should say fifty distinct portions."
"*Q.* Did it appear smooth or rough?"
"*A.* It appeared rough and scaly."
"*Q.* Had it ears, horns, or any other appendages?"
"*A.* I perceived none."
"*Q.* How did its tail terminate?"
"*A.* He seemed to taper towards (what I thought) his tail, though I had no distinct view of his tail."
"*Q.* Did it utter any sound?"
"*A.* Not in my hearing."
"*Q.* Did it appear to pursue, avoid, or notice any thing?"
"*A.* It appeared to me to avoid the boat where I was, though afterwards, I saw him make towards a boat, in which was Mr. Gaffney and others."
"*Q.* Did you see more than one?"
"*A.* I did not."
"*Q.* How many persons saw it?"
"*A.* Twenty or thirty persons were in view of me."
"*Q.* Did he open his mouth when you saw him, and if so, how wide?"
"*A.* Yes, when I looked at him from the shore with a glass at about two hundred yards distance, his mouth appeared to be open about ten inches. I had no glass, when I saw him from the boat."
"*Q.* Did he carry his head above the surface of the water?"
"*A.* Yes, at times, about two feet, then again he would carry the top of his head just on the surface of the water."
"*Q.* Did he turn short and quick, and what was the form of the curve that he made?"
"*A.* He turned short and quick, and the first part of the curve that he made in turning resembled the link of a chain; but when his head came parallel with his tail, his head and tail appeared near together.
"Solomon Allen 3d."

"Essex. ss. August 21, 1817. Personally appeared Solomon Allen the third, and made oath that the foregoing facts by him subscribed, are true, according to his best knowledge and belief."
"Cor. Lonson Nash, Jus. Pacis."

As we have already seen, Mr. Lonson Nash wrote in his letter to the Committee: "I am confident, from my own observation, that Mr. Allen is mistaken, as to the motion of the animal. His motion is vertical." And:

"I think Mr. Allen is likewise mistaken as to the distinct portions of the animal, that were visible, at one time. I saw at no time more than eight distinct portions; though more may have been visible; still I cannot believe that *fifty* distinct portions were seen at one time."

As to the motion of the animal I believe that Mr. Allen was really mistaken. When the animal was nearest to him, there was still a distance of a hundred and fifty yards between Mr. Allen and the animal. As to the number of the bunches which Mr. Allen reports, viz. fifty, I believe that he has not *counted* them; he says: I should say fifty. Pontoppidan tells us that the greatest number ever seen was twenty-five, and I believe that this is indeed the case.

Moreover its length of from eighty to ninety feet, the size of the visible part to be that of a half barrel, the resemblance of the head to a rattle-snake's, say a common snake's, the size of it to be that of a horse's, say two feet, &c., &c., are all common statements. Of course Mr. Allen is also mistaken as to its scaly surface. The roughness, however, may have been the result of the rippling of the water. When the animal disappeared it sunk directly down, like a rock, a statement which we have met with and shall meet with several times. That the teeth of the animal were not visible at a distance of two hundred yards cannot surprise us. In the animal's turning its flexibility again is mentioned: head and tail approaching, nay, nearly touching each other.

41—1817, August 14.—See also no 41 on p. 164.—(*Report of a Committee*, 1817).

"I, Epes Ellery, of Gloucester, in the County of Essex, shipmaster, depose and say; that on the 14th. day of August, 1817, I saw a sea animal that I thought to be a serpent, in the harbour in said Gloucester. I was on an eminence, near low water mark, and about thirty feet above the level of the sea, when I saw him. I should judge that he was about one hundred and fifty fathoms from me. I saw the upper part of his head, and I should say about forty feet of the animal. He appeared to me to have joints, about the size of a two-gallon keg. I was looking at him with a spyglass, when I saw him open his mouth, and his mouth appeared like that of a serpent; the top of his head appeared flat. His motion when he turned was quick, but I will not express an opinion of his velocity. The first part of the curve that he made in turning was of the form of a staple, and as he approached towards his tail, he came near his body with his head, and then ran parallel with his tail, and his head and tail then appeared together."

"*Q.* At what time of the day did you see him?"

"*A.* It was a little after sun set."

"*Q.* What parts of it were above the surface of the water, and how high?"

"*A.* I did not count the number of bunches, but they appeared about six inches above the surface of the water."

"*Q.* Were its sinuosities vertical or horizontal?"

"*A.* Vertical."

"*Q.* Did it appear to pursue, avoid, or notice any thing?"

"*A.* It did not appear to avoid any thing. He appeared to be amusing himself, though there were several boats not far from him."

"*Q.* Did you see more than one?"
"*A.* I did not."
"*Q.* How many persons saw it?"
"*A.* There were fifteen or twenty persons near where I was."
"Epes Ellery."

"Essex ss. August, 25, 1817. Personally appeared Epes Ellery, and made oath to the truth of the foregoing facts by him subscribed.
"Cor. Lonson Nash, Jus. Pacis."

Not a single fact which has not been stated before.

41—1817, August 14.—(See also n°. 41 on p. 164 and n°. 41 on p. 167.)—(*Report of a Committee*, 1817).

"I, William H. Foster, of Gloucester, in the county of Essex, merchant, depose and say: That on the fourteenth day of August, A. D. 1817, I first saw an uncommon sea-animal, that I believe to have been a serpent, in the harbour in said Gloucester. When I first discovered him, his head was above the surface of the water, perhaps ten inches, and he made but little progress through the water. He was apparently shaded with light colours. He afterwards went in different directions, leaving on the surface of the water, marks like those made by skating on the ice. Then he would move in a straight line west, and would almost in an instant, change his course to east, bringing his head, as near as I could judge, to where his tail was; or in fact, to the extreme hinder part visible, raising himself as he turned, six or eight inches out of water, and shewing a body at least forty feet in length."

Its being shaded with light colours is already mentioned by Pontoppidan. Its leaving a wake behind it has already been stated many times, and will often be stated afterwards. Also its mode of turning, giving to its body the form of a staple."

41.—1817, August 14.—(See also n°. 41 on p. 164, p. 167, p. 168.)—Report of a Committee, 1817.).

"I, Matthew Gaffney, of Gloucester, in the County of Essex, ship carpenter, depose and say: That on the fourteenth day of August, A. D. 1817, between the hours of four and five o'clock in the afternoon, I saw a strange marine animal, resembling a serpent, in the harbour in said Gloucester. I was in a boat, and was within thirty feet of him. His head appeared full as large as a four-gallon keg, his body as large as a barrel, and his length that I saw, I should judge forty feet at least. The top of his head was of a dark colour, and the under part of his head appeared nearly white, as did also several feet of his belly, that I saw. I supposed and do believe that the whole of his belly was nearly white. I fired at him, when he was the nearest to me. I had a good gun, and took good aim. I aimed at his head, and think I must have hit him. He turned towards us immediately after I had fired, and I thought he was coming at us; but he sunk down and went directly under our boat, and made his appearance at about one hundred yards from where he sunk. He did not turn down like a fish, but appeared to settle directly down, like a rock.

My gun carries a ball of eighteen to a pound; and I suppose there is no person in town, more accustomed to shooting than I am. I have seen the animal at several other times, but never had so good a view of him, as on this day. His motion was vertical, like a caterpillar."

"*Q*. How fast did it move?"

"*A*. I should say he moved at the rate of a mile in two, or at most three minutes"

"*Q*. Did it appear smooth or rough?"

"*A*. I thought it smooth, when I was endeavouring to take aim at him, and will not say positively, that he was smooth, though that is still my belief."

"*Q*. Does he turn quick and short, and if so, what is the form of path that he makes, in turning?"

"*A*. He turns quick and short, and the first part of the curve that he makes in turning, is in the form of the staple; but his head seems to approach rapidly towards his body, his head and tail moving in opposite directions, and when his head and tail came parallel, they appear almost to touch each other."

"*Q*. Did he appear more shy, after you had fired at him?"

"*A*. He did not; but continued playing as before."

"*Q*. Who was in the boat with you, when you fired at the serpent?"

"*A*. My brother Daniel, and Augustin M. Webber.

"Matthew Gaffney."

"Essex, ss. August 28, 1817. Then Matthew Gaffney made oath that the foregoing, by him subscribed, is true according to his best knowledge and belief.

"Before Lonson Nash, Jus of Peace"

As we have already seen Mr. Lonson Nash in his letter to the Committee wrote:

"His manner of turning is well described in Mr. Gaffney's description..... I have questioned Daniel Gaffney, who was in the boat with his brother Matthew when he fired at the animal, and Daniel's answer corroborate Matthew's testimony."

We read here that the underpart of the head appeared almost white, and several feet of its belly too (read of the underpart of its neck, or of its throat). Further Mr. Gaffney goes on: "I supposed and do believe that the whole of his belly was nearly white". This is very remarkable, for Mr. Gaffney seems to be familiar with sea-animals, as porpoises, &c., and a very good observer, and his conclusion is quite right from a zoological point of view. Very remarkable is the animal's demeanor after the shot. Apparently furious, it directed itself suddenly to the shooter, but when very near to him, it sank down like a rock and appeared again far away. This manner of acting will afterwards be described again in Norway. Again its manner of disappearing is described as sinking like a rock. The mode of turning too is just the same as is mentioned every where.

41—1817, August 14.—(See also n°. 41 on p, 164, p. 167, p. 168, p. 168.) (*Report of a Committee*, 1817.)

We read in the letter from Mr. Lonson Nash to the Committee that he himself saw the animal:

"I saw him on the 14th. instant, for nearly half an hour. I should judge he was two hundred and fifty yards from me, when the nearest. I saw him twice with a glass for a short time, and at other times, with the naked eye. At that distance, I could not take in the two extremities of the animal, that were visible, at one view with a glass..... His motion is vertical..... His manner of turning is well described in Messrs Pearson's and Gaffney's descriptions..... I saw, at no time, more than eight distinct portions; though more may have been visible..... I believe the animal to be straight, and that the apparent bunches were caused by his vertical motion."

The Chairman of the Committee, the Hon. John Davis immediately wrote to Mr. Lonson Nash the following letter:

"Boston, September 2, 1817."
"Sir",
"Your letter of the 28th. ult. to the Committee of the Linnaean Society, and the accompanying depositions, were duly received, and were yesterday communicated to the Society. The Committee are greatly obliged to you for your ready compliance with their request. In these sentiments the Society unite, and I am charged with the agreeable office of communicating to you their vote of thanks for your very acceptable labours. What you have thus accomplished will go far in giving some precise and accurate conceptions on a subject, peculiarly exposed to exaggeration and mistake. This evidence, with some additional documents, will probably be published. The Committee will not make their final report on the subject of their Commission until evidence shall be procured respecting some other reputed appearances of like description, particularly one at Plymouth in 1815."

"We have been informed that the animal at Gloucester was once seen, and it was said by a woman, lying dormant very near the shore. The Committee wished this intimation to be given to you, that if it should point to any material circumstances, the evidence might be taken."

"The last we hear of the object of our inquiry is of his appearance off East Point on the 28th. ult. This we gather from the testimony of captain Toppan, and his crew, of the schooner Laura, coming from Newburyport to Boston."

"It appears by your letter, that you had sight of the animal. A letter from you, giving a detailed account of your observations, would be particularly acceptable."

"We understand that a gentleman in Gloucester, (Captain Beach) has a drawing; supposed to be a good representation of the animal. Some information respecting this drawing would be agreeable; how far it is considered by those who had the best view of the animal as a correct representation, and whether the person possessing it would be disposed to permit an engraving from it to be annexed to the publication of the evidence, and on what terms. Yours very respectfully,
"Jno Davis."

"We have already read the report of the appearance of 1815 (n°. 34 and 35); the intelligence of the encounter on the 28th. of August we will communicate afterwards (n° 48). The answer of Judge Nash, omitting the intelligence about the animal reposing on the rocks (this report has been discussed some pages further on, n°. 45) runs as follows (See *Report of a Committee*, 1817): 'Gloucester, September 9, 1817.'

"Sir",
"Your favoured of the 2d. inst. has been received. The vote of thanks of the Linnaean Society for my services was highly gratifying to me, not simply on

account of the high consideration I entertain for the members of that laudable institution; but likewise for the agreeable manner, and respectable channel, through which their vote of thanks was communicated to me."

"You request a detailed account of my observations, relative to the serpent. I saw him on the fourteenth ultimo, and when nearest, I judged him to be about two hundred and fifty yards from me. At that distance I judged him (in the largest part) about the size of a half barrel, gradually tapering towards the two extremes. Twice I saw him with a glass, only for a short time, and at other times, with the naked eye, for nearly half an hour. His colour appeared nearly black—his motion was vertical. When he moved on the surface of the water, the track of his rear was visible, for at least half a mile."

"His velocity, when moving on the surface of the water, I judged was at the rate of a mile in about four minutes. When immersed in the water, his speed was greater, moving, I should say, at the rate of a mile in two or at most three minutes. When moving under water, you could often trace him by the motion of the water, on the surface, and from this circumstance, I conclude he did not swim deep. He apparently went as straight through the water, as you could draw a line. When he changed his course, he diminished his velocity but little—the two extremes that were visible appeared rapidly moving in opposite directions, and when they came parallel, they appeared not more than a yard apart. With a glass, I could not take in, at one view, the two extremes of the animal, that were visible. I have looked at a vessel, at about the same distance, and could distinctly see forty five feet. If he should be taken, I have no doubt that his length will be found seventy feet, at least, and I should not be surprised, if he should be found one hundred feet long. When I saw him I was standing on an eminence, on the sea shore, elevated about thirty feet above the surface of the water, and the sea was smooth."

"If I saw his head, I could not distinguish it from his body; though there were seafaring men near me, who said that they could distinctly see his head. I believe they spoke truth; but not having been much accustomed to look through a glass, I was not so fortunate."

"I never saw more than seven or eight distinct portions of him above the water, at any one time, and he appeared rough; though I supposed this appearance was produced by his motion. When he disappeared, he apparently sunk directly down like a rock."

"Captain Beach has been in Boston for a week past, and I am informed that he is still there. An engraving from his drawing of the serpent has been, or is now, making at Boston, but I have not been able to ascertain how far his drawing is thought a correct representation. "

"Respectfully, Sir,
Your most obedient,
    Lonson Nash."

Mr. W. D. Peck says of this declaration (*Mem. Am. Acad. Arts Sc.* Vol. IV. Pt. 1.)

"The account of it by Lonson Nash Esq. Justice of the Peace in Gloucester, from his own observation, is perfectly free from prejudice, and as clear and satisfactory as can be expected of an object at a distance of two hundred and fifty yards."

Remarkable in this testimony is again the considerable wake the animal leaves behind it when swimming rapidly. Easy it is to explain why the speed is greater under water than when partly visible above the surface of the water. Those parts viz. which are above the surface must be borne by the body hidden under water, consequently this carries a burden, and the speed, it is evident, cannot be so rapid as when the animal is quite under water, in which position each part of the animal's body is carried by the water itself, and not by the individual. It has no burden to carry, it is specifically lighter, and the speed can reach its maximum.— Remarkable too is the fact that the animal, when swimming under water, does so just below the surface, and causes the rippling of it. This is a habit of Pinnipeds.

Where Mr. Nash thinks that the apparent roughness is produced by its motion, I am convinced that he is right. He could not distinguish its head from its body, which cannot surprise us; both are of the same thickness, when seen from aside, and I believe too that the seafaring men, more accustomed to look with a glass, distinctly saw the difference between head and neck. Moreover the mode of turning, its length of more than seventy feet, its sinking down like a rock, when disappearing, need not be spoken of; they were mere repetitions of former statements.

I am sorry I have not been able to get a look at Mr. Beach's figure.

42.—1817, August 15.—(*Report of a Committee*, 1817).

"I, James Mansfield, of Gloucester, in the county of Essex, merchant, depose and say: That I saw a strange creature, of enormous length, resembling a serpent. I think this was on the 15th. of August, A. D. 1817. I should say he was from forty to sixty feet in length, extended on the surface of the water, with his head above the water about a foot. He remained in this position but a short time, and then started off very quick, with much greater velocity than I have seen him move with at any other time. I saw bunches on his back about a foot in height, when he lay extended on the water. His colour appeared to me black or very dark. It was a little before six o'clock P. M. when I saw him. I should say, he moved a mile in five or six minutes."

"*Q.* How near the shore was the serpent?"

"*A.* About one hundred and eighty yards from the shore where I stood."

"*Q.* Were its sinuosities vertical or horizontal?"

"*A.* Vertical."

"*Q.* What were the size and shape of its head; and had it ears, horns, or any other appendages?"

"*A.* His head appeared to be about the size of the crown of a hat, at the distance from whence I saw him. The shape of his head I cannot describe, and I saw no ears, horns, or other appendages. I had no spy glass, and cannot describe him so minutely as I otherwise could. I have seen him at other times, but my view of him was not so good, as on this day."

"James Mansfield."

"Essex, ss. August 27, 1817. Then James Mansfield made oath to the truth of the foregoing deposition by him subscribed."

"Before Lonson Nash, Jus. Pacis."

We have here again the statement that the animal is able to keep its bunches, when it lies extended on the water.

43.—1817, August 17.—(*Report of a Committee,* 1817.) The second part of the affidavit of Mr. William H. Foster runs as follows:

"On the seventeenth of August instant, I again saw him. He came into the harbour, occasionally exhibiting parts of his body, which appeared like rings or bunches. As he drew near, and when opposite to me, there rose from his head or the most forward part of him, a prong or spear about twelve inches in height, and six inches in circumference at the bottom, and running to a small point."

"*Q.* Might not the prong or spear that you saw, have been the tongue of the serpent?"
"*A.* I thought not; as I saw the prong before I saw his head; but it might have been."
"*Q.* At what distance were you, when you saw the spear of the serpent?"
"*A.* I should judge forty rods; I had a spyglass when I saw the prong or spear."
"*Q.* Did the animal appear round?"
"*A.* He did."
"*Q.* Did he appear jointed, or only serpentine?"
"*A.* He appeared jointed."
"*Q.* Were its sinuosities vertical or horizontal?"
"*A.* Vertical."
"*Q.* What was its colour?"
"*A.* It appeared brown."
"*Q.* Did it appear smooth or rough?"
"*A.* It appeared smooth."
"*Q.* What was the size and shape of his head?"
"*A.* At the distance where I was, his head appeared as large as a man's head; but I cannot describe its shape."
"*Q.* Did it appear to pursue, avoid or notice objects?
"*A.* I thought it appeared to notice objects."
"*Q.* How fast did it move?
"*A.* At the rate of a mile in a minute, at times, I have no doubt."
"William H. Foster."

"Essex ss. August 27, 1817. Personally appeared William H. Foster, and made oath that the foregoing deposition, by him subscribed, is true, according to his best knowledge and belief."
"Before Lonson Nash, Jus. of Peace."

The first statement that strikes us is the prong or spear, seen by Mr. Foster. I am convinced that this instrument, seen by him at a distance of forty rods, and with a spy-glass, rising from the foremost part of the head, about 12 inches, or a foot, in length, pointed at its end, and having six inches in circumference, or two in diameter, at the bottom, was nothing else but the animal's tongue.

43.—1817, August 17.—See also n°. 43 on p. 175.—(*Report of a Committee,* 1817).—

"I, John Johnston, jun, of Gloucester, in the County of Essex, of the age of seventeen years, depose and say: That on the evening of the seventeenth day of August, A. D. 1817, between the hours of eight and nine o'clock, while passing from the shore in a boat, to a vessel lying in the harbour of said Gloucester, I saw a strange marine animal, that I believe to be a serpent, lying extended on the surface of the water. His length appeared to be fifty feet at least, and he appeared straight, exhibiting no protuberances. Capt. John Corliss and George Marble were in the boat with me. We were within two oars length of him. We immediately rowed from him, and at first concluded to pass by his tail; but fearing we might strike it with the boat, concluded to pass around his head, which we did, by altering our course. He remained in the same position, till we lost sight of him. We approached so near to him that I believe I could have reached him with my oar. There was not sufficient light to enable me to describe the animal."

"John Johnston, jun."

"Essex, ss. August 25, 1817. Personally appeared John Johnston, jr. and made oath that the foregoing deposition, by him subscribed, is true according to his best knowledge and belief."

"Before Lonson Nash, Jus of Peace."

This account is as interesting as all the other ones; though no further particulars are described, it is again mentioned that more than fifty feet of the animal's back part were visible, lying perfectly still on the surface of the water, showing no bunches at all.

44.—1817, August 18.—In the letter of Mr. S. G. Perkins to Mr. E. Everett, dated Boston Aug. 20, 1817, we read:

"But on Saturday, the day before yesterday, a vessel arrived at Beverly from the bank of New-foundland. The captain and the crew report that, off Cape Ann Harbour, they saw a Sea Monster of the Snake kind, lying on the water, of immense length. That the crew were so much alarmed, that they got away as soon as they could, and that they estimated it at 100 feet long."

44.—1817, August 18.—See also n°. 44 hereabove.—(*Report of a Committee, 1817*).—

"I, William B. Pearson, of Gloucester, in the County of Essex, merchant, depose and say: That I have, several times, seen a strange marine animal, that I believe to be a serpent, of great size. I have had a good view of him, only once, and this was on the 18th. of August, A. D. 1817. I was in a sailboat, and when off Webber's cove (so called) in the harbour of said Gloucester, I saw something coming out of the cove; we hove to, not doubting but that it was the same creature that had been seen several times in the harbour, and had excited much interest among the inhabitants of Gloucester. James P. Collins was the only person with me. The serpent passed out under the stern of our boat, towards *Ten Pound Island*; then he stood in towards us again, and crossed our bow. We immediately exclaimed: 'here is the snake!' From what I saw of him, I should say that he was nothing short of seventy feet in length. I distinctly saw bunches on his back, and once he raised his head out of water. The top of his head appeared flat, and was raised seven or eight inches above the surface of the water. He passed by the bow of the boat, at about thirty yards distance. His colour was a dark brown. I saw him at this time about two minutes. His motion was vertical. His velocity at this time was not great, though at times, I have seen him move with great velocity, I should say at the rate of a mile in three minutes, and perhaps faster. His size I judged to be about the size of a half barrel. I saw Mr. Gaffney fire at him, at about the distance of thirty yards. I thought he hit him, and afterwards he appeared more shy. He turned very short, and appeared as limber and active as the eel, when compared to his size. The form of the curve when he turned in the water, resembled a staple; his head seemed to approach towards his body for some feet; then his head and tail appeared moving rapidly, in opposite directions, and when his head and tail were on parallel lines, they appeared not more than two or three yards apart."

"*Q*. At what time in the day was this?"
"*A*. Between the hours of five and six in the afternoon."
"*Q*. How many distinct portions of it were out of water at one time?"
"*A*. Ten or twelve distinct portions."
"*Q*. Can you describe his eyes and mouth."
"*A*. I thought and believe, that I saw his eye at one time, and it was dark and sharp."
"*Q*. How did its tail terminate?"
"*A*. I had not a very distinct view of his tail; I saw no bunches towards, what I thought the end of the tail, and I believe there were none. From where I judged his navel might be, to the end of his tail, there were no bunches visible."
"William B. Pearson.
"*Essex.* ss. August 27, 1817. Then William B. Pearson made oath to the truth of the above."
"Before Lonson Nash, Jus. of Peace."

In this account too there is not a single fact which has not been mentioned before, except that the tail did not show bunches, while the back did. From that point of the body where Mr. Pearson judged his navel might be towards the end of the tail, the animal had no bunches. It is probable that we are meant to read: from the middle of the visible part, where the animal seemed to be thickest. It is also probable that the animal's external characters, though Mr. Pearson says he believed it to be a serpent, made on him the impression of a mammal.

44.—1817, August 18.—See also n°. 44 p. 176 and hereabove.—In the above-mentioned letter from Mr. S. G. Perkins to Mr. B. Everett we read:

"My Brother—Colonel Perkins—went down to Cape Ann two days ago to see it. He says that he is satisfied that such an animal is there. As he stood on the shore, it came within the eighth of a mile of him, but as he did not see it so distinctly, as to be able to state all its points, he has not said any thing to the public about it."

Fortunately Col. T. H. Perkins wrote down his experiences in a letter, dated Oct. 13, 1820, when on board the ship *Ann Marie*, to his friend Jno P. Cushing. He published it in the *Boston Daily Advertiser* of Nov. 25, 1845, after the excitement caused by the appearance of the sea-serpent seen by the *Daedalus* (n°. 118). The whole is reprinted in the *Zoologist* of 1849, p. 2358, which I had the opportunity to consult. The part of the letter, treating of his visit runs as follows:

"Boston, November, 1848."
"In the paper called the "Illustrated London News" of 28th. October, is an account given by Capt. M'Quhae, of H. R. M. ship Daedalus, of a sea-serpent, seen from his ship in August last, on her passage from the East-Indies, and between the Cape of Good Hope and St. Helena. The perusal of several articles on the subject leads me to send you a letter written by me on my passage from England to the United States, in August, 1820, to Jno. P. Cushing, my friend and then partner, residing at Canton in China. I also send you a memorandum from Commander Bolton, of the U. S. Navy, giving the report of the gentlemen of the Navy who were on board a tender called the Lynx, and who had a very favourable opportunity of satisfying themselves of the existence of the animal which had caused so much excitement. The serpent was seen in 1817, '19, and '20, from the *shore*, and the reports show the bunches to be produced by the vertical motion of the body when in action. From the drawings which accompany the letter of Capt. M'Quhae, there are none of the protuberances, and which would lead to the opinion that the animal seen on the other side of the Equator differs in genus from that which has been seen on our coast. The drawings of the sea-serpent seen on the coast of Norway, given in the report of the Bishop Pontoppidan, are identical with the appearance of the animal which has been so often spoken of as visiting our northern seas. T. H. Perkins."
"On board the ship Ann Marie, at sea, lat. 46, long. 44, Oct. 13, 1820."
"My dear sir,—When on shore I have little time to spare from business to devote to details which I am now to communicate."
"During the past three years you will have seen accounts in the newspapers, or reports will have met you in another form of an immense sea-serpent having infested our shores in Boston Bay. The first appearance he made in the summer of 1817, in the harbour of Cape Ann. Wishing to satisfy myself on a subject on which there existed a great difference of opinion, I myself visited Gloucester with Mr. Lee. On our way down we met several persons returning, who had visited the place where he was said to have exhibited himself, and who reported to us that he had not been seen for two or three days past. We however, continued our route to Gloucester, though with fears that we should not be gratified with the sight of the monster which we sought. I satisfied myself, from conversation with several persons who had seen him, that the report in circulation was not a fable. All the town were, as you may suppose, on the alert; and almost every individual, both great and small, had been gratified, at a greater or less distance, with a sight of him. The weather was fine, the sea perfectly smooth, and Mr. Lee and myself were seated on a point of land which projects into the harbour, and about twenty feet above the level of the water, from which we were distant about fifty or sixty feet ......
"Whilst thus seated, I observed an agitation in the water at the entrance of the harbour, like that which follows a small vessel going five or six miles an hour through the water. As we knew there was no shoal where the water was thus broken, I immediately said to Mr. Lee that I had no doubt that what I had seen was the sea serpent in pursuit of fish. Mr. Lee was not directing his attention to the

spot which I speak of, and had not seen the foam of the water, the animal having immediately disappeared."

"In a few moments after my exclamation, I saw on the opposite side of the harbour, at about two miles distance from where I had first seen, or thought I saw, the snake, the same object, moving with a rapid motion up the harbour, on the western shore. As he approached us, it was easy to see that his motion was not that of the common snake, either on the land or in the water, but evidently the vertical movement of the caterpillar. As nearly as I could judge, there was visible at a time about forty feet of his body. It was not, to be sure, a continuity of body, as the form from head to tail (except as the apparent bunches appeared as he moved through the water) was seen only at three or four feet asunder. It was very evident, however, that his length must be much greater than what appeared, as, in his movement, he left a considerable wake in his rear. I had a fine glass, and was within from one-third to half a mile of him. The head was flat in the water, and the animal was, as far as I could distinguish, of a chocolate colour. I was struck with an appearance in the front part of the head like a single horn, about nine inches to a foot in length, and of the form of a marlinespike. There were a great many people collected by this time, many of whom had before seen the same object, and the same appearance. From the time I first saw him until he passed by the place where I stood, and soon after disappeared, was not more than fifteen or twenty minutes."

"I left the place fully satisfied that the reports in circulation, although differing in details, were essentially correct. I returned to Boston, and having made my report, I found Mrs. Perkins and my daughters disposed to make a visit to Gloucester with me when the return of the animal should be again announced. A few days after my return I went again to Cape Ann with the ladies; we had a pleasant ride, but returned ungratified in the object which carried us there."

The reader knows already that I don't agree with Col. T. H. Perkins as to the generic difference of the sea-serpent.—It is the second time that the tongue of the animal is seen to be thrown out.

All these reports of course greatly alarmed the people, and divided them into believers and unbelievers. Letters were written to Europe. As it is of interest to know the public opinion about the subject, it is perhaps not unnecessary to communicate here the letters which I found, especially those hitherto unpublished. On the 20th. of August of 1817 Mr. S. G. Perkins wrote a letter to Mr. E. Everett, then at Paris; this letter is preserved in the Library of the Royal University of Göttingen. An extract from it, respecting the sea-serpent, here printed for the first time, runs as follows:

"You will except me to give you some account of the extraordinary monster, which is now the subject of universal conversation here. So far as we know anything of it, I will give it you, but we have yet to learn its Genus, species and character. About a fortnight since, two women, who live near the entrance of the Harbour of Cape Ann, reported that they saw a Sea-Monster come into the Harbour, that it had the appearance of a Snake, was of great length, &c. But little attention, however, was paid to this report, and it gained no public circulation. Within a week the Country has been agitated with reports of the existence of the monster, and men of reputation and character have made known, that they have distinctly seen the animal. Many have gone off in search of him in Boats, and muskets have been fired at him, without any other effect than alarming him and deterring him from suffering the approach of the boats. He is represented to be from 50 to 100 feet long, of the size of a barrel about the body, which is formed into parallel rings, which—when he is on the top of the water—are so prominent, that they resembled buoys attached to each other. Its motions, when in pursuit of its prey, are very rapid, and create a wake like a small vessel passing thro' the water. My Brother—Colonel Perkins—went down to Cape Ann two days ago to see it. He says that he is satisfied that such an animal is there. As he stood on the shore, it came within the eighth of a mile of him, but as he did not see it so distinctly as to be able to state all its points, he has not said any thing to the public about it. Many persons—who are well known as men of character—have assured me they have seen 30 or 40 feet of it out of water at once. These reports have created various opinions and sensations, many disbelieving the whole story, and others not doubting it, in the least. My brother goes again to morrow morning to pass a week at Cape Ann. It comes into the harbour daily, in pursuit of the herrings, which resort here in great quantities. All these facts, however, were loose, and from the variety of Reports, people had gotten to doubt their foundation, and supposed it was only a number of porpuses following each other, in rapid succession. But on Saturday, the day before yesterday, a vessel arrived at Beverly from the banks of Newfoundland. The captain and crew report that, off Cape Ann Harbour, they saw a Sea-Monster of the Snake kind, lying on the water, of immense length. That the crew were so much alarmed, that they got away as soon as they could, and that they estimated it, at 100 feet long. Other particulars were stated, which I do not recollect. This had revived the belief, in its existence, and great efforts will be made to take it dead or alive. I heard today that a subscription was on foot, and that an express has been sent to Nantucket for twenty whale men to come up with their boats and apparatus to destroy it. The Linnean Society have appointed a Committee to go down and investigate it, of which Judge Davis is Chairman."

45.—1817, August 22?—We have already seen that the Chairman of the Committee asked Judge Nash to give, if possible, an evidence of the fact that a woman saw the animal lying dormant very near the shore. In speaking of Mr. Nash's answer we skipped this evidence to insert it here. It runs as follows:

"I have seen and conversed with the woman, who was said to have seen the serpent dormant on the rocks, near the water, to whom you refer in yours; but she can give no material evidence. She says that she saw something, resembling a large log of wood, on the rocks, on the extreme eastern point of Ten Pound Island, (a small island in our harbour), resting partly on the rocks, and partly in the water. The distance was about half a mile. She took a glass, looked at the object and saw it move. Her attention was for a short time arrested, by some domestic avocation, and when she looked for the object again, it had disappeared."

The letter from the Hon. John Davis, the Chairman of the Committee, was dated Sept. 2, 1817. The appearance, therefore, took place before this date. Fortunately we have another testimony of this position of the animal. In the letter from Col. T.

H. Perkins, dated Oct. 13, 1820, and published by him in the *Boston Daily Advertiser* of Nov. 25, 1848, we read that he visited the harbour of Gloucester. This must have been on the 18th. of August 1817 (see n°. 44. p. 178.); after having described this visit the Colonel goes on:

"A few days after my return I went again to Cape Ann with the ladies; we had a pleasant ride, but returned ungratified in the object which carried us there."

"Whilst at Cape Ann I talked with many persons who had seen the serpent, and among others with a person of the name of Mansfield, one of the most respectable inhabitants of the town. His account to me was, that a few days before, as he was taking a ride with his wife in a chair, the road taking them close to a bank which overlooks the harbour (and is nearly a perpendicular precipice), he saw an uncommon appearance, which induced him to descend from the carriage, when he saw the sea-serpent, in which until then he had been an unbeliever. The animal was stretched out, partly over the white sandy beach, which had four or five feet of water upon it, and lay partly over the channel. He desired his wife to get out of the chair, which she did. He said he had made up his mind as to the length of the snake, but wished the opinion of his wife on the same subject. He asked her what she should consider his length; she answered that she could not undertake to say how many feet in length he was, but that she thought him as long as the wharf behind their house, an object with which she had always been familiar. Mr. Mansfield said he was of the same opinion. The wharf is one hundred feet in length. It is to be observed that the person above spoken of had been such an unbeliever in the existence of this monster, that he had not given himself the trouble to go from his house to the harbour when the report was first made of such an animal being there."

Consequently I may fix the appearance of the animal resting on a bank, or beach, or rock, on the 22th. of August, 1817. This is the only report I have found of this way of reposing of the animal, but I cannot believe that these reports are contrary to truth.

46.—1817, August, 23.—(*Report of a Committee*, 1817). Mr. Amos Story after having made affidavit of his having seen the animal on the tenth of August, goes on:

"I likewise saw, what I believe to be the same animal this day, viz. the twenty third of August, A. D. 1817. This was in the morning, about seven o'clock. He then lay perfectly still, extended on the water, and I should judge that I saw fifty feet of him at least."

"I should judge that I was forty rods from him this day. I had a good spy glass both days when I saw him. I continued looking at him about half an hour, and he remained still and in the same position, until I was called away. Neither his head nor tail were visible. His colour appeared to be a dark brown, and when the sun shone upon him, the reflection was very bright. I thought his body was about the size of a man's body."

"Amos Story."

"Essex ss. Aug. 23, 1817. Personally appeared Amos Story, and made oath that the foregoing deposition by him subscribed is true, according to his best knowledge and belief."

"Cor. Lonson Nash, Jus. Pacis."

As we read that the animal lay perfectly still, and as Mr. Story does not mention that bunches were visible, we may conclude that it lay with its body in a straight line. Fifty feet of its length at least were visible. Its head and tail were not visible, says Mr. Story, and yet the animal remained about half an hour in this position, which I think may thus be accounted for: the animal's head, neck and back were in a straight line just above the surface of the water, so that its nose was also above it, which enabled the animal to breathe and to remain motionless, but at the distance of forty rods, though with a good spy glass, these particulars cannot have been distinctly seen by one who was not acquainted with the animal's external features, and so he believed its head was invisible. That its tail was under water, I will believe with him.

47.—1817, August 24?—In the letter from Col. T. H. Perkins to Mr. Cushing, dated Oct. 13, 1820, Col. P. mentions the appearance of the sea-serpent as seen by Mr. and Mrs. Mansfield on the 22th. of Aug., 1817 (n°. 45), and he continues:
"Subsequent to the period of which I have been speaking, the snake was seen by several of the crews of our coasting vessels, and in some instances within a few yards."
I have therefore chosen the above date.

48.—1817, August 28.—(*Report of a Committee*, 1817).
"Sewell Toppan, Master of the schooner Laura, declares: That on thursday morning the 28th. day of August, at about 9 o'clock A. M. at about two miles, or two and half miles east of the eastern point of Cape Ann being becalmed, I heard one of my men call to the man at the helm, 'what is this coming towards us'; being engaged forward, I took no further notice till they called again.—I then got on top of the deck load, at which time I saw a singular kind of animal or fish, which I had never before seen, passing by our quarter, at distance of about forty feet, standing along shore. I saw a part of the animal or fish ten or fifteen feet from the head downwards including the head; the head appeared to be of the size of a ten-gallon keg, and six inches above the surface of the water. It was of a dark colour. I saw no tongue, but heard William Somerby and Robert Bragg, my two men, who were with me, call out, 'look at his tongue'. The motion of his head was sideways and quite moderate; the motion of the body, up and down. I have seen whales very often; his motion was much more rapid than whales or any other fish I have ever seen; he left a very long wake behind him; he did not appear to alter his course in consequence of being so near the vessel. I saw him much less time than either of the others, and not in so favourable a position to notice his head."
"I have been to sea many years, and never saw any fish that had the least resemblance to this animal. Judging from what I saw out of water, I should judge the body was about the size of a half barrel in circumference."
"Sewell Toppan".

"Suffolk ss. Boston, September 1, 1817. Personally appeared captain Sewell Toppan, and made solemn oath, that the foregoing declaration by him subscribed is true."
"Before me, Jos. May, Jus. Pacis."

"Robert Bragg, of Newburyport, mariner, of the schooner Laura, of Newburyport, Sewell Toppan Master, testifies: That on thursday last, about ten o'clock A. M. coming in said schooner bound from Newburyport to Boston, off Eastern Point, (Cape Ann), about a mile and a half from the shore, I being on deck, the vessel being becalmed, looking at the windward, I saw something break the water, and coming very fast towards us, I mentioned it to the man at helm, William Somerby; the animal came about 28 or 30 feet from us, between the vessel and the shore, and passing very swiftly by us; he left a very long wake behind him. About six inches in height of his body and head were out of water, and as I should judge about 14 or 15 feet in length. He had a head like a serpent, rather larger than his body and rather blunt; did not see his eyes; when astern of the vessel about 30 feet, he threw out his tongue about two feet in length; the end of it appeared to me to resemble a fisherman's harpoon; he raised his tongue several times perpendicularly, or nearly so, and let it fall again. He was in sight about ten minutes. I think he moved at the rate of 12 or 14 miles an hour; he was of a dark chocolate colour, and from what appeared out of water I should suppose he was two and a half feet in circumference; he made no noise; his back and body appeared smooth; a small bunch on each side of his head, just above his eyes; he did not appear to be at all disturbed by the vessel; his course was in the direction for the Salt Islands; his motion was much swifter than any whale that I have ever seen, and I have seen many—did not observe any teeth; his motion was very steady, a little up and down."

"To this account I am willing to make oath."

"Robert Bragg."

"I, William Somerby of the Schooner Laura, testify and say: That on thursday last about 10 o'clock, A. M. as I was coming in said schooner from Newburyport, bound to Boston, off Brace's cove, a little eastward of Eastern Point, (Cape Ann) about two miles from land, the sea calm, I was at helm. Robert Bragg, one of the crew, asked me if that was not the snake coming, pointing out a break in the water, south of us; a strange animal of the serpent form passed very swiftly by us—the nearest distance I should judge to be between 30 and 40 feet—the upper part of his head and back was above water—the length that appeared was about 12 or 15 feet, his head was like a serpent's tapering off to a point. He threw out his tongue a number of times, extended about two feet from his jaws—the end of it resembled a harpoon—he threw his tongue backwards several times over his head, and let it fall again—I saw one of his eyes as he passed; it appeared very bright, and about the size of the eye of an ox. The colour of all that appeared was very dark, almost black. He did not appear to take any notice of the vessel, and made no noise. There appeared a bunch above the eye.—Should judge him to be about two and a half feet in circumference. Have often seen whales at sea. The motion of this animal was much swifter than that of any whale. The motion of the body was rising and falling as he advanced, the head moderately vibrating from side to side. The colour of his tongue was a light brown."

"To this account I am willing to make oath."

"William Somerby."

"*Commonwealth of Massachusetts*, August 30, 1817. Then appeared Robert Bragg and William Somerby, and made oath to the truth of the above declarations, by them respectively subscribed."

"Before me, Jos. May, Jus Pacis."

In these three depositions we find the same observation. As the head was moving moderately sideways, we may conclude that the animal, though it was also moving up and down, used it flappers too, so that with the use of the right fore-flapper its head went a little to the left, and otherwise went a little to the right by the motion of the left fore-flapper.—For Robert Bragg's "larger" in "the head was rather larger than the body", we don't hesitate to read "broader".—It is the third time that the animal's tongue was observed. The tongue most probably was rather pointed, which led the two mariners to compare it with a harpoon.—Remarkable is the statement of the animal having a small bunch on each side of the head just above its eyes. This is the heavy eye brow figured by Bing (fig. 19) and so often described afterwards.

In a letter from Col. T. H. Perkins dated Oct. 13, 1820, and published in the *Boston Daily Advertiser* of Nov. 25, 1848, we read:

"Captain Tappan, a person well known to me saw him with his head above water two or three feet, at times moving with great rapidity, and at others slowly. He also saw what explained the appearance which I have described, of a horn on the front of the head. This was doubtless what was observed by Captain Tappan to be the tongue, thrown in an upright position from the mouth, and having the appearance which I have given to it."

I quite agree with Col. T. E. Perkins as to the explanation of the horn (see n°. 44, p. 180.)—In the *Report* of 1817 the name is spelt Toppan, whilst Col. Perkins writes Tappan; but as the details of the two accounts of the prong, or spear, or horn, or tongue are the same, I am convinced that these two names identify the same person. So the statement of Captain Toppan, William Somerby and Robert Bragg is substantiated by Col. Perkin's letter.

49.—1817, August 30?—In the same letter from Col. Perkins we read:
"One of the revenue cutters, whilst in the neighbourhood of Cape Ann, had an excellent view of him at a few yards' distance; he moved slowly; and upon the approach of the vessel, sank and was seen no more."

50.—1817, October 3.—In a letter from Mr. Thos. Herttell, to Mr. Silvanus Miller, printed in the *Report of a Committee*, 1817, a passage runs as follows:
"Understanding that Mr. James Guion, a gentleman of character and respectability, had seen what was supposed to be the same animal, I yesterday conversed with him on the subject. He states that on Friday the 3d. inst. while on the point of land on the east side of the mouth of Mamaroneck harbour, he saw a little distance from the rocks, usually called the Scotch Caps, which lie at the extremity of Rye Point, a large marine animal, going with great rapidity up sound. He judged his speed to be little or no less than a mile in a minute. He describes the irregularity and unevenness of his back, about fifty feet of which appeared above the surface of the water, much in the way in which I have done."

51.—1817, October 5.—The abovesaid letter runs as follows:

"Rye-Neck, Oct. 21, 1817"
"Silvanus Miller, Esq."
"Sir, I observed in the Columbian of the 15th. inst. a paragraph stating that an animal had been seen in Long Island sound, corresponding with the description of the serpent lately seen in Gloucester harbour. That communication probably resulted from some observations which I made to you, and several other gentlemen, on the subject alluded to. When I spoke on that occurrence, I had no idea that it would become the subject of a newspaper remark; but since it has been publicly noticed, perhaps a more particular detail of the circumstances may not be deemed improper.

"On Sunday, the 5th. inst. at 10 o'clock A. M. while standing a few rods from my house on Rye-Neck, I observed at a small distance to the southward and eastward of Mr. Ezekiel Halsted's dwelling on Rye Point, and perhaps not more than a half mile from the shore, a long, rough, dark looking body, progressing rapidly up sound (towards New York) against a brisk breeze, and a strong ebb tribe. Viewing it with my glass convinced me it was a large living animal.—His back, forty to fifty feet of which was seen above the surface of the water, appeared to be irregular, uneven, and deeply indented. I did not at this time remark that his head was more elevated above the water than the ridges or humps on his back. Some trees standing near the water, Rye Point soon intercepting my view of him, I hastened to a situation from which I obtained another sight of him as he passed that part of the sound opposite Hempstead bay. At this time he appeared to be nearly in the middle of the sound—his body more depressed below and his head more elevated above the water, going with increased velocity in the direction of Sand's point, creating a swell before him not unlike that made by a boat towed rapidly at the stern of the vessel. From the time I first saw him till I lost sight of him perhaps could not have exceeded ten minutes, in which short time he had gone probably not less than six or seven miles."

"I was yesterday informed on creditable authority, that on the day on which I saw the above mentioned animal, he was seen by some persons at or in the vicinity of the light house on Sand's Point."

"That it was a sea animal of great bulk, to me is certain.—That it is what is usually called a Sea-Serpent, and the same which appeared in Gloucester harbour, is only probable."

"With much respect, Sir, yours, &c."
"Thos. Herttell."

Though the usual statement that the animal had bunches on its back is here expressed in other terms, viz.: that its back was irregular, uneven, deeply indented, it may be seen at a glance that no new feature gave rise to these terms. The animal may moreover have had a mane, extending all over the back.

N°. 20 of the *Report* is, as we have seen above, an account of a serpent said to have been frequently seen in the North-Sea, extracted from the "History of Norway" written by the Right Rev. Erich Pontoppidan. Here is an extract from the matter given by that Bishop about the sea-serpent, and the whole affidavit of Capt. von Ferry.

After this the Committee goes on:

"We have seen and heard sundry other statements of various authority relating to similar animals, said to have been seen at sea by different persons, but do not insert them in our report, because we consider the foregoing testimony sufficient to place the existence of the animal beyond a doubt; and because they do not appear so minute and so well authenticated as the preceding documents."

Poor Committee! Could they have foreseen that *seventy* years afterwards the existence of the sea-serpent was *not* beyond a doubt, at least among learned persons, they would not only have published all those sundry other statements, but have exerted themselves more in the matter than they did now. They would have gone to have a look at the animal and made an affidavit of their observations, and—even then they would not have been believed!

I would kindly beg the Linnaean Society of Boston, or that learned Society which has inherited its archives, either to publish *all* reports, accounts and letters in their hands, or to send them all to me, that I may enlarge, correct and rectify this work in case a second edition is called for.

The Committee, after having published the various exceedingly interesting reports, was of course morally bound to explain the phenomenon. What kind of beast could it be!? And before the question had become embarrassing, a *deus ex machina* in the form of a sick, illformed and lame little snake presented itself suddenly in a field near Loblolly Cove. It was killed by a labourer at that place. And as the people believed that this was a spawn of the great sea-serpent, it was bought by a certain Dr. and presented to the Committee to examine it. The Committee really examined and dissected it, and gave a full account of their experience in their *Report*. They considered the little snake to be new to science, closely allied to the *Coluber constrictor* or Black Snake, a species common in those regions, and gave it the name of *Scoliophis atlanticus*. This account is followed by "two documents relating to the appearance of the *Scoliophis*, while living, and to the circumstance under which it was killed."

Next they gave "a few remarks on the question" (raised by the public) "whether the great Serpent, seen in the Harbour of Gloucester, be the *Scoliophis atlanticus*". These "few remarks" fill three pages and a half, and end with their conclusion that this is indeed the case, "until a more close examination of the great Serpent shall have disclosed some differences of structure, important enough to constitute a specific distinction."

Now, my readers will probably say that I have not yet explained why none of the eye-witnesses of the animal seen near Cape Ann saw a mane. I hope my readers will be satisfied when I tell them that I am convinced that the female Sea-Serpent has no mane, and that the mane is only a character of full grown males. So most of the eye-witnesses saw a female. It is only the individual witnessed by Messrs James Guion and Thos. Hertell, which was most probably a male and had a mane. Seen from a distance its back was uneven, and deeply indented.

Dr. Hamilton in his *Amphibious Carnivora*, 1839, "Groep III", devoted a few pages to the "*Report of a Committee*", giving a very short extract from it.

I will insert here an extract from a letter written by Edward Everett, Esq., Nov. 13, 1817, then in Paris, to the "Obermedicinal rath und Ritter" Blumenbach in Göttingen. This extract, here printed for the first time, is preserved in the Library of the Royal University of Göttingen; it runs as follows:

"With Respect to the monstrous Serpent, of which I furnished you some account, before leaving Göttingen, I am sorry to say that the Reports, which circulated in the newspapers of his capture, were incorrect, and that he has escaped. Great attempts were made, and large sums of money offered, in Vain. I begun to collect a full account of him out of 300 American Newspapers, which I intended for You, but as I hear that a pamphlet, on the subject, is preparing by our Linnaean Society, which will contain depositions made on Oath, I have prefered waiting, till this appears, and I shall have it sent to you immediately. I have received to-day a letter of Oct. 25 from my brother, in which he informs me, that—a few days after the Serpent disappeared—a Young Serpent, 3 feet long, corresponding with the large one in appearance, was taken. This was brought to Boston, has been dissected, and pronounced a Non-descript, by the Connoisseurs there. This will also be described in the pamphlet of the Linnaean Society. Upon the subject of the Serpent four letters have been written by Gen. Humphreys of Boston—a member of the Royal Society—to Sir Joseph Banks; so that it is possible something may appear in the Philosophical Transactions about it."

Afterwards we shall read more of the attempts to catch the Sea-Serpent. It is a pity that Mr. Everett never published his collection! Most probably it has gradually disappeared in the paper-basket! Apparently Mr. Everett and Mr. Blumenbach corresponded much about the serpent: I also found a list of ancient works in which the sea-serpent and large snakes are mentioned, forwarded by the former to the latter, and in the above-mentioned letter Everett calls the Sea-Serpent "Our old friend the Serpent."

As soon as the *Report* reached Europe, Mr. H. M. Ducrotay de Blainville made an extract from it in his *Journal de Physique, de Chimie et d'Histoire Naturelle*, Vol. 86, (Paris, 1818). Apparently he too believed the little snake to be a new species, and therefore paid more attention to it than to the large marine animal, which he doubtlessly could not explain, and about which he did not trouble himself much. In one respect Mr. De Blainville tried to throw ridicule on two reports, viz. those of Robert Bragg and William Somerby: "and the imagination of some sailors is cause that they saw a tongue or spear coming out of his mouth, to which they gave a length of twelve feet, a circumference of 6 inches at the bottom and a termination as a lancet". As we saw, the two sailors only mentioned a *tongue* of *two* feet; they did not use the expression of spear, they neither gave the circumference at the bottom, nor did they describe the termination as a *lancet's* but as a *harpoon's*. It was Mr. Foster who saw a *prong* or *spear*, but only of twelve *inches* and terminating in a *small point*. At all events Mr. De Blainville has read badly!

But on the other hand he is a believer. His extract ends thus:
"If we were now to scrutinize the existence of the Great Sea-Serpent, we must confess that it would he difficult to deny the appearance of an animal of very great length, very slender, and swimming with rapidity, in the sea near Cape Ann, but that it is a true snake, this is doubtful; that it is of the same genus as the *Scoliophis*, this assertion is still more doubtful, and finally that it is of the same species, here the number of probabilities still diminishes, and becomes totally null, if one believes that such an immense animal, as that which is observed in the sea has gone ashore to lay its eggs."

For this is firmly believed by the Committee!

Prof. W. D. Peck in his dissertation on the Sea-Serpent (*Mem. Am. Acad. Arts Sc.* Vol. IV. Pt. I, 1818) says:
"The testimony is ample of the existence of such a serpent, in the portion of the Atlantic which washes our shores."

After having mentioned some early accounts Prof. Peck says:
"These are the earliest notices I can find of this animal on our shores, and their truth is rendered undubitable by the evidence lately brought together by the Committee of the Linnaean Society, of men of fair and unblemished character in Gloucester."

After having given an extract from these evidences, Prof. Peck says:
"The accounts of all these persons are very consistent; to the greater part it appeared to be straight, or without gibbosities or protuberances on the back; one person thought it had protuberances, but it seems probable that the upper flexures of its undulations occasioned this opinion."

"Its velocity is variously estimated; by some it was thought to move a mile in a minute, by others in three, four, or five minutes. It has great lateral flexibility, as is shewn by its turning short and moving in an exactly contrary direction, advancing the head in a line parallel with the body; hence its undulations when under water and equally surrounded by the medium, may be either vertical or horizontal at the will of the animal. The judgment of its velocity, however, without knowing its precise distance and without instruments to observe it, is extremely liable to err."

"In the testimonies above referred to, the imagination seems to have had no influence, and we certainly know from them, that the existence of the animal to which they relate is indisputable; we know that it moves by vertical undulations, at least while near the surface of the sea; that it is laterally as flexible as other serpents; and that its motion, at times, is very swift; but our knowledge is circumscribed by these limits. It is to be hoped, that if it again visits our shores, some successful means may be devised of taking it and presenting an opportunity of completing our knowledge of so interesting a link in the chain of animated beings."

"It has been seen in Long Island sound, progressing southward; it seems from this circumstance to be migratory, like the Coluber natrix in Hungary, and may pass the winter season in Mexico or South America."

A remarkable fact is it that Prof. Peck really believes that it was a sea-snake of enormous dimensions!

The *Journal of Science and the Arts*, edited at the Royal Institution of Great Britain, republished in its fourth Vol. (London, 1818) the affidavits of Mssrs Lonson Nash and William B. Pearson, (n°. 41 and n°. 44) and the writer of the article declares: "the existence of the animal is placed beyond doubt." Now we are in 1892, and yet it is doubted!

52.—1818 June.—(*Quart. Journ. Sc. Litt. Arts R. Inst. Gr. Britt.* VI, 1818.)

"The *Commercial Advertiser* of June 9th. contains a letter from a Captain of the brig *Wilson*, of Salem, bound to Norfolk, wherein he states, that during his passage, off Cape Henry, he fell in with, as he at first supposed, the wreck of a vessel, when he ordered his boat to be lowered; but to his great astonishment he found it to be the sea-serpent; he says, he then examined it, and such an object he never before witnessed; he believed it to be 190 feet in length, and its mouth and head were of an enormous size. After returning to the ship they bore off, fearing the consequences that might result from its coming in contact with the vessel."

The only characters mentioned here are the enormous head and the length of about 190 feet. Both may be exaggerated though greater dimensions are mentioned in later trustworthy reports.

53.—1818, June 19.—(*Quart. Journ. Sc. Litt. Arts R. Inst. Gr. Brit.* VI, 1818).—
"On the 19th of June he appeared in Sag-Harbour, and rewards were offered to the whalers to secure it."

54.—1818, June 21.—(*Ibidem*).

"S. West, of Hallowell, master of the Packet *Delia*, describes it as seen on the 21st. of June, engaged with a whale."

The writer does not mean to say that it was a whale-bone-whale or a sperm-whale, but a whale of the smaller kind, viz. a dolphin, a grampus, or a porpoise. We shall come across an account stating that the eye-witnesses saw a panic amongst a shoal of porpoises, evidently caused by a sea-serpent pursuing them (n°. 97); and across another account, stating that a sea-serpent was seen seizing a porpoise in one of its lateral-fins (n°. 151). It is evident that when the opportunity offers, a sea-serpent also preys on the grampuses, porpoises and dolphins.

55.—1818 July 2.—(*Ibidem*).

"and on July 2d. two persons, J. Webber and R. Hamilton, saw it about seven miles from Portland, between Cranch Island point and Marsh-Island."

56.—1818 July.—(*Phil. Mag.* LIV, 1819). The second Sea Serpent described by Mr. Rafinesque Schmaltz (for he believes there are several species) is called by him:
"*Capt. Brown's Sea-Serpent*. This fish was observed by Capt. Brown in a voyage from America to St. Petersburg, in July 1818, near 60° N. latitude and 8° W. longitude, or north of Ireland. In swimming the head, neck and forepart of the body stood upright like a mast: it was surrounded by porpoises and fishes. It was smooth, without scales, and had eight gills under the neck; which decidedly evinces that it is not a snake, but a new genus of fish belonging to the eighth order *Tremapnea*, 28th. family *Ophictia*, and 3d. subfamily *Catremia*, along with the genera *Sphagebranchus* and *Symbranchus* of Bloch, which differ by having only one or two round gills under the neck. I shall call this new genus *Octipos* (meaning eight gills beneath); head depressed, mouth transverse, large, eight transverse gills under the neck, and its specific name and definition will be *Octipos bicolor*. Dark brown above, muddy white beneath: head obtuse. Capt. Brown adds, that the head was two feet long, the mouth fifteen inches, and the eyes over the jaws, similar to the horse's; the whole length might be 58 feet."

Immediately we recognize our well-known Sea-Serpent, an individual of which the length is estimated at 58 feet, which held its head and very long neck upright whilst swimming. Captain Brown says: "and the forepart of the body"; of course, for he thought to see a snake; if he had really seen the forepart of the body, (trunk) he would have seen the shoulders and the fore-flappers. It was surrounded by porpoises and fishes. Evidently the animal swam between them with the purpose to snatch one of them. It had a smooth skin, no scales, and eight gills under its neck. Dark brown above (i. e. on the dorsal part of head and neck), muddy white beneath (i.e. on its throat); head obtuse (read rather obtuse, seen from above or from below, or in front; just from aside it is rather pointed). The head was two feet long, the mouth fifteen inches (of course estimated dimensions), and the eyes over the jaws similar to those of a horse (this definition was caused by the heavy eyebrows and by the little bunch above each eye). The whole description is exactly that of our animal in the above-mentioned position and seen from a certain direction. For "eight gills" we may safely read "eight gillsplits", or eight splits caused by and lying between nine folds or wrinkles, which in their turn are caused by the animal bending its head rectangularly towards the throat. Such folds or wrinkles are also seen in sea-lions, when they make the same motion, and stout corpulent persons will know what is meant by a double chin!

57.—1818, July?—Mr. A. de Capell Brooke in his *Travels through Sweden* in 1820, p. 187, says:—"The fishermen at Sejerstad said a sea-serpent was seen two years ago in the Folden Fjord, the length of which, as far as it was visible was 60 feet. This had been told them by those who had seen it in the Folden."

58.—1818, August?—At p. 203 the same author mentions:
"On being asked (viz. the merchant of Fieldvigen) his opinion respecting the serpent, he said he had never seen it himself, though others had in that neighbourhood."

59.—1818, August 19.—In 1818 in the United States many rewards were offered to whalers to catch the animal, and many attempts were made to do this, and to bring it home, dead or alive. Amongst others this was the case at Boston. In the copy of the *Report of a Committee* of 1817, which I borrowed from the Library of the Royal University of Göttingen, there was a paragraph from a newspaper of August 21, 1818, the head or title of which was not noted down; the cutting runs as follows:

"Boston Aug. 21."
"Transmitted by our N. Y. correspondents."
"Capt. Rich, who went from here a few days since, in pursuit of the sea-serpent, writes the concern as follows:
"*Squam River, Aug. 20th.*, 12 *o'clock.*—After several unsuccessful attempts, we have at length fastened to this strange thing called the sea-serpent. We struck him fairly, but the harpoon soon drew out. He has not been seen since, and I fear the wound he received will make him more cautious how he approaches these shores. Since my last, yesterday, we have been constantly in pursuit of him; by day he always keeps a proper distance from us, to prevent our striking oars. But a few hours since, I thought we were sure of him, for I hove the harpoon into him as fairly as ever a whale was struck; took from us about 20 fathoms of warp before we could wind the boat, with as much swiftness as a whale. We had but a short ride when we were all loose from him to our sore disappointment."
"Rich'd. Rich."

"*Gloucester, Aug. 20.*—As I thought it would be interesting to you to hear from Capt. Rich, and as he is at some distance, I will give you some particulars of his cruise. On Monday last he sailed from this in a large whale boat, and two smaller ones well manned. My brother commanded one of the boats. Yesterday they met the Serpent off Squam, and chased him about seven hours, when they closed with him. He passed directly under the bows of Capt. Rich's boat; he immediately threw the harpoon, which pierced him about two feet; he drew the boat a considerable distance but went with such a velocity that he broke that part of the boat through which the rope passed and drew out the harpoon. I hope they will have another opportunity before they give up the chase."
"He has *no* scales on him, and no bunches on his back, but his skin is smooth, and looks similar to an eel. In the attack, Capt. Rich had one of his hands wound. These particulars I have in a letter from my brother."
"Saml. Dexter."

As far as I can judge after having read what I could find about the Sea-Serpent, this is the only time that the animal was struck with a harpoon. Evidently the animal then swam with its body in a straight line. Interesting to us are the words: "He has *no* scales on him, and no bunches on his back, but his skin is smooth, and looks similar to an eel".

The attempts mentioned above were continued, and, as my readers already read in my Chapter on hoaxes, ended with a hoax; at last a large tunny was brought in, and many persons believed it to be the animal! Among those who were present there was a Mr. Andrews Norton; he wrote, Sept. 11, 1818, a letter about this affair to Mr. George Bancroft, an extract from which is also inserted in our Chapter on hoaxes. I will repeat here his last words:

"I have only to add that if you should learn that any one of the German literati is writing a volume upon Sea-Serpents, I beg you will assure him that we" (Mr. Norton and Prof. Peck) "do not consider the circumstance connected with the deception just mentioned, as affecting the evidence before obtained for their real existence."—

The Quarterly Journal of Literature, Science and the Arts R. Inst. Gr. Brit. repeats in its Vol. VII, London, 1819, the whole paper of Prof. Peck, and a translation into German appeared in Oken's Isis of 1819.

The well-known Rafinesque Schmaltz, when in America, made the sea-serpent a subject of study and inquiry as Prof. Peck had done. He too wrote a paper about it, entitled: *Dissertation on Water-Snakes, Sea-Snakes, and Sea-Serpents.* It seems that his dissertation appeared in an American Journal or in American Transactions, and that it was afterwards reprinted in the *Philosophical Magazine,* Vol. LIV, 1819. He is a believer in Sea-Serpents, is evidently convinced that several species exist, belonging to the family of the *Hydrophidae,* or real Sea-Snakes.

After having mentioned 9 species of real Sea-Snakes, of which the last was 8 to 10 feet long, he goes on:

"This last species appears to be the largest real Sea-Snake which has fallen under the personal observation of naturalists as yet. But larger species still have been noticed at different periods. If I had the time and opportunity of perusing all the accounts of travellers and historians, I could probably bring many into notice; but this tedious labour must be postponed, and I must warn those who may be inclined to inquire into the subject, not to be deceived by the imperfect and exaggerated accounts of ancient and unknown writers. Whenever they mention neither the scales nor tail of their Sea-Serpents, or when they assert they had no scales, or had gills or fins, you must in all those instances be certain that they are real fishes rather than serpents. There might, however, be found some Sea-Snakes without scales, since there are such land snakes; and there are fishes with scales and yet without fins but there are no fishes without gills, and no snakes or serpents with gills!—in that important character the classical distinction consists."

"Nearly all the writers whom I can remember, have been unacquainted with that obvious distinction; and they have, in imitation of the ancient Greek and Roman writers, given the name of Sea-Snakes to the large eels or fishes they happened to observe. This I apprehend is the case with Pontoppidan, in his Natural History of Norway; with Mongitore in his Remarkable Objects of Sicily; with Leguat, in his Travels to Rodriguez Island, &c. Their observations, and the facts they record, are notwithstanding equally valuable, since they relate to monstrous unknown fishes, which seldom fall under the observation of men. The individuals of huge species are not numerous in nature, either on land or in water, and it is probable they often become extinct for want of food or reproduction."

"Among the four different animals which have lately been observed by Americans, and named Sea-Serpents, only one (the Massachusetts Serpent) appears to be such; another is evidently a fish, and two are doubtful. I shall refer a few remarks on each."

"1. *The Massachusetts Sea Serpent.* From the various and contradictory accounts given of this monster by witnesses, the following description may be collected.—It is about 100 feet long; the body is round and nearly two feet in diameter, of a dark brown, and covered with large scales in transverse rows; its head is scaly, brown mixed with white, of the size of a horse's and nearly the shape of a dog's; the mouth is large with teeth like a shark; its tail is compressed, obtuse, and shaped like an oar. This animal came in August last into the bay of Massachusetts in pursuit of shoals of fishes, herrings, squids, &c. on which it feeds. Its motions are very quick: it was seen by a great many; but all attempts to catch it have failed, although 5000 dollars have been offered for its spoils. It is evidently a real Sea Snake, belonging probably to the genus *Pelamis*, and I propose to call it *Pelamis megophias*, which means Great Sea Snake Pelamis. It might however be a peculiar genus, which the long equal scales seem to indicate and which a closer examination might have decided: in that case the name of *Megophias monstrosus* might have been appropriated to it."

We observe that Mr. Rafinesque gives here some characters to the Massachusetts's Sea-Serpent, with which we have met nowhere else, apparently only for the purpose of rendering his supposition more plausible: 1. "The scales". It is true that some of the eyewitnesses have declared the skin to be rough and scaly, but against *one* who says so, there are *twenty* who deny it, describing the skin to be smooth and having no scales. 2. "The scales are in transverse rows." This assertion is made nowhere else. 3. "Its head brown mixed with white." A new statement. The head is only described as white on its throat and lower Jaws. 4. "The head of the shape of a dog's." I did not find this expression any where else; on the contrary all agree in its resembling a serpent's or a snake's head. 5. "The teeth like a shark's, the tail compressed, obtuse, shaped like an oar." Nobody saw either teeth or tail! Indeed a splendid description after the reports given of the animal's external features!

60.—1819, June 6.—(Silliman's *American Journal of Science and the Arts*, Vol. II, Boston 1820.)

"I, Hawkins Wheeler, of Fairfield, in the County of Fairfield, and state of Connecticut, mariner, Commander of the sloop Concord, of said Fairfield, in her late passage from New York to Salem, in the County of Essex and Commonwealth of Massachusetts, on oath declare, that during the said passage from New York to Salem, to wit, on Monday, the 6th. day of June instant, at about five o'clock in the morning, the sloop being as near as I could judge, 15 miles N. W. of Race Point, and within sight of Cape Ann, I was at the helm of the sloop, and saw directly ahead, (the course of the vessel being N. W.) something that resembled a snake, about 100 yards distance from the sloop, moving in a S. W. direction. The animal moved in that direction, till he had passed athwart the course of the sloop, and appeared directly over the weather bow, when he altered his course to S. E. At this time he had been visible about five minutes, when he sunk, and in about six or eight minutes after, appeared again directly over the weather quarter, about the same distance from the sloop—he continued in that course about five or six minutes, when he sunk again, and I saw him no more. His motion was at the rate of about four miles an hour, when he passed ahead; but after he appeared again on the quarter, his motion was less rapid. To the best of my judgment he was not more than 100 yards of the vessel—the weather was good and clear—it was almost calm, with a light air of wind from the S., the vessel was going about two knots—I had a fair and distinct view of the creature, and from his appearance am satisfied that it was of the serpent kind. The creature was entirely black; the head, which perfectly resembled a snake's; was elevated from four to seven feet above the surface of the water, and his back appeared to be composed of bunches or humps, apparently about as large as, or a little larger than a half barrel; I think I saw as many as ten or twelve, but did not count them; I considered them to be caused by the undulatory motion of the animal—the tail was not visible, but from the head to the last hump that could be seen, was, I should judge, 50 feet. The first view I had of him appeared like a string of empty barrels tied together, rising over what little swell of the sea there was. What motion I could discern in the body of the animal was undulatory, but he evidently moved his tail under water, and the ripples produced by it indicated a sweeping motion, making a wake as large as that made by the sloop."

"Hawkins Wheeler."

"Essex, ss. June 9th. 1819.—Then Hawkins Wheeler personally appeared, and made oath that the foregoing affidavit by him subscribed, contains the truth, the whole truth, and nothing but the truth. Before me
"Theodore Eames, Justice of the Peace."

"I, Gersham Bennet, of Fairfield, in the County of Fairfield, and State of Connecticut, mariner, on oath declare, that I was mate of the sloop Concord, Hawkins Wheeler, master, in her late passage from New York to Salem, Mass., that on Monday, the 6th. day of June inst., at seven o'clock in the morning, I was on the deck of the sloop, sitting on the hatches—the vessel was steering N. W. and was then about eighteen miles from Race Point—the man at the helm made an outcry, and said there was something alongside that he wanted me to look at. I looked, and saw something on the larboard side of the vessel, about twelve rods, certainly not exceeding fourteen, from the vessel, that resembled a serpent or snake. I immediately arose and went to the side of the vessel, and took a position on the rough tree, holding on by the shrouds; I there saw a serpent of an enormous size and uncommon appearance, upon the water; his head was about the length of the anchor stock above the surface of the water, viz. about seven feet. I looked at the anchor stock at the time, and formed my opinion by comparing the two objects. The weather was very clear and good and the water almost calm; and I had, I think, as good a view of the animal as if I had been within two rods of him. The colour of the animal throughout, as far as could be seen, was black, and the surface appeared to be smooth, without scales—his head was about as long as a horse's and was a proper snake's head—there was a degree of flatness, with a slight hollow on the top of his head—his eyes were prominent, and stood out considerably from the surface, resembling in that respect the eyes of a toad, and were nearer to the mouth of the animal than to the back of the head. I had a full view of him for seven or eight minutes. He was moving in the same direction with the sloop, and about as fast. The back was composed of bunches about the size of a flour barrel, which were apparently about three feet apart—they appeared to be fixed, but might be occasioned by the motion of the animal, and looked like a string of casks or barrels tied together—the tail was not visible, but the wake of his tail which he evidently moved under water, showed a horizontal or sweeping motion, producing a wake as large as the vessel made. He turned his head two or three times slowly round towards and from the vessel, as if taking a view of some object on board. I went up on the rigging, for the purpose of taking a view of him from above; but before I had reached my station, he sunk below the surface of the water, and did not appear again. Gersham Bennett."

"Essex ss. June 9th. 1819.—Then Gersham Bennett personally appeared and made oath that the foregoing affidavit by him subscribed, contains the truth, the whole truth, and nothing but the truth. Before me,

"Theodore Eames, Justice of the Peace."

It is probable that Mr. Bennett is right in considering the "wake as large as the vessel made" was produced by a horizontal or sweeping motion of the tail, but it is far more probable that it was caused by the motion of the hind-flappers, supposed the animal nearly touched the surface of the water with the hinder part of the body.

New characters to us are these: that there is a slight hollow on the top of its head, that its eyes are prominent, and stand out considerably from the surface, resembling in that respect the eyes of a toad, and that they are nearer to the mouth of the animal than to the back of the head.

61.—1819, July.—A. De Capell Brooke in his *Travels through Sweden, in the Summer of* 1820, says at p. 187:

"As I had determined, on arriving at the coast, to make every inquiry respecting the truth of the accounts, which had reached England the preceeding year, of the sea-serpent having recently seen off this part of Norway, I shall simply give the different reports I received of it during my voyage to the North Cape, leaving others to their own conclusions, and without expressing, at least for the present, any opinion respecting them."

and at p. 198:

"From him (the postmaster Mr. Schilderup) I learned some curious particulars respecting the sea-serpent, which had caused so much alarm and wonder in Norway, and the report of which, as I have said, had even reached England. From having formerly been in the Norwegian sea service, he was called Captain Schilderup; and seemed a quick intelligent man. It appeared, that the serpent had actually been off the island for a considerable length of time during the preceding summer, in the narrow part of the Sound, between this island (Ottersum) and the continent; and the description he gave of it was as follows."

"It made its appearance for the first time in the month of July, 1819, off Ottersum, in the sound above mentioned. Previous to this he had often heard of the existence of these creatures, but never before believed it. During the whole of that month the weather was excessively sultry and calm; and the serpent was seen every day, nearly in the same part of the Sound. It continued there while the warm weather lasted, lying motionless, and as if dozing in the sun-beams.—This part of his account reminded me of the monster of the deep, so finely described by Milton."

"The number of persons living on the island, he said, was about thirty; the whole of whom, from motives of curiosity, went to look at it while it remained. This was confirmed to me by subsequent inquiries among the inhabitants, who gave a similar account of it. The first time that he saw it, he was in a boat, at a distance of about 200 yards. The length of it he supposes to have been about 300 ells, or 600 feet. Of this he could not speak accurately; but it was of very considerable length; and longer than it appeared, as it lay in large coils above the water to the height of many feet. Its colour was greyish. At the distance at which he was, he could not ascertain whether it were covered with scales; but when it moved, it made a loud crackling noise, which he distinctly heard. Its head was shaped like that of a serpent, but he could not tell whether it had teeth or not. He said it emitted a very strong odour, and that the boatmen were afraid to approach near it, and looked on its coming as a bad sign, as the fish left the coast in consequence. Such were the particulars he related to me. Thanking him for his information, I took my leave of him, and proceeded on my voyage."

And at p. 200:

"Near Ottersum is the small Island of Krogoën", (upon which a merchant lived, who hearing that Mr. Brooke was an Englishman, who travelled to North-Cape, put to him numberless questions.) "Having answered all these questions as well as I could, and a momentary pause ensuing I seized the opportunity now to have my turn; and wishing to hear something still farther respecting the sea-monster, I began to overwhelm him with interrogations, as to its length, colour, appearance, time it staid, by whom seen, and many others that occurred to me. However ludicrous the earnest loquacity on both sides might have been, I had the satisfaction of hearing him confirm, in every particular, the account of Capt. Schilderup at Ottersum; and that many of the people at Krogoën had also witnessed it. It did not appear, however, that any one had ventured very near it, from the dread that was entertained of it."

Of course the length of the animal, estimated from a distance of 200 yards, is exaggerated. The greyish colour is that which the animal obtains when drying in the sunshine, as I have already explained before. For the first time we meet with the statement that the animal emits a very strong odour, which is twice stated here. As we shall once more come across this statement, we must needs believe it. In my last chapter I will return to this fact, proving that it is not an impossible character of sea-serpents.

62.—1819, August 12?—Mr. Smith informed us the sea-serpent had been seen the evening before at Nahant-beach". (Part of the following report.)

---

164   The Great Sea-Serpent

63.—1819, August 13?—There appeared an interesting account of an eye-witness about a sea-serpent in the *Boston Daily Advertiser* of 19th. August, 1819. I have not been able to consult this journal. The report was translated in Oken's *Isis* of 1819, p. 1754, accompanied by the figure, made by the eye-witness. Happily I found the same in Silliman's *American Journal Sc. Arts*, Vol. II, Boston, 1820, but without the figure. It runs as follows:

"The recent appearance of this animal at Nahant, in the view of several hundred persons, has furnished, perhaps, more conclusive proof of his existence, than any that has before been made public. For the satisfaction of our readers, we have procured a copy of the following letter, which gives a very clear and intelligible description of his appearance and movements. We have heard verbal statements from a great number of gentlemen, all of whom agree in substance with what is here related."

"*Copy of a letter from* James Prince, *Marshal of the District, to the Hon. Judge Davis, dated*":
"Nahant, Aug. 16th., 1819."
"Dear Sir,"
"I presume I may have seen what is generally thought to be the sea-serpent—I have also seen my name inserted in the evening newspaper printed at Boston on Saturday, in a communication on this subject. For your gratification, and from a desire that my name may not sanction any thing beyond what was presented and passed in a review before me, I will now state that which, in the presence of more than two hundred other witnesses, took place near the long beach of Nahant, on Saturday morning last."

"Intending to pass two or three days at Nahant, with my family, we left Boston early on Saturday morning. On passing the halfway house, on the Salem turn pike, Mr. Smith informed us the sea-serpent had been seen the evening before at Nahant-beach, and that a vast number of people from Lynn, had gone to the beach that morning, in hopes of being gratified with a sight of him: This was confirmed at the hotel. I was glad to find I had brought my famous mast-head spy-glass with me, as it would enable me, from its form and size, to view him to advantage, if I might be so fortunate as to see him. On our arrival on the beach, we associated with a considerable number of persons, on foot and in chaises, and very soon an animal of the fish-kind made his appearance. His head appeared about three feet

Fig. 26.—The sea-serpent as delineated by Mr. Prince.

out of water; I counted thirteen bunches on his back: my family thought there were fifteen—he passed three times at a moderate rate across the bay, but so fleet as to occasion a foam in the water—and my family and myself, who were in carriage, judged he was fifty feet in length, and, at the extend, not more than sixty; whether, however, the wake might not add to the appearance of his length; or whether the undulation of the water, or his peculiar manner of propelling himself, might not cause the appearance of protuberances, I leave for your better judgment. The first view of the animal occasioned some agitation, and the novelty perhaps prevented that precise discrimination which afterwards took place—as he swam up the bay, we and the other spectators moved on, and kept abreast of him; he occasionally withdrew himself under water, and the idea occurred to me that this occasionally raising his head above the level of the water, was to take breath, as the time he kept under water was of an average about eight minutes; after being accustomed to view him, we became more composed; and made the annexed figure of his outlines. Mrs. Prince and the coachman having better eyes than myself, were of great assistance to me in marking the progress of the animal; they would say he is now turning, and by the aide of my glass I saw him distinctly in this movement; he did not turn without occupying some space, and taking into view the time and space which he found necessary for his ease and accommodation, I adopted it as a criterium to form some judgment of his length—I had seven distinct views of him from the long beach so called, and at some of them the animal was not more than a hundred yards distance. After being on the long beach about an hour, the animal disappeared, and I proceeded on towards Nahant; but on passing the second beach, I met Mr. James Magee, of Boston, with several ladies in a carriage, prompted by curiosity to endeavor to see the animal, and we were again gratified beyond even what we saw in the other bay; which I concluded he had left in consequence of the number of boats in the offing in pursuit of him—the noise of whose oars must have disturbed him, as he appeared to us to be a harmless timid animal. We had more than a dozen different views of him, and each similar to the other; one however so near, that the coachman exclaimed: 'Oh, see his glistening eye'. Thinking I might form some calculation of his length by the time and distance of each turn; and taking an angle with my two hands of the length he exhibited, that is to say, from his head to his last protuberance, and applying the same angle to other objects, I feel satisfied of the correctness of my decision that he is sixty feet long, unless the ripple of his wake deceived me—nor my dear sir, do I undertake to say he was of the snake or eel kind, though this was the general impression on my family, the spectators and myself. Certainly it is a very strange animal. I have been accustomed to see whales, grampuses, porpoises, and other large fishes, but he partook of the appearance of none of these. The whale and the grampus would have spouted—the shark never raises his head out of water, and the porpoise skips and plays; neither of these has such appearances on the back or such a head as this animal. The shark it is true, has a fin on his back, and often the fluke of his tail is out of water; but these appendages would not display the form, and certainly not the number of protuberances, which this animal exhibited; nor is it the habit of the shark to avoid a boat. The water was extremely smooth, and the weather clear: we had been so habituated to see him, that we were cool and composed—the time occupied was from a quarter past eight to half past eleven—a cloud of witnesses exceeding two hundred, brought together for a single purpose, were all alike satisfied and united as to appearances, and as to the length and size of the animal; but you must deduct the influence which his passage through the water and the manner he propelled himself might have as to the apparent protuberances on his back, and the ripple occasioned by his motion on his real length, of all which you can judge equally well and better than myself. I must conclude there is a strange animal on our coast—and I have thought an unvarnished statement might be gratifying to a mind attached to the pursuit of natural science, and aid in the inquiries on a controverted question, which I knew to have interested you. I have ventured on the description, being also induced to hope, that if anything on the marvellous is stated as coming from me, you will correct it.

"Accept the respects and attention of
"Dear Sir, yours sincerely
   "James Prince."

We see that Mr. Prince uses many words to give a very short description of the animal. Yet we are able to gather the following details. Its head appeared about three feet out of the water, there were 13 or 15 bunches on its back, sometimes the rapidity was moderate, occasioning, however, a foam in the water; length 50 to 60 feet; the animal left behind it a wake; sometimes it withdrew itself under water; it appeared to be a harmless timid animal; its eyes were glistening. All these characters, external features and habits are long known to us. Mr. Prince first said the animal belonged to the fish-kind; afterwards, however, he dared not say whether it was of the snake or eel-kind; yet his figure shows large scales and a fish-tail. It is astonishing that the person who is so careful in his expressions, is so inaccurate when handling the pencil. The head of the animal in his figure is more that of a young duck than of a serpent or snake, which the head of the sea-serpent is said to resemble closely. The coils are badly drawn, and though 13 to 15 bunches were seen, only six are delineated. The rippling of the water on the animal's left side and before it is well represented, on its right side, however, it is quite wrong. The two racked-formed wings are certainly the representation of the foam, caused in the water by the animal's rapid motion. And finally the scales and the fish-tail are drawn by Mr. Prince though he has not seen them! I am obliged to state again that this figure is a facsimile of that which I found in Oken's *Isis*; the very one of the *Boston Daily Advertiser* I have had no opportunity to see.

The letter from Mr. Prince is translated into Dutch in the *Vaderlandsche Letteroefeningen voor* 1820, *Tweede Stak, Mengelwerk*.

On the same day it was seen by Mr. Cabot, who wrote the following letter (Silliman's *Am. Journ. Sc. Arts*, II, 1820) to our well known

"Col. T. H. Perkins"
"Brookline, August 19, 1819.
"Dear Sir"

"I very willingly comply with your request to state what I saw of the *Sea-Serpent* at *Nahant*, on Saturday last, particularly as I happened to see it under favourable circumstances to form a judgment, and to considerable adventage in point of position and distance."

"I got into my chaise about seven o'clock in the morning to come to Boston, and on reaching the long Beach observed a number of people collected there and several boats pushing off and in the offing. I was speculating on what should have occasioned so great an assemblage there without any apparent object, and finally had concluded that they were embarking in those boats on a party of pleasure to Egg Rock, or some other point."

"I had not heard of the *Sea-Serpent* being in that neighbourhood, and I had not lately paid much attention to the evidences which had been given of its existence, the idea of this animal did not enter my mind at the moment.

"As my curiosity was directed towards the boats to ascertain the course they were taking, my attention was suddenly arrested by an object emerging from the water at the distance of about one hundred or one hundred and fifty yards, which gave to my mind at the first glance the idea of a horse's head. As my eye ranged along I perceived at a short distance eight or ten regular bunches or protuberances, and at a short interval three or four more. I was now satisfied that the *Sea-Serpent* was before me, and after the first moment of excitement produced by the unexpected sight of so strange a monster taxed myself to investigate his appearance as accurately as I could."

"My first object was the Head, which I satisfied myself was serpent shaped, it was elevated about two feet from the water, and he depressed it gradually, to within six or eight inches as he moved along. I could always see under his chin, which appeared to hollow underneath or to curve downward. His motion was at that time very slow along the Beach, inclining towards the shore; he at first moved his head from side to side as if to look about him. I did not see his eyes, though I have no doubt I could have seen them if I had thought to attend to this. His bunches appeared to be not altogether uniform in size, and as he moved along some appeared to be depressed, and others brought above the surface, though I could not perceive any motion in them. My next object was to ascertain his length. For this purpose I directed my eye to several whale boats at about the same distance, one of which was beyond him, and by comparing the relative length, I calculated that the distance from the animal's head to the last protuberance I had noticed, would be equal to about five of those boats. I felt persuaded by this examination that he could not be less than eighty feet long; as he approached the shore and came between me and a point of land which projects from the eastern end of the Beach, I had another means of satisfying myself on this point."

"After I had viewed him thus attentively for about four or five minutes, he sunk gradually into the water and disappeared; he afterwards again made his appearance for a moment at a short distance."

"My first reflection after the animal was gone, was, that the idea I had received from the description you gave of the animal you saw at *Gloucester*, in 1817, was perfectly realized in this instance; and that I had discovered nothing you had not before described. The most authentic testimony given of his first appearance there seemed to me remarkably correct; and I felt as if the appearance of this monster had been already familiar to me."

"After remaining some two or three hours on the Beach, without again seeing him, I returned towards Nahant; and in crossing the small beach, had another good view of him, for a longer time, but at a greater distance. At this time he moved more rapidly, causing a white foam under the chin, and a long wake, and his protuberances had a more uniform appearance. At this time he must have been seen by two or three hundred persons on the beach and on the heights each side, some of whom were very favourably situated to observe him."

"I am very respectfully"
"your obedient servant"
"Samuel Cabot."

The Editor of the American Journal, Prof. Benjamin Silliman, adds:
"It is almost superfluous to add, that Mr. Cabot and his friend Col. Perkins, are gentlemen of the fixst standing and consideration."

In Oct. 13, 1820, Col. T. H. Perkins, when on board the *Ann Marie*, wrote a letter to his friend Mr. Jno. E. Cushing; he published it in the *Boston Daily Advertiser* of 1848, Nov. 25; a passage of it runs as follows:

"Besides the instances I have mentioned, there were many others reported of his having been seen the same year. In that year, 1817, although there were several reports of his having been seen, yet they were not well authenticated, nor do I place any confidence in them."

"In the month of August, in the last year, he again made his appearance in our vicinity, and under very satisfactory circumstances. The weather being hot, many of our citizens resorted to Nahant to pass a few weeks. On the number were Mr. and Mrs. Cabot and their children. Mr. Cabot had a view of him for more than half an hour at one time. He was in a chair, and had reached what is termed the long beach, when he saw several persons collected half a mile from him, which called his attention to the object which occupied them. Mr. C. had heard me often describe the view I had had of the serpent in 1817 and recognized in what was visible just without the brakers, and within a quarter of a mile, the monster which was supposed by many to exist nowhere but in the imaginations of those who had reported to have seen him. Mr. Cabot immediately rode back to Nahant; took Mrs. Cabot into his chair and returned to the beach; but the animal was no longer visible. By this time the inhabitants of Lynn had assembled to the number of some hundreds, on and near the beach, and all the visitors of Nahant were upon the alert. Having given over the hope of seeing him, Mr. Cabot was returning to leave his wife at her lodgings, when, to their mutual delight, he came in view just without the surf of the little beach, and within a quarter of a mile or less of where they stood."

"Marshal Prince, James Magee, and many persons of my acquaintance had a fine sight of him, and all agreed in their account of him in the principal particulars. They all agreed as to the rapidity of his movements, being very much beyond anything living they had ever seen. The apparent bunches on his back they consider as arising from the construction of his body, and that the movement was vertical and not horizontal. At one time his head was about two or three feet above water, but soon depressed to the level of the sea. When not swimming to be in persuit of his prey, his motion was not rapid. They saw him turn and bring his body into a letter S, the head being at right angles with the tail. From fifteen to twenty three bunches, or apparent bunches, were counted by the different persons who saw him, and his size round they thought to be that of a common firkin or half barrel".

"No one thought they saw the whole of the body at a time, the tail seeming always to be considerably under water. The greatest length given to him was one hundred feet and no one who had a good sight of him thought him less than eighty feet in length. If the number of protuberances is twenty-three (and it seems there are at least this number), and calculating them to be distant from centre to centre four feet (and I think, considering their thickness, they cannot be less than this), he would be ninety two feet long. They all agreed, too, as to the colour being quite dark, approaching to black."

In a letter from Dr. Boott to Dr. Hooker dated London, Nov. 4, 1826, part of which was published in the *Edinb. Journ. of Sc.*, we read that he visited Boston to gather testimony from eye-witnesses. He then sais:

"During this visit I distinctly remember the news coming from Nahant one morning, of the Serpent being in the bay of that place, distant about sixteen miles from Boston. Many hurried down to see it, and among them my brother Mr. James Boott. I was prevented from some cause leaving Boston. My brother reported that he distinctly saw a large serpent, about a mile from the shore; and that thousands were watching its motion on the beach and rocks. The first idea that occurred to my brother was that it was a horse swimming, its head at the time bearing a resemblance to that of the latter creature. He afterwards saw the undulating line of its back, and remained several hours watching the animal. Colonel Perkins of Boston, his wife, and family, were present at this time, as far as I recollect."

So we have of this appearance three different statements of respectable persons, who distinctly saw the animal on the same spot.

This appearance of the sea-serpent near Nahant is also mentioned in Dr. Hamilton's *Amphibious Carnivora*, 1839.

64.—1819, August.—Mr. A. de Capell Brooke says in his *Travels through Sweden*, &c., at p. 207:

"I there" (Stenesöen) "obtained from his" (Peder Greger's) "son John Greger, a young man, who employed himself in the fishery, still further information respecting the sea-serpent; it was in August of the preceding year, while fishing with others in the Vieg or Vegfjord, that he saw it; at that time they were on shore, hauling in their nets, and it appeared about sixty yards distant from them, at which they were not a little alarmed, and immediately retreated. What was seen of it above water, he said, appeared six times the length of their boat, of a grey colour, and lying in coils a great height above the surface. Their fright prevented them from attending more accurately to other particulars. In fact they all fairly took to their heels, when they found the monster so near them. The weather at the time was very hot and calm. Farther to the south (at Stenesöen) he said it was seen several times, and it remained there for a considerable period."

65.—1819, August.—The same author at p. 216 of his volume relates:

"My honest boatmen who had brought me all the way from Leköe, a distance of near sixty miles, now left me. Previous to their departure they gave me the following account of the sea-serpent, which is here inserted as they related it, without the least variation. They were fishermen and had been up at the North Cape. During the time they remained there they saw the serpent twice, once at no very great distance from them. It was of a grey colour; the head blackish, with teeth. What they discerned of it they judged to be at least five times the length of their boat, which is about thirty feet. It moved in large folds on the water; and when they saw it, they rowed away from it as fast as they could. The weather was very calm at the time."

This is the most northern appearance of the sea-serpent. The teeth are mentioned here, though not described.

66.—1819? August?—The same author at p. 222 of his *Travels* tells us:

"To the testimony of others respecting the existence of the sea-serpent, I shall now add that of the bishop" (of the Nordlands and Finmark) "himself, who was eye-witness to the appearance of two in the bay of the Shuresund, or Sorsund, in the Drontheim *fjord*, about eight Norway miles from Drontheim. He was but a short distance from them, and saw them plainly. They were swimming in large folds, part of which was seen above the water, and the length of what appeared the largest he judged to be about 100 feet. They were of a darkish grey colour; the heads hardly discernable, from their being almost under water; and they were visible for only a short time. Before that period he had treated the account of them as fabulous; but it was now impossible, he said, to doubt their existence, as such numbers of respectable people, since that time had likewise seen them on different occasions."

Not a single fact that need astonish us. That *two* were seen together is not reported for the first time, as the reader will remember. The swimming "in large folds, part of which was seen above water", is a very accurate description of the effect made by the swimming animals. The colour is described as a darkish grey, which is exactly the colour of the animal, when seen at a short distance. Their holding their heads very low, only just above the surface of the water, is a common habit of them too.

67.—1819? August?—The same author relates (p. 403):

The last account respecting the existence of the sea-serpent I received from him" (the sexton of Maasöe) "during our journey. He was fishing, as he said, with others in the Mageröe-Sund, when they discerned the monster of the deep, stretching out his bulk in many a spiral fold, and basking on the surface of the water. Its colour was dark and as to its length, he assured me, with looks of wonder and almost of alarm, that it nearly reached from the Mageröe side to the mainland opposite. In this measurement fear, doubtless, was the principal agent; for as to any accurate observations made by himself, they were out of the question. My friend the sexton was much too prudent a man, to hasard any at such a juncture. A glance was sufficient for him to commence his flight forthwith, as fast as his arms would enable him."

Of course I agree with Mr. de Capell Brooke as to the exaggerated dimensions attributed to the animal by the sexton of Maasöe. The words "spiral folds", of course, are wrong, the author meant the sinuosities in which the animal moves. Its colour is here described dark, which corresponds with so many other testimonies.

68.—1819? August?—At page 406 of the volume of this author we read in a note:

"The account of the serpent, received by him" (Prösten Deinbolt of Vadsöe) "from several persons on that part of the coast, agreed with those which have been already given."

This, of course, is only a report of the appearance of the sea-serpent near Vadsöe.

69.—1819, Aug. 26.—"*Extract of a letter from* Mr. Cheever Felch, Chaplan to the United States' ship Independance of 74 guns, to the Editor of the Boston Centinel." (Silliman's *Am. Journ. Sc. Arts*, Vol. II).

"Gloucester, August 26, 1819.
"Dear Sir.
"Others having taken in hand to give some account of the Sea-Serpent, I know not why I should not have the same liberty. Being on this station, in the United States' schooner Science, for the purpose of surveying this harbor, we were proceeding this morning down the harbor, in the schooner's boat; when abreast of Dallivan's Neck, William T. Malbone, Esq. Commander of the Schooner, seeing some appearance on the water, said—"*there is your sea-serpent*", meaning it is a laugh on me, for believing in its existence; but it prooved to be no joke. The animal was then between thirty and forty yards distance from us. Mr. Malbone, Midshipman Blake, myself, and our four boatmen, had a distinct view of him. He soon sunk; but not so deep but we could trace his course. He rose again within twenty yards distance of us, and lay sometime on the water. He then turned, and steered for Ten Pound Island; we pulled after him; but finding that he was not pleased with the noise of our oars, they were laid in, and the boat skulled. We again approached very near him. He continued some length of time, playing between Ten Pound Island and Stage Point. As he often came near the Point, we thought we could get a better view of him there, than from the boat, of which he seemed conspicuous. Mr. Malbone and myself landed; and the boat was sent to order the schooner down, for the purpose of trying what effect a twelve pound carronade would have upon him. He did not remain long after we landed, so that I was unable to effect my intention, of ascertaining, accurately, his length, with my instruments. From my knowledge of aquatic animals, and habits, and intimacy with marine appearances, I could not be deceived. We had a good view of him, except the very short period while he was under water, for half an hour.—His colour is a dark brown, with white under the throat. His size, we could not accurately ascertain, but his head is about three feet in circumference, flat and much smaller than his body. We did not see his tail; but from the end of the head to the fartherest protuberance, was not far from one hundred feet. I speak with a degree of certainty, from being much accustomed to measure and estimate distances and length. I counted fourteen bunches on his back, the first one, say ten or twelve feet from his head, and the others about seven feet apart. They decreased in size towards the tail. These bunches were sometimes counted with, and sometimes without a glass. Mr. Malbone counted thirteen, Mr. Blake thirteen and fourteen, and the boatman about the same number. His motion was sometimes very rapid, and at other times he lay nearly still. He turned slowly, and took up considerable room in doing it. He sometimes darted under water, with the greatest velocity, as if seizing prey. The protuberances were not from his motion, as they were the same whether in slow or rapid movement. His motion was partly vertical and partly horizontal, like that of fresh water snakes. I have been much acquainted with the snakes in our interior waters. His motion was the same. I have given you in round numbers, one hundred feet, for his length, that is, what we saw; but I should say he must be one hundred and thirty feet in length, allowing for his tail. There were a considerable number of birds about the sea-serpent as I have seen them about a snake on shore. That there is an aquatic animal in the form of a

snake, is not to be doubted. Mr. Malbone, till this day, was incredulous. No man would now convince him, there was not such a being. The sketch or picture of Marshal Prince, is perfectly correct. I could not, with my own pencil, give a more correct likeness."

"With respect"
"Your obedient servant"
  "Cheever Felch"
  "Major B. Russell."

I will not contest Mr. Felch's opinion about Mr. Prince's figure! As to the letter itself there is not a single statement which can detract from or add to our present notions of the sea-serpent.

In 1846 Col. T. H. Perkins, of whom we have spoken more than once, requested Mr. Bolton, who was first Lieutenant of the *Independence* in 1819, to send him some particulars about this appearance. Mr. Bolton promptly replied under date of July 14, 1846. This letter, published by Col. Perkins in the *Boston Daily Advertiser* of Nov. 25, 1848, runs as follows:

"In the year 1817 I was the first lieutenant of the Independence, of 74 guns, then lying in the harbour of Boston."

"In the course of the spring or summer a party of officers were detailed, by order of Commodore Bainbridge, to survey the coast of the bay, to a limited extent northeastward and outside of the light-house."

"The officers selected for this duty were the sailingmaster of the ship, Wm. T. Malbone, and the Rev. Cheever Felch, the instructor of the midshipmen."

"To assist in the service several of the most competent and elder midshipmen were designated. As they alternated periodically with other gentlemen of the same grade, I cannot with any degree of precision venture to name them. I hope that some of them are yet living, and, further, that they have advanced in professional distinction. There were also added a sufficient number of seamen and boys."

"Commodore Bainbridge, Mr. Malbone and Mr. Felch died some years ago."

"I recollect that on the first occasion, when the Lynx returned to the Independence, of which ship she was the tender, that Mr. Malbone reported as having seen a monstrous sea-animal, not before known to him, of the snake species; the length doubtful, but estimated at some eighty or more feet; and added as an accident, that the officers and men employed in a small boat to carry out the soundings had returned in haste, and indeed alarm, to the Lynx, which was at anchor."

"These statements were corroborated by Mr. Felch, the officers and crew."

"Subsequently it was seen several times, by some of the party, who, being soon satisfied that it was harmless approached comparatively near, and no doubt gave me a minute description of its appearance as it presented itself to them; but if so, the particular details have escaped my memory."

"These facts are all that I can with distinctness and certainty mention. Wm. Compton Bolton, Captain in the Navy of the United States, Saratonga Springs, July 14, 1846; to Hon. T. H. Perkins, Boston."—

It cannot surprise us that in some particulars, as "in the year 1817", and in some others this letter does not agree with the foregoing Letter from the Rev. Cheever Felch himself, as twenty-seven years had since elapsed.

Various Accounts

70.—1819, September?—Dr. Francis Boott in a letter to Dr. Hooker, dated London, Nov. 4, 1826, and published in the *Edinb. Journ. Sc.*, VI, 1827, says:
"I remember also that a letter appeared in the *Boston Centinel*, soon after, published by an officer in the American Navy, who reported that, on his return from a survey of some part of the coast, he saw, when out of sight of land, a large serpent. He was so near that he drew an outline of it, and that outline accompanied the paragraph. When you showed me Mr. Warburton's figure on the card, I at first thought it was a copy of that of the *Centinel*. I can only add, for your own satisfaction, that *I* have no doubt of the existence of this remarkable animal."

As Dr. Boott is speaking of a visit at Boston in August 1813, the words "soon after" of course signify in the latter part of August or in the beginning of September. As the officer was "on his return" and published his encounter in the *Boston Centinel*, the appearance most probably occurred not far from Boston. The reader will find Mr. Warburton's drawing further on (n°. 83).

71.—1819, September 13?—(*Phil. Mag.* LIV, 1819).
"The great Sea-Snake has been seen again towards the middle of September, in the bay of Massachusetts, and three yellow collars observed on his neck, which has led some to believe it might be another individual and species; but this circumstance might have been overlooked before. It is not stated whether it had streaks of a lighter hue on the body, as the first was represented to have by some witnesses. It is therefore likely that the two characters of "streaks of a lighter hue on the body and three yellow collars on the neck", may be added to its description. The collars are described as about two inches broad, and one foot apart."

The three yellow collars observed on its neck may be explained as follows: The animal has a hairy skin, as we have already seen, like a seal-skin. Now, when the neck is wet and contracted by the animal, its skin gets wrinkles, of course running round the neck, as is also the case in sea-lions. Those parts of these wrinkles, which are deepest, remain wet for a very long time, because they are not exposed to the air; those, however, which are highest, if we may use this expression, are not only most exposed to the air, but the hairs on those parts diverge and dry as soon as possible; and—when dry, they have a yellow greyish colour. If the animal now stretches its neck, it may show one, two, &c., even eight or more yellow-coloured collars round its dark brown neck, which may have a breadth of about two inches and a distance of one foot between them. This phenomenon or appearance, as already stated, is often to be seen in our zoological gardens on sea-lions and seals.

In the *Philosophical Magazine*, Vol. LIV, 1819, Dr. Rafinesque says:
"Dr. Mitchill informs me that General Hawkins has written a memoir on the sea-serpent of Massachusetts, which he has sent, with a drawing, to Sir Joseph Banks; it is a paper of some length and much interest, as it relates facts, and all the circumstances attending the appearance and natural history of those huge animals, taken upon oath of eye-witnesses. He attempts to prove, with much probability, that several individuals have been seen, and two at least, if not three species; one with three collars, another without any, and a smaller one."

In Silliman's *Am. Journ. Sc. Arts*, Vol. II, 1820, I have found the following extract from a letter to the Editor, dated Boston, April 8, 1820.

"I have lately received a letter from Sir Joseph Banks, written by his own hand, in which he expresses his full faith in the existence of our Serpent in the Sea, and not only as it regards himself, but his friends, and he is grateful for every new communication I have given him on that subject, and writes with the same enthusiasm that he did several years ago. Although he is now very infirm."

Evidently this was a letter from General Hawkins.

Professor Benjamin Silliman, the Editor of this journal adds:

"Sir Joseph Banks, President of the Royal Society of London, the Companion of Capt. Cook, is now at a very advanced age but still vigourous in his intellectual powers, and ardent in the promotion of every species of useful knowledge."

In Mr. A. de Capell Brooke's *Travels through Sweden*, we find at p. 411:

"For a length of time the most extraordinary accounts were circulated relating to it, till at last the whole story was generally considered as the fabric of American invention; and there are many, I believe, in this country" (Great Britain) "who do not consider it in any other light than that of a hoax. Judging, however, from the detailed accounts of the circumstance which are preserved among the papers of sir Joseph Banks, the principal facts appear to be these."

And at p. 413:

"The repeated accounts of the serpent's appearance having attracted the attention of the Linnaean Society at Boston, one of its members was deputed to visit the spot and to examine into the truth of them. This was accordingly done; and the above is the general substance of the various depositions sworn to before General Humphreys. This gentleman, who was a corresponding member of the Society, despatched to Sir Joseph Banks copies of the whole of these, which are still preserved in his library. Sir Joseph entered with warmth into this curious investigation; and the minuteness, with which every particular was supplied, showed how greatly he felt interested in the question."

In Nov. 4, 1826, Dr. Francis Boott wrote a letter to Dr. Hooker, a part of which was published in the *Edinburgh Journal of Science*, Vol. VI, 1827. Dr. Boott, after some general remarks, goes on to express himself in the following terms:

"All that I could collect upon the subject was sent to Sir Joseph Banks, with whom I had repeated conversations about the animal, and the respectability of the individuals who affirmed to the sight of him. The great mass of evidence is to be found in the pamphlet published by the Linnaean Society of New England. The question as to the real appearance of a large serpent off the coast of Massachusetts, was put to rest by that publication. There could be no doubt of the fact, and the testimony of thousands who saw the animal *for one or two years afterwards*, must have been sufficient to satisfy the most incredulous."

"I believe I was one of the first who mentioned to Sir Joseph Banks, that a large serpent had been seen on the American coast; at all events, I distinctly remember that when I first spoke to him on the subject, he was incredulous, and showed me a Plate of a similar animal in Pontoppidan's *History of Norway*. I myself had no doubt of the truth of the assertions of the early observers of it; for many of them were known to me, and I was anxious to convince Sir Joseph of the discovery of a new and remarkable animal. I therefore was in the habit of sending him every information I could collect respecting it. In one of my last visits to Boston, I gathered testimony from individuals, and from the public papers, and was happy to find on my return to Europe, that Sir Joseph was satisfied of the existence of the serpent, though he continued doubtful of the relationship between the small snake (figure 1 of the Linnaean pamphlet) and the large serpent."

In October, 1828, Mr. Mitchill, read a paper before the New. York Lyceum, which paper will be found in our Chapter on Hoaxes. As we have already observed, this paper also contains a particular account concerning the letters addressed by General Humphreys to Sir Joseph Banks.

Again Dr. Hamilton, in his *Amphibious Carnivora*, 1839, asserts:

"General Humphreys, by whom the affidavits were taken, transmitted a copy of them, and a detail of the whole circumstance, to the late Sir Joseph Banks, in whose Library the documents are still preserved."

Remarkable fact! Nowhere I have found a paper of Sir Joseph Banks himself, neither in the *Transactions of the Royal Society of London*, nor anywhere else. I beg the present members of this Very Learned Body to give me the loan of all the papers about the subject, or to publish them in their next volume.

72.—1820, July?—Mr. A. de Capell Brooke in his *Travels through Sweden, during the Summer of* 1820, relates at p. 263:

"During the time I remained at Hundholm a curious circumstance occurred: One day when at dinner at Mr. Blackhall's house, and thinking little of the sea-serpent, concerning which I had heard nothing for some time, a young man, the master of a small fishing yacht, which had just come in from Drontheim, joint our party; in the course of conversation, he mentioned that a few hours before, whilst close to Hundholm, and previous to his entering the harbour, two sea-snakes passed immediately under his yacht. When he saw then, he was on the deck, and, seizing a handspike, he struck at them as they came up close to the vessel on the other side, upon which they disappeared. Their length was very great, and their colour greyish; but from the very short time they were visible, he could not notice any other particulars. He had no doubt of their being snakes as he called them, and the circumstance was related entirely of his own accord."

73.—1820, August.—In the *Zoologist* of 1849, p. 2361, we read:

"He was several times seen in the month of August, 1820, from the piazza of the house of Col. Perkins, at Nahant."

74.—1820?—The following report was published in the *Zoologist* of 1849, p. 2460.

"What degree of confidence the following story may gain is to me a subject of very little consideration; for as I can have no view of gaining anything by it, so it certainly will appear that it would hardly be worth the trouble of invention; but as a story of this sort has made its appearance among our transatlantic friends, without being at all credited, it is as likely in Europe this may have the same fate; yet if it can afford any amusement or information for intelligent and scrutinizing minds, for their gratification I freely give it to the press, assuring them, on my sacred honour, of the truth of what I am about to describe. On Sunday, about 5. P. M., being then in latitude 46, longitude 3, by dead reckoning, observed an immense body on the surface of the water, apparently without motion, but water spouting from it, not unlike the blowing of a whale. I immediately got my glass; and, from its rugged appearance and showing nothing where the water issued from, I began to entertain some doubts, that this must have been the vigia laid down for Barenethy's rocks or the three chimneys, and, so prepared in my own mind, I directed the steering sails to be taken in and the ship prepared for going about. Some of my ship's company were of opinion it was a ship-bottom up: this I thought not unlikely, and went into the main cat harpens to look more distinctly at it: the appearance then was still steady, but irregular. I saw neither head nor tail above the water, but a hump from one extreme resembling the rise or point of rather a triangular rock: this tapered to a distance,—I certainly believe 70 or 100 feet, and the water broke over it, a little beyond it: it discharged the spout; but nothing showing itself, undetermined in mind what it could be, or whether I should tack the ship, it all at once disappeared, and, to my great astonishment, a head and neck—resembling something of a serpent's—made its appearance, erected about six feet above the surface of the water. After taking a survey towards the vessel, it all at once vanished, leaving us full of conjecture and surprise. It gives me more confidence in making the above statement, as one of the seamen, whose name in Jonathan Townsend, was in the main top, and saw the creature I have described, and would feel no hesitation in taking an oath to it.—George Sanford, Lieutenant R. N."

["Copied from a memorandum-book of Lieut. Sanford, and communicated by Dr. Scott, of Exeter. There is no date to the above statement, but it is presumed to have been written about the year 1820. Lieut. Sanford then commanded a merchant-ship, the Lady Combermere.—E. N."]

No doubt the latitude of 46 degrees is northern lat., so that the appearance occurred in the Bay of Biscay.—The act of breathing of the sea-serpent, after having remained for some time under the surface of the water, just as in whales, has an appearance generally called "spouting". Apparently the animal held its head just at water-level, and so it showed "nothing where the water issued from". The rugged appearance may have been caused by the animal lying with several bunches on its back, as afterwards was also reported by the Lloydsteamer *Kätie* (n°. 154) or by its having a mane, extending all along the neck and back. The "hump from one extreme resembling the rise or point of rather a triangular rock" must have been the animal's head which it lifted up just above the surface. Nearly the same appearance will be observed in the figure of one of the officers of H. M. S. *Plumper* (fig. 81). Let the dimensions moreover be somewhat exaggerated, the "head and neck resembling something of a serpent's erected about six feet above the surface of the water", the "taking a survey towards the vessel", and the vanishing at once, makes all comment superfluous; all these characters have more than once been reported of this creature.

In the *Philosophical Magazine and Journal*, Vol. LVII, 1821, we find an extract from the numerous reports communicated by Prof. Bigelow in Silliman's *American Journal of Science and the Arts,* Boston, Vol. II, 1820, May.

We have already quoted Milton, who in his *Paradise Lost*, printed in 1667, compares Satan with some huge monsters, amongst others the sea-serpent. Parts of these verses have been more than once cited by writers of articles on the sea-serpent. I cannot but express my surprise at this custom, for there is not one single word or expression in Milton's verses, which is taken from accounts, reports, or tales of the sea-serpent itself. Walter Scott, however, in his *Pirate*: which was published in 1821, vol. I, chapt. II, says a few words about the animal, which are so correct, that they must have been taken from some or other report:

"The Ocean also had its mysteries, etc."

"The Sea-Snake was also known, which arising out of the depths of Ocean, stretches to the skies his enormous neck, covered with a mane like that of a war-horse, and with its broad glittering eyes, raised mast-head high, looks out, as it seems, for plunder or for victims."

The large glittering eyes, the enormous neck, covered with a mane are known characters, and the rising from the depths high into the air, standing nearly upright and viewing for a moment all around, evidently taking a survey, is a habit observed more than once.

75.—1821, Summer.—Col. T. H. Perkins on the 13th. Of Oct. 1820, when on board the *Ann Marie*, wrote a letter to his friend Jno P. Cushing, which he published in the *Boston Daily Advertiser* of 25th. Nov. 1848, after the excitement caused by the appearance of an individual on the 6th. of August, 1848. The different parts of this letter are inserted partly in our Chapter on Hoaxes and partly in n°. 44, 45, 47, 48, 49, 63. The Editor of the *Boston Daily Advertiser* now goes on:

"In addition to this interesting narrative our venerable correspondent gives letters from several members of his family, who *the next summer* had opportunity to see the sea-serpent, in which the appearance of the animal is minutely described. This correspondence is very interesting; the description of the animal agrees entirely with that given above, and we regret that want of space must prevent the insertion of it."

It is a great pity that all these letters have not been published. Perhaps they are now lost for ever!

76.—1821.—In a letter from William Warburton to Robert Barclay, Esq. printed in the *Edinburgh Journal of Science*, Vol. VI, 1827, p. 130, and dated 20th. September 1826, we read: "I dined one day at the Hôtel of New York with Sir Isaak Coffin, who discredited the existence of such an animal, which was reported to have been seen by Captain Bennett of Boston, about five years back."

Of course the occurrence took place near the coast of the U. S.

77.—1821 , September 25? In Froriep's *Notizen* of Jan. 1822, I, we read:

"The Sea-Serpent, of which much has been spoken of late years, has been clearly seen again this year by many persons with spyglasses, and it is described by all of them and the descriptions agree pretty well with each other: on Sept. 27 last a distinguished merchant of Nantucket, Mr. Francis Joy, jun. made a declaration of it on oath before the justice of the peace."

78.—1821?—Dr. Hibbert in his *Description of the Shetland Islands* says at p. 565:
"I have heard, in Shetland, of a sea-serpent being seen off the Isle of Stenness, Vailey Island and Dunrossness."
This report is also quoted by Dr. R. Hamilton in his *Amphibious Carnivora*, 1839.

79.—1822.—Mr. A. de Capell Brooke in his *Travels through Sweden, &c.*, 1823, says in a note, p. 416:
"In some very recent accounts I have received from Finmark, founded on respectable authority, the sea-serpent is stated to have appeared off Soröe this last summer (1822) and to have been seen by many of the inhabitants of that Island. The length of the animal is described as about a fourth of an English mile, its size that of a full grown ox; the colour of a greyish brown; and the weather when it made its appearance, calm and fine."
Fear must have enlarged its length: the diameter, the colour, the calmness of the weather, however, are all correct.

Mr. A. de Capell Brooke in his *Travels through Sweden &c.*, 1823, at p. 403 tells us a remarkable fact, viz. the striking agreement of the fabulous tales of the sea-serpent of those days (1820) with those, related by Pontoppidan. The passage runs as follows:
"The following information, however, which he" (the sexton of Massöe) "gave me concerning this animal deserves a greater share of attention. It is the practise of the fishermen, he said, when at any time they found themselves suddenly surrounded by the folds of the serpent, and obliged to pass over a part of it, never to attempt making their way between the openings, caused by part of the body of the animal being concealed under water, for fear of its raising and upsetting the boat. On the contrary, they rowed with all their strength against one of the visible folds, as the serpent, as soon as he feels the touch of the boat, naturally sinks down and enables it thus to pass over in safety. It will appear perhaps as a striking circumstance, that looking afterward into Pontoppidan, I found the foregoing particulars the very substance of what is related in his work, which may be said to be unknown in Finmark, and even of his name my informant had never heard."
Indeed, this is remarkable, but it is only a proof of the scrupulousness with which fables are told unchanged! The passages from Pontoppidan referred to by our traveller have been discussed by me.
For history's sake, as well as to acquaint my readers with all that has been written for or against the subject, I am obliged to insert all that Mr. Brooke further

says about it. After having repeated nearly all what Pontoppidan mentioned about it, he goes on:

"Taking upon the whole a fair view of the different accounts related in the foregoing pages respecting the sea-serpent, no reasonable person can doubt the fact of some marine animal of extraordinary dimensions, and in all probability of the serpent tribe, having been repeatedly seen by various persons along the Norway and Finmark coasts. These accounts, for the most part, have been given verbally from the mouths of the fishermen; an honest and artless class of men who, having no motive for misrepresentation, cannot be suspected of a wish to deceive. Could this idea, however, be entertained, the circumstance alone, of their assertions having been so fully confirmed by others in more distant parts, would be sufficient to free them from any imputation of this kind. The simple facts are these: In traversing a space of full 700 miles of coast, extending to the most northern point, accounts have been received from numerous persons respecting the appearance of an animal, called by them a sea-serpent. This of itself would induce some degree of credit to be given to it; but when these several relations as to the general appearance of the animal, its dimensions, the state of the weather, when it has been seen, and other particulars are so fully confirmed, one by the other, at such considerable intervening distances, every reasonable man will feel satisfied of the truth of the main fact. Many of the informants, besides, were of superior rank and education; and the opinions of such men as the *Amtmand* (Governor) of Finmark, Mr. Steen of Carlsöe, *Prösten* (Dean) Deinbolt of Vadsöe, and the Bishop of Nordland and Finmark, who was even an eye witness, ought not to be disregarded. There does not appear the least probability, or even possibility, that any other marine animal at present known on the northern coast, could have been confounded with the sea-serpent. The finners, a species of whale already mentioned, are too well known to occasion any mistake; and the total want of similarity in shape, appearance, and size, if they were even rare, would be sufficiently obvious."

Remarkable is the fact that Mr. de Capell Brooke considers the animal to be "in all probability of the serpent tribe", with which he of course means *snakes*.

"The strongest confirmation of the fact appears to be the account received at the island of Otersun. There it will be recollected, the serpent made its appearance in July, 1919, being visible a short distance from the shore, nearly every day, during the greater part of that month, and having been seen during that time by the whole of the population of the island. The information collected, indeed, is scantier than might have been expected, from its remaining so considerable a time; but the talent of observation in fishermen is far from considerable, and their curiosity is easily gratified. To these circumstances, and the general dread entertained of this animal, may be attributed the want of any attempt to take it. At the neighbouring island of Krogöen also, it will be remembered, that its having appeared was confirmed; and this would be sufficient at least to cause a wavering in the minds of those naturalists, who have treated former accounts as the mere offspring of imagination."

We may add: not only their curiosity is easily gratified, but their fear to approach the animal too closely withholds them from investigating it nearer, or from observing it, as a naturalist or more curious person would do!

Further he discusses the subject historically, first comparing the Leviathan in the Book of Job with it, to which idea evidently Milton's *Paradise Lost* led him. I am far from admitting any relation between the story in Holy Writ and the sea-serpents. He further quotes Knud Leems, Olaus Magnus (n°. 1), Hans Egede (n°. 5), Eric Pontoppidan, and speaks of the letters written to and preserved in the library of Sir Joseph Banks, then president of the Royal Society, by General Hawkins and General Humphreys.

I am also obliged to repeat here *in extenso* his plea for the sea-serpent (p. 415-419):

"In the belief of the possibility of events, men are too generally guided by the limited knowledge of things they may possess; and there are doubtless many among the more uninformed classes, who, if told of the existence of an animal attaining the height of eighteen feet, such as the giraffe or camelopard, or that the ocean produced one like the whale, more than 100 feet in length, would not only stare with astonishment, but would as much doubt the truth of these assertions, as if informed of the sea-serpent. This is but natural; their knowledge of the world and its productions, deprived as they are of other means of attaining it, must be confined to the narrow sphere they live in; and the ideas they possess of life must necessarily be contracted."

"The naturalist, however, whose views of creation are bounded by no country, and whose field of inquiry is the globe itself, sees with admiration though without surprise the rich kingdom of nature gradually unfolding itself to the researches of science, and finds his imperfect catalogue almost daily swelled by proofs of the existence of some new and extraordinary animal, which before was unknown to the world, or considered as living in the imagination alone. By the exertions of the present age, he has become acquainted with many creatures, in their forms and habits the most singular and strange; and thus he is taught never to deny the existence of any thing rashly; assured, as he is, by whatever he beholds, of the unlimited power of the great Creator; and conscious, that all which the utmost zeal of man can attain is a knowledge of but a very small portion of his works. When he considers the various discoveries of modern times, and the astonishing effects produced by the ingenuity of man in the united application of chemistry and mechanism, it gives him but a more exalted idea of that great superior force, which not only sets in motion this master machine, and indues it with powers of sense and reflection, but causes it to act in so extraordinary a manner in the creation and reproduction of matter. In fine the philosopher, whether his researches regard the minuteness or magnitude of creation, is equally prepared for the wonders that are displayed to his eye. The aid of the mikroscoop makes known to him the existence of myriads of living creatures, some of such incredible smallness, that the utmost powers of the magnifier can with difficulty render them visible; and of which thousands if put together, would not equal a grain of sand in bulk. He finds even, that the human body itself is filled with them; and that the structure of their own internal parts is equally complex and curious. When, however, he reflects, that each of these beings, diminutive as they are, may perhaps contain a countless number of other, visible but to the minuter tecture of their eyes, he is lost and bewildered, and can only look forward to the period, when his purer existence will be permitted to comprehend the great secrets of nature, and the mysteries of the universe. If, on the other hand, he directs his steps to the deep gloom of the African forests, tenanted by their various wild inhabitants, he sees, on a sublimely enlarged scale the works of the Creator; whether he meets with the elephant supporting its enormous bulk with peaceful and dignified steps, or views the huge trunk of the stupendous boa serpent, extended to the length of fifty feet, and viing in size with the stately trees, between which it glides, the terror of all, and the sovereign of the forest. The secrets of the great deep alone are veiled from his inquiring eyes; and he regrets, that his structure prevents him from cleaving, like the finny tribe, the watery fluid, and gazing on the wonders below. Phenomena the most extraordinary, nay even a new world, would there be opened to his inspection, did not the grosser materials of his composition obstruct his pursuit. From the marine animal productions, notwithstanding, that come under his observation, he finds, on comparing them with those of the land, that they are larger, proportionably to the vast space allotted them; and he reasonably concludes, that in the existence of unknown regions of the ocean, compared with which the land we inhabit may be deemed but as a spot, and the depth of which is not merely that of some miles, but extends, for any thing that is known to the contrary, even from pole to pole; there may be a variety of animals, greatly exceeding in size even those which, on this account alone, have been deemed fabulous: yet that their bulk may, nevertheless, be fairly proportioned to the space they inhabit; and that living midway in this world of waters, without ever rising even to the surface, or seeing the light of heaven, they may be made, by the hand that fashoned them, and in ways unknown to us, subservient to the use and benifit of man."

"Here let me pause; for though the subject appears the more interesting and inexhaustible the more it is pursued, yet I feel insensible, that I have wandered very far, and that the thoughts, to which the sea-serpent gave rise, have already comprised the whole globe."

The most remarkable accounts mentioned by Mr. A. de Capell Brooke are translated in Froriep's *Notizen*, 1823, IV, 84, p. 273.

80.—1824 January.—In the *American Journal of Science and Arts* conducted by Prof. Benjamin Silliman, Vol. 28, July, 1835, we read:

"The following statement having been made by a gentleman of great intelligence and candor, a cool and judicious observer, who has travelled very extensively and traversed the seas in many climates, the editor desired a written notice of the facts which he is permitted to publish without the name of the author; with him he is, however, well-acquainted and reposes full confidence in his integrity and in his freedom from any influence of imagination."

"Boston, April, 5th., 1835."

"To Prof. Silliman,—Dear Sir,—On my passage from the River La Plata to this country in January, 1824, latitude 34 1/2° South, and 48° West longitude, I saw what was first supposed to be a fish called an Albicore; but, on further examination it was discovered to be a serpent of which I cannot give a clearer description than to say that a common dark coloured land snake is, in miniature, a perfect representation. A light breeze prevailed at the time and the sea was quite smooth. It first appeared within ten feet of the vessel, its head was, perhaps, two feet above the water and appeared as large as a ten gallons keg; the eye was distinctly seen. The whole length of the serpent was about half the length of the vessel, say 40 feet. The size and circumference of the body, was nearly as large as a barrel; nothing like a fin was seen. I could not make out the distinct appearance of the tail. The serpent remained almost motionless while in sight, the head above water and eyes directed towards the vessel."

Prof. Benjamin Silliman adds to it a

"*Remark of the Editor.*—The distance of the place of observation being several hundred miles from the nearest coast, this serpent must have been a denizen of the ocean; for the huge land snake of South America could not navigate so far out to sea if indeed they ever take to the ocean at all. The snake was perfectly quiet, and appeared quite comfortable and at home on the waves. We must therefore consider this case as settling the question of the real existence of a Sea-Serpent. The absence of paddles or arms forbids us from supposing that this was a swimming saurian."

We may observe here that all the characters of the sea-serpent of Prof. Silliman's acquaintance agree with those which are already known to us, and that the supposition or negative explanation of Prof. Silliman, that this sea-serpent was not a swimming saurian is at least premature, for the assertion of the eye-witness that "nothing like a fin was seen" does not prove an "absence of paddles or arms", which of course remained hidden under water!

81.—1824, Summer.—In Froriep's *Notizen* of Oct. 1824, Vol. VIII, n°. 168, p. 218, we read:

"The American Sea-Serpent is said to have appeared again this summer. A Mr. Ruggles in Bristol County, has, as is mentioned by the Newburyport Journal, seen it off Plum-Island and in Shad Cove at a distance of about 100 feet. The head was two feet long and of a brown colour. Mr. R. could distinctly observe the teeth in the mouth when opened. He could not discern the tail, but several times, about thirty feet behind the head, he observed parts of the animal in an undulating motion".

Though this is not the first time that the teeth are mentioned to have been seen, yet now again no description of them is given.

82.—1825?—In a paper by Dr. T. S. Traill, printed in n°. 44, May, 1854, of the *Proceedings of the Royal Society of Edinburgh*, we read:

"That in the ocean such animals do exist, have been affirmed by persons worthy of credit. I shall notice an unpublished instance related to me many years ago by my intelligent friend, the late Mr. Andrew Strang, a gentleman of unblemished honour." "Once, when on a deep-sea fishing, he saw pass below his boat, at the depth of eight or ten feet, an enormously long fish, of an eel-shape. It was swimming slowly with a vermicular motion, and appeared to be at least sixty feet in length." It appeared to take no notice of them; but they hastily removed from what they considered a dangerous neighbourhood. He stated that he was shy in mentioning this circumstance, "lest the sceptical public should class him with the fableloving Bishop of Bergen." "There is considerable reason to believe that a similar fish has appeared more than once on the western coasts of Scotland."

Neither date nor locality is mentioned. I don't hesitate to put the date at nearly thirty years back, and to choose the year 1825, and to fix the locality on the western coasts of Scotland, because of all the coasts of Great Britain only the western ones are frequented by these animals. I know but one occurrence on the eastern coast of Scotland, of which I have three observations (n°. 141, 142, 143). I am convinced that the animal seen by Mr. Andrew Strang was a sea-serpent. Its enormous length of at least sixty feet, its *vermicular* motion, its eel-shape, at once betray it. Evidently the animal moved only by vertical undulations, holding its four flappers pressed against its body, otherwise Mr. Strang would have compared it with "an alligator with flappers like those of a sea-turtle and with a long neck," as did Captain Hope (n°. 119.)

83.—1826, June 16.—*New York Advertiser* of June 21, 1826, and *American Journal of Science and Arts*, Vol. XI, 1826.

"Capt. Holdrege, of the ship Silas Richards, which arrived yesterday from Liverpool, states that in passing George's Bank, five days since, he had a fair view of the sea-serpent. It was about ten rods from the ship, the sea perfectly calm, and that part which appeared out of water about sixty feet in length. The head and protuberances were similar to the representations which have frequently been given to him by persons who had seen him near Cape Ann. He was going at a very slow rate, and appeared unmindful of the ship. He was visible about seven minutes to the passengers and crew, who were on deck at the time. A certificate has been drawn up and signed by the passengers, which, with a drawing made by one of the gentlemen, gives a minute description of the serpent as seen by them. The number and credibility of the witnesses, place beyond all doubt the existence of such an animal as a sea-serpent."

Of this occurrence we learn more in the *Edinb. Journ. Sc.*, Vol. VI, 1827, where we read in a paper by Dr. Hooker:

"That which has been the principal inducement for us to present this imperfect paper to the public, is a letter which we have had the pleasure of seeing addressed to Robert Barclay Esq. of Bury Hall, Surry, from Mr. Warburton, a gentleman belonging to the house of Barclay, Brothers, and Company, London. That gentleman, proceeding in his passage to America, on board the Silas Richards, New York packet, Captain Holdrege, had an opportunity of beholding this sea-monster on Friday the 16th of June off St. George's Banks. But his own plain statement must be presumed far more satisfactory to every candid mind than any account extracted from his letter."

"Pentonville, 20th September 1820"

"Dear Sir,"

"Having been informed by your grandson, Mr. Robert Reynolds, that you were desirous of possessing a sketch of the sea-serpent as seen by me in crossing the Atlantic, and to have some account of the same; in compliance with your wishes, I have inclosed a rough pencil drawing of the monster as it appeared during the time when its head was elevated above the water, and I shall state the particulars attending this novel exhibition."

"The captain and myself were standing on the starboard side of the vessel, looking over the bulwark, and remarking how perfectly smooth was the surface of the sea. It was about half-past six o'clock P. M., and a cloudless sky. On a sudden we heard a rushing in the water a-head of the ship. At first we imagined it to be a whale spouting, and turning to the quarter whence the sound proceeded, we observed the serpent in the position as it appears in the sketch, slowly approaching at not more than the rate of two miles an hour, in a straight direction. I suppose we were hardly going through the water so fast, for there was scarcely a breath of wind. I must premise that I had never heard of the existence of such an animal. I instantly exclaimed, why, there is a *sea-snake!* 'That is the sea-serpent', exclaimed the captain, 'and I would give my ship and cargo to catch the monster'. I immediately called to the passengers, who were all down below, but only five or six came up, among whom was Miss Magee, the daughter of a merchant in New York. The remainder refused to come up, saying there had been too many hoaxes of that kind already. I was too eager to stand parleying with them, and I returned to the captain. In the same slow style the serpent passed the vessel at about the distance of 50 yards from us, neither turning his head to the right or left. As soon as his head had reached the stern of the vessel, he gradually laid it down in a horizontal position with his body, and floated along like the mast of a vessel. That there was upwards of 60 feet visible, is clearly shown by the circumstance, that the length of the ship was upwards of 120 feet, and at the time his head was off the stern, the other end (as much as was above the surface) had not passed the main mast. The time we saw him, as described in the drawing, was two minutes and a half. After he had declined his head we saw him for about twenty minutes a-head, floating along like an enormous log of timber. His motion in the water was meandering like that of an eel, and the rake he left behind was like that occasioned by the passing of a small craft through the water. We had but one harpoon on board, and the ship's long-boat was, for the time being converted into a *cow-house*. We had two guns on board, but no ball..... I dined one day at the Hotel of New York with Sir Isaac Coffin, who discredited the existence of such an animal, which was reported to have been seen by Captain Bennet of Boston about five years back; but as I assured him I had never heard previously even the report of such a monster, and that I was an *Englishman*, he gave full credit to it. The sketch I gave him also corresponded with the description that was circulated at that time. The humps on the back resembled in size and shape those of the dromedary. I remain, Dear Sir, yours respectfully,

"William Warburton."

I give in fig. 27 a facsimile of the figure, accompanying the paper of Mr. Hooker (*Edinb. Journ. Sc.* Vol. VI, 1827, Pl. I. fig. 10).

The description of the sea-serpent given here, may be summed up in the following words: When it came to the surface a rushing of the water was heard. The part which appeared out of water was about sixty feet in length. It held its head some feet above the surface of the water, swimming at a rate of two miles an

FIG. 27.—THE SEA-SERPENT AS SEEN BY MR. WARBURTON.

hour, and showing bunches on its back. After some moments it gradually laid down its bead in a horizontal position with its body, and floated along like the mast of a vessel, evidently swimming with its body in a straight line, using its flappers. The wake which it left behind was equal to that of a small vessel. Nothing is said of the skin, which evidently was smooth, otherwise the scales would have been seen and mentioned, for the animal appeared not far from the vessel. Nor does the sketch show any scales. The position of the head in the sketch, making nearly a right angle with its neck, may have led others to say it resembled that of a horse, if we take moreover in consideration that some individuals have a mane. The individual seen by Captain Holdrege and Mr. Warburton evidently had no mane.

84.—1826, June 18.—In the same letter from Mr. Warburton to Robert Barclay there is a passage which we have omitted above and which runs as follows:

"Two days after we saw him he was seen by another vessel off Cape Cod, about 200 miles from where he made his appearance to us. This intelligence reached New York about four days after we arrived there, and the description given exactly corresponds with the foregoing."

Evidently this was the same individual, or one of the same sex.

In 1827 Dr. Hooker wrote the following paper for the *Edinburgh Journal of Science*, Vol. VI:

"When we remember the numberless impositions concerning Natural History, which at various periods have been detected, it is not surprising that doubt should be a principal, nay, a necessary, qualification of the student of Nature. Yet we cannot but think that the scientific world in general has been too incredulous concerning the sea-serpent, seeing the mass of concurrent testimony which has been adduced to prove its existence. It is certainly true that vague reports had been spread abroad with regard to this enormous animal long ere any just foundation was afforded for them, and indeed before we had heard of any who professed to have seen it. This may have very far conduced to produce that scepticism which now is perfectly unwarrantable. We are so accustomed, whenever the subject is introduced in conversation, to couple it with the preposterous fables of the *Kraken*, that it would be extremely difficult to break down the barriers against belief which prejudice has so long assisted to support. The accounts of the most credible witnesses have thus been rejected, although, 'to make assurance doubtly sure', the generality of them have been taken upon oath."

"So many wonderful discoveries, both in the arts and Sciences, have been made within the last century, that it is astonishing how the existence of the sea-serpent has been supposed either so marvellous or impossible. Time has satisfactorily proved the veracity of Bruce, and we must leave it to time to do the same office with reward to the beholders of this 'wonder of the deep.' Is this monster more disproportionate to the extent of the sea than the elephant to that of the land? Or, it may be asked, has it a solid bulk, (even according to late most extravagant accounts), nearly approaching in magnitude to that of the whale? Geology has been infinitely more fortunate than zoology in many respects; theories only partially sustained have been received; and while the recent discoveries of the *Plesiosaurus* and *Megalosaurus* have made demands upon our powers of credence far greater than the *serpent*, the descriptions of the latter animal have received very little trust, and even much ridicule and contempt. In general, however, it must be confessed, that people do not object to the extraordinary proportions of such a creature, so much as to what they consider the want of respectable and satisfactory evidence. We trust to advance, in the sequel, such additional evidence to that already presented, and of such respectability, as to confirm entirely the truth of the existence of such an animal,—an animal concerning which so many contradictory opinions have been hazarded as to its more immediate nature and structure; and which, from the mystery in which it has hitherto been wrapped, must be interesting to the most casual admirer of nature:— which must be interesting even from the element in which it lives; so vast, so unexplored in its inmost recesses. We can have so little information with regard to an animal which has so mighty an habitation, that it acquires a grandeur in our estimation far surpassing those which inhabit the earth. The monsters of the deep appear so independent of our influence, and so far removed from any connection with us, that any increase of our knowledge in reference to them must be highly gratifying."

"It was during the year 1817 that it began to be correctly reported, that in the neighbourhood of Boston and Gloucester in America, an animal, in general construction nearly resembling a serpent, had been frequently seen. These rumours created a good deal of excitement, insomuch that, at a meeting of the Linnaean Society of New England, it was determined more fully to investigate the matter. The Honourable Lonson Nash of Gloucester was appointed by a Committee to gather together all the information which might be obtained."

"It is unnecessary here to dwell at any length upon the evidence which his unremitting and meritorious exertions procured. From different quarters, individuals of the highest respectability communicated all the information which it was in their power to proffer, and all declared themselves prepared to take an oath upon the accuracy of their narrations. No testimony was received, excepting from those who professed to have been personal witnesses of the monster: no weight was given to their accounts deduced from the reports which were everywhere circulated:—the unadorned and unexaggerated style in which their statements were worded is of itself perfectly sufficient to win over to all unqualified trust. The witnesses for the most part, unite in ascribing a vertical motion to the creature. Fifty or sixty yards was no uncommon distance between it and the spectators, and it was never seen except in weather the most calm and bright. But these facts, along with the various depositions, have been long laid before the public in the 'Report of the Committee of the Linnaean Society of New England', and it is our part now merely to adduce some corroborative circumstances which have lately occurred, and which *we* think puts the matter for ever beyond the possibility of a doubt;—facts which have already completely satisfied some highly scientific gentlemen, who before were entirely sceptical."

He next gives the letter from Mr. Warburton, of which we have spoken above, and the letter from Mr. Boott, parts of which we have inserted in n°. 63 and 70. After the different passages from various transactions and journals referring to the papers in Sir Joseph Banks' library, Dr. Hooker goes on:

"We sincerely hope that these few bare facts may satisfy all upon this much agitated question; at least we think they must remove the ideal connection between our serpent, and
"That sea-snake, enormous curled,
"Whose monstruous circle girds the world."
"It can now no longer be considered in association with hydras and mermaids, for there has been nothing said with regard to it inconsistent with reason. It may at least be assumed as a sober fact in Natural History quite unconnected with the gigantic exploits of the God Thor, or the fanciful absurdities of the Scandinavian mythology. We cannot suppose, that the most ultra-sceptical can now continue to doubt with regard to facts attested by such highly respectable witnesses."

It is a deplorable fact that all the endeavours of such an eminent scientist to convince zoologists of the existence of sea-serpents, have been in vain!

German translations of the whole of Dr. Hooker's paper as well as of the letters from Dr. Boott and Mr. Warburton are in Froriep's *Notizen*, of April, 1827, Vol. XVII, n°. 356, p. 49.

In the *American Journal of Science and Arts*, Vol. XII, June 1827, the editor, Prof. Benjamin Silliman, says:

"To us it seems a matter of surprise, that any person who has examined the testimony, can doubt the existence of the Sea-Serpent; the documents communicated by Dr. Bigelow of Boston, and published in the second volume of this Journal, in 1820, were in our judgment alone sufficient, to settle the question: the following letter is an important additional document."

This is the letter from Mr. Warburton to Mr. Barclay, reprinted evidently from the *Edinb. Journal* (n°. 83, 84).

85.—1827, August 24.—According to Froriep's *Notizen* Vol. XIX, n°. 409, p. 193,

"the *Norwegische Handelszeitung*" (apparently of the 3d. or 4th. of September, 1827), "contains fresh intelligence of the Sea-Serpent, which confirms what has been published by Captain de Capell Brooke."

"In the last days of the last month an animal was seen by several trustworthy men in Christianiafjord, which, according to the description, appears to be a sea-serpent of extraordinary dimensions. On the 1st of this month five eyewitnesses were heard before the justice of peace, and according to their agreeing declarations, the animal held its head, which was dark and black, above the surface of the water, and showed at least ten coils; there was a distance of about twenty ells" (60 feet) "between each two coils, and the coils themselves were about six ells" (18 feet) "so that the total length of the animal may be estimated at 250 ells" (750 feet). It moved with about the swiftness of a common boat, rowed by a man in still water, and caused a heavy rushing, like a strong motion in the water. The thickness was about that of a large wine-barrel or pipe. No tail, nor fins were observed. The rushing, it is believed, was caused by the head. The coils were movable, i. e. what was above the water one moment, was under it the next. Two eye-witnesses also declared, that what they saw, was one coherent whole and were not several animals. On Friday, the 24th. of August, at 10 o'clock A. M. the animal was seen moving from the Vakkerö-Bay into the Bonnefjord. The animal was seen from a distance of 200 fathoms."

Although the dimensions are exaggerated, the other features of the animal, viz. the head which is dark and black, and held above the water, the undulating motion of the animal, its visible coils, the rushing sound made by it, the apparent want of fins and the tail, which were hidden under water, are correct and known to us.

86.—1827, August 26.—(The same journal, the same issue).
"And on Sunday, the 26th. of August at 7 o'clock in the evening it came again from the fjord and swam towards the shipwharf, passing Liob-, and Principal-Islands.—It was then seen from a distance of 120 fathoms. The eye-witnesses declared, that, if asked, they were ready to make oath to those declarations."

87.—1827, September 3.—(The same journal, the same issue).—
Christiania, Sept. 5.—The sea-serpent, mentioned in the Monday-number, has been seen again the day before yesterday off Nusodden."

88.—1827, September 5.—(The same journal, the same issue).
"and to-day, off Lepager, by persons just a trustworthy as those who were heard before the justice. Their affidavit in principal points agrees with that of the former. A reward is offered to whoever will kill it and bring it home."

89.—1827, September 59.—(The same journal, the same issue).
"Christiania, September 15.—Sunday last the sea-serpent appeared also off Dröbak. Last week several persons saw large shoals of porpoises, and therefore supposed that the alleged presence of the former could not be true. But as among those who saw the sea-serpent, are many fishermen and seamen, who know very well how to distinguish the several sea-animals, and as it is not at all uncommon, that porpoises and whales of the smaller kind appear here in the fjord, so there is no reason to condemn the judicial concurrent testimonies."

90, 91.—1828? The well-known Mr. Heinrich Rathke, when on a journey in Norway, noted down the following evidence, which he published in the *Archiv für Naturgeschichte* of 1841.
"Nils Roe, workman at Mr. William Knutszon's, an elderly and simple man, relates: I saw the serpent twice, once at noon, and two days afterwards towards the evening, in the fjord" (near Christiansund) "at the back of Mr. Knutszon's garden. The first time, when it was nearest to me, it was about a hundred feet distant. It swam first along the fjord, afterwards over against the spot, where I stood. I then observed it for more than half an hour. Some strangers, who were on the opposite shore, fired at it, when it disappeared."

"The second time it was farther from me. It was small, perhaps twice as long as this room (about forty-four feet); while swimming it made serpentine movements, some to left and right, others up and down. I cannot state its correct thickness, but it appeared to be about as a common snake in proportion to its length. It was much thinner towards the tail. Several times it raised its head wholly above the water, but so, that it was just above the surface; the neck, however, and the other part of the body were but partly visible above the surface. The front of the head was rather pointed: the eyes were very large and glistened like those of a cat. I did not see a tongue and did not observe that it opened its mouth. I cannot state that the neck just behind the head is much thinner than the head itself, for from the back of the head commenced a mane like that of a horse, which waved to and fro in the water. Just behind the head the mane was thickest and got thinner further backwards; in general it was not very long. The colour of the animal was a blackish brown."

Again we meet with no character that is not known to us. All of them have already been stated.

92.—1829?—The following is an evidence given before the same Mr. Rathke, being at Christiansund, and published by him in the journal mentioned above.

"Lars Johnöen, a fisherman at Smölen, about 50 years of age. I have seen the sea-serpent several times, but for the longest time and nearest to me, twelve years ago in the dog-days in the fjord not far from here (Christiansund), when I was alone, one noon, angling in a boat. Then I saw it within two hours three times for a considerable time, quite near to me. It came close to my boat, so that it was only about six feet from me. (He placed himself in the room at a distance of nearly six feet from the wall, and said, this was about the distance between him and the serpent.) I became alarmed, recommended my soul to God, laid myself down in the boat, and only held my head so far over it, that I could observe the serpent. It swam now past the boat, that was vehemently agitated by the ripple caused by its movements in the water, which was previously smooth as a mirror, and afterwards took itself off. After it had swam a considerable distance from me, I wound my angling line round the little instrument commonly used (a frame, moving on an axis) and I began again to fish. Not long afterwards, however, the serpent came again quite close to the boat, which again was violently agitated by the movements made by it in the water. I lay down again, and remained quite still, keeping, however, a watchful eye on the animal. Again it passed me, disappeared far off, and returned, though not so close as before, and at last disappeared, when a light wind rose, and ruffled the water. Notwithstanding my fright I yet observed the animal very accurately. Its length was about five to six fathoms, and the body, which was as round as a snake's, was about two feet in diameter. (Lars Johnöen measured on a table before him with his hands a space of about two feet). The tail too appeared to me to be round. The head was about as long and as thick as a brandy anker (a ten gallon cask), it was not pointed but bluntly round. The eyes were very large and glistening. Their size (or diameter) was about that of this box here (five inches), and they were as red as my neckerchief (crimson). The animal did not open its mouth, therefore I cannot give its size. It constantly held its head above the surface of the water in an acute angle; not so high, however, that the nose should come over the board of a boat. Close behind the head, a mane like a horse's commenced, extending rather far down the neck, and spreading on both sides; floated on the water; it was of tolerably long hair. The mane as well as the head and the rest of the body was brown as this looking glass frame (dark brown of old mahogany). I could not observe spots, or stripes of other colours, nor were there any scales; it seemed as if the body was quite smooth. The movements of the serpent were by turns fast and slow; they were also slow when the animal approached my boat. At the moment in which I could observe it best, its movements were serpentine, up and down. The few undulations, made by those parts of the body and the tail that were out of the water, were scarcely a fathom in length. These undulations were not so high, that I could see between them and the water.—When Lars Johnöen had given this declaration, the drawing which Pontoppidan had given of the animal was shown to him. He looked at it with astonishment, smiled and said that he saw a great resemblance between it and the animal he had seen. He likewise said, that some of the other sea-serpents he had seen were a great deal longer than the one described above."

This unvarnished account describes very well the animal's general doings, and accurately pictures its curiosity and harmlessness.

93.—1829, July.—We shall soon be acquainted with the appearance of the sea-serpent seen by Captain M'Quhae of the *Daedalus*, in Aug. 6, 1848. Prof. Richard Owen, questioned whether this animal could be a snake or not, gave his answer in an article published in the *Times* of Nov. 11, 1848, wherein he expresses his opinion that it must have been a large seal. This article seems to have been reprinted in the *Bombay Bi-monthly Times*. In the same journal for January, 1849, appeared the following statement and objections against Professor Owen's suggestions.

"I see, in your paper of the 30th December, a paragraph in which a doubt is expressed of the authenticity of the account given by Captain M'Quhae of the 'great sea-serpent'. When returning to India, in the year 1829, I was standing on the poop of the *Royal Saxon*, in conversation with Captain Petrie, the commander of that ship. We were at a considerable distance south-west of the Cape of Good Hope, in the usual track of vessels to this country, going rapidly along (seven or eight knots) in fine smooth water. It was in the middle of the day, and the other passengers were at luncheon; the man at the wheel, a steerage passenger, and ourselves, being the only persons on the poop. Captain Petrie and myself, at the same instant, were literally fixed in astonishment by the appearance, a short distance ahead, of an animal of which no more generally correct description could be given than that by Captain M'Quhae. It passed within thirty-five yards of the ship, without altering its course in the least; but as it came right abreast of us, it slowly turned its head towards us. Apparently about one third of the upper part of its body was above water, in nearly its whole length; and we could see the water curling up on its breast as it moved along, but by what means it moved we could not perceive. We watched it going astern with intense interest until it had nearly disappeared, when my companion, turning to me with a countenance expressive of the utmost astonishment, exclaimed, 'Good heavens! what can that be?' It was strange that we never thought of calling the party engaged at luncheon to witness the extraordinary sight we had seen; but the fact is, we were so absorbed in it ourselves, that we never spoke, and scarcely moved, until it had nearly disappeared. Captain Petrie, a superior and most intelligent man, has since perished in the exercise of his profession. Of the fate of the others then on deck I am ignorant; so the story rests on my own unsupported word, but I pledge that word to its correctness. Professor Owen's supposition, that the animal seen by the officers of the *Daedalus* was a gigantic seal, I believe to be incorrect, because we saw this apparently similar creature in its whole length, with the exception of a small portion of the tail, which was under water; and, by comparing its length with that of the *Royal Saxon* (about six hundred feet), when exactly alongside in passing, we calculated it to be in that, as well as in its other dimensions, greater than the animal described by Captain M'Quhae. Should the foregoing account be of any interest to you, it is at your service; it is an old story, but a true one. I am not quite sure of our latitude and longitude at the time, nor do I exactly remember the date, but it was about the end of July.—R. Davidson, Superintending Surgeon, Nagpore Subsidiary Force, Kamptee, 3d January 1849."

At present we have only to fix our attention on the animal's appearance, and not on Mr. Davidson's objections. As the reader will observe, the whole description agrees with other accounts already given. There is nothing in it that is new or unknown to us.

94.—1830?—The well-known Mr. Heinrich Rathke, on his journey in Norway, being in Christiansund, noted down the following evidence, to publish it in the *Archiv für Naturgeschichte* of 1841.

"John Johnson, merchant, about 60 years of age, says in German: I saw the animal some years ago in the fjord" (of Christiansund); "it was about a thousand paces distant, when nearest to me; I observed it for more than half an hour. It swam very swiftly, for in the same time that we rowed about a quarter of a mile aside of it, it had swum about one half of a mile. I saw it best when it swam in a semicircle round a tolerable large rock that obstructed its passage, coming to that side of it which was turned towards me; in doing this it partly raised itself above the surface of the water. Its colour was blackish; its length was about that of this house (55 feet). Except the head, I did not observe much of its body, as it appeared but little above the surface. Judging from what I observed now and then, I think its thickness to be that of a stout man's body. Its head was apparently as large as a hat. It was not pointed, but seemed rather blunt; in general, however, in comparison with its thickness, it was not very long. It was held but little above the surface of the water, making an acute angle with it; and it remained above the surface, as long as I saw it. Owing to the distance I could not discern the eyes. Also on account of the distance or because the neck was seldom elevated above the surface, I could observe nothing of a mane. The agitation which it caused in the water was very strong. The movements of the animal itself were serpentine, up and down, like those of a swimming leech. When the animal had reached a spot, where the water was ruffled by a rising gentle wind, it disappeared. Moreover, I believe, that the animal is not much to be feared and that it would not easily harm men."

95.—1831?—The same Mr. Rathke also noted down the following declaration (published in the above mentioned journal.)

"Mr. William Knutszon and Candidatus Theologiae Booklune gave the following written account: We together saw the sea-serpent in a narrow fjord, at a distance of about one sixteenth of a mile" (about 515 yards) "for about a quarter of an hour; afterwards it dived, and came up so far from us, that we could not see it plainly. The water was as smooth as a mirror, and the animal had, as it moved on the surface, quite the appearance of a worm, or of a snake. Its motions were in undulations, and so strong that white foam appeared before it, and waves were caused at its sides, which extended over several fathoms. It did not appear very high above the water, and it was principally its length, which was quite considerable. Once, however, it stretched its head quite erect in the air. The body was somewhat dark, and the head nearly black; the body had nearly the form of an eel or of a snake, a length of about fifty ells" (above one hundred feet) "and in proportion to it an inconsiderable thickness. The breadth diminished considerably from the head to the tail, so that the latter ended in a point. The head was long and narrow in proportion to the throat, as the latter appeared much greater than the former, which probably was the consequence of its being provided with a mane. The details of the head were not to be discerned, as the distance was too great."

I may observe here that if these eye-witnesses declare that the head seemed to be narrower than the throat, this may probably also be the consequence of the animal's contracting its neck. This may be often seen in seals and sea-lions. If a common seal has contracted its neck, it appears as if the animal has no neck, as if the head is immediately connected with the body. In reality the neck is shortened, and has become thicker than the head. If stretched, the neck on the contrary is very well visible, and narrower than the head. The same in sea-lions. If contracted, several rings of blubber surround the hind part of the head, which appears smaller than the neck; if stretched, the neck immediately gets much narrower and the head is broader than the neck. The expression "which probably was the consequence of its being provided with a mane" distinctly shows that the eye-witnesses, knowing that others at other times saw a mane, intended to explain the phenomenon they observed by the presence of this mane, which they could impossibly see, "as the distance was too great."

96.—1832, Summer.—(Froriep's *Notizen*, XXXV, n . 750). "There is again question in Norway of the sea-serpent. It is said to have appeared and remained rather a long time in the Rödö- and Södelöw fjords this summer, and to have been seen by many persons. Distinct traces of it are said to have been found in the fields (??)."

We observe that Mr. Froriep adds two notes of interrogation after the last words. Evidently he is unable to explain them. I am convinced of the truth that the sea-serpent appeared in the fjords above mentioned. As to the traces of it, I must tell my readers that the superstition of the Norwegian people has forged this fable ever since they first became aware that the sea-serpent frequented their fjords. We have already met with this tale in Pontoppidan's *Natural History of Norway*, and probably the Norwegians will tell it us again, if we ask them now!

97.—1833, May, 15.—(*Zoologist* p. 1714, 1847).

"On the 15th. of May, 1833, a party, consisting of Captain Sullivan, Lieutenants Maclachlan and Malcolm of the Rifle Brigade, Lieutenant Lyster of the Artillery, and Mr. Ince of the Ordnance, started from Halifax in a small yacht for Mahone Bay, some forty miles eastward, on a fishing excursion. The morning was cloudy, and the wind at S. S. E., and apparently rising. By the time we reached Chebucto Head, as we had taken no pilot with us, we deliberated whether we should proceed or turn back; but, after a consultation, we determined on the former, having lots of ports on our lee. Previous to our leaving town, an old man-of-war's-man we had along with us busied himself in inquiries as to our right course; he was told to take his departure from the Bull Rock, off Pennant Point, and that a W. N. W. course would bring us direct on Iron Bound Island, at the entrance of Mahone or Mecklenburgh Bay. He, however, unfortunately told us to steer W. S. W., nor corrected his error for five or six hours; consequently we had gone a longe distance off the coast. We had run about half the distance, as we supposed, and were enjoying ourselves on deck, smoking our cigars, and getting our tackle ready for the approaching campaign against the salmon, when we were surprised by the sight of an immense shoal of grampuses, which appeared in an unusual state of exitement, and which in their gambols approached so close to our little craft, that some of the party amused themselves by firing at them with rifles. At this time we were jogging on at about five miles an hour, and must have been crossing Margaret's Bay. I merely conjecture where we were, as we had not seen land since a short time after leaving Pennant Bay. Our attention was presently diverted from the whales and 'such small deer', by an exclamation from Dowling, our man-of-war's-man, who was sitting to leeward, of, 'Oh sirs, look here!' We were started into a ready compliance, and saw an object which banished all other thoughts, save wonder and surprise."

"At the distance of from a hundred and fifty to two hundred yards on our starboard bow, we saw the head and neck of some denizen of the deep, precisely like those of a common snake, in the act of swimming, the head so far elevated and thrown forward by the curve of the neck, as to enable us to see the water under and beyond it. The creature rapidly passed, leaving a regular wake, from the commencement of which, to the fore part, which was out of water, we judged its length to be about eighty feet, and this within, rather than beyond the mark. We were, of course, all taken aback at the sight, and, with staring eyes and in speechless wonder, stood gazing at it for full half a minute. There could be no mistake, no delusion, and we were all perfectly satisfied that we had been favoured with a view of the 'true and veritable sea-serpent', which had been generally considered to have existed only in the brain of some Yankee skipper, and treated as a tale not much entitled to belief. Dowling's exclamation is worthy of record. 'Well, I've sailed in all parts of the world, and have seen rum sights too in my time, but this is the queerest thing I ever see!' and surely Jack Dowling was right. It is most difficult to give correctly the dimensions of any object in the water. The head of the creature we set down at about six feet in length, and that portion of the neck which we saw at the same; the extreme length, as before stated, at between eighty and one hundred feet. The neck in thickness equalled the bole of a moderate-sized tree. The head and neck of a dark brown or nearly black colour, streaked with white in irregular streaks. I do not recollect seeing any part of the body."

"Such is the rough account of the sea-serpent, and all the party who saw it are still in the land of the living,—Lyster in England, Malcolm in New South Wales with his regiment, and the remainder still vegetating in Halifax."

"W. Sullivan, Captain, Rifle Brigade, June 21, 1881.
"A. Maclachlan, Lieutenant, ditto, August 5, 1824.
"G. P. Malcolm, Ensign, ditto, August 13, 1830.
"B. O'Neal Lyster, Lieut. Artillery, June 7, 1816.
"Henry Ince, Ordnance Storekeeper at Halifax."

Mr. Newman, the editor of the *Zoologist* adds between parentheses:
"The dates are those on which the gentlemen received their respective Commission, I am not aware of their present rank. I am indebted to Mr. W. H. Ince for this interesting communication: this gentleman received it from his brother, Commander J. M. R. Ince, R. N. It is written by their uncle, Mr. Henry Ince, the Ordnance store-keeper at Halifax, Nova Scotia."—

We observe that the colour of the head and neck is described as "streaked with white in irregular streaks", and that evidently the sea-serpent hunted after the grampuses "which appeared in an unusual state of excitement".

This account translated into German is in Froriep's *Notizen*, Third Series, III, n°. 54, p. 148.

98, 99.—1833, July.—In Froriep's *Notizen* of June 1834 we read that Prof. Benjamin Silliman in a note to Mr. Bakewell's *Introduction to Geology*, stated that

"since 1820 nearly each year the mass of evidences has increased, and that the current year 1833 has been particularly fertile in such reports."

Dr. Hamilton in his *Amphibious Carnivora*, 1839, says:

"The last notice we have seen of this American animal bears date July 1833. The Boston and New York papers of that date state, that the Sea-Serpent had again appeared off Nahant. 'It was first seen on Saturday afternoon, passing between Egg-Rock and the Promuntory, winding his way into Lynn-Harbour, and again on Sunday morning, heading for South-shores. He was seen by forty or fifty ladies and gentlemen, who insist that they could not have been deceived'."

It is evident that many reports of great sea-serpents have been published here and there, especially in Norwegian and North American newspapers, which I have had no opportunity to consult, and which probably will never come within my reach. As we learn from Mr. Froriep's *Notizen*, Vol. XL, n°. 879, p. 328, "Mr. R. Bakewell in the latest edition of his Introduction to Geology (1833?) states: that there are descriptions of the sea-serpent, wherein it is ascertained that it 'has flappers like sea-turtles'." I have not been able to consult Mr. Bakewell's work, but I insert this statement here, because we shall observe afterwards more than once this comparison of the flappers with analogous members of turtles.

100.—1834, Summer.—In Captain Shibbles' report (n°. 101) a passage runs as follows:
"One of the crew told us that his appearance and motion are precisely like that he saw last summer while in the bay" (of Gloucester) "which was said to be a sea-serpent."
Though no particulars are mentioned, I am convinced that the appearance took place.

101.—1835, March or April.—(*Amer. Journ. Sc. Arts* Vol. 28, 1835, July.—)
"Captain Shibbles, of the brig Mangehan, of Thomastown, from Boston, for New-Orleans, which arrived here (Gloucester, Mass., March or April, 1835) on Saturday last, states that he saw when about nine or ten miles from Race Point light, what he, as well as the whole crew, supposed to be a sea-serpent,—he could distinctly see it with the naked eye, but to be certain, he took his glass and saw his eyes, neck and head, which was about as large as a barrel—the neck had something that looked like a mane upon the top of it; several times he raised his head seven or eight feet above the water, and for thirty or forty minutes he swam backward and forward with great swiftness. There were two other vessels near, the crews of which were in the rigging looking at the same object. Capt. S. states that it was very long, and that his head, neck and tail and his motion in the water, was exactly like those of a snake; every time he put his head out of water, he made a noise similar to that of steam escaping from the boiler of a steam-boat..... The Captain and crew attest to the correctness of this statement."
As to the swimming backward and forward, I think that Captain Shibbles meant that the animal swam to and fro, and that he used these expressions in reference to the direction of the brig.

102.—1836?—Mr. Heinrich Rathke published in the *Archiv für Naturgeschichte* the following evidence, which he noted down when being in Christiansund in Norway:
"The *Sorenskriver* Gaeschke (a kind of judge of the same rank as the German country-judges, or the British sheriffs) gave me the following evidence: I saw the sea-serpent for a considerable time in a small fjord, first from a boat, afterwards from the beach, and from there during several minutes, at a distance of from thirty to thirty-six feet. In the beginning it swam round the fjord at Torvig, afterwards it went towards the mouth of the fjord. I saw its head stretched considerably out of the water. I noticed as well two or three undulations of the forepart of the body. Its motion was not like that of an eel, but consisted in vertical undulations. They were so strong, that they caused rather large waves; they were largest at the forepart of the animal and gradually lessened towards the back. The traces of them I discerned in a length of eight to ten fathoms, and in a breadth of two or three fathoms. The head, apparently blunt in front, had the size and nearly also the shape of an anker (ten-gallon cask) and the visible coils of the body were round and their thickness was that of a good timberstock (twelve to fourteen inches square). I could not judge the entire length of the animal, as I could not discern the animal's hindpart. The colour of the animal seemed to me to be a very dark

grey one. What I believed to be the eyes, had according to my estimation the size of the outlines of a tea-cup (3 1/2 inches). At the back of the head there was a mane, which had the same colour as the rest of the body."

103.—1837, end of July.—(Froriep's *Neue Notizen*, Vol. IV, n°. 67, p. 7, October, 1837).

"About the much mentioned Sea-Serpent the Drontheim Newspaper contains, as is ascertained, from an enlightened and trustworthy gentleman, the following statement: "Uncommonly early in this Summer our coasts and fjords were blessed with a mass of fat herrings, of which till to-day very few were cleaned and pickled, because the uncommon greasiness of the herrings made it difficult to preserve them in the warm air, which, however, was so beneficient to agriculture. Since the beginning of the dog-days the sea-serpent appeared on different spots in this country; one of these sea-monsters seems to have constantly remained near Storfosen and the Krovaag Isles; several fishermen were terrified in the highest degree, when the sea-serpent suddenly came down so near to them, that they had no time to think, to which side they should fly. It is true this terrible visitor properly has not made an attack, but it has followed the boat for a long distance, when one has tried to fly in a great hurry, so that the men overworked themselves, and some of the runaways fell ill afterwards. It is ascertained by quite trustworthy persons, that the length of the sea-serpent may be estimated from 600 to 800 ells, or perhaps still more, because if one was near its head, the other end of the sea-animal was not to be discerned distinctly. The sea-serpent is thickest just behind the head, apparently as thick as a large horse; its black and dark eyes are as large as an ordinary plate, without being glossy or very movable; the skin is smooth and of a dark colour; on the nose there are thick hairs, as on a seal's, two or three quarters of an ell long, also on the neck there is something movable, which resembles the mane of a horse; the mouth, as far as the writer knows, has not been seen distinctly, and it is quite uncertain whether the animal is a beast of prey or not. Rarely does the sea-serpent appear but in calm weather; its motions and shape are serpentine. These observations are distinctly made in these days, amongst others by a trustworthy and intelligent gentleman, who with his two sons had reached a small islet, where the sea-serpent, after having followed their boat, passed closely and slowly."

Those who made the statement that when they were near the head, the tail could not be discerned distinctly, of course, spoke the truth, for the tail is very seldom above water, but they who afterwards thereby imagined that the animal therefore must have a length of from 600 to 800 ells, exaggerated in a most ridiculous manner. Again we observe that the Norwegian fishermen are in great dread of the sea-serpent, and the description of their behaviour is quite the same as told us Pontoppidan a century ago. Again we read of the habit of the sea-serpent of following boats, but never attacking them, which may only be the effect of mere curiosity. The description, moreover, given by the not mentioned trustworthy and intelligent observer is quite correct. All the characters given by him are already known to us, and where he states that the eyes are not glossy, apparently in contradiction with former statements, it is natural that in a certain direction and in certain moments they need not give the impression of being so. Remarkable is the statement of the animal having bristles on its upper-lips, as in seals.

In Dr. Hamilton's *Amphibious Carnivora*, 1839, we read:

"The most recent account of this monster we have noticed, appeared in the public Newspapers of Drontheim, in the autumn of 1837, and we confess we cannot regard it as a sheer fabrication".

And he further cites the above mentioned report and tells us that it was the *Adis* of Drontheim which contained those particulars. The Krovaag Islands are called by Dr. Hamilton the Kerchvang Islands, and strange enough, the very interesting particulars about the skin, the eyes and the bristles on the upper lips near the nose are omitted.

104.—1838?—The reader will soon be made acquainted with the well known report of Captain M'Quhae, of the *Daedalus*. As the report was published in the newspapers of Oct., 1848, Captain Beechy, of the *Blossom*, "one of the most scientific officers and ablest naval surveyors", wrote a letter to Mr. Francis Beaufort, F. R. S., Admiralty Hydrographer. An extract from this letter appeared in the *Illustrated London News* of Oct. 28, 1848, and runs as follows:

"What an extraordinary creature the *Daedalus* seems to have fallen in with! The description recalls to my mind an extraordinary appearance we witnessed in the *Blossom*, in crossing the South Atlantic: I took it for the trunk of a large tree, and before I could get my glass upon deck it had disappeared, and I could nowhere find it—fresh breezes at the time."

As Captain Beechy writes "recalls to my mind", the "extraordinary appearance" must have taken place some time ago, say ten years; so I have chosen the year 1838, as the year in which it happened. If I may ever get the opportunity to learn the exact year or date, I shall be glad to correct my supposition in an eventual second edition. But for the present I am sure that the "trunk of a large tree" which had so suddenly disappeared, really was a sea-serpent.

Repeatedly we have already quoted Dr. Hamilton's work about the *Amphibious Carnivora*, which appeared in the year 1839. The writer sums up numerous reports and accounts, which he cited from other works, or from which he gave only short extracts. One would say that Dr. Hamilton is an unbeliever, for he ends his chapter on this animal with the words:

"With these extracts, and without farther comment, we close our account of the Great Sea-Serpent, only remarking, that till favouring circumstances bring the animal under the examination of Naturalists, the satisfaction, which is desiderated respecting it, is scarcely to be expected."

I only ask, what then was the reason that he spoke of it, and that he published these extracts in a book, which properly treated of Amphibious Carnivora or the Pinnipeds (seals, walrusses, sea-lions and sea-bears)? May it be, that he observed any relation between them and the sea-serpent? I cannot believe it, for after the sea-serpent he treats of the Kraken in the same volume. And why did he end in such a vague way? May it be, because he could not give an explanation, or because he hesitated to show the public that he was really a believer?

105.—1839, August?—According to Froriep's *Neue Notizen*, vol. XII, n°. 248, of Oct., 1839, the *Boston Mercantile* mentions that Mr. Bubier, Lieutenant of the U. S. Navy affirms to have seen the sea-serpent on his way from Daims Island to Nahant, near Boston, and estimated its length at 120 to 135 feet.

106.—1839.—In the same periodical on the same page we read that Captain Smith who had been a long time in the whale fishery, asserts in the *Kennebek Journal*, that he never before saw such a creature, and that if he had had a harpoon and lines on board, he would have harpooned it.

106, A.—1840, April 21.—(*Journal du Havre*, 1840, Sept. 15, *Zoologist*, 1847, p. 1716).—As I have not had the opportunity to consult the first paper, I give the account as I have found it in the *Zoologist*.

"A French captain has just related to us a remarkable circumstance, which he has himself witnessed, and his recital exhibits a degree of cautious reserve, which is well calculated to shake the obstinacy of the most sceptical. We shall preface his narrative by the remark that the sea serpent has been recently alleged to have been seen at different points along the whole line of the American coast. Captain d'Abnour, commander of the Ville de Rochefort, makes the following statements:

"On the 21st. of April, 1840, while we were in 24 deg. 13 min. N. latitude, and 89 deg. 52 min. W. longitude (calculated from the meridian of Paris), in the gulf of Mexico, we were running under a light breeze from E. N. E. with beautiful weather. In a few hours we distinguished something like a long chain of rocks, falling off by a gentle inclination at the two extremities, and elevated at the middle by only a few feet over the level of the sea. Against this object the sea broke softly. As we approached we remarked that its different parts changed their position, and even their form, and we became perfectly certain that it was not a reef. A little later, we distinguished by the assistance of a telescope a long chain of enormous rings, resembling a number of barrels linked together, and in form very like the back of a silk worm. It was a three quarter view of the object which we had first obtained. As the ship approached, these appearances became more distinct, and we presently saw the extremity of an enormous tail, longitudinally divided into two sections, white and black. This tail appeared to wind itself up, and repose on a part of the object itself. Then, at the other extremity, we saw a membrane rising to the height of about two *metres* from the water, and inclining itself at a considerable angle upon the mass (without leaving it, however); and this led me to conjecture that the monster before us was provided with an apparatus for the purpose of respiration, like the lampreys. At last we perceived something like an *antenna* rising from the water, to the great height of nearly eight *metres*, terminated by a crescent of at least five *metres* from one extremity to the other. We could not approach sufficiently near to acquire any very positive idea as to what we had seen; but everything led us to believe that it was an enormous serpent of at least 100 *metres* in length."

Although the editors of the *Journal du Havre* believed that Captain D'Abnour by his "exhibiting a degree of cautious reserve would shake the obstinacy of the most sceptical", I think that on the contrary his narrative has had quite another effect. Every sceptic, I think, will smile or even laugh when he reads this report, for who can help laughing when he reads of a "membrane which led me to conjecture that the monster before us was provided with an apparatus for the purpose of respiration, like the lampreys", and of an "antenna of eight metres, terminated by a crescent of at least five metres from one extremity to the other." We find here several limbs enumerated, and mentioned by the names of the corresponding limbs of different classes of the animal kingdom. A "membrane" in my opinion is a thin and transparent or nearly transparent planely extended object. If what the captain saw was one, I don't know what it could be. If not, if untransparent, how could they see from such a great distance, that it was thin; what reason was there to call it a "membrane"?

I am convinced that Captain d'Abnour really saw a sea-serpent. The animal lay extended on the surface of the water, nearly still, showing numerous bunches; head and tail being under water and invisible. Quite the same thing was afterwards witnessed by Captain Weisz, of the *Kätie* (n°. 154, fig. 50). We know that sea-serpents lying still may show coils or bunches or hillocks. It resembled "a long chain of rocks, falling off by a gentle inclination at the two extremities, and elevated at the middle by only a few feet over the level of the sea". The sea broke gently against it. As they approached, the animal seen through a telescope had the appearance of "a long chain of numerous rings, resembling a number of barrels linked together". We remember that this comparison has often been made by different witnesses. The other comparison of the captain, viz.: "in form very like the back of a silk worm" is also tolerably well chosen. "As the ship approached, these appearances became more distinct" and the sea-serpent raised in a playful manner "its enormous tail, longitudinally divided into two sections, white and black". We know that the animal's head and neck are longitudinally divided into two sections, dark brown or nearly black above, and white beneath. It is, therefore, probable that also the trunk has a dark back and a light coloured belly. The supposition of this division of colours had already been made by Mr. Matthew Gaffney (n°. 41, p. 169). It is, therefore, very remarkable that Captain d'Abnour really saw that the tail too is coloured black above and white beneath! The animal curled its tail and let it for a moment "repose on a part of" its body. Then, "at the other extremity" the animal elevated its foreflapper to the height of about two metres (six feet) from the water. The flapper "inclined itself at a considerable angle upon the" body, consequently the animal made the same movement with its foreflapper as the individual afterwards witnessed by Captain Weisz (n°. 154, fig. 50). At last a tail of a spermwhale or of a finwhale elevated above the water, "an antenna terminating in a crescent" "to the height of nearly eight metres" (about 25 feet), which tail of course has nothing at all to do with the sea-serpent. Captain d'Abnour says: that it rose "from the water" and he says nothing as to its relative position to the animal, nor whether it was close to or far from it. The length of at least 100 metres (about 320 feet) is at all events exaggerated. Evidently head and neck remained constantly under the water.

The above mentioned account, translated into German, is in Froriep's *Notizen, Third Series,* Vol. III, n°. 54, p. 148, 1847.

106B.—1840, June?—In the *Journal du Havre*, of 15th September, 1840, (see *Zoologist*, 1847, p. 1716,) we read:

"Not long since the *Boston Daily Advertiser* announced a new appearance of this marine monster, about whose existence the world is so naturally incredulous."

I do not think that I am wrong in fixing this appearance in the month of June of that year.

107.—1840, July?—In his Postscript Mr. Rathke (*Archiv für Naturgeschichte*, 1841, Vol. I) says:

"According to a letter addressed to me by Dr. Hoffmann, a respectable physician in Molde, which is situated several miles south of Christiansund on one of the largest fjords, the school-inspector Hammer, the adjunct Kraft, and some other persons, who in 1840 made together an excursion in a boat on this fjord, saw very distinctly a so-called sea-serpent of considerable length."

107 A.—1840, August?—The Editor of the *Journal du Havre* before publishing Capt. D'Abnour's report (n°. 106 A) says, (see *Zoologist*, 1847, p. 1715):

"We shall preface his narrative by the remark, that the sea-serpent has been recently alleged to have been seen, at different points along the whole line of the American coast."

The Editor would have done better if he had published all the reports of the sea-serpent, that had come within his reach. The reader must know that with the terms "the whole line of the American coast" the Editor can only have meant the east coast of British America and of the United States, from Newfoundland to Cape Canaveral, Florida.

108.—1841.—In a Postscript to his paper (*Archiv für Naturgeschichte*, 1841, Vol. I) Mr. Rathke tells us:

"According to a letter which I received some time ago from Mr. Soern Knutszon, a sea-serpent is again seen there some weeks after I had left Christiansund, by several persons."

The well known Mr. Heinrich Rathke in 1841 published in the *Archiv für Naturgeschichte*, 7th year, Vol. I, his dissertation "On the Sea-Serpent of the Norwegians". I am obliged to give a translation of his paper:

"On a journey which I made through Norway I availed myself of the opportunity of making inquiries after a hitherto problematical and even doubted animal, the so-called sea-serpent (Soe Orm in the language of the Norwegians). The most favourable opportunity offered in Christiansund, in the neighbourhood of which this animal is said to have often been observed. The general notices which I received about the sea-serpent, agree in the following points: It is mostly seen in the larger fjords of Norway, but seldom in the open sea. In the fjord of Christiansund, which has such a considerable extent, manifold ramifications, and in which numerous islets are found, it appears almost every year. It is said to have been especially observed in that part of the fjord on which the village of Lorvig is situated. This only happens in the warmest part of the year, viz. in the dog days, and only then when the weather is quite still and the surface of the water smooth. When after its appearance the water is ruffled, however slightly, it immediately disappears. Great is the dread of it, so that in the dog days many fishermen, otherwise intrepid, don't go far into the sea, without taking with them asa foetida, which is said to drive away the animal by its smell, when thrown into the water. Moreover the fishermen advise to be very quiet, when a sea-serpent approaches, and therefore rowing must be avoided, because the least noise attracts it still more."

"To have, however, more accounts than those general ones which are spread amongst the people, I wrote to several persons who were said to have seen it with their own eyes. Some of them who at the request of Soeren and Wilhelm Knudtszon Brothers, two distinguished and very intelligent merchants, paid me a visit, I questioned personally; for others I had put down several questions to which I received a written answer. I will communicate here the result of my inquiry."

Now Mr. Rathke publishes the affidavits which I have inserted above (n°. 90, 91, 92, 94, 95, 102), and his Postscript (see n°. 107 and 108).

"If one" Mr. Rathke goes on, "were to submit the above mentioned evidences to an inquiry, one would soon observe, that they not only contain several contradictory statements, but also that each evidence by itself cannot pretend to accuracy. Yet I believe, that we may at least admit so much of them, to be right, that what those persons who bear the evidences, took for a long animal, was really such a one. For I should not know, what could be the cause of the illusion, which had created the belief in such an animal. Some persons, as I know, believe that what has been taken for a so-called sea-serpent, was nothing else but a row of porpoises, swimming in a line. But all those persons by whom the above mentioned evidences are borne were too familiar with the sea, and had observed porpoises together too often to be deceived by a row of such animals swimming on the surface of the water. If this, however, had been the case, all the observations related to me of the sea-serpent holding its head above the surface, and about its size, must have been mere fictions, and this I cannot believe. According to all this, it evidently cannot be doubted that there is a long serpentine animal in the sea of Norway, which may grow to a considerable length."

Now Mr. Rathke weighs and considers to what kind of animals the sea-serpent may belong. This, however, we omit here, as we have partly discussed these views in our Chapter on Would-be Sea-Serpents, where we spoke of the Animal of Stronsa, and as we shall once more refer to it in our Chapter of Explanations.

Every one, I think, will agree with me, that Mr. Rathke has committed two faults. 1. He criticises the correctness of the statements in question, apparently without having taken the trouble to read all that had been written about the subject. If he had done so, he would never have said that the particulars of the evidences collected by him in Norway were sometimes contradictory; on the contrary, he would have observed that they completed one another! 2. He was the first scientific man and zoologist who had an opportunity to see the sea-serpent, probably even to kill it, and yet he returns to Germany without having made one single effort either to kill or to see it!

Immediately after Mr. Heinrich Rathke's dissertation, the Editor of the *Archiv für Naturgeschichte*, the well-known Prof. Dr. W. F. Erichson, wrote a paper, in which he gave full details of the Animal of Stronsa and descriptions of the saved bones. He ends this extract with the words:

"Consequently the Animal of Stronsa has no relation at all with the sea-serpent of the Norwegians; the animal, however, seen by the Rev. Maclean" (n°. 31) "might be considered as such an animal."

These words convince me of the fact that Mr. Erichson, like Mr. Rathke firmly believed that there are in the Norwegian seas animals still unknown to them, which are called "sea-serpents".

109.—1842?— (*Times*, Nov. 4, 1848).—

"A parish priest residing on Romsdal fjord, about two days journey south of Drontheim, an intelligent person, whose veracity I have no reason to doubt, gave me a circumstantial account of one, which he had himself seen. It rose within 30 yards of the boat in which he was, and swam parallel with it for a considerable time. Its head he described as equalling a small cask in size, and its mouth, which it repeatedly opened and shut, was furnished with formidable teeth; its neck was smaller, but its body—of which he supposed that he saw about half on the surface of the water—was not less in girth than that of a moderate sized horse." (Part of a letter from "Oxoniensis").—

110. 1842?— "Another gentleman, in whose house I stayed, had also seen one, and gave a similar account of it: it also came near his boat upon the fjord, when it was fired at, upon which it turned and pursued them to the shore, which was luckily near, when it disappeared" (Also a part of the letter from Oxoniensis, *Times*, Nov. 4, 1848).

111.—1843, Summer.—In Froriep's *Neue Notizen*, Vol. XXVIII, n°. 606, p. 184, Nov. 1843, we read:

"Some months ago the sea-serpent again appeared between the islets and inlets of the fjord of Christiansund."

111 A.—1843, October?—(Froriep's *Neue Notizen*, Vol. 28, n°. 606, p. 184).

"The Editors of the *Christiansands Posten* add the following remarks: "This whole description accurately fits on an appearance, which the writer of these lines has witnessed a few times in the North Sea, and when the inhabitants of the coast near Ibbestad, if not withheld by their fear of the supposed sea-monster, had rowed with their boats towards the animal, they would soon have observed without any doubt that the supposed intervals between the coils were nothing else but water."

The number of the *Christiansands Posten* was most probably one of the beginning of November or of the end of October. Consequently the appearance spoken of must have taken place some days before. At all events this is a proof of an appearance of the sea-serpent, swimming in vertical undulations, near Ibbestad, in Norway, at that time.

112, 113.—1845.—The report of Captain M'Quhae, which we shall meet with a little further on, induced Mr. J. D. Morries Stirling to write a letter on the sea-serpent to the Admiralty.

"By the courtesy" says the Editor of the *Illustrated London News* in his number of Oct., 28, 1848, "of the Secretary to the Admiralty, we have been favoured with the following letter from a gentleman long resident in Norway."

"13, Great Cumberland Street, October 25, 1848."

"My dear Sir,—I regret that I have not found the volumes referred to in our conversation respecting the recent authentication of the existence of the sea-serpent by Captain M'Quhae, of H. M. frigate Daedalus, but I will give you that part of the information which I remember best. Several years ago, a museum was established at Bergen, in Norway, the directors of which have, amongst other subjects of interest, turned their study to Natural History in general, and to the elucidation of some of its more doubtful or less known subdivisions. The question of the sea-serpent's existence had previously attracted the attention of several scientific men in Northern Europe; and my friend, the late Dr. Newmann, Bishop of Bergen—a man much and justly respected for his learning, research and energy—made it the subject of inquiry within the last twenty or twenty-five years among his clergy and those of the adjoining dioceses. The amount of proof thus collected was sufficient to convince any one, however sceptical, as it is not mere hearsay evidence, but the testimony of known and respectable persons in various walks of life. One of the most striking statements is made by some fishermen, who saw the animal quite close to them, and of whom one more hardy than the rest struck it with a boat-hook, upon which it immediately gave them chase; and, had they not been very near a small island or rock, on which they took refuge, in all probability they would have been destroyed."

"The size of the sea-serpents seen in the Norwegian fjords varies much; and I do not now remember what the dimensions of the largest are said to be. As far as I can tax my memory, none of them lately seen are larger than that described by Capt. M'Quhae. The one seen by the fishermen above alluded to, was, I think, not above 70 feet long. I have written to my colleagues in the direction of the Bergen Museum, and as soon as their answer arrives I will give you a more full account."

"There are I believe, several varieties of the reptile, known as the sea-serpent, but almost all the accounts agree as to the existence of a mane, and as to the great size of the eye. In several of the fossil reptiles somewhat approaching the sea-serpent in size and other characteristics, the orbit is very large; and in this respect, as well as having short paws or flappers, the descriptions of the northern sea-serpents agree with the supposed appearance of some of the antidiluvian species. A great part of the disbelief in the existence of the sea-serpent has arisen from its being supposed to be the same animal as the Kraken, or rather from the names having been used indiscriminately."

"In concluding this hurried statement, allow me to add my own testimony as to the existence of a large fish or reptile of cylindrical form. (I will not say sea-serpent.) Three years ago, while becalmed in a yacht between Bergen and Sogn in Norway, I saw (at about a quarter of a mile astern) what appeared to be a large fish ruffling the otherwise smooth surface of the fjord, and, on looking attentively, I observed what looked like the convolutions of a snake. I immediately got my glass, and distinctly made out three convolutions, which drew themselves slowly through the water. The greatest diameter was about ten or twelve inches. No head was visible; and from the size of each convolution, I supposed the length to be about thirty feet. The master of my yacht (who, as navigator, seaman, and fisherman, had known the Norwegian coast and North Sea for many years), as well as a friend who was with me, an experienced Norwegian sportsman and porpoise shooter, saw the same appearance at the same time, and formed the same opinion as to form and size. I mention my friend being a porpoise shooter, as many have believed that a shoal of porpoises following each other has given rise to the fable, as they called it, of the sea-serpent."

114.—1845 or 1846, Summer.—(Copied in the *Illustrated London News* of June, 13, 1857, from the *Cape Argus* of March, 14, 1857).

"Sir,—I inclose a letter addressed to me by a friend Dr. Biccard (with a drawing) containing an interesting account of the sea-serpent seen by him and others off the old lighthouse at the entrance of Table Bay on the 16th. of last month. It savours not a little of presumption to maintain that such a marine monster does exist, in the face of the deliberately recorded opinion of the greatest living Zoologist, Professor Owen, yet I venture to do so upon the simple testimony of my own eyes. In the year 1845, or 6, Mr. G. D. Brunette (of St. George's-street, the conveyancer) and myself were fishing at Camp's Bay one bright, clear summer day. There was not a breath of air, and the water was as smooth as the surface of a pond. About midday we were leaving the rocks to proceed to the marine villa, when Mr. Brunette suddenly directed my attention to what he at first thought was a whale. A moment's inspection was sufficient, however, to detect the real nature of the animal. At about a mile from the shore we saw a line of shining black objects, like a string of large casks, floating on the surface of the water, lying parallel with the shore. It kept gently bobbing up and down, and on one occasion we saw the whole length for a few seconds above the water. Judging from the size of an Indiaman, 1000 tons, at a similar distance, I should say the animal's length was from 150 to 200 feet. Of its girth I can form no estimate; but, from the show it made at so great a distance, it must have been at least three feet above the level of the sea. Nor could we distinguish head from tail, though near one extremity we saw what looked like foam or froth, as though the animal was blowing water in a lateral direction. It seemed to be basking in the warm sun, with no other motion than that I have described, or dipping under occasionally. After watching it for about a quarter of an hour we started for the villa, for the purpose of borrowing a telescope, but we had scarcely walked ten yards when we observed the animal turn slowly round and then made off in a straight line to seawards, towards the N. W. It moved at a rapid rate; so much so that when we got to the house and procured the glass it had reached such a distance that we could not distinguish it better than we had done with our naked eyes while on the rocks. The motion while moving off was undulatory, the cask like substances submerging and emerging from time to time, and glittering in the sun till we lost sight of them altogether, which was about an hour after first seeing the animal. That this animal was a sea-serpent I never had the slightest doubt; yet, knowing the general incredulity on this subject, neither Mr. Brunette nor myself cared much to boast of what we had seen, so we said nothing about it; but as Dr. Biccard has obligingly, at my request, furnished me with particulars, for general information, of the animal seen by him under such favourable circumstances, I am induced to add my own poor testimony to the many facts now on record, proving conclusively the existence of a great marine saurian or some similar animal. I would point out that a gentleman as Dr. Biccard's well known scientific attainments is not likely to mistake a seal for a serpent; and that the six or seven individuals who witnessed the evolutions of the animal at so short a distance as 200 yards could scarcely have been misled by a piece of seaweed, or by a seal."

"The narrative of Dr. Biccard will be read with interest, and I beg to refer those who feel any interest in it to an article on the Great Sea-Serpent in the Westminster Review for January 1849."

"Yours, &c.," "Chas. A. Fairbridge."
"Cape Town, 13th. March, 1857."

The above mentioned letter will be inserted in its right place hereafter, (n°. 130). It is clear enough that we have here an unvarnished account of an appearance of a true sea-serpent. The appearance of a line of shining black objects, like a string of large casks is a common one. Its length, estimated at upwards of 150 feet, is surely not exaggerated, as we shall observe afterwards. As the animal raised itself at least three feet above the level of the sea, its diameter may have been some fifteen feet. The animal evidently lay with its nostrils just at water-level, so that in exhaling it caused "a foam or froth, as though blowing water in a lateral direction". I think, that the observer was a little mistaken as to the direction, which cannot have been quite a lateral one.

115.—1845, July 28.—(*Zoologist*, 1847, p. 1606).
"The Rev. Mr. P. W. Deinbolt, Archdeacon of Molde, gives the following account of one, which was seen last summer near Molde. The 28th. of July, 1845, J. C. Lund, bookseller and printer; G. S. Krogh, merchant; Christian Flang, Lund's apprentice, and John Elgenses, labourer, were out on Romsdale-fjord, fishing. The sea was, after a warm, sunshiny day, quite calm. About seven o'clock in the afternoon, at a little distance from the shore, near the ballast place and Molde Hove, they saw a long marine animal, which slowly moved itself forward, as it appeared to them, with the help of two fins, on the fore-part of the body nearest the head, which they judged by the boiling of the water on both sides of it. The visible part of the body appeared to be between forty and fifty feet in length, and moved in undulations, like a snake. The body was round and of a dark colour, and seemed to be several ells (an ell two feet) in thickness. As they discerned a waving motion in the water behind the animal, they concluded that part of the body was concealed under water. That it was one connected animal they saw plainly from

its movement. When the animal was about one hundred yards from the boat, they noticed tolerably correctly its fore-part, which ended in a sharp snout; its colossal head raised itself above the water in the form of a semi-circle; the lower part was not visible. The colour of the head was dark brown and the skin smooth; they did not notice the eyes, or any mane or bristles on the throat. When the serpent came about a musket-shot near, Lund fired at it, and was certain the shots hit it in the head. After the shot it dived, but came up immediately. It raised its neck in the air, like a snake preparing to dart on his prey. After he had turned and got his body in a straight line, which he appeared to do with great difficulty, he darted like an arrow against the boat. They reached the shore, and the animal, perceiving it had come into shallow water, dived immediately and disappeared in the deep. Such is the declaration of these four men, and no one has cause to question their veracity, or imagine that they were so seized with fear that they could not observe what took place so near them. There are not many here, or on other parts of the Norwegian coast, who longer doubt the existence of the sea-serpent. The writer of this narrative was a long time sceptical, as he had not been so fortunate as to see this monster of the deep; but after the many accounts he has read, and the relations he has received from credible witnesses, he does not dare longer to doubt the existence of the sea-serpent."
"P. W. Deinbolt."
"Molde, 29th. Nov. 1845."

I need scarcely observe that the eye-witnesses of this appearance were deceived as to their opinion that the "boiling of the water on both sides of the head" was caused by "two fins on the forepart of the body, nearest the head". The two fore-flappers of the sea-serpent are situated at rather a great distance from the head. The animal has a very long neck. This assertion is proved by their own words: "it raised its neck in the air". If there were two fins near the head, large enough to cause any boiling of water, they would have been seen then by the persons, who would have mentioned them. The so called boiling of the water was nothing but the commonly observed rushing caused by the animal's motion through the water.

117.—1846, August 8.—(*Zoologist*, 1847, p. 1608).
"Sunds Parsonage, August 31, 1846."
"On Saturday, the 8th. inst., in the course between the islands of Sartor Leer and Tös, a sea-monster, supposed to be a sea-serpent, was seen by several persons. Early on this day as the steamer Biörgvin passed through Rognefjord towing a vessel to Bergen, Daniel Salomonson, a cotter, saw a sea-monster, whose like he declares he never met with although accustomed to the sea and its inhabitants from his earliest years. The animal came swimming from Rognefjord in a westerly direction towards his dwelling at Grönnevigskioeset, in the northern part of the parish of Sund. The head appeared like a Foering boat (about twenty feet long) keel uppermost, and from behind it raised itself forward in three, and sometimes four and five undulations, each apparently about twelve feet long: its rate appeared to be that of a light boat rowed by four active men. When it reached Grönnevigskioeset at a distance of two rifle-shots it turned with considerable noise and continued its course towards Lundenoes. Later about eleven o'clock on the

same day his wife Ingeborg, in Daniel's absence, heard a loud noise in the sea, and she and two little children saw a great sea monster, such as described above, take a northerly course, close by their place at such a rate that the waves were dashed on the shore in the same way as when a steamer is passing by. Neither of them say that they saw anything like eyes or fins, or indeed anything projecting from its round form, but they declare that the colour of the animal was dark brown, and that it often rose up with gentle undulations, sometimes, however, sinking below the surface so that merely a stripe indicated the rapid course of the gigantic body.— On the same morning a lad, by name Abraham Abrahamsen Hagenoes, was out fishing in the Rognefjord, not far from Lundenoes, and just ready to throw out his line, when he, as he asserts, became aware that on about one hundred fathoms a monster with a head as large as a Foering boat (about twenty feet long) and a long body lay upon the sea like large kegs and was nearing his boat: seized with a panic he exerted all his strength to reach the shore, and as the animal, apparently following him, was only about forty fathoms off, he leaped ashore, drew up the boat and ran up the bank, whence he viewed the monster which had by this time approached the shore within twenty fathoms. He says that that part of the body which was visible was about sixty feet in length, and that its undulating course was similar to the eel: that the colour of the back was blackish, shining strongly, and as far as he could distinguish there was a whitish stripe under the belly."

"Report also says that the sea-serpent was seen by several persons in Biornfjord causing a great deal of dread, hut of this our informants want authentic accounts. Our informant further says that he has no reason whatever to doubt the truth of the story of the man and his wife, or the truthworthiness of the lad Abraham, except as far as that his fears may have caused him to see several things through a magnifying glass."

I am convinced that by a head as large as a Foering boat (about twenty feet long) must be meant the head and a great part of the neck. The other characters are mere repetitions of what we have so often observed. Very interesting again is the statement of the lad that the animal had a white stripe "under the belly". As the lad cannot have seen the proper belly of the animal, it must have been the throat; the boy thought that he saw a snake and I think that he, being questioned, would tell me that a snake has a head, a trunk and a tail, and hardly any neck and throat. I am also convinced, that the boy has not seen with a magnifying glass: the measurements, he gives, are not exaggerated.

In 1847, Mr. Edward Newmann, the Editor of the *Zoologist* had the courage to open the columns of his Journal to all kinds of reports and discussions about the great sea-serpent. He says (p. 1604):

"It has been the fashion for so many years to deride all records of this very celebrated monster, that it is not without hesitation I venture to quote the following paragraphs in his defence. A month only has elapsed since I had occasion to quote with approbation, a very marked passage from the pen of Sir J. W. Hershell (Zool. 1586): I may apply it with equal propriety to the enquiry of the era of the Irish deer, or of the existence of the Great Sea-Serpent. Naturalists, or rather those who choose thus to designate themselves, set up an authority above that of fact and observation, the gist of their enquiries is whether such things *ought to be,* and whether such things *ought not to be;* now fact-naturalists take a different road to knowledge, they enquire whether such things *are,* and whether such things *are not.* The *Zoologist,* if not in itself the fountain-head of this *fact* movement, may at least claim to be the only public advocate of that movement; and it is therefore most desirable, that it should call the attention of its readers to the following remarkable paragraphs. They are quoted from one of our daily papers, which gives them as literal translations from the Norse papers, in which they originally appeared; the localities mentioned are intimately known to all travellers in Norway; and the witnesses are generally highly respectable and of unimpeachable veracity. The very discrepancies in the accounts prove the entire absence of any preconcerted scheme of deception. The only question therefore for the fact-naturalists to decide, is simply, whether all of the records now collected, can refer to whales, fishes, or any other marine animals with which we are at present acquainted."

I have no reason to doubt Mr. Newman's veracity, and so I am willing to believe that the five reports which follow this introduction "are quoted from one of" the British "daily papers, which gives them as literal translations from the Norse papers, in which they originally appeared". I only ask why Mr. Newman did not mention the daily paper? For the assertion of this daily paper that they are "literal translations from *Norse* papers in which they originally appeared" is at all events a fabrication, as the reports which Mr. Newman published here are the evidences which Mr. Heinrich Rathke took, when on a journey in Norway, near Christiansund, apparently in the year 1840, and which he published in the *Archiv für Naturgeschichte* of 1841, six years later! I have inserted them above (n°. 90, 91, 92, 94, 95, 102). As to the "discrepancies in the accounts" I have already showed that there are, in fact, hardly any discrepancies, but that the accounts complete one another. I must also observe here that the accounts are not translated *literally.* Many, and among them very interesting passages, are omitted. The reader, who will convince himself of the truth of my assertion, has only to compare the accounts, as they are inserted in the *Zoologist* with my translations of the German originals, or with the originals themselves.

Mr. Gosse, too, in his *Romance of Natural History,* 1860, writes: "The public papers of Norway, during the summer of 1846, were occupied with statements of the following effect", and he too publishes extracts from the evidences printed in the *Archiv für Naturgeschichte* of 1841!

Also Mr. Lee, in his *Sea-Monsters Unmasked,* 1883, says: "In 1847 there appeared in a London daily paper a long account translated from the Norse journals of fresh appearances of the sea-serpent."

And Mr. John Ashton in his *Curious Creatures in Zoology,* 1889, asserts: "In 1847 a sea-serpent was seen frequently in the neighbourhood of Christiansund and Molde, by many persons, and by one Lars Johnöen, fisherman at Smölen, especially."

All these writers have copied Mr. Newman, and have therefore quite overlooked the fact that the originals were in the *Archiv für Naturgeschichte* of 1841, and that the appearances took place long before the year 1847!

The last number of the *Zoologist* for 1847 appeared in October of that year. The reader must know that the matter of this journal is arranged according to the class of the animals, treated of in each article. This I must mention for the better understanding of the following passage which Mr. Newman wrote in his preface to the above mentioned volume of the *Zoologist*.

"In Reptiles, the communications and quotations about "the Sea-Serpent" are well worthy of attentive perusal: it is impossible to suppose all the records bearing this title to be fabricated for the purpose of deception. A natural phenomenon of some kind has been witnessed: let us seek a satisfactory solution rather than terminate enquiry by the shafts of ridicule. The grave and learned have often avowed a belief that toads can exist some thousands of years without food, light or air, and immured in solid stone: surely it is not requiring too much to solicit a suspension of judgment on the question whether a monster may exist in the sea which does not adorn our collections."

Mr. Newman, viz. believed that the sea-serpent belonged to the class of Reptiles. The "communications and quotations" spoken of here, have already been inserted above (n°. 25, 90, 91, 92, 94, 95, 97, 102, 106 A, 115, 116, 117.).

118.—1848, August 6.—No report of the sea-serpent has ever more shaken the incredulity of hundreds and thousands than that generally known as the account of the *Daedalus*, after the frigate from which the sea-serpent was seen.

The *Times* newspaper of October, 9, 1848, published the following paragraph:

"Intelligence from Plymouth, dated 7 Oct."
"When the *Daedalus* frigate, Captain M'Quhae, which arrived at Plymouth on the 4th. instant, was on her passage home from the East Indies, between the Cape of Good Hope and St. Helena, her captain, and most of her officers and crew, at four o'clock one afternoon, saw a sea-serpent. The creature was twenty minutes in sight of the frigate, and passed under her quarter. Its head appeared to be about four feet out of the water, and there was about sixty feet of its body in a straight line on the surface. It is calculated that there must have been under water a length of thirty-three or forty feet more, by which it propelled itself at the rate of fifteen miles an hour. The diameter of the exposed part of the body was about sixteen inches; and when it extended its jaws, which were full of large jagged teeth, they seemed sufficiently capacious to admit of a tall man standing upright between them".

The Admiralty instantly inquired into the truth of the statement, and in the *Times* of the 13th. the gallant captain's official reply was published in the following terms:

"Her Majesty's Ship Daedalus, Hamoaze, Oct. 11."
"Sir,—In reply to your letter of this date, requiring information as to the truth of a statement published in *The Times* newspaper, of a sea-serpent of extraordinary dimensions having been seen from Her Majesty's ship *Daedalus*, under my command, on her passage from the East Indies, I have the honour to acquaint you, for the information of my Lords Commissioners of the Admiralty, that at five o'clock P. M., on the 6th. of August last, in latitude 24° 44' S., and longitude 9° 22' E., the weather dark and cloudy, wind fresh from the N. W., with a long ocean swell from the S. W., the ship on the port tack heading N. E. by N., something very unusual was seen by Mr. Sartoris, midshipman, rapidly approaching the ship from before

the beam. The circumstance was immediately reported by him to the officer of the watch, Lieutenant Edgar Drummond, with whom and Mr. William Barrett, the master, I was at the time walking the quarterdeck. The ship's company were at supper."

"On our attention being called to the object, it was discovered to be an enormous serpent, with head and shoulders kept about four feet constantly above the surface of the sea, and, as nearly as we could approximate, by comparing it with the length of what our main-topsail yard would show in the water, there was at the very least sixty feet of the animal *à fleur d'eau*, no portion of which was, to our perception, used in propelling it through the water, either by vertical or horizontal undulation. It passed rapidly, but so close under our lee quarter, that had it been a man of my acquaintance, I should easily have recognized his features with the naked eye; and it did not, either in approaching the ship or after it had passed our wake, deviate in the slightest degree from its course to the S. W., which it held on at the pace of from twelve to fifteen miles per hour, apparently on some determined purpose."

"The diameter of the serpent was about fifteen or sixteen inches behind the head, which was, without any doubt, that of a snake; and it was never, during the twenty minutes that it continued in sight of our glasses, once below the surface of the water; its colour a dark brown, with yellowish white about the throat. It had no fins, but something like a mane of a horse, or rather a bunch of seaweed, washed about its back. It was seen by the quartermaster, the boatswain's mate, and the man at the wheel, in addition to myself and officers above-mentioned."

"I am having a drawing of the serpent made from a sketch taken immediately after it was seen, which I hope to have ready for transmission to my Lords Commissioners of the Admiralty by to-morrow's post."

"Peter M'Quhae, Captain."

"To Admiral Sir W. H. Gage, G. C. H., Devonport."

In the *Literary Gazette* of Oct. 21st., 1848, the Editor published an engraving of Pontoppidan's representation, and adds some accompanying conclusions, appended to copious extracts from the learned Bishop's work:

"We have now only to point to the very remarkable resemblance between Captain M'Quhae and Pontoppidan's description. One might fancy the galant Captain had read the old Dane, and was copying him, when he tells of the dark brown colour and white about the throat, and the neck clothed as if by a horse's mane or a bunch of sea-weed—the exact words of the historian. This snake, however, did not seem to care for the fresh wind and ruffish weather, but kept, as in the calm, its head several feet above the water, and stretched out its length so as to be visible for some sixty or eighty feet. The motion was not perceptibly impelled by vermicular or lent-serpent action! Had it then large fins? There must be some power. The picture engraved in the folio represents it like a series of six barrels, or risings, with the intermediate parts under the sea."

In the *Illustrated London News* of Oct. 28st. was reprinted all that has been mentioned above, and there appeared three representations of the sea-serpent, as seen from the *Daedalus*, which I here show my readers in fig. 28, 29 and 30, omitting, however, the ship's stern, because the drawings would be too large for our pages. The Editor of the *Illustrated London News* adds:

"The drawing above-named have been received by the Lord Commissioners to the Admiralty, and by the courtesy of Capt. M'Quhae, our artist has been permitted

Various Accounts 211

FIG. 28.—THE SEA-SERPENT, AS SEEN BY THE OFFICERS OF THE DAEDALUS.

FIG. 29.—ANOTHER SKETCH OF THE SAME INDIVIDUAL.

212   The Great Sea-Serpent

to copy this pictorial evidence, as well as further to illustrate the appearance of the Serpent, under the supervision of Captain M'Quhae, and with his approval of the Authenticity of their details as to position and form."

On the 28th. of October Lieutenant Drummond, the officer of the watch, mentioned in the report of Captain M'Quhae, published his own impressions of the animal, in the form of an extract from his own journal. As far as I can discover it did not appear before the 1st. of December, in the *Zoologist* (p. 2306) and runs as follows:

"I beg to send you the following extract from my journal."

"H. M. S. *Daedalus*, August, 6, 1848, lat. 25° S., long 9° 37' E., St., Helena 1015 miles. In the 4 to 6 watch, at about five o'clock, we observed a most remarkable fish on our lee quarter, crossing the stern in a S. W. direction; the appearance of its head, which, with the back fin, was the only portion of the animal visible, was long, pointed, and flattened at the top, perhaps ten feet in length, the upper jaw projecting considerably; the fin was perhaps twenty feet in the rear of the head, and visible occasionally; the captain also asserted that he saw the tail, or another fin about the same distance behind it; the upper part of the head and shoulders appeared of a dark brown colour, and beneath the under jaw a brownish

FIG. 30.—A SKETCH OF THE HEAD OF THE SAME INDIVIDUAL.

white. It pursued a steady undeviating course, keeping its head horizontal with the surface of the water, and in rather a raised position, disappearing occassionally beneath a wave for a very brief interval, and not apparently for purposes of respiration. It was going at the rate of perhaps from twelve to fourteen miles an hour, and when nearest, was perhaps one hundred yards distant. In fact it gave one quite the idea of a large snake or eel. No one in the ship has ever seen anything similar, so it is at least extraordinary. It was visible to the naked eye for five minutes, and with a glass for perhaps fifteen more. The weather was dark and squally at the time, with some sea running."

The following article appeared in the *Times* of Nov. 2d.:

"Amidst the numerous suggestions of those of your correspondents who are disposed to admit the account given by Captain M'Quhae of the marine monster seen by him and several of his brother officers, on the 6th. of August last, as not altogether imaginary, it appears surprising that it should not have occurred to any one to suggest an explanation of some apparent anomalies in the account, which have no doubt tended to stagger the belief even of some readers who are not disposed to assume (any more than myself) that a number of officers in Her Majesty's navy would deliberately invent a falsehood, or could have been deceived in an appearance which they describe with such precise details."

"One of the greatest difficulties on the face of the narrative and which must be allowed to destroy the analogy of the motions of the so called 'sea-serpent' with those of all known snakes and anguilliform fishes, is that no less than sixty feet of the animal were seen advancing *à fleur d'eau* at the rate of from twelve to fifteen miles an hour, without it being possible to perceive, upon the closest and most attentive inspection, any undulatory motion to which its rapid advance could be ascribed. It need scarcely be observed that neither an eel nor a snake, if either of those animals could swim at all with the neck elevated, could do so without the front part of its body being thrown into undulation by the propulsive efforts of its tail."

"But, it may be asked, if the animal seen by Captain M'Quhae was not allied to the snakes or to the eels, to what class of animals could it have belonged? To this I would reply, that it appears more likely that the enormous reptile in question was allied to the gigantic Saurians, hitherto believed only to exist in the fossil state, and, among them, to the Plesiosaurus."

"From the known anatomical characters of the *Plesiosauri*, derived from the examination of their organic remains, geologists are agreed in the inference that those animals carried their necks (which must have resembled the bodies of serpents) above the water, while their progression was effected by large paddles working beneath—the short but stout tail acting the part of a rudder. It would be superfluous to point out how closely the surmises of philosophers resemble, in these particulars, the description of the eye-witnesses of the living animal, as given in the letter and drawings of Captain M'Quhae. In the latter we have many of the external characters of the former, as predicated from the examination of the skeleton. The short head, the serpent-like neck, carried several feet above the water, forcibly recall the idea conceived of the extinct animal; and even the bristly mane in certain parts of the back, so unlike anything found in serpents, has its analogy in the *Iguana*, to which animal the *Plesiosaurus* has been compared by some geologists. But I would most of all insist upon the peculiarity of the animal's progression, which could only have been effected with the evenness, and at the rate described, by an apparatus of fins or paddles, not possessed by serpents, but existing in the highest perfection in the *Plesiosaurus*."—F. G. S.—

In the number of the *Illustrated London News* of November 4, 1848, the letter of Captain M'Quhae was published in which he expresses his special approbation of the figures:

"I have observed with very great satisfaction the Engravings of the 'Sea-Serpent' in the *Illustrated London News* of the 28th. inst.; they most faithfully represent the apearance of the animal, as seen from Her Majesty's ship *Daedalus* on the 6th. of August last; and it is evident that much care has been bestowed upon the subject by the artist employed, to whom I beg to acknowledge myself greatly indebted for the patience and attention with which he listened to the various alterations suggested by me during the progress of the drawings."

In the *Times* of Nov. 4th., we find the following remark:

"As some interest has been excited by the alleged appearance of a sea-serpent, I venture to transmit a few remarks on the subject, which you may or not may think worthy of insertion in your columns. There does not appear to be a single well authenticated instance of these monsters having been seen in any southern latitudes; but in the north of Europe, notwithstanding the fabulous character so long ascribed to Pontoppidan's description, I am convinced that they both exist and are frequently seen. During three summers spent in Norway I have repeatedly conversed with the natives on this subject."

Here follow the descriptions of two appearances which I have inserted above, (n°. 109, 110).

"They expressed great surprise at the general disbelief attaching to the existence of these animals amongst naturalists, and assured me that there was scarcely a sailor accustomed to those inland lakes, who had not seen them at one time or another."—Oxoniensis.

An unknown writer in one of the daily papers, after suggesting, whether the animals in question might not be full grown specimens of the *Saccopharynx flagellum* of Mr. Mitchill (described in the *Annals of the New York Lyceum of Natural History*, for March, 1824), or of the *Ophiognathus ampullaceus* of Dr. Harwood (Phil. Trans., 1827), gives Captain M'Quhae the benefit of a further conjecture, viz., whether some land species, as the boas, among which are individuals "forty feet" in length, may not sometimes betake themselves to the sea, or even "transport themselves from one continent to another" (See *Zoologist*, 1848; p. 2320).

Some days after the figures of Captain M'Quhae were published, a nobleman, whose name is not mentioned, wrote to Prof. Owen to know his opinion about the animal seen by the Captain. The Professor, it would seem, did not answer the nobleman directly, but sent his answer to the Editor of the *Times*, evidently with a view of bringing his opinion under the eyes of thousands. This letter is too important to be abridged; I therefore give it in extenso; it appeared in the *Times* of November 11, 1848.

The Great Sea-Serpent.

"Sir,—Subjoined is the answer to a question relative to the animal seen from the *Daedalus*, addressed to me by a nobleman distinguished in literature, and taking much interest in science."

"As it contains the substance of the explanation I have endeavoured to give to numerous inquirers, in the Hunterian Museum and elsewhere, and as I continue to receive many applications for my opinion of the 'Great Sea Serpent,' I am desirous to give it once for all through the medium of your columns, if space of such value may be allotted to it."

"I am, Sir, your very obedient servant
  "Richard Owen."
  "Lincoln's Inn Fields, Nov. 9."

"The sketch (this was a reduced copy of the drawing of the head of the animal seen by Captain M'Quhae; attached to the submerged body of a large seal, showing the long eddy produced by the action of the terminal flippers) will suggest the reply to your query, 'Whether the monster seen from the *Daedalus* be anything but a saurian?' If it be the true answer, it destroys the romance of the incident, and will be anything but acceptable to those who prefer the excitement of the imagination to the satisfaction of the judgment. I am far from insensible to the pleasures of the discovery of a new and rare animal; but before I can enjoy them, certain conditions—e. g. reasonable proof or evidence of its existence—must be fulfilled. I am also far from undervaluing the information which Captain M'Quhae has given us of what he saw. When fairly analized, it lies in a small compass, but my knowledge of the animal kingdom compels me to draw other conclusions from the phenomena than those which the gallant captain seems to have jumped at. He evidently saw a large animal moving through the water, very different from anything he had before witnessed—neither a whale, a grampus, a great shark, an alligator, nor any of the larger surface swimming creatures which are fallen in with in ordinary voyages. He writes:—'On our attention being called to the object, it was discovered to be an enormous serpent' (read 'animal'), 'with the head and shoulders kept about four feet constantly above the surface of the sea. The diameter of the serpent' (animal) 'was about fifteen or sixteen inches behind the head; its colour a dark brown, with yellowish white about the throat'. No fins were seen (the captain says there were none; but from his own account, he did not see enough of the animal to prove the negative). 'Something like the mane of a horse, or rather a bunch of sea-weed, washed about its back.' So much of the body as was seen was 'not used in propelling the animal through the water, either by vertical or horizontal undulation.' A calculation of its length was made under a strong preconception of the nature of the beast. The head, e. g., is stated to be, 'without any doubt, that of a snake;' and yet a snake would be the last species to which a naturalist conversant with the forms and characters of the heads of animals, would refer such a head as that of which Captain M'Quhae has transmitted a drawing to the Admirality, and which he certifies to have been accurately copied in the *Illustrated London News* for October 28, 1848, p. 265. Your Lordship will observe that no sooner was the captain's attention called to the object, than 'it was discovered to be an enormous serpent', and yet the closest inspection of as much of the body as was visible, *à fleur d'eau*, failed to detect any undulations of the body, although such actions constitute the very character which would distinguish a serpent or serpentiform swimmer from any other marine species. The foregone conclusion, therefore, of the beast's being a sea-serpent, notwithstanding its capacious vaulted cranium, and stiff, inflexible trunk, must be kept in mind in estimating the value of the approximation made to the total length of the animal, as '(at the very least) sixty feet'. This is the only part of the description, however, which seems to me to be so uncertain as to be inadmissible, in an attempt to arrive at a right conclusion as to

the nature of the animal. The more certain characters of the animal are these:—
Head with a convex, moderately capacious cranium, short obtuse muzzle, gape of
the mouth not extending further than to beneath the eye, which is rather small,
round, filling closely the palpebral aperture; colour, dark brown above, yellowish
white beneath; surface smooth, without scales, scutes, or other conspicuous modifications or hard and naked cuticle. And the captain says, 'Had it been a man of my
acquaintance, I should have easily recognized his features with my naked eye.'
Nostrils not mentioned, but indicated in the drawing by a crescentic mark at the
end of the nose or muzzle. All these are the characters of the head of a warm-
blooded mammal—none of them those of a cold-blooded reptile or fish. Body long,
dark brown, not undulating, without dorsal or other apparent fins; 'but something
like the mane of a horse, or rather a bunch of sea-weed, washed about its back.'
The character of the integuments would be a most important one for the zoologist
in the determination to the class to which the above defined creature belonged. If
an opinion can be deduced as to the integuments from the above indication, it is
that the species had hair, which, if it was too short and close to be distinguished
on the head, was visible where it usually is the longest, on the middle line of the
shoulders or advanced part of the back, where it was not stiff and upright like the
rays of a fin, but 'washed about.' Guided by the above interpretation, of the 'mane of
a horse, or a bunch of sea-weed', the animal was not a cetaceous mammal, but
rather a great seal. But what seal of large size, or indeed of any size, would be
encountered in latitude 24° 44' south, and longitude 9° 22' east—viz. about three
hundred miles from the western shore of the southern end of Afrika? The most
likely species to be met with are the largest of the seal tribe, e. g. Anson's sea
lion, or that known to the southern whalers by the name of the sea-elephant, the
Phoca proboscidea, which attains the length of from twenty to thirty feet. These
great seals abound in certain of the islands of the southern and antarctic seas, from
which an individual is occasionally floated off upon an iceberg. The sea lion exhibited in London last spring, which was a young individual of the *Phoca proboscidea*
was actually captured in that predicament; having been carried by the currents that
set northwards towards the Cape, where its temporary resting-place was rapidly
melting away. When a large individual of the *Phoca proboscidea* or *Phoca leonina* is
thus borne off to a distance from its native shore, it is compelled to return for rest to
its floating abode, after it has made its daily excursions in quest of the fishes or
squids that constitute its food. It is thus brought by the iceberg into the latitudes
of the Cape, and perhaps farther north, before the berg was melted away. Then the
poor seal is compelled to swim as long as strength endures, and in such a predicament I imagine the creature was that Mr. Sartoris saw rapidly approaching the
Daedalus from before the beam, scanning, probably, its capabilities as a resting-
place, as it paddled its long stiff body past the ship. In so doing, it would raise a
head of the form and colour described and delineated by Captain M'Quhae, supported on a neck also of the diameter given; the thick neck passing into an inflexible trunk, the longer and coarser hair on the upper part of which would give rise
to the idea, especially if the species were the *Phoca leonina*, explained by the similes above cited. The organs of locomotion would be out of sight. The pectoral fins
being set on very low down, as in my sketch, the chief impelling force would be the
action of the deeper immersed terminal fins and tail, which would create a long
eddy, readily mistakable, by one looking at the strange phenomenon with a sea-
serpent in his mind's eye, for an indefinite prolongation of the body."

"It is very probable, that not one on board the *Daedalus* ever before beheld a gigantic seal freely swimming in the open ocean. Entering unexpectedly from that vast and commonly blank desert of waters, it would be a strange and exciting spectacle, and might well be interpreted as a marvel; but the creative powers of the human mind appear to be really very limited, and, on all the occasions where the true source of the 'great unknown' has been detected—whether it has proved to be a file of sportive porpoises, or a pair of gigantic sharks—old Pontoppidan's sea-serpent with the mane has uniformly suggested itself as the representative of the portent, until the mystery has been unravelled."

"The vertebrae of the sea-serpent described and delineated in the *Wernerian Transactions*, vol. I., and sworn to by the fishermen who saw it off the Isle of Stronsa (one of the Orkneys), in 1808, two of which vertebrae are in the Museum of the College of Surgeons, are certainly those of a great shark, of the genus *Selache*, and are not distinguishable from those of the species called 'basking-shark', of which individuals from thirty to thirty-five feet in length have been from time to time captured or stranded on our coasts."

"I have no unmeet confidence in the exactitude of my interpretation of the phenomena witnessed by the captain and others of the *Daedalus*. I am too sensible of the inadequacy of the characters which the opportunity of a rapidly passing animal, 'in a long ocean swell', enabled them to note, for the determination of its species or genus. Giving due credence to the most probably accurate elements of their description, they do little more than guide the zoologist to the class, which, in the present instance, is not that of the serpent or the saurian."

"But I am usually asked, after each endeavour to explain Captain M'Quhae's sea-serpent, 'Why should there not be a great sea-serpent?'—often, too, in a tone which seems to imply, 'Do you think, then, there are not more marvels in the deep, than are dreamt of in your philosophy?' And, freely conceding that point, I have felt bound to give a reason for scepticism as well as faith. If a gigantic sea-serpent actually exists, the species must, of course, have been perpetuated through successive generations, from its first creation and introduction into the seas of this planet. Conceive, then, the number of individuals that must have lived, and died, and have left their remains to attest the actuality of the species during the enormous lapse of time, from its beginning, to the 6th. of August last! Now, a serpent, being an air breathing animal, with long vesicular and receptacular lungs, dives with an effort and commonly floats when dead; and so would the sea-serpent, until decomposition or accident had opened the tough integument, and let out the imprisoned gases. Then it would sink, and, if in deep water, be seen no more until the sea rendered up its dead, after the lapse of the aeons requisite for the yielding of its place to dry land,— a change which has actually revealed to the present generation the old saurian monsters that were entombed at the bottom of the ocean, of the secondary geological periods of our earth's history. During life the exigencies of the respiration of the great sea-serpent would always compel him frequently to the surface; and when dead and swollen—

"Prone on the flood, extended long and large,"
he would
"Lie floating many a rood; in bulk as huge,
"As whom the fables name of monstrous size,
"Titanian, or Earth-born, that warr'd on Jove."

"Such a spectacle, demonstrative of the species if it existed, has not hitherto met the gaze of any of the countless voyagers who have traversed the seas in so many directions. Considering, too, the tides and currents of the ocean, it seems still more reasonable to suppose that the dead sea-serpent would be occasionally cast on shore. However, I do not ask for the entire carcase. The structure of the back-bone of the serpent tribe is so peculiar, that a single vertebra would suffice to determine the existence of the hypothetical Ophidian; and this will not be deemed an unreasonable request, when it is remembered that the vertebrae are more numerous in serpents than in any other animals. Such large blanched and scattered bones on any sea-shore, would be likely to attract even common curiosity; yet there is no vertebra of a serpent larger than the ordinary pythons and boas in any museum in Europe."

"Few sea-coasts have been more sedulously searched, or by more acute naturalists (witness the labours of Sars and Lovén), than those of Norway. Krakens and sea serpents ought to have been living and dying thereabouts from long before Pontoppidan's time to our day, if all tales were true; yet they have never vouchsafed a single fragment of the skeleton to any Scandinavian collector; whilst the great denizens of those seas have been by no means so chary. No museums, in fact, are so rich in skeletons, skulls, bones and teeth of the numerous kind of whales, cachelots, grampuses, walrusses, sea unicorns, seals, etc., as those of Denmark, Norway, and Sweden; but of any large marine nondescript or indeterminable monster they cannot show a trace."

"I have inquired repeatedly whether the natural history collections of Boston, Philadelphia, or other cities of the United States, might possess any unusually large ophidian vertebrae or any of such peculiar form as to indicate some large and unknown marine animal; but they have received no such specimens."

"The frequency with which the sea-serpent has been supposed to have appeared near the shores and harbours of the United States, has led to its being specified as the 'American sea-serpent;' yet, out of the two hundred vertebrae of every individual that should have lived and died in the Atlantic since the creation of the species, not one has yet been picked up on the shores of America. The diminutive snake, less than a yard in length, 'killed upon the sea-shore', apparently beaten to death, 'by some labouring people of Cape Ann,' United States (see the 8vo pamphlet, 1817, Boston, page 38), and figured in the *Illustrated London News*, October 28, 1848, from the original American memoir, by no means satisfies the conditions of the problem. Neither does the *Saccopharynx* of Mitchill, nor the *Ophiognathus* of Harwood—the one four and a half feet, the other six feet long: both are surpassed by some of the congers of our own coasts, and, like other muraenoid fishes and the known small sea snake (*Hydrophis*), swim by undulatory movements of the body."

"The fossil vertebrae and skull which were exhibited by Mr. Koch, in New York and Boston, as those of the great sea-serpent, and which are now in Berlin, belonged to different individuals of a species which I had previously proved to be an extinct whale; a determination which has subsequently been confirmed by Professors Müller and Agassiz. Mr. Dixon of Worthing has discovered many fossil vertebrae, in the Eocene tertiary clay at Bracklesham, which belong to a larger species of an extinct genus of serpent (*Palaeophis*), founded on similar vertebrae from the same formation in the Isle of Sheppey. The largest of these ancient British snakes was twenty feet in length; but there is no evidence that they were marine."

"The sea saurians of the secondary periods of geology have been replaced in the tertiary and actual seas by marine mammals. No remains of *Cetacea* have been found in lias or oolite, and no remains of Plesiosaur, or Ichthyosaur, or any other secondary reptile, have been found in Eocene or later tertiary deposits, or recent, on the actual sea-shores; and that the old air-breathing saurians floated when they died has been shown in the *Geological Transactions* (vol. V., second series, p. 512). The inference that may reasonably be drawn from no recent carcase or fragment of such having ever been discovered, is strengthened by the corresponding absence of any trace of their remains in the tertiary beds."

"Now, on weighing the question, whether creatures meriting the name of 'great sea serpent' do exist, or whether any of the gigantic marine saurians of the secondary deposits may have continued to live up to the present time, it seems to me less probable that no part of the carcase of such reptiles should have ever been discovered in a recent or unfossilized state, than that men should have been deceived by a cursory view of a partly submerged and rapidly moving animal, which might only be strange to themselves. In other words, I regard the negative evidence from the utter absence of any of the recent remains of great sea serpents, krakens, or *Enaliosauria*, as stronger against their actual existence, than the positive statements which have hitherto weighed with the public mind in favour of their existence. A larger body of evidence from eye-witnesses might be got together in proof of ghosts than of the sea-serpent."

What speaks for itself, this letter appeared in several journals and newspapers. So I have found it in the *Annals and Magazine of Natural History*, 2d. Ser. Vol. II, p. 458 (15? Nov. 1848), in Galignani's *Messenger* of Nov. 23, 1848, in the *Illustrated London News* of Nov. 25, 1848, and in the *Zoologist*, of Nov. 27, 1848. As it came from such a quarter it is not surprising that many persons were willing to acquiesce in the decision.

Captain M'Quhae, however, promptly replied to Professor Owen. His answer was also addressed to the Editor of the *Times* (*Times*, Nov. 21, 1848):

"Sir,—Will you do me the very great favour to give a place in your widely-circulating columns to the following reply to the animadversions of Professor Owen on the serpent or animal seen by me and others from Her Majesty's ship *Daedalus* on the 6th. of August last, and which were published in the Times of the 14th. inst.?

"I am, Sir, your obedient servant

"P. M'Quhae.

"Late Captain of Her Majesty's ship *Daedalus*.

"London, November 18.

"Professor Owen correctly states that I 'evidently saw a large creature moving rapidly through the water very different from anything I had before witnessed, neither a whale, a grampus, a great shark, an alligator, nor any of the larger surface-swimming creatures fallen in with in ordinary voyages'. I now assert, neither was it a common seal nor a sea elephant; its great length, and its totally differing physiognomy, precluding the possibility of its being a *Phoca* of any species. The head was flat, and not a 'capacious vaulted cranium;' nor had it 'a stiff inflexible trunk'—a conclusion to which Professor Owen has jumped, most certainly not justified by the simple statement, that 'no portion of the sixty feet seen by us was used in propelling it through the water, either by vertical or horizontal undulation'."

"It is also assumed that the 'calculation of its length was made under a strong preconception of the nature of the beast;' another conclusion quite contrary to the fact. It was not until after the great length was developed by its nearest approach to the ship, and until after that most important point had been duly considered and debated, as well as such could be in the brief space of time allowed for so doing, that it was pronounced to be a serpent by all who saw it, and who are too well accustomed to judge of lengths and breadths of objects in the sea to mistake a real substance and an actual living body, coolly and dispassionately contemplated, at so short a distance too, for the 'eddy caused by the action of the deeper immersed fins and tail of a rapidly moving gigantic seal raising its head above the water,' as Professor Owen imagines, in quest of its lost iceberg."

"The creative powers of the human mind may be very limited. On this occasion they were not called into requisition; my purpose and desire being, throughout, to furnish eminent naturalists, such as the learned Professor, with acurate facts, and not with exaggerated representations, nor with what could by any possibility proceed from optical illusion; and I beg to assure him that old Pontoppidan's having clothed his sea-serpent with a mane could not have suggested the idea of ornamenting the creature seen from the *Daedalus* with a similar appendage, for the simple reason that I had never seen his account, or even heard of his sea-serpent, until my arrival in London. Some other solution must therefore be found for the very remarkable coincidence between us in that particular, in order to unravel the mystery."

"Finally, I deny the existence of excitement, or the possibility of optical illusion. I adhere to the statement, as to form, colour, and dimensions, contained in my official report to the Admiralty; and I leave them as data whereupon the learned and scientific may exercise the 'pleasures of imagination' until some more fortunate opportunity shall occur of making a closer acquaintance with the 'great unknown',— in the present instance assuredly no ghost."

It also appeared in the *Illustrated London News* of Nov. 25, 1848.

And a gentleman, who signed his letter with the initials J. C., wrote a letter to the Editor of the *Illustrated London News* (see this Journal of Nov. 25, 1848) to rectify another statement of the learned Professor:

"The very interesting account of the sea-serpent seen by Captain M'Quhae, and the drawing in your paper, are to my mind quite satisfactory as to the existence of the animal, and I have no doubt we shall hear of his being again seen sooner or later. But my object in writing to you is to remark on the conclusions come to by Mr. Owen, in his letter to the Editor of the *Times*, of November 9th., that it was *not* of the serpent species, because 'they failed to detect any undulations of the body', whereas the fact of there being "no vertical or horizontal undulations perceptible" stamps the character of the animal; for it is well known by all observers of snakes in India, that when the animal is in chase of game, small or great, or when scared away, and moving at a *rapid* pace, he is propelled entirely by the tail, or the smaller half of the body, while the other portion, with a curve of the head, is kept quite *stiff*—and this exactly corresponds with the Captain's account, that it held on at the pace of twelve to fifteen miles an hour, *apparently on some determined purpose.*"

In May, 1854, Dr. T. S. Traill read a paper before the Royal Society of Edinburgh, comparing the animal of the *Daedalus*, with the Animal of Stronsa. The part of his dissertation concerning the present occurrence runs as follows:

"In their statements there are no suspicious affectations of minute detail. Their simple narrative appears to deserve more attention than it has yet received from naturalists; and I strongly incline to the belief, that the animal seen by the crew of the *Daedalus* was an analogue of, if not the very same species, as the animal cast ashore in Orkney in 1808."

"Considering the derision with which, in this country, the subject of the sea-serpent has been treated, and the ridicule attempted to be thrown on all who were bold enough to assert that they had seen such an animal, nothing but a consciousness of his unimpeachable veracity could have tempted the gallant Captain M'Quhae to encounter the sneers of his incredulous countrymen. From all I have heard of his character for sagacity and veracity, from those who intimately knew him, I have not the smallest doubt that he has faithfully described what he and his crew saw distinctly, and at a short distance from the ship."

"'It was seen rapidly approaching before the *beam.*' Captain M'Quhae says: On our attention being called to the object, it was discovered to be an enormous serpent, with head and shoulders kept about four feet constantly above the surface of the sea. The diameter of the serpent was about fifteen or sixteen inches behind the head; its colour of a dark brown, with yellowish-white about the throat."

"The Captain could discover no fins, but 'something like the mane of a horse, or rather a bunch of sea-weed, washed about its back.' He thought that its head did certainly resemble that of a snake; but the drawing which he transmitted to the Admiralty has not, to the eye of a naturalist, the form of that of any snake. The figure published in the *Illustrated London News* for October 28, 1848, is said to be an accurate copy of that drawing."

"Captain M'Quhae estimates the length of its body at the surface of the water, '*à fleur d'eau,*' at the very least equal to sixty feet! no part of which was to our perception used in propelling it through the water, either by vertical or horizontal undulations. It passed rapidly, but so close under our quarter, that had it been a man of my acquaintance, I should easily have recognized his features with the naked eye, and it did not, either in approaching the ship, or after it had passed our wake, deviate in the slightest degree from its course to the S. W., which it held on at the pace of twelve or fifteen miles an hour, apparently on some determined purpose."

"If we may judge from the engraving, the cranium is very convex, of moderate size, with a short obtuse muzzle, a mouth reaching beyond the eye; which last organ is round, and of a moderate size. The surface of the body is represented as smooth, and destitute of scales—of which they were enabled to judge, because it passed close under the *quarter* of the ship. It was in sight for twenty minutes."

"The description certainly does not belong to any Ophidian; and as certainly militates against an opinion thrown out by Mr. Owen, that it might be a specimen of the *leonine seal*, which has, it is alleged, occasionally reached those latitudes. The leonine seal never exceeds twenty-five feet in length, and such would have a circumference at its shoulders of twenty feet, while this appears to be eel-shaped, with a diameter of not more than fifteen or sixteen inches behind the head; the mane too, of the male of the leonine seal extends only over the head and neck; but in the other, it extended down the back."

"With all deference to so eminent a naturalist as Mr. Owen, I humbly conceive that his conjecture respecting the identity of Captain M'Quhae's animal with the leonine seal, is not more probable than Home's identification of the Basking shark with the Orkney animal."

"Both M'Quhae's and the Orkney animal would appear to be a cartilaginous fish, totally different from any genus known to naturalists."

Three years afterwards Captain Harrington's report (n°. 131) was published in the *Times*. Some days afterwards Captain Frederic Smith published his encounter with a sea-serpent, which after being harpooned and hoisted on board, proved to be a piece of a gigantic sea-weed, and the sea-serpents of the *Daedalus* and of Captain Harrington were in his opinion undoubtedly pieces of the same kind of weed.

Now "An Officer of Her Majesty's Ship *Daedalus* felt obliged to state again that it was a living animal. As in this letter further particulars of the animal are mentioned, I insert it here *in toto,* (The Times of Febr. 16th., 1868):

"Sir,—Observing in your paper of yesterday's date a letter from a correspondent to the marine animal commonly called the 'sea-serpent', in the concluding paragraph of which he mentions that he has no doubt the object seen from Her Majesty's Ship *Daedalus* in the month of August, 1848, when on the passage from the Cape of Good-Hope to St. Helena, was a piece of the same sea-weed observed by himself, I beg to state that the object seen from her Majesty's ship was, beyond all question, a living animal, moving rapidly through the water against a cross sea, and within five points of a fresh breeze, with such velocity that the water was surging under its chest, as it passed along at a rate probably of ten miles per hour. Captain M'Quhae's first impulse was to tack in pursuit, ourselves being on a wind on the larboard tack, when he reflected that we could neither lay up for it nor overhaul it in speed. There was nothing to be done, therefore, but to observe it as accurately as we could with our glasses, as it came up under our lee quarter and passed away to windward, at its nearest position being not more than two hundred yards from us; the eye, the mouth, the nostril, the colour and form, all being most distinctly visible to us. We all felt greatly astonished at what we saw, though there were sailors among us of thirty and forty years' standing, who had traversed most seas and seen many marvels in their day. The captain was the first to exclaim: 'This must be that animal called the sea-serpent', a conclusion which, after sundry guesses, we all at last settled down to. My impression was that it was rather of a lizard than a serpentine character, as its movement was steady and uniform, as if propelled by fins, not by any undulatory power. It was in sight, from our first observing it, about ten minutes, as we were fast leaving one another on opposite tacks with a freshening breeze and the sea getting up."

"I feel, Sir, I have already occupied more of your time and space than is justiable, and have the honour to remain your obedient servant,

"An Officer of Her Majesty's ship *Daedalus*."

Now let us run over all the prominent important particulars in the reports of the appearance of the sea-serpent as seen from the *Daedalus*. The first report, which appeared in the *Times* of October, 9, 1848, contains the description of the mouth: "and when it extended its jaws, which were full of large and jagged teeth, they seemed sufficiently capacious to admit of a tall man standing upright between them." It is not said from whom the report came, nor is it signed. All the details, except this last, were afterwards substantiated by Captain M'Quhae himself and by Lieutenant Drummond. To me it seems quite impossible that the head was longer than three feet; as the neck is estimated at 16 inches in diameter, or one foot and a third, the breadth of the head, according to what we already know of the relative dimensions, cannot have been more than about two feet, and the length not more than about three feet. So the jaws, when extended, may open the mouth to about one and a half or two feet, a space which never can admit "of a tall man standing upright between them!"

The animal seen by the captain and some of the officers and crew of the *Daedalus*, was as follows: It swam with its body in a straight line. About sixty feet of its body were visible. Its head appeared to be about four feet out of the water. The part of the body hidden under water was estimated at thirty feet at least. The diameter of the neck behind the head was estimated at one foot and a third. When the animal opened its mouth, large jagged teeth were seen. "It moved with such velocity that the water was surging under its chest" (read throat, for the very chest, situated between the foreflappers, was invisible and much farther back). The head and a portion of the neck (Captain M'Quhae says, though without any reason, shoulders) were kept above the surface of the sea. The animal was, during the time it was in sight, never once below the surface. Lieutenant Drummond, however, says: the head disappeared occasionally beneath a wave for a very brief interval. The colour of the animal was a dark brown, with yellowish white under the throat. Something like the mane of a horse, or rather like a bunch of sea-weed, washed about its back. Though the Captain says: it had no fins, Lieutenant Drummond stated, that there was "a backfin which was perhaps twenty feet in the rear of the head, "and visible occasionally". If this were a true back-fin, it ought to have been constantly visible. As, however, it was only occasionally seen, we conclude that it was nothing else but one of the animal's foreflappers, occasionally coming above the surface of the water. "The captain also asserted that he saw the tail, or another fin about the same distance behind it." This of course must have been one of the animal's hind flappers. Lieutenant Drummond must have been mistaken as to the length of the head, which he described as "perhaps ten feet." His calculation evidently includes a portion of the neck. The head moreover was rather pointed, rather blunt, flattened at the top; the upperjaw projecting considerably. He too, uses the terms of shoulders in saying: "the upper part of the head and shoulders appeared of a dark brown colour, and beneath the under-jaw a brownish-white."

The three figures are tolerably well drawn; in fact they are the best of all the sketches ever made of this animal. They are as if they were delineated after the description above, but they were in reality "made from a sketch taken immediately after the animal was seen." Here, as in foregoing reports, the figures and the text complete one another. The head is not that of a serpent, but that of a mammal. The proportions of length and height, the outlines of the jaws, the length of the mouth-split, the exact place of the eye, even the flattened appearance of forehead and nose are true mammalian characters. No whiskers or bristles on the upper-lips, and no ears or earholes are drawn, or mentioned. The distance, when nearest, was about one hundred yards. It is clear that they were not visible at that distance. The nostrils are indicated in the drawing by a crescentic mark at the end of the nose or muzzle, and are afterwards mentioned as having been visible.

In short, the descriptions as well as the figures agree with our present notion of the external appearance of the animal, known as the sea-serpent. I only wish to point out here that in none of the three figures the head can boast of great correctness; for such a head would never have been described as resembling that of a snake. It is clear that it is drawn too high, too short and not flat enough.

I will insert here a single remark on a passage in Prof. Owen's reply. It is the following: Prof. Owen rejects the existence of the sea-serpent in the Norwegian Seas. "Few sea-coasts have been more sedulously searched, or by more acute naturalists (witness the labours of Sars and Loven) than those of Norway. Krakens and sea-serpents ought to have been living and dying thereabouts from long before Pontoppidan's time to our day, if all tales were true; yet they have never vouchsafed a single fragment of the skeleton to any Scandinavian collector." It may be true that Mssrs Sars and Loven often navigated along the coasts of Norway and yet never saw a sea-serpent. Prof. Owen forgets that his own countryman, Mr. Morries Stirling, saw one with his own eyes! Is this proof not decisive enough? The absence of remains is not a proof of the non-existence of the sea-serpent, as there are whales with two backfins, which are *seen* by three different *naturalists*, yet not one single bone has ever fallen under the notice of zoologists. Prof. Owen also mentions the Kraken. Now my readers know well enough that the Krakens are abundant enough, being gigantic calamaries; it is, however, possible that before the year 1848 there was no official report of such a calamary. At present, however, they may be found by scores! It may be remarked here, too, that it was not before the year 1861, that a piece of a Kraken, or gigantic calamary, was brought to Paris by the commander of the *Alecton, nota bene* notwithstanding Prof. Owen's assertion that they did not exist, as else the naturalists of Norway, and amongst them especially Sars and Loven, would have found them!

Of course it was impossible that the statement of Capt. M'Quhae agreed in details with that of Lieutenant Drummond, because the latter was immediately written after the appearance of Aug. 6th., whilst the letter of Captain M'Quhae was addressed to the Admiralty on the 11th. of October, two months afterwards and apparently written from memory.

Mr. Andrew Wilson in his *Leisure Time Studies* says of the "fin" mentioned by Lieutenant Drummond:

"This fin evidently corresponds to the structure described in the captain's report as 'something like a mane of a horse', and which the introduction of the word 'like' (as I have inserted it in parentheses after the word 'rather' in his description) serves to correlate with the 'bunch of sea-weed' which 'washed about its back'."

I believe to have clearly shown that the "fin" of Lieutenant Drummond was nothing but one of the animal's fore-flappers and the other fin, "twenty feet more backward", was one of the animal's hind-flappers, and I believe that I may express my conviction that Mr. Andrew Wilson was just as wrong in supposing this, as in his conviction that the sea-serpent of Captain M'Quhae was merely an extraordinarily developed sea-snake! A few pages further on, viz., the writer of *Leisure Time Studies*, quoting the report of Captain M'Quhae says:

"The idea that the animal observed in this instance was a huge serpent, seems to have been simply slurred over without that due attention, which this hypothesis undoubtedly merits."(!)

And on the following page:

"Suppose that a sea-snake of gigantic size is carried out of ordinary latitude, and allow for slight variations and inaccuracies in the accounts given by Captain

M'Quhae, and I think we have in these ideas the nearest possible approach to a reasonable solution of this interesting problem." (!!)

Though they don't touch our subject directly, the following words of Mssrs. H. E. Strickland and A. G. Melville, treating of the Dodo, are well worth our notice; they say *(Annals and Magazine of Natural History* 2d. Series, Vol. II, p. 444, Nov. 15 ?, 1848):
"In proof of the existence of the Dodo we have—unlike the assumed evidence of the existence of some other anomalous monsters of which we have lately heard much—every canon of cautious truthseeking fully satisfied. With no traditional superstition or belief to give an origin to such a story (a point of no little importance in such an investigation), we have here fifteen or sixteen seperate and independant authorities all alluding incidentally to the Dodo, each different in language and description, yet each of which has points of resemblance that cannot be mistaken as referring to similar objects. We have moreover drawings of the creature itself, made by different hands, and at different times, and with different objects; some of them rude and coarse to grotesqueness, other finished works of art. Yet throughout all these there run characters which it is impossible to mistake, and which satisfy us that the draughtsmen drew, not from imagination, but from something real, and from individuals of one and the same species."
I am obliged to remark here that the proof of the existence of the *Dodo,* quoted by them, is *not* unlike the proof of the existence of great sea-serpents. If they, however, had known and mentioned that a head and a foot of the Dodo are preserved in Kopenhague, they would have been right. This is *not* the case with the sea-serpent. As far as I know, there is not one *material* proof of the existence of sea-serpents. But it is with the sea-serpent just as with the different accounts and pictures of the Dodo, "throughout all which run characters which it is impossible to mistake, and which satisfy us, that the draughtsmen drew, not from imagination, but from something real, and from individuals of one and the same species".
I hope that every-one who has read all the accounts I have collected and published in this volume, and thoroughly studied the figures, will grant that there is no question of "assumed evidences of the existence of some anomalous monsters".

119.—1848?—In the *Zoologist* of 1849, p. 2356, we read: "Enormous undescribed animal apparently allied to the Enaliosauri, seen in the Gulf of California.—Captain the Hon. George Hope states that when in H. M. S. 'Fly', in the Gulf of California, the sea being perfectly calm and transparent, he saw at the bottom a large marine animal with the head and general figure of the alligator, except that the neck was much longer, and that instead of legs the creature had four large flappers, somewhat like those of turtles, the anterior pair being larger than the posterior; the creature was distinctly visible, and all its movements could be observed with ease; it appeared to be pursuing its prey at the bottom of the sea; its movements were somewhat serpentine, and an appearance of annulations, or ring-like divisions of the body, was distinctly perceptible. Captain Hope made this relation in company, and as a matter of conversation. When I heard it from the gentleman to whom it was narrated, I enquired whether Captain Hope was acquainted with those remarkable fossil animals *Ichthyosauri* and *Plesiosauri*, the supposed forms of which so nearly correspond with what he describes as having seen alive, and I cannot find that he had heard of them; the alligator being the only animal he mentioned as bearing a partial similarity to the creature in question."

Mr. Newman, the Editor of this Journal, considers this testimony "in all respects, the most interesting natural-history-fact of the present century" (*Zoologist*, 1849, Preface, Nov. 11).

Though I think that all reports of sea-serpents are very interesting natural-history facts, it is indisputable that this testimony is a very important one. If the reader for a moment brings before his mind the animal of the *Daedalus*, about eighty feet long, with a head of about three feet, a neck like the body of a serpent, the thickness behind the head being somewhat smaller than that of the head itself; at twenty feet in the rear of the head the body becoming at once much broader and provided there with two flappers; twenty feet more backwards again two flappers, and then a tail of about forty feet, ending in a point. If the reader now imagines this animal to be on the bottom of the sea, whilst he himself is placed on the deck of a vessel, the sea perfectly calm, is it not true that such an animal must make the impression of an alligator with a long neck, and having instead of paws flappers like those of a sea-turtle? If moreover the animal moved in vertical undulations, is it not very well conceivable and clear that, by the light and shadow falling on the animal from above, the curves of the animal's back (called *bunches* when it swims on the surface) must be taken as distinctly perceptible annulations or ringlike divisions of the body? I think that there can be no question but this animal was a sea-serpent. The reader will remember that Pontoppidan relates an account of a very young sea-serpent, eighteen feet in length, entangled in a fisherman's net, "a worm with four paws on the belly", and that the learned Bishop himself made the comparison: "thus it resembled a crocodile"!

120.—1848, December 31.—(*Illustrated London News* of 1849, April 14)
"To the Editor of the *Illustrated London News*."
"H. M. S. *Plumper*, Plymouth Harbour, April 10, 1849."
"Not having seen a sketch of the extraordinary creature, we passed between England and Lisbon, and being requested by several gentlemen to send you the rough one I made at the time, I shall feel much obliged by your giving it publicity in your instructive and amusing columns."

"On the morning of the 31th. December, 1848, in lat. 41° 13'N., and long 12° 31' W., being nearly due West of Oporto, I saw a long black creature with a sharp head, moving slowly, I should think about two knots, through the water, in a north westerly direction, there being a fresh breeze at the time, and some sea on I could not ascertain its exact length, but its back was about twenty feet if not more above water; and its head, as near as I could judge, from six to eight. I had not time to make a closer observation, as the ship was going six knots through the water, her head E. half S., and wind S. S. E. The creature moved across our wake towards a merchant barque on our lee-quarter, and on the port tack. I was in hopes she would have seen it also. The officers and men who saw it, and who have served in parts of the world adjacent to whale and seal fisheries, and have seen

them in the water, declare they have neither seen nor heard of any creature bearing the slightest resemblance to the one we saw. There was something on its back that appeared like a mane, and, as it moved through the water, kept washing about, but before I could examine it more closely, it was too far astern.—I remain, yours very truly
"A Naval Officer."

FIG. 31.–THE SEA-SERPENT AS SEEN BY AN OFFICER OF H. M. S. *PLUMPER*.

Evidently the Naval Officer did not send the description of the appearance and the figure, before he was repeatedly requested by several gentlemen to do so. These gentlemen would not have been so pressing, if an appearance like that of the *Daedalus* had not happened very recently. How many written testimonies of the existence of sea-serpents will not be found in log books and private journals of navigators!

121.—1849, February 18.—In the *Zoologist* of 1849 we read, p. 2459:
"Captain Adams, of the schooner Lucy and Nancy, which arrived at Jacksonville, Florida, on the 1st of April, from New York, had sight of a monster in many respects resembling the sea-monsters described by many others. Captain Adams states that on the morning of Sunday, the 18th. of February, about nine o'clock, when off the south point of Cumberland Island, about twelve miles from the St. John's (Florida) bar, the attention of himself, crew and passengers, was suddenly rivetted upon an immense sea monster, which he took to be a serpent. It lifted its head, which was that of a snake, several times out of the water, seemingly to take a survey to the vessel, and at such times displayed the largest portion of its body, and a pair of frightful fins or claws, several feet in length. His tail was not seen at any time; but, judging from the dimensions of the body, the captain supposes the leviathan to be about 90 feet in length. Its neck tapered small from the head to the body and it appeared to measure about seven feet across the broadest part of the back. The colour was that of a dirty brown. When first seen it was moving towards the mouth of the St. John's. The monster moved from the side of the vessel, and placed itself athwart its track, in front of her bows; but Captain Adams, not feeling

partial to an encounter with his snakeship, ordered the vessel to be kept off. A boy on the deck, not knowing his antagonist, had seized a harpoon, and was in the act of striking, when he was prevented by the vessel's moving off"—*"Boston Atlas"*.

At a glance we recognize the sea-serpent, as it appeared to Hans Egede. "The largest portion of its body" was seen, "and a pair of frightful fins or claws, several feet in length". The reader may compare the fig. 19 in our report n°. 5.—

122.—1849, May 30.—(*Illustrated London News*, 1850, January, 19.—)

"The following is an extract from the private log of Captain Edwards of the *Alpha*.—'Wednesday, May 30, P. M., strong breezes at N. N. W., and a sharp sea on; about 1.15 I felt a strange shaking of the ship. Mr. Thomson, my chief officer; Mr. George Park, civil engineer, cabin passenger on board, ran on deck as well as myself, when we beheld immediately under our lee quarter a monster of huge dimensions. It had no fins or broad tail, as whales have. It was of a light fawn colour, with large brown spots behind the shoulders; the head pointed like that of a porpoise. It had large glossy eyes; the shoulder was much darker than the rest of the body, which was the thickest part of it, (say twenty feet in diameter), from thence diminishing to the tail, to about the size of our mainyard in the slings (say twenty-four inches diameter). He took a turn round, and we afterwards saw him astern, and he went away in a S. E. by S. direction, at about thirty miles an hour.'—*Melbourne Daily News*, Juli, 1.—('A correspondent, who sends us the above, adds that he believes this to be the first time the sea-serpent is stated to have been seen so far south')."

Evidently the animal remained under water for a long time, and struck the vessel in coming to the surface. Seen from very near the colour evidently did not seem dark brown, but of a lighter hue. The absence of visible fins, the pointed tail, the brown spotted skin (no scales are mentioned, so it must have been smooth), the pointed head, the appearance of shoulders, the large eyes, its astonishing rapidity in swimming, all these statements characterize the sea-serpent. Alarmed at its having struck the vessel, off it went! Evidently Captain Edwards did not see the tip of the tail, which is rather pointed; he described, it is clear, what he took for the end of it, the extreme end being under water. No latitude is given in this report, but we may conclude that the appearance took place more towards the south than Melbourne is situated. This town is situated at about 38° S. lat., so the appearance may have taken place between 40° and 45° S. lat., and of course between 110° and 145° W. longitude, in the common track of vessels.

123.—1849, September 15.—(*Illustrated London News* for 1850, January 12).— Extract from a letter, dated "H. M. S. *Cleopatra*, Singapore, Oct. 26, 1849", from an officer of that ship:—"Sept. 15. This evening they reported the *Sea-Serpent*: several of the men, as well as the officer of the, forecastle, saw the monster; and they all ran aft to see it from the stern: they say it was about *thirty feet long*. After the report, all hands came to deck; but the evening was fast drawing to a close, and the ship going at eight knots, soon left the monster astern, going through the water very quickly to the N. W."—*(From a Correspondent.)*

Most probably this appearance took place in the Indian Ocean between latitude 10 and 20 S. and longitude 50 and 70 E.

If one of the gentlemen of the *Cleopatra* is still in the land of the living, he will greatly oblige me by sending me some more details of the external appearance of the animal, and of the place where the animal was seen.

"The Rev. Alfred Charles Smith, M. A., an excellent naturalist, who passed the three summer months of 1850 in Norway, and who published" his *Notes on Observations in Natural History during a Tour in Norway* "in the *Zoologist* for that and the following year, thus alludes to his own inquiries, which, if they add nothing to the amount of fact accumulated, add weight to the testimonies already adduced". (Gosse, *Romance of Natural History*, 13th. Ed., Vol. I., p. 282.)

"Being in the country of the renowned Bishop Pontoppidan, and in the fjords which are generally claimed as the home, or, at any rate, as one of the habitations of the sea-serpent, whose existence seems yet to be a disputed point in England, I lost no opportunity of making inquiries of all I could see, as to the general belief in the country regarding the animal in question; but all, with one single exception— naval officers, sailors, boatmen, and fishermen—concurred in affirming most positively that such an animal did exist, and had been repeatedly seen off their coasts and fjords, though I was never fortunate enough to meet a man who could boast of having seen him with his own eyes. All, however, agreed in unhesitating belief as to his existence and frequent appearance; and all seemed to marvel very much at the scepticism of the English, for refusing credence to what to the minds of the Norwegians seemed so incontrovertible. The single exception to which I have alluded, was a Norwegian officer, who ridiculed what he called the credulity or gullibility of his countrymen; though I am bound to add my belief, that he did this, not from any decided opinion of his own, but to make a show of superior shrewdness in the eyes of an Englishman, who, he at once concluded, must undoubtedly disbelieve the existence of the marine monster. That Englishman, however, certainly partakes of the credulity of the Northmen, and cannot withhold his belief in the existence of some huge inhabitant of those northern seas, when, to his mind, the fact of his existence has been so clearly proved by numerous eye-witnesses, many of whom were too intelligent to be deceived, and too honest to be doubted."

The reader will remember the splendid hoax of the *New York Tribune* (1852); now Mr. Robert Froriep in his *Tagsberichte über die Fortschritte der Natur- und Heilkunde*, no 486, already doubted this report. After some time (n°. 491) he communicated to his readers that according to the *Philadelphia Bulletin*, the whole was a hoax, but to show them how firm a believer Mr. Froriep, nevertheless, remained, he adds:

"This, however will not prevent us from bestowing further attention on the subject of the Sea-Serpent."

124.—1850?—The following evidence may be called one of the more interesting which tell about the habits of the sea-serpent. In the *Zoologist* of 1862, p. 7850, we read:

"Off Madeira, on board R. M. S. *Thames*. Made acquaintance with a Captain Christmas, of the Danish Navy, a proprietor in Santa Cruz, and holding some office about the Danish Court. He told me he once saw a sea-serpent between Iceland and the Faroe Islands. He was lying in to a gale of wind, in a frigate of which he had the command, when an immense shoal of porpoises rushed by the ship, as if pursued, and lo and behold a creature with a neck moving like that of a swan, about the thickness of a man's waist, with a head like a horse, raised itself slowly and gracefully from the deep, and seeing the ship it immediately disappeared again, head foremost, like a duck diving. He saw it only for a few seconds; the part above water seemed about eighteen feet in length. He is a singularly intelligent man, and by no means one to allow his imagination to run away with him.— *Stephen Cave, M. P. for Shoreham;* 35, *Wilson Place, April* 29, 1861, *in a letter to Mr. Gosse."*

It is a very remarkable fact that we meet here the sea-serpent between Iceland and the Far-Oer, a place situated between the two most frequented parts of the North Atlantic, i. e. the coasts of Norway and the coasts of the United States. But it is not the first time; the readers will remember the report of Hans Egede (n°. 5) and that of Capt. Brown (n°. 56). Remarkable, too, is the fact that the sea-serpent now made its appearance in a gale of wind. Is this not a matter of surprise as everywhere else is stated that it appears only in fine weather? Is it not reasonable therefore, to conclude that the animal feels comfortable in fine weather, but that, being an air-breathing animal it must come to the surface from time to time and may consequently be seen at times when there is wind? There is the statement of Captain M'Quhae, who speaks of a "breeze" and here we meet with "a gale of wind". It is also worthy of our notice that Capt. Cristmas mentions the immense shoal of porpoises rushing by the ship, as if pursued, and a sea-serpent making its appearance. I need not remind my readers of the same observation of some gentlemen near Nova Scotia (n°. 97). Later on we shall have the report in which a sea-serpent gripped "a whale" (of the smaller kind) in its fin, and we have already learned that a sea-serpent (n°. 54) was engaged with "a whale" (of the smaller kind).

Not less important is the description of the long neck, moving like that of a swan, and disappearing head foremost like a duck diving. Nearly exactly the same thing was observed in 1879, April 5.

The thickness of the neck was that of a man's waist, the part above the water measured eighteen feet in length, and yet the foreflappers remained hidden under water. The head is described as resembling that of a horse, which may be the result of the animal bearing a mane, and when first rising out of the water, holding its head in a nearly right angle with the neck. Moreover the nostrils might have been widely opened. The animal of Capt. M'Quhae had also a neck of one foot and a third in diameter; head and neck had a length of about twenty feet, for at about twenty feet in the rear of the head was seen the animal's fore flapper. So we may conclude that these two individuals were of the same or nearly of the same length.

125.—1853?—Dr. Traill says in the *Proceedings of the Royal Society at Edinburgh*, n°. 44, May, 1854, that it "is said to have been seen lately in some of their fjords."

126.—1854, September 4.—(*Illustrated London News*, for 1855, February 17.—)
"It is reported by the British Brig *Albeona*, arrived at Liverpool, that on the 4th. of September last, about five in the afternoon, in lat. 38 S., long 13 E., while the ship was under a light wind and in smooth water, a sea-monster of great size and singular appearance was descried. Attention was first directed to it by the broken action of the water, which otherwise was smooth all around. The animal was discovered protruding its head above water to the length of about 30 feet, at an angle of 60 degrees to the horizon. His head was about 12 feet long and was marked by a white stripe or streak down each side. At about six feet from the termination of the streaks, which were presumed to be its jaws, there was a protuberance on its back like a small water-cask. The creature kept its mouth shut, but its eyes were plainly visible. At the point of contact with the water the body seemed about as much as the ship's long-boat round. The general colour of the body was black, but under the jaw was a quantity of loose skin, like a pouch, of a lighter colour than the rest of the animal. While under observation he dipped under water three times, remaining submerged about a minute each time. From the broken action of the water at different points, it seemed as if protuberances, similar to that on the back existed on various parts of the body. From the best conjecture that could be made, it was computed at 180 feet in length over all."

The length of the head may be somewhat exaggerated, the largest dimensions admissible are 6 feet in breadth and about 8 feet in length, as we shall afterwards observe from one of the most recent reports. It is a remarkable fact that here mention is made of a white stripe or streak down on each side of the head, presumed to be its jaws. In the deposition of Captain Finney (n°. 34) too, we read "It had a white stripe extending the whole length of the head just above the water, there where the underjaw must have been". And in the figures of the animal seen by the gentlemen of the *Daedalus* (fig. 28, 29, 30) the underjaw is drawn white, and described whitish brown or yellowish white. The protuberance on its back (read on the back of its neck) was a fold in the animal's skin, as may be seen in the sea-lions in our Zoological Gardens, when they contract their long necks, and then the other "protuberances, similar to that on the back" were of the same character. This character of having bunches occasionally, is well known to us. Or all these protuberances were merely vertical undulations.

Attention was first paid to it by the broken action of the water, which otherwise was smooth all around. So the animal first swam for a moment just below the surface, a habit which we have often observed in foregoing reports. The general colour of the body was black, but under the jaw was a quantity of loose skin, like a pouch, of a lighter colour than the rest of the animal. As to the description of the colour of the animal's throat, it agreed with foregoing statements. As to the loose skin, and the pouch, this is also only explicable by the animal's having a skin just like sea-lions. It is so loose and folds so easily, that if the head is bent a little downward, or if the neck is somewhat contracted, several folds are seen, which led Captain Brown (n°. 56) to mention "eight gills under the neck". He had better have written "gillsplits", meaning the furrows between the folds.—The length of 180 feet may be somewhat exaggerated, though we will afterwards prove that individuals of still greater length must exist.

127.—1855, August;—In the letter from Capt. G. H. Harrington to Rear-Admiral W. A. B. Hamilton, dated Liverpool, February 8, 1858, which letter will be inserted afterwards, we read:

"I am informed by Messrs Lamport and Holt, shipowners of this place, that one of their captains reported a similar thing about two years ago, off the Island of St. Helena, but they took no further notice of it, supposing that he might have been deceived."

I am convinced that the captain really saw a sea-serpent. The reader will, I hope, be convinced of it himself, after having read Captain Harrington's report (n°. 131).

128.—1856, March 30.—(*Illustrated London News* of the 3d. of May, 1856).
"To the Editor of the Illustrated London News."
"*Imogen*, Channel, 15th. April, 1856."
"Sir.—We beg to hand you the enclosed Sketch of a Sea-Serpent we had the good fortune to sight on the 30th. of March last."
"Imogen, from Algoa Bay, towards London. Sunday 30th. March, 1856. Lat. 29 deg., 11 min. N., Long. 34 deg., 36 min. W., bar. 30.50; calm and clear. Four vessels visible to southward and westward."
"About five minutes past eleven A. M., to helmsman drew our attention to something moving through the water, and causing a strong ripple about 400 yards distant from our starboard quarter."
"In a few moments it became more distinct, presenting the appearance in fig. 1., and showing an apparent length of about forty feet (above the surface of the sea), the undulations of the water extending on each side to a considerable distance in its wake: Mr. Statham immediately ascended to the maintopsailyard, Captain Guy and Mr. Harries watching the animal from the deck with the telescope. After passing the ship about half a mile, the serpent 'rounded to' and raised its head, seemingly to look at us (fig. 2), and then steered away to the northward (N. E.), possibly to the neighbourhood of the Western Islands, frequently lifting its head (fig. 3). We traced its course until nearly on the horizon, from the topsailyard, and lost sight of it from deck about 11 h. 45 m. A. M. No doubt remained on our minds as to its being an immense snake, as the undulations of its body were clearly perceptible, although we were unable to distinguish its eyes."
"The weather being fine and the glossy surface of the sea only occasionally disturbed by slight flaws (catspaws) of wind, we had a perfect opportunity of noticing its movements."
"In conformity to your regulations we inclose our references, and remain,
"Sir, your obedient servants,
"James Guy, Commander,
"J. H. Statham, Julian B. Harries, D. J. Williamson, Passengers."

Various Accounts 233

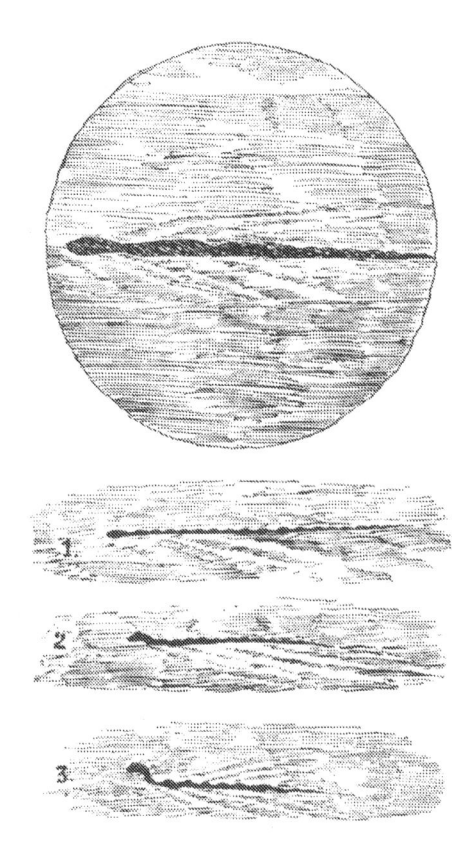

FIG. 32, 33, 34 AND 35.—THE SEA-SERPENT AS SEEN BY CAPT. GUY OF THE IMOGEN.
FIG. 32 = FIG. 33, SEEN WITH A TELESCOPE.

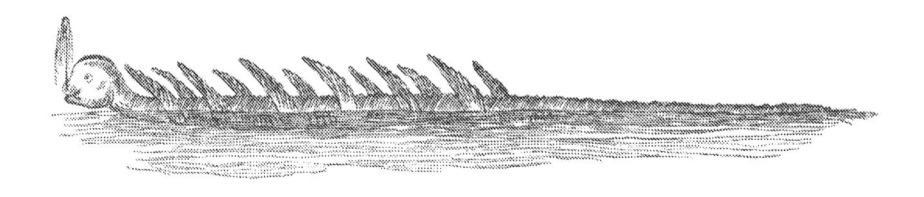

FIG. 36.—THE SEA-SERPENT AS SEEN BY CAPTAINS TREMEARNE AND MORGAN.

After the figures of Capt. M'Quhae of the *Daedalus* (n°. 118, fig. 28, 29, 30), which show the animal swimming with its body in a straight line, these four figures of the animal are the best we have, but here it is swimming with vertical undulations. To the description I can add nothing, nor need I explain anything. Description and figures complete each other and give an accurate and very natural idea of a sight of the animal seen from afar.—

129.—1856, July 8.—(The *Illustrated London News* of the 4th. of October, 1856.)
"To the Editor of the Illustrated London News."
"Colonial Agency, 4, Cullum-street, London, September 25th. 1856."
"We hand you the following extract from the log-book of our ship *Princess*, Captain A. R. N. Tremearne, in London Docks 15th. inst., from China, viz:—
"'Thuesday, July 8, 1856.—Latitude accurate 34° 56' S.; Longitude accurate 18° 14' E. At one P. M. saw a very large fish, with a head like a walrus, and twelve fins, similar to those in a black fish, but turned the contrary way. The back was from 20 to 30 feet long; also a great length of tail. It is not improbable that this monster has been taken for the great sea-serpent. Fired and hit it near the head with rifle-ball. At eight, fresh wind and fine.'"
"We submit that the repeated accounts of seeing a marine monster, whatever be its correct name or kind, yet harmonising in some leading descriptions forbid longer doubt of one such creature existing, and we inclose you a rough sketch as this one appeared, signed by Captain Tremearne, who has been six years in our employ, and is otherwise well known. His own private log contains a similar record, and we have interrogated others of the *Princess* crew, who assert the fact of such appearance."
"Captain Tremearne states that Captain Morgan, a passenger by the *Princess*, but who at St. Helena joined the ship *Senator*, to command her to Liverpool (where she is daily expected), also saw this monster, and can corroborate the statements."
"Until 13th. of October the *Princess* will be at London Dock jetty, loading for Melbourne, and naturalists and other scientific persons can there make further inquiries, provided they do not subject Captain Tremearne to correspondence or interrupt ship's duties, which are urgent for her speedy departure. The ship's log-book and the rough sketch of the fish can also be inspected at our office."
"Edmund J. Wheeler and Co."

Though the description is very short, the figure enables us to make the following conjecture. Captain Tremearne really saw a sea-serpent, swimming with extraordinary speed, most probably because, on coming to the surface, it was alarmed by the unexpected presence of the ship. Having remained under water a long time it suddenly exhaled on coming to the surface, and blew like a whale, as the figure shows.

The extreme velocity of its motion is cause that the impression of the head was that of a walrus. But this is a remarkable fact. We have already observed that a Norwegian fisherman described the head as resembling that of a seal (n°. 8), and that Mr. Cummings (n°. 29), too described at first sight the head to resemble that of a seal. Afterwards Mr. Kriukof (n°. 36) better acquainted with sea-lions, described it as resembling a sea-lion's; more than once the bristles on the upper lip are mentioned; one of the gentlemen of the *Daedalus* drew a head distinctly that of a Pinniped, and Captain Tremearne declares that it had the head of a walrus. Most probably he has seen the animal close to him and in its face, and saw the upper-lip with bristly whiskers, though this is neither mentioned nor figured. The same uncommonly rapid motion of the animal caused the captain to draw the neck too short and to see "twelve fins". He was the dupe of an optical illusion, resulting from the very rapid paddling of the animal's fore-flappers. But he has very well observed that the posture of the flappers when directed as upward as possible is "turned the contrary way to those in a black fish". The head is described by him as that of a mammal, belonging to the order of Pinnipeds, the posture of the flappers is exactly that which pinnipedian mammals, as sea-lions and walruses, would exhibit, when swimming with extreme velocity. No reptile is able to lift up its fore-limbs to such a height. The animal in this position, but seen from behind, would have the external features as shown in the figure of Lieutenant Haynes (fig. 45, n°. 148). And captain Tremearne has also very well observed and delineated that six of the fins were on the left, and six on the right sight of the animal as if rising out of the water, and that the twelve were not situated on the animal's back. The rough back, too, is a proof that the animal had a mane. The violent motions of the flappers must have caused a severe splashing and foaming of the water; it is clear that this is omitted by captain Tremearne when drawing his figure. So this report, though apparently of no worth, is, with the figure, one of the most valuable reports of an appearance of the sea-serpent, throwing light upon its rank in the system of nature. Remarkable is the fact that captain Tremearne writes: "it is not improbable that this monster has been taken for the great sea-serpent".

130.—1857, February 16.—The following letter was forwarded by Dr. Biccard to his friend Mr. Fairbridge, at his request, was then published in the *Cape Argus* of the 14th. of March, 1857, and reprinted, with the figure, in the *Illustrated London News* of 1857, June 13.—

"Cape Town, 11th. March, 1857.
"My dear Fairbridge,—According to your wish, I give you a short description of the Sea-Serpent seen by me and others opposite the old light-house at Green Point."
"On Monday, the 16th. of February last, I went out to Green Point in the afternoon. At about 5 p. m., or a little after, I was called by Mr. Murray, the light-house-keeper, to 'come and see a sea monster'. I proceeded to the light-house, and from thense I saw on the water, about 150 yards from the shore, the serpent, of which some details have already appeared in print. It was lying in the position shown in the accompanying sketch n°. 1. I borrowed a rifle from Mr. Hall (Mr. Murray's father-in-law), and fired at the animal. The ball fell short in front of it by about four yards, as shown in the sketch. The animal did not move, and I then fired a second shot, the ball striking about a foot and a half from it. The serpent, then apparently startled, moved from his position, straightened himself out, and went under water, evidently getting out of the way. He was invisible for about ten minutes, at the expiration of which interval he reappeared at about two hundred yards distance, and I should say about forty yards further off. He then came right

on towards the place where I first saw him; but, before arriving there, my son, who had joined me, fired at the animal. Unlickly, the discharge broke the nipple of the rifle, and I was thus prevented from further firing. Upon reaching the place he had first occupied, the serpent formed himself into the position delineated in Sketch n°. 2. He then stood right into the bay, and soon afterwards we lost sight of him altogether."

"As I have stated, the distance the animal kept from shore was not more than 200 yards; its length was about 200 feet, but its thickness I cannot tell, the upper part of the body only being visible. The head could be seen but indistinctly, as he raised it at intervals, as shown in the sketch. I consider the protuberance to be the upper part of the head, but I could not discover the eyes, notwithstanding the short distance, and the telescope which was a pretty good one. The colour of the animal was a dark dull colour, except the head, which was maculated with large white spots. The weather at this time was very calm, with a light northwesterly breeze. Besides myself, the serpent was seen by Mr. Hall, Mr. Murray, Mrs. and Miss Biccard, my two sons, and my coachman, who all saw it distinctly."

"Yours, &c.,
"Biccard."

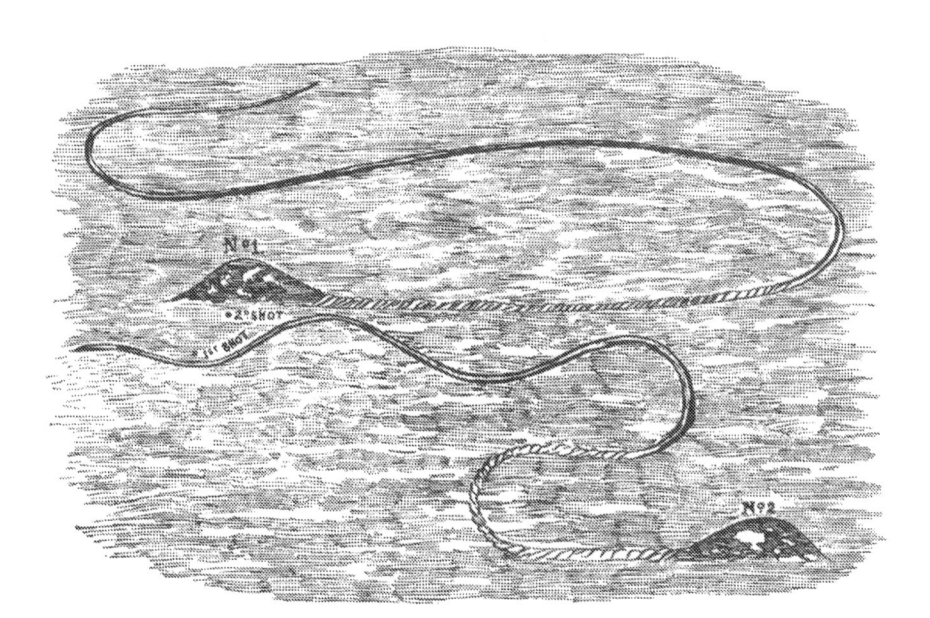

FIG. 37 AND 38.–TWO POSITIONS OF THE SEA-SERPENT AS SEEN BY DR. BICCARD.

Nobody can help laughing when he sees this figure, representing something very much like a black buoy, with white streaks and spots, and glittering in the sun, having a long rope attached to it! It is, however, pretty well done for one who cannot draw. As in so many other instances the figures and the text complete each other. The animal appears here nearly in the same position as it did in the Harbour of Gloucester, in 1817. The same astonishing lateral flexibility! "It lay down, in turning, in the form of a staple or horse-shoe" we have learned on that occasion, and "in doing so it nearly touched its head with its tail", "the tail and the head then appeared only to be a few yards one from another", once "it lay down in the form of an S", &c. Though the Doctor does not describe this position, his figures tell it us. As the second ball apparently startled it, it changed its position, straightened itself out, disappeared, and came up after ten minutes, about forty yards further off. It behaved in the same way in the Harbour of Gloucester. The length may again be somewhat exaggerated, though I do not think such to be the case. The white streaks and spots on the head may have been the shining reflexion of day or sunlight, the head being thoroughly wet, as the animal raised and dropped it at intervals, which made the water run down every time, but it is also very possible that the individual was really spotted on its head.

131.—1857, December 12.—(The *Times* of February 5, 1858; the *Zoologist* for 1858, p. 5989.).

"I beg to enclose you a copy of an extract from the meteorological journal kept by me on board the ship *Castilian*, on a voyage from Bombay to Liverpool. I have sent the original to the Board of Trade, for whom the observations have been made during my last voyage. I am glad to confirm a statement made by the commander of Her Majesty's ship *Daedalus*, some years ago, as to the existence of such an animal as that described by him.—G. H. Harrington; 14 and 14 1/2, South Castle Street, Liverpool, February 2, 1858.—"

"Copy of an Extract from the Board of Trade Meteorological Journal, kept by Captain Harrington, of the ship *Castilian*, from Bombay to Liverpool."

"Ship *Castilian*, December 12, 1857, north-east end of St. Helena, bearing north-west, distance 10 miles."

"At 6.30 p. m., strong breezes and cloudy, ship sailing about twelve miles per hour. While myself and officers were standing on the lee-side of the poop, looking towards the island, we were startled by the sight of a huge marine animal, which reared its head out of the water within twenty yards of the ship, when it suddenly disappeared for about half a minute, and then made its appearance in the same manner again, showing us distinctly its neck and head about ten or twelve feet out of the water. Its head was shaped like a long nun-buoy, and I suppose the diameter to have been seven or eight feet in the largest part, with a kind of scroll, or tuft of loose skin, encircling it about two feet from the top; the water was discoloured for several hundred feet from its head, so much so that, on its first appearance, my impression was that the ship was in broken water, produced, as I supposed, by some vulcanic agency since the last time I passed the island; but the second appearance completely dispelled those fears, and assured us that it was a monster of extraordinary length, which appeared to be moving slowly towards the land. The ship was going too fast to enable us to reach the mast-head in time to form a correct estimate of its extreme length, but from what we saw from the deck we conclude that it must have been over two hundred feet long. The boatswain and several of the crew who observed it from the top-gallant forecastle, state that it was more than double the length of the ship, in which case it must have been five hundred feet. Be that as it may, I am convinced that it belonged to the serpent tribe; it was of a dark colour about the head, and was covered with several white spots. Having a press of canvas on the ship at the time, I was unable to round to without risk, and therefore was precluded from getting another sight of this leviathan of the deep."

"George Henry Harrington, Commander."
"William Davies, Chief Officer."
"Edward Wheeler, Second Officer."

The animal seen by Captain Harrington was no doubt a sea-serpent, of which at first sight, only the head and a small portion of the neck were exposed to the eyes of the spectators. Afterwards, when the animal moved slowly towards the land, its whole length must have been visible, and estimated at about two hundred feet. The head was seen in such a direction that it resembled a "nun-buoy". The diameter of the head may have been six feet. At a moment that the animal contracted its neck, an annular fold was formed round the neck just behind the head, as may be seen in our sea-lions, and which led Captain Harrington to write "with a kind of scroll, or tuft of loose skin, encircling it about two feet from the top" of the head, i. e. somewhat behind the occiput. The discolouring of the water has of course nothing at all to do with the animal or its appearance.

Some days afterwards (*Times* of February 13, 1858; *Zoologist* for 1858, p. 5990) this document was followed by an account of Frederic Smith, who stated that on December 28th., 1848, commanding the ship Pekin, they saw an extraordinary creature, which, when harpooned, and hoisted on board, proved to be a piece of a gigantic sea-weed, twenty feet long. So like a huge living monster did this appear, that, had circumstances prevented my sending a boat to it, I should certainly have believed I had seen the great sea-snake." Captain Smith firmly believes that the animals of the *Daedalus* and of the *Castilian* were pieces of the same weed.

Hereupon, "An officer of H. M. S. *Daedalus*" wrote an apology in the *Times* of 16th. February, which we have inserted in n°. 118. This letter was immediately followed in the same paper of the same date by the two following:

"Sir.—A letter appears in the *Times* of to-day signed 'Frederic Smith' on the subject of the sea-serpent.

"The writer has this advantage over others who have reported the occasional appearance of what he fairly calls 'this queer fish'—that he has handled as well as seen it. Still there would seem to be a considerable variety in the genus, for, while the specimen obtained by the *Pekin* in 1848 was 4 inches in diameter and 20 feet in length, that seen from the *Circassian* is described, if I remember rightly, in your paper of 4th. inst. as 10 feet or 11 feet in diameter, and upwards of 200 feet in length."

"In this latter instance it was seen only, and but a passing sight; and testimony of this kind is just that which naturalists may be slow to receive as evidence of any new fact; nevertheless the practised vision of the *Circassian's* commander should go for something, and as it would appear from the following letter that

Captain Harrington is to be in town next week and ready to answer any questions, it might be worth the while of some of our philosophers to examine a little into the question of what Capt. Harrington and his officers really did see."
"I have the honour to be, Sir, your most obedient servant
"Blackheath, February 12." "W A. B. Hamilton"

For *Circassian* of course read *Castilian*.

"14, South Castle Street, Liverpool, February 8.
"Dear Sir,—I am in receipt of your favour of the 6th. of February, and should be glad if my communication to the *Times* might be instrumental in dispelling many doubts respecting the existence of such a monster as that described by myself and my officers."
"I communicated it to Capt. Schomberg, R. N., of this place, in the course of conversation, who advised me by all means to send a copy of it to the *Times*."
"Notwithstanding the assertions of men of science to the contrary I am now sure that such animals exist. I could no more be deceived than (as a seaman) I could mistake a porpoise for a whale. If it had been at a great distance it would have been different, but it was not above 20 yards from the ship."
"I am of opinion that this animal makes its appearance at the surface at long intervals only. I am informed by Messrs. Lamport and Holt, shipowners of this place, that one of their captains reported a similar thing about two years ago, off the Island of St. Helena, but they took no further notice of it, supposing, as your friend seems to do, that he might have been deceived."
"Twenty people, including Mrs. Harrington and my two officers, saw it as distinctly as I now see the gas light which I am writing by. I am well known in London, having commanded a steam transport during the Russian war belonging to the North of Europe Steam Navigation Company."
"Captain Claxton, R. N., of the Priory, Battersea, is a personal friend of mine. I am also well known to Sir Colin Campbell, who is now in the East. My present ship is 1604 tons new measurement, and a new ship, of which I own a good part myself. There are, therefore, many reasons (in addition to my holding a firstclass certificate in the mercantile marine) to hinder me from propagating a report which can do me no good, and, if untrue, do injury to science in the room of assisting it to elicit the truth in so important a matter as the discovery of the inhabitants of the deep."
"I shall be in town for three or four days in the early part of next week. A letter addressed to me at the Jerusalem Coffee-House will meet with attention, and, if my limited time permit, I should be glad to have an interview with yourself, or any of your friends who might wish to have a verbal explanation in this matter."
"I have the honour to remain, Sir, your obedient servant
"G. H. Harrington."
"To Rear-Admiral W. A. B. Hamilton"

This letter was again answered in a very witty way in the *Times* of Febr. 23, 1858; this however, will be inserted in our chapter on Explanations.
In the *Zoologist* for 1858, p. 6015, Mr. Alfred Charles Smith, an old acquaintance of ours (p. 299) now wrote the following remark:
"To one who firmly believes in the existence of some huge marine monster of the serpent-form, such as the Northmen love to descant upon (and I am not ashamed

to own to such credulity, as I have already declared in my Notes on Norway (Zool. 3229), the clear and minute account of Capt. Harrington, on the sea-monster which he and twenty people saw on the 12th of December last, off the coast of St. Helena, was exceedingly interesting; nor did the subsequent letter of Mr. F. Smith tend to shake my belief in the accuracy of Capt. Harrington's statement, the particulars of the two alleged appearances being so very different. I am not, however, about to argue the point, the premises before us being far too unsatisfactory and vague to argue from. I merely write to express my hope that as you have admitted the first correspondence on the subject to the pages of the *Zoologist*, you will give both parties fair play, and insert the remaining letters, which appeared in the *Times* of February 16th and 23 respectively, copies of which I enclose, so that naturalists may have an opportunity of studying the case in all its bearings, before they form their conclusions.—Alfred Charles Smith; Yatesbury Rectory, Calne, March 5, 1858."

Of course, it was but natural that also foreign newspapers should take great delight in this polemic. So we find in the *Revue Britannique*, of 1858, n° 2, Febr. p. 496, an article full of erroneous statements:

"Amongst the grave questions of the day, we did not think of meeting again, in the newspapers, with the famous sea-serpent, the problematic existence of which seemed to be bannished to the world of apocryphal, or at least antediluvian animals; but no! three new eye-witnesses declare to have seen it, and very well too. Now a Captain Smith, of Newcastle, writes that he is convinced that these witnesses have been illuded, as he himself was on the 28th. of December, 1848, when after believing to see through his telescope an extraordinary monster, and after lowering the great net of the ship, he drew in only a gigantic sea-weed of twenty feet in length, which really had the form, attributed to the fantastic reptile. This indirect refutation, however, does not discourage the Rear-Admiral Harrington (imagine, a Rear-Admiral!) who in a second article in the *Times*, repeats that he is sure of the fact, that he has seen the sea-serpent twenty fathoms from his ship, that he has recognized it, as if he would have recognized a whale on the side of a porpoise, that his wife, who was on board, has seen it with him, as had his two officers, in short, that he will come to London, as soon as he has terminated his business at Liverpool, and will furnish all evidences demanded by science and scepticism. If he had only brought home the animal's tail or one of its fins!"

132—1858, January 26,—The *Illustrated London News* of March 20, 1858, mentions:

"The following is a report made by Captain Suckling, of the ship *Carnatic*, of London, of a Sea Serpent seen by him between the Cape of Good Hope and St. Helena:—On the 26th of January, in latitude 19° 10' S., long 10° 6' W., about 5 minutes after noon, my attention was called by Captain Shuttleworth, a passenger on board the *Carnatic* to a large spar sticking out of the water one end some thirty feet above the level of the sea. It appeared to me to be the lower mast of some wrecked vessel, and having the glass in my hand, with which I had been looking at an American vessel in sight, I examined it narrowly. It seemed to be passing very rapidly to the eastward, having altered its bearings several points in the course of a few minutes, when it suddenly disappeared, and came up shortly afterwards astern of the ship. It was seen by all those on deck at the time, and it is their opinion, as well as my own, that it was an enormous sea-serpent. The American ship *A. B. Thompson* from Bombay to London, was in company at the time—wind light and variable, with clear weather".—We have not space for the Sketch obligingly send with this account".

The comparison with a spar, an unwrought spar, or spruce, a log of timber, etc., has been made more than once, as the reader will remember, and when we compare the figures, drawn by an officer of H. M. S. *Plumper* (fig. 31), and by Major Senior (fig 46), we can easily imagine, that in this position the animal must have illuded the observers more than once. It is a pity that the sketch has not been published. How many interesting drawings have in this way got into the paperbasket!

In 1860 Mr. P. H. Gosse published his *Romance of Natural History*, First Series. The last chapter of this volume is entitled "the Great Unknown" and is entirely devoted to the Great Sea-Serpent. His manner of teaching Natural History to his readers was, as the able writer says himself, a poetical one. "In my many year's wandering through the wide field of Natural History, I have always felt towards it something of a poet's heart, though destitute of a poet's genius". I can recommend every zoologist and botanist to read his work in his leasure hours; I have read it with great interest and pleasure, increasing my knowledge, wandering with the writer from north to south and from east to west, from one pole to the other and from continents to the greatest depths of the ocean!

The sea-serpent's question was such a favourite one of this romantic naturalist, that in his preface he wrote the following about it:

"If I may venture to point out one subject on which I have bestowed more than usual pains, and which I myself regard with more than common interest, it is that of the last chapter in this volume. An amount of evidence is adduced for the existence of the sub-mythic monster popularly known as 'the sea-serpent', such as has never been brought together before, and such as ought almost to set doubt at rest. But the cloudy uncertainty which has invested the very being of this creature; its home on the lone ocean; the fitful way in which it is seen and lost in its vast solitudes; its dimensions, vaguely gigantic; its dragon-like form; and the possibility of its association with beings considered to be lost in an obsolete antiquity;—all these are attributes which render it peculiarly precious to a romantic naturalist. I hope the statisticians will forgive me if they cannot see it with my spectacles."

His chapter on the sea-serpent will also be read with great interest. But there are several facts which he seems not to have been able to explain. In describing the animal, seen near Cape Ann, 1817, he writes: *"no appearance of mane was seen by any"*, without giving any explanation; he has evidently underlined these words to draw the readers' attention to this evidence, which is so quite contradictory to others, mentioned before and afterwards. On the same page (p. 284) when repeating the expression of one of the eye-witnesses "the mode of progression was like that of a caterpillar", Mr. Gosse inserts his opinion in the following terms: "probably a looping or geometric caterpillar". Now my readers will be at one with me, that the motion of the geometric caterpillar is the last with which that of the sea-serpent can be compared! The rapid motion of a common caterpillar of some butterfly, when tickled on its back part, will give the best idea."

The writer further tries to throw discredit on reports of Americans. He says (p. 287):

"Though the position and character of some of these witnesses add weight to their testimony, and seem to preclude the possibility of their being either deceived or deceivers, on a matter which depended on the use of their eyes, yet, owing to a habit prevalent in the United States, of supposing that there is somewhat of wit in gross exaggerations, or hoaxing inventions, we do naturally look with a lurking suspicion on American statements, when they describe unusual or disputed phenomena."

I, however, am of the contrary opinion, and may turn his words in the following way: Though we generally and naturally look with a lurking suspicion on American statements, when they describe unusual or disputed phenomena, owing to a habit prevalent in the United States, of supposing that there is somewhat of wit in gross exaggerations, or hoaxing inventions, we are bound to admit all that is stated by such persons of unimpeachable character as Col. Perkins and others, whose testimonies we have inserted in our papers. They evidently communicated what they saw, without any exaggeration and without any tendency to crack a joke or to hoax.

Again p. 318 of his work, after having treated of only a few of the different reports, that had come in up to his days (1860) Mr. Gosse goes on in the following terms:

"A large mass of evidence has been accumulated; and I now set myself to examine it. In so doing, I shall eliminate from the inquiry all the testimony of Norwegian eye-witnesses, that obtained in Massachusetts in 1817, and various statements made by French and American captains since. Confining myself to English witnesses of known character and position, most of them being officers under the Crown, I have adduced the following testimonies."

Here again I must point out that there is not a single reason to exclude all testimonies not coming from British navigators. With such reasoning Mr. Gosse makes himself ridiculous in the eyes of all reasonable persons of his own and of other nations!

That it is wrong to exclude reports, because they are of Americans or Norwegians, the reader himself will be ready to admit, I think, after having read the different reports mentioned in this volume.

"The following testimonies" now, alluded to by Mr. Gosse, are:

"1. That of five British officers, who saw the animal at Halifax, N. S., in 1833" (n°. 97).

"2. That of Captain M'Quhae and his officers, who saw it from the *Daedalus* in 1848," (n°. 118).

"3. That of Captain Beechy, who saw something similar from the *Blossom*" (n°. 104).

"4. That of Mr. Morries Stirling, who saw it in a Norwegian fjord" (n°. 113).

"5. That of Mr. Davidson, who saw it from the *Royal Saxon*, in 1829" (n°. 93).

"6. That of Captain Steele and others, who saw it from the *Barham*, in 1852." (See our Chapter on Would-Be Sea-Serpents, 1852, August 28).

"7. That of Captain Harrington and his officers, who saw it from the *Castilian*, 1857" (n°. 131).

To our great astonishment Mr. Gosse also alludes to n°. 6: That of Captain Steele, who saw it from the *Barham*, in 1852. Some pages before, Mr. Gosse himself throws great doubt on this report, believing that the animal seen by Captain Steele and his officers was a scabbard-fish, (the reader, I hope, will take the trouble to look up the report of 1852, August 28, in my Chapter on Would-Be Sea-Serpents, to read there again Mr. Gosse's own opinion of this report), and now he uses this report amongst others to examine to which of the recognized classes of created beings this rover of the ocean can be referred!

Now Mr. Gosse passes to this inquiry: first, he asks, is it an animal at all? And he comes to the conclusions that this must be so, for else the being could not move with that astonishing rapidity. Further he examines the sea-weed hypothesis, the seal-hypothesis, &c., and winds up with: "my own confident persuasion, that there exists some oceanic animal of immense proportions, which has not yet been received into the category of scientific zoology; and my strong opinion, that it possesses close affinities with the fossil *Enaliosauria* of the lias."

All the above-mentioned views will be considered in Chapter V.

To our great surprise we see that Mr. Newman, the editor of the *Zoologist*, who ever was a warm defender of the sea-serpent, and like Mr. Gosse firmly believed that there are still living *Plesiosauri*, is of another opinion in 1860. In this year, a very large riband fish was captured on the Bermuda Isles. Three descriptions of this fish appeared in the *Zoologist* (p. 6934, p. 6986, p. 6989), the last by Mr. Newman himself, who, thinking that it was a new species, gave it the name of *Regalecus Jonesii*. The second description was by Mr. Jones; the naturalist on the Bermudas, at whose deposal the fish was placed by Mr. Trimingham, the captor. Mr. Jones, after his description, points out some striking peculiarities, which this riband-fish and the sea-serpent seen by captain M'Quhae, had in common, and concludes that a part of the reports of the great sea-serpent must have been caused by the appearance of riband fishes. Now, Mr. Newman, after the description of his new species *Regalecus Jonesii*, as I have already said, seems to waver in his opinion, for he adds:

"In reference to the last question mooted by Mr. Jones, the similarity of *Regalecus Jonesii* to Capt. M'Quhae's sea-serpent, I do not consider myself competent to express an opinion. I am quite willing for the present to allow every sea-serpent to hold on its own course; hereafter a better opportunity may be afforded on comparing and arranging the conflicting evidence already published in the 'Zoologist'."

133, 134.—1861? August.—(*Zoologist*, 1862, p. 7850).—

"On a Sunday afternoon, in the middle of August, above a hundred persons, at that time in and about the hotel, were called on to observe an extraordinary appearance in the sea, at no great distance from the shore. Large shoals of small fish were rushing landwards in great commotion, leaping from the water, crowding on each other, and showing all the common symptoms of flight from the pursuit of some wicked enemy. I had already more than once remarked this appearance from the rocks, but in a minor degree; and on these occasions I could always distinguish the shark, whose ravages among the 'manhaidens' was the cause of such alarm. But the particular case in question was far different from those. The pursuer of the fugiting shoals soon became visible; and that it was a huge marine monster, stretching to a length quite beyond the dimensions of an ordinary fish, was evident to all observers. No one, in short, had any doubt as to its being the sea-serpent, or one of the species to which the animal or animals so frequently before seen belonged. The distance at which this one was, for ten minutes or a quarter of an hour, visible, made it impossible to give a description of its apparent dimensions so accurate as to carry conviction to the sceptical. For us who witnessed it, it was enough to be convinced that the thing was a reality. But one of the spectators, Dr. Amos Binney, a gentleman of scientific attainments, drew up a minute account of it, which is deposited in the archives of one of the Philosophical Societies of Boston. I was and am quite satisfied that on this occasion I had a partial and indistinct but positive view of this celebrated nondescript; but had the least doubt rested on my mind it would have been entirely removed by the event of the day following the one just recorded. On that day, a little before noon, my wife was sitting, as was her wont, reading on the upper piazza of the hotel. She was alone. The gentlemen, including myself and my son, were, as usual, absent at Boston, and the ladies were scattered in various directions. She was startled by a cry from the house of 'The sea-serpent! the sea-serpent!' But this had been so frequent, by the way of joke, since the event of the preceding day, and was so like 'The wolf! the wolf!' of the fable, that it did not attract her particular attention for a moment or two, until she observed two women belonging to the family of the hotel keeper running along the piazza towards the corner nearest the sea, with wonder in their eyes, and the cry of 'The serpent! the serpent! he is turning! he is turning!' spontaneously bursting from their lips. Then my wife did fix her looks in the direction they ran; and sure enough she saw, apparently quite close beyond the line formed by the rising ground above the rocks, a huge serpent, gliding gracefully through the waves, having evidently performed the action of turning round. In an instant it was in a straight line, moving rapidly on; and after coasting for a couple of minutes the north west front of the hotel, and (as accurately as the astonished observer could calculate) looking as it stretched at full-length about the length of the piazza,—that is to say, about ninety feet,—it sank quietly beneath the surface, and was seen no more. The person who was thus so lucky as to get this unobstructed view is one so little liable to be led astray by any imaginary impulse, that I may reckon on her statement with entirely as much confidence as if my own eyes had demonstrated its truth."—Grattan's *Civilized America*, p. 39.—

Mr. Newman, the editor of the *Zoologist*, ought to have mentioned the writer of the article, the date of it and the locality where the appearance took place. It was most probably Nahant, the well known watering place near Lynn, Mass. I have had no opportunity to consult Grattan's *Civilized America*, therefore I have placed the note of interrogation after the above-mentioned year.

In this report only a few words are devoted to the description of the animal, yet the description itself is given as well as possible by the lady who saw it from the upper piazza of the hotel.

135.—1863, May 16th.—(*Zoologist*, 1863, p. 8727).

"The following is a copy of a letter from an officer of the African mail steamer *Athenian*, addressed to a gentleman in this town:—'African Royal Mail Screw

Steamer *Athenian*, Cape Palmas, May, 16, 1863.—My dear Sir,—All doubts may now be set at rest about the great sea-serpent. On the 6th. of May the African Royal Mail Steam Ship *Athenian* on her passage from Teneriffe to Bathurst, fell in with one. At about 7 a. m. John Chapple, quartermaster, at the wheel, saw something floating towards the ship. He called the attention of the Rev. Mr. Smith and another passenger, who were on deck at the time, to it. On nearing the steamer it was discovered to be a large snake about 100 feet long, of a dark brown colour, head and tail out of water, the body slightly under. On its head was something like a mane or sea-weed. The body was about the size of our mainmast. You are at liberty to publish this'."

The reader will observe that this too is a very insignificant description, but it mentions one of the very few cases that the tail of the animal was visible above the surface of the water.

The same report was published in the *Illustrated London News* of 1863, June, 13.—

136.—1871.—(G. Verschuur, *Eene reis om de wereld in vier honderd tachtig dagen*).—After an appearance of a would-be sea-serpent on board the *Grenada*, which caused a dispute between those who saw it and those who were not so fortunate,

"the second officer, who joined in the quarrel, declared to have seen in 1871, near the coast of Australia a sea-serpent, which was several meters in length."

137, 138, 139,140.—1872, August 20th., 21st., 23d. and 24th.—In the *Zoologist* of May 1873, p. 3517, the following statements of high respectable gentlemen are published.

"Appearance of an Animal, believed to be that which is called the Norwegian Sea-Serpent, on the Western Coast of Scotland, in August, 1872. By the Rev. John Macrae, Minister of Glenelg, Invernesshire, and the Rev. David Twopeny, Vicar of Stockbury, Kent."

"On the 20th. of August, 1872, we started from Glenelg in a small cutter, 'the Leda', for an excursion to Lochourn. Our party consisted, besides ourselves, of two ladies, F. and K., a gentleman G. B., and a Highland lad. Our course lay down the Sound of Sleat, which on that side divides the Isle of Skye from the mainland, the average of breadth of the Channel in that part being two miles. It was calm and sunshiny, not a breath of air, and the sea perfectly smooth. As we were getting the cutter along with oars we perceived a dark mass about two hundred yards astern of us, to the north. While we were looking at it with our glasses (we had three on board) another similar black lump rose to the left of the first, leaving an interval between; then an other and an other followed, all in regular order. We did not doubt its being one living creature: it moved slowly across our wake, and disappeared. Presently the first mass, which was evidently the head, reappeared, and was followed by the rising of the other black lumps, as before. Sometimes three appeared, sometimes four, five, or six, and then sank again. When they rose, the head appeared first, if it had been down, and the lumps rose after it in regular order, beginning always with that, next the head, and rising gently; but when they sank, they sank all together, rather abruptly, sometimes leaving the head visible. It gave the impression of a creature crooking up its back to sun itself. There was no appearance of undulation: when the lumps sank, other lumps did not rise in the intervals between them. The greatest number we counted was seven, making eight with the head, as shown in the sketch N°. 1. The parts were separated from each other by intervals of about their own length, the head being rather smaller and flatter than the rest, and the nose being very slightly visible above the water; but we did not see the head raised above the surface either this or the next day, nor could we see the eye. We had no means of measuring the length with any accuracy, but taking the distance from the centre of one lump to the centre of the next to be six feet, and it could scarcely be less, the whole length of the portion visible, including the intervals submerged, would be forty-five feet."

"Presently, as we were watching the creature, it began to approach us rapidly, causing a great agitation in the sea. Nearly the whole of the body, if not all of it, had now disappeared, and the head advanced at a great rate in the midst of a shower of fine spray, which was evidently raised in some way by the quick movement of the animal—it did not appear how,—and not by spouting. F. was alarmed and retreated to the cabin, crying out that the creature was coming down upon us. When within about a hundred yards of us it sank and moved away in the direction of Skye, just under the surface of the water, for we could trace its course by the waves it raised on the still sea to the distance of a mile or more. After this it continued at intervals to show itself, careering about at a distance, as long as we were in that part of the Sound, the head and a small part only of the body being visible on the surface; but we did not again on that day see it so near nor so well as at first. At one time F. and K. and G. B. saw a fin striking up at a little distance back from the head, but neither of us were then observing."

"On our return the next day we were again becalmed on the north side of the opening of Lochourn, where it is about three miles wide, the day warm and sunshiny as before. As we were dragging slowly along in the afternoon the creature again appeared over towards the south side, at a greater distance than we saw it the first day. It now showed itself in three or four rather long lines, as in the sketch N° 2, and looked considerably longer than it did the day before: as nearly

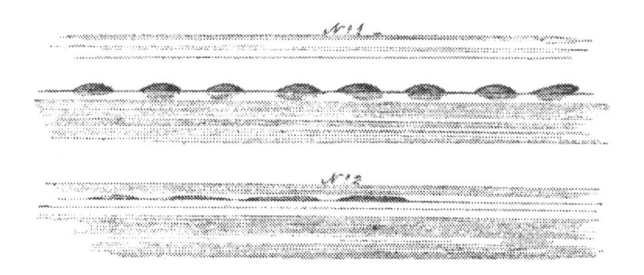

FIG. 39 AND 40.—TWO POSITIONS OF THE SEA-SERPENT AS SEEN BY THE REV. JOHN MACRAE AND THE REV. TWOPENY.

as we could compute, it looked at least sixty feet in length. Soon it began careering about, showing but a small part of itself, as on the day before, and appeared to be going up Lochourn. Later in the afternoon, when we were still becalmed in the mouth of Lochourn, and by using the oars had nearly reached the Island of Sandaig, it came rushing past us about a hundred and fifty yards to the south, on its return from Lochourn. It went with great rapidity, its black head only being visible through the clear sea, followed by a long trail of agitated water. As it shot along, the noise of its rush through the water could be distinctly heard on board. There were no organs of motion to be seen, nor was there any shower of spray as on the day before, but nearly such a commotion in the sea as its quick passage might be expected to make. Its progress was equable and smooth, like that of a log towed rapidly. For the rest of the day, as we worked our way home northwards through the Sound of Sleat, it was occasionally within sight of us until night fall, rushing about at a distance, as before, and showing only its head and a small part of its body on the surface. It seemed on each day to keep about us, and as we were always then rowing, we were inclined to think it might perhaps be attracted by the measured sound of the oars. Its only exit in this direction to the north was by the narrow Strait of Kylerhea, dividing Skye from the mainland, and only a third of a mile wide, and we left our boat, wondering whether the strange creature had gone that way or turned back again to the south."—

"We have only to add to this narration of what we saw ourselves the following instances of its being seen by other people, of the correctness of which we have no doubt:

"The ferrymen on each side of Kylerhea saw it pass rapidly through on the evening of the 21st., and heard the rush of the water: they were surprised, and thought it might be a shoal of porpoises, but could not comprehend their going so quickly."

"Finlay Macrae, of Bundaloch, in the parish of Kintail, was within the mouth of Lochourn on the 21st., with other men in his boat, and saw the creature at about the distance of one hundred and fifty yards."

"Two days after we saw it, Alexander Macmillan, boat-builder at Dornie, was fishing in a boat in the entrance of Lochduich, between Druidag and Castledonan, when he saw the animal near enough to hear the noise and see the ripple it made in rushing along in the sea. He says, that what seemed its head was followed by four or more lumps, or 'half-rounds', as he calls them, and that they sometimes rose and sometimes sank all together. He estimated its length as not less than sixty and eighty feet. He saw it also in two subsequent days in Lochduich. On all these occasions his brother Farquhar was with him in the boat, and they were both much alarmed and pulled to the shore in great haste."

"A lady at Duisdale, in Skye, a place overlooking the part of the Sound which is opposite the opening of Lochourn said that she was looking out for the glass when she saw a strange object on the sea which appeared like eight seals in a row. This was just about the time we saw it"

"We were also informed that about the same time it was seen from the island of Eigg, between Eigg and the mainland about twenty miles to the south-west of the opening of Lochourn."

"We have not permission to mention the names in these two last instances."

"John Macrae"

"David Twopeny"

"P. S. The writers of the above account scarcely expect the public to believe in the existence of the creature which they saw. Rather than that, they look for the disbelief and ridicule to which the subject always gives rise, partly on account of the animal having been pronounced to be a snake, without any sufficient evidence, but principally because of the exaggerations and fables with which the whole subject is beset. Nevertheless they consider themselves bound to leave a record of what they saw, in order that naturalists may receive it as a piece of evidence, or not, according to what they think it is worth. The animal will very probably turn up on these coasts again, and it will be always in that 'dead season', so convenient to editors of newspapers, for it is never seen but in the still warm days of summer or early autumn. There is a considerable probability that it has visited the same coasts before. In the summer of 1871 some large creature was seen for some time rushing about in Lochduich, but it did not show itself sufficiently for any one to ascertain what it was. Also some years back a well-known gentleman of the west coast, now living, was crossing the Sound of Mull, from Mull to the mainland, 'on a very calm afternoon, when', as he writes, 'our attention was attracted to a monster which had come to the surface not more than fifty yards to our boat. It rose without causing the slightest disturbance of the sea, or making the slightest noise, and floated for some time on the surface, but without exhibiting its head or tail, showing only the ridge of the back, which was not that of a whale, or any other sea-animal that I had ever seen. The back appeared sharp and ridgelike, and in colour very dark, indeed black, or almost so. It rested quietly for a few minutes, and then dropped quietly down into the deep, without causing the slightest agitation. I should say that above forty feet of it, certainly not less, appeared on the surface.' It should be noticed that the inhabitants of that western coast are quite familiar with the appearance of whales, seals and porpoises, and when they see them, they recognize them at once. Whether the creature which pursued Mr. Maclean's boat off the Island of Coll in 1808, and of which there is an account in the Transactions of the Wernerian Society (Vol. I, p. 442); was one of these Norwegian animals, it is not easy to say. Survivors who knew Mr. Maclean say that he could quite be relied upon for truth."

"The public are not likely to believe in the creature till it is caught, and that does not seem likely to happen just yet, for a variety of reasons,—one reason being that it has, from all the accounts given of it, the power of moving very rapidly. On the 20th., while we were becalmed in the mouth of Lochourn, a steam launch slowly passed us, and, as we watched it, we reckoned its rate at five or six miles an hour. When the animal rushed past us on the next day at about the same distance, and when we were again becalmed nearly in the same place, we agreed that it went quite twice as fast as the steamer, and we thought that its rate could not be less then ten or twelve miles an hour. It might be shot but would probably sink. There are three accounts of its being shot at in Norway; in one instance it sank, and in the other two it pursued the boats, which were near the shore, but disappeared when it found itself getting into shallow water."

"It should be mentioned that when we saw this creature and made our sketches of it, we had never seen Pontoppidan's 'Natural History', or his print of the Norwegian sea-serpent, which has a most striking resemblance to the first of our own sketches. Considering the great body of reasonable Norwegian evidence, extending through a number of years, which remains after setting aside fables and exaggerations, it seems surprising that no naturalist of that country has ever applied himself to make out something about the animal. In the meantime, as the public will most probably be dubious about quickly giving credit to our account, the following explanations are open to them, all of which have been proposed to me, *viz*:—porpoises, lumps of sea-weed, empty harring-barrels, bladders, logs of wood, waves of the sea, and inflated pig-skins; but as all these theories present to our minds greater difficulties than the existence of the animal itself, we feel obliged to decline them."

"D. Twopeny."

We observe at a glance that the figures show nearly exactly the same outlines as the figure of Mr. Benstrup (fig. 24). The reappearing and disappearing of the animal is well pictured and evidently recalls to my readers' mind the 'sinking down like a rock' of American reports. The reader will observe that the appearance took place nearly in the same locality as that of 1808, June (n°. 31, 32). Moreover we need not add anything to the unvarnished reports. As to the appearances of the large creatures in 1871 and 'some years back', communicated in the post-scriptum, their descriptions, are too vague for me to see in them sea-serpents.—The fin striking up at a little distance from the head, of course, was one of the animal's fore-flappers.—

Mr. Edward Newman, the Editor of the *Zoologist*, who first was a firm believer in the sea-serpent, and expressed his opinion that it might be a still living *Plesiosaurus* or an animal closely allied to it, and who afterwards evidently wavered in his opinion, after his description of the *Regalecus Jonesii*, a ribbandfish, (see above p. 319), now suddenly adds to the evidences of the Rev. John Macrae and the Rev. David Twopeny, the following note:

"I have long since expressed my firm conviction that there exists a large marine animal unknown to us naturalists; I maintain this belief as firmly as ever. I totally reject the evidence of published representations; but do not allow their imaginary figures to interfere with a firm conviction, although I admit their tendency is always in that direction: the figures and exaggerated descriptions of believers are far more damaging to a faith in such an animal than the arguments, the ridicule on the explanatory guesses of unbelievers. The guess that a little seal was magnified by Captain M'Quhae into a monster several hundred feet in length is simply incredible: we smile at the conceit, and that is all."

So he is again converted into a firm believer, but he does not now express any supposition as to the kind of animal that it may be.

141, 142, 143.—1873, November 16?, 17?, 18?—I have not been able to get a sight at the *Times* of Nov. 20th. of this year, but I have found an extract from an account in it, in the *Zoologist* of December of that year, p. 3804, running as follows:

"Mr. Joass, an eye-witness, writing in the *Times* of November 20, says, 'the ears seemed to be diaphanous and nearly semicircular flaps or valves over-arching the nostrils, which were in front. The cavity of the eye appeared to be considerably further back, and a peculiar glimmer in it, along with the sudden disappearance of the creature, presented, indeed, the only signs of its vitality, as far as I could see, while I watched it for half an hour, apparently drifting with the rising tide, but always keeping about the same distance off shore..... Dr. Soutar and I are more or less familiar with the forms of the porpoise, seal, halibut, conger, and even shark, both in and out of the water'."

In the same journal and on the same page we read the following "Extract from a letter from Mr. Joass, of Golspie, to the Rev. John Macrae, of Glenelg:"

"On Thuesday afternoon last, lady Florence Leveson Gower and the Hon. Mrs. Coke, driving near the sea, about eight miles east from Dunrobin, saw what seemed to them a large and long marine animal; on Wednesday morning Dr. Soutar, of Golspie, saw a large creature rushing about in the sea, about fifty yards from shore: it frequently raised what seemed a neck seven feet out of the water, and from the length of troubled water behind it appeared to be fifty or sixty feet long. He said to his family on meeting them at breakfast, 'If I believed in sea-serpents, I should say I had seen one this morning'. I may mention that this gentleman is a most trustworthy observer and cautious man. On Thursday I saw what seemed some drift sea-weed. When your report was published Dr. Tayler, the author of 'Thanatophidia of India' was at the castle; I asked him what he thought of the matter, and he said he was quite prepared to believe in such a monster. Mr. Vernon Harcourt told me that he was in a small yacht off Glenelg on the evening of the day mentioned in your report, and about six miles from the locality and that he and his crew saw what seemed a great moving mass, which, but for some engagement or the lateness of the hour, they would have examined."

It is evident that the greater part of the account of the *Times* is not reprinted in the *Zoologist*.

The above given descriptions are poor, giving no approximative measurements of the diameter of the neck, &c.

This is the only appearance of the animal on the *eastern* coasts of Great Britain!

Again I am obliged to express my astonishment that Mr. Newman does not mention any date, neither of the appearances. nor of Mr. Joass' letter.

114.—1875, July 8.—In the *Illustrated London News* of November 20th., 1875, appeared the following engraving and account:

"Our Engraving is an exact representation of a sketch we have received, with the following letter from the Rev. E. L. Penny, M. A., Chaplain to H. M. S. *London*, at Zanzibar, Oct. 21:—

"I send you herewith a sketch of the great sea-serpent attacking a spermwhale, which I have made from the descriptions of the captain and crew of the barque *Pauline*, and they have, after careful examination, pronounced it to be correct. The whale should have been placed deeper in the water, but I should then have been unable to depict so clearly the manner in which the animal was attacked."

"Captain Drevar, of the barque *Pauline*, bound with coals for her Majesty's naval stores at Zanzibar, when in lat. 5 deg. 13 min. S., long. 35 deg. W., on July 8 last, observed three very large sperm whales, and one of them was gripped round the body, with two turns, by what appeared to be a huge serpent. Its back was of a darkish brown and its belly white, with an immense head and mouth, the latter always open; the head and tail had a length beyond the coils about 30 ft.; its girth was about 8 ft. or 9 ft. Using its extremities as levers, the serpent whirled its victim round and round for about fifteen minutes, and then suddenly dragged the whale down to the bottom, head first. The other two whales, after attempting to release their companion, swam away upon its descent, exhibiting signs of the greatest terror."

"On July 13 this or another sea-serpent was again seen, about 200 yards off the stern of the vessel, shooting itself along the surface, 40 ft. of its body being out of the water at a time. Again, on the same day, it was seen once more, with its body standing quite perpendicular out of the water to the height of 60 ft. This time it seemed as if determined to attack the vessel, and the crew and officers armed themselves with axes for self defence."

"Captain Drevar is a singularly able and observant man, and those of the crew and officers with whom I conversed were singularly intelligent; nor did any of their descriptions vary from one another in the least—there were no discrepancies."

This report translated into German appeared in the *Illustrirte Zeitung* of Dec. 4th. 1875.

We observe that the so-called fight between the sea-serpent and the spermwhale took place in 5° 13' S. lat., 35° W. long, i. e. near Cape San Roque (Eastern coast of Brazil), and that the barque *Pauline* on October 21 of that year was at Zanzibar, laden with coals. The reports were evidently copied from the Captain's journal or log-book, and the figure was drawn by the Rev. E. L. Penny, at Zanzibar. The barque did not return directly to England, but steered for Akyab (British Burmah); from where she sailed home, for we read in the *Illustrated London News* of January 13, 1877 (p. 35, third column):

"The great sea-serpent will not be ignored. He has now appeared, by affidavit, in a police court. The captain and crew of a vessel called the *Pauline* which has arrived in the Mersey from Akyab, report that in July, 1875, off Cape San Roque, on the north-east coast of Brazil, they saw the great sea-serpent. On Thuesday, the captain, whose name is Drevar, appeared before the stipendiary magistrate of Liverpool, Mr. Raffles, and expressed a wish, on his own behalf and that of his crew, to make a declaration affirming the truth of their statements respecting the serpent. Mr. Raffles desired Captain Drevar to prepare a written declaration and bring it before him. This captain Drevar did, on Wednesday, accompanied by a number of his crew. The declaration is to the effect that he and others on board the *Pauline*, on July 8, 1875, while in latitude 5 deg. 13 min. S., longitude 35 deg. W., observed three large spermwhales, one of which was gripped round the body with two turns of what appeared to be a huge serpent. The head and tail appeared to have a length, beyond the coils, of about thirty feet, and the girth seemed to be eight or nine feet. The serpent whirled its victim round and round for about fifteen minutes, and then suddenly dragged the whale to the bottom head first. Again, on July 13, a similar serpent was seen about 200 yards off the *Pauline*, shooting itself along the surface, its head and neck being several feet out of the water. Subsequently the head of the animal was shot sixty feet into the air. The declaration was signed by Captain Drevar, Horatio Thompson (chief officer), John Henderson Landells (second officer), William Lewarn (steward) and Owen Baker (seaman).

I am so fortunate as to be able to communicate the account as it appeared in the newspapers of the 10th. and 11th. of January, 1877. I have found it in Andrew Wilson's *Leisure Time Studies*:

"The story of the mate and crew of the barque *Pauline*, of London, said to have arrived in port from a twenty months' voyage to Akyab,—about having seen 'a

FIG. 41.—THE SO-CALLED "FIGHT BETWEEN A SEA-SERPENT AND A SPERM-WHALE".

sea-serpent' while on a voyage in the Indian seas, was declared to on oath before Mr. Raffles, the stipendiary magistrate, at the Liverpool Police-Court. The affidavit was made in consequence of the doubtfullness with which anything about the 'sea-serpent' has hitherto been received; and to show the genuine character of the story it has been placed judicially on record. The following is a copy of the declaration, which will be regarded as unprecedented in its way:—

"Borough of Liverpool, in the County Palatine of Lancaster, to wit.

"We, the undersigned, captain, officers, and crew of the barque *Pauline* (of London), of Liverpool, in the county of Lancaster, in the United Kingdom of Great Britain and Ireland, do solemnly and sincerely declare that on July 8, 1876, in Lat. 5° 13' S., long 35° W., we observed three large sperm whales, and one of them was gripped round the body with two turns of what appeared to be a huge serpent. The head and tail appeared to have a length beyond the coils of about thirty feet, and its girth eight or nine feet. The serpent whirled its victim round and round for about fifteen minutes, and then suddenly dragged the whale to the bottom, head first."

George Drevar, *Master.*
Horatio Thompson.
John Henderson Landells.
Owen Baker.
Wm. Lewarn.

"Again, on July 13, a similar serpent was seen about two hundred yards off, shooting itself along the surface, the head and neck being out of the water several feet. This was seen only by the captain and one ordinary seaman, whose signatures are affixed."

George Drevar, *Master.*
Owen Baker.

"A few moments after it was seen elevated some sixty feet perpendicularly in the air by the chief officer and the following able seamen, whose signatures are also affixed."

Horatio Thompson.
William Lewarn.
Owen Baker.

"And we make this solemn declaration conscientiously, believing the same to be true, and by virtue of the provisions of an Act made and passed in the sixth year of the reign of his late Majesty, entitled 'An Act to repeal an Act of the present Session of Parliament, entitled an Act for the more effectual abolition of oath and affirmations, taken and made in various departments of the State, and to subtitute declarations in lieu thereof, and for the more entire suppression of voluntary and extrajudicial oaths and affidavits, and to make other provisions for the abolition of unnecessary oaths.' Severally declared and subscribed at Liverpool aforesaid the tenth day of January, one thousand eight hundred and seventy-seven."

George Drevar, *Master.*
William Lewarn, *Steward.*
Horatio Thompson, *Chief Officer.*
J. H. Landells, *Second Officer.*
Owen Baker.

"Severally declared and subscribed at Liverpool aforesaid, the tenth day of January, one thousand eight hundred and seventy-seven, before T. S. Raffles, J. P. for Liverpool."

In *Nature* of February 10th., 1881, we read that "Captain Drevar has circulated a printed account of the conflict which he witnessed, and of the subsequent appearance of the animal rearing its long neck out of the water."

Evidently this circular was a letter addressed by Captain Drevar, when in Chittagong (Bengal), to the Editor of the *Calcutta Englishman*, in January, 1876. I have had no opportunity to consult this paper, but I have found an extract from it in the *Graphic* of January 27, 1877, and a partial translation of it in the *Illustrirte Zeitung* of Febr. 3, 1877. What I have found in the *Graphic* runs as follows:

"Captain George Drevar, master of the barque *Pauline*, has furnished us a sketch of the Sea-Serpent (from which the annexed engraving is taken), which he encountered off the coast of South America. The occurrence took place on the 8th. July, 1875, at eleven A. M., the *Pauline* being at that time off Cape San Roque, lat. 5° 13' N., long 35° W., the north-east coast of Brazil being twenty miles distant. Captain Drevar says:—The weather fine and clear, wind and sea-moderate. Observed some black spots on the water, and a whitish pillar, about thirty feet high above them. At the first glance I took all to be breakers as the sea was splashing up fountain-like about them, and the pillar a pinnacle rock, bleached with the sun; but the pillar fell with a splash, and a similar one rose. They rose and fell alternately in quick succession, and good glasses showed me it was a monstrous sea-serpent coiled twice round a large sperm-whale. The head and tail parts, each about thirty feet long were acting as levers, twisting itself and victim round with great velocity. They sank out of sight about every two minutes, coming to the surface still revolving; and the struggles of the whale and two other whales, that were near, frantic with excitement, made the sea in their vicinity like a boiling cauldron; and a loud and confused noise was distinctly heard. This strange occurrence last some fifteen minutes, and finished with the tail portion of the whale being elevated straight in the air, then waving backwards and forwards, and lashing the water furiously in the last death struggle, when the body disappeared from our view, going down head foremost to the bottom, where no doubt it was gorged at the serpent's leisure; and that monster of monsters may have been many months in a state of coma, digesting the huge mouthful. Then two of the largest spermwhales that I have ever seen moved slowly thence towards the vessel, their bodies more than usually elevated out of water, and not spouting or making the least noise, but seeming quite paralized with fear; indeed, a cold shiver went through my own frame on beholding the last agonizing struggle of the poor whale that had seemed as helpless in the coils of the vicious monster as a small bird in the talons of a hawk. Allowing for two coils round the whale, I think the serpent was about 160 or 170 feet long, and 7 or 8 feet in girth. It was in colour much like a conger-eel; and the head, from the mouth being always open, appeared the largest part of its body. I wrote thus far, little thinking I would ever see the serpent again, but at seven A. M., July 13, in the same latitude, and some eighty miles east of San Roque I was astonished to see the same or a similar monster. It was throwing its head and about 40 feet of its body in a horizontal position out of water as it passed onwards by the stern of our vessel."

"This narrative is extracted from a letter addressed from Chittagong to the editor of the *Calcutta Englishman* in January 1876. It seems that Captain Drevar's

FIG. 42.–ANOTHER REPRESENTATION OF THE SO-CALLED "FIGHT BETWEEN A SEA-SERPENT AND A SPERM-WHALE".

FIG. 43.–THE SPERM-WHALE GOING DOWN HEAD FOREMOST TO THE BOTTOM.

friends advised him to say nothing about this strange spectacle. 'My relatives wrote saying that they would have seen a hundred sea-serpents and never reported it, and a lady also wrote that she pitied any one that was related to any one who had seen the sea-serpent.' On the 10th. of this month Captain Drevar and four of the crew attended before Mr. Raffles, the magistrate at Liverpool, and made a solemn declaration in support of the foregoing narrative."

The two figures, 42 and 43, are facsimiles of those accompanying the account in the *Graphic*.

I will try to translate again into English, what the *Illustrirte Zeitung* has published about this curious case, taken for granted that the German translation was correct, and laying all responsibility on the German writer.

"The Barque *Pauline* was on July 8th, 1875, about twenty miles distant from the north-eastern coast of Brazil, in lat. 5° 13' S., long. 35° W., near Cape San Roque. At 11 o'clock a. m., the weather fine and clear"..... etc., word for word as in the *Graphic* up to the passage..... "head foremost to the bottom, where no doubt it was gorged at the serpent's leisure".

"As the serpent was twice wound round the body of the whale, Captain Drevar estimated its length to be 160 or 170 feet; it was about seven or eight in girth. The mouth was always open; the head was very large."

"On the 13th. of July at 7 o'clock a. m. the barque was still in the same latitude, but about eighty miles from San Roque; then the same or a similar monster raised out of the water. Its head and about forty feet of its body were thrown horizontally out of the water and passed our stern."

"As I was still reflecting on the cause, why this strange guest so often paid us a visit, and concluded that it was the white stripe of two feet breadth, which went round our ship above the copper work and which the serpent probably thought to be one of its colleagues, the cry of 'There he is again' roused me. At a short distance from the ship I really saw the Leviathan, balancing about sixty feet high in the air, looking angrily at our vessel. As I was not sure, whether it was only looking at the white stripe on the ship's hull, probably thinking to see one of its colleagues, or whether it was preparing to attack the vessel, we kept ready all our axes, to give it a warm reception. But the animal dived and disappeared."

The German translator is convinced that the story contains truth, but he suggests that the whale was playing with a large tree or with a broken mast, "for it is known that whales like to gambol with violent motions". The author further presents to his readers a reduced copy of the sketch of the Rev. Penny, (our fig. 41).—

Mr. Lee, who usually explains every sea-serpent after each report quoted by him, says, in his *Sea Monsters Unmasked*, p. 90, the following about these reports.

"It is impossible to doubt for a moment the genuineness of the statement made by Captain Drevar and his crew, or their honest desire to describe faithfully that which they believed they had seen; but the height to which the snake is said to have upreared itself is evidently greatly exaggerated; for it is impossible that any serpent could 'elevate its body some sixty feet perpendicularly in the air'—nearly one third of the height of the Monument of the Great Fire of London. I have no desire to force this narrative of the master and crew of the *Pauline* into conformity with any preconceived idea. They may have seen a veritable sea-serpent; or they may have witnessed the amours of two whales, and have seen the great creatures rolling over and over that they might breathe alternately by the blow-hole of each coming to the surface of the water; or the supposed coils of the snake may have been the arms of a great calamary, cast over and around the huge cetacean. The other two appearances—1st., the animal 'seen shooting itself along the surface with head and neck raised', and 2nd., the elevation of the body to a considerable height, as in Egede's sea monster, would certainly accord with this last hypothesis; but taking the statement as it stands, it must be left for further elucidation".

It is remarkable that Mr. Lee who generally explains sea-serpents by calamaries, cannot give an explanation of *this* sea-serpent, with which he himself is satisfied. "They may have seen a veritable sea-serpent". This phrase is very surprising, for Mr. Lee has not yet explained what is a veritable sea-serpent. Or did he mean a veritable sea-snake? This is improbable, for he knows very well that the largest snake which frequents the sea, the *Eunectes murina*, does not measure above 25 feet, so that it is not able to encircle a spermwhale, whose circumference is about forty feet. "Or they may have witnessed the amours of two whales, and have seen the great creatures rolling over and over that they might breathe alternately by the blow-hole of each coming to the surface of the water". This phrase, however, does not give any explanation of the long neck, the tail, the mouth being constantly open, the thick coils, which were coloured longitudinally, partly black, partly white, so that the captain spoke of a black back and a white belly!" "Or the supposed coils of the snake may have been the arms of a great calamary, cast over and around the huge cetacean." This too is impossible, for the circumference of the serpent was estimated at seven or eight feet, and no arm of a calamary has a greater circumference than about sixteen inches, even that of the largest known specimens, which have a total length of eighty feet! For a moment I will leave Mr.

Lee in his supposition that the animal, seen on the 13th. of July, was a swimming calamary or a similar individual standing upright with its tail in the air, and pass to his last phrase: "but, taking the statement as it stands, it must be left for further elucidation". This, now, I will try to do. But first I beg the reader to direct his attention to the sperm whales.

The sperm-whales may attain a length of 60 to 70 feet, with a circumference of 40 feet at the thickest part. The females are smaller, growing from 30 to 40 feet. It is reported that sometimes, though very seldom, a male measures 90 feet. The head occupies the third part of the body-length, in mass, however, it is larger, for it is quadrangular in shape and in front just as thick and high as behind, whilst the bulky body tapers to the tail. The mouth lies wholly on the under side of the head. It is a terrible cavity when opened and may be up to fourteen feet in depth. The upper-jaw is toothless, but the under-jaw has from forty to fifty four formidable teeth, comparatively as sharp as the canines of a dog.

The sperm-whales live in troops, numbering from a very few to some hundreds, and containing many females and young ones, under the command of some old males. The young males remain in this family till they are strong enough to command their own family. Some old males wander about solitary, wild and angry. To become the sole proprietor of some females, these males fight each other vehemently, and indescribably grand is the sight of two troops meeting! The wild and warlike nature and the untamable muscular strength of the sperm-whale makes its presence even dangerous. The greatest hatred exists between them and the whale-bone-whales, or the fin-fishes, or rorquals, and when a shoal of sperm-whales meets with a shoal of whale-bone-whales, the latter are immediately attacked with the greatest fury and cruelty. The fight between two such squadrons is terrible, but grand, and commonly ends in the flight of the whale-bone-whales, pursued by the sperm-whales, not, however, without leaving many dead and terribly wounded companions, on which the frightful effects are visible of the bites of the sperm-whales, animals that might be called "mouth and teeth".

Knowing the wild and angry nature of the warlike and pitiless sperm-whale, and the rather harmless character of the sea-serpent, we cannot believe that a sea-serpent has ever or will ever attack such a formidable antagonist. Every one will rather believe that a sperm-whale, when meeting with a sea-serpent, would suddenly attack it. Moreover, if the sea-serpent was the attacker, it would not have had "its mouth always open",—an unfailable sign of great pain—but would have bitten repeatedly the whale! And so I firmly believe that one of the three spermwhales, had seized with its colossal mouth a sea-serpent by the trunk. The poor defenseless sea-serpent with its enormous flexible body wound round the upper jaw and forepart of the quadrangular head of the spermwhale. We know that the sea-serpent has a rather dorso-ventral flexibility, for it can swim in vertical undulations, but we know too that its lateral flexibility is astonishing. I refer to the American reports from 1817 to 1819, wherein the animal in turning bent its body in the form of a staple, so that its head nearly touched its tail, and to the figures of Dr. Biccard (fig. 37, 38.).

The sea-serpent, seized by the sperm-whale by the trunk, did not bend itself dorsally round the spermwhale's head, for if this had been the case, the captain would have seen the underpart of the animal and described its colour as being white. It did not bend itself ventrally, for if this had happened, the colour would have been described as dark, or black. On the contrary the coils are described as longitudinally divided into two sections white and black. Consequently the sea-serpent had bent itself laterally. Captain Drevar was right in his statement that the colour of the belly (under part) was white, and that the back (upper part) of the animal was black.

The sea-serpent in its violent pain raised its long neck high in the air and extended its jaws; it is even probable that it uttered a roaring sound or shriek, this is not mentioned; it may have been drowned by the dreadful noise caused by the fight of these two huge monsters, for we may suppose that the sea-serpent was not destitute of muscular strength, and must have been a formidable antagonist. Though it is not mentioned, I am convinced that the "two turns" of the sea-serpent were not always wound closely round the whale, but from time to time were loosened to be tightened again a moment afterwards. Nor do I set great value on the repeated assertion that there were *two* turns; it is impossible that this has always been seen clearly through such a "boiling of the water like a cauldron". The dimensions of the head and tail part being each about thirty feet beyond the coils are certainly not exaggerated, as is the circumference or girth "about eight or nine feet". The sea-serpent in its agony evidently paddled with its formidable flappers, which caused the water to be thrown like a fountain into the air. They therefore cannot have been visible with the glasses. The rolling over and over is, in my opinion, very natural in animals of such dimension, fighting in the water, and cannot be a result of the serpent "using its extremities as levers". And so they were rolling for about fifteen(?) minutes and at last the spermwhale (and not the sea-serpent) dragged its victim down to the depths, head foremost. It is a habit of spermwhales, which is to be ascribed to their attachment to members of their family and to their warlike character and hatred of their enemies, to help each other in danger, and so the captain's statement is quite correct: "the two others attempted to release their companion" and after the disappearance of the combatants "swam away, exhibiting signs of the greatest terror"; here we may safely read "fury", probably they followed on the surface their companion which was beneath it, perceptible to them, but invisible to the spectators of the *Pauline*.

It is, however, more probable that the sea-serpent, feeling itself free for a moment, suddenly escaped, dived and was followed by the sperm-whale.

It is now the right moment to say some words about the figures. I will be short, only observing that they are not worth our attention. The sketches were evidently drawn in October and December, consequently more than three and five months after the encounter. It is impossible that they can give an exact representation.

Mr. Andrew Wilson in his *Leisure Time Studies* is of another opinion than I, as to the fight; for he declares: "to my mind, the only feasible explanation of the narrative of the crew of the *Pauline* must be founded on the idea that the animals observed by them were gigantic snakes. The habits of the animals in attacking the whales, evidently point to a close correspondence with those of terrestrial serpents of large size, such as the boas and pythons". The reader will understand that I do not wish to contest Mr. Wilson's opinion.

145.—1875, July 13.—Now we come to the second statement of the same report, viz. the encounter with the animal on the 13th. of July.

On that day another or the same individual was seen again shooting itself along the surface horizontally, forty feet of its body being out of the water at a time. Consequently the animal swam with its body in a straight line, and not with vertical undulations. Again on the same day, it was seen once more, with its body standing quite perpendicular some sixty feet in the air, and evidently taking a survey towards the vessel. This case is nearly the same as that which Egede witnessed in 1734 near Gothaab. As it is often reported that whales and sperm-whales, when coming from the depths, do so with such an astonishing force and rapidity that they leap clear out of the water, I am convinced that the sea-serpent sometimes elevates its fore part to a considerable height as was seen by Egede (n° 5), Captain Adams (n° 121) and Captain Drevar. If the height of the sea-serpent rising in the air was really sixty feet, Captain Drevar must have seen the animal's fore-flappers, though he did not mention them. Else I think that he exaggerated, that the height did not surpass forty feet and that the flappers remained under water. See also N° 31.—

146.—1876, September 11.—In the number of the 15th. Of January, 1877, of the *Echo* appeared an article by Mr. R. A. Proctor entitled "Strange Sea-Monsters", wherein he quotes the following report. I have not been able to consult the *Echo*, but I have found it cited in Mr. Wilson's *Leisure Time Studies*. Here no date, except that of September 11th., is given, but as the report appeared in the January number of 1877 of the *Echo*, I conclude that the appearance took place in September of 1876.

"Soon after the British steamship *Nestor* anchored at Shanghai, last October, John K. Webster, the captain, and James Anderson, the ship's surgeon, appeared before Mr. Donald Spence, Acting Law Secretary in the British Supreme Court, and made affidavit to the following effect:

"On September 11, at 10.30 a. m., fifteen miles north-west of North Sand Lighthouse, in the Malacca Straights, the weather being fine and the sea smooth, the captain saw an object which had been pointed out by the third officer as 'a shoal!' Surprised at finding a shoal in such a well-known track, I watched the object, and found that it was in motion, keeping up the same speed with the ship, and retaining about the same distance as first seen. The shape of the creature I would compare to that of a gigantic frog. The head, of a pale yellowish colour, was about twenty feet in length, and six feet of the crown were above the water. I tried in vain to make out the eyes and mouth; the mouth may, however, have been below water. The head was immediately connected with the body, without any indication of a neck. The body was about forty-five or fifty feet long, and of an oval shape, perfectly smooth, but there may have been a slight ridge along the spine. The back rose some five feet above the surface. An immense tail, fully one hundred and fifty feet in length, rose a few inches above the water. This tail I saw distinctly from its junction with the body to its extremity; it seemed cylindrical, with a very slight taper, and I estimate its diameter at four feet. The body and tail were marked with alternate bands of stripes, black and pale yellow in colour. The stripes were distinct to the very extremity of the tail. I cannot say whether the tail terminated in a fin or not. The creature possessed no fins or paddles so far as we could perceive. I cannot say if it had legs. It appeared to progress by means of an undulatory motion of the tail in a vertical plane (that is, up and down).

"Mr. Anderson, the surgeon, confirmed the captain's account in all essential respects. He regarded the creature as an enormous marine salamander. 'It was apparently of a gelatinous (that is, flabby) substance. Though keeping up with us, at the rate of nearly ten knots an hour, its movements seemed lethargic. I saw no legs or fins, and am certain that the creature did not blow or spout in the manner of a whale. I should not compare it for a moment to a snake. The only creatures it could be compared with are the newt or frog tribe'."

As the captain asserts that the animal kept up the same speed as the ship, and Mr. Anderson that "though keeping up with us, at the rate of nearly ten knots an hour, its movements seemed lethargic", we must conclude that the animal moved by paddling with its flappers, and that with this simple mechanism it is able to propel itself at a rate of ten knots an hour, steadily and uniformly. The tail of the animal, which trailed inactively behind the trunk, must of course have been brought in motion by the action of the water, so that it is easy to understand that the captain thought that "it appeared to progress by means of an undulatory motion of the tail in a vertical plane (that is, up and down)". It is also very natural that the captain declared that "the creature possessed no fins or paddles as far as we could perceive. I cannot say if it had legs", and that the surgeon Anderson confirmed it: "I saw no fins"; the flappers of the animal being entirely hidden under water.—The captain says: "The shape of the creature I would compare to that of a gigantic frog". According to his description, however, the shape might have been better compared with that of a gigantic newt. This is done by Mr. Anderson, as we have seen above, who says at the end of his statement, "the only creatures it could be compared with are the newt or frog tribe"; he "should not compare it for a moment to a snake". This is one of the few reports of the animal having been observed swimming in full length on the surface of the water. This I think very comprehensible. Generally the animal is swimming with the head and a part of the neck raised some feet out of the water, and in this case the trunk and the tail must carry their weight, so that the trunk will be visible only a few inches above the water, and the tail hidden for a greater part under it. But as soon as the animal drops its neck and head so that only the upper part of both remain above the surface, their weight is carried by the water itself, and body and tail will become more visible, lying almost *à fleur d'eau* (to use Captain M'Quhae's term). I firmly believe that this is also one of the few occasions that the animal swam with its neck contracted. In this situation it is very difficult to decide whether the animal has a neck or not, and so the captain's assertion "the head was immediately connected with the body, without any indication of a neck" is very conceivable. From the hind part of the head the contracted neck gradually grows thicker towards the shoulders, where the animal seems to have its largest diameter, and from here it tapers towards the hind flappers, so that seen from the ship, both neck and body, being visible only a few feet above the surface, must have given rise to the description of the captain "the body was of an oval shape". Again the position was very favourable to observe the exact place where the tail begins, and that the animal has there its pelvis and hind flappers, so that, being there broader than at the tail-root, the captain observed "this tail I saw distinctly from its junction with the body to its extremity". The colour of the head being described as a pale yellowish one, and that of the body and the tail alternately black and pale yellow, I conclude that the animal having swum for some time in this manner, had been partly dried up in the sun, while "catspaws" washing over it again coloured it black here and there. As to its length I am inclined to believe that Mr. Webster is mistaken. I cannot admit that "the head was twenty feet, and six feet of the crown were above the water", nor can I set much value upon his assertion that the tail was "fully one hundred and fifty feet in length". I willingly admit that the head measured eight or nine feet, and the tail about one hundred feet. As the animal swam just at the surface it is clear to me that no mouth was visible, and I think that even the nose tip will only have been a few inches above the water. As no eyes were seen, the distance must have been rather great; but this is not mentioned. The body was perfectly smooth but there may have been a slight ridge along the spine. Probably this was the mane, not quite discernable on account of the distance. The tail is described as cylindrical, tapering to its end, and estimated at four feet in diameter (at its junction, evidently).—It is clear that the extreme end of the tail was under water, for Mr. Webster "cannot say whether the tail terminated in a fin or not". As to the supposition of Mr. Anderson that the animal was "apparently of a gelatinous (that is, flabby) substance", I cannot attach much importance to this, as it is impossible to decide this of an animal swimming at some distance, even of a calamary. The body was smooth, and that's all. That the creature did not blow or spout like a whale, is very natural, as there was evidently no reason for doing so, the nose being constantly above the surface, and the animal swimming without diving from time to time. A whale, sleeping on the surface, does not spout either, as in that case the spout-holes are above the surface, and the breathing is regular and without puffing. So I think I have shown that all the parts of the statement are correct, except the estimated length.

Mr. Andrew Wilson relying upon the statement of Mr. Anderson, adds in a note:

"It is just possible that the 'flabby' or 'gelatinous' creature mentioned in this narrative was a giant cuttle-fish, whose manner of swimming, colour, absence of limbs, etc., would correspond with the details of the narrative. The 'immense tail' might be the enormous arms of such a creature trailing behind the body as it swam backwards, propelled by jets of water from the breathing, 'funnel'."

My objections against this supposition are first, that, as I have already stated above, it is impossible to decide whether an animal is gelatinous or flabby, until we have touched and handled it, and secondly, that the manner of swimming of a calamary is not so as Mr. Wilson believes; for the enormous arms of such a creature are not trailing behind the body, when it is swimming backwards, but are coiled up and retracted into two peculiar arm pockets, and thirdly, that the colour of a calamary does not correspond with the colour stated in the report, but is a very light grey one, mixed with red or crimson, intermixed with purple.

In the number of February 3d, 1877 of the *Illustrirte Zeitung*, an article entitled "Zur Geschichte der Seeschlange" appeared, written by an anonymous writer. Evidently the report of Captain Drevar, which appeared in the Liverpool newspapers of the 10th. of January of that year, was the stimulus to this essay. The writer superficially treats of several already known accounts and reports of sea-serpents viz: our nos. 144, 145, and 5, the tales of Pontoppidan, the animal of Stronsa, the appearances quoted by the Boston Linnaean Society (1817), our n°. 118, the hoax of the *Daphne* (1848, Oct. 21), our nos. 129 and 130, the cheat of Dr. Koch (1845), and the true sea-snakes (*Hydrophidae*). In two of his assertions this anonymous author is incorrect, viz. It was not Captain M'Quhae who asserted that the animal's mouth was large enough to admit of a tall man standing upright in it, but an anonymous contributor to the *Times*; Mr. Henderson was master of the ship *Mary Ann*, and not of the *Daphne*; the master of this ship was called Trelawney. I consider these four names as fictive (see my Chapter on hoaxes.)

147.—1877, May 21.—In Mr. Andrew Wilson's *Leisure Time Studies* we read in a note (p. 111):

"An instance of a large sea-snake being seen in its native seas is afforded by the report of the master of the barque *Georgina* from Rangoon, which (as reported in the newspapers of September 4, 1877) put into Falmouth for orders on the 1st. September. On May 21, 1577, in latitude 2° N. and longitude 90° 53' E., a large serpent about forty or fifty feet long, grey and yellow in colour, and ten or eleven inches thick, was seen by the crew. It was visible for twenty minutes, during which time it crossed the bow, and ultimately disappeared under the port-quarter."

The dimensions are clearly those of the visible part of the animal. The colour being stated as grey and yellow makes me conclude that the animal had swam for a long time with its body in a straight line, without diving and that the part, exposed to the sunbeams, had dried up.

Mr. Andrew Wilson adds: "There can be little doubt that this sea-serpent was simply a largely developed marine snake". I'll not contest his opinion.—

148.—1877, June 2.—Not less important than others is the report of the *Osborne*. In Mr. Lee's *Sea Monsters Unmasked* we read p. 93 the following about this occurrence:

"In June, 1877 Commander Pearson reported to the Admiralty that on the 2nd. of that month, he and other officers of the Royal Yacht *Osborne*, had seen, off Cape Vito, Sicily, a large marine animal, of which the following account and sketches were furnished by Lieutenant Haynes, and were confirmed by Commander Pearson, Mr. Douglas Haynes, Mr. Forsyth, and Mr. Moore, engineer."

"Lieutenant Haynes writes, under date, 'Royal Yacht *Osborne*, Gibraltar, June 6': On the evening of that day, the sea being perfectly smooth, my attention was first called by seeing a ridge of fins above the surface of the water, extending about thirty feet, and varying from five to six feet in height. On inspecting it by means of a telescope, at about one and a-half cables' distance, I distinctly saw a head, two flappers, and about thirty feet of an animal's shoulder. The head, as nearly as I could judge, was about six feet thick, the neck narrower, about four to five feet, the shoulder about fifteen feet across, and the flappers each about fifteen feet in length. The movements of the flappers were those of a turtle, and the animal resembled a huge seal, the resemblance being strongest about the back of the head. I could not see the length of the head, but from its crown or top to just below the shoulder (where it became immersed), I should reckon about fifty feet. The tail end I did not see, being under water, unless the ridge of fins to which my attention was first attracted, and which had disappeared by the time I got a telescope, were really the continuation of the shoulder to the end of the object's body. The animal's head was not always above water, but was thrown upwards, remaining above for a few seconds at a time, and then disappearing; there was an entire absence of 'blowing' or 'spouting'. I herewith beg to enclose a rough sketch, showing the view of the "ridge of fins", and also of the animal in the act of propelling itself by its two fins."

Evidently Mr. Lee has not communicated the whole account as it was in the original periodical, nor did he mention the name of the periodical.

The *Times* of June 14th., 1877 mentions:

"The *Osborne*, 2, paddle royal yacht, Commander Hugh L. Pearson, which arrived at Portsmouth from the Mediterranean on Monday, and at once proceeded to her moorings in the harbour, has forwarded an official report to the Admiralty, through the commander-in-chief (Admiral Sir George Elliot, K. C. B.), respecting a sea-monster which she encountered during her homeward voyage. At about five o'clock in the afternoon of the 2nd. instant, the sea being exceptionally calm, while the yacht was proceeding round the north coast of Sicily towards Cape Vito, the officer on the watch observed a long ridge of fins, each about six feet long, moving slowly along. He called for a telescope, and was at once joined by other officers. The *Osborne* was steaming westward at ten and a half knots an hour, and, having a long passage before her, could not stay to make minute observations. The fins were progressing in an eastwardly direction, and as the vessel more nearly approached them, they were replaced by the foremost part of a gigantic sea-monster. Its skin was, so far as could be seen, altogether devoid of scales, appearing rather to resemble in sleekness that of a seal. The head was bullet-shaped, with an elongated termination, being somewhat similar in form to that of a seal, and was about six feet in diameter. Its features were only seen by one officer, who described them as like those of an alligator. The neck was comparatively narrow, but so much of the body as could be seen, developed in form like that of gigantic turtle, and from each side extended two fins, about fifteen feet in length, by which the monster paddled itself along after the fashion of a turtle. The appearance of the monster is accounted for by a submarine volcano, which occurred north of Galita, in the Gulf of Tunis, about the middle of May, and was reported at the time by a steamer which was struck by a detached fragment of submarine rock. The disturbance below water, it is thought probable, may have driven up the monster from its 'native element', as the site of the eruption is only one hundred miles from where it was reported to have been seen".

The *Graphic* of June 16, 1877, tells us p. 563, 3d. column:

"The Sea-Serpent has once more made his appearance, and this time the officers of the Royal Yacht *Osborne* are the witnesses to his existence. The Commander, says the *Portsmouth Times and Navel Gazette*, has sent an official report to the Admiralty, stating that on the 2nd. inst. a curious creature was seen off the coast of Sicily in a smooth sea. The serpent was "of immense length, with a smooth scaleless skin, and a ridge of fins, 15 feet in length, and 6 ft. apart along the back, a bullet-shaped head, and a face like an alligator. It moved slowly, and was distinctly seen by all the officers."

The same Journal of the 30th. of June publishes the following account and sketch by Lieutenant Haynes:

"We are indebted to Lieut. W. P. Haynes, of H. M. S. *Osborne*, for the sketch of the sea-monster seen by the officers and crew of that vessel off the north coast of

264 The Great Sea-Serpent

FIG. 44.—THE RIDGE OF FINS MENTIONED IN THE REPORT OF THE *OSBORNE*.

FIG. 45.—THE SEA-SERPENT AS SEEN BY COMMANDER PEARSON AND LIEUTENANT HAYNES OF THE *OSBORNE*.

Sicily on the 2nd. inst. In a letter accompanying the sketch, he says:—'My attention was first called by seeing a long row of fins appearing above the surface of the water at a distance of about 200 yards and 'away on our beam'. They were of irregular heights, and extending about 30 or 40 feet in line (the former number is the length I gave, the latter the other officers), in a few seconds they disappeared, giving place to the foremost part of the monster. By this time it had passed astern, swimming in an opposite direction to that we were steering, and as we were passing through the water at 10 1/2 knots, I could only get a view of it, 'and on', which I have shown in the sketch. The head was bullet-shaped, and quite six feet thick, the neck narrow and its head was occasionally thrown back out of the water, remaining there for a few seconds at a time. It was very broad across the back or shoulders, about 15 or 20 feet, and the flappers appeared to have a semi-revolving motion, which seemed to paddle the monster along. They were about 15 feet in length. From the top of the head to the part of the back where it became immersed, I should consider 50 feet, and that seemed about a third of the whole length. All this part was smooth, resembling a seal. I cannot account for the fins, unless they were on the back below, where it was immersed'."

According to Mr. Henry Lee a Mr. Frank Buckland has suggested (where? this is not mentioned) that "the ridge of dorsal fins might, possibly, belong to four basking sharks, swimming in line, in close order." Mr. Lee himself seems to be of this opinion too. As to me, I don't believe it, for the simple reason that the basking sharks only live in the Arctic Sea, and are never observed farther south than the coasts of Great-Britain and of Massachusetts. So Mr. Frank Buckland's whole supposition falls to the ground.

At all events the fins have nothing to do with the sea-serpent. This is also the opinion of Mr. Lee, who asserts: "The combination of them with long flippers, and the turtle-like mode of swimming, forms a zoological enigma which I am unable to solve."

We will first speak of the account Lieutenant Haynes wrote on the 6th. of June, when at Gibraltar. The sea was perfectly smooth, and he saw the ridge of fins. He took his glasses and instead of fins he distinctly saw something quite different. In the short time that he fixed his glasses, the ridge of fins had no doubt disappeared, and the huge animal emerged. The owners of the fins were evidently frightened at the approach of the sea-serpent. Lieut. Haynes "distinctly saw a head, two flappers, and about thirty feet of an animal's shoulder". We may safely add: and a long neck connecting this head with the shoulder, and we may safely read for shoulder: a part of its back. The head was about six feet thick, the neck narrower, about four or five feet; consequently the animal had stretched its neck as forward as possible. The back, on the level of the flappers, was about fifteen feet broad, "and the flappers each about fifteen feet in length. The movements of the flappers were those of a turtle." I should like to say: were those of a sea-lion, for a sea-turtle cannot possibly elevate its flappers so high above the surface of the water, while sea-lions are able to do so. Moreover the fashion is the same, that is to say, the paddling happens alternately, i. e. when the right flapper is brought as forward as possible to commence the act of paddling, the left one is kept as backward as possible, nearly touching the trunk, having just brought the act of paddling to an end. "The animal resembled a huge seal, the resemblance being strongest about the back of the head." This is in my opinion the most remarkable statement of this report. We have more than once met with the comparison of the head or face of the animal with that of a seal, but Lieutenant Haynes clearly states the *animal* (seen from behind) resembled a seal. "I could not see the length of the head, but from its crown or top to just below the shoulder (where it became immersed) I should reckon about fifty feet." Going by known descriptions and figures, we may suppose that the length of the head may have been between eight and nine feet. When from the top of the head to just below the shoulder the length is estimated at about fifty feet, I reckon that the neck of the animal must have been one of forty feet, reckoning two feet from the top of the head to the occiput, and eight feet from the flappers to where the animal became immersed, i. e. the visible part of its back. The estimated measurements of the individual of captain M'Quhae (n°. 118) were: length of the head about three feet, breadth about two feet; diameter of neck below the head about one foot and a third; length of the neck to the fore-flappers about twenty feet; length of the trunk from the fore-flappers to the hindflappers about twenty feet, length of the tail about forty feet, length of the whole animal between eighty and ninety feet. Let us now repeat those of the individual of the *Osborne*, which seems to be about *three times* larger. The breadth of the head is about six feet, consequently the length of the head about nine feet; the diameter of the neck below the head about four or five feet, say four feet, i. e. *three times* one foot and a third; the distance from the occiput to the flappers—forty feet, according to my calculation given above but,—comparing the dimensions of the individual of Captain M'Quhae with the present, I don't hesitate a moment to put down sixty feet for the distance from the head to the fore-flappers. The officers of the *Daedalus* were in a more favourable situation to estimate this distance, the distance from the fore-flappers to the hind-flappers and the whole length of the animal they saw,—than Lieutenant Haynes; for the former saw the animal from aside, whilst the latter beheld it from behind, and was consequently in a bad situation to estimate the different lengths of the animal, but in a more favourable to estimate its different breadths. The length of the neck must really have been formidable, for though the animal (see drawing) showed hardly any neck at all, (resembling an enormous ball just visible above the surface of the water, with another smaller bullet on its top,) Lieutenant Haynes estimated the distance from the top of the head to the part of its back, where it became immersed, at fifty feet! The remaining part of the back and the animal's tail and hind-flappers were entirely invisible. I have already expressed my firm conviction that the ridge of fins has nothing at all to do with the animal. It is evident that Lieutenant Haynes himself had his doubts about this point, for else he would not have written: "unless the ridge of fins..... were really the continuation of the shoulder to the end of the object's body". Evidently the animal elevated its head from time to time some feet into the air to take a survey before it. Evidently it never dropped its head so as to come with its nostrils below water, for "there was an entire absence of blowing or spouting".

In the account of the *Times* only the following sentences are interesting. The ridge of fins moved *slowly* along. They were *replaced* by the foremost part of a sea-serpent. In my opinion this statement is very correct. Its skin was altogether devoid of scales, appearing rather to resemble in sleekness that of a seal. This is a remarkable statement, for in the foregoing account the animal is said to resemble a huge seal! Again: the head was bullet-shaped (seen from behind) with an elongated termination (read snout) being somewhat similar in form to that of a seal, and was about six feet in diameter. The assertion of one of the officers who saw the animal's features and described them as like those of an alligator, cannot surprise us, as this comparison has been made more than once. As much of the body as could be seen was developed in form like that of a gigantic turtle. Evidently this reporter did not observe that the head and trunk were connected by a long neck, as did Lieutenant Haynes. I cannot approve of the supposition that the animal would have been started by the volcanic disturbance, which took place a hundred miles more southward and a fortnight ago!!

The rough account of the *Portsmouth Times and Naval Gazette* partly reprinted in the *Graphic*, is as the reader will already have observed himself, for the greater part, wrong: the fins of the ridge were estimated to be from five to six feet high, and not 15 feet in length. They were never seen along the back". Lieutenant Haynes clearly doubted of it, and I believe that nobody of my readers will admit the possibility of such a position! It was the ridge of fins that moved slowly, and not the animal. Though it is not expressed *in words*, the figure shows us that the sea-serpent moved with the greatest velocity, paddling so violently, that it lifted up its flappers as high as possible.

In the letter which Lieutenant Haynes forwarded to the Editor of the Graphic, we read that the animal passed the stern, swimming in an opposite direction to that they were steering to; consequently the animal could have been seen for a few seconds only from aside, and then only from behind. Most probably in passing the yacht, the animal turned its face once towards it, for we read in the *Times* of 14th. June: "its features were seen only by one officer." The breadth of the back is now stated to be about 15 or 20 feet. "The flappers appeared to have a semi-revolving motion," which is indeed a nearly exact expression for this motion. The length of 50 feet is now considered by the gallant officer to seem to be about a third of the whole length. The reason of this estimation is not mentioned; probably it was the rippling of the water behind the back of the animal, which led to it. I firmly believe that this individual was more than two hundred feet in length. Again, the Lieutenant seems not to have had the least idea of what could have been the ridge of fins! No wonder!

Of the second sketch (fig. 45) I will only say that it is partly wrong; for only *one* flapper must have been visible *at one time*, though it may be that the animal was paddling with such a rapidity that it *seemed* as if the two flappers were visible together. And when seen from aside in this position it would appear that the animal had more than two flappers, had a row of them, as is shown in our fig. 36.—It is also clear that the severe splashing and foaming of the water, which *must* have been caused by the movements of the flappers, is omitted in the figure.

Mr. Andrew Wilson in his *Leisure Time Studies* notes that the details furnished in the account of the Times appear to be explicable by a tape-fish (*Gymnetrus* or *Regalecus*). I need not say that I am not at all at one with him. There is not one simple character either in the ridge of fins, or in the animal described, which agrees in the least with that of a tape-fish! Moreover tapefishes are deep-sea fishes, and only rise to the surface, dying or dead!

Mr. Searles V. Wood, Jun's comparison of the animal with a manatee (*Nature*, 1880, Nov. 18) is better at first view, but the length of the neck, the form of the flappers and the dimensions of both animals differ in such a degree, that it is superfluous to dwell any longer on it.

In January 1879, Mr. Andrew Wilson published his *Leisure Time Studies*, a very interesting and captivating book. His fifth chapter is entitled. "The sea-serpents of Science". As might be expected the author treats of the various explanations of the sea-serpent given by men of science as well as by others, and declares himself to be a firm believer of the fact that large unknown animals exist. I wish to quote here the most interesting parts, or better-said, those parts which are, at present, of great interest. In considering the authenticity of the reports and the admission that really "something" must have been seen, the author says:

"Can we, after perusing the mass of evidence accumulated during past years, dismiss the subject *simpliciter*, as founded on no basis of fact? The answer to such a question must be an emphatic negative; since the evidence brought before our notice includes the testimony of several hundreds of sane and reasonable persons, who in frequent cases have testified on oath and by affidavit to the truth of their descriptions of curious marine forms, seen and observed in various seas. The second supposition, that all of these persons have simply been deceived, is one which must also be dismissed. For, after making all due allowance for exaggeration and for variations in accounts arising from different modes of expression and even from mental peculiarities in the witnesses, there remains a solid body of testimony, which, unless there is some special tendency to mendacity on the part of persons who travel by sea, we are bound, by all the rules of fair criticism and of evidence, to receive as testimony of honest kind. As I have elsewhere observed: There are very many calmly and circumstantially related and duly verified accounts of serpentine, or at any rate of anomalous marine forms, having been closely inspected by the crew and passengers of vessels. Either, therefore, we must argue that in every instance the senses of intelligent men and women must have played them false, or we must simply assume that they are describing what they have never seen. The accounts in many instances so minutely describe the appearance of such forms, inspected from a near standpoint, that the possibility of their being mistaken for inanimate objects, as they might be if viewed from a distance, is rendered entirely improbable. We may thus, then, affirm firstly that there are many verified pieces of evidence on record, of strange marine forms having been met with,—which evidences, judged according to ordinary and common sense rules, go to prove that certain hitherto undescribed marine organisms do certainly exist in the sea-depths."

"The first issue I must therefore submit to the reader, as representing one of a large and impartial jury, is, that the mass of evidence accumulated on the sea-serpent question, when weighed and tested, even in a *prima facie* manner, plainly shuts us up to the belief that appearances, resembling those produced by the presence in the sea of huge serpentine forms, have been frequently noted by competent and trustworthy observers. Unless we are to believe that men and women have deliberately prevaricated, and that without the slightest excuse or show of reason, we must believe that they have witnessed marine appearances, certainly of unwonted and unusual kind. That 'something' has assuredly been seen, must be the verdict on this first issue. What that "something" is or was, and whether or not the evidence will support the opinion that the appearances described bear out the existence of a 'sea-serpent' in the flesh, form points for discussion in the next instance."

Mr. Andrew Wilson mentions some pages further on a curious case of fear of popular ridicule in telling that, "one ship-captain related that when a sea-serpent had been seen by his crew from the deck of the vessel, he remained below; since, to use his own words, "had I said I had seen the sea-serpent, I should have been considered to be a warranted liar all my life after!"

In examining whether that "something" was a dead or living organism, Mr. Wilson concludes that:

"Numerous cases exist in which the object, presumed to be a living being, has been scrutinized so closely that, save on the supposition that senses have played their owners false, or that minds have given way to an unaccountable impulse for lying, we must face and own the belief that living animals have been seen."

He now speaks of a few accounts, viz. the various reports of the animal seen by the officers of the *Daedalus* (n°. 118), by the crew of the *Pauline* (n°. 144, 145), and by the captain and the surgeon of the *Nestor* (n°. 146), and explains them in his own way, believing that these sea-serpents were gigantically developed sea-snakes, or a great, calamary. Next he treats of the appearance of the animal as reported by the officers of the *Osborne* (n°. 148), explaining it to be a tape-fish. Finally he defends his hypothesis of gigantically developed sea-snakes and ribbon-fishes. These parts, however, I have inserted in my Chapter on various explanations.

In a review of Mr. Andrew Wilson's *Leisure Time Studies*, which I have found in *Nature* of the 30th. of January, 1879, Vol. XIX, the following is written about the chapter on the sea-serpent:

The lecture on "The Sea-Serpents of Science" is interesting, both as giving a very fair summary of the most recent evidence on this subject, and as showing that the age of incredulity is past, and that naturalists are now prepared to admit that several distinct kinds of oceanic monsters probably exist, of which no single specimen has yet been obtained. Recollecting, however, the number of clever hoaxes to which this subject has given rise we think that the newspaper account at p. 104, of the declaration before a Liverpool J. P., made by the master and crew of a merchant-ship, to the effect that they had seen a huge serpent twice coiled round a sperm-whale, and a similar serpent with its head raised "sixty feet perpendicularly in the air," should not have been inserted as evidence without first ascertaining that such a declaration was actually made before the magistrate named. The troubling of writing a single letter would probably have been sufficient, and would have settled the preliminary question of whether, from beginning to end, it was not a newspaper *canard*."

I am convinced that, after having attentively read what they find in this book about the appearance of the sea-serpent as seen by the crew of the *Pauline* (n°. 144, 145) my readers will be convinced that the report of Captain Drevar was not a *canard*. We read moreover in *Nature* of Febr. 10, 1881, that Captain Drevar has circulated a printed account of the conflict which he witnessed, and of the subsequent appearance of the animal rearing its long neck out of the water. Mr. Wood, the writer of the article in which this is communicated, adds: "This is satisfactory as showing that the declaration was no hoax". I quite agree with him.

149.—1879, January 28.—The *Graphic* of April, 19, 1879, says:

"The following is an extract from the account given by our correspondent, Major H. W. J. Senior, of the Bengal Staff Corps, to whom we are indebted for the sketch from which our engraving is taken.—'On the 28th. of January, 1879, at about 10 a. m., I was on the poop deck of the steamship *City of Baltimore* in lat. 12° 28' N., long 43° 52' E. I observed a long black object abeam of the ship's stern on the starboard side, at a distance of about three-quarters of a mile, darting rapidly out of the water, and splashing in again with a sound distinctly audible, and advancing nearer and nearer at a rapid pace. In a minute it had advanced to within half a mile, and was distinctly recognizable as the veritable 'sea-serpent'. I shouted out 'Sea-serpent! sea-serpent! call the captain!' Dr. C. Hall, the ship's surgeon, who was reading on deck, jumped up in time to see the monster, as did also Miss. Greenfield, one of the passengers on board. By this time it was only about 500 yards off, and a little in the rear, owing to the vessel then steaming at the rate of about ten knots an hour in a westerly direction. On approaching the wake of the ship the serpent turned its course a little away, and was soon lost to view in the blaze of sunlight reflected on the waves of the sea. So rapid were its movements that when it approached the ship's wake, I seized a telescope, but could not catch a view as it darted rapidly out of the field of the glass before I could see it. I was thus prevented from ascertaining whether it had scales or not but the best view of the monster obtainable when it was about three cables' length, that is about 500 yards' distant, seemed to show that it was without scales. I cannot, however, speak with certainty. The head and neck, about two feet in

FIG. 46.–THE SEA-SERPENT AS SEEN BY MAJOR SENIOR OF THE *CITY OF BALTIMORE*.

diameter, rose out of the water to a height of about twenty or thirty feet, and the monster opened its jaws wide as it rose, and closed them again as it lowered its head and darted forward for a dive, reappearing almost immediately some hundred yards ahead. The body was not visible at all, and must have been some depth under water, as the disturbance on the surface was too slight to attract notice, although occasionally a splash was seen at some distance behind the head. The shape of the head was not unlike pictures of the dragon I have often seen, with a bull-dog appearance of the forehead and eyebrow. When the monster had drawn its head sufficiently out of the water it let itself drop, as it were, like a huge log of wood, prior to darting forward under the water. This motion caused a splash of about fifteen feet in height on either side of the neck, much in shape of a pair of wings."

"Major Senior's statement is countersigned by the two persons whom he mentions as co-witnesses, and he expresses his willingness to answer any questions which may be put to him by any one interested in the subject. His address while on furlough is Rosebank Villa, Southfield Rode, Cotham, Bristol."

The appearance took place in the Gulf of Aden, as pointed out by the latitude and longitude. The account here is very correct as I now will try to show. The colour of the animal is called black and the appearance of the skin was that it was without scales. The head and neck, about two feet in diameter, rose out of the water to a height of about twenty or thirty feet, and the animal opened its jaws wide as it rose, evidently swallowing some fish, captured under water in its pursuit of a shoal of them, and closed them again as it lowered its head and darted forward for a dive, reappearing almost immediately some hundred yards ahead. The body was not visible at all, and must have been some depth under water, as the disturbance on the surface was too slight to attract notice. This is very natural, as I have already pointed out on a former occasion: if the head and neck are above the surface, the remaining parts of the body must carry their weight and sink a little below the surface. Not very much, however, for the foreflappers, as well as the hindflappers, paddling very rapidly caused a splash distinctly visible on the base of the neck (or on the shoulders), and "occasionally a splash was seen at some distance behind the head". Examining the figure, which is very exact, we may take it that the foremost splash was caused by the foreflappers, about twenty-five feet in the rear of the head, the very same place where the officers of the *Daedalus* (n°. 118) "occasionally saw a fin", and that about twenty-five feet more backward the hindmost splash was caused by the hindflappers, the place, where Captain M'Quhae (n°. 118) "occasionally saw another fin". The animal seen from the *Daedalus* seems to have been a little smaller than that seen from the *City of Baltimore*. The comparison of the head with a dragon's is a little far-fetched. The animal furiously pursuing its prey, sometimes opening its jaws, knitting its heavy eye-brows, which as we know are a little prominent, in short, expressing in its features hurry and a wild longing for its prey, may under these circumstances have had a feature terrible enough to cause Mr. Senior's expression "the shape of the head was not unlike pictures of the dragons I have often seen, with a bull-dog appearance of the fore-head and eye-brow". We have learned already that on such occasions the animal curved its neck swan-like and diving head foremost like a duck, disappeared. Here we have another habit of pursuing: "when the monster had drawn its head sufficiently out of water it let itself drop, as it were, like a huge log of wood, prior to darting forward under the water. This motion caused a splash of about fifteen feet in height on either side of the neck, much in shape of a pair of wings". This last might have been fairly omitted as every one can imagine the splash of water, caused by a log of wood falling into it. I think this comparison also far-fetched: such a splash cannot be compared with an object.

Our figure is taken from Mr. Lee's often quoted work. It is the middle third of the one which illustrated the text in the *Graphic*, but as it is drawn on the same scale, I saw no reason to give my readers the whole illustration of the *Graphic*.

150.—1879, March 30th.—*Nature* of the 24th. of July, 1879, contains the following of Surgeon Barnett, respecting the appearance of a sea-serpent near Cape Naturaliste in Australia.

"In *Nature*, Vol. XIX, p. 286, I observed some remarks respecting sea-serpents, and especially noted one passage which stated that 'The age of incredulity is past, and naturalists are now prepared to admit that several distinct kinds of oceanic monsters probably exist'."

"I was pleased to read this statement, as I have for many years been convinced that some of the accounts published from time to time in the newspapers are accurate descriptions of what has actually been witnessed, but I little expected that I should so soon be able to forward to you a description of one of these creatures, as given by an eye-witness, of whose accuracy there can be no question, and whose observations were made when very close to the animal."

"Busselton is a little seaport about 150 miles south of Fremantle, on the west coast of Australia, situated on the shore of Geographe Bay, which is sheltered by Cape Naturaliste; the northern point of that singular projection on the south-west corner of Australia."

"During the greater part of the year the water of Geographe Bay is as smooth as a lake, though it is a portion of that vast Indian Ocean which extends unbrokenly to the African coast. The beach is of smooth white sand, so hard at the water's edge that it is frequently used as a road for riding or driving from Busselton to Lockville; the latter place, a few miles to the north, is the station of the Ballarat Timbre Company, containing their steam saw mills, the termination of their railway, and the jetty from which large quantities of that imperishable and valuable timber called jarrah is exported to be used as piles, railway sleepers, etc."

"Last month I heard a report that the sea-serpent had been seen near Busselton, and that the resident clergyman had been one of the spectators. Having the pleasure of personal acquaintance with that gentleman, I wrote to him on the subject, and received from him such an interesting account, that I applied to him for permission to communicate the facts to your paper, and verify them by publishing his name. It is fortunate that the principal eyewitness was an educated gentleman, who has for twenty seven years been a Colonial chaplain in this colony, and whose description of what he saw is clear, simple, and free from exaggeration."

"I copy from the letters of the Rev. H. W. Brown the following extracts:

"On Sunday, March 30, I left Lockville just as the sun was setting, on my way home by the beach".

"The afternoon had been oppressively hot, not a breath of wind, and the sea was as smooth as a glass. I met C. M'Guire and his wife walking towards Lockville."

"Soon afterwards, when abreast of the track to Richardson's, I noticed ahead of me what looked like a black log of wood in the water a stone's throw from the shore, nearly end-on to me, and apparently more buoyant at that end; getting nearer, I noticed that it was *drifting* apparently towards Lockville, and soon discovered that it was moving, leaving behind it a very long, narrow ridge on the smooth water. I then turned my horse's head, and, at a walking pace kept just abreast of it, unnoticed apparently till I had gained sufficiently on M'Guire to make him hear. I then coo-eed *once*; he turned and came back to meet me; but at the sound of my coo-ee the fish started off seawards out of sight (under water), and doubled again in shore, but so rapidly as to leave both outward and inward 'ridge' on the water distinctly visible at once, like a wide V with quite a sharp corner. It gave me the idea of two fishes, the one darting outward, the other crossing its track inward at the same moment."

"Not knowing where it might show up next, but satisfied that it had come in-shore again, I tried by pointing seaward to direct M'Guire's attention that way"

"Just as I met him the fish again came to the surface, showing gradually more and more of his length, till, when he was almost at rest, and all apparently was in view, I estimated the length to be 60 feet, straight and taper, like a long spar, with the butt end, his head and shoulders, showing well above the surface."

"I can only describe the head as like the end of a log, bluff, about two feet diameter; on the back we noticed, showing very distinctly above water, several square-topped fins."

"I here make an exact tracing from Mr. Brown's letter of his sketch:

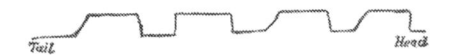

FIG. 47.—OUTLINE OF THE BACK OF THE SEA-SERPENT AS SEEN BY THE REV. H. W. BROWN.

"It was now getting rather too dark to see details distinctly. The fish proceeded toward Lockville, and I turned homeward. M'Guire said he would go on to Lockville jetty and look out for him there."

"Whether he saw him again I know not, but M' Mullan, the fisherman, told me next morning that he had seen it about fifty yards from that jetty, and it looked to him about twenty feet long. So it did to me while in motion; only when at rest for a moment did its whole length show up sufficiently. What its propelling power was I cannot say from observation; I saw no lateral fins and no fish-tail."

"When it started away at the sound of my voice, it was with the rapid movement of a pike or sword-fish, and yet the thick bluff head had but little resemblance to a snake."

"There was an unusual abundance of fish close in shore the same afternoon, yet when I saw the stranger there were certainly no fish of which it could be in pursuit."

"Since the year 1848, when the captain and officers of a British man-of-war gave evidence that they passed within 100 yards of a snake, which they estimated to be 60 feet in length above water, with probably 40 feet beneath, I do not know of any more clear account than the above. Many independant accounts of the existence of marine monsters have been placed on record, and it seems mere folly to treat these repeated reports with ridicule."

"I trust that your readers will no longer doubt that the 'age of credulity' is past."

"H. C. Barnett."

"Fremantle, W. Australia, May 19." "Colonial surgeon."

I need not tell my readers that the figure is very rude, and only gives a very indistinct representation of four "bunches", or visible parts of vertical undulations, called "fins" in the narrative. The blunt head, compared with the end of a log, the imperfect description, and the so-called square appearance of the bunches must be ascribed to the falling darkness. The other details of the report: the swimming of the animal in bunches, its causing the "ridges" in the water in the shape of a wide V, its holding its head well above the surface, its length, its resemblance with a spar, straight and taper, are in my opinion convincing enough to call this "fish" a sea-serpent.

151.—1879, April 5.—In the *Graphic* of July, 19th., 1879, and in *Nature* for November 18th., 1880, we find the following statement:

"The accompanying engraving is a *fac-simile* of a sketch sent to us by Captain Davison, of the steamship *Kiushia-maru*, and is inserted as a specimen of the curious drawings which are frequently forwarded to us for insertion in the pages of this journal. Capt. Davison's statement, which is countersigned by his chief officer, Mr. Mc Kechnie, is as follows:—Saturday, April 5th., at 11.15 a. m. Cape Satano distant about nine miles, the chief officer and myself observed a whale jump clear out of the sea, about a quarter of a mile away. Shortly after it leaped out again, when I saw there was something attached to it. Got glasses, and on the next leap distinctly saw something holding on the belly of the whale. The latter gave one more spring clear of the water, and myself and chief then observed what appeared to be a large creature of the snake species rear itself about thirty feet out

FIG. 48 AND 49.–TWO POSITIONS OF THE SEA-SERPENT AS SEEN BY CAPTAIN DAVISON OF THE *KIUSHIU MARU*.

of the water. It appeared to be about the thickness of a junk's mast and after standing about ten seconds in an erect position, it descended into the water, the upper end going first. With my glasses I made out the colour of the beast to resemble that of a pilot fish."

It is clear that the Editor of the *Graphic* is an unbeliever, else he would not have called these figures "specimens of the curious drawings which are frequently forwarded to us for insertion in the pages of this journal". I think that there is nothing curious in these figures, which are as correct as possible.

Cape Satano is the most southern point of Japan, or better, of the Isle of Kiu Siu. It is also called Satano Misaki, of which "Saki" or "Misaki" signifies "cape". The Russian call it Cape Chichakoff. This is the third time that we read of the seaserpent being seen in the Pacific Ocean (see n°. 36 and 119).

The most remarkable fact mentioned in this report is the gripping the whale. The reader will remember the report of a sea-serpent engaged with a whale, of course one of the smaller kind (n°. 54). In 1833 some British officers saw a shoal of grampuses near Halifax, Nova Scotia, which appeared in an unusual state of excitement" and a little while afterwards the sea-serpent appeared, evidently hunting after the grampuses (n°. 97). Again in 1850 (?) Captain Christmas saw "an immense shoal of porpoises rushing by the ship, as if pursued" and soon afterwards a sea-serpent made its appearance, curving its neck swan-like, evidently keeping a lookout and disappearing "head foremost like a duck diving" (n°. 124). Also Captain Brown saw it "surrounded by porpoises" (n°. 56). And now we have for the fifth time the sea-serpent pursuing whales, and a second time that it is engaged with one which it had evidently gripped in its pectoral fin. I am convinced that the description "holding on the belly of the whale" is incorrect. The dimensions of the neck estimated at thirty feet in length and of about the thickness of the mast of a junk are certainly not exaggerated. After the whale's escape, the seaserpent for about ten seconds stood in an erect position, like the animal of Captain Brown (n°. 56), taking evidently a survey all around, then bent its neck swan-like as in shown in the figure and finally "descended into the water, the upper end going first", exactly the way in which the animal behaved seen by Capt. Christmas (n°. 124). The description of the colour as "resembling that of a pilot-fish", is very vague, for the different pilot-fishes (*Naucrates*) have different colours, generally grey with some hue of blue, brown, or purple. The vague definition may be the result of a damp atmosphere, or it must be that the throat was turned towards the spectators, and not the back-part of the neck, which is nearly black. As the seaserpent has a very long and pointed tail, the fan-shaped or double finned tail in fig. 49 must be accounted for. This I think may be done in the following four ways: 1. The tail represents the whale, disappearing in the water, which in so doing caused a severe splash as is shown in the figure. 2. The tail is an optical illusion and the two fins of it were in fact the animal's hindflappers paddling furiously, which may be explained as an expression of the animal's emotion, as the whale escaped, and in doing so, the flappers caused the violent splash. 3. Not the flappers but the tail of the animal was lashing the water vehemently, and caused the optical illusion and the immense splash and foam. 4. The drawer, believing that the animal had a cetacean tail or a fish-tail, drew one, lashing the water, and so represented more his own imagination than the reality; but in no case a double finned tail has ever belonged to an animal with a long swan-like curved neck, as is really believed by Mr. Searles V. Wood in that number of *Nature!*

152.—1879, August 5.—(*Times* of September 24, 1879).

"Capt. J. F. Cox, master of the British ship *Privateer*, which arrived at Delaware breakwater on the 9th. inst. from London, says:—'On the 5th. ult., 100 miles west of Brest (France), weather fine and clear, at 5 p. m., as I was walking the quarter deck, looking to windward, I saw something black rise out of the water about twenty feet, in shape like an immense snake about three feet in diameter. It was about 300 yards from the ship, coming towards us. It turned its head partly from us, and went down with a great splash, after staying up about five seconds, but rose again three times at intervals of ten seconds, until it had turned completely from us and was going from us with great speed, and making the water all boiling round it. I could see its eyes and shape perfectly. It was like a great eel or snake, but as black as coal tar, and appeared to be making great exertions to get away from the ship. I have seen many kinds of fish in five different oceans, but was never favoured with a sight of the great sea-snake before'."

Of this unvarnished account Mr. Wood says with reason (*Nature*, February 10, 1881), that it is "almost a duplicate of that of Major Senior" (n°. 149). The colour of the animal is called black, the head and neck, like those of a snake, were elevated about twenty feet in the air. The animal stood so about five seconds, went down with a great splash, but rose again three times at intervals of ten seconds, thus behaving in the same way as the individual seen from the *City of Baltimore* (n°. 149). The thickness here is estimated at three feet. The animal moved from the vessel with great speed. Consequently the captain could not discern four different splashes, two of the fore and two of the hind-flappers, but he reports that the water was boiling all around it. I think that the animal here again was pursuing a shoal of fish and not trying to escape the vessel.—

152A.—1881, Nov. 12?—The Zuid-Afrikaan, of Nov. 17, 1881, mentions:

"In the *Argus* we read the following:—'Mr. C. M. Hansen, functionary to the harbour-office, mentions, that on Saturday evening a little after six o'clock, being occupied in his garden near Monillepoint, he perceived near the spot where the *Athens* was wrecked, a great sea-serpent, and that he immediately drew the attention of his wife and children, and several of his neighbours to this appearance. After viewing the coast at its ease for half an hour the monster turned its head seaward and disappeared. Mr. Hansen describes this sea-monster as being about 75 feet long, of a dark colour and with a head of the size of a 54 gallon hogshead, resembling that of a bull-dog, and provided with a long and brown mane, hanging down'."

Undoubtedly the length of 75 feet is that of the part visible above the surface of the water. It is not mentioned whether the animal swam with its body in a straight line or in vertical undulations. It is not for the first time that we hear of the sea-serpent near Cape-Town, (for *Argus* must no doubt be read *Cape Argus*). I pass the dimension of the head as I don't know that of a 54 gallon hogshead. Remarkable is the comparison of the head with a bull-dog's; it must have been seen in front, in order to make this impression. Again a mane was present and its colour is now called brown.

153.—1882, May 28th.—In the next account we read:
"At our arrival in Newcastle, I learned that some days before some fishermen of Lewis had observed the same or a similar animal."

154.—1882, May 31.—(*Illustrirte Zeitung* of 1st. of July, 1882).—
"The following report, with the accompanying engraving, has been forwarded to us by Mr. Weisz, Captain of the Stettin Lloyd Steamer *Kätie*."

"When the Stettin Lloyd Steamer *Kätie*, on her return from New-York to Newcastle, on the 31st. of May of this year, shortly after sunset and in that clear light which in this season takes place in fine weather in high northern latitudes, was about eight miles W. N. W. of Butt of Lewis (Hebrides), we observed on starboard before us, at a distance of about two miles a dark object lying on the surface, which was only slightly moved by the waves; first we took it for a wreck, as the highest end resembled the bow and the forepart of a ship, and the remaining hilly part resembled the broken waist-cloth of a ship filled with water. As we got nearer we saw with a glass on the left of the visible object, the water moving in a manner, as if the object extended there under the water, and this motion was of the same length as the part of the object, visible above the surface. Therefore we took care, not to steer too near, lest the screw should be damaged by some floating pieces of the wreck. But on getting nearer observed that the object was not a wreck, and, if we had not known with certainty that on these coasts there are no shallows, we should have taken this dark connected row of hills for cliffs. When we, however, changed our course obliquely from the object, which lay quite still all the time, to our astonishment there rose, about eighty feet from the visible end a fin about ten feet in height, which moved a few times, whilst the body gradually sunk below the surface. In consequence of this the most elevated end rose, and could distinctly be made out as the tail of a fish kind of immense dimensions."

"The length of the visible part of this animal which had in no case any resemblance with the back of a whale, measured, according to our estimation, about 150 feet, the hills, which were from three to four feet in height, and about six or seven feet distant from each other, were smaller on the tail end, than on the head end, which withdrew from our observation."

"At our arrival at Newcastle, I learned that some days before some fishermen of Lewis had observed the same or a similar animal. Had I directly recognized the object before us, to be one of these creatures, which for so long time belonged to the fables, I should certainly have neared it with the *Kätie* as much as possible."

It is obvious that captain Weisz saw, and Mr. Andrew Schultz sketched the animal, ignorant of its being a sea-serpent. It became clear to them, when they arrived at Newcastle where they learned that a "sea-serpent" was seen by some fishermen of Lewis.

Here we have again the assertion that the animal showed bunches, though it lay still or nearly still, an observation already reported more than once, as the reader will remember. I am convinced that the dimensions are exaggerated, and that the disturbance of the water was caused by the length of the tail, and not of the head of the animal, which evidently was searching for food in a playful manner,

278 The Great Sea-Serpent

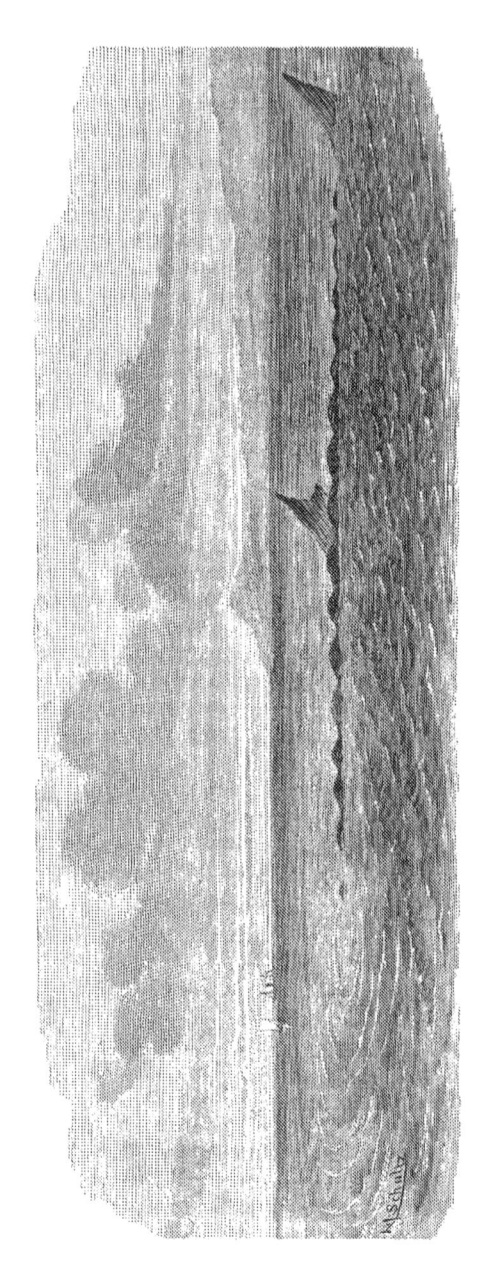

FIG. 50.—THE SEA-SERPENT, AS SEEN FROM THE STETTIN LLOYD STEAMER *KÄTIE*, NEAR THE HEBRIDES. DRAWN UNDER THE SUPERVISION OF THE CAPTAIN MR. WEISZ, BY THE AMERICAN ANIMAL-PAINTER MR. ANDREW SCHULTZ.

as we may observe in seals and sea-lions in our Zoological Gardens, and in doing so turned for a moment its body round, and raised once or twice first one of its hindflappers "which it moved a few times", and then raised one of its foreflappers, which was taken for a tail by the captain and the drawer. The long neck here commences, but was, with the head, constantly under water, evidently directed downwards, for there was no disturbance of the water visible here. It is clear that the *Kätie* remained at a good distance from the animal, so that Mr. Schultz, a well-known animal painter, could not obtain a better view of the flappers. The outlines of the flappers, however, are as correct as possible.

155.—1882, September 3.—(*Nature*, 1883, January 25). "Believing it to be desirable that every well-authenticated observation indicating the existence of large sea-serpents should be permanently registered, I send you the following particulars."

"About 3 p. m. on Sunday, September 3, 1882, a party of gentlemen and ladies were standing at the northern extremity of Llandudno pier, looking towards the open sea, when an unusual object was observed in the water near to the Little Orme's Head, travelling rapidly westwards towards the Great Orme. It appeared to be just outside the mouth of the bay, and would therefore be about a mile distant from the observers. It was watched for about two minutes, and in that interval it traversed about half the width of the bay, and then suddenly disappeared. The bay is two miles wide, and therefore the object, whatever it was, must have travelled at the rate of thirty miles an hour. It is estimated to have been fully as long as a large steamer; say 200 feet; the rapidity of its motion was particularly remarked as being greater than that of any ordinary vessel. The colour appeared to be black, and the motion either corkscrew like or snake-like, with vertical undulations. Three of the observers have since made sketches from memory, quite independently of the impressions left on their minds, and on comparing these sketches, which slightly varied, they have agreed to sanction the accompanying outline as representing as nearly as possible the object which they saw. The party consisted of W. Barfoot, J. P. of Leicester. F. J. Marlow, solicitor, of Manchester, Mrs. Marlow, and several others. They discard the theories of birds or porpoises as not accounting for this particular phenomenon."

"F. T. Mott."

"Bristal Hill, Leicester, January 16."

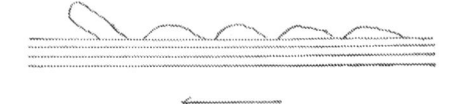

FIG. 51.–OUTLINE OF THE SEA-SERPENT SEEN NEAR LITTLE ORME'S HEAD, DRAWN BY MR. F. T. MOTT AFTER THREE DIFFERENT SKETCHES.

The appearance took place, as is stated, near Orme's Head, a headland of the Northern coast of Wales, projecting in a northwestern direction into the Irish Sea. The great rapidity of the movement through the water, estimated at thirty miles an hour, its great length of about 200 feet, its black colour, its vertical undulations and the whole external appearance of the animal, outlines of which are represented in the figure, at once betray the sea-serpent.

Another correspondent of *Nature* immediately wrote to the Editor as follows: "I have seen four or five times something like what your correspondent describes and figures, at Llandudno, and have no doubt whatever that phenomenon was simply a shoal of porpoises. I never, however, saw the *head* your correspondent gives." There! It is just the head which shows that the animal seen by the party of gentlemen and ladies above mentioned, was one single animal and not a row of porpoises!

And therefore, one of the eye-witnesses, Mr. W. Barfoot, promptly answered in *Nature* of Febr. 8, 1883:

"Like your correspondent, Mr. Sidebotham (in *Nature* Vol. XXVII, p. 315), I have frequently seen a shoal of porpoises in Llandudno Bay, as well as in other places, and on the occasion referred to by Mr. Mott, in *Nature*, Vol. XXVII, p. 293, the idea of porpoises was at first started but immediately abandoned. I will venture to suggest that no one has seen a shoal of these creatures travel at the rate of from twenty five to thirty miles an hour. I have seen whales in the ocean, and large flocks of seabirds, such as those of the eider-duck, skimming its surface; but the strange appearance seen at Llandudno on September 3 was not to be accounted for by porpoises, whales, birds, or breakers, an opinion which was shared by all present."

"William Barfoot."

In 1883 Mr. Henry Lee published his *Sea Monsters Unmasked*, one of the Series of publications of the International Fisheries Exhibition. This delightful book treats of the Kraken and the sea-serpent.

In the Preface Mr. Lee remarks:

"In treating of the so-called 'sea-serpent', I have been anticipated by many able writers. Mr. Gosse, in his delightful book 'The Romance of Natural History', published in 1862, devoted a chapter to it; and numerous articles concerning it appeared in various papers and periodicals."

"But, for the information from which those authors have drawn their inferences, and on which they have founded their opinions, they have been greatly indebted, as must be all who have seriously to consider this subject, to the late experienced editor of the *Zoologist*, Mr. Edward Newman, a man of wonderful power of mind, of great judgment, a profound thinker, and an able writer. At a time when, as he said, 'the shafts of ridicule were launched against believers and unbelievers in the sea-serpent in a very pleasing and impartial manner', he, in the true spirit of philosophical inquiry, in 1847, opened the columns of his magazine to correspondence on this topic, and all the more recent reports of marine monsters having been seen are therein recorded. To him, therefore, the fullest acknowledgements are due."

I too am under obligations to Mr. Newman, as to one who has collected so many reports of the sea-serpent and published them in his journal, but I fail to see in him what Mr. Lee asserts him to be.

As to the contents of Mr. Lee's "Great Sea-Serpent", the second part of his *Sea-Monsters Unmasked*, I may be allowed to note the following.

First he mentions the various great snakes of antiquity and believes them to be merely boas (read pythons) and real sea-snakes. Next he represents a figure, found on a sarcophagus or coffin in the Catacombs of Rome, and tells us that it corresponds in many respects with some of the descriptions of the sea-serpent given several centuries afterwards. I, however, don't observe any resemblance in them. I consider this monster as a singular combination of a horse and a fish, badly drawn, as one of the representations of those wonderful ideas or beliefs of antiquity concerning the existence of such monsters as sirens, tritons, the minotaurus, etc.

Further he treats of Olaus Magnus, Bishop Pontoppidan, Hans Egede, the Animal of Stronsa, and of various reports of the sea-serpent, and it is obviously a favoured idea of his that the sea-serpent is only to be accounted for by a great calamary; to prove this, he makes himself guilty of all kinds of misrepresentations and improbabilities, he considers every one as having been the dupe of optical deceptions, or as having made exaggerations, and their observations to be "full of error and mistakes"! And he who has never seen a sea-serpent, but sits pen in hand in his chair at his desk, knows it best of all: all sea-serpents were calamaries, except a very few, which were a row of porpoises! But the more Mr. Lee has to deal with more recent reports, the less he is able to explain the various sea-serpents by reference to his favoured calamary. Of the animals seen in the Harbour of Gloucester in 1817 he says: "Of this I can offer no zoological explanation". He neither gives an explanation of the sea-serpent seen in 1833 by British officers (n°. 97), nor of that in Lochourn (n°. 137, 138, 139, 140). Then he says: "Many other accounts have been published of the appearance of serpent-like sea-monsters, but I have only space for two or three more of the most remarkable of them". Truly, an easy way to get rid of them! One of these two or three more remarkable reports is the fight between the whale and the sea-serpent (n°. 144) of which he proposes several explanations (I beg to refer the readers to that account), ending with the words: "it must be left for further elucidation". The sea-serpent of the *City of Baltimore* (n°. 149) was misunderstood by him. He compares the *splash of the water*, caused by the animal's dropping its neck like a log of wood into it, with the *caudal fins of a calamary* (just imagine!) but ends: "but, as one with a bull-dog expression of eyebrow, visible at 500 yards distance, does not come within my ken, I will not claim it as much." And of the animal of the *Osborne* he says:

"It seems to me that this description cannot be explained as applicable to any one animal yet known. The ridge of dorsal fins might, possibly, as was suggested by Mr. Frank Buckland, belong to four basking sharks, swimming in line, in close order; but the combination of them with long flippers, and turtle-like mode of swimming, forms a zoological enigma which I am unable to solve."

Nevertheless, in answering the question: "To which of the recognized class of created beings can this huge rover of the ocean be referred?" he says: "I reply: To the Cephalopoda" (i. e. calamaries). Such a contradiction I do not understand.

And notwithstanding his cherished great-calamary-hypothesis, and after having said some words about Mr. Newman's Plesiosaurus theory and Mr. Wilson's ideas of the extraordinary development of snakes, he ends his work with the following conclusions:

"I arrive, then, at the following conclusions: 1st. That, without straining resemblances, or casting a doubt upon narratives not proved to be erroneous, the various appearances of the supposed 'Great Sea-Serpent' may now be nearly all accounted for by the forms and habits of known animals; especially if we admit, as proposed by Dr. Andrew Wilson, that some of them, including the marine snakes, may, like the cuttles, attain to an extraordinary size."

"2nd. That to assume that naturalists have perfect cognizance of every existing marine animal of large size, would be quite unwarrantable. It appears to me more than probable that many marine animals, unknown to science, and some of them of gigantic size, may have their ordinary habitat in the great depths of the sea, and only occasionally come to the surface; and I think it not impossible that amongst them may be marine snakes of greater dimensions than we are aware of, and even a creature having close affinities with the old sea-reptiles whose fossil skeletons tell of their magnitude and abundance in past ages."

I am unable to follow out such a reasoning.

156.—1883, October 15?—The *Graphic* of 20th. October, 1883, mentions, p. 387:
"The inevitable sea-serpent has turned up again. This time he has been seen going down the Bristol Channel towards the Atlantic at the rate of twenty-five miles per hour, and afterwards he was noticed off the north coast of Cornwall. The monster was about half a mile long, and left a greasy trail behind him."

I have no doubt about the appearance of a sea-serpent in Bristol Channel, and a few hours or a day afterwards off the north coast of Cornwall, as several individuals have already been reported on the west coast of Great Britain. The greasy trail left behind it is not an improbability, but the length of half a mile is most probably an invention of the incredulous Editor of the *Graphic!*

Mr. C. Honigh in his *Reisschetsen uit Noorwegen* in *de Gids* for 1884, p. 300 speaking of strange and violent motions in the water of the lake of Mjösen in Norway during perfectly calm weather tells us as a specimen of Norwegian superstition:

"People ascribe these motions to sea-serpents, in which many persons in Norway firmly believe upon the authority of undeniable witnesses and their observations. One of the most famous of these monsters lived some centuries ago in the lake of Mjösen, in the neighbourhood of Hamar, where it became entangled in the shallow. A monk killed it with arrow-shots in its eye, and the monster then floated to near the 'Holy-Isle' to a place which is still called 'Pilestöa'. And yet there is still a sea-serpent in the lake, which has coiled itself round the great bell of Hamar, which in the time of the seven years' war was lowered to the bottom."

Mr. Honigh adds:

"After all I heard and saw at Bergen, I don't doubt in the least that in the Atlantic and on the coasts of Norway really appear from time to time immensely large mammals of the seal-kind, known by the name of 'great sea-serpent', though I therefore don't admit all fabulous tales about it."

The words "mammals of the seal-kind" are explained by the following circumstance. In November, 1881, appeared from my pen, then a student's pen, a little article on the sea-serpent, in which I tried to show that a sea-serpent is a yet undescribed long marine animal, closely allied to the pinnipeds, with a long neck and a long tail. Mr. Honigh, in preparing his paper for the *Gids* requested me to let him have a copy of my article, which I sent him, and he evidently accepted my supposition.

In a letter Mr. Honigh tells me:

"In the literature of the Norwegians the sea-serpent or soe-orm is repeatedly mentioned, and in such an indisputable manner, that in my opinion there is no doubt of its existence."

"On my return I learned from a gentleman of Bergen, that some time ago there was a part of the skeleton of a sea-serpent in the Museum of Natural History of Bergen."

Though I begged Mr. Honigh, teacher at the National Agricultural School at Wageningen, to communicate to me further particulars about the sea-serpent and about its literature, learned by him on his travels through Norway, and repeated this my question in February 1889, I am still waiting for an answer.

157.—1885, August 16.—(*Nature* of September 10, 1885).

"It was hardly to be expected that the season should pass without the appearance of the sea-serpent somewhere, and if we are to believe the information forwarded to us from a correspondent in Norway, it has just visited the coast of Nordland. Three sundays ago some lads were returning to the Island of Röd from the church at Melö, in the middle of the day, when they saw far out in the fjord a streak in the sea which they believed to be a flock of wild ducks swimming. On proceeding further, however, they heard a whizzing as of a rushing fountain and in a few moments perceived a great sea-monster with great velocity making straight for the boat. It appeared to be serpentine in shape, with a flat scaly head, and the lads counted seventeen coils on the surface of the water just as it passed the stern of the boat so closely that they could have thrown a boathook into it. By subsequent measurements on land the length of the animal was estimated at about 200 feet. It pursued its course on the surface of the sea until close behind the boat when it went down with a tremendous noise, but reappeared a little after, shaping its course for the Melö, where it disappeared from view. Naturally, the lads were greatly frightened. The weather at the time was hot, calm, and sunny. Our informer states that the lads are intelligent and truthful, and that there is no reason to discredit their unanimous statement, made, as it were, in a terribly frightened condition. It might be added that the waters in which the animal was seen are some of the deepest on the Norwegian coast, and that it is not the first time fishermen have averred having seen the sea-serpent here. The existence of the sea-serpent is fully believed in along the coast of Norway."

The sea-serpent in its rapid motion made, as is often stated, the water curl before its throat, which rushing sound was distinctly heard by the lads. Notwithstanding their great fright they yet saw the head was flat, but they were mistaken as to its being scaly. Moreover the account is unvarnished and the description of the animal's motions is correct.

Mr. W. E. Hoyle, busy on the article "Sea-Serpent" for the 9th. Edition of the Encyclopedia Britannica, published in 1886 (June?) a number of titles of books and journals, which came in his way while studying the subject. This bibliography contains 89 numbers. They were printed, as the author says: "in the hope that they might be the means of saving time and labor on the part of others". Alas, his hope has not been realized on my part, for I had nearly finished my work when I happened to find Mr. Hoyle's paper quoted in the decennial Register of the *Zoologischer Anzeiger*. Only 25 of the numbers published by Mr. Hoyle were new additions to my "Literature on the subject", and I could consult only three of them, amongst which Mr. Hoyle's article "Sea-Serpent" in the *Encyclopedia Brittannica* quoted above.

Though Mr. Hoyle states: "no satisfactory explanation has yet been given of certain descriptions of the sea-serpent", among others of "the huge snake seen by certain of the crew of the Pauline" (n°. 144, 145) and of "Lieutenant Hayne's account" (n°. 148), and though he ends his article with the words: "It would thus appear that, while, with very few exceptions, all the so-called sea-serpents can be explained by reference to some well-known animal or other natural object, there is still a residuum sufficient to prevent modern zoologists from denying the possibility that some such creature may after all exist", he himself was evidently taken in by the different persons who explained the sea-serpent by reference to the most impossible suppositions! He enumerates eight different explanations and seems fully to agree with them. It is evident that his only purpose was to satisfy the request of writing an article on the Sea-Serpent for an Encyclopedia.

158.—1886, August.—In the *Graphic* of September, 25, we read:

"The sea-serpent has now crossed the Atlantic, and has suddenly appeared near Kingston Point, on the Hudson. It was seen by two young men, who were rowing in a boat, and who, it seems, the monster fruitlessly chased. They describe the animal as growing furious, when it found them escaping. 'It lashed the water with its tail, which seemed to be about seventy-five feet distance from its head' The head was as large and round as a flour-barrel; and its eyes of a greenish hue, looked 'devilish'. Before resuming its journey up the Hudson, it squirted from its mouth a stream of foamy stuff resembling long shavings from a pine plank."

I have no reason to consider this account as a hoax, though it almost reads like one. In the Norwegian accounts it is said that the sea-serpent very often follows boats. I have explained this by the animal's curiosity, mixed with some fear. The young men may have observed the animal paddling with its hind flappers, a possible expression of some emotion, as I have also explained when speaking of the animal seen from the *Kiushiu Maru* (n°. 151), and they may have ascribed the foam to the lashing of its tail; or it really lashed its tail, as I also supposed on that occasion (n°. 151). The length between head and tail estimated at seventy-five feet, is certainly not exaggerated. As the head is described round as a flour-barrel, it was evidently seen in its face. I refer to the animal of the *Osborne* (n°. 148) where the head seen from behind is also described and figured round as a bullet. Of the young men's description that the eyes "looked devilish", and also that of their colour being "of a greenish hue" I will only say that it is unique. The "stream of foamy stuff resembling long shavings from a pine plank" was of course nothing but a sudden exhalation, probably held for some time from curiosity and fear, and then suddenly sent forth. The locality where the sea-serpent appeared, may be apparently strange, it is, however, very well explicable, owing to the animal's habit of frequenting shores, and to the habit of other pinnipeds of frequenting brackish water and even mouths of large rivers.—

159.—1886, August?—In the same number of the *Graphic* it says:
"The serpent was also seen by the captain of a steamer, who 'gave it the right of way'."

160.—1886, August?—(On the same page):
"And yet another man (appropriately) named Jonah, who at first took the monster to be an immense tree floating with the tide—a notion which was quickly dispelled by the supposed tree throwing twenty feet of its length out of water."

As the reader will remember, the comparison of the sea-serpent, swimming or lying on the surface, with a floating tree or log of wood, has been made more than once; evidently the animal raised its enormous neck for a moment out of water, to take a look-out.

161.—1889, May.—In the *Haagsche Courant* of June 6, of this year, I read:
"The sea-serpent has again appeared, and been seen by a captain sailing from Liverpool to Philadelphia, who hitherto obstinately refused to believe in its existence."

Of course I immediately wrote to the Editor, begging him for the name of the journal, from which this statement had been taken. The Editor courteously answered that one of his correspondents had forwarded him a written copy of the account taken from the 38th. number of the *Grondwet* of May 21st., of this year, published in Holland, Michigan, but the written copy had already disappeared in the paper-basket, and the correspondent requested to send the original, answered that he was unable to do so for the same reason.

In the first days of December 1889, Mr. John Ashton published his *Curious Creatures in Zoology*. Pages 268-278 of his volume treat of the sea-serpent. The illustrations which accompany this part are: 1. A representation of a piece of sculpture on a wall of the Assyrian palace at Khorsabad, which as I believe, has nothing at all to do with the sea-serpent, but which is a bad drawing of a *Hydrophis*. 2. The drawing of Gesner (our fig. 16) twice reduced. 3. Egede's sea-serpent, as it was published in Pontoppidan (our fig. 22). 4. An eel-kind taken from Aldrovandus' work, and 5. A reduced copy of Captain M'Quhae's sea-serpent (our fig. 28).—

Curious is Mr. Ashton's assertion, when speaking of the sea-serpent of Khorsabad-palace and of Aristoteles: "These...... were doubtless marine snakes, which are still in existence, and are found in the Indian Ocean, but the larger ones seem to have been seen in more northern waters". Consequently he believes, like

Mr. Andrew Wilson that the *Hydrophidae* may develop gigantically and when in this condition make little trips from their common tropical residences to more northern latitudes!

Further he quotes Olaus Magnus, Gesner, Topsell, Aldrovandus, Pontoppidan, and Egede, but all by the way.

More space is devoted to the accounts of Walter Scott, and to the observations of Mr. Maclean (n°. 31), of a party of British officers (n . 597), of Lars Johnöen (n . 92), of Captain M'Quhae (n°. 118), and of Lieutenant Haynes (n°. 148). All this, however, without giving the least explanation, and ending with these words:

"I think the verdict may be given that its existence although belonging to 'Curious Zoology', is not impossible, and can hardly be branded as a falsehood."

162.—1890, June.—*De Amsterdammer, Weekblad voor Nederland*, of July 12th. of this year, mentions:

"The sea-serpent again.—Captain David Tuits, of the British schooner *Anny Harper*, has been favoured with a sight of it, near Long Island, not far from the coast of Connecticut. He is a perfectly trustworthy gentleman, who hitherto has never believed in sea-serpents, but who has now seen one on a clear day; the tail which was coloured brown with black spots, was about forty feet out of the water. The captain estimates the total length of the monster at over one hundred feet."

I think it not too bold to consider this report almost a duplicate of our n°. 135. There the sea-serpent is called "a large snake about 100 feet long, of a dark brown colour, head and tail out of water, the body slightly under". Most probably captain Tuits also saw only the head and the tail of the animal, and not the trunk. The tail is described here to be brown with black spots. It is evident that only the upper part of the tail was seen.

I immediately enquired of the Editor of the *Amsterdammer* about the source of this article; he, however, promptly answered me that his correspondent did not remember from which of the five or six German newspapers daily read by him, he had copied it.—

"To what class of known beings does this monster of the deep belong?" This question has caused various suppositions, to which we will turn our attention in the next chapter.—

5 The various explanations hitherto given.

I have found the **first** explanation given about the Sea-Serpent in the *Report* of the Committee of 1817, where we read an extract from a M. S. journal of the Rev. William Jenks, which he communicated in a letter to the Hon. Judge Davis, and which letter is printed there. It runs as follows.

"A gentleman of intelligence (Rev. Alden Bradford of Wiscasset, now Secretary of the Commonwealth,) inquired of Mr. Cummings, whether the appearance might not be produced by **a number of porpoises, following each other** in a train.

This passage from the private journal was written in Sept. 10, 1809; but after having consulted Silliman's *American Journal of Science and the Arts*, Vol. II, Boston 1819 (1820), we are convinced that Mr. Bradford's inquiry of Mr. Cummings took place before Aug. 1803.

Fig. 52 shows my readers a porpoise.

As we read in Schlegel's *Essai sur la physionomie des Serpens*, p. 517, note, Peter Ascanius in his *Icones rerum nataralium* Cahier V, Copenhague, 1805, says:

"In summer porpoises approach the coasts and the fjords. They often meet in the open sea in troops of several scores, and when the weather is calm and fine, they range in a line after each other to play and to tumble: they then have the appearance of a chain of little eminences floating on the surface of the water; some fishermen of the North, seeing them at a great distance, took this resemblance for an immense animal and gave it the name of sea-serpent."

Again in the letter from Mr. S. Perkins to Mr. E. Everett, dated August 20, 1817, we read:

"All these facts, however, were loose, and from the variety of reports, people had gotten to doubt their foundation, and supposed it was only a number of porpuses following each other in rapid succession.

For the fourth time we read in Froriep's *Notizen*, Vol. XIX, p. 193:

"Christiania, September 5, 1827. Last week several persons saw large shoals of porpoises, and therefore uttered the supposition that the alleged presence of the sea-serpent was not right."

Mr. Mitchill's paper, of 1828, which we have inserted *in toto* in our Chapter on hoaxes, also ends with the supposition that the "gambols of porpoises" have given rise to all the tales of the sea-serpent.

Schlegel in his *Essai sur la physionomie des Serpens*, La Haye, 1837, p. 105, in his chapter on Fables respecting snakes says:

"We are surprised to hear of a sea-serpent, monstrous in shape and size",

and he refers to his chapter on true sea-snakes, the *Hydrophidae*. There p. 517 he ends his chapter with the following words:

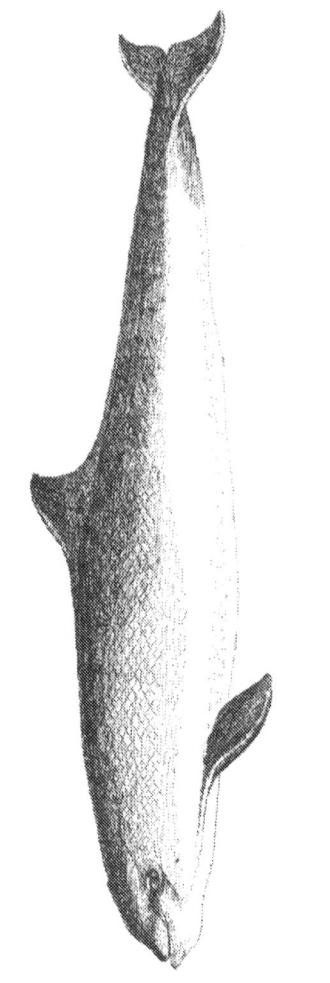

FIG. 52.—Phocaena phocoena (Linné).

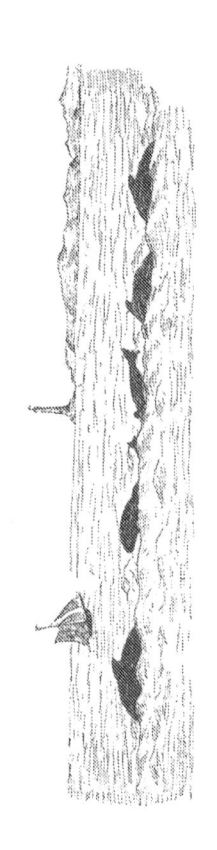

FIG. 53.—A row of porpoises.

Various Explanations

"Before ending the history of the interesting beings of which I have treated, I cannot help saying a few words about an animal, observed through centuries by many people of all ranks, and known to every one from the tales which are spread about it, but which is still ignored by naturalists. I mean the monstrous sea-serpent of the North, which in reality has nothing to do either with the sea-snakes, of which we have treated in the foregoing pages, or with my work. The numerous evidences given by very respectable persons to prove the existence of this enormous sea-animal, have imposed silence upon naturalists; I too should be silent, when the doubt which I always felt had not been turned into certainty by a little observation I made in the spring of 1826. Once when hunting on a stormy day along the coasts of the sea, I suddenly saw a sea-animal of great size swimming before the mouth of the Rhine-river. I was about to fire at this animal which I took for a shark, when I distinguished through the fog several others closely following each other. For the greater part hidden by the water, the upper part of this creature could be distinctly seen only for the short moment, when it was carried on the top of a wave, and plunged down into the precipice formed before it. The illusion caused by the continuous agitation of the waves indeed contributed to make doubtful the appearance of a great number of black objects, appearing together out of the water, disappearing the moment afterwards, and the whole of which deceitfully represented the simultaneous movements of the undulations of one single body. Convinced that the animals were unable to swim in vertical undulations, I kept looking at this spectacle, till I knew this monstrous creature to be composed of a little troop of porpoises."

In the *Archiv für Naturgeschichte*, of 1841, Mr. Rathke, who published in it seven accounts of sea-serpents, gathered by him on his journey in Norway, says:

"If we submit the above mentioned evidences to an inquiry, we shall soon observe that they not only contain several contradictory statements, but that each of the evidences itself cannot even pretend to accuracy. Yet we may believe that what those persons took for a long animal, was really such a one. For I should not know, what else could be the cause of the illusion which has created the belief in such an animal. Truly, I know that some believe, that what has been taken for a so-called sea-serpent, to be nothing else but a row of porpoises, swimming in line. But all those persons, by whom the above-mentioned evidences are given were too familiar with the sea, and have too often observed porpoises together, to be deceived by a row of such animals swimming on the surface of the water. If this, however, had been the case, all the observations related to me of the sea-serpent's holding its head above the surface, and about the size of it, must have been mere fiction, and this I cannot admit. According to all this, it evidently cannot be doubted, that there is a long serpentine animal in the sea of Norway, which may grow to a considerable length."

Again, as we learn in Froriep's Neue *Notizen*, Vol. XXVIII, n°. 606, p. 184, Nov. 1843, the Editors of the *Christiansand's Posten* after an account of a new appearance of the sea-serpent in the fjord of Christiansand, inserted in their columns, add the following remarks:

"This whole description tallies well with an appearance, which the writer of these lines has witnessed a few times in the North Sea, and if the inhabitants of the coast near Ibbestad, if not withheld by their fear of the supposed sea-monster, had rowed their boats to near the animal, they would undoubtedly have soon observed that the supposed intervals between the coils were nothing else but water.

This great sea-serpent in reality consists of a row of porpoises, which in a shoal of from eight to twelve often swim after each other in line. As each of these brown animals, eight or ten feet long, when swimming, appears above the surface of the water at proportionably short intervals, in such a way, as if they were about to tumble head first, so every one, who sees such a row swimming, must at first sight believe to see the coils of an immense snake."

In a letter from Mr. J. D. Morries Stirling to Captain Hamilton, R. N., Secretary to the Admiralty, we find the passage (see *Ill. Lond. News* of October 28, 1848, and our n°. 113):

"I mention my friend being a porpoise shooter, as many have believed that a shoal of porpoises following each other has given rise to the fable, as they called it, of the sea-serpent."

In Andrew Wilson's *Leisure Time Studies* we read, 1879:

"The instance already alluded to, of a shoal of porpoises swimming in line, with their backs and dorsal fins appearing now and then, with a kind of regular alternating motion above the surface of the water, presents an example of a deceptive appearance brought about by a somewhat unusual habit of familiar animals."

Mr. Lee in his *Sea Monsters Unmasked*, 1883, treating of the figure of Mr. Benstrup (see our fig. 24), says:

"The supposed coils of the serpent's body present exactly the appearance of eight porpoises following each other in line."

I have treated of his explanation in the right place (n°. 10). And on the following page he also asserts:

"I believe that in every case so far cited from Pontoppidan, as well as that given by Olaus Magnus, the supposed coils or protuberances of the serpent's body were only so many porpoises swimming in line in accordance with their habit before mentioned. If an upraised head, like that of a horse, was seen preceding them, it was either unconnected with them, or it certainly was not that of a snake; for no serpent could throw its body into those vertical undulations."

I repeat here what I have said above (n°. 10): If Mr. Lee wishes to explain the coils by reference to porpoises, he ought to tell me what was the head that resembled a horse's head.

Again on p. 96 of his work, after having concluded that the great calamaries "have played the part of the sea-serpent in many well-authenticated incidents", he says: "In other cases, such as some of those mentioned by Pontoppidan, the supposed vertical undulations of the snake seen out of water have been the burly bodies of so many porpoises swimming in line—the connecting undulations beneath the surface have been supplied by the imagination."

After an alleged appearance of a sea-serpent near Great Orme's Head (n°. 155), Mr. Sidebotham, a correspondent of *Nature* writes in this journal (1883, Febr. 1):

"I have seen four or five times something like what your correspondent describes and figures, at Llandudno, crossing from the Little Orme's Head across the bay, and have no doubt whatever that the phenomenon was simply a shoal of porpoises. I never, however, saw the head your correspondent gives, but in other respects what I have seen was exactly the same; the motions of porpoises might easily be taken for those of a serpent; once I saw them from the top of the Little Orme, they came very near the base of the rock, and kept the line nearly half across the bay."

Here we have a remarkable assertion: "I never, however, saw the head." I remind here my readers of Mr. Cummings' question "who ever saw a row of porpoises with a head of a seal?"

I need not say that porpoises swimming in line, do so very irregularly. They are in the habit of continually throwing up their bodies half above the surface of the water, and so their backfin is clearly visible, but nowhere the sea-serpent is said to have on each coil a backfin. Sometimes one porpoise is only visible, a moment afterwards three, eight, or more, but never the whole row is seen at once, while the undulations of the sea-serpent are constantly visible above the surface, moving with the greatest regularity. Every one will feel that this explanation is not satisfactory; it does not even explain a single observation. Besides, how to explain the swan-like neck, so often seen by reference to porpoises? To avoid repetitions, I beg the reader to refer to the testimonies of Mr. Cummings (n°. 29) and Mr. Prince (n°. 63), in which they clearly bring to light the difference between the appearance of the sea-serpent and that of a row of porpoises.

And where a naturalist, like Mr. Schlegel, describes the effect caused by a row of porpoises, he has no right to assert that those persons who declare to have seen the sea-serpent, were the dupe of an optical illusion. Mr. Schlegel should have said: "On one occasion I was nearly deceived by a row of porpoises, but alas, I never saw a sea-serpent!"

The **second** explanation is that of the Committee of the Linnaean Society of New England (Boston). This Committee consisted of the Hon. Judge Davis, Prof. Jacob Bigelow, and Mr. Francis C. Gray. This learned body after having published, 1817, exceedingly interesting reports, was of course morally bound to explain the phenomenon. What kind of beast could it be!? and before they began to feel puzzled, a *deus ex machina* in the form of a sick, illformed and lame little snake presented itself suddenly in a field near Loblolly Cove. It was killed by a working man at that place, bought by Dr. So and So, and presented to the Committee to examine it, because people believed that this animal was a spawn of the great sea-serpent. The Committee really examined and dissected it and gave a full account of their experience in their *Report*. They considered the little **snake** to be **new to science**, closely allied to the *Coluber constrictor* or Black Snake, a common species of North-America, and gave it the name of *Scoliophis atlanticus*. This account is followed by two documents describing how the *Scoliophis* looked while it was alive, and the circumstance under which it was killed. I present here to my readers the *Scoliophis atlanticus* reduced to 1/6 of its size, and a separate full-sized figure of its head, showing the two wounds caused by the pitchfork with which the animal was killed.

Next they gave: "A few remarks on the question" (broached by the public) "whether the great serpent, seen in the Harbour of Gloucester be the Scoliophis Atlanticus." These "few remarks" fill three pages and a half and end with the words:

"On the whole, as these two animals agree in so many conspicuous, important and peculiar characters, and as no material difference between them has yet been clearly pointed out, excepting that of size, the Society will probably feel justified in considering them individuals of the same species, and entitled to the same name, until a more close examination of the great Serpent shall have disclosed some difference of structure, important enough to constitute a specific distinction."

FIG. 54.–SCOLIOPHIS ATLANTICUS; ONE SIXTH OF ITS FULL-SIZE.

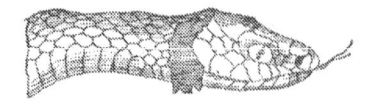

FIG. 55.–ITS HEAD; FULL-SIZE.

It is quite astonishing that scientific men could come to the conclusion that the large animal, that gave rise to the 51 accounts which the Committee could have gathered up to their days, was a full grown individual of the species they called *Scoliophis atlanticus*! If they had collected all these accounts, if they had seriously compared them, they would have come most probably to the conclusion that they did not know precisely what it was, but that it could never be a snake.

Also from another point of view it is hard to explain that the Committee believed the sea-serpent to be of the same species as the little *Scoliophis*. Three persons mentioned the tongue, which was not bifid, while the tongue of *Scoliophis* is so! And the most accurate testimonies agree that the skin was smooth and had *no* scales!

The newspapers brought the accounts of 1817 to Europe and no doubt drew the attention of many zoologists, but only Mr. H. M. Ducrotay de Blainville dared handle the subject publicly. As soon as the *Report* of the Committee of 1817 reached him, he made an extract from it in his *Journal de Physique*, etc., Vol. 86, 1818, Paris. He, however, made much more of the little curious snake, apparently believing too that it was a new species, than of the large marine animal of which he was unable to give any explanation. Mr. de Blainville does not hesitate to express his astonishment that the Committee concluded the sea-serpent to be a real snake and an adult of their *Scoliophis atlanticus*, and ended his extract:

"If we will now scrutinize severely the existence of the Great Sea-Serpent, we must avow that it would be difficult to deny the appearance in the sea near Cape Anne, of an animal of very great length, very slender, and swimming with rapidity, but that it is a true snake, is doubtful; that it is of the same genus as the *Scoliophis*, is an assertion still more doubtful; and finally to hold that it is of the same species, reduces the number of probabilities which become null, if one is to believe that such an immense animal as that observed in the sea, goes ashore to lay its eggs!"

For this is firmly believed by the members of the Committee!

For Mr. de Blainville who did not give himself the trouble to collect as many accounts as possible, to read Olaus Magnus, Pontoppidan, Egede, etc., it was of course impossible to conceive what animal had been seen near Cape Ann, nor was he, for the same reason, able to explain the very different declarations of the witnesses concerning the length of the animal.

Mr. A. Lesueur, who was a companion of the celebrated Mr. Péron, and who, in 1818, lived at Boston, wrote to Mr. de Blainville to say that he had not only seen the little snake, but had dissected the same portion of the vertebral column as did the members of the Committee, together with several inches of another portion of the snake, and concluded that the figure of the little snake published by the Committee was very well drawn, but that the figure of the portion of the vertebral column was very badly done; of this he gave another figure, and furthermore asserted that the little snake not only was nothing else but a true snake, closely allied to the Black Snake (*Coluber constrictor*), but that it was in a state of disease and notably difformed. Of the great Sea-Serpent he said nothing, because he had not seen it himself.

The dissertation of Mr. de Blainville and the extract from Mr. Lesueur's letter translated into German are in Oken's *Isis*, 1819.

Mr. Froriep in his *Notizen*, Vol. 4, 1823, expresses himself about this explanation in the following manner:

"As long as the Linnaean Society, to prove their explanation, cannot depose an accurate observation or a dissection, we may be allowed to entertain modest doubt about their explanation."

Of this little *Coluber* we find also the following passage in Schlegel's *Essai sur la physionomie des Serpens*. La Haye, 1837, p. 80:

"In the same country a snake has been found, probably of the species called *Coluber constrictor*, of which all parts were disfigured by sickness much so, that they believed to recognize in this kind of monster the famous Sea-Serpent of the North, so well-known for its enormous size. The extract from the dissertation, published in Boston, will be found in the *Journal de Physique* Vol. 86, p. 297."

Dr. Hamilton, in his *Amphibious Carnivora*, 1839, apparently believes that the little *Scoliophis atlanticus* was the spawn of the Great Sea-Serpent, at least he heads his Group III:

"The Great Sea-Serpent."

"Scoliophis atlanticus? Linn. Soc. of Boston".

We see that he is not quite sure of it, as he puts a note of interrogation after the scientific name.

Without any doubt the *Scoliophis atlanticus* was a difformed specimen of *Coluber constrictor*. It was the bunches on its back, which induced the Committee to suppose this little snake to be a spawn of the sea-serpent, which had also bunches on its back. After the discovery that the little snake was a difformed one, the explanation falls to the ground. Moreover the smooth skin and the presence of four flappers of the sea-serpent, are proofs against this supposition.

The **third** explanation. In the Chapter on Hoaxes I have already inserted the letter from Prof. T. Say, of Philadelphia, to Prof. Leach, of London, in which the former, relying upon a trick of the crew of the vessel commanded by captain Richard Rich, firmly believed and declared the Sea-Serpent to be nothing but **a large tunny**. Prof. Say's letter is also printed in Thomson's *Annals* of January, 1819. We have inserted a figure of a tunny in the above mentioned Chapter, fig. 1.

Prof. Bigelow's indignation rose against this explanation; in Silliman's *Am. Journ. Sc. Arts*. Vol. II, Boston, 1820, we read:

"In some of the Scientific Journals remarks have been published, in which the testimony of these witnesses" (of Gloucester and elsewhere), "is announced to be an 'absurd story', attributable to a 'defective observation connected with an extravagant degree of fear' (See Thomson's *Annals*, for January 1819)".

"In the American Journal of Science Vol. I, p. 260, is a note from the same author, on the identity of *Scoliophis* with *Coluber constrictor*. As this gentleman probably received his knowledge on the subject from p. 40th. of the Linnaean Society's Report, it might have been decorous in him to have noticed the source from which he got his information."

"As the friends of Science can have no object in view more important than the attainment of truth, it is proper to submit to the public consideration some additional evidence in regard to the size and shape of this marine animal which has come to light since the publication of Captain Rich's letter on the subject. This evidence is partly the result of observations during the present year, and partly the contents of a communication made to the American Academy of Arts and Sciences fifteen years ago, but which, having been mislaid, has not before been published. The reader will judge whether it is a 'defective observation' which has produced a remarkable coincidence between witnesses in different periods and places, unknown to each other; or whether it was 'an extravagant degree of fear' which induced the commander of an American fregate to man his boats and go with his mariners in pursuit of this unknown animal. It may be proper to add that the original letters constituting the communication last alluded to, are in the hands of the corresponding Secretary of the Academy, where they may be seen. It is hoped that the unsuccessful termination of Capt. Rich's cruise will not deter others from improving any future opportunities which may occur for solving what may now perhaps be considered the most interesting problem in the science of Natural History."

How to make the animal's head (which is like that of a snake, a seal, a walrus, a sea-lion), its long neck, its four flappers, its enormous long pointed tail, agree with the general outlines of a tunny, even of nine or ten feet in length!?

The **fourth** explanation. Mr. Constant Samuel Rafinesque Smaltz, in his *Dissertation on Water-Snakes, Sea-Snakes, and Sea-Serpents* (*Philosophical Magazine*, Vol. 54, 1819.), is evidently convinced of the fact that there are several kinds of sea-serpents, which are merely **sea-snakes of a very large size**, (Family *Hydrophidae*), of which I give a figure representing the *Hydrophis pelamidoides*, and Mr. Rafinesque classes two different sea-serpents under this head, proposing for them the names of *Pelamis megophias* (*Megophias monstrosus*) and *Pelamis monstrosus s. chloronotis*.

Mr. Gosse, in his *Romance of Natural History*, after discussing the question whether the sea-serpent may be an optical illusion caused by a huge stem of seaweed, or a large seal, a cetacean, a basking shark, a ribbon fish, or a large kind of eel, continues his considerations in the following terms:

"To the Reptiles, however, popular opinion has pretty uniformly assigned this denizen of the sea, and his accepted title of 'sea-serpent' sufficiently indicates his zoological affinities in the estimation of the majority of those who believe in him. Let us, then, test his claims to be a serpent."

"The marine habit presents no difficulty. For, in the Indian and Pacific Oceans, there are numerous species of true snakes (*Hydrophidae*), which are exclusively inhabitants of the sea. They are reported to remain much at the surface, and even to sleep so soundly there, that the passing of a ship through a group sometimes fails to awaken them."

"None of these are known to exceed a few feet in length, and so far as we know, none of them have been found in the Atlantic."

Mr. Andrew Wilson on the contrary in September, 1878, declares in *Nature* (Vol. XVIII, Sept. 12) that:

"As a firm believer from the standpoint of Zoology the large development of the marine ophidians of warm seas offers the true explanation of the sea-serpent mystery,...."

But a few lines further on he also tells us:

"I am far from contending that a sea-snake developed in the ratio of a giant 'cuttle fish', presents the only solution of this interesting problem. A long tape fish, or even a basking shark of huge dimensions, might do duty in the eyes of non-zoological observers for a 'sea-serpent'."—

In his *Leisure Time Studies*, the same writer returns to his favourite idea:

"The only group of animals to which our attention may be specially directed with the view of finding a zoological solution of the problem, is that of the *Vertebrata*,—the highest group of animals, which possesses the fishes as its lowest, and man and quadrupeds as its highest representatives. Laying aside the class of birds, as including no form at all allied to our present inquiry, we are left with, speaking generally, three groups of animals, from the ranks of which various forms may be selected to aid us in solving the sea-serpent mystery. These three groups are the fishes, reptiles, and mammalia, and it may be shown that from each of these classes, but more notably from among the fishes and reptiles, various animals, corresponding more or less closely with the descriptions given of strange marine monsters, may be obtained. An important consideration, however, must not be overlooked at this stage, namely, that too frequently the attempt to reconcile the sea-serpent with some *known* animal of serpentine form and nature, has limited the perceptions and foiled the labours of naturalists. Starting with the fixed idea that the unknown form must be a serpent, and not widening their thoughts to admit of the term 'serpentine' being extended to groups of animals other than the reptilia, naturalists soon exhausted the scientific aspect of the subject, and the zoological solution of the problem was almost at once given up. Then, also, as far as I have been able to

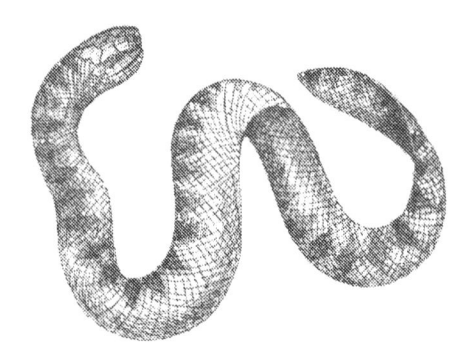

FIG. 56.–HYDROPHIS PELAMIDOIDES.

ascertain, zoologists and other writers on this subject have never made allowance for the *abnormal and huge development of ordinary marine animals*. My own convictions on this matter find in these two considerations, but especially in the last idea, the most reasonable and likely explanation of the personality of the sea-serpent, and also the reconciliation of such discrepancies as the various narrations may be shown to evince. If we thus fail to find in the ranks of ordinary animal life, or amongst the reptiles themselves, the representatives of the 'sea-serpents', I think we may nevertheless build up a most reasonable case both for their existence and for the explanation of their true nature, by taking into account the facts, *that the term 'sea-serpent', as ordinarily employed, must be extended to include other forms of vertebrate animals which possess elongated bodies; and that cases of the abnormally large development of ordinary serpents and of serpent-like animals will reasonably account for the occurrence of the animals collectively named sea-serpents.*"

"The idea that the animal observed in this instance" (n°. 118) "was a huge serpent, seems to have been simply slurred over without that due attention which this hypothesis undoubtedly merits. Whilst to my mind, the only feasible explanation of the narrative of the crew of the *Pauline*" (n°. 144, 145) "must be founded on the idea that the animals observed by them were gigantic snakes. The habits of the animals in attacking the whales, evidently point to a close correspondence with those of terrestrial serpents of large size, such as the boas and pythons; whilst the fact of the animal being described in the various narratives as swimming with the head out of water, would seem to indicate that, like all reptiles, they were air-breathers, and required to come more or less frequently to the surface for the purpose of respiration. The difficulties which appear to stand in the way of reconciling the sea-serpent with a marine snake, in this or in other cases, are two in number. The great majority of intelligent persons are unaware of the existence of serpents of truly and exclusively marine habits; and thus the mere existence of such snakes constitutes an apparent difficulty, which, however, a slight acquaintance with the history of the reptilia would serve at once to remove. Mr. Gosse speaks of these marine snakes,—the *Hydrophidae* of the naturalist,—which inhabit the warmer seas, possess compressed fin-like tails adapted for swimming, and are frequently met with far out at sea. Whilst, as regards the claims of the 'sea-serpent' to belong to the true serpent order, naturalists have dismissed their idea, simply because it has never occurred to them that a gigantic development of an ordinary species of sea-snake would fully correspond with most of the appearances described, and would in the most natural manner explain many of the sea-serpent tales. Suppose that a sea-snake of gigantic size is carried out of its ordinary latitude, and allow for slight variations or inaccuracies in the accounts given by Captain M'Quhae, and I think we have in these ideas the nearest possible approach to a reasonable solution of this interesting problem".

"It will be asked how I account for the apparent absence of motion of the fore part of the body, and for the existence of a dorsal or back fin. I may suggest, in reply, that the simple movements of the laterally compressed tail, altogether concealed beneath the surface, would serve to propel the animal forward without causing the front portion of the body to exibit any great or apparent motion; whilst the appearance of a fin may possibly be explained on the presumption that sea-weed may have become attached to the animal, or, that the upper ridge of the vertically compressed tail extended far forward and appeared as a fin-like structure."

"The most important feature in my theory, however, in which I may be desired to lead evidence, and that which really constitutes the strong points of this explanation, is the probability of the development to a huge or gigantic size of ordinary marine serpents. This point is one in support of which zoology and physiology will offer strong and favourable testimony. There is no single fact, so far as I am aware, which militates in the slightest degree against the supposition that giant members of the sea-serpents may be occasionally developed. The laws which regulate human growth and structure, and in virtue of which veritable 'sons of Anak', like Chang the Chinese giant, and the Russian giant, differing widely in proportions from their fellow-mortals, are developed, must be admitted to hold good for the entire animal kingdom. There is, in fact, no valid reason against the supposition that a giant serpent is occasionally produced, just as we familiarly observe almost every kind of animal to produce now and then a member of the race which mightily exceeds the proportions of its neighbours. But clearer still does our case become when we consider that we have proof of the most absolute and direct kind of the giant development of such forms as cuttle-fishes, which have thus appeared as if in realisation of Victor Hugo's 'devil-fish', which plays so important a part in that strange weird tale, the 'Toilers of the Sea'. At the present time we are in full possession of the details of several undoubted cases of the occurrence of cuttle-fishes of literally gigantic proportions,—developed, in fact, to an extent justly comparable to that of the supposed 'sea-serpent', when the latter is compared with its ordinary representatives of the tropical oceans."

"Is there anything more improbable, I ask, in the idea of a gigantic development of an ordinary marine snake into a veritable giant of its race—or, for that matter, in the existence of distinct species of monster sea-serpents—than in the production of huge cuttle-fishes, which, until within the past few years, remained unknown to the foremost pioneers of science! In the idea of gigantic developments of snakes or snake-like animals, be they fishes or reptiles, I hold we have at least a feasible and rational explanation of the primary fact of the actual existence of such organisms."

Mr. Lee in his *Sea Monsters Unmasked* (1883) also says:

"As marine snakes some feet in length, and having fin-like tails adapted for swimming, abound over an extensive geographical range, and are frequently met with far at sea, I cannot regard it as impossible that some of these also may attain to an abnormal and colossal development. Dr. Andrew Wilson, who has given much attention to this subject, is of the opinion that "in this huge development of ordinary forms we discover the true and natural law of the production of the giant serpent of the sea." It goes far, at any rate, towards accounting for its supposed appearance".

But by this supposition the smooth skin, the four flappers, the mane, and the pointed tail of the sea-serpent are not explained. Further, true snakes cannot possibly throw their bodies into vertical undulations. It is moreover very improbable that large *Hydrophidae*, supposing that they do exist, should visit Great Britain, the United States, the coasts of Norway, the North-Cape, Greenland and the Aleutes, as their geographical distribution only extends over the tropical seas.

The **fifth** explanation. The same Mr. Rafinesque believed the sea-serpent seen by Capt. Brown to be a fish (n°. 56), closely allied to the genera *Symbranchus*

(Fam. *Symbranchidae*) and *Sphagebranchus* (Fam. *Muraenidae*); consequently **belonging to the eel tribe**.

Mr. Gosse, in his *Romance of Natural History*, after having shown that in some instances the sea-serpent may have been an optical illusion caused by a huge stem of sea-weed, or a large seal, a cetacean, a basking shark, or a ribbon-fish, says:

"A far greater probability exists, that there may be some oceanic species of the eel tribe, of gigantic dimensions. Our own familiar conger is found ten feet in length. Certainly, Captain M'Quhae's figures remind me strongly of an eel; supposing the pectorals to be either so small as to be inconspicuous at the distance at which the animal was seen, or to be placed more than commonly far back."

And Mr. Andrew Wilson in his *Leisure Time Studies* is also inclined to this hypothesis:

"Amongst the fishes, we may find not a few examples of snakelike animals, which, admitting the fact of the occurrence of gigantic developments, may be supposed to mimic very closely the appearance of marine serpents. Any one who has watched the movements of a large conger-eel, for example, in any of our great aquaria, must have remarked not only its serpentine form, but also the peculiar gliding motion, which seems frequently to be produced independently of the active movements of the tail or pectoral fins. I do not doubt, however, that a giant eel might by most persons be readily enough referred to its proper place in the animal sphere, although, when viewed from some distance, and seen in an imperfect and indistinct manner, the spectators—all unprepared to think of an eel being so largely developed—might report the appearance as that of a marine snake."

Mr. Lee in his *Sea-Monsters Unmasked*, too, asserts:

"An enormous conger is not an impossibility."

As the common eel and the conger or sea-eel are well enough known to all my readers, I have not given a figure of it. The *Symbranchus* has nearly the same external features, it has, however, no pectoral or ventral fins, and the right and left gill-aperturus, or gill-splits, are united together on its throat. The *Sphagebranchus* has also nearly the same external features; it has no ventral fins and the very end of its tail is destitute of a fin.

The four flappers of the sea-serpent and its vertical flexibility are strong proofs against this hypothesis.

The **sixth** explanation is that which I have accidentally found mentioned in Dr. Hibbert's *Description of the Shetland Islands*, 1822. The passage runs as follows:

"The faith in the Edda of the great Serpent that Thor fished for, did not, as Dr. Percy conceives, give rise to the notion of the sea-snake, but a real sea-snake was the foundation of the **fable**."

I am convinced that Dr. Hibbert is right. All fables have their foundation in facts, or in objects of nature, and it is plausible that the Norwegians had met with the sea-serpent before the fable of Thor's great Serpent was inserted in their Eddas.

Dr. Percy's explanation that the notion of the Sea-Serpent springs from the faith in the Edda, is repeated by Messrs. H. E. Strickland and A. G. Melville in a note to their dissertation on the Dodo, in the *Annals and Magazine of Natural History*, 2nd. series, Vol. 2, p. 444, Nov. 15? 1848:

"It has always seemed to us that the fable of the Great Sea-Serpent, which first spread in modern times from Norway, was to be traced to the myth, in the fine Old Northern Mythology, of that fell offspring of Loki, Jormungandr,—the great world surrounding serpent, whom Thor fished up with the bull's-head bait, and whom, at the great day of Ragnarokr, he shall slay. It is curious by the way, that we are expressly told how Jormungandr rearing his head, poured out fountains of venom upon Thor, very much as old Bishop Egede tells us of the great sea-serpent raising up its head and spouting out water."

At present every one is convinced of the fact that the reports of the great sea-serpent are no fables.

The **seventh** explanation, viz. that the "slow motions of **basking sharks**" evidently caused a deceitful appearance, will be found at the end of Mr. Mitchill's dissertation, printed in 1828, with which the reader will remember to have been made acquainted in our Chapter on Hoaxes. A basking shark is delineated in our fig. 8, in the Chapter on Would-be Sea-Serpents.

Again this suggestion is made by the well-known palaeontologist Mantell, in a P. S. to a letter addressed by him to the Editor of the *Illustrated London News*, and published there in the number of November 4, 1848:

"P. S. With regard to the existence of the so-called sea-serpent, I would beg to remark, that, although it is highly improbable that an ophidian, or true snake, of the dimensions and marine habits described by our voyagers now exists, yet there is nothing to forbid the supposition that there are unknown living forms of cartilaginous fishes presenting the general configuration and proportions of the animals figured in the last Number of the Illustrated London News."

Evidently he meant a shark, of which individuals of more than thirty feet are no rarity in the species called basking shark (*Squalus maximus* of Linné). The figures referred to are those of the sea-serpent seen by Captain M'Quhae, (fig. 28, 29, 30).

In the fifth explanation we have learned that Mr. A. G. Melville was of opinion that there does not exist a sea-serpent in reality, but only in fables, and that these fables originated in the Northern mythology. Now, he seems to have changed his opinion in a fortnight, for in a letter to Dr. Cogswell, part of which is published "with permission of both gentlemen" in the *Zoologist*, number of November 27th., 1848, he says:

"I have never entertained a doubt regarding the existence of some unknown animal of vast dimensions, whose angel visits have astonished the fortunate observers or excited the incredulous smile of the authorities of science."

"No one inclined, I believe, to give due importance to the known facts of geology, can entertain the probability of any relationship between "the great sea-serpent" and the extinct Plesiosauri; nor do the recorded phenomena require such a hypothesis."

"Reasoning from the known occurrence of a huge cartilaginous fish (Squalus) on our Orcadian shores, I am of opinion that when caught the sea-serpent will turn out to be a shark, and I conceive it is just as probable that a shark may carry the head for short periods out of the water, as that the flying fishes should occasionally step aboard to look at us land monsters."

"It is always unsafe to deny positively any phenomena that may be wholly or in part inexplicable; and hence I am content to believe that one day the question will

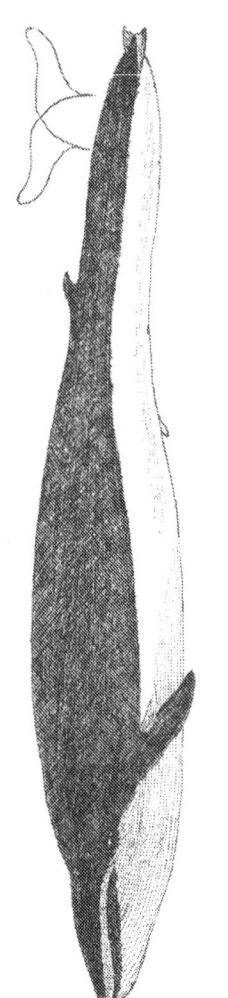

FIG. 57.—BALAENOPTERA PHYSALUS, (LINNÉ).

FIG. 58.—SKELETON OF ICHTHYOSAURUS COMMUNIS.

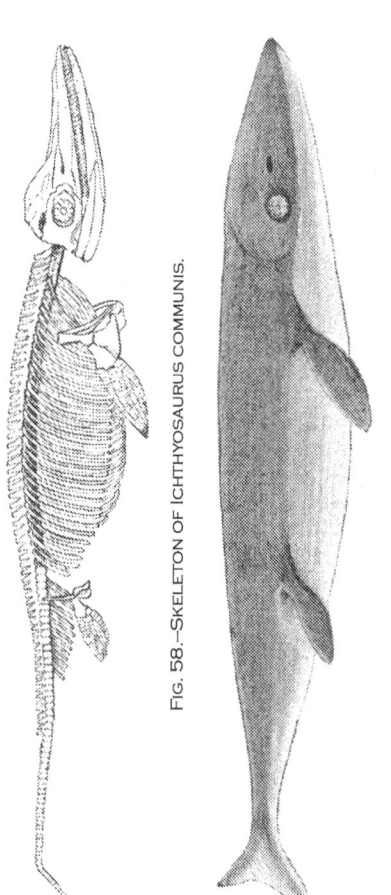

FIG. 59.—ICHTHYOSAURUS COMMUNIS, RESTORED.

be satisfactorily solved. Might we not obtain some information from the accurate Sars regarding the Norwegian tradition? Could not the surgeon of the Daedalus throw some light on the subject?"

Mr. Gosse, in his *Romance of Natural History*, after having treated of the probability of the sea-serpent being an optical illusion caused by huge stems of sea-weed, or being a large seal, or some cetacean, expresses his opinion about the basking-shark theory in the following terms:

"As to its place among fishes, Dr. Mantell and Mr. Melville consider that the *Daedalus* animal may have been one of the sharks; and there is no doubt that the celebrated Stronsa animal, which was considered by Dr. Barclay as the Norwegian sea-serpent, was really the *Selache maxima* or basking-shark. But the identification of Captain M'Quhae's figure and description with a shark is preposterous."

Mr. Andrew Wilson, however, in *Nature* (1878, Sept. 12, Vol. XVIII) is of the opinion that:

"A long tape fish, or even a basking shark of huge dimensions, might do duty in the eyes of non zoological observers for a 'sea-serpent'."

Mr. Lee, in his *Sea Monsters Unmasked*, 1883, also believes that "the dorsal fins of basking sharks, as figured by Mr. Buckland, may have furnished the 'ridge of fins'." Here he evidently means the ridge of fins as seen in fig. 44.

None of the observers of the sea-serpent mention fins on its back, so that this explanation is not untenable either.

The **eighth** explanation is given by Mr. Mitchill in his paper "*On Sea-Serpentism*", printed in 1828; (See our Chapter on Hoaxes), at the end of which he supposed that also the appearances of **balaenopterous whales** may have given rise to reports of the sea-serpent. He says: "which have fins on their back", and yet he cannot show me one single account of the sea-serpent, in which there is question of backfins. Moreover, who has ever heard of fin-fishes which bend their body in such a manner as to show bunches on their backs, or coils like a string of buoys? Fig. 57 shows the readers a finfish (*Balaenoptera physalus* (Linné). It is the largest kind of whales, it may obtain a length of 106 feet. An outline of the tail, seen from above, is added above the hindmost part of the main-figure.

Mr. Gosse in his *Romance of Natural History*, after having considered and upset the sea-weed hypothesis and the seal-theory says:

"It is by no means impossible that the creature may prove to belong to the *Cetacea* or whale tribe. I know of no reason why a slender and lengthened form should not exist in this order. The testimony of Colonel Steele, who represents his animal as spouting, points in this direction."

The sea-serpent seen by Colonel Steele, however was not a cetacean, although it was observed spouting, for it had a red back-fin like a saw (see our Chapter on Would-be Sea-Serpents, 1852, Aug. 28).—

The **ninth** explanation is Mr. R. Bakewell's. In Froriep's *Notizen*, Vol. 40, n°. 879, of June, 1834, we read:

"With regard to the often mentioned and much questioned great American Sea-Serpent Mr. R. Bakewell, in the latest edition of his Introduction to Geology, Chapt. 16, p. 312, has expressed the opinion that the great sea-serpent often seen on the coasts of the United States of America probably belonged to a genus of reptiles which may be analogous to the fossil **Ichthyosaurus**, and that the description, given of the sea-serpent, as having flappers like sea-turtles, and formidable mandibles like a crocodile, was agreeing more with that of a saurian than with that of a snake. Some of the people who saw the sea-serpent state that the body was very long and as thick as a water-cask."

Though in 1872 the majority apparently believed the sea-serpent to be a living *Plesiosaurus*, yet we meet with the following suggestion, in the September number of *Nature* of that same year.

"The following extract from an evening contemporary well illustrates the hazy ideas prevalent as to the extinct Saurian monsters of which the sea-serpent is supposed to be a descendant:—'If the sea-serpent continues in its present sociable state of mind, we may perhaps have an opportunity of deciding the vexed question regarding the formation of that portion of his figure which, according to English observers, he keeps concealed under the water. The legend of the Lambton Worm, a popular tale in the North of England, describes the worm as a serpent of enormous size, who used to coil himself round a hill overhanging the River Wear, just as thread is wound round a reel, but a very ancient stone effigy of the creature which lately existed at Lambton Castle, represents it with ears, legs and a pair of wings. If this effigy was made, as it probably was, *from some recollection* on recent tradition of the Lambton Worm, these adjuncts would indicate that the beast was one of the *winged land monsters* which existed at the same time as the *Ichthyosaurus*, but would naturally become an extinct species far sooner than the *fish-lizard*, which can conceal itself in the depth of the ocean from the curiosity and violence of man'."

The *Ichthyosaurus* must have been destitute of scales, or better the scales must have been of a microscopic minuteness, and so I have ventured to sketch my fig. 59, showing the *Ichthyosaurus communis*, as it most probably looked, and of which fig. 58 represents the skeleton.

Here we have an animal of really huge dimensions. Some may have had a length of from forty to fifty feet. Their skin was smooth, the tail was very long and four flappers resembling the foreflappers of whales, were the organs of locomotion. Most probably, however, the tail was provided with a vertical fin, as I have delineated. The neck was very short, as in whales. Now the sea-serpent has a pointed tail, and a very long neck. Especially this last character is enough to drop the supposition that the sea-serpents are still living *Ichthyosauri*. Moreover, the *Ichthyosaurus* was unable to move in vertical undulations.

The **tenth** explanation.—In Froriep's *Notizen*, Vol. 40, (1834), n°. 879, p. 328, we read that, in a note to Mr. Bakewell's latest (1834?) edition of his *Introduction to Geology*, above mentioned, Prof. Benjamin Silliman adds:

"Mr. Bakewell's very sensible conjecture that the sea-serpent may be a Saurian, agrees still more with the supposition, that it is a **Plesiosaurus**, than an Ichthyosaurus, as the short neck of the latter does not agree with the common appearance of the sea-serpent."

Plesiosaurians, as well as the *Icthyosaurians*, are reptiles only known in a fossil state. Only the bones of the skeleton of these animals are found in Europe as well as in America and in Australia in *liassic* and *oolitic* formations. Of these remains geologists are able to build up or to "restore" the whole skeleton, of which I show my readers a sketch in fig. 60.—If this is done, it will not be difficult to imagine how the animal must have looked, the more so as it is a well-known fact that these animals must have been destitute or nearly destitute of scales. The figures drawn by Gosse, Figuier and Andrew Wilson, don't please me, as the necks are delineated too slender, and the head of the animal in Mr. Gosse's drawing, in my opinion, is wrongly represented. So I venture to present to my readers my fig. 61, showing how I think that the animal must have looked.

Mr. Rathke, in the *Archiv für Naturgeschichte*, of 1841, after publishing some accounts of the sea-serpent, collected by himself during a journey in Norway, and after declaring that he himself is a firm believer in it, goes on:

"To which group of known animals, however, this being belongs, cannot of course be asserted with any certainty. The supposition, however, is very near, that it is closely related to that animal which in 1816" (read 1808) stranded in Stronsa, one of the Orkney's," &c.

After a short description of this animal with which the reader will remember to have been made acquainted in the Chapter on Would-be Sea-Serpents, Mr. Rathke concludes: "that this animal resembled a *Plesiosaurus*, and that it thus belonged to the *Amphibia*, viz. to the *Saurians*. Now if such were the case, and if the creature found in Stronsa were closely related to the sea-serpent of the Norwegians, and we have every reason to believe this, it is astonishing that the latter has not been more observed, than has been the case. For being an Amphibium, which, according to its organization, can only breathe by lungs, the sea-serpent necessarily must have come very often to the surface of the water, to renew the inhaled air. It is, however, conceivable and probable that stretching out its long neck, it generally comes only with the nose tip and only for a very short time on the surface of the water, remaining under it with the rest of the body, in which circumstances it will not be easy to observe it amongst the beating of the waves."

We observe that Mr. Rathke, like Prof. Silliman, inclines to believe that the sea-serpent is, or is allied to the *Plesiosaurus*.

Mr. Edward Newman, the Editor of the *Zoologist*, in 1847, on the wrapper of the 54th. number of this Journal made the suggestion that sea-serpents may belong to one of the *Enaliosaurians*.

I have not seen this wrapper so that I am unable to give the words in which this supposition was written.

Most probably Mr. Newman took this suggestion from Mr. Rathke's above mentioned dissertation, all the accounts of which he inserted (N. B.!) *in the same number* of the *Zoologist*; but it is, of course, *possible* that this supposition really was the product of his own brain. We hope that the latter was the case; but I only ask: why did he insert the accounts of Mr. Rathke in the *columns* of the issue, and why not the above-mentioned suggestion; what was the reason to communicate it on the *wrapper*? It makes on me the impression as if Mr. Newman waited to see if some one or other would perhaps find out that *both accounts and supposition* were *already six years old!* But, of course, I may be mistaken!

Immediately after reading this suggestion on the above mentioned wrapper, Mr. Charles Cogswell wrote for the same Journal his *Plea for the Sea-Serpent*. For history's sake I repeat here his whole paper. It runs as follows:

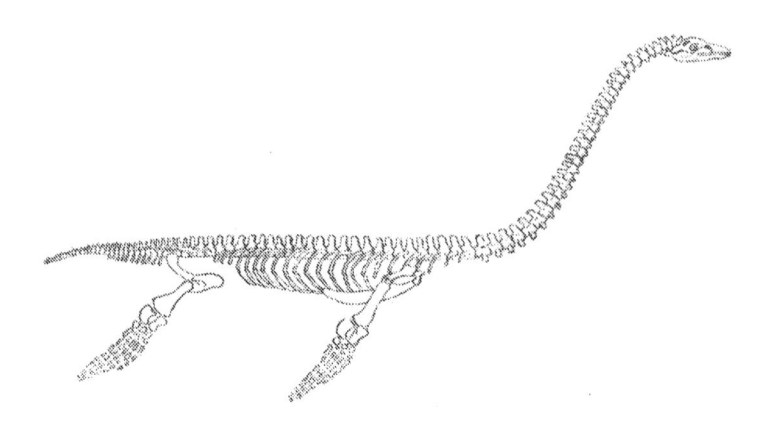

FIG. 60.—SKELETON OF PLESIOSAURUS DOLICHODEIRUS.

FIG. 61.—PLESIOSAURUS DOLICHODEIRUS, RESTORED.

"*A Plea for the North-Atlantic Sea-Serpent.* By Charles Cogswell, M. D."

> "Every generation of man is born to stare at something, which so long as it eludes their understanding, is a very African fetish to the many, and a Gordian knot to the few."
>
> Hawkin's *Memoirs of Ichthyosauri and Plesiosauri.*

"Of the numerous contributions supplied through the press to support the cause of the subject of this article, one of the most recent has arrested my attention, because of the particulars having been long since familiar to me by oral communication from the writer in person. I allude to the interesting narrative contained in the 'Zoologist' for May last, describing a meeting with such an animal off the coast of one of the British provinces, stretching out into the Atlantic to the north-east of New England. It is worthy of notice that several animals of the Cetaceous kind (sometimes conjectured to have been a source of deception) were seen and scanned *in limine*, and an opportunity was thus afforded for immediate descrimination. Immediately subjoined is another statement, copied from a foreign newspaper, being the tribute of a French sea-captain to the same object, but qualified with so much of the characteristic national precision in the detail of certain forms and measurements, as rather to display an elaborate view of disjoined parts, than represent them all in harmony together as belonging to one individual. It betrays the caution of a witness, who would fain keep an opening in reserve for escape from a precarious position. The former adventure took place in 1833, the latter in 1840, and now they are related almost simultaneously within the last few months."

"Nor is this delay to be wondered at, when we consider how much the reserve of unbiassed is the tribunal of public opinion, before which they appear. It will hardly be denied that there is no debateable point in the modern records of observation more complacently devoted to ridicule by all but universal consent, than that of the existence of huge serpent-like animals in the North Atlantic Ocean. The very mention of the name of sea-serpent in the singular number with the definite article prefixed, suggests to most minds an idea of some anomalous monster, without parentage or congeners, feigned to haunt the recesses of the deep, and, like the ghost of vulgar superstition, manifesting itself now and again for the sole conceivable end of adorning some wonderful legend. This impression, favoured by the circumstance of no actual specimen having ever occurred to the observation of a naturalist, much less been obtained for deliberate examination, has caused the subject of our notice to rank with the mermaid, the unicorn, the griffin, and other prodigies of the olden faith. It does not fail to be objected that Norway, a locality most fruitful in accounts of the appearance in question, has been immemorially distinguished for a vivid perception of the marvellous. Nor, after hearing the other side of the Atlantic, are we much better able to divest our minds of suspicion with regard to the trustworthy character of the witnesses; our relative in the West having acquired nearly as much celebrity for the endowment of a grand inventive genius as his Scandinavian ally in the cause of sea-serpents. They defer indeed, in so far as the latter believes and venerates his own creations, while the American indulges his fancy for the purely benevolent purpose of what is called 'hoaxing' the unwary public. Not many years since, it may be recollected, one of these pleasant philosophers enlightened his fellow-mortals with a 'true and peculiar' description of certain winged inhabitants assumed to have been discovered in the moon by an eminent living astronomer, giving the details with so much simplicity and effected candour with regard to some particulars, in the manner of 'Gulliver's Travels', that many readers were not aware of its being a fabrication. Such proof of a disposition to practise on the public credulity, too often repeated, necessarily communicate a colouring of insincerity to all other reports of strange events emanating from the same source, and certainly demand the exercise of an unusual amount of circumspection, though they do not justify scepticism, in the case now before us."

"Making due allowance for these peculiarities in the testimony, we may, nevertheless, proceed in a spirit of induction to examine into the tendency of the collateral evidence. The question after all, when reduced to its simplest form comes to be little more than one of geographical distribution. That is to say, that even if we chose to confine the animal to the true serpents, which has been the ordinary conception heretofore, there is no obvious impediment to oppose it, either on the score of want of analogy, or of structural incapacity. Amphibiousness, to commence with, in its popular acceptation, or the capability of spending a considerable time in the water, is one of the most familiar properties of serpents, as illustrated in the common snake (*Coluber natrix*) and the viper, the only two species, if we except the blindworm, ascertained to be indigenous to these islands. 'Snakes', observes Professor Bell ('History of British Reptiles') 'are extremely fond of the water, taking to it readily, and swimming with great elegance and ease, holding the head and neck above the surface. It is extremely probable that they resort to the water in search of frogs.' In the learned System of Schlegel, translated by Prof. Traill—'Physiognomy of Serpents'—members of various ophidian-groups are characterised as living near and inhabiting lakes and rivers. Some belong to the genera *Tropidonotus* (which here includes the first named British species), and *Homalopsis*, comprised under the head of *Fresh Water-Serpents*. Of the Boas, this author says: 'several species frequent fresh water, and there are some of them essentially aquatic,' among them the *Boa murina*, the largest of known serpents, and his two species of *Acrochordus*."

"Further, and what completely sets at rest the part of the case we are now considering, there are swarms of *marine* ophidians inhabiting the warm latitudes of the pacific. These appear to have been partly known to the ancients. Aelian informs us that Hydrae with flat tails were found in the Indian Seas, and that they also existed in the marshes. He also tells us that these reptiles had very sharp teeth, and appeared to be venomous. According to Ctesias, 'the serpents of the river Argada in the province of Sittacene, remain concealed at the *bottom of the water* during the day, and by night they attack persons who go to bath or wash linnen' (Griffith in Cuvier). Schlegel has no less than seven species collected under the generic name of Hydrophis, constituting his family of *Sea-Snake*—; they are especially fitted for aquatic life, having the nostrils directed vertically and furnished with valves, and the tail flattened like an oar; they reside in the sea exclusively, never going on land, and are supposed to prey on fishes. Their limits belong to the intertropical regions of the Indian Seas, or of the Great Pacific Ocean."

"The existence of *bona fide* sea-serpents being therefore a matter of notoriety, (and preserved specimens are to be seen at any time on the shelves of the British Museum), we have but to address ourselves to the subordinate inquiry, whether there be sufficient reason for assigning to any of the family a habitat in the North

Atlantic Ocean. And here it is necessary to put away all that idea of deviation from the common order of *Nature*, which could connect the evidence heretofore given with some isolated excrescence so to speak, of the animal kingdom. The great size attributed to them has doubtless, served very materially to produce an infavourable impression. Schlegel limits the extreme length of the greatest known serpent to twenty-five feet, although such naturalists as Cuvier and Milne-Edwards allow an extension of thirty or forty feet to some of the Boas. These estimates do not fall so far short of those contended for in the present instance as to form an insuperable ground of objection. Many witnesses whose character and station in life command respect, whatever judgment may be formed of their powers of correct observation, profess to be fully persuaded that they have seen immense creatures, resembling serpents, in the vicinity of the European or the American shores. The several depositions from Norway that appeared in the 'Zoologist' of February last, comprised the testimony not only of fishermen, drawing their subsistence from the sea, and familiar with the more prevalent forms of the inhabitants, but of a class commonly presumed to be well educated, as merchants, clergymen, and a surgeon. Their observations indeed vary on the subject of length (varying between forty and one hundred feet), and likewise on some of the details of outline, so that they may either relate to different specimens, or to deceptive phenomena producing dissimilar impressions, whichever alternative decretic may be inclined to profer. The first notice transmitted by an English gentleman, holding a responsible appointment under the crown in one of our transatlantic dependencies, is calculated to supply any deficiency on the part of the new hemisphere, so far as a faithful representation of what was submitted to the eye alone may remain a desideration. But for the resolution manifested in this periodical to allow the question a fair hearing on its sterling merits, there can be little doubt that this testimony, would not have been forthcoming; like in all probability, more of the same ingenious stamp, which the unwillingness of the principals to oppose the current of public opinion, directly proportioned to the value of the character they run the risk of compromizing for no obvious use, induces them to withhold."

"But it may be asked, how it is possible to explain the circumstance of these *monstra natantia* being encountered no farther South than about the sixtieth or fifty-fifth parallel on the European boundary, while in the American water their domain approaches so much nearer the Equator, as Nova Scotia (or New Scotland) and New England? By a curious and happy coincidence, of like significance to many that are constantly springing up to confirm the results of independent research, such for instance as the print of the piscivorous gavials in a prior leaf of the 'Stonebook' to the mammalivorous crocodiles; it happens that precisely a line swerving from Norway in a southerly direction to Massachusetts is the boundery likewise of other marine animals of corresponding types. Among the divisions of the North Atlantic, recently marked out by Professor Edward Forbes as determined by the presence of similar forms of animal life, occurs what is called the 'arctic and boreal' province, which "sweeps across the northernmost part of the North Atlantic from Europe, extending down the coast of North America as far as Massachusetts, but nothing like so far on the European side as the American." (Lecture at the Royal Institution, May 14, 1847).''

"Thus copiously backed by the most affirmative evidence, both positive and circumstantial, all contributing to establish the lawful claim to entity, the 'great unknown' of the North Atlantic has still to overcome the strong feeling of discredit so widely associated with his past history, before he can hope to be understood as seriously claiming to be a subject of the animal kingdom. If men of the highest name in science condescend to notice him at all, it is most probably with a smile at the expense of what they consider a crude invention, to which no importance should be attached. But authority, however exalted, has no patent of final adjudication in cases where its means of information are confessedly imperfect, as compared with those enjoyed by the supporters of a disputed position. The learned world was centuries in believing the story of Herodotus about little birds resorting to feed on insects within the 'stretched jaws' of the crocodile. Bruce all but ruined his credit for a time by relating that he had seen the Abyssinians eat the raw flesh cut from one of the haunches of a living cow; and there are some who, with no more reason, pretend to doubt the good faith of a contemporary traveller, who declares that he once made a brief excursion on the back of an alligator. The conflicts of discovery and opinion engross indeed no small share of the history of human knowledge. There are cases, no doubt, in which the senses and the judgment of incompetent persons are liable to be imposed upon by irrelevant facts created or qualified for the occasion. But here there is no hypothesis concerned requiring nature to be tortured into its service; physiology can have no latent objections, ready to start up unawares and make a mockery of belief, because some of the serpent kind are indubitably organized for an aquatic medium; the laws of geographical distribution deduced irrespectively, yield their consent, and the integrety of not a few of the narrator is unimpeachable. Are we justified in rejecting the text, because the interpretation may not harmonize with our views; in imputing willful dishonesty to those who merely describe to the best of their hability what their eyes have disclosed to them? We do not despice the mermaid, the triton and siren, as altogether imaginary but endeavour to reconcile at least their physical attributes with those of the seal or oriental dugong. The unicorn is supposed to have original in the narwhal; and the griffin is recognized as a well-known friend in an antiquated garb, being no other than the tapir, somewhat disfigured by travellers, and further indebted to the artist for a pair of wings and an architectural style of tail. Even the ghost-seer is seldom suspected of intentional fraud, however justly we may believe to be the dupe of an imagination acted on by some positive phenomenon. The collateral truths which testify on the affirmative side have been dwelt upon to some extent, and shall again be adverted to presently. On the other hand, surely there must be something peculiar in the economy of a vast air-breathing race, frequenting well-known tracts and yet never visible but by the merest accident; nor is it any sufficient answer to refer to the construction of the breathing apparatus, distinctive of the marine ophidians, enabling them to live long under water, and respire air with an almost imperceptible exposure above the surface, because the like provision does not prevent the Pacific denizens from being abundantly subject to observation. The want of conformity in some of the reported particulars of form and dimensions is of insignificant moment, and may easily be converted into a proof of innocence of design. Above all, the objections, be it understood, are not *of the kind* which the public at large appear to imagine them. There is nothing ridiculous or abnormal in the idea of a sea-serpent. So far from this the philosopher should rather be required to give a reason why at least the warmer situations of the Atlantic are unprovided with occupants corresponding to those which dwell in the opposite region of the globe."

"If the diversity of detail be accounted too serious an objection to be so lightly dismissed, is there no other organization within our cognizance which more satisfactorily embodies the several conditions rather loosely intimated than prescribed throughout the problem? The portraits given in authors of the restored Plesiosaurus, albeit conceived to represent beings that 'filled up the measure of their years long before Eden was planted, and the dominions of man made of the red earth, acknowledged' (Hawkins), offer several particulars answering to those ascribed in most of the notices on record to the sonamed sea-serpent,—the long, over-arched neck, the huge trunk, the protracted tail, and sometimes (see the deposition of Archdeacon Deinbolt, 'Zoologist' 1606) an appearance of fins or paddles. This coincidence is the more remarkable, because no one can suppose it to have been preconcerted. Hence the ingenious suggestion of the Editor of the 'Zoologist', that the animals may belong to one of the Enaliosaurian types, seems to supply the only deficient link in the chain of demonstration, before we arrive at the final proof, a spectacle open to all observers. The neck of the Plesiosaurus (presuming this to be the genus indicated) 'is composed of upwards of thirty bones, a number far exceeding that of the cervical vertebrae in any other known animal. This reptile combines in its structure the head of a lizard with teeth like those of a crocodile, a neck *resembling the body of a serpent*, a trunk and tail of the proportions of those of a quadruped, with paddles like those of turtles' (Mantell's Wonders of Geology). If this seemingly whimsical coaptation of incongruous members, which the dictum of science has consigned to the doom of pre-Adamic extinction, can be suspected without unpardonable heresy to be yet among the living, what is more allowable than to surmise that persons even of cultivated intellect, but quite unconscious that such things had ever existed, may have all honestly striven, more or less, to mould their visual perception into accordance with the familiar notion suggested by its general outline; and thus have given rise to the confusion objected to in their reports. Be this as it may, the discovery of Mr. Darwin of *marine* saurians, though but three or four feet long, about some of the south sea islands, contradicts any assumption that animals approaching to it in character are no longer extant. To account upon this supposition likewise for the hide-and-seek sort of life which those in question seem to lead, it may be observed that 'the breathing holes of the Plesiosaurus differ from those of all other existing reptiles, and resemble those of whales'. They are placed 'near the highest part of the head, where they would enable the animal most readily to breathe without exposing anything more than the apertures themselves above the water, corresponding admirably with the marine habits of the animal as indicated by the structure of its extremities.' (Ansted's Ancient World, 1847).

"Without committing myself to anything more than a belief that the subject is one fairly entitled to be considered an open question—open to the unrestrained testimony of future casual observers, equally with the criticism of the scientific—I feel assured that I cannot better express the opinion which every candid peruser of what has been stated must be prepared to arrive at, than by using the words of a naturalist who has given his attention to these remarks: 'The argument appears to me perfectly satisfactory in favour of at least a suspension of judgment on the subject. The question is whether the evidence is such as would induce any man to believe, whose mind was prepossessed with no notions at all respecting it. Should we credit the testimony, if the animal to which it relates were claimed to be a mere variety? I think we should'."—

I am obliged to make a few notes or observations on this paper. The account, namely, of which Mr. Cogswell speaks in the beginning of his "Plea", which arrested his attention, because of the particulars having been long since familiar to him by oral communication, is that of the party of British officers (n°. 97).—That "other statement" is that made by Capt. D'Abnour (n°. 106 a).—I beg the reader to look over the above-mentioned passages.—Mr. Cogswell had better done to omit his observation, that the account of the French sea-captain "was qualified with so much of the characteristic national precision in the detail of certain forms and measurements". The reader himself will in most of the accounts of the sea-serpent, which fill this volume, have observed the same "precision in details" indifferently whether the account was recorded by a Norwegian, a German, an English, a French or an American witness.—His observation that the sea-serpent only occurs "in the North Atlantic no farther south than a line swerving from Norway in a southerly direction to Massachusetts" is incorrect, as the reader may already have observed himself. If he had read all the accounts of the sea-serpent up to his days, he would, of course, not have written this. The "deposition of Archdeacon Deinbolt, Zool. 1606" is of the 28th. of July, 1845 (n°. 115). Mr. Cogswell cites here the passage in which he will find "an appearance of paddles". The reader will probably remember that there was no question of paddles, but of a boiling of the water, which the witnesses *thought* to have been caused by a pair of fins nearest the head, and which I have explained in another way.—Mr. Cogswell calls Mr. Newman's suggestion, that the sea-serpents may belong to the *Enaliosaurian* type, "ingenious". I think that the reader, after having read only the accounts of the sea-serpent up to the days of Mr. Newman's suggestion, i. e. up to 1847, will not be inclined to call this suggestion "ingenious", with regard to the sea-serpent being so often reported as having a mane and whiskers, and swimming with vertical undulations. Moreover it is the question whether this suggestion was Mr. Newman's or Mr. Rathke's.

Mr. J. D. Morries Stirling too, seemed to believe that the sea-serpents are allied to the extinct *Plesiosauri*, for he writes in a letter to Captain Hamilton, R. N., Secretary to the Admiralty (See *Illustrated London News* of 28th. October, 1848):

"There are I believe, several varieties of the reptile known as the sea-serpent but almost all the accounts agree as to the existence of a mane, and as to the great size of the eye. In several of the fossil reptiles somewhat approaching the sea-serpent in size and other characteristics, the orbit is very large; and in this respect. as well as having short paws or flappers, the description of the Northern sea-serpents agree with the supposed appearance of some of the antediluvian species. A great part of the disbelief in the existence of the sea-serpent has arisen from its being supposed to be the same animal as the kraken, or rather from the names having been used indiscriminately."

Another gentleman, who signed his article in the *Times* of November 2nd., 1848, with the initials F. G. S., came to the same suggestion. His letter will be found in its right place, after the statements of Captain M'Quhae (n°. 118).

Dr. Cogswell who perhaps feared that in spite of his "Plea" the story of the sea-serpent was on a fair way to be forgotten, once more took the subject in hand, and sent a second paper to the *Zoologist* of December 1848. This dissertation is at least better than the first, being partly critical, partly historical. Again, for history's sake, I am obliged to repeat nearly his whole paper.

"It grows more and more necessary every day to acknowledge the *existence* of a vast form of marine animal bearing some resemblance to a serpent. The recent letter of Captain M'Quhae to the Admiralty allows of no other alternative than either to admit the evidence, or invent some still more extraordinary hypothesis to explain it away. The forms of bearings of the strangers have been duly reported at head quarters, and no more deserve to be called in question, as regards the fidelity of the narrator, than the existence of any commissioned 'Snake' or 'Anaconda', whose station and appointments we find recorded in the daily press. No preternatural messenger in 'the shape that tempted Eve',—he passes by on the other side without manifesting the slightest degree of interest in human affairs; no phantom progeny of light and air, although affecting literally the same haunts as the 'Flying Dutchman',—he steers himself by compass, and is the herald of no signal disaster; no herd of porpoises disporting all in a row, and joined together by some *Daedalian* process of imagination into the semblance of unity—his head is 'decidedly that of a snake',—he carries it for twenty minutes at a time out of the water; and his body is seen for a continuous length of sixty feet on a level with the surface. From the standard jest of the witty, and the discarded problem of the wise, he has shown himself likely to be 'no joke' for his physical powers, and well deserving the gravest scientific inquiry."

"To show what a formidable and unyielding front has been heretofore opposed to him, I shall quote a passage from the article under the head of 'Serpents' in the last edition of the 'Encyclopedia Britannica' (1842): 'No proper proof has yet been adduced of any of these species (sea-serpents) inhabiting the 'American Ferry', as we see that world of waters now named since the steaming days of the British Queen and the Great Western.' Mr. Schlegel characterizes the statement as an assertion *que je puis contredire avec certitude*: and the author adds: 'we shall content ourselves by stating that sea-serpents have not yet been observed in the Atlantic Ocean'. The following notice occurs in a popular compilation of the animal kingdom just issued from the press (1848): 'Sea-serpent (or the Kraken). The appearance of this *fabulous* monster is thus accounted for by Mr. A. Adams. In the Sooloo seas I have often watched the phenomenon which first gave rise to the marvellous stories of the great sea-serpent, viz., lines of rolling porpoises resembling a long string of buoys oftentimes extending seventy, eighty, or one hundred yards. These constitute the so-named protuberances of the monster's back, keep in close single file progressing rapidly along the calm surface of the water.' &c. Had the *fabulous* serpent in Aesop, who complained of being 'a multis hominibus pessumdatus', been aware of what laid up in the fates for his aquatic relative, no doubt he would have ceased to repine at his own hard lot."

"The official corroboration of the fundamental truth of these 'marvellous stories' is important, not only because the author under the circumstances must at least receive credit for the most entire sincerety, but from the encouragement thus given to other credible witnesses to bring forward their evidence. There is no reason to suppose that even this would have been readily laid before the public, but for the desire expressed by the Board of Admiralty to learn the truth of an accidental rumour. As regards any additional light thrown on the natural history of the animal, it is not more satisfactory than many of the accounts we already possess. Indeed the paragraphs which precede the captain's letter in the 'Zoologist' viz., the extract from the Journal of Lieut. Drummond, and the first public rumour as it appeared in the 'Times', tend rather to confuse the official statement, and will no doubt be used to create suspicious of its accuracy. The communication which follows it, purporting to give a report of another specimen seen by an American captain, is supposed to be 'a hoax', and as such is worthy of preservation from the ingenuity it displays."

"When a doctrine is assumed to be fanciful, people seldom take the trouble to inquire into its history and merits. This may account for the sea-serpent being commonly confounded with a very different prodigy, too exacting in its claims for the most extravagant credulity of modern days to regard with favour. As seen above, its name and that of Kraken are popularly used as synonymous. And nevertheless, Pontoppidan, Bishop of Bergen, whose 'Natural History of Norway' (translated into English in 1755) is the usual standard of authority on both subjects, treats of them separately in appropriate sections of his work. Of the Kraken he says, 'I come now to the third, and incontestably the largest sea-monster in the world: it is called Kraken, krasen, or, as some name it, krabben, that word being applied by way of eminence to this creature'. Its back or upper part he described as truly gigantic, being a mile and a half or more in circumference, and it is provided with limbs so strong as to be able to pull boats and the smaller sailing crafts under water. Some deem the original of this story to have been a Sepia or Medusa of enormous size; others set it down for an optical illusion; Pontoppidan himself thinks that 'in all probability it may be reckoned of the polypi or of the starfish kind'. One cannot help being reminded, on reading the above, of the passage in Milton where he compares Satan, 'prone on the flood', to 'That sea beast'"..... &c.—

"Commentators have been divided in opinion whether Milton supposed the leviathan to be a crocodile or a whale. The former idea derives little support from the text; the whale, which has only lately been divested of its 'scaly rind', puts forward more plausible pretentions: nevertheless, the vast bulk of the creature alluded to, and its position, 'slumbring in the Norway foam', suggest the inquiry whether the poet may not have had in his mind a tradition of the kraken. I may mention here that the Norwegian Bishop believed that the Leviathan of Job and Isaiah had been detected in the *sea-serpent*. Of the latter animal Pontoppidan says: 'The soe-ormen'"..... &c.

"It would serve little purpose to occupy these pages with mere copies of the published narratives and depositions tending to prove the existence of the animal under our consideration. Whatever discrepancies may perplex us with regard to subordinate details, it is important to remember that the one ruling form, that of a serpent, is the foundation of all the descriptions. The form may vary—in length, perhaps, from forty to a hundred feet and upwards; in the relative dimensions of the head and different parts of the body; in the presence or absence of a mane or paddles; and more particularly with respect to an appearance of dorsal arches or elevations, rising above the water like a row of casks or buoys. The greater part of the evidence on the subject is contained, I believe, in Pontoppidan's 'Natural History of Norway' (1755), the 'Report of a Committee of the Linnaean Society of New England relative to a large Marine Animal, supposed to be a Sea-Serpent, seen near Cape Ann, Massachusetts, in August, 1817' (Boston 1817), and the last volume of 'The Zoologist' (1847). In the Scandinavian work the principal witness is Captain L. de Ferry, of the Navy, who thus describes an individual which he saw while in a boat, rowed by eight men, within six miles of Molde, in a calm hot day of August, 1747. 'The head of the snake'"..... &c.

"The Report of the Linnaean Society of New England contains the result of an inquiry"..... &c.

"The tenor of the late observations in Norway recorded in the 'Zoologist' (Zool. 1604) certainly might justify the inference that these so remarkable prominences are not persistent, but depend, as suggested by the American functionary, on the mode of progression practised at the moment. Anybody that had watched the lithe and varied curves of an otter in the water can have no difficulty in recording together the different kinds of undulations to the sea-serpent. There is one particular of rare occurrence worthy of notice, in one of these later accounts, calling to mind a peculiarity in the description of the animal seen by Mr. Egede, a Greenland missionary and furnished to us with a copy of the figure, by Pontoppidan. This creature, of the unusual length of 600 feet, 'had under its body two flappers, or perhaps two broad fins'. One of the recent narratives also states of the progressive movement, that it appeared to be produced 'by the help of two fins' (Zool. 1607). Thus is offered a possible solution of the difficulty occasioned by captain M'Quhae's specimen having advanced at a rapid rate, with 60 feet of the body à fleur d'eau, without any visible undulation." (I, however, refer the reader to the report of 1845, July 28).

"Here I may refer to 'The Description of an Animal stranded on the Island of Stronsa, in the year 1808' given in the first Volume of the 'Wernerian Transactions' by the late eminent Dr. Barclay. Evidently disposed to believe that this animal was a sea-serpent, Dr. Barclay indignantly repudiates the opinion of Mr. Home, that it was nothing more than a shark (*Squalus maximus*). Figures of the two are shown in juxtaposition, for the purpose of constrasting them, and to all appearance their respective peculiarities are quite sufficient to distinctive appellations. The Orkney animal, in fact, bears a curious resemblance to a *Plesiosaurus*, with six legs. Nevertheless, anatomists have decided that a shark it really was, the anomalies being accounted for by the circumstance of the drawing having been taken from hearsay and under the supervision of persons who only saw the original in a very imperfect state. The 'Animal of Stronsa' and the '*Scoliophis atlanticus*' leave us equally in the dark with regard to the physical economy of the sea-serpent; that is, unless the solution offered by Drs. Mantell and Melville (Zool. 2310) shall prove to be correct." (See our 7th. explanation.)

"From what precedes it is evident, *First*, that the notion of the sea-serpent is not a mere growth of unlettered and credulous superstition, since it has been repeated and confirmed by parties than whom it would be difficult to select any more worthy of confidence, with this sole objection—that none of them have been naturalists. The critical eye of a Müller or an Owen would determine its true affinities in a moment. *Secondly*, that if we do the justice of rejecting all extraneous ideas, and confine ourself to what strictly relates to the object in question, there is a consistent tendency in nearly all the different narratives to invest it with the true characters of the reptilian class. *Thirdly*, that if there be any truth in the idea that the animal spends most of its time under water, only rising to the surface in calm weather during the summer months, this—however difficult to conceive of an air-breathing creature—in a great measure accounts for the infrequency of its occurrence. But are there no other forms, even of the highest stage of organization, which have been able to conceal themselves from the scrutinizing of naturalists? Not to speak of the minor accessions of unknown species, coming in to adorn our collections and extend the limits of science, it deserves to be borne in mind that perhaps the very chief of all the quadrumana (*Troglodytes gorilla* of Savage), the being that holds the foremost rank in the scale next to man, is one of the most recent contributions of the African Fauna. At the beginning of this century a cetaceous animal (*Physeter bidens* of Sowerby), sixteen feet long, was cast ashore on the coast of Elginshire, the species has been previously undescribed, and not another example is *commonly* believed to have since occurred. From the difficulty of assigning it a place, it has been the subject of no fewer than four or five generic appellations, and it is finally referred, by my friend Dr. Melville, to the *Delphinorhynchus micropterus* of Dumortier, two other specimens of which only exist, the one *stranded* at Havre, the other at Ostend. Were this animal known only by tradition, it is improbable that naturalists would have refused it their sanction, under an impression that a species of such individual magnitude could not possibly have escaped being captured and subjected of their criticism? And yet the recognition of the great *Physeter bidens* is purely the result of an accident!"

"If the reptilian nature of this mysterious creature be supposed to have been established, it becomes an interesting speculation to consider how far the stories of terrific dragons, transmitted to us by the ancients, had their origin in realities with which they were more conversant than ourselves. The sea-serpent, if a real existence, is of no modern creation. Our forefathers must have seen it. The utmost length at present allowed to land-snakes is twenty-five feet (Schlegel). Nevertheless, the very important part sustained by the serpent in the old mythologies,—its imposing magnitude and powers, and celebrated by historians and poets,—and its consequence in the romantic animals of the middle ages, will unstill a suspicion that, perhaps, not the biographers of snakes were mendacious, but their heroes, like those of 'the last minstrel', have changed or disappeared in the progress of civilization. It is without the slightest idea of attaching any overstrained importance to the following passages that I venture to quote them, as proving that the idea of serpents frequenting and traversing the sea was at least not repugnant to ancient prejudices. The avenging ministers of Minerva, crossing the Aegean on their mission to destroy Laocoon, might be vindicated by an ardent classic as the model from which the moderns have often plagiarised their descriptions of the sea-serpent.

"Ecce autem gemini a tenedo *tranquilla* per alta
"(Horresco referens) *immensis orbibus* angues
"Incumbunt pelago, pariterque ad litora tendunt:
"Pectora quorum iter fluctus arrecta, jubaeque
"Sanguineae exuperant undas; pars caetera pontum
"Pone legit, sinuatque immensa volumine terga.
"Fit sonitus spumante salo".— *Virgil.*—[1].

---

1) Look, from Tenedos there come down through the *quiet* see (I shudder in telling it) two serpents in *enormous coils*, moving through the sea, and together they direct themselves to the strand: their chests, held up between the waves, and their blood-red *mane* are held above the waves; the remaining part lashes the sea, and they bent their immense backs in coils. There arises a noise, whilst the ocean skims.—Vergilius, Aeneis, II, 203, sqq.

"The poet, too, is sustained by the naturalist, for here we have Pliny (whose facts by the way deserve to have inspired the apophthegm that 'truth is stranger than fiction') telling how the African *dracones* were wont to club together and brave the perils of the Red Sea, in quest of the more luxurious diet of Arabia: 'Narratur in maritimis eorum quaternos quinosque inter se cratium modo implexos erectis capitibus velificantes, ad meliora pabula Arabiae vehi fluctibus.' (Plin. Hist. Nat. VIII, 13).[1]

"On a former occasion (Zool. 1841) I took advantage of the rare opportunity afforded for the discussion of the subject by the conductor of this journal, for the purpose of showing, first, that sea-serpents as a family have long been perfectly recognized in science, and that therefore the name itself should inspire no sentiment of ridicule; and next, of remarking that strange as are the properties attributed to the great sea-serpent, there are remains of a former world in our museums which in their perfect state united them all or nearly all. Encouraged by the Editor's referring them to the Enaliosauri [Zool. LIV. Wrapper] I ventured to name the Plesiosaurus as the marine animal of our acquaintance to which they bear the nearest resemblance. This, although admitted at the time to be a daring breach of the *Draconic* laws of geology,—laws, which, having once consigned an organized form to extinction, have very rarely relaxed their rigour,—seemed to be a necessary result to the argument *pàr voie d'exclusion*: if not a Plesiosaurus what else is it likely to be, allowing the descriptions to be at all correct? Is it an anomolous shark? and does the 'animal of Stronsa' after all furnish the real key to the problem? The affirmative side of the question is not without at least two very able supporters (see Zool. 2310); and yet how to reconcile the characteristics of any possible shark with the sea-serpent-like head, curved neck, mane, or certainly very equivocal dorsal fin, and the protuberances so often mentioned, it is difficult to imagine. A recent correspondent of the 'Times' (Zool. 2311) calls attention to the striking resemblance between the sea-serpent and the Plesiosaurus, and is surprised at its never having occurred to any one before. If the signature F. G. S. implies that the writer is a Fellow of the Geological Society, it is satisfactory to find a member of that particular body, whose favour was least to be expected, so pleased with the idea as to be willing to adopt it for his own. It had, however, been repeated and widely circulated by other periodicals. In the words of an elegant contributor in 'Chambers' Edinburgh Journal' who alludes to it one would almost suppose that among the buried learning of the earlier nations there lurked some knowledge of geology, seeing how their ideas about dragons came to such a conformity in some respects, with the realities of these preadamite reptiles."

"The determination of a great marine species, however, and even a knowledge of its habits and influence on the other inhabitants of the deep, are not, as I conceive, the most obvious advantages to be desired from the settlement of this question. Let it be admitted that a huge unknown creature of any description,

---

1) "And (the Asachaeans) tell that near their coasts every time four or five of these (dragons) twisted together in the way of a twisted work, and sailing with their heads erected in the air, sail on the waves towards a better provender place of Arabia."

provided its general appearance is such as to redeem the various historians of the great sea-serpent from the charge of wilful deception, does 'swim the ocean stream', and the value of the result cannot be too easily over-estimated. The *cui-bono* philosopher, the bugbear of naturalists, will no doubt have been highly amused with the recent excitement about a discovery that at first sight appears of no practical consequence to the interests of man. I know of no subject of research he would be likely to seize upon with more secure self-complacency—or of one which, though indirectly, supplies a more triumphal answer. To have our failing confidence in the value of human testimony reassured (and no evidence can be more solemn than that which relates to the sea-serpent), is surely no trifling gain of itself. But more than this: no circumstance has tended so emphatically to stamp the 'Yankee' character with the stain of a bold and unscrupulous love of fiction and exaggeration as the story of the sea-serpent. Perhaps, on the principle of Mr. Warren's 'man about town', who, being called a *splendid sinner*, made it his pride to deserve the title, the thoughtless portion of our Trans-atlantic family (the generous tribute of an Agassiz is sufficient warrant for the *savans*) may have thence been led to indulge in a dangerous style of humour, through a spirit of bravads. This source of misunderstanding once removed, the American character may afterwards be regarded with more respect, and the people themselves—no longer excited to defy the ridicule they were not able to escape—may sober down to the legitimate standard of reason."

Mr. Newman, the Editor of the *Zoologist*, too, could not forego the pleasure to publish a second time his favourite explanation of the *Enaliosaurians*. In the Preface to the year 1848 of his Journal, which appeared together with Mr. Cogswell's above mentioned dissertation, he filled some pages about the subject:

"The communications made to the Admiralty by Captain M'Quhae has turned public attention to the possibility of the existence of a *Sea-Serpent* (Zool. 2307). My own views on this subject have long been known: two years have elapsed since I expressed an opinion (Zool. 1604), that although the evidence then before the public was perhaps insufficient to convince those who had hypotheses on their own to support, yet that it was far too strong for the fact-naturalist, the inquirer after truth, to dismiss without investigation. To advance such an opinion as this,— to admit the possibility of the existence of a sea-serpent in so enlightened an age as the nineteenth century,—of course led to my being loaded with ridicule; loaded, but not overwhelmed, for I immediately afterwards ventured on expressing a still bolder opinion,—no less than that of suggesting its affinity to a tribe of animals supposed to be extinct. I stated on the wrapper of n°. 54 that the Enaliosauri of authors would, if living, present the appearances described. Almost immediately after this I published the statement of Captain Sullivan and five other British officers, who deliberately assert (Zool. 1715) that they saw—while on a fishing excursion on the coast of British America—a sea-serpent, which they supposed to be eighty or a hundred feet in length; its head, six feet in length, and its neck, also six feet in length, were the only part constantly above water, and resembled those of a common snake: the creature passed them with great rapidity, 'leaving a regular wake'. Nothing is said of any undulating movement, or of any appearance of portions or coils of the body. The statement of Captain M'Quhae (Zool. 2307), and that obligingly furnished expressly for the 'Zoologist' by Lieut. Drummond (Zool. 2306), essentially corroborate the evidence of Captain Sullivan and his companions: the length and position of the head and neck, and their being kept constantly above water, closely correspond; the estimated total length corresponds; the non-observance of any undulation corresponds,—indeed Captain M'Quhae expressly states that no portion of the animal appeared to be used in 'propelling it through the water, either by vertical or horizontal undulation'. Thus we have separate statements closely corresponding with each other, and each statement is vouched for by several British officers whose veracity has never been called in question: under these circumstances we may afford to dismiss from this inquiry all those assertions of American captains, which have been treated in this country with such contempt. Resting the evidence solely on the authority of British officers, I then wish to state my unhesitating conviction that a marine animal of enormous size does exist, and that it differs essentially from any living animal described in our systematic works; and here I cannot refrain from expressing my regret that the statement of captain Sullivan should have been so entirely neglected as it has been: it appears to me in all respects equally trustworthy with the official statement of captain M'Quhae."

"The next question which occurs is this—to what class of vertebrate animals must we refer this monster of the deep? Is it a mammal, bird, reptile, or fish? All these classes include animals whose home is the ocean. To commense with placental mammals;—we have otters, seals, walrusses and sea-cows, all of which breathe atmospheric air, and, therefore, when swimming on the surface usually keep their nostrils—often their heads—above the water: they also propel themselves by means of submerged fins or paddles, and, when inclined, can move along the surface with rapid direct and continuous motion. Professor Owen (Zool. 2312), in accordance with these views, declares the animal to be a seal; Phoca proboscidea or P. leonina, but his reasoning on the point appears to me very inconclusive: he assigns the animal a 'capacious vaulted cranium', whereas Lieutenant Drummond (Zool. 2307) declares the head was 'long, pointed, and *flattened* at the top', adding that it was, 'perhaps ten feet in length, the upper jaw projecting considerably.' Captain M'Quhae, also, subsequently to Professor Owen's paper, repeats (Zool. 2333) that 'the head was *flat*, and not a *capacious vaulted cranium*'. The captain, who must be annoyed at the insinuation that in an official report he had magnified a seal into a sea-serpent, emphatically declares that 'its great length and its totally differing physiognomy preclude the possibility of its being a Phoca of any species.' This idea must therefore be abandoned; the other marine mammals still remaining open for future consideration."

"Among Birds we have no approach to the animal described."

"The Enaliosauri next claim our attention, and, for the present purpose, I could wish to separate them from the Reptiles, because I feel doubtful of their Reptilian nature. For this doubt I could urge many reasons in connection with the views I have long since published in the System of *Nature*, but, waiving all considerations which may be considered speculative, I would invite the intention of naturalists to the figure of Ichthyosaurus as restored by geologists, to the shape of the beak, the situation of the blow-holes, the character of the paddles, the mammalian structure exhibited by a section of the vertebrae, the extraordinary conformation of the sternum, and the smoothness of the skin; and when they have well-considered these important points, I would inquire whether these distinguishing features are not rather mammalian than reptilian; and, again, whether they are not rather marsupial than placental? I have already pointed out the manupedine, ferine, glirine and brutine groups of marsupials; why should we not also have a cetine group? Without making any other use of this suggestion than that of temporarily separating the Enaliosaurians from the Reptiles, I now request the readers' attention to the arguments of Mr. Morries Stirling (Zool. 2309) and of F. G. S. (Zool. 2311), both of whom support the opinion which I had previously broached as to the Enaliosaurian character of the Sea Serpent,—a view controverted by Dr. Melville (Zool. 2310) and Prof. Owen (Zool. 2316), on the ground that the Enaliosaurians are extinct; but here I may perhaps be permitted to remark that this fact, being only assumed, does not touch the main question."

"Proceeding to Reptiles proper, and referring to the suggestion of an anonymous contributor to the 'Times', quoted by Dr. Cogswell (Zool. 2321 note), we find it questioned whether the animal may not have been a boa; and I may observe that the evidence concerning the head, which has been repeatedly described as precisely resembling that of a snake or serpent, together with the fact of the animal holding its head clear of the water, are so many points in favour of its belonging to the Ophidia; but, on the other hand, we must place the non-observance of that undulating mode of progression which every snake must employ,—and it amounts to more than non-observance, for Captain M'Quhae, who directed his attention to this point especially, declares that such undulation did not exist. Again, the enormous length—three times that of a boa—militates against this hypothesis. Professor Owen lays great stress on the non-existence of ophidian vertebrae; but as only two Ophidians have yet entered the arena as competitor for the title of sea-serpent,—Saccopharynx flagellum, which I have heard is a *bona fide* black snake, and Boa constrictor, which is received on all kinds as a veritable serpent,—I think the absence of ophidian vertebrae is of no great moment. The Sauria offer similar coincidences with the Ophidia, and present a similar discrepancy: their heads and necks might readily be described by general observers as those of snakes or serpents, but the undulating motion with which they swim is almost precisely similar to that of snakes, and holds equally good as an objection to our marine monster entering their ranks. The Crocodilia and Chelonia have next to be considered, and these truly possess the submerged limbs requisite for propulsing in a direct course along the surface of the water; moreover, natatorial undulation of the vertebral column in crocodiles is highly improbable, in turtles absolutely impossible; hence: as far as aquatic progression is concerned, these reptiles agree more aptly than any other known living animal with the recently-published descriptions of so-called sea-serpents. Yet the comparatively compact form of both crocodiles and turtles, and especially the orbicular figure of the latter quite preclude the idea of their being described—even by the veriest tyro in observation—as snakes of a hundred feet in length; again in both crocodiles and tortoises floating on the surface of water, the back, and not the head and neck, must be the part most prominently and permanently visible. It is therefore manifest that no existing groups of reptiles answers the conditions required by the recently—recorded descriptions of the sea-serpent."

"Finally, among fishes, the mind turns very willingly to the sharks as offering a solution of the problem, and the record respecting the sea-serpent of Stronsa (Zool. 2320) has given great weight to this view, adopted as it has been by such eminent naturalists as Drs. Mantell and Melville (Zool. 2310). With regard to the Stronsa animal, I entertain very great doubts of the decision in question; it certainly does not seem to have possessed the vertebrae of an ophidian, but then no naturalist desires to make it one; the boa hypothesis is applied only to the sea-serpent of the *Daedalus*. Leaving, however, this Orcadian monster to its own merits,

I may observe, *first*, that all analogy contravenes the idea of a shark having a neck, and *secondly*, I would beg of those gentlemen who advocate this hypothesis, to take their pencils and depict a shark with a head and shoulders clear out of the water, and his body hanging almost perpendicularly below. I think the most brilliant fancy could scarcely imagine a shark maintaining such a position for twenty minutes at the time, and, what is stranger still, while in this position, ploughing the ocean at the rate of twenty miles an hour."

"After maturely considering these various views, it will be found that the Enaliosaurian hypothesis presents the fewest difficulties,—in fine, one only, the supposition that these wonderful creatures have become extinct. It will be the object of a separate essay, now preparing for the press, to adduce evidence from other sources of the existence—in sea-serpents seen off the Norwegian coast—of two large flappers or paddles, closely corresponding in situation with the anterior paddles of Ichthyosaurus, and also of enormous eyes, exactly as indicated by the fossil remains of that animal; but this, not being deducible from recent observations, may be reserved for a more complete and careful review of the entire history of these enormous creatures which in all probability will eventually be found to constitute several genera and species."

"In throwing open the pages of the 'Zoologist' to communication on a subject so uniformly tabooed by the scientific,—in claiming for that subject a calm and dispassionate investigation,—in expressing my unhesitating belief that the various narratives, although often conflicting, are nevertheless, according to the belief of the narrator, perfectly true,—and in attempting to assign the sea-serpent a place in the System of *Nature*,—I feel convinced that all true naturalists will approve the course I have taken, and will be willing to abide the result. Discussion must ever have the tendency to dissipate error and establish truth; and he who believes himself right need never shun the ordeal. In this spirit I invite discussion, and shall feel obliged for any communications tending to elicit or establish truth."

Here again I am obliged to make some remarks.

The communications made by Captain M'Quhae and Lieutenant Drummond are inserted in the foregoing Chapter (n°. 118).—The statement of Captain Sullivan and five other British officers is that of 1833, May 15th., inserted above. (n°. 97.)

Ever and anon Mr. Newman shows that the statements referred to by him are those of *British* officers. Why so? Is a British officer more trustworthy than an officer of any other nation?

What zoologist or palaeontologist has ever shared Mr. Newman's doubt of the reptilian nature of the Enaliosaurians!? Who would like to bring these extinct creatures under a newly founded order of Cetacean Marsupials! Did not Mr. Newman's suggestion originate in the two facts 1. That he himself thought the sea-serpent to be an Enaliosaurian, and 2. That Prof. Owen asserted that the sea-serpent of Captain M'Quhae, according to his description and figures, must be a mammal? I think Mr. Newman reasoned further: "well, why should the Enaliosaurians not be mammals?"

"The enormous length of the animal, three times that of a boa, militates against this hypothesis", viz. of being a boa. This is no argument. In the time that only calamaries were known of 6 or 7 feet length, with arms of 10 or 11 feet, nobody had ever dreamt that there existed really individuals of 30 feet in length with long arms of 50 feet!

It is evident that Mr. Newman was wrongly informed about the *Saccopharynx flagellum*, for this animal is a kind of *fish*, belonging to the eel-tribe, however not in the least resembling an eel in its external characters, and not a black *snake*!

The "separate essay, now preparing for the press" as far as I know has never been published.

The quotation of the *Ichthyosaurus* shows us that Mr. Newman was unwilling to give up his first suggestion. The evidence, referred to by him, where the sea-serpent had apparently two flappers near the head, is the same as that referred to by Dr. Cogswell, (see pp. 409, 411, and n°. 115.).

After observing that other sea-serpents, e. g. that of Captain M'Quhae don't come up to his Ichthyosaurian suggestion, Mr. Newman concludes that "the enormous creatures in all probability will eventually be found to constitute several genera and species!!!

The favourite Plesiosaurian hypothesis is also spoken of by the writer of the *"Reply to Mr. Newman's Inquiries respecting the bones of the Stronsa Animal"* (which I have inserted in my Chapter on Would-be sea-serpents). He says:

"But we must now conclude with the single remark, that if the Stronsa Animal was not a shark, it was certainly not the great sea-serpent, which, if it does exist, will most likely be allied to the Plesiosauri of by-gone days, and to which the animal seen by the Rev. Mr. Maclean, Eigg Island (Wern. Mem. I. p. 442), seems to have borne a strong resemblance." Jas. C. Howden.

As to the animal of Mr. Maclean, see our no. 31.

Mr. Newman in the Preface to the *Zoologist* for 1849, wrote the following about the Reptiles mentioned in this volume. The words are worth quoting.

"In British *Reptiles* nothing remarkable has occurred; but I have been favoured with a communication, published in the February number (Zool. 2366), announcing the present existence of huge marine animals closely related to the Enaliosauri of by-gone ages, that appears to me in all respects the most interesting Natural History-fact of the present century, completely overturning as it does some of the most favourite and fashionable hypotheses of geological science. The published opinion of Mr. Agassiz (Zool. 2395) certainly favours the idea that Enaliosaurians may still exist: he says: it would be in precise conformity with analogy that an animal should exist in the American seas which has long been extinct and fossilized in the Eastern hemisphere: he instances the gar-pike of the western rivers, and says that, in a recent visit to Lake Superior, he has detected several fishes belonging to genera now extinct in Europe."

The communication mentioned here is that of Captain Hope, who saw the sea-serpent in the Gulf of California (n°. 119). In fact, since this opinion was expressed by Agassiz, (where?) numerous animals, even of tolerably large size, have been discovered in Australia as well as in the great depth of the ocean, the allies of which are only found in a fossilized state.

The favourite *Plesiosaurus* hypothesis is also treated of and finally adopted by Mr. Gosse, in his *Romance of Natural History*. After rejecting the hypotheses of the sea-serpent being only a deceitful huge stem of sea-weed, or a large seal, a cetacean, a basking shark, a large ribbon-fish, some large kind of the eel tribe, a large specimen of true sea-snakes, a strayed large land-snake as the boas, he goes on in the following manner:

"It yet remains to consider the hypothesis advanced by Mr. E. Newman, Mr. Morries Stirling, and "F. G. S.", that the so called sea-serpent will find its closest affinities with those extraordinary animals, the *Enaliosauria*, or Marine Lizards, whose fossil skeletons are found so abundantly scattered through the oolite and the lias. The figure of *Plesiosaurus*, as restored in Professor Ansted's *Ancient World*, has a cranium not less capacious or vaulted than that given in Captain M'Quhae's figures; to which, indeed, but that the muzzle in the latter is more abbreviate, it bears a close resemblance. The head was fixed at the extremity of a neck composed of thirty to forty vertebrae, which, from its extraordinary length, slenderness, and flexibility, must have been the very counterpart of the body of a serpent. This snake-like neck merged insensibly into a compact and moderately slender body, which carried two pairs of paddles, very much like those of a sea-turtle, and terminated behind in a gradually attempted tail".

"Thus, if the *Plesiosaur* could have been seen alive, you would have discerned nearly its total length at the surface of the water, propelled at a rapid rate, without any undulation, by an apparatus altogether invisible,—the powerful paddles beneath; while the entire serpentine neck would probably be projected obliquely, carrying the reptilian head, with an eye of moderate aperture, and a mouth whose gape did not extend beyond the eye. Add to this a covering of the body not formed of scales, bony plates, or other form of solidified integument, but a yielding, leathery skin, probably black and smooth, like that of a whale; give the creature a length of some sixty feet or more, and you would have before you almost the very counterpart of the apparition that wrought such amazement on board the *Daedalus*.The position of the nostrils at the summit of the head indicates that on first coming on the surface from the depths of the sea, the animal would spout in the manner of the whales,—a circumstance reported by some observers of the sea-serpent."

"I must confess that I am myself far more disposed to acquiesce in this hypothesis than in any other that has been mooted. Not that I would identify the animal seen with the actual *Plesiosaurs* of the lias. None of them yet discovered appear to exceed thirty-five feet in length, which is scarcely half sufficient to meet the exigencies of the case. I should not look for any species, scarcely even any genus, to be perpetuated from the oolitic period to the present. Admitting the actual continuation of the order *Enaliosauria*, it would be, I think, quite in conformity with general analogy to find important generic modifications, probably combining some salient features of several extinct forms. Thus the little known Pliosaur had many of the peculiarities of the *Plesiosaur*, without its extraordinarily elongated neck, while it vastly exceeded it in dimensions. What if the existing form should be essentially a *Plesiosaur*, with the colossal magnitude of a *Pliosaur*?"

"There seems to be no real structural difficulty in such a supposition except the 'mane', or waving appendage, which has so frequently been described by those who profess to have seen the modern animal. This, however, is a difficulty of ignorance, rather than of contradiction. We do not *know* that the smooth integument of the *Enaliosaurs* was destitute of any such appendage, and I do not think there is any insuperable unprobability in the case. The nearest analogy that I can suggest, however, is that of the *Chlamydosaur*, a large terrestrial lizard of Australia, whose lengthened neck is furnished with a very curious plaited frill of thin membrane, extending like wings or fins to a considerable distance from the animal."

(*Foot-note*:) ["It was not till after this paragraph was written that I noticed the very close similarity of the fins with which Hans Egede has adorned his figure of the sea-serpent (copied in the Illustrated London News, Oct. 28, 1848), to the frill of the *Chlamydosaurus*."]

"Two strong objections, however, stand in the way of our acceptance of the present existence of *Enaliosauria*; and these are forcibly presented by Professor Owen. They are,—1. The hypothetical improbability of such forms having been transmitted from the era of the secondary strata to the present time; and 2. The entire absence of any parts of the carcases or unfossilized skeletons of such animals in museums."

"My ignorance of the details of palaeontology makes me feel very diffident in attempting to touch the former point, especially when so great an authority has pronounced an opinion; still I will modestly express one or two thoughts on it."

"There does not seem any *à priori* reason why early forms should not be perpetuated; and examples are by no means rare of animals much anterior, geologically, to the *Enaliosaurs*, being still extant. The very earliest forms of fishes are of the *Placoid* type, and it is remarkable that not only is that type still living in considerable numbers, but the most gigantic examples of this class belong to it,—viz. the sharks and rays; and these exhibiting peculiarities which by no means remove them far from ancient types. The genus *Chimaera* appears in the oolite, the wealden, and the chalk; disappears (or rather is not found) in any of the tertiary formations, but reappears, somewhat rarely, in the modern seas. It is represented by two species inhabiting respectively the Arctic and Antarctic Oceans."

"Now, this is exactly a parallel case to what is conjectured of the *Enaliosaurs*. They appear in the oolite and the chalk, are not found in the tertiary strata, but reappear, rarely, in the modern seas, represented by two or more species inhabiting the Northern and Southern Oceans."

"Among Reptiles, the curious family of river tortoises named *Trionychidae*, distinguished by their long neck, and a broad cartilaginous margin to the small back-shell, appears first in the wealden. No traces occur of it in any subsequent formation, till the present period, when we find it represented by the large and savage inhabitants of the Mississipi, the Nile, and the Ganges."

"What is still more to the purpose is, that the *Iguanodon*, a vast saurian which was contemporary with the *Plesiosaur* and *Ichthyosaur*, though transmitting no observed representative of its form through the tertiary era, is yet well represented by the existing *Iguanadae* of the American tropics."

"It is true the *Iguana* is not an *Iguanodon*; but the forms are closely allied. I do not suppose that the so-called sea-serpent is an actual *Plesiosaur*, but an animal bearing a similar relation to that ancient type. The *Iguanodon* has degenerated (I speak of the type, and not of the species) to the small size of the *Iguana*; the *Plesiosaurus* may have become developed to the gigantic dimensions of the sea-serpent."

"A correspondent of the *Zoologist* (2395) adduces the great authority of Professor Agassiz to the possibility of the present existence of the *Enaliosaurian* type. That eminent palaeontologist is represented as saying, that 'it would be in precise conformity with analogy that such an animal should exist in the American seas, as he had found numerous instances in which the fossil forms of the Old World were represented by living types in the New. He instances the gar pike of the Western rivers, and said he had found several instances in his visit to Lake Superior, where he had detected several fishes belonging to genera now extinct in Europe.'"

"On this point, however, an actuall testimony exists, to which I cannot but attach a very great value."

Here Mr. Gosse cites the report of Captain Hope (n°. 119), and goes on:

"Now, unless this officer was egregiously deceived, he saw an animal which could have been no other than an *Enaliosaur*,—a marine reptile of large size, of sauroid figure, with turtle-like paddles. It is a pity that no estimate, even approximate, of the dimensions is given; but as the alligator affords the comparison as to form, it is most probable that there was a general agreement with it in size. This might make it some twelve or fifteen feet in length."

"I cannot, then, admit that either the *general* substitution of *Cetacea* for *Enaliosauria* in our era, or the absence of remains of the latter in the tertiary deposits, is sufficient evidence of their non-existence in our seas; any more than the general replacement of *Placoid* and *Ganoid* fishes by the Cycloids and Ctenoids, or the absence of the former two from the tertiaries, is proof of *their* present non-existence."

"It must not be forgotten, as Mr. Darwin has ably insisted, that the specimens we possess of fossil organisms are very far indeed from being a complete series. They are rather fragments accidentally preserved, by favouring circumstances, in an almost total wreck. The *Enaliosauria*, particularly abundant in the secondary epoch, may have become sufficiently scarce in the tertiary to have no representative in these preserved fragmentary collections, and yet not have been absolutely extinct."

"But Professor Owen presses also the absence of any recognised recent remains of such animals. Let us test this evidence first by hypothesis, and then by actual fact."

"It may be that a true serpent, with large vesicular lungs, would float when dead, and be liable to be seen by navigators in that condition, or to be washed ashore, where its peculiar skeleton would be sure to attract notice. But, as I have before said, I do not by any means believe that the unknown creature is a *serpent* in the zoological sense. Would a *Plesiosaurus* float when dead? I think not. It is supposed to have had affinities with the whales. Now, a whale sinks like lead as soon as the blubber is removed; the surface-fat alone causes a whale to float. But we have no warrant for assuming that the *Plesiosaur* was encased in a thick blanket of blubber; no geologist has suggested any such thing, and the long neck forbids it; and if not, doubtless it would sink, and not float, when dead. Therefore the stranding of such a carcase, or the washing ashore of such a skeleton, would most probably be an extremely rare occurrence, even if the animal were as abundant as the sperm whale; but, on the supposition that the species itself is almost extinct, we ought not to expect such an incident, perhaps, in a thousand years. If we add to this the recollection, how small a portion of the border of the ocean is habitually viewed by persons able to discriminate between the vertebrae of an *Enaliosaur* and those of a *Cetacean*, we shall not, I think, attach great importance to this objection."

"The only region of the globe in which the unknown monster is reputed to be in any sense common, is the coast of Norway. Now this, it is true, is fortunately within the ken of civilized and scientific men; and, confessedly, no enormous ophidian or saurian carcases have ever been recognised on that shore. But the shore of Norway is, perhaps, the least favourable in the world for such a *jetsam*. Such a thing as a sand or shingle beach is scarcely known; the coast is almost exclusively what is called iron-bound; the borders of the deeply indented fjords rise abruptly out of the sea, so that there is generally from fifty to three hundred fathoms' depth of water within a boat's length of the shore. How could a carcase or a skeleton be cast up here, even if it floated?"

"But, secondly, as to facts. Is it true, that of all the larger oceanic animals we find the carcases or skeletons cast up on the shore? Is it true even of the *Cetacea*, whose blubber-covered bodies invariably ensure their floating, and whose bones are so saturated with oil that they are but little heavier than water?"

"In September 1825, a cetacean was stranded on the French coast, which was previously unknown to naturalists. It was so fortunate as to fall under the examination of so eminent a zoologist as De Blainville; and hence its anatomy was well investigated. It has become celebrated as the Toothless Whale of Havre (*Aodon Dalei*). Yet *no other example of this species is on record*; and, but for this accident, a whale *inhabiting the British Channel* would be quite unrecognised."

"Of another Whale (*Diodon Sowerbyi*), *likewise British, our entire knowledge rests on a single individual* which was cast on shore on the Elgin coast, and was seen and described by the naturalist Sowerby."

"There is a species of sperm whale (*Physeter tursio*) affirmed to be frequently seen about the Shetland Islands; a vast creature of sixty feet in length, and readily distinguishable from all other *Cetacea* by its lofty dorsal, and, according to old Sibbald, by other remarkable peculiarities in its anatomy. Yet *no specimen of this huge creature has fallen under modern scientific observation*; and zoologists are not yet agreed among themselves whether the high-finned Cachelot is a myth or a reality!"

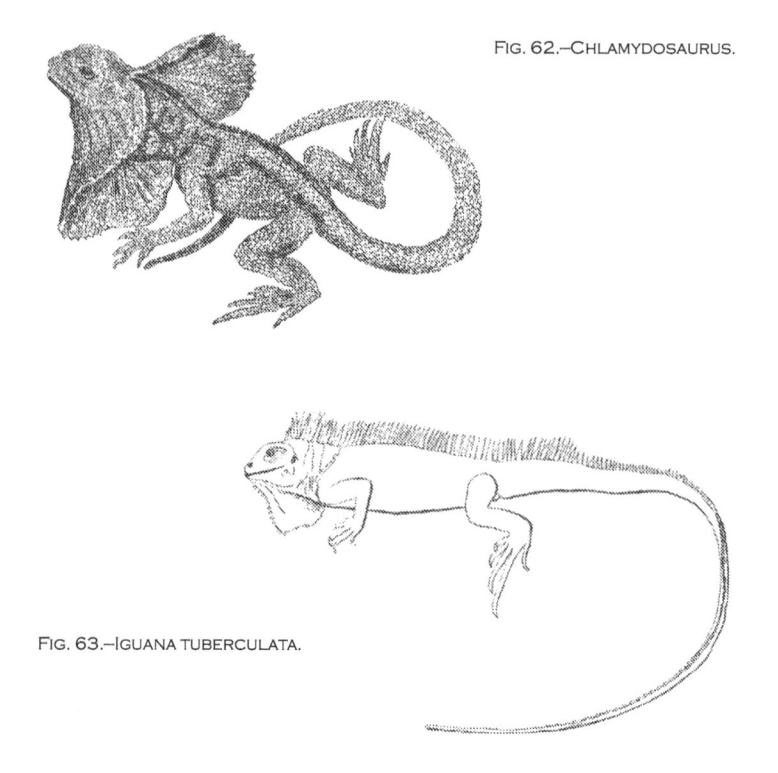

FIG. 62.—CHLAMYDOSAURUS.

FIG. 63.—IGUANA TUBERCULATA.

"Mr. Rafinesque Schmaltz, a Sicilian naturalist, described a Cetacean which, he said, he had seen in the Mediterranean, possessing *two dorsals*. The character was so abnormal that his statement was not received; but the eminent zoologists attached to one of the French exploring expeditions,—MM. Quoy and Gaimard,— saw a school of cetacea around their ship in the South Pacific, having this extraordinary character,—the supernumerary fin being placed on the back of the head. Here is the evidence of competent naturalists to the existence of a most remarkable whale, *no carcase* of which—*no skeleton—has ever been recognised.*"

"The last example I shall adduce is from my own experience. During my voyage to Jamaica, when in lat. 19° N., and long. from 46° to 48° W., the ship was surrounded for *seventeen continuous hours* with a troop of whales, of a species which is certainly undescribed. I had ample opportunity for examination, and found that it was a *Delphinorhynchus*, thirty feet in length, black above and white beneath, with the swimming paws wide on the upper surface, and isolated by the surrounding black of the upper parts,—a very remarkable character. This could not have been the Toothless Whale of Havre; and there is no other with which it can be confounded. *Here, then, is a whale of large size, occurring in great numbers in the North Atlantic, which on no other occasion has fallen under scientific observation.*"

"Are not these facts, then, sufficiently weighty to restrain us from rejecting so great an amount of testimony to the so-called sea-serpent, merely on the ground that its dead remains have not come under examination?"

"In conclusion, I express my own confident persuasion, that there exists some oceanic animal of immense proportions, which has not yet been received into the category of scientific zoology; and my strong opinion, that it possesses close affinities with the fossil *Enaliosauria* of the lias."

We only observe that Mr. Gosse is evidently inclined to believe that there are "two or more species inhabiting the Northern and Southern oceans." It is not at all plain what circumstance has led him to this supposition.

Curious is the comparison of the flappers, figured by Mr. Bing (fig. 19) with the frill of the *Chlamydosaurus*. I give here a figure of such an animal.

Mr. Gosse gets clearly entangled in his own considerations of the affinity of the sea-serpent with the *Plesiosaurus* when he comes to the fact of the existence of a mane. It is a pity that he has not mixed up with his considerations the well-known *Iguana tuberculata*, a lizard belonging to the same family as the *Chlamydosaurus*, but which has a comb extending over the whole length of the neck, the back and the tail!

Mr. Lee in his *Sea Monsters Unmasked*, considering the *Plesiosaurus* hypothesis, says:

"I think this theory is not forced upon us."

Of the probability of living *Plesiosauri*, however, he says:

"Only a geologist can fully appreciate how enormously the balance of probability is contrary to the supposition that any of the gigantic marine saurians of the secondary deposits should have continued to live up to the present time. And yet I am bound to say, that this does not amount to an impossibility, for the evidence against it is entirely negative. Nor is the conjecture that there may be in existence some congeners of these great reptiles inconsistent with zoological science. Dr. J. E. Gray, late of the British Museum, a strict zoologist, is cited by Mr. Gosse as having long ago expressed his opinion that some undescribed form exists which is intermediate between the tortoises and the serpents."

"Prof. Agassiz, too, is adduced by a correspondent of the *Zoologist* (p. 2395), as having said concerning the present existence of the Enaliosaurian type that 'it would be in precise conformity with analogy that such an animal should exist in the American Seas, as he had found numerous instances in which the fossil forms of the Old World were represented by living types in the New'."

It is obvious that of all animals, now living or extinct, the outlines of the *Plesiosaurus* fit best to the descriptions and figures of the great sea-serpent. Abandoning the possibility of still living *Plesiosauri*, I reply to the question "Why cannot the sea-serpent be a *Plesiosaurus*?"

Plesiosauri with such an enormous tail as the sea-serpent has, are hitherto unknown to palaeontologists, but, as to me, this cannot be of much importance; for there is no reason why in the course of ages this appendage should not have been developed to gigantic dimensions. The difference between the place of the nostrils in the two animals cannot claim any weight either (the *Plesiosaurus* had its nostrils both before its eyes and not at the end of its snout, as is the case in the sea-serpent) for this place may have changed in process of time. But there are two other differences which are of very great importance, and settle the question: 1. The neck of the *Plesiosaurus* must have been fit to be bent in all directions, but I think no palaeontologist will ever admit that its trunk or backbone could be bent in such vertical undulations, as is the case with the sea-serpents. 2. The *Plesiosaurus* may have been destitute of scales, and may have had a smooth skin, it can never have been provided with a hairy skin as seals have, and at all events it had no mane, and no whiskers.

An **eleventh** explanation is properly a negative one. In the *American Journal of Science and Arts*, of 1835, viz: Prof. Benjamin Silliman, the Editor, published a report of one of his acquaintances, wherein the eye-witness declared: "nothing like a fin was seen". Now Prof. Silliman in a *Remark of the Editor* says: "The absence of paddles or arms **forbids us from supposing that this was a swimming saurian**."

I need not observe that this explanation was premature, and that the assertion "nothing like a fin was seen" does not exclude the presence of flappers, hidden under water. The flappers of a swimming sea-lion or seal are not generally seen either. If not a saurian, what kind of animal could it be then, a fish or a mammal?

The **twelfth** explanation, viz: **a row of spermwhales**, which is found in Prof. Schlegel's *Essai sur la physionomie des Serpens*, 1837, p. 518, is better than that of a row of porpoises or of basking sharks, with their plainly visible backfins, for there is a species of spermwhales, viz. the *Catodon macrocephalus* the backfin of which is so small as to be almost invisible. The other species, *Physeter tursio* has a rather large and erected backfin.

Professor Schlegel, after describing the appearance of a row of porpoises swimming in line, goes on saying: "This habit is also common to the larger cetaceans, which, however, only accidentally frequent our" (the Dutch) "coasts. The coasts of North-America, where the monstrous sea-serpent has so often been observed, swarm with them, and I confess that from a vessel, for instance, the unexpected appearance

Various Explanations 327

FIG. 64.—CATODON MACROCEPHALUS.

FIG. 65.—SKELETON OF BASILOSAURUS.

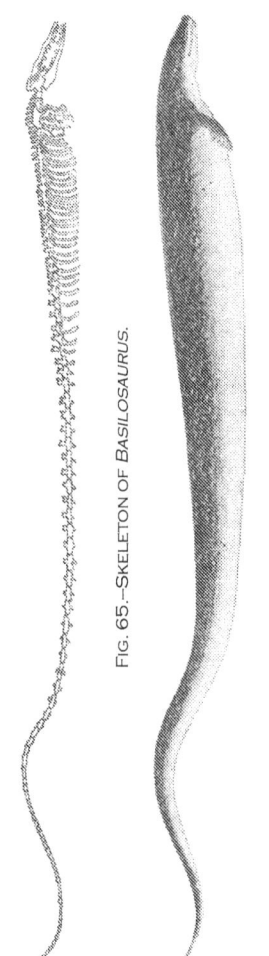

FIG. 66.—BASILOSAURUS RESTORED.

of a family of spermwhales swimming in line, with the eldest at the head, must offer a spectacle striking enough and fit to call forth at once superstition, imagination and fear."

It is true that a row of spermwhales must offer a striking spectacle, but in none of the accounts of the sea-serpent the "bunches" or visible parts of the vertical undulations surpassed the length of a fathom, whilst the visible parts of the backs of spermwhales measure several fathoms, and the distance between two of these backs in a row of spermwhales is enormous. The supposition, moreover, does not explain the head resembling that of a snake, and kept constantly above water, neither the long neck accidentally observed, the long and pointed tail, &c.

The **thirteenth** explanation supposes that the sea-serpent may be a still living **Basilosaurus**, an extinct marine mammal, first described by Harlan in the year 1824; afterwards the name was changed to that of *Zeuglodon* by Prof. Richard Owen. Fig. 65 represents the skeleton of a *Basilosaurus*. This animal lived in the tertiary periods. Almost all the characters of the skeleton remind us of Pinnipeds, only a few of Cetaceans, and so it is still doubtful to which order it belongs. Professor D'Arcy W. Thompson rejects all association with the Cetacea (*Studies from the Museum of Zoology in University College, Dundee*, Vol. I. N°. 9.) The length of the largest skeletons measured seventy-five feet. The teeth and molars are nearly exactly those of seals. The nostrils were situated at the tip of the nose, as in seals, most probably, however, they were directed upwards. The bones of the rather short fore-extremities resemble those of seals. Most probably these limbs were provided with nails, as in seals. But, on the other hand, of some of the known skulls the remaining part shows an affinity to cetaceans. The vertebrae again are seal-like. Till now it is unknown whether the animal had hind-extremities or not, for the bones of them are not yet discovered. The body must have been rather slender and cylindrical. I venture to represent to my readers in fig. 66, a *Basilosaurus* restored. As the bones of the fore-extrimities closely resemble those of seals, it is probable that small hind-extremities were not wanting. If the former resembled those of dolphins, the existence of hind-flappers would be problematic. Yet I have omitted them, because the bones of them are not yet discovered, as far as I know.

The reader will remember that Dr. Koch (see our Chapter on Hoaxes and Cheats) exhibited a large skeleton in Broadway, New York, under the name of *Hydrarchos Sillimanni*. This skeleton was made by him out of several bones of the extinct *Basilosaurus*. The imposture was soon discovered by Prof. Wyman, and, of course, immediately published in all kinds of newspapers, which also reached Europe. In Froriep's *Neue Notizen*, of February, 1846, is one of these articles translated into German. Consequently we may conclude that the translator of this article knew that the *Hydrarchos Sillimanni* was, in fact, made up of bones of the *Basilosaurus*. Now we find in Froriep's *Notizen*, Third Series, Vol. III, n°. 54, p. 148, 1847, a suggestion of a writer who wrote under the initials M. J. S. (evidently the Editor, the well-known Professor Matthias Jacob Schleiden: I have searched the *Bibliotheca Zoologica* of Carus and Engelmann, and not found another author whose name has these initials):

"Is the sea-serpent perhaps identical with the *Hydrarchus*, viz. a still living species, a still present remainder, though in a few individuals, of former periods?"

I think that this means: "Are there perhaps still living *Basilosauri*, and is the sea-serpent perhaps one of these creatures?"

Mr. Searles V. Wood, Jun. wrote in *Nature* of 18th. of November, 1880, Vol. 23, a paper, entitled: "*Order Zeuglodontia*", in which he tries to show that the sea-serpent most probably belongs to this Order. The contents of his paper are as follows:

"In August 1848 H. M. S. *Daedalus* encountered off St. Helena a marine animal, of which a representation appeared in the *Illustrated News* of the latter part of that year. It is thirty-two years since I saw this figure, but I recollect that it was one of a blunt-nosed animal with a neck carried about four feet above the water, which was so long as to present the appearance of a serpent; and I remember that Prof. Owen, in combating at the time the idea that this was a sea-serpent, pointed out that the position of the gape in relation to the eye, as shown in the figure in the *Illustrated News*, was that of a mammal, and not that of a reptile; in consequence of which he argued that the animal seen was probably only a leonine seal, whose track through the water gave an illusory impression of great length. This idea, however, seemed to me untenable in the face of the representation in the *Illustrated News*; but it was obvious that to afford the buoyancy necessary for the support above the water of so long a neck (estimated on that occasion as sixty feet though only the part near the head was actually out of the water), the submerged portion of the animal could not have had the shape of a serpent."

"To or three years after this, on reading the description of *Zeuglodon cetoides*, from the Tertiary (probably Upper Eocene) formations of Alabama, it struck me that the animal seen from the *Daedalus* may have been a descendant of the order to which *Zeuglodon* belonged; and I have ever since watched with interest for reports of the "great sea-serpent"."

"Three years ago the following appeared in the newspapers."

Here Mr. Searles Wood copies the whole affidavit of the crew of the *Pauline* (n°. 144), and adds:

"The locality here specified was about thirty miles off the northern coast of Brazil."

And he goes on:

"In this account I thought that I recognized the grip of the whale by the long neck of the attacking animal, the appearance being confounded into the double coil of a serpent by the distance and motions of the objects; but in face of the general ridicule which has been attached to this subject, and being without any assurance that the declaration so purporting to be made was genuine, I did not venture to ventilate my long-cherished idea. A relative of mine, however, just returned from India, chancing to say that two of the officers to the steamer in which she went out had on the previous voyage witnessed an immense animal rear its neck thirty feet out of the water, and that a sketch of the object had been instantly made, and on reaching port sent to the *Graphic*. I obtained the number of that paper for July 19, 1879, and I inclose a tracing of the figures in it, which are accompanied by the following statement in the *Graphic*:—

The statement of the *Kiushiu Maru* is further copied, accompanied by the two figures (see n°. 151, figg. 48 and 49), and he continues saying:

"As I have not been able to find any description of the skeleton of the *Zeuglodon*, I venture to draw attention to the subject through your columns, in the hope that among your many readers in America this letter may attract the notice of some one who will tell us whether what is known of the osseous structure of *Zeuglodon cetoides* is or is not consistent with the representation in the *Graphic*. The remains of the cetacean, supposed to be extinct, indicate, according to Sir Charles Lyell, that it was at least seventy feet in length, (He observes in the third edition of his 'Manual of Elementary Geology', 1851, p. 208, that he visited the spot where a vertebral column of this length belonging to *Zeuglodon* had been dug up.) while its great double-fanged but knife-edged molars show that it was carnivorous; and as we are not so far removed from the period of the Alabama Tertiaries as to render it improbable that members of what must once have been a great Order of carnivorous cetacea, totally distinct from the orders of cetacea hitherto known as living, may still survive, I have braved the ridicule attaching to this subject so far as to invite attention to it."

"The second of the two figures in the *Graphic* shows the long necked animal to possess the cetacean tail, and its head there seems to have been turned from the observer, so that the underside of it only is presented. The first figure shows that the whale had been seized on its flank by the powerful bite of its agressor, and that to escape from this it had thrown itself out of the water. Having succeeded in this object the second figure shows the agressor rearing its head and neck out of the water to discover the direction which its prey had taken, in order that it might follow it up; and so far from the charge of curious drawing made by the editor of the *Graphic* being justified, the representation of the whale can be at once recognized as fairly correct; while that of the tail of the unknown animal (which probably prompted this charge), so far from being curious, forms an important piece of evidence as showing the animal in question to be cetacean."

This paper had already been sent to the Editors of *Nature*, when Mr. Searles V. Wood, Jun., observed that he was mistaken as to the report, and as soon as possible he sent a Postscript to the Editors, which appeared appended to his paper. The postscript runs as follows:

"P. S. Since sending to you the above I have again seen my relative, and find that the cut in the *Graphic* of July 19, 1879, is not that of the instance observed from the steamer in which she came home, which was the *City of Washington*; but of a separate instance which occurred to another ship. I have not been able yet to procure the *Graphic* containing the figure of the animal seen from the *City of Washington*, but she tells me that it was pasted up in the saloon and represented only the head and long neck of the animal, which was raised to a great height out of the water, and near to the ship; and had been drawn for the *Graphic* by a lady passenger immediately after the occurrence. These repeated and independent notices of the same long necked are, however, the more confirmatory of its existence."

"I find that Prof. Owen in his article on Palaeontology in the *Encyclopedia Britannica* (Vol. XVII, p. 166), in giving a description of *Zeuglodon cetoides*, says that "the skull is very long and narrow *and the nostril single*", that Dr. Harlan obtained the teeth on which, correcting Harlan's reptilian reference of them, he founded the order *Zeuglodontia*, from the Miocene of Malta; and that the teeth discovered by Grateloup in the Miocene beds of the Gironde and Herault, and described by him also to a reptile under the name of *Squalodon*, are those of a smaller species of *Zeuglodon*. The remains of *Squalodon*, along with those of the shark with huge teeth, *Carcharodon megalodon*, and of numerous cetaceans assigned to orders all still living, and of which some, such as *Delphinus*, belong to living genera, occur in the 'Sables inférieures' of Antwerp; which, though long called Miocene, are by Mr. Van den Broeck regarded as older Pliocene, and as the base of that series of deposits of which the middle and upper divisions are respectively represented by the Coralline and Red Crags of England; and with these 'Sables inférieures' the so called Miocene of Malta, in which *Zeuglodon* is associated with *Carcharodon*, is probable coeval. Dr. Gibbes (Jour. Acad. Nat. Sc., 2d. ser., vol. I, p. 143), figures and describes teeth of the Antwerp species of *Carcharodon* from both the Eocene of South Carolina and Miocene of Alabama. These various references bring the *Zeuglodonts*, with their *Carcharodon* associates, down to a late geological period during which they co-existed with Delphinian prey; and of this prey the whale in the woodcut (which looks like a *Grampus*) seems an example".

"It is most likely that Bishop Pontoppidan, a copy of the English (1755) edition of whose work I possess, concocted his two figures (one of which is that of a huge snake undulating on the waves, and the other that of a serpent-like animal with pectoral flappers or fins, resting almost on the surface of the sea, with head and tail erect out of the water like the letter U, and spouting water or steam from its mouth *in a single column*), from accounts given him by Norwegian seamen, some of whom had seen the animal in the position in which it was observed from the *Daedalus*, and others in that in which it is represented in the cut as seen from the *Kiushiu-maru*; for in the long narrative which he gives of the descriptions received from observers at numerous times, some of these agree with the one, and some with the other, though both of the Bishop's figures represent only preposterous conceptions of his own."

"[The animal seen from the *Osborne*, and figured in the *Graphic* of June 30, 1877, as the 'Sea-Serpent', is quite a different thing from the one in question, and may have been a manatee.]"

I shall take the liberty to make some remarks on his paper.

The reader will remember (see n°. 118) that it was *not* the *long neck* of the animal, which caused the comparison of a snake, made by the officers of the *Daedalus*, but the roundness of its neck, the apparent roundness of the body, and the resemblance of the animal's head with that of a snake.

In their reports there is not a single estimation of the length of the neck. It is only said that the length of the visible part of the animal was about sixty feet; and now Mr. Searles V. Wood says: "a neck, estimated on that occasion as sixty feet". I don't see the reason of such a deduction!

As I have not read the "description of *Zeuglodon cetoides*" I am not able to discover the reason *why* it struck Mr. Wood that the animal seen from the *Daedalus* may have been a descendant of the order to which *Zeuglodon* belonged.

We observe that Mr. Wood really believes that it was the sea-serpent which attacked "the whale by the long neck, the appearance being confounded into the double coil of a serpent by the distance and motions of the object" (See n°. 144). I will not contest his opinion!

I do not know what to think of Mr. Wood, when he speaks of the *Kiushiu Maru* in connection with a relative of his. I may suppose that his relative had told him she repatriated by the *City of Baltimore* through the Indian Ocean, and that the "previous voyage" of that vessel was also from India to England; notwithstanding this he cites the account of the *Kiushiu Maru* reporting the appearance of a sea-serpent near the isle of Kiu Siu (Japan) in the Van Diemen's Straits. Most probably the *City of Baltimore* never was there!

In short, the error took place, and Mr. Wood sees clearly in the figures of the *Graphic* his *Zeuglodon* pointing out that this figure shows a bifurcated or fan-shaped

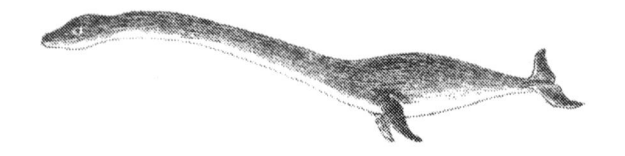

FIG. 67.–*BASILOSAURUS*, AS IMAGINED BY MR. SEARLES V. WOOD JUN.

tail, and that consequently the animal must be a cetacean! It is evident, that Mr. Wood was convinced that the *Zeuglodon* (read *Basilosaurus*) had the following outlines!

It is clear that, before writing his postscript, he had already had the opportunity to read "a description of *Zeuglodon cetoides*". Yet he holds to his idea, and does not show the great difference between the extremely *short* neck of *Basilosaurus* and the extraordinarily *long* neck of the Sea-Serpent. This at all events *must* have struck him.

At last I am obliged to say some words about his considerations of Pontoppidan's *Natural history of Norway*. It is clear that he has not read a single word of it! He says: "it is most likely that the Bishop concocted his two figures from accounts given him by Norwegian seamen", whilst the Bishop clearly states that the first figure is a copy of a sketch of Mr. Benstrup, and the second a copy of the drawing of Mr. Bing. Of the latter figure Mr. Wood says "it is that of a serpent-like animal almost resting on the surface of the sea". I shall be greatly obliged to any person who can show me a passage either in Pontoppidan's or in Egede's work, stating that the animal presented itself in this way "resting on the surface". I refer my readers to the account itself (n°. 5), where it is clear that the animal must have been seen in this position for only the fraction of a second!

Mr. Wood, describing the drawing of Mr. Bing underlines the words: *in a single column*, speaking of the animal's "spouting water or steam from its mouth". Now I ask my readers (drawing their attention to the fact that the figure represents the animal's head seen from aside), whether a column, spouted from the animal's nose or mouth, when seen from aside could ever have been decided to be single or double! If we look at the breath of a horse, standing just on one side of him, it will be observed to be single. This optical illusion will be dispelled as soon as we stand in front of the horse. Bing's figure would have been incorrect, if he had drawn two columns, though in reality—if the animal exhaled through its nostrils,—the column must have been double.—It is remarkable that Mr. Wood does not say anything of the great difference between the figure of the *Kiushiu Maru* (with a cetacean tail) and that of Mr. Bing, (with a long and pointed one).—Again, he asserts that both the Bishop's figures represent only preposterous conceptions of his own description!

Finally he compares the animal seen from the *Osborne* with a manatee! Surely we must be a Mr. Searles V. Wood Jun. to find this conception *not* preposterous!

In a second paper in *Nature* of February 10, 1881, Mr. Wood quotes the report of the *City of Baltimore*, and correcting his second error, writes in parentheses "not *City of Washington*, as I had misunderstood."—In treating of this report and of the accompanying figure he is again mistaken, for the figure shows the animal moving at a rapid rate with its neck high in the air, and the two splashes were evidently caused by the animal's fore-flappers and hind-flappers, whilst the splash "like a pair of wings" described in the report, is caused by the dropping of the immense neck like a log of wood in the act of disappearing suddenly in the water. This act, and consequently this splash too, is not represented in the figure! According to his idea of the sea-serpent being a dolphin or porpoise with a very long neck (called by him *Zeuglodon*), he ascribes the splash, caused by the hind flappers, to his "cetacean tail" of the animal. Remarkable is his third error; for after having first confounded the foremost splash, drawn in the figure, with that described in the report as caused by the dropping of the neck, he now writes: "the foam around the neck may be due to the splash of the humeroid" (i. e. fore) "paddles which a cetacean should possess."

Mr. Wood further sees in the figure of the head of the *Daedalus* animal (fig. 30) the alleged "bulldog appearance of the forehead and eye-brow". I can only express my opinion that this comparison is far fetched.

Of the report of Captain Cox (n°. 152) Mr. Wood says:

"In this account we have almost a duplicate of that of Major Senior in the dropping of the animal with a great splash into the water prior to its darting forward under it; while the boiling of the water around, which is so inconsistent with the motion of a snake in water (which I have more than once seen) evidently resulted from the strokes of the cetacean tail, and possibly also from those of the paddles, as in the case witnessed by Major Senior. The black colour also is described in both cases."

In treating of this report I have already expressed my opinion that the boiling of the water must have been caused by the four flappers together. It is very natural that Mr. Wood who represents the sea-serpent as a dolphin-shaped animal, without a backfin, and with a long neck, sets much value on the cetacean tail. Finally he says:

"Judging from the figures which accompany this and my previous letter" (figg. 48, 49, 46, and reduced sketches of figg. 28 and 30), "it appears to me that the external form of the animal must resemble the well-known *Plesiosaurus*, if we imagine the hinder (femuroid) paddles of that *Enaliosaurian* to be absent, and a cetacean tail (which is their homologue), to be present in their stead. Since in the direction of the *Porpesse* the cetacean in external form so closely simulates the fish, so it may in another direction simulate this Mesozoic marine saurian, or the gigantic *Elasmosaurus* of the American cretaceous formation, of which a nearly perfect skeleton is described by Prof. Cope as forty-five feet in length, the neck constituting twenty-two of this length."

And he expresses his firm opinion:

"There ought, I submit, to remain no longer with naturalists any doubt that a hitherto unknown group of carnivorous cetaceans, with necks of extraordinary length, inhabit the ocean."

In the middle of November, 1881, appeared the first number of the *Album der Natuur* for 1882, and in this issue the author of the present Volume treated of the probability of the existence of the great sea-serpent. Unfortunately he, who at that time was only a student of Natural History at the Utrecht University, really believed the animal of Stronsa, of 1808, to be a sea-serpent, and was misled by the hoax of Captain Seabury of which he only knew the last part, found by him in the Illustrated London News. In his firm belief, however, he examined such characters, taken from these tales and from nearly 60 reports then known to him, as were possible from a zoological point of view, and came to the conclusion that the sea-serpent must be a mammal, with *four* flappers, a *long* neck and a *long* and *pointed* tail, and that the position of this marine mammal is between dolphins and pinnipeds. Was there such an animal known? Yes, the *Zeuglodon cetoides* of Prof. Richard Owen. Well, as the sea-serpent has the outlines of a *Plesiosaurus*, with an enormous tail, he called it *Zeuglodon plesiosauroides*. At that time he was the dupe of the Stronsa animal and of the alleged capture of 1852, because, like so many other writers on the subject, he believed that he could solve the difficult question without reading, if not all that had been written about the animal, at least much more than some few reports!

The **fourteenth** explanation is that of an anonymous writer in one of the public papers of about the sixth of November, 1848. Amidst the excitement, caused by the reports of Capt. M'Quhae and Lieutenant Drummond, he asks whether or not the animal could be a full grown specimen of **Saccopharynx flagellum** of Dr. Mitchill or the **Ophiognathus ampullaceus** of Harwood. I have only to tell my readers that these two names are given to two different species of the same genus, that the former attains a length of about five, the latter of about six feet, and to give the next figure, in order to enable them to judge themselves, whether such an animal could ever have shown itself in the form of a sea-serpent! They belong to the family of the *Muraenidae*.

The figure represents the *Eurypharynx pelecanoides* of Vaillant, taken from Filhol's *la vie au fond des mers*. Günther, in his *Deepsea-fishes of the Challenger* says on p. 262 of *Saccopharynx Bairdii* (synonym with *Saccopharynx flagellum*): "It is uncertain whether these specimens are specifically distinct from *Saccopharynx pelecanoides* Vaillant." I therefore don't hesitate to put before my readers the above figure as a representation of the general outlines of *Saccopharynx flagellum*.

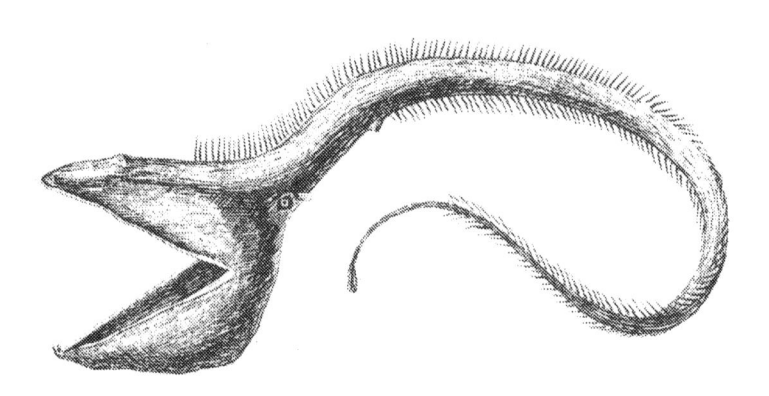

FIG. 68.—*EURYPHARYNX PELECANOIDES*, VAILLANT.

The **fifteenth** explanation is suggested by the same anonymous writer on the same occasion, who wishing to explain the appearance of the sea-serpent near the coasts of Africa, asks whether "some land species, as the **boas**, among which are individuals of forty feet in length, may not sometimes betake themselves to the sea, or even transport themselves from one continent to another".

Probably he "adduced" this suggestion "of a large boa constrictor having been conveyed to the island of St. Vincent, twisted round the trunk of a cedar tree, carried away, as is supposed, from the banks of some South-American river. This occurrence is quoted by Sir Charles Lyell from the *Zoological Journal* of December, 1827. (Principles of Geology.)"

Mr. Gosse in his *Romance of Natural History* after having shown that the sea-serpent cannot be a kind of true sea-snake (Family *Hydrophidae*) because "none of these are known to extend a few feet in length and, so far as we know, none of them have been found in the Atlantic", goes on saying: "It is remarkable, however, that a record exists of a serpent having been seen in the very midst of the North Atlantic". And instead of relating now the historical fact of the boa constrictor, above mentioned, he quotes the report of the sea-serpent seen from the *General Coole*, (n°. 25) and goes on saying:

"It augments very considerably the value of this incident, that no suggestion of identity with the Norwegian dragon appears to have occurred to the observer; he speaks of it of 'a snake', and nothing more; the dimensions alone appear to have excited surprise, 'sixteen or eighteen feet', and these are by no means extravagant."

"On the whole I am disposed to accept this case as that of a true serpent—perhaps the *Boa Murina*, one of the largest known, and of very aquatic habits—carried out to sea by one of the great South American rivers, and brought by the Gulf Stream to the spot where it was seen. If I am warranted in this conclusion it affords us no help in the identification of the *great unknown*."

"I do not attach much value to the assertions of observers, that the head of the animal seen by them respectively was 'undoubtedly that of a snake.' Such comparisons made by persons unaccustomed to mark the characteristic peculiarities which distinguish one animal from another, are vague and unsatisfactory. Their value, at all events, is rather negative than positive. For example, if a person of liberal education and general information, but no naturalist, were to tell me he had seen a creature with a head 'exactly like that of a snake', I should understand him, that the head was not that of an ordinary beast, nor of a bird, nor that of the generality of fishes; but I should have no confidence at all that it was not as like that of a lizard as of a serpent, and should entertain doubt whether, if I showed him the form of head, even of certain fishes, he would not say, 'Yes, it was something like *that*'."

"There does not seem, then, any sufficient evidence that the colossal animal seen from the *Daedalus*, and on other occasions, is a serpent, in the sense in which zoologists use that term. A lengthened cylindrical form it seems to have; but, for anything that appears, it may as well be a monstrous eel, or a slender cetacean, as anything. All analogies and probabilities are against its being an ophidian."

It is remarkable that Mr. Gosse is disposed to believe that the sea-serpent of the *General Coole* was a boa, because the report speaks of "a snake", and that he cannot believe that the sea-serpent of the *Daedalus* was a boa, though the captain, Mr. M'Quhae, clearly tells that he saw "a serpent, the head of which, without any doubt, was that of a snake". Now I ask what is the difference between "a snake" and "a serpent with a head of a snake"!? What, in short, is the difference between a *snake* and a *serpent?* Though he attaches a considerable value to the assertion of the captain of the *General Coole* who speaks of *"a snake, and nothing more"*, Mr. Gosse "does not attach much value to the assertions of observers, that the head of the animal seen by them was *undoubtedly that of a snake*". How to make this agree?

Mr. Lee in his *Sea Monsters Unmasked* says: "a marine snake of enormous size may, really, have been seen". As I think he means in this instance, a land-snake which occasionally frequents the sea, as the *Boa murina*, I have placed this supposition here, and I have not considered it as identical to the fourth explanation.

As a snake has no paddles or flappers, and is unable to undulate vertically, the sea-serpent cannot be such an animal. Moreover the boas are only inhabitants of tropical America and adjacent seas.

The **sixteenth** explanation is given by Professor Richard Owen, viz.: that the sea-serpent is a swimming **large seal**. I refer my readers to his answer to a nobleman's question, what Captain M'Quhae could have seen, inserted in our foregoing Chapter (n°. 118). After having enumerated all the characters of the animal seen by captain M'Quhae, taken from the figures as well as from the descriptions, Professor Owen comes to the conclusion: "All these are the characters of the head of a warm-blooded mammal..... Guided by the above interpretation, of the "mane of a horse, or a bunch of sea-weed", the animal was not a cetacean mammal, but rather a great seal. But what seal of large size, or indeed of any size, would be encountered in latitude 24° 44' south, and longitude 9° 22' east?" Professor Owen further concludes: *Phoca proboscidea* or *Phoca leonina*. Very remarkable is the fact that a few lines before, the Professor said of the animal's length: "This is the only part of the description, however, which seems to me to be so uncertain as to be inadmissable, *in an attempt to arrive at a right conclusion as to the nature of the animal"*. (The italics are mine).

In fig. 69 I show my readers the *Macrorhinus leoninus*, Linné, or sea-elephant, of which *Phoca leonina*, Linné, and Phoca proboscidea, Péron, are synonyms. The adult males have an elongated tubercular proboscis, the young ones and the females, one of which is seen in the background of my drawing, have the common features of seals.

Mr. H. E. Strickland and Mr. A. G. Melville in the note added to their dissertation on the Dodo, in the *Annals and Magazine of Natural History*, 2d. series, Vol. II, p. 444, Nov. 15? 1848, say of Prof. Owen's letter that it "gives a simple and clear explanation of the circumstances that have recently attracted attention, and briefly, but conclusively, discusses the question of existence of the Great Sea-Serpent generally."

Captain M'Quhae, on the contrary, at once rejects the idea of a seal. His letter is interesting enough to be read over again; I therefore refer my readers to it (n°. 118).

Mr. Froriep, in his *Notizen*, Third Series, X. p. 97, of July, 1849, after having inserted in his columns extracts from the statement of Lieutenant Drummond, from that of Captain M'Quhae, from the hoax of the *Daphne*, from the suggestion of Mr. Mantell, from that of Prof. Owen, &c. &c. finally concludes:

FIG. 69.–*MACRORHINUS LEONINUS* (LINNÉ).

"We therefore observe from all these articles that nothing is still fixed about the existence or non-existence of the great sea-serpent; yet so much seems inquestionable now, that there must be a large sea-animal, still unknown, and not quite unlike a snake; but whether this monster is a snake, nay even belongs to the family of the amphibians, this gets more and more doubtful after the objections of Prof. Owen."

Mr. Gosse, in his *Romance of Natural History* treats of the seal-hypothesis in the following manner:

"Among animals, the *Vertebrata* are the only classes supposable. But of these, which? Birds are out of the question; but *Mammalia, Reptilia, Pisces*,—there is no antecedent absurdity in assigning it to either of these. Each of these classes contains species of lengthened form, of vast dimensions, of pelagic habit; and to each has the creature been by different authorities, assigned."

"Let us, then, look at the *Mammalia*. Here Professor Owen would place it; and his opinion on a zoological question has almost the force of an axiom. I trust I shall not be accused of presumption if I venture to examine the decision of one whom I greatly respect. It is true, his reasoning applies directly only to the creature seen from the *Daedalus*; but we are bound to consider the exigencies not only of that celebrated case, but of all the other well-authenticated cases."

"Prof. Owen thus draws up the characters of the animal:—"Head with a *convex, moderately capacious cranium*, short obtuse muzzle, *gape not extending farther than the eye;* eye rather small, round, *filling closely the palpebral aperture;* colour, dark brown above, yellowish white beneath; surface smooth, *without scales, scutes,* or other conspicuous modifications of hard and naked cuticle; nostrils not mentioned, but indicated in the drawing by *a crescentic mark at the end of the nose or muzzle;* body long, dark brown, not undulating, without dorsal or other apparent fins; "but something like the mane of a horse, or rather a bunch of sea-weed, washed about its back."

"The earlier of these characters are those 'of the head of a warm-blooded mammal; none of them those of a cold-blooded reptile or fish'. The comparison of the dimly-seen something on the back to a horse's mane or sea-weed, seems to indicate a clothing of hair; and, guided by this interpretation, the Professor judges that the animal was not a cetacean, but rather a great seal."

"Now, it is manifest that it was from the pictorial sketches, more than from the verbal description of Captain M'Quhae, that this diagnosis was drawn up. And if the drawings had been made *from the life,* under the direction of a skilful zoologist, nothing could be more legitimate than such a use of them. But surely it has been overlooked that they were made under no such circumstances. Only one of the published representations was original; and this was taken 'immediately *after* the animal was seen'. That is, one of the officers, who could draw, went below immediately, and attempted to reproduce what his eye was still filled with. Now, what could one expect under such conditions? Of course, the artist was not a zoologist, or we should have had a zoologist's report. Would the drawing so produced be of any value? Surely yes; of great value. It would doubtless be a tolerably faithful representation of the *general appearance* of the object seen, but nothing more; its form, and position, and colour, and *such* of the details *as the observer had distinctly noticed, and marked down,* so to speak, *in his mind,* would be given; but a great deal of the details would be put in by mere guess. When a person draws from an object before him, he measures the various lines, curves, angles, relative distances, and so on, with his eye, one by one, and puts them down *seriatim;* ever looking at the part of the original on which he is working, for correction. But no possibility of doing this was open to the artistic midshipman; he had merely his vivid, but necessarily vague, idea of the whole before him as the original from which he drew. Who is there that could cary all the details of an object in the memory, after a few minutes' gaze, and that, too, under strong excitement? This was not the case even of a cool professional artist, called in to view an object for the purpose of depicting it; in all probability the officer had not thought of sketching it till all was over, and had made no precise observations, his mind being mainly occupied by wonder. He sits down, pencil in hand; he dashes in the general outline at once; now he comes to details,—say the muzzle, the facial angle;—of course, his figure must have *some* facial angle, *some* outline of muzzle; but probably he had particularly noticed that point. What shall he do? there is no original before him, a glance at which would decide; he sketches on a scrap of paper by his side two or three forms of head; perhaps he shows the paper to a brother officer, with a question, 'Which of these do you think most like the head?' and then he puts the one selected in his sketch, and so of other details."

"Those who are not used to drawing will think I am making a caricature. I am doing no such thing. I have been accustomed for nearly forty years to draw animals from the life; and the public are able to judge of my power of representing what I see; but I am quite sure that if I were asked to depict an object unfamiliar to me, which I had been looking at for a quarter of an hour, without thinking that I should have to draw it, I should do, in fifty points of detail, just what I have supposed the officer to have done. Let my reader try it. Get hold of one of your acquaintances, whom you know to be a skilful, but non-professional artist, whose attention has never been given to flowers; take him into your greenhouse, and show him some very beautiful thing in blossom; keep him looking at it for some ten minutes without a hint of what you are thinking of; then take him into your drawing-room, put paper and colours before him, and say, 'Make me a sketch of that plant you have just seen!' When it is done, take it to a botanist, and ask him to give you the characters of the genus and species from the sketch; or compare it yourself with the original, and note how many and what ludicrous blunders had been made in details, while there was a fair general correctness."

"Viewed in this light, it will be manifest how inefficient the sketch made on board the *Daedalus* must be for minute characters; and particularly those which in the diagnosis above I have marked with italics. Yet these are the characters mainly relied on to prove the mammalian nature of the animal. Some of these characters could not possibly have been determined at two hundred yards' distance. I say '*mainly* relied on'; because there is the manelike appendage yet to be accounted for. This is a strong point certainly in favour of a mammalian, and of a phocal nature; whether it decides the question, however, I will presently examine."

"The head in either of the large sketches (those, I mean, in which the creature is represented in the sea) does not appear to me at all to resemble that of a seal; nor do I see a 'vaulted cranium'. The summit of the head does not rise above the level of the summit of the neck; in other words, the *vertical* diameter of the head and neck are equal, while there are indications that the occiput considerably exceeds the neck in *transverse* diameter. This is not the case with any seal, but it is eminently characteristic of eels, of many serpents, and some lizards. Let the reader compare the lower figure (*Illustrated London News*, Oct. 28, 1848) with that of the Broadnosed Eel in Yarrell's *British Fishes* (ed. ii. Vol. ii. p. 396). The head of some of the scincoid lizards (the Jamaican *Celestus ociduus*, for instance) is not at all unlike that represented; it is full as vaulted, and as short, but a little more pointed, and with a flatter facial angle. On this point the Captain's assertion corrects the drawing; for, in reply to Professor Owen, he distinctly asserts that 'the head was *flat*, and not a capacious vaulted cranium;' and the description of Lieutenant Drummond, *published before any strictures were made on the point*, says, 'the head... was long, pointed, and flattened at the top, perhaps ten feet in length, the upper jaw projecting considerably'."

"With regard to the 'mane'. The great *Phoca proboscidea* is the only seal which will bear comparison with the *Daedalus* animal in question, reaching from twenty to thirty feet. H. M. officers declare that upwards of sixty feet of their animal were visible at the surface; but Mr. Owen supposes, not improbably, that the disturbance of the water produced by progression induced an illusive appearance of a portion of this length. But how much? Suppose all behind thirty feet, the extreme length of the elephant seal. Then it is impossible the animal could have been such a seal, for the following reason. The fore paws of the seal are placed at about one-third of the total length from the muzzle; that is, in a seal of thirty feet long, at ten feet behind the muzzle. But *twenty* feet of the "serpent" were projected from the water, and yet no appearance of fins was seen. Lieutenant Drummond judges the head to have been ten feet in length (with which the lower figure, assuming sixty or sixty-five feet as the total length drawn; well agrees); and besides this, at least an equal length of neck was exposed."

"But the great *Phoca proboscidea* has no mane at all. For this, we must have recourse to other species, known as sea-lions. Two kinds are recognized under this name, *Otaria jubata* and *Platyrhynchus leoninus*; though there is some confusion in the names. Neither of these ever exceeds sixteen feet in total length, of which, about five feet would be the utmost that could project from the water in swimming. Suppose, however, the eyes of the gallant officers to have magnified the leonine seal to sufficient dimensions; I fear even then it will not do. For the mane in these animals is a lengthening and thickening of the hair on the occiput and on the neck, just as in the lion. But the 'serpent's' mane was not there, but 'perhaps twenty feet in the rear of the head' says Lieutenant Drummond; it 'washed about its back,' says Captain M'Quhae."

"I do not hesitate to say, therefore, that on data we at present possess, the seal hypothesis appears to me quite untenable."

I think that the reader will easily see that Mr. Gosse in discussing the mammalian character of the sea-serpent, and we may add: *especially of the sea-serpent seen by Captain* M'Quhae, was prepossessed with his idea of the sea-serpent being an Enaliosaurian.—Mr. Gosse points out that the vertical diameter of the head and neck are equal, but he does *not* fix the reader's attention to the fact that if this were really the case, the estimation of the length of the head by Lieutenant Drummond at "ten feet" and that of the diameter of the neck by Captain M'Quhae at "sixteen inches" don't agree at all!—In none of the reports of the animal of the *Daedalus* there is question of the "serpent" being "twenty feet projected from the water"; it is only stated that the head was kept four feet above the water.—Neither do the reports mention *how much* of the neck was exposed, besides the head: Mr. Gosse says "an equal length".—Lieutenant Drummond did *not* say that the *mane* was "perhaps twenty feet in the rear of the head": the gallant officer, on the contrary, did not mention the mane at all!—

Prof. Owen relying upon the descriptions of Captain M'Quhae and drawings of one of the midshipmen, and admitting all their statements to he true and their sketches to be as accurate as possible, absolutely rejects the estimation of the length of the animal at "sixty-feet at least"; in doing so he of course could not possibly come to another conclusion than that the animal was a mammal, and to the question: "which mammal could it have been? his reply could not be otherwise than: "a large seal". It is evident that for this reason he recalled to his mind all the sea-mammals known to him, but he seems to have totally overlooked the possibility of the existence of sea-mammals unknown to him!!! The conclusion: "the animal was a large seal" leads the Professor to write: "A larger body of evidences from eye-witnesses might be got together in proof of ghosts than of the sea-serpent". The Professor would never have expressed such an opinion, if he had examined *all* the reports about the animal, and *all* that had been written about it up to his time. It is evident that, without a thorough investigation a sceptic *must* remain a sceptic.

I need not say, why the sea-serpent cannot be a sea-elephant. The latter has a proboscis, the sea-serpent has none, the sea-elephant has no long neck, no long tail, no mane, whereas these characters are very prominent in the sea-serpent.

The **seventeenth** explanation is the following: the sea-serpent is nothing else but a gigantic **sea-weed**, detached from the bottom of the sea. In 1849 we meet for the first time with this suggestion. In the Zoologist of that year, p. 2541, we read the following statement of Captain Herriman:

"Mr. J. A. Herriman, commander of the ship *Brazilian*, now lying near the principal entrance of the London Dock, makes the following curious and interesting statement:—

"He left the Cape on the 19 of February, running with a strong south-easterly wind for four days. On the morning of the 24th. the ship was becalmed in latitude 26° South, longitude 8° East, being about forty miles from the place in which Captain M'Quhae, R. N., is said to have seen the Great Sea-Serpent. About eight o'clock on that morning, whilst the captain was surveying the calm, heavy, rippleless swell of the sea through his telescope, the ship at the same time heading N. N. W., he perceived something right abeam, about half a mile to the westward, stretched along the water to the length of about twenty-five or thirty feet, and perceptibly moving from the ship with a steady, sinuous motion. The head, which seemed to be lifted several feet above the waters, had something resembling a mane, running down to the floating portion, and within about six feet of the tail it forked out into a sort of double fin. Having read at Colombo the account of the monster said to have been seen by Captain M'Quhae in nearly the same latitude, Mr. Herriman was led to suppose that he had fallen in with the same animal, or one of the genus; he immediately called his chief officer, Mr. Long, with several of the passengers, who, after surveying the object for some time, came to the unanimous conclusion that it must be the sea-serpent seen by Captain M'Quhae. As the *Brazilian* was making no headway, Mr. Herriman, determining to bring all doubts to an issue, had a boat lowered down, and taking two hands on board, together with Mr. Boyd, of Peterhead, near Aberdeen, one of the passengers, who acted as steersman under the direction of the captain, they approached the monster, Captain Herriman standing on the bow of the boat armed with a harpoon, to commence the onslaught. The combat, however, was not attended with the danger which those on board apprehended; for on coming close to the object it was found to be nothing more than an immense piece of sea-weed, evidently detached from a coral reef, and drifting with the current, which sets constantly to the westward in this latitude, and which, together with the swell left by the subsidence of the gale, gave it the sinuous, snake-like motion."

"But fore the calm, which afforded Captain Herriman an opportunity of examining the weed, we should have had an other 'eyewitness' account of the great sea-serpent,—Mr. Herriman himself admitting that he should have remained under the impression that he had seen it. What appeared to be the head, crest, and mane of the *immensum volumen*, was but the large root which floated upwards, and to which several pieces of the coral reef still adhered. The Captain had it hauled on board, but as it began to decay, was compelled to throw it over. He now regrets that he had not preserved it in a water-butt for the purpose of exhibition in the Thames, where the conflicting motion produced by the tide and steamers would in all probability give it a like appearance."

Again we read in the *Times* of February 13th., 1858, republished also in the *Zoologist* for 1858, p. 5990:

"In your paper of the 5th. inst. is a letter from Captain Harrington, of the ship *Castilian*, stating his belief that he had seen the great sea-serpent near St. Helena. His confidence is strengthened by the fact of something similar having been seen by H. M. Ship Daedalus near the same position. The following circumstance which occurred on board the ship *Pekin*, then belonging to Mrrs. T. & W. Smith, on her passage from Moulmein, may be of some service respecting this 'queer fish.' On December 28th., 1848, being then in lat. 26° S., long. 6° E., nearly calm, saw, about half a mile on port beam, a very extraordinary looking thing in the water, of considerable length. With the telescope we could plainly discern a huge head and neck, covered with a long shaggy-looking kind of mane, which it kept lifting at intervals out of the water. This was seen by all hands, and declared to be the great sea-serpent. I determined on knowing something about it, and accordingly lowered a boat, in which my chief officer and four men went, taking with them a long small line in case it should be required. I watched them very anxiously, and the monster seemed not to regard their approach. At length they got close to the head. They seemed to hesitate, and then busy themselves with the line, the monster all the time ducking its head, and showing its great length. Presently the boat began pulling towards the ship, the monster following slowly. In about half an hour they got alongside; a tackle was got on the mainyard and it was hoisted on board. It appeared somewhat supple when hanging, but so completely covered with snaky-looking barnacles, about eighteen inches long, that we had it some time on board before it was discovered to be a piece of gigantic sea-weed, twenty feet long, and four inches diameter; the root end appeared when in the water like the head of an animal, and the motion given by the sea caused it to seem alive. In a few days it dried up to a hollow tube, and as it had rather an offensive smell, was thrown overboard. I had only been a short time in England when the *Daedalus* arrived and reported having seen the great sea-serpent,—to the best of my recollection near the same locality, and which I have no doubt was a piece of the same weed. So like a huge living monster did this appear, that, had circumstances prevented my sending a boat to it. I should certainly have believed I had seen the great sea-snake. Frederic Smith, New-castle-on-Tyne, February 10, 1858."—

The Editor of the *Zoologist* adds the following quotation from Harvey's *British Algae*, p. 27, however, not as an explanation of the appearances of the sea-serpent, for he was a firm believer in its existence, but only as a note to the statement of Captain Smith and to increase the knowledge of his readers as to the existence of these large weeds. We do the same.

"The plants of this family (*Laminariaceae*) are almost all of large size, and many of them gigantic, greatly exceeding in bulk any other marine vegetables. The Oarweeds and Tangles of our own coasts have frequently stems six or eight feet long, and fronds expanding from their summits to as great a length; and the Sea-thong (*Chorda*) often measures forty feet in length. But these dimensions are small, compared with their kindred on the shores of the Pacific ocean. The *Nereocystis*, a plant of this family inhabiting the north-western shores of America, has a stem, no thicker than whipcord, but upwards of 300 feet in length, bearing at its apex a huge vesicle, six or seven feet long, shaped like a barrel, and crowned with a tuft of upwards of fifty forked leaves, each from 30 to 40 feet in length. The vesicle being filled with air, buoys up this immense frond, which lies stretched along the surface of the sea: here the sea-otter has his favoured lair, resting himself upon the vesicle, or hiding among the leaves while he pursues his fishing. The cord-like stem which anchors this floating tree must be of considerable strength; and, accordingly, we find it used as a fishing-line by the natives of the coast."

As soon as this suggestion was published, "an officer of H. M. S. *Daedalus*" and Captain Harrington repeated their assurances that the creatures they saw were living animals. Nay, even Rear Admiral Hamilton took up the cudgels for Captain Harrington, upon which Captain Frederic Smith wrote the following paper (*The Times* of 23 February 1858):

"Sir,—I beg to explain, in answer to Rear-Admiral Hamilton, that in the water, before being divested of its extraordinary-looking appendages, the diameter of my marine capture was above three feet. Some buckets full of splendidly-coloured blue and crimson crabs, varying from the size of a shilling to that of a man's hand, were collected from it, and that this quantity of such animal life could be furnished with a refuge in the mats of snaky-looking creatures which constitued the moving monstrous-looking external will assist those who read my account in believing what I before stated that even when the object was laid on deck we had difficulty in making out what it was. Now, sea-weeds of gigantic growth abound near the islands of the group of Tristan d'Acunha. From decay or other causes, these will from time to time be detached at the roots, and with their living attachment will then, floating horizontally, be carried by the well-known currents, into the very positions where the sea-serpent delights in exhibiting himself. It is not disputed that such was the monster picked up by the boat's crew of my ship. I do not doubt that more monstrous specimens may be seen from time to time, and I expect that your insertion of this correspondence will cause more attention to be given to their capture than, as on board of Her Majesty's Ship *Daedalus*, to the forming of 'sundry guesses', causing the observers to 'settle down' to the conclusion: 'This must be the animal called the sea-serpent.' Had the monster I described not been taken, I should have believed, as firmly as Captain Harrington does, that I could confirm the statement of the commander of the *Daedalus* and that 'the animal belonged to the serpent tribe'."

"Everybody knows what different notions are generated by momentary and unexpected appearances of things as compared with the things themselves when examined. Perhaps the nostril of the *Daedalus* sea-serpent was seen in the recollection of one spectator, the mouth in that of another, and so on. I take leave to question the possibility of these being 'most distinctly visible', when the object at its 'nearest position' was 200 yards distant, the sea getting up, and the observers travelling in an opposite direction, the passing of the two being apparently at the rate of 20 miles an hour. Naturalists will say whether an animal to answer to the habits and attributes of that in question would have a nostril."

"I am sure that Captain Harrington, of the *Castilian*, saw an extraordinary object, and described it according to his impression, and having a great respect for 'a first-class certificate in the mercantile marine' (as I hold a 'first-class extra' myself), and also for 'Sir Colin Campbell, now in the East', to whom Capt. Harrington is so well known, I feel equally sure that, so accredited, he has published his account with no other than a good object. Nevertheless, these circumstances do not prove to me that Captain Harrington saw the sea-serpent, because that 'queer fish' so very nearly and completely took me in until I took him in."

"I am, Sir, your most obedient servant
"Fred. Smith."

Mr. Gosse, in his *Romance of Natural History*, p. 320, inquiring whether the sea-serpent is an animal at all, treats of the sea-weed hypothesis. We will let him reason himself.

"To which of the recognised classes of created beings can this huge rover of the ocean be referred? And, first, is it an animal at all? That there are immense algae in the ocean, presenting some of the characters described, has been already shown; and on two occasions an object supposed to be the 'sea-serpent' proved on examination to be but a sea-weed floating; the separated and inverted roots of which, projecting in the role of the swell, seemed a head, and the fronds (in the one case), and (in the other) a number of attached barnacles, resembled a shaggy mane washed about in the water."

"But surely it must have been a very dim and indistinct view of the floating and ducking object, which could have mistaken this for a living animal; and it would be absurd in the highest degree to presume that of such a nature could be the creatures, going rapidly through the water at ten or twelve miles an hour, with the head and neck elevated, so distinctly seen by Captain M'Quhae and Mr. Davidson, the former at two hundred, the latter at thirty five yards' distance. We may fairly dismiss the sea-weed hypothesis."

Again in *Nature* of the 12th. of September, 1872, appears the following passage which also clearly shows that by some unbelievers the sea-weed hypothesis is admitted.

"The 'dead season' has brought up its usual crop of reports of the reappearance of the sea-serpent, mostly easily resolvable into masses of floating sea-weed."

Mr. Andrew Wilson in his *Leisure Time Studies* speaking of this hypothesis says:

"That a long and connected string of sea-weed, extending for some fifty or sixty feet along the surface of a sea, slightly disturbed by a rippling breeze, may be moved by the waves in a manner strongly suggestive of the movements of a snake in swimming, is a statement to the correctness of which I can bear personal testimony, and to the truth of which even observant sea-side visitors may testify. The movements of an unusually long frond or group of fronds of tangle, attached to a rock, and set in motion at low water, by a light swell, has before now, and when seen indistinctly, suggested the idea of the existence at the spot of some large denizen of the sea, browsing on the sea-weeds, with the fore part of its body, represented by the tangle fronds, occasionally appearing at the surface of the water."

Though the writer of the following story which originally appeared in the *Madras Mail*, but which I take from *Nature* of 13th. October, 1881, does not assert that the sea-serpent may be explained in this way, I firmly believe that such was, indeed, his purpose. I also think that this was the intention of the contributor who inserted it in the columns of *Nature*, of the man who sent a Dutch translation of it to the *Nieuws van den Dag*, of 26th. Nov., 1881, and of Professor P. Harting who republished this translation in the *Album der Natuur*, of 1882, p. 66.

"In a letter to the *Madras Mail* of September 8, on the use of gigantic sea-weed as a protective agent for shores, Capt. J. H. Taylor, the Master-superintendent of Madras, gives the following interesting 'sea-serpent'-story:—'A notable incident connected with this sea-weed, is recalled to my recollection, by Dr. Furnell's letter. About fifteen years ago, while I was in my ship at anchor in Table Bay, an enormous monster, as it appeared, was seen drifting, or advancing itself round Green Point, into the harbour. It was more than one hundred feet in length, and moved with an undulating snake-like motion. Its head was crowned with what appeared to be long hair, and the keen-sighted among the affrighted observers declared they could see its eyes and distinguish its features. The military were called out, and a brisk fire poured into it at a distance of about five hundred yards. It was hit several times, and portions of it knocked off. So serious were its evident injuries, that on its rounding the point it became quite still, and boats went off to examine it and complete its destruction. It was found to be a specimen of the sea-weed above mentioned, and its stillness after the grievous injuries inflicted was due to its having left the ground swell and entered the quite waters of the Bay'."

It will not be necessary to point out that this hypothesis is not deserving of any notice on our part.

The **eighteenth** explanation is attempted by Mr. A. G. More (see *Zoologist* for 1856, p. 4948). He writes as follows:

"The sea-serpent having again risen phoenix-like from the deep, in the pages of the 'Zoologist', it may perhaps be pardonable to sollicit insertion for the following attempt at explaining his reality, in some at least of the many instances of his reported appearance. Any one who has looked at the preserved remains of the great **ribband or scabbard fishes**, or who has ever read the striking accounts of the huge size they sometimes attain, as well as their extreme rarity, may, like myself, have been thus reminded of those mysterious sea-monsters which are occasionally observed by the unlearned to be no less a puzzle to learned opinion. When, too, we know that these fishes are supposed often to swim at the surface, and thus to be driven ashore more readily, when the only example of whose healthy life we have a credible account, is described as advancing head above water, and by the undulating movement of his body (Yarrell, Vol. 1. p. 177), may we not reasonably suppose that there exists other and more gigantic forms of this most interesting race at yet uncaptured, and such as might easily simulate, in the waving of their long dorsal fin, the so called 'mane' of the great sea-snake."

The ribband or scabbard fish theory is briefly treated of by Mr. Gosse in his *Romance of Natural History* in the following terms:

"There are, however, the ribbon-fishes; and some of these, as the hair-tail, the *Vaegmaer*, and the *Gymnetrus*, are of large size, and slender sword-like form. Several kinds have been found in the North Atlantic, and, wherever seen, they invariably excite wonder and curiosity. All of these are furnished with a back-fin; but in other respects they little correspond with the descriptions of the animal in question. One of their most striking characteristics, moreover, is, that their surface resembles polished steel or silver."

In 1860 a ribbon-fish of large dimensions was captured on Bermudas Isles. Mr. Trimingham, the captor, placed it at the disposal of Mr. J. Matthew Jones, a naturalist living there. This gentleman described the animal for the *Zoologist*, in which his paper appeared in the volume of that year (p. 6986). Now Mr. Jones ended his article as follows:

"The most notable fact however, in connection with the capture of the present specimen, will doubtless be the interest and attraction it will produce on the scientific world, for most assuredly we have in the specimen now before us many of the peculiarities, safe size, with which the appearance of that hitherto apocryphal monster 'The Great Sea-Serpent', as detailed by navigators, is invested. The lengthened filaments crowning the caput, joined anteriorly by the connecting membrane, and extending to the shoulders, would, viewed from a vessel's deck, present to the spectator the mane so accurately described as a singular feature in the gigantic specimen seen by Capt. M'Quhae, R. N., and officers of H. M. S. *Daedalus*. Then again, the rapidity with which that individual specimen moved through the water, would coincide with the capabilities of a member of this genus, for the motive power produced by such an extent of tail, coupled with the extremely compressed form of body from the head throughout, must be immense."

"Here then we have a partial elucidation of the various statements which have at intervals appeared in the columns of the united presses of England and America, emanating from the pens of travelers, and usually headed—'Occurrence of the Sea-Serpent'— criticised, however, in an ungenerous manner, and always exposed to an unmerited ridicule at the hands of the many, but, nevertheless, firmly believed in by the few, who have patiently waited to see the day when the mystic cloud which has hitherto veiled the existence of the maned denizen of the deep should vanish with the suspicion of the sceptic, and exhibit more clearly the truth of the assertions of those ill-used men, who, endeavouring like useful members of society to extend the cause of natural knowledge by publishing candid accounts of what their eyes have seen, have always met with an amount of contempt and reproach, sufficient to silence for ever the pen of many a truthful writer."

"I am sorry I have not the numero of the Illustrated London News at hand in which Capt. M'Quhae's graphic statement appeared, as it would have afforded me an opportunity of particulirising other features in connection with his specimen and the present one. The facts, however, regarding the mane-like appendage, and the rapidity of motion to which I have alluded, are still fresh in my memory."

Mr. Newman, the Editor of the *Zoologist*, thinking this ribbon-fish a new species, gave a detailed description of it, and honoured it with the name of *Regalecus Jonesii*, but to our great astonishment, he, who firmly believed the sea-serpent to be an *Enaliosaurus* (as we have observed above) now seems to be in doubt about the matter, for he ends his article with the following words:

"In reference to the last question mooted by Mr. Jones, the similarity of *Regalecus Jonesii* to Capt. M'Quahae's serpent, I do not consider myself competent to express an opinion. I am quite willing for the present to allow every sea-serpent to hold on its own course; hereafter a better opportunity may be afforded on comparing and arranging the conflicting evidence already published in the '*Zoologist*'."

The ribbon-fish hypothesis gradually takes a firmer hold on the unbelievers, no doubt, at it *seems* more plausible than the *Plesiosaurus*-one. An inhabitant of Cape Town wrote the following note which I have found in *Nature* of the 1st. August, 1872:

"The South-African Museum, Cape Town, recently received a specimen of the Ribbon Fish (Gymnoterus) fifteen feet long without the tail. It appears that this fish is known to distant inland fishermen as being forty feet long, and from its slender shape and snake-like movement is probably the 'sea-serpent' of late years so minutely described by navigators. From its head there is erected a plume of flexible, rose-coloured spines, and from head to tail along its back there is a conspicuous mane-like fin. Its general colour is like burnished silver. The eye is large and silvery, and the profile of the head comports well with that of the horse. The specimen could not be preserved, but there are two smaller specimens in the Museum."

Mr. Andrew Wilson in his turn believes (see *Nature* of Sept. 12, 1878) that:

"A long tape-fish" (which is the same as a ribbon-fish) "might do duty in the eyes of non zoological observers for a sea-serpent."

In his *Leisure Time Studies* he returns to his idea:

"A visit paid to the Newcastle Museum of Natural History, on which occasion I had the pleasure of inspecting a dried and preserved ribbon or tape-fish of large size, forcibly confirmed an idea that such an animal, developed to a gigantic size, and beheld from a distance by persons unskilled in natural history,—and who would, therefore, hardly dream of associating the elongated being before them with their ordinary ideas of fish-form and appearance,—might account for certain of the tales of sea-serpents which have been brought under our notice. I had been specially struck with the mention, in several accounts of sea-serpents, of a very long back fin, sometimes termed a 'mane', and of a banded body covered with tolerably smooth skin; whilst in several instances the description given of the heads of the sea-monsters closely correspond with the appearance of the head of the tape-fishes. These fishes have further been described by naturalists as occasionally having been seen swimming with an undulating or serpentine motion close to the surface of the water, the head being somewhat elevated above the surface,— this latter feature, as we have observed, forming a remark of frequent occurrence in sea-serpent tales. I found, on making inquiry into the history of these fishes, that their serpentine form had struck previous observers, but, as far as I could ascertain, their merits as representatives of sea-serpents had never before been so persistently advocated."

"These views and the dimensions of the specimen at Newcastle, I communicated to the *Scotsman* and *Courant* newspapers in June, 1876. The measurements of the ribbon-fish at Newcastle are given as 12 feet 3 inches in length, the greatest depth being 11 1/4 inches, and the greatest thickness only 2 3/4 inches; the small dimensions in thickness, and the relatively long length and depth, giving to these fishes the popular names of ribbon and tape-fishes. The species was the well-known *Gymnetrus* or *Regalecus Banksii* of naturalists; and by the Museum attendent at Newcastle, I was informed that a still larger specimen of the same species was recently obtained of the Northumberland coast, the length of this latter being 13 1/2 feet, the depth 15 inches, and the thickness 5 inches. These fishes possess a greatly compressed body. The breast fins are very small, and the ventral or belly fins are elongated and spine-like. The first rays of the dorsal or back fin are very long, whilst the fin itself extends the whole length of the back, and obtains an average breadth of about three inches."

"Curiously enough, the publication of these views regarding the ribbon-fishes drew forth from the head of a well-known firm of fish merchants in Edinburgh, a remarkable confirmation of the idea that gigantic specimens of these fishes might be occasionally developed. The gentleman in question wrote to inform me that about thirty years ago he engaged the smack *Sovereign*, of Hull, Baillie commander, to trawl in the Frith of Forth for Lord Norbury, then residing at Elie Lodge, Fifeshire. Whilst engaged in their trawling operations, the crew of the *Sovereign* captured a giant tape-fish, which, when spread out at length on the deck, extended beyond the limits of the vessel at stem and stern. The smack was a vessel of forty tons burthen; and the length may therefore be safely estimated at sixty feet,—this measurement being exceeded by the ribbon-fish. The breadth of the fish measured from five to nine inches, and the dorsal fin was from six to seven inches in depth. Unfortunately, Lord Norbury seemed inclined to view the giant he had captured with distrust and ordered the fish to be cut in pieces and thrown overboard; but it is also worthy of remark that the trawlers seemed to express no great surprise at the size of Lord Norbury's specimen, since they asserted that they had met with one much larger, this latter being coloured of a dirty-brown hue."

He also explains the animal of the *Osborne* (n°. 148) by reference to a ribbon-fish in the following terms:

"I thought the opportunity a favourable one for offering a reasonable explanation of the circumstance, and I communicated my views to the *Times* in the following terms, the letter appearing in that journal for June 15, 1877:—'About a year ago I ventilated in the columns of several journals the idea that the 'sea-serpents' so frequently seen, were in reality giant tape-fishes or ribbon-fishes. While not meaning by this statement to exclude the idea that other animals,—such as giant sea-snakes themselves,—may occasionally personate the 'sea-serpent', I am, as a zoologist, fully convinced that very many of the reported appearances of sea-serpents are explicable on the supposition that giant tape-fishes—of the existence of which no reasonable doubt can be entertained—have been seen. The report of Captain Pearson, of the royal yacht *Osborne*, appears, as far as zoological characters are concerned, to be fully explained on the 'ribbon-fish' theory. The long back fins, the scale-less skin, the rounded head, and lastly, the two great side (or pectoral) fins, each measuring many feet in length, all form so many details corresponding exactly to the appearance of a great tape-fish. I offer these observations with the view of showing that, given a recital founded, as I believe the present narrative to be, on fact, we possess in the lists of living and of well-known animals adequate representatives of the great unknown'."

"The imperfect view obtained of the body renders the expression contained in the report, that the body was 'like that of a gigantic turtle', somewhat problematical as to its correctness; and in the absence of more defined information, does not necessarily invalidate the views expressed above as to the personality of this strange tenant of the Mediterranean Sea."

"In an article entitled 'Strange Sea Creatures,' which appeared in the *Gentleman's Magazine* for March, 1877, Mr. R. A. Proctor, speaking of my views regarding the sea-serpent, remarks that I offer as an alternative only the ribbon-fish. This observation being hardly correct, I may point out that in the article in *Good Words*, from which Mr. Proctor quotes my views, I distinctly refer to the probability of giant sea-snakes being occasionally developed and appearing as the modern sea-serpent. The use of the word 'only' in Mr. Proctor's remark is misleading; since I offer the ribbon-fishes simply as explanatory of certain sea-serpent narratives, and not as a sole and universal representative of the modern leviathan."

"Thus, then, with the ribbon-fishes at hand, and with the clear proof before us that these and other animals may be developed to a size which, compared with their ordinary dimensions, we can only term enormous, I think the true and valid explanation of the sea-serpent question is neither far to seek nor difficult to find. To objectors of a practical turn of mind, who may remind me that we have not yet procured even a single bone of a giant serpent, I would point out that I by no means maintain the frequent development of such beings. The most I argue for and require is their occasional production; and I would also remind such objectors of the case of the giant cuttle-fishes which, until within the past few years, remained in the same mysterious seclusion affected at present by the great serpentine unknown. I need only add that I have as firm faith in the actual discovery of a giant serpent of the sea, as that in the giant tape-fish we find its representative, or that in the huge development of ordinary forms we discover the true and natural law of its production."

"To sum up my arguments by way of conclusion, I respectfully submit, as does a pleading counsel to his jury, —"

"Firstly: That many of the tales of sea-serpents are amply verified, when judged by the ordinary rules of evidence; this conclusion being especially supported by the want of any *prima facie* reason for prevarication;"

"Secondly: That, laying aside appearances which can be proved to be deceptive and to be caused by inanimate objects or by unusual attitudes on the part of familiar animals, there remains a body of evidence only to be explained on the hypothesis that certain gigantic marine animals, at present unfamiliar or unknown to science, do certainly exist; and"

"Thirdly: That the existence of such animals is a fact perfectly consistent with scientific opinion and knowledge, and is most readily explained by recognizing the fact of the occasional development of gigantic members of groups of marine animals already familiar to the naturalist."

Mr. Lee, in his *Sea Monsters Unmasked*, too, supposes that "the dorsal fins.... of ribbon-fishes, as suggested by Dr. Andrew Wilson, may have furnished the "ridge of fins".

I have only to direct my readers' attention to the fact that a ribbon-fish has only *one* connected dorsal *fin*, and not a *ridge of fins*, (compare fig. 13 with fig. 44). The dorsal fin of a ribbon-fish is quite red, the mane of the sea-serpent is dark brown, nearly black; the colour of the fish is silvery, that of the sea-serpent dark brown above, nearly black, and when having swum for a long time in the sun on the surface of the water, a greyish yellow; the under parts are of a dirty white. The fish has no flappers, which are the organs of locomotion of the sea-serpent. The breadth of a ribbon-fish is only a few inches, while that of the sea-serpent, as is clearly pointed out in the animal of the *Osborne* (n°. 148), may grow to more than fifteen feet. But I need not sum up the differences between ribbon-fishes and sea-serpents. We have only to ask the opinion of one of the most able ichthyologists of our days, and the whole hypothesis has not a leg to stand upon:

Mr. Günther says in his *Introduction to the study of Fishes*, 1880, p. 520:

"The 'Ribbon-fishes' are true deep-sea fishes, met with in all parts of the oceans, generally found when floating dead on the surface, or thrown ashore by the waves....."

"When these fishes reach the surface of the water, the expansion of the gases within their body has so loosened all parts of their muscular and bony system, that they can be lifted out of the water with difficulty only, and nearly always portions of the body and fins are broken and lost..... At what depths ribbon-fishes live is not known; probably the depths vary for different species; but although none have been yet obtained by means of the deep-sea dredge, they must be abundant at the bottom of all oceans, as dead fishes or fragments of them are frequently obtained. Some writers have supposed from the great length and narrow shape of these fishes that they have been mistaken for 'Sea-Serpents'; but as these monsters of the sea are always represented by those who have had the good fortune of meeting with them as remarkably active, it is not likely that harmless Ribbon fishes, which are either dying or dead, have been the objects described as "Sea-Serpents"."

The **nineteenth** explanation is that of Mr. Arthur Adams (see *Zoologist*, 1860, p. 7237) who believes that **a floating dead tree** "might have become a source of error, and given rise to yet another sea-serpent". His article runs as follows:

"An incident occurred on board the vessel of which I am surgeon, which, I think, deserves to be recorded as an illustration of optical delusion that might have become a source of error, and given rise to yet another sea-serpent. We were sailing among the Islands of the Miatan group, at the entrance of the Gulf of Pe-Chili. There was little wind, and the gentle ripples covered the surface of the sea. I was sipping my Congo at the open port of the ward room on the main deck, admiring the setting sun, and watching the rounded outlines of the blue mountains and distant islands against the sky, and the numbers of sea-birds 'wheeling rockwards to their nests', when my eye rested on a long dark object apparently making its way steadily through the water. After observing it some time in silence I was sorely puzzled and could make nothing of it. It was neither a seal nor a diver nor a fishing cormorant, for with their forms I was familiar; so I went on deck and consulted other eyes than mine. Sundry glasses were brought to bear on the suspicious object, and the general scrutiny seemed to decide that it was a large snake, about ten feet long (or much longer according to some), working its way vigorously against the tide by lateral undulations of the body. So strong was this conviction that the course of the ship was altered, and a boat got ready for lowering. With a couple of loaded revolvers, some boathooks and a fathom or so lead-line, I made ready for the encounter, intending to range up alongside, shoot the reptile through the head, make him fast by a clove-hitch, and tow him on board in triumph! By this time, however, a closer and more critical inspection had taken place, and the supposed sea-monster turned himself into a long dark root, gnarled and twisted, of a tree, secured to the moorings of a fishing net, with the strong tide passing it rapidly, and thus giving it an apparent life-like movement and serpentine aspect."

After Mr. Drew had published in *Nature* a case, in which he and many others were deceived by a large mass of flying shags, another contributor Mr. E. H. Pringle wrote the following (*Nature*, September 12, 1878):

"If you have space for the following, it is so confirmatory of Dr. Drew's experience of an opera-glass dispelling "fond deceits" concerning a sea-serpent, that it may be worth recording."

"One morning in October, 1869, I was standing amid a small group of passengers on the deck of the ill-fated P. and O. ss. *Rangoon*, then steaming up the straits of Malacca to Singapore. We were just within sight, so far as I remember, of Sumatra. One of the party suddenly pointed out an object on the port bow, perhaps half a mile off, and drew from us the simultaneous exclamation of 'The sea-serpent!' And there it was, to the naked eye, a genuine serpent, speeding through the sea, with its head raised on a slender curved neck, now almost buried in the water, and anon reared just above its surface. There was the mane, and there were the well-known undulating coils stretching yards behind."

"But for an opera-glass, probably all our party on board the *Rangoon* would have been personal witnesses to the existence of a great sea-serpent, but, alas for romance! one glance through the lenses and the reptile was resolved into a bamboo, root upwards, anchored in some manner to the bottom—a 'snag' in fact. Swayed up and down by the rapid current, a series of waves undulated beyond it, bearing in their crests dark coloured weeds or grass that had been caught by the bamboo stem."

"Ignorance of the shallowness of the straits so far from land, and of the swiftness of the current, no doubt led us to our first hasty conclusion, but the story, with Dr. Drew's shows how prone the human mind is to accept the marvellous, and how careful we should be in forming judgments even on the evidence of our senses."

Mr. Andrew Wilson, in his *Leisure Time Studies*, speaking of this hypothesis says:

"Floating trunks and roots of trees, serving as a nucleus around which sea-weed has collected, and to which barnacles and sea-acorns—producing a variegated effect by reason of their light colour—have attached themselves in great numbers, have also presented appearances closely resembling those of large marine animals, swimming slowly along at the surface of the water. In one instance of this latter kind, related to me by a friend who was an actual spectator, the floating piece of timber assumed a shape imitating in the closest and most remarkable manner the head of some reptile,—by the same rule, I suppose, that in the gnarled trunks and branches of trees one may frequently discern likenesses to the human face and to the forms of other living things. In this latter instance, the floating object was perceived at some miles' distance from the deck of a yacht; and even when seen through a telescope, and carefully scrutinized by men accustomed to make out the contour and nature of objects at sea, the resemblance to the head of some animal was so close that the course of the vessel was changed and the object in due time overhauled. This latter, therefore, presents an example of a case, the details of which, when related, tempt people to maintain without further parley, that sea-serpents always resolve themselves into inanimate objects of one kind or another."

The extreme rapidity which is reported of the sea-serpent, banishes at once the idea of a dead organism.

The **twentieth** explanation is: **a mass of flying birds**, of Mr. Joseph Drew, who wrote in *Nature* of the 5th. of September, 1878:

"On Monday, August a, a number of geologists crossed in the Folkestone boat to Boulogne, to study the interesting formations of that neighbourhood, and, when about three or four miles from the French coast, one of these gentlemen suddenly exclaimed, 'Look at that extraordinary object passing across the bow of the steamer about a mile or a mile and a-half in advance of us!' On turning in this direction there was seen an immense serpent apparently about a furlong in length, rushing furiously along at the rate of fifteen or twenty miles an hour; it was blackish in front and paler behind; its elongated body was fairly on the surface of the water and it progressed with an undulating or quivering motion, mirum erat spectaculum sane."

"Of course many suppositions were immediately started to account for this extraordinary phenomenon, but they quickly changed and settled into the fixed idea that the object before them could be nothing less than the great sea-serpent himself; for—

"Prone on the flood, extended long and large,
"Lay floating, many a rood, in bulk as huge
"As whom the fables name of monstrous size,
"Leviathan, which God of all his works
"Created hugest, that swim the ocean stream."

"The writer fortunately had with him one of Baker's best opera-glasses, and, after a few moment's use of this little instrument, the wonder was satisfactorily resolved. The first half of the monster was dark and glittering and the remainder of fainter hue, gradually, fading towards the tail. The glass did not determine the matter until the extreme end was reached, and then it was seen to consist of a mass of birds in rapid motion; those that were strong on the wing were able to keep well up with the leaders, and to make the head appear thicker and darker by their numbers, whilst those that had not such power of flight were compelled to settle into places nearer and nearer the tail. Doubtless these birds were shags *(Pelecanus cristatus)* returning to their homes for the night from the distant waters in which they had been fishing, during the day; perchance it may be wrong to assert positively as to the variety of bird, but in as much as the writer has often seen shags on the Cornish coast in smaller numbers returning in single or double file to their roosting places, and since it is stated in works of natural history that they have been noticed accasionally flying in this peculiar manner to the number of a thousand or more, it does not appear an unwarranted liberty in supposing that they really were *Pelecani cristati*."

"It is to be feared some of the geological gentlemen still doubt the interpretation of the lorgnette, preferring the fond deceit of a large and unknown serpent; but as in this case individual birds (scores of them) were distinctly seen flapping their wings, the writer has thought it his duty to report the circumstance to you that your readers who voyage across the seas may keep their opera-glasses in their pockets and verify for themselves, on the first opportunity this interpretation of the great sea-serpent."

This story induced Mr. Bird (*Nature*, of 12th. September, 1878) to make a similar avowal:

"Dr. Drew's letter in *Nature*, Vol. XVIII, p. 489, recalls to my mind a similar phenomenon witnessed by myself and a friend on August 3, while crossing from Grimsby to Rotterdam. It was towards evening, when, looking ahead, we saw a low, black hull, without masts or funnel, moving through the water at enormous speed. After a minute or two it undulated and rose from the surface, and we saw that it was a flight of birds."

"The deception was so complete that I can well believe that at least many of the stories of the sea-serpent have so originated, though I doubt whether *all* can be explained in this manner."

Mr. Andrew Wilson, on the contrary wrote the following against this suppositions (*Nature*, in the same number):

"The communication of Dr. Joseph Drew in your issue of yesterday regarding the serpentine appearance of a flock of shags in the English Channel is extremely interesting even as a mere fact regarding the habits of these birds. Will you kindly permit me, however, to point out that Dr. Drew's statement cannot be regarded as explanatory of the sea-serpent's personality? At the most the incident only explains one of a number of *serpentine appearances* of which porpoises and sun-fishes swimming in line, pieces of wood with trains of sea-weed, &c., are also good examples. There have been placed on record numerous incidents of serpentine forms having been closely expected (as in the well-known case of the *Daedalus*, or later still of H. M. S. *Osborne*) where the hypothesis of the serpentine appearances assumed by flocks of birds or fishes could not be held as explanatory in any sense. It is with the view of showing that the exact personality of the 'sea-serpent' cannot be accounted for by such an incident as Dr. Drew relates, that I venture to pen these remarks; and as a firm believer from the standpoint of zoology that the large development of the marine ophidians of warm seas offers the true explanation of the 'sea-serpent' mystery, I would also ask your readers to distinguish carefully between cases in which serpentine appearances have been assumed by ordinary animals, and those in which *one* animal form has presented itself in the guise of the 'great unknown'. I am far from contending that a sea-snake developed in the ratio of a giant 'cuttle-fish', presents the only solution of this interesting problem. A long tape-fish, or even a basking shark of huge dimensions, might do duty in the eyes of non-zoological observers for 'a sea-serpent'."..... "At the same time zoologists cannot but feel indebted to Dr. Drew, and to those who, like that gentleman, note unwonted appearances in ordinary animal life, and communicate such incidents to your columns."

A week afterwards the following article bearing upon the foregoing descriptions of flying sea-birds, appeared in the same journal from the pen of Mr. C. M. Ingleby:

"The letters of Dr. Drew and others remind me of what I witnessed at Sandgate twenty four years ago. I was staying at a cottage on an elevation which commanded an extensive sea-view. One morning my attention was called to a large, dark, undulating body, which moved rapidly through the sea. As it was some way out from shore, I naturally concluded it to be of enormous length. I lost no time in making inquiries as to the nature of this phenomenon, and was so fortunate as to discover a fisherman who had witnessed it. He told me it was a flight of petrels. But for this I should certainly have believed that I had seen the Great Unknown. I have often seen a similar phenomenon, but nothing nearly so striking as this."

In *Nature* of January 25, 1883, an alleged appearance of a sea-serpent is published. In the following number of Febr. 1st., a correspondent says that he often has witnessed a row of porpoises in the same locality; 'I never, however, saw the *head*'. Now another correspondent thinking that *he* had solved the problem, wrote the following article in the next issue of the same journal:

"In the summer of 1881 I was staying for some weeks at Veulettes, on the coast of Normandy. While there, on several occasions, several members of my party, as well as myself, saw, at a distance of three or four miles out at sea, what had the appearance of a huge serpent. Its length was many times that of the largest steamer that ever passed, and its velocity equally exceeded that of the swiftest. What seemed its head was lifted and lowered, and sometimes appeared to show signs of an open mouth. The general appearance of the monster was almost exactly similar to that of the figure in your correspondent's letter published on the 25th. ult. Not the slightest appearance of this continuity in its structure could be perceived by the eye, although it seemed incredible that any muscular mechanism could really drive such an enormous mass through the water with such a prodigious velocity. I carefully watched all that any of us caught sight of, and one day, just as one of these serpent forms was nearly opposite our hotel, it instantaneously turned through a right angle, but instead of going forward in the new direction of its length, proceeded with the same velocity broad side forward. With the same movement it resolved itself into a flock of birds."

"We often saw the sea-serpent again without this resolution being effected, and, knowing what it was, could with difficulty still perceive that it was not a continuous body; thus having a new illustration of Hershell's remark, that it is easier to see what has been once discovered than to discover what is unknown.

Possibly this experience may afford the solution of your correspondent's difficulty.— W. Steadman Aldis.—

As to the figure, it is our fig. 51.—In the next issue of *Nature* again another correspondent asserts:

"On reading the letter of W. Steadman Aldis in *Nature* yesterday, I was reminded by a person present that some years ago, when in Orkney, I pointed out an appearance that most people unaccustomed to witness it might have taken for a great sea-monster. This was nothing more or less than some hundred of cormorants or 'skarps' flying in a continuous line close to the water, the deception being increased by the resemblance of a head caused by several 'skarps' in a cluster *heading* the column, and by the *'lumpy'* seas of a swift tideway frequently intervening and hiding for an instance part of the black lines, causing the observer to—not unnaturally—imagine that the portions so hidden had gone under water. The speed of the cormorant on the wing may be fairly estimated at thirty miles an hour or more."—J. Rae.

It would be superfluous to compare the sea-serpent with a mass of flying birds. The descriptions and figures of the former are the most striking proofs against this hypothesis.

The **twenty-first** explanation was proposed by Dr. Andrew Wilson in his *Leisure Time Studies*, 1879. He presents a frontispice to his work "embodying the chief representations of the various theories of the sea-serpent question." On the left side of the foreground is delineated **a large turtle.** Of this supposition Mr. Lee says in his *Sea Monsters Unmasked:*

"A giant turtle may have done duty, with its propelling flippers and broad back."

The largest sea-turtle does not surpass the length of six feet, including the neck and head when stretched as much as possible. The breadth of the shell of such an individual may be about three and a half in diameter. It is impossible that sea-faring people would have been deceived by a swimming turtle. They know these animal well enough. Even a giant turtle would immediately be recognized by its broad shell. No sea-turtles occur near the Norwegian shore.

The **twenty-second** explanation. I don't know whether the note p. 106 of the third edition, 1884, of Mr. Andrew Wilson's *Leisure Time Studies*, also appeared in the first edition, January, 1879, and so I don't know whether this author, or Mr. Lee, (1883), has a superior claim to the supposition that the great sea-serpent might be in some or in most instances **a giant cuttle-fish or calamary.**

Mr. Andrew Wilson, quoting the report of Messrs Webster and Anderson (n°. 146), in which the latter says: "the creature was apparently of a gelatinous (that it flabby) substance", writes in a note:

"It is just possible that the 'flabby' or 'gelatinous' creature mentioned in this narrative was a giant cuttle-fish, whose manner of swimming, colour, absence of limbs, etc., would correspond with the details of the narrative. The 'immense tail' might be the enormous arms of such a creature trailing behind the body as it swam backwards, propelled by jets of water from the breathing 'funnel.'"

Mr. Lee in his *Sea Monsters Unmasked* tries to explain all accounts of the sea-serpent by reference to large calamaries. Of one of the figures of Olaus Magnus' work (our fig. 14) he says: "the presumed body of the serpent was one of the arms of the squid" (which snatched the man from the vessel) "and the two rows of suckers thereto belonging are indicated in the illustration by the medial line traversing its whole length (intended to represent a dorsal fin) and the double row of transverse septa, one on each side of it." I have discussed this explanation in its right place.

The "monster of Egede" he also explained by reference to a great calamary. Mr. Lee does not doubt of the accuracy of Egede's description, but as to Mr. Bing's figure he says: "The high character of the narrator would lead us to accept his statement that he had seen something previously unknown to him (he does not say it was a sea-serpent) even if we could not explain or understand what it was that he saw. Fortunately however, the sketch made by Mr. Bing, one of his brother-missionaries, has enabled us to do this". And Mr. Lee has the boldness to figure a large calamary, with the words: "the animal which Egede probably saw", of which figure I give a facsimile in fig. 70. —

Well! It looks convincing enough, and there is a savour of ingenious acuteness of wit in it, that might lull the suspicions of a doubting zoologist! What more could be required? And yet, the whole fabric falls to pieces as soon as we compare Egede's description and Bing's drawing with the greater part of descriptions and figures given as well before as after Egede. His idea is far fetched and thereby impossible: 1. When a calamary propels itself with great velocity to the surface and raises its tail high out of the water, all its arms are turned and stretched downwards; not one is visible above the surface. 2. When a calamary is in this position and falls down in consequence of its weight, it will fall to the side where its body is nearest the water, in our figure to left, and not to right, as Mr. Egede saw very distinctly; he says: 'backwards" that is towards the tail; and 3. A calamary in the position

FIG. 70.–POSITION OF A GIGANTIC CALAMARY, BY WHICH MR. HENRY LEE EXPLAINS MR. BING'S DRAWING.

above delineated, spouting through its locomotor tube, spouts in a direction contrary to that which Mr. Lee has figured. The locomotor tube may be somewhat flexible, when at rest; it is stretched by its own muscular wall towards the head, and not towards the tail, nor in a direction perpendicularly to the body, when the act of spouting takes place. Moreover Hans Egede saw the sea-serpent spouting (exhaling) through its nostrils or its mouth, and not on or below the surface of the water, as the calamary of Mr. Henry Lee!

Of Mr. Maclean's report (n°. 31) he says: "His description of it is exceedingly vague, but is strongly indicative of a great calamary". If I may beg my readers to read Mr. Maclean's report again, they will observe that *nothing* in it indicates a calamary!

About the report of Mr. J. C. Lund (n°. 115) he writes:

"We may at once accept most fully and frankly the statements of all the worthy people mentioned in this series of incidents. There is no room for the shadow of a doubt that they all recounted conscientiously that which they saw. The lastquoted occurrence, especially, is most accurately and intelligently described—so clearly indeed, that it furnishes us with a clue to the identity of the strange visitant."

"Here let me say—and I wish it to be distinctly understood—that I do not deny the possibility of the existence of a great sea-serpent, or other great creatures at present unknown to science, and that I have no inclination to explain away that which others have seen, because I myself have not witnessed it. 'Seeing is believing', it is said, and it is not agreeable to have to tell a person that, in common parlance, he 'must not trust his own eyes'. It seems presumptuous even to hint that one may know better what was seen than the person who saw it. And yet I am obliged to say, reluctantly and courteously, but most firmly and assuredly, that these perfectly credible eye-witnesses did not correctly interpret that which they witnessed. In these cases, it is not the eye which deceives, nor the tongue which is untruthful, but the imagination which is led astray by the association of the thing seen with an erroneous idea. I venture to say this, not with any insolent assumption of superior acumen, but because we now posses a key to the mystery which Archdeacon Deinbolt and his neighbours had not excess to, and which has only within the last few years been placed in our hands. The movements and aspect of their sea-monster are those of an animal with which we are now well acquainted, but of the existence of which the narrators of these occasional visitations were unaware; namely, the great calamary, the same which gave rise to the stories of the kraken, and which has probably been a denizen of the Skandinavian seas and fjords from time immemorial. It must be remembered, as I have elsewhere said, that until the year 1873, notwithstanding the adventure of the *Alecton* in 1861, a cuttle measuring in total length fifty or sixty feet was generally looked upon as equally mythical with the great sea-serpent. Both were popularly scoffed at, and to express belief in either was to incur ridicule. But in the year above mentioned, specimens of even greater dimensions than those quoted were met with on the coasts of Newfoundland, and portions of them were deposited in museums, to silence the incredulous and interest zoologists. When Archdeacon Deinbolt published in 1846 the declaration of Mr. Lund and his companions of the fishing excursion he and they knew nothing of there being such an animal. They had formed no conception of it, nor had they the instructive privilege, possessed of late years by the public in England, of being able to watch attentively, and at leisure, the habits and movements of these strangely modified mollusks living in great tanks of sea-water in aquaria. If they had been thus acquainted with them, I believe they would have recognized in their supposed snake the elongated body of a giant squid."

"When swimming, these squids propel themselves backwards by the outrush of a stream of water from a tube pointed in a direction contrary to that in which the animal is proceeding. The tail part, therefore, goes in advance, and the body tapers towards this, almost to a blunt point. At a short distance from the actual extremity two flat fins project from the body, one on each side, so that this end of the squid's body somewhat resembles in shape the government 'broad arrow'. It is a habit of these squids, the small species of which are met with in some localities in teeming abundance, to swim on the smooth surface of the water in hot and calm weather. The arrow-headed tail is then raised out of water, to a height which in a large individual might be three feet or more; and, as it precedes the rest of the body, moving at the rate of several miles an hour, it of course looks, to a person who has never heard of an animal going tail first at such a speed, like the creature's head. The appearance of this 'head' varies in accordance with the lateral fins being seen in profile or in broad expanse. The elongated, tubular-looking body gives the idea of the neck to which the 'head' is attached; the eight arms trailing behind (the tentacles are always coiled away and concealed) supply the supposed mane floating on each side; the undulating motion in swimming, as the water is alternately drawn in and expelled, accords with the description, and the excurrent stream pouring aft from the locomotor tube, causes a long swirl and swell to be left in the animal's wake, which, as I have often seen, may easily be mistaken for an indefinite prolongation of its body. The eyes are very large and prominent, and the general tone of colour varies through every tint of brown, purple, pink, and grey, as the creature is more or less excited, and the pigmentary matter circulates with more or less vigour through the curiously moving cells."

"Here we have the 'long marine animal' with 'two fins on the forepart of the body near the head', the 'boiling of the water', the 'moving in undulations', the 'body round, and of a dark colour', the 'waving motion in the water behind the animal', from which the witnesses concluded that 'part of the body was concealed under water', the 'head raised, but the lower part not visible', the 'sharp snout', the 'smooth skin', and the appearance described by Mr. William Knudtzon, and Candidatus Theologiae Bochlum, of 'the head being long and small in proportion to the throat, the latter appearing much greater than the former', which caused them to think 'it was *probably* furnished with a mane'. Not that they *saw* any mane, but as they had been told of it, they thought they *ought to have seen it*. Less careful and conscientious persons would have persuaded themselves, and declared on oath, that they *did see it*."

"I need scarcely point out how utterly irreconcileable is the proverbially smooth, gliding motion of a serpent, with the supposition of its passage through the water causing such frictional disturbance that 'white foam appeared before it, and at the side, which stretched out several fathoms', and of 'the water boiling around it on both sides of it'. The cuttle is the only animal that I know of that would cause this by the effluent current from its 'syphon tube.' I have seen a deeply laden ship push in front of her a vast hillock of water, which fell off on each side in foam as it was parted by her bow; but that was of man's construction. *Nature* builds on better lines. No swimming creature has such unnecessary friction to overcome. Even the seemingly unwieldy body of a porpoise enters and passes through the water without a splash, and nothing can be more easy and graceful than the feathering action of the flippers of the awkward-looking turtle."

Again I beg my readers to read the above-mentioned account, that they may decide for themselves, whether the animal was a sea-serpent or a great calamary. Mr. Lee's last views of the motion of sea-animals is also wrong; I make bold to contradict here all his assertions; for instance, he says: "*Nature* builds on better lines". I say: If nature built on better lines, men would long ago have imitated them. All creatures, when swimming rapidly on the surface, cause a splash. Swans, when moving as rapidly as possible, cause heavy undulations before the chest, and I have observed myself the common porpoises in the Zuider Zee, which when coming to the surface to breathe, caused a splash and a rushing of water, which all who were on board distinctly saw and heard.

The sea-serpent of Mr. Morries Stirling (n°. 113) appeared, according to Mr. Henry Lee also "to have been, like the others from the same locality, a large calamary."

Of the sea-serpent seen by Captain M'Quhae and his officers he says:

"Of course neither Professor Owen, nor any one else, doubted the veracity or *bona fides* of the captain and officers of one of Her Majesty's ships; and their testimony was the more important because it was that of men accustomed to the sights of the sea. Their practised eyes would, probably, be able to detect the true character of anything met with afloat even if only partially seen, as intuitively as the Red Indian reads the signs of the forest or the trail; and therefore they were not likely to be deceived by any of the objects with which sailors are familiar. They would not be deluded by seals, porpoises, trunks of trees, or Brobdingnagian stems of Algae; but there was one animal with which they were not familiar, of the existence of which they were unaware, and which, as I have said, at that date was generally believed to be as unreal as the sea-serpent itself—namely, the great calamary, the elongated form of which has certainly in same other instances been mistaken for that of a sea-snake. One of these seen swimming in the manner I have described, and endeavoured to portray, would fulfil the description given by Lieutenant Drummond, and would in a great measure account for the appearances reported by Captain M'Quhae. *'The head long, pointed and flat on the top'*, accords with the pointed extremity and caudal fin of the squid. *'Head kept horizontal with the surface of the water, and in rather a raised position, disappearing occasionally beneath a wave for a very brief interval, and not apparently for purposes of respiration.'* A perfect description of the position and action of a squid swimming. *'No portion of it perceptably used in propelling it through the water, either by vertical or horizontal undulations.'* The mode of propulsion of a squid—the outpouring stream of water from its locomotor tube—would be unseen and unsuspected, because submerged. Its effect, the swirl in its wake, would suggest a prolongation of the creature's body. The numerous arms trailing astern at the surface of the water would give the appearance of a mane. I think it not impossible that if the officers of the *Daedalus* had been acquainted with this great sea-creature the impression on their mind's eye would not have taken the form of a serpent. I offer this, with much diffidence, as a suggestion arising from recent discoveries; and by no means insist on its acceptance; for Captain M'Quhae, who had a very close view of the animal, distinctly says that 'the head was, without any doubt, that of a serpent', and one of his officers subsequently declared that the eye, the mouth, the nostril, the colour, and the form were all most distinctly visible."

And of the sea-serpent of Mr. R. Davidson (n°. 93) he asserts: "The features of this incident are consistent with his having seen one of the, then unknown, great calamaries."

The sea-serpent, seen by Lieutenant Sanford (n°. 74) is also explained by him to be "evidently a great squid seen under circumstances similar to those described by Hans Egede".

Captain Harrington's sea-serpent (n°. 131), according to Mr. Lee, "was evidently, again, a large calamary raising its caudal extremity and fin above the surface, and discolouring the water by discharging its ink."

Considering and weighing various explanations hitherto given, Mr. Lee concludes: "I am convinced that, whilst naturalists have been searching amongst the vertebrata for a solution of the problem, the great unknown, and therefore unrecognized, calamaries by their elongated cylindrical bodies and peculiar mode of swimming, have played the part of the sea-serpent in many a well-authenticated incident."

In answering, again, Mr. Gosse's question: "To which of the recognized classes of created beings can this huge rover of the ocean be referred?" he says: "I reply: To the Cephalopoda. There is not one of the above judiciously summarized characteristics that is not supplied by the great calamary, and its ascertained habits and peculiar mode of locomotion."

With these "above summarized characteristics" are meant those which Mr. Gosse enumerates in his *Romance of Natural History* (see p. 318 of the present volume), but which, as we know, are taken by him from only six reports of true sea-serpents, and from a report of a would-be sea-serpent!

The reader will remember that, on one occasion, I explained a would-be sea-serpent by reference to a large calamary, because the head was described "acute" and the colour "crimson". All true sea-serpents are brownish black, and only in case the animal had swam for a long time in the sun and partly above the surface of the water, the colour is yellowish, grey or greyish. It is true that this colour partly agrees with that of a calamary, when quite at rest or when dead; but generally, when the animal is in motion, and especially in emotion, the colour becomes a reddish-purple or crimson-red. Moreover the long neck, the mane, the extraordinary long tail, the four flappers, are not explained by reference to a calamary.

The **twenty-third** explanation is proposed by Mr. Searles V. Wood, Jun. in *Nature* of November 18th., 1880. His article on the "Order Zeuglodontia" closes with the following parenthesis:

"[The animal seen from the *Osborne*, and figured in the *Graphic* of June 30th., 1877, as "the sea-serpent", is quite a different thing from the one in question, and may have been **a manatee**.]"

This figure is our figure 45. Evidently Mr. Wood did not read the account accurately, and so came to a hasty supposition based on a figure only. The length of the visible part of the animal seen from the *Osborne*, i. e. "from its crown or top to just below the shoulders, where it became immersed", was "about fifty feet", and the length of the flappers "each about fifteen feet". So this animal had an enormous neck. Now the manatee or sea-cow has a total length of ten feet, the length from the crown or top to just below the shoulders is not more than four feet. and there is no question of a neck, as our figure will show. Mr. Wood committed the mistake, like so many others, that he explained *one* sea-serpent, instead of first comparing *all* the reports of it before giving an opinion.

FIG. 71.—*THRICHECHUS MANATUS* LINNÉ.

Let us now place all these explanations side by side. According, to different authorities, the sea-serpent may be:
1. A row of porpoises. (Rev. Alden Bradford, 1803).
2. *Scoliophis atlanticus*, a new species of snake with bunches on its back. (Hon. John Davis, Prof. Jacob Bigelow, Mr. C. F. Gray, 1817).
3. A large tunny. (Prof. Thomas Say, 1818).
4. A true sea-snake (*Hydrophis*) of very large size. (Mr. Constant Samuel Rafinesque Schmaltz, 1819).
5. A gigantic individual of the eel-tribe. (Mr. Constant Samuel Rafinesque Schmaltz, 1819).
6. A fable, arisen from Northern Mythology. (Dr. Percy, 1820?).
7. A basking shark, or a row of sharks. (Mr. Samuel L. Mitchill, 1828).
8. A balaenopterous whale, or a row of them. (Mr. Samuel L. Mitchill 1828).
9. An *Ichthyosaurus*, or a saurian allied to it. (Mr. R. Bakewell, 1830?).
10. A *Plesiosaurus*, or a saurian allied to it. (Professor Benjamin Silliman, 1830?).
11. Not a saurian. (Prof. Benjamin Silliman, 1835).
12. A row of spermwhales. (Professor Hermann Schlegel, 1837).
13. A *Basilosaurus*. (Professor Matthias Jacob Schleiden, 1847).
14. A *Saccopharynx* or an *Ophiognathus*. (Anonymous writer in one of the daily papers, 1848, Nov. 6?).
15. A large boa. (Anonymous writer in one of the daily papers, 1848, Nov. 6?).
16. A *Macrorhinus leoninus*, or sea-elephant. (Professor Richard Owen , 1848 , Nov. 9).
17. A large sea-weed. (Commander J. A. Herriman, of the Brazilian, 1849).
18. A large ribbon-fish, *Gymnetrus* or *Regalecus*. (Mr. A G. More, 1856).
19. A floating dead tree, or bamboo, or a weed-laden log of wood. (Mr. Arthur Adams, 1860).
20. A mass of flying birds. (Mr. Joseph Drew, 1878).
21. A large sea-turtle. (Mr. Andrew Wilson, 1879).
22. A gigantic calamary. (Mr. Andrew Wilson, 1879? or Mr. Henry Lee, 1883).
23. A manatee. (Mr. Searles Valentine Wood Jun., 1880).

I have bracketed the names of the authors who, as far as I could discover, were the first to express the supposition to which their name is added. The dates are those at which they published their supposition.

Of all these explanations those are the best, which are not the result of reading *one single* report (1, 3, 4, 5, 11, 14, 15, 16), which are not mere suppositions without any foundation (6, 7, 8, 12, 13, 21, 23), which are not offered by persons who a moment ago saw a deceitful object or animal (17, 18, 19, 20, 22), but which are the result of a *study* of several accounts and reports. They are those marked 2, 9 and 10. And of these n°. 10 is the most admissible, because the *Plesiosaurus* in its outlines most resembles the sea-serpent. Why, however, is the sea-serpent not a *Plesiosaurus?* I have already summed up some reasons, when treating of this explanation, but the principal reasons are the mammalian characters, habits and behaviour of the sea-serpent; I will try to prove this in the next chapter.

6 Conclusions.

The Libraries from which I borrowed the greater part of the works treating of the subject were:

The Royal Library at the Hague,
The Library of the Leiden University,
The Library of the Utrecht University,
The Library of the Groningen University,
The Library of the Amsterdam University,
The Library of the Royal University at Göttingen,
The Library of the Royal Zoological Society "Natura Artis Magistra" at Amsterdam,
The Library of the Royal Academy of Sciences at Amsterdam,
The Library of the Museum of Natural History at Leiden,
The Library of the Dutch Zoological Society at den Helder, and
The Library of the Dutch Entomological Society at Leiden.

In the part headed *Literature on the Subject* I have given an idea of the mass of works and articles written about it. I here present to my readers a list of the different appearances found by me in the works which I have consulted. Of each appearance I have noted down as far as possible, the date, the locality and the names of the observers. The numbers correspond with those in the 4th. Chapter.

1.—1522.—Near the Isle of Moos, Norway.
2.—1640.—Most probably in the Sound between Sweden and Denmark.—Burgomaster of Malmö.
3.—1687.—Damsfjord in Norway.—Several persons, and at one time eleven persons together.
4.—1720.—A little inlet near Kobbervueg, in Norway.—Thorlack Thorlacksen.
5.—1734, July 6.—Before the harbour of Gothaab in Davis' Straits, west of Greenland, at 64° N.—Rev. Hans Egede, Rev. Bing.
6.—1743?—Cliffs near Amund in Nordfjord, in Norway.
7.—1744?—Isle of Karmen, in Norway.
8.—1745?—Near Sundsland, two miles from Bergen, in Norway.—A fisherman.
9.—1746, August.—Jule-Naess, six miles from Molde, in Norway.—The Hon. Lorenz von Ferry, Niels Petersen Kopper, and Niels Nielsen Anglewigen.
10.—1747?—Coast of Norway.—Commander Benstrup.

11.—1748?—Coast of Norway.—Mr. Reutz.
12.—1749?—Coast of Norway.—Mr. Tuchsen.
13.—1750?—Coast of Norway.—A north-sailor.
14.—1751?—Near Sundsmöer.—Some fishermen.
15.—1751—Near Muscongus-Island and Round Pond in Broad Bay, Maine, U.S.A.—Mr. Joseph Kent.
16.—1770?—East coast of U. S. A.—Captain Paul Reed.
17.—1777 or 1778.—Penobscot Bay, Maine, U.S.A.—Captain Eleazar Crabtree.
18.—1779?—Penobscot Bay, Maine, U.S.A.—Mr. Stephan Tuckey.
19.—1780, May.—Near Muscongus Island and Round Pond, in Broad Bay, U.S.A.—Captain George Little, of the *Boston* frigate.
20.—1781?—Off Meduncook, east coast of U.S.A.
21.—1782?—East coast of U.S.A?—The British on their expedition to Bagadusa.
22.—1783?—Near the Isle of Mount Desert, east of Penobscot Bay, Maine, U.S.A.—Inhabitants of this isle.
23.—1784?—Near Ash Point on Fox and Long Island, Maine, U.S.A.—Mr. Crocket.
24.—1785?—Penobscot Bay, Maine, U.S.A.—Mr. Miller.
25.—1786, August 1.—Lat. 42° 44' N., long. 23° 10' W., north-east of the Azores.—On board the *General Coole*.
26.—1787?—East coast of U.S.A.—Captain Lillis.
27.—1794?—Near Fox and Long Islands, Maine, U.S.A.—Two inhabitants of these islands.
28.—1799?—Near Fox and Long Islands, Maine, U.S.A.—Two inhabitants of these islands.
29.—1802, July.—Between Cape Rosoi and Long Island, Maine, U.S.A.—The Rev. Abraham Cummings, Mrs. Cummings, Miss Cummings, Miss Martha Spring.
30.—1805?—Near Cape Breton and Newfoundland.—Mr. W. Lee.
31. —1808, June.—Coast of Coll, west of Scotland.—Rev. Donald Maclean.
32.—1808, June.—Coast of Canna and Rum, west of Scotland.—The crew of thirteen fishing boats.
33.—1810?—?—A mariner.
34.—1815, June 20.—Warren's Cove, near Plymouth, in Cape Cod Bay, Mass., U.S.A.—Captain Elkanah Finney, his son, and some house carpenters.
35.—1815, June 21.—Warren's Cove, near Plymouth, in Cape Cod Bay, Mass., U.S.A.—Captain Elkanah Finney.
36.—1816?—Near Behring's Island.—Mr. Kriukof.
37.—1817, August 6.—Harbour of Cape Ann.—Two women.
38.—1817, August 10.—Near Ten Pound Island in the Harbour of Gloucester, Mass., U.S.A.—Mr. Amos Story.
39.—1817, August 12.—Harbour of Gloucester, Mass., U.S.A.—Mr. Salomon Allen, 3d.
40.—1817, August 13.—Harbour of Gloucester, Mass., U.S.A.—Mr. Salomon Allen, 3d.
41.—1817, August 14.—Harbour of Gloucester, Mass., U.S.A.—Mr. Salomon Allen 3d., Mr. Epes Ellery, Mr. William H. Foster, Mr. Matthew Gaffney, Mr. Daniel Gaffney, Mr. Augustin M. Webber, and the Hon. Lonson Nash.
42.—1817, August 15.—Harbour of Gloucester, Mass., U.S.A.—Mr. James Mansfield.

43.—1817, August 17.—Harbour of Gloucester, Mass., U.S.A.—Mr. William H. Foster, Mr. John Johnston, jun., Captain John Corliss, Mr. George Marble.

44.—1817, August 18.—Off Cape Ann Harbour, Mass., U.S.A.—The Captain and crew of a vessel.—Webber's Cove in the Harbour of Gloucester, Mass., U.S.A.—Mr. William B. Pearson, Mr. James P. Collins, Colonel T. H. Perkins, Mr. Lee.

45.—1817, August 22? Harbour of Gloucester, Mass., U.S.A.—A woman, Mr. Mansfield and Mrs. Mansfield.

46.—1817, August 23.—Harbour of Gloucester, Mass., U.S.A.—Mr. Amos Story.

47.—1817, August 24?—Harbour of Gloucester, Mass., U.S.A.—Several of the crews of coasting vessels.

48.—1817, August 28.—Two miles east of the eastern point of Cape Ann, Mass., U.S.A.—Captain Sewell Toppan, of the schooner *Laura*, William Somerby, Robert Bragg, mariners on board the same schooner.

49.—1817, August 30?—In the neighbourhood of Cape Ann, Mass., U.S.A.—One of the revenue cutters.

50.—1817, October 3.—In the sound between Long Island and the State New York, U.S.A.—Mr. James Guion.

51.—1817, October 5.—Long Island Sound, N. York, U.S.A.—Mr. Thomas Hertell.

52.—1818, June.—Off Cape Henry, Virg., U.S.A.—The Captain and crew of the brig *Wilson*.

53.—1818, June 19.—In Sag Harbour, Long Island, N. Y., U.S.A.

54.—1818, June 21.—East coast of U.S.A.—S. West, master of the Packet *Delia*.

55.—1818, July 2.—Between Cranch Island Point and Marsh Island, about seven miles from Portland, Maine, U.S.A.—Mssrs. J. Webber and R. Hamilton.

56.—1818, July.—60° N. latitude and 8° W. longitude, between Far Oer and Hebrides.—Captain Brown.

57.—1818 July.—Folden fjord, Norway.—Some fishermen of Folden fjord.

58.—1818 August ?—Near Fieldvigen, Norway.—Fishermen of Fieldvigen.

59.—1818 August 19.—Harbour of Gloucester, Mass., U.S.A.—Captain Richard Rich.

60.—1819, June 6.—About 15 miles north-west of Race Point, Mass., U.S.A.—Captain Hawkins Wheeler, of the sloop *Concord*, and Gersham Bennett.

61.—1819, July.—Sound between the Island of Ottersum and the continent, Norway.—Captain Schilderup and about thirty other persons.

62.—1819, August 12?—At Nahant Beach, Mass., U.S.A.

63.—1819, August 13?—Near Nahant, Mass., U.S.A.—Mr. James Prince, Mr. Smith, Mrs. Prince, Mr. James Magee, Mr. Samuel Cabot, Mrs. Cabot, Mr. James Boott, Colonel T. H. Perkins, Mrs. Perkins, and family.

64.—1819, August.—Vieg or Veg fjord, Norway.—John Gregar.

65.—1819, August?—At the North Cape.—Some fishermen.

66.—1819, August?—Bay of Shuresund or Sorsund in the Drontheim fjord, Norway.—The Right Rev. Bishop of the Nordlands and Finmark.

67.—1819? August?—In the Magerōe-Sund near North Cape, Norway.—The sexton of Maasōe.

68.—1819, August.—Near Vadsōe, Norway.—Several persons.

69.—1819, August 26.—Harbour of Gloucester, Mass., U.S.A.—The Rev. Cheever Felch, Captain William T. Malbone, of the schooner *Science*, Midshipman Blake, four boatsmen.

70.—1819, September?—Near Boston, Mass., U.S.A.—An Officer of the American Navy.

71.—1819, September 13?—Bay of Massachusetts, U.S.A.
72.—1820, July?—Near Hundsholm, Norway.—A young man, master of a small fishing yacht.
73.—1820, August.—Near Nahant, Mass., U.S.A.—Several members of the family of Colonel T. H. Perkins.
74 —1820?—About latitude 46°, longitude 3°, Bay of Biscay.—Lieutenant George Sandford, Captain of the *Lady of Combermere*.
75.—1821, Summer.—Several members of the family of Colonel T. H. Perkins.
76.—1821.—Near the east coast of U.S.A.—Captain Bennett.
77.—1821, September 25?—Near Nantucket Isle.—Many persons, Mr. Francis Joy Jun.
78.—1821.—Off the Isles of Stenness, Vaily and Dunrossness (Shetland Islands).
79.—1822—Summer.—Off Soröe, Norway.—Many inhabitants of Soröe.
80.—1824, January.—Lat. 34° 31' South, long. 48° West, about sixty miles east of Uruguay.
81.—1824, Summer.—Off Plum Island and in Shad Cove (Rhode Island?), U.S.A.—Mr. Ruggles.
82. — 1825?—West coast of Scotland?—Mr. Andrew Strang.
83.—1826, June 16.—George's Bank, South of Newfoundland.—Captain Holdrege of the ship *Silas Richards*, Mr. Warburton, Miss. Magee.
84.—1826, June 18.—Off Cape Cod, Mass., U.S.A.—Captain and crew of a vessel.
85.—1827, August 24.—Christiana fjord, Norway.—Five persons.
86.—1827, August 26.—Christiania fjord, Norway.—Several persons.
87.—1827, September 3.—Off Nusodden, Norway (Christiania fjord?).
88.—1827, September 5.—Off Lepager (Christiania fjord?), Norway.
89.—1827, September 9.—Off Dröbak, Christiania fjord, Norway.—Several persons.
90.—1828?—Christiansund fjord, Norway.—Nils Roe.
91.—1828?—Christiansund fjord, Norway.—Nils Roe.
92. — 1829? July.—Christiansund fjord, Norway.—Lars Johnöen.
93.—1829, the end of July.—A considerable distance southwest of the Cape of Good Hope.—Captain Petrie, of the *Royal Saxon*, and Mr. R. Davidson.
94.—1830?—Christiansund fjord, Norway.—John Joeinson.
95.—1831?—In a narrow fjord near Christiansund, Norway.—Mr. William Knudtzon, Mr. Booklune.
96.—1832, Summer.—Rödö and Södelöw fjords, Norway.—Many persons.
97.—1833, May, 15.—Some miles from Margaret's Bay, Nova Scotia.—Captain W. Sullivan, Lieutenants A. Maclachlan, G. P. Malcolm, B. O' Neal Lyster, Mr. Henry Ince.
98.—1833, July, on a Saturday.—Off Nahant, Mass., U.S.A.—Several persons.
99.—1833, July, the next Sunday.—Lynn Harbour, Mass., U.S.A.—Forty or fifty ladies and gentlemen.
100.—1834, Summer.—Bay of Gloucester Mass., U.S.A.—One of the crew of the Brig *Mangehan*.
101.—1835, March or April.—A few miles from Race Point Light, near Gloucester, Mass., U. S. A.—Captain Shibbles, and the crew, of the brig *Mangehan*.
102.—1836?—In Christiansund fjord, at Torvig, Norway.—Mr. Gaeschke.
103.—1837, end of July.—Near Storfosen and the Krovaag Isles (Drontheim) Norway.—A trustworthy and intelligent gentleman, with his two sons, and numerous people.

104.—1838?—The South Atlantic.—Captain Beechy, of the *Blossom*.
105.—1839, August?—Near Boston.—Captain Bubier.
106.—1839, September?—Coast of Maine, U.S.A.—Captain Smith.
106 A.—1840, April 21.—24° 13' N. latitude, 89° 52' W. longitude, in the Gulf of Mexico.—Captain D'Abnour.
106 B.—1840, June?—Near Boston?
107.—1840, July?—Molde fjord, Norway.—Mr. Hammer, Mr. Kraft, and some other persons.
107 A.—1840, August ?—"Along the whole line of the American coast", i. e. of the east coast of the U.S.
108.—1841.—Christiansund fjord, Norway.—Several persons.
109.—1842?—Romsdal fjord, Norway.—A parish priest.
110.—1842?—Romsdal fjord, Norway.—A gentleman.
111.—1843, Summer.—Christiansund fjord, Norway.
111A.—1843, October?—Near Ibbestad, not far from Christiansand, Norway.— Some fishermen.
112.—1845?—Near Bergen? Norway.—Some fishermen.
113.—1845.—Between Bergen and Sogn, Norway.—Mr. J. D. Morries Stirling, and two other gentlemen.
114.—1845 or 1846, Summer.—Camp's Bay, near Cape Town.—Mr. G. D. Brunette, Mr. Charles A. Fairbridge.
115.—1845, July 28.—Romsdale fjord, Norway.—Mr. J. C. Lund, Mr. G. S. Kroch, Christian Flang and John Elgenses.
117.—1846, August 8.—Between the islands of Sartor Leer and Tös, and in Bjornfjord, near Bergen, Norway.—Several persons, Daniel Salomonson, his wife Ingeborg, Abraham Abrahamsen Hagenoes.
118.—1848, August 6.—Lat. 24° 44' S., long 9° 22' E., between the Cape of Good Hope and St. Helena.—Mr. Sartoris, midshipman, Lieutenant Edgar Drummond, Captain Peter M'Quhae, Mr. William Barrett, master, and most of the officers and crew of H. M. S. *Daedalus*.
119.—1848?—The Gulf of California.—Captain the Hon. George Hope.
120.—1848, December 31.—Lat. 41° 13' N., long. 12° 31' W., west of Oporto.— An officer of H. M. S. *Plumper*.
121.—1849, February 18.—Off the south point of Cumberland Island, about twelve miles from the St. John's bar, Florida.—Captain Adams, of the schooner *Lucy and Nancy*, and the crew and passengers of it.
122.—1849, May 30.—South of Australia, between 40° and 45° S. lat., and 110° and 145° W. long.—Captain Edwards, of the *Alpha*, Mr. Thomson, Mr. George Park.
123.—1849, September 15.—Indian Ocean, between lat. 10° and 20° S., and long. 50° and 70° E.—An officer of H. M. S. *Cleopatra*.
124.—1850?—Between Iceland and the Far Oer.—Captain Cristmas.
125.—1853?—Fjords of Norway.
126.—1854, September 4.—Lat. 38° S., long. 13° E.—The Brig *Albeona*.
127.—1855, August?—Off St. Helena.—A Captain.
128.—1856, March 30.—Lat. 29° 11' N., long. 34° 26' W.—Mr. J. H. Statham, Captain James Guy, of the *Imogen*, Mr. Julian B. Harries, Mr. D. J. Williamson.
129.—1856, July 8.—Lat. 34° 56' S., long. 18° 41' E.—Captain A. K. W. Tremearne of the ship *Princess*, Captain Morgan, of the ship *Senator*.

130.—1857, February 16.—In Table Bay, Cape Town.—Dr. Biccard, his wife, daughter and two sons, Mr. Murray and Mr. Hall.

131.—1857, December 12.—North east end of St. Helena distant 10 miles.— Captain George Henry Harrington, of the ship *Castilian*, William Davies, chief officer, Edward Wheeler, second officer.

132.—1858, January 26.—Lat. 19° 10' S., long. 10° 6' W., between the Cape of Good Hope and St. Helena.—Captain Suckling of the *Carnatic*, Captain Shuttleworth.

133.—1861? August, on a Sunday.—Nahant?—Dr. Amos Binney, and above a hundred persons.

134.—1861? August, the following Monday.—Nahant? from the piazza of the hôtel.

135.—1863, May 16.—Between the Isles of Canary and the Cape Verde Isles.— Mr. John Chapple, Rev. Mr. Smith, on board the Screw Steamer *Athenian*.

136.—1871.—Near the coast of Australia.—A second officer.

137.—1872, August 20.—The Sound of Sleat between the Isle of Skye and the west coast of Scotland, and between Eigg and the mainland.—Rev. John Macray, Minister of Glenelg, Rev. David Twopeny, Vicar of Stockbury, two ladies, F. and K., a gentleman, G. B., and a Highland lad, on board the cutter *Leda*; also a Lady at Duisdale, in Skye.

138.—1872, August 21.—On the north side of the opening of Loch Hourn, west coast of Scotland, and in the same Strait of Kylerhea, dividing Skye from the mainland.—The same witnesses as of n°. 137; the ferrymen on each side of Kylerhea, Finlay Macrae, and other people.

139.—1872, August 23.—In the entrance of Lochduich.— Alexander Macmillan and his brother Farquehar.

140.—1872, August 24.—In the same locality.—The same witnesses.

141.—1873, Nov. 10?—Near Dunrobin castle, east coast of Sutherland, Scotland.— Lady Florence Leveson Gower and the Hon. Mrs. Coke.

142.—1873, Nov. 17?—Near Golspie, east coast of Sutherland, Scotland.—Dr. Soutar.

143.—1873, Nov. 18?—The same locality.—Mr. James.

144.—1875, July 8.—Lat. 5° 13' S., long. ,35° W., twenty miles from Cape San Roque.—Captain Drevar, of the barque *Pauline*, Horatio Thompson, John Henderson Landells, William Lewarn, Owen Baker.

145.—1875, July 13.—Lat. 5° S., long 34° 10' W., eighty miles from Cape San Roque.—The same witnesses.

146.—1876, September 11.—Fifteen miles north west of North Sand Lighthouse, in the Malacca Straits.—John K. Webster, Captain of the British s. s. *Nestor*, and Mr. James Anderson.

147.—1877, May 21.—Lat. 2° N., long. 90° 53' E., Indian Ocean.—The master of the barque Georgina.

148.—1877, June 2.—Off Cape Vito, Sicily.—Commander Pearson of H. M. Yacht *Osborne*, Mr. Douglas Hanes, Mr. Forsyth, and Mr. Moore.

149.—1879, January 28.—Lat. 12° 28' N., long 43° 52 E., Gulf of Aden.—Major H. W. J. Senior, Dr. C. Hall, Miss. Greenfield, on board the s. s. *City of Baltimore*.

150.—1879, March 30.—In Geographe Bay, Australia, near Lockville and Busselton.—Rev. H. W. Brown, Mr. C. M'Guire and his wife, Mr. M'Mullan.

151.—1879, April 5.—Cape Satano, the most southern point of Japan, distant about nine miles.—Captain Davison, Mr. Mc. Kechnie, of the *Kiushiu Maru*.

152.—1879, August 5.—100 miles west of Brest, France.—Captain J. F. Cox, of the *Privateer*.

152 A.—1881, Nov. 12?—Near Monillepoint, not far from Cape Town.—Mr. C. M. Hansen, his wife and children, and several of his neighbours.

153.—1882, May 28.—About six miles W. N. W. of Butt of Lewis (the northern point of the Hebrides or Western Islands).—Some fishermen.

154.—1882, May 31.—The same locality.—Mr. Weisz of the Lloydsteamer *Kätie*, Mr. Andrew Schultz.

155.—1882, September 3.—Near Orme's Heads, northern coast of Wales? Irish Sea.—Mr. W. Barfoot, Mr. F. J. Marlow, Mrs. Marlow, and several other ladies and gentlemen.

156.—1883, October 15.—Bristol Channel.

157.—1885, August 16.—Between Rödö and Melö Isles, Nordland, Norway, at lat. 66° 35' N., long. 13° 21' E.—Some lads.

158.—1886, August.—Near Kingston Point on the Hudson, New Jersey, U.S.A.— Two young men.

159.—1886, August.—Near the east coast of U.S.A.

160.—1886, August.—Near the east coast of U.S.A.—Jonah.

161.—1889, May.—In the common track from Liverpool to Philadelphia.—A captain.

162.—1890, June.—Near Long Island, not far from the coast of Connecticut.— Captain David Tuits of the schooner *Anny Harper*.

In these reports nearly all is very probable from a zoological point of view, and there is but little that must be looked upon as fabulous.

Some statements, which at first seem to us to be exaggerations, we unhesitatingly accept as truths, when we have taken a review of all the reports together; either because they are constantly repeated, or because they are confirmed by highly respectable testimonies of recent date.

What now follows is an abstract of the 166 reports, enumerated above. The numbers in brackets correspond with those placed in the List given above, consequently also with those in my 4th. Chapter. Let us first speak of the improbable things.

A. Fables, Fictions, Exaggerations and Errors.

At present nobody believes that the appearance of a strange animal on the coast is a bad sign! In the sixteenth and the seventeenth century, however, this was not uncommon. So we read that an appearance of a sea-serpent portended a change in Norway (1), and that the appearance of one in 1522 was followed by the banishment of King Christiernus and by a great persecution of the Bishops; it also foretold the destruction of the country (1). The snatching away of a man from a ship did not happen without a terrible event in the Kingdom, without a change being at hand, either that the princes would die or be banished, or that a war would soon break out. The Norwegian fishermen looked upon its coming as a bad sign, for the fish would leave the coast (61). Curious are also the characters described to the animal. It lives in rocks and holes, and it comes out of its caverns only in summernights and fine weather, to devour calves, lambs and hogs. The eating of cuttles, lobsters and all kinds of sea-crabs may also be a story, though this is not quite improbable. The fables, often told of Kraken and Spermwhales, that when sleeping on the surface of the water they are taken for an islet, are also related of sea-serpents: "and when it is slumbering on the Norway foam, the seamen deeming it some island, fixed their anchor in its scaly rind".

It is also said to enclose ships by laying itself round them in a circle; and to upset the ship if the seamen do not try to escape, which they can manage to do when they row over its body there where a coil is visible, for that when they reach the coil, it sinks, while on the contrary the invisible part rises. Arend Berndsen tells us that sea-serpents, as well as spermwhales, often run down whole ships with all aboard, and some north sailors know that it had occasionally thrown itself across a yacht of several hundred tons and dragged it to the bottom. Mr. Lee has sufficiently shown in his *Sea Monsters Unmasked*, that large calamaries really sometimes snatch a man from a rowing boat; for a long time this was considered to be a fable; now, however, zoologists unconditionally accept it as truth. Such incidents, if happened, are generally, but falsely, attributed by the Northern fishermen to sea-serpents.

It is not astonishing that by such people the sea-serpent is called dangerous to seamen and that they are very much afraid of it (7, 14, 61, 64, 65, 67, 92, 103, 139, 157), and will never forget to take with them asa foetida or castoreum, the smell of which the animal cannot bear. Moreover the fishermen advise to be very quiet when a sea-serpent approaches, and to avoid rowing, because the least noise attracts the animal. Some believe that it casts its skin, as common snakes do, and that it is born on land, and lives in forests and mountains till it can no longer hide its enormous body in it; then it seeks some river and floats down to the sea. When swimming, sea-serpents don't show their tail above the surface. Fishermen, in their fear, would say: if one was near the head, the other end of the animal could not be seen (103). I am convinced that this is one of the reasons that the animal is sometimes said to be at least a cable in length. The animal leaves behind itself a considerable wake, which may be another reason that the witnesses exaggerated its length. So we find: it is three hundred feet long (21), about 320 feet (106 A), six hundred and seventy feet (61), about a fourth of an English mile (79), about 750 feet (85), from six hundred to 800 ells, i. e. from 1340 to 1780 feet (103), more than 500 feet (130) or half a mile long (156).

The thickness too is sometimes exaggerated (twenty feet); the head is described in some instances to be as large as a foering boat, i. e. about twenty feet long (117, 146), or twelve feet long (126), or perhaps ten feet long (118), and the tail fully a hundred and fifty feet in length (146). The jaws are said to be of such an enormous size that, if extended, they seemed sufficiently capacious to admit of a tall man standing upright in them (118). It may be that the alleged serpentine shape of the animal caused some writers to give scales to the sea-serpent, or that the distance was too large for a closer examination, so that the observers thought it might have a hard skin (5), or a rough coating (41, 51), or even a scaly one (39), or it was the fear which made them see scales (157) which in reality did not exist. Scales are also occasionally delineated (fig. 26) though the eye-witness does not mention them, and even believed it belonged to the eel-tribe (63). No wonder that such a terrible animal is often called Leviathan, an animal which raises its coils so high above the water that a ship can go through one of them. Norwegian fishermen really believe that the animal sometimes comes on land as Olaus Magnus and Pontoppidan tell us, and as is stated afterwards, when even distinct traces of it were said to have been found in the fields (96).

In my opinion it is an error to believe that there are *two* species of sea-serpents or that there are several species of them all belonging to the same genus (112). And also that the animal ever takes a boat for one of the other sex, which induces it to follow the boat. This is a habit of the animal, but as it is a quite harmless one, it is an error to believe that it grows furious when the pursued are so fortunate as to escape (158), or that it may ever destroy them, even after being struck with a boat-hook (112). That the shores of Norway are the only in Europe, which are frequented by this monster is a positive error, since the animal is known to appear also on the coasts of Great Britain, France, and even in the Mediterranean.

From what we now know of the division of the colours of the animal's body, I don't hesitate to say that they are wrongly represented in one of the drawings (fig. 31). The cetacean tail delineated in fig. 49 is explained in n°. 151, the fish tail of fig. 26 in n°. 63. The definition that the eyes were of a greenish hue and looked devilish (158) is certainly the result of an observation made in great fright. I am sure that in cases wherein the colour of the head and neck are described as a bluish green (29), or of a blue colour (29), or as blue as possible (29), and that of the back of a dark green (30), these definitions are the result of optical illusion, or the observers may have been colour-blind.

The twelve fins (129, fig. 36) of which six are drawn on the left side and six on the right side of the body emerging from the water, are undoubtedly the result of an optical deception, as I have explained in n°. 129.—In the same way I have explained why the animal has a head connected with the body without any indication of a neck, so that it resembled a gigantic salamander (146), and that it seemed to be of a gelatinous, that is flabby, substance (146), and that the motion of it was apparently corkscrew-like (155).

In no case the antenna, ending in a crescent (106A) or the ridge of fins (148), or the discolouring of the water (131) observed, have anything to do with the animal or with its appearance.

But let us now pass to the *facts* which may be inferred from what is reported of the animal.

B. Facts.

These are so numerous that I am obliged to bring them together under several heads.

1. External Characters.
a. Dimensions.

The length of what was visible of the animal above the surface of the water was estimated to be: from sixteen to eighteen feet (25), several meters (136), about twenty feet (150), from twenty to thirty feet (35), thirty feet (113, 123), about thirty-six feet (92), about forty feet (26, 41, 42, 44, 80, 91, 128, 145), forty-five feet (137), between forty and fifty feet (115, 147), fifty feet at least (43, 46, 50, 51, 60), about fifty-five feet (94), from fifty to sixty feet (63), sixty feet (57, 83, 117, 118, 129, 138, 150), seventy-five feet (152 A), eighty feet at least (97), a hundred and fifty feet (154), and, though estimated by the eye-witnesses at about fifty feet, the visible part must, according to my reckoning, have been eighty feet at least in n°. 148. These enormous differences in the statements cannot surprise us of an animal which may attain a length of more than two hundred feet. As a rule the animal swims with head and neck above the water-surface, commonly the back too is partly visible, but of the tail only a small portion. In n°. 154 as we see, a length of 150 feet of the animal was visible; in this instance it lay nearly perfectly still; only the long neck and head were under water, and the back and a great length of tail were above the surface.

The *whole length of the animal* is spoken of as: great (37, 152), large (119), very large (2), considerable (107), immense (36), astonishing (1), enormous (132), as a yacht of fifty tons (8), three or four times larger than the ship (5), eighteen feet (14), from fifty to fifty-five feet (19), from fifty to sixty feet (18), sixty feet (17, 28, 56), at least sixty feet (82), more than sixty feet (29), from sixty to seventy feet (24), from sixty to eighty feet (139, 142), about seventy feet (29), not above seventy feet (109), at least seventy feet (41), from seventy to eighty feet (31), from seventy to one hundred feet (74), seventy five feet (1, 158), about eighty feet (63), from eighty to ninety feet (39, 118), about ninety feet (121, 134), one hundred feet (17, 33, 41, 44, 45, 63, 66, 69, 135), at least a hundred feet (34), more than one hundred feet (95), greater than the animal of Captain M'Quhae, consequently probably more than one hundred feet (93), one hundred and twenty feet (34), from one hundred and twenty to one hundred and thirty feet (105), one hundred and thirty feet (69), about one hundred and fifty feet (65), from one hundred and fifty to two hundred feet (114), from one hundred and sixty to one hundred and seventy feet (34, 144), one hundred and eighty feet (126), one hundred and ninety feet (52), about 200 feet (130, 155, 157), more than two hundred feet (30, 131), and though estimated by the eye witnesses (see n°. 148) as to be at least one hundred and fifty feet, the individual seen by them must have been, according to my reckoning, more than two hundred feet long.—Such a length needs no explanation: it is *a fact*, established by the declarations of highly respectable men, and of men who are accustomed to estimate the length of objects floating in the water from afar and at any short distance. Moreover it is the enormous tail which apparently enlargens these dimensions. The elephant is of a great bulk and of an enormous weight, but the giraffe astonishes us by its enormous legs and its enormous neck, though its body and its head are smaller than that of a moderate sized horse. So the colossal spermwhales, fin whales and whalebone whales surprise us by their bulk and weight, but the sea-serpent deprived of its neck and immense tail is only a child to them. Moreover a zoologist has not one single reason to deny the possibility of the existence of sea-animals with a body of no more than sixty feet, a neck of sixty feet, and a tail of hundred and twenty feet.

The *length of the head* is, according to the different declarations: nearly as that of a man (19, 43), about the size of the crown of a hat (42), larger than that of any dog (38), as large as a hat (94), about as that of a pail (29), full as large as a four gallon keg (42), equal to a small cask (109), nearly as large as the head of a horse (39, 60), rather larger than that of a horse (29), two feet long (56, 81), of the size of a ten gallon keg (48, 80, 92, 102), as large as a barrel (101), as large as a flour barrel (158), of the size of a 54 gallon hogshead (152 A), long (118), with regard to its thickness not very long (94), long in proportion to the throat (95), about six feet in length (97), about six or eight feet long (34, 120), as large as a little boat (32), colossal (115). The head of the individual seen by the officers of H. M. S. *Daedalus* cannot have been longer than three feet, as the neck is estimated sixteen inches in diameter, though it is called long (118) or even ten feet long (118); evidently a portion of the neck was included in the calculation. The head of the individual seen by the officers of the royal yacht *Osborne* must have been from eight to nine feet long, as its breadth is estimated at six feet (148).

The *length of the neck* is said to be: long (31, 56, 119, 124), enormous, a length of ten feet was visible (48), about eighteen feet (124), about twenty feet (118), at least twenty feet (160), the neck together with the body fifty or forty-five feet, i. e. the neck alone must have been about twenty-five feet (146), about twenty five feet (149), at least twenty five feet (152), about thirty feet (151), about sixty feet (145); "from its crown or top to just below the shoulder where it became immersed, I should reckon about fifty feet", but as the eye-witness saw the animal from behind, the length of the neck could not be estimated with accuracy; as to me, I am convinced that the neck of the individual measured about sixty feet (148). The long neck is delineated in fig. 46, 48 and 49.

The length of the trunk has never been actually estimated, as nearly all the observers believed that the animal was serpent-shaped, and therefore estimated only its total length or the part exposed to their eyes. Yet we may put down the length of the trunk of the individual seen by the officers of H. M. S. *Daedalus* to be about twenty feet, as one of the hindflappers was occasionally seen at about twenty feet distant from the point where one of the foreflappers was also occasionally seen. And as this fore-flapper was visible at about twenty feet in the rear of the head, we may conclude that the length of the trunk equals that of the neck (118). Consequently we may decide that the individual observed by the Captain and the surgeon of the *Nestor*, who saw the animal swimming evidently with its neck contracted, had a neck and a trunk each of about forty feet (146). In the same way we may conclude that the individual observed by the captain and crew of the *Pauline* (145) and that seen by the officers of the royal yacht *Osborne* (148) had both a neck and a trunk of each about sixty feet.

The *tail* delineated in fig. 19, has only three times been actually estimated. Once it is called thirty five feet long (8), then forty feet long (162), and once a hundred and fifty feet long (146). In my opinion the animal's tail in this last instance cannot have been longer than about eighty feet, i. e. as long as the animal's head, neck and trunk together. The length of the individual observed by the officers of the *Daedalus* was estimated by them to be at least eighty feet. As we have reckoned above about forty three feet for head, neck and trunk together, its tail consequently must have been about forty feet long. So the animal's hind flappers are situated almost in the middle of the whole length. And therefore Egede and Bing did not observe them, because the middle part of the whole length remained hidden from them (fig. 19). Captain Hope states (119) that the animal seen from above on its back resembles an alligator with an enormous neck. If the animal had not an immense tail, he would never have made this comparison. When Captain Tremearne says "also a great length of tail" he seems to me to have included in his estimation a portion of the animal's trunk (129). The individuals seen by the officers of the *Osborne* (148), of the *Pauline* (145), and of the *Kätie* (154), undoubtedly had a tail of about one hundred or even of one hundred and twenty feet in length. Captain D'Abnour called the tail enormous (106 A).

Twice (14, 119) it has been stated that the *four flappers* were seen together; the two *fore flappers* were seen four times (5, 121, 129, 148); and delineated in fig. 19, 36, and 45; it is possible that the two *hind flappers* were twice seen (151,158), and delineated in fig. 49. Four times one of the fore-flappers was visible above the surface (106 A, 118, 137, 154) and twice one of the hindflappers (118, 154). The foreflappers are called broad and large (5), frightful, several feet in length (121), larger than the posterior (119), about fifteen feet in length (148), and of immense dimensions (154); judging from the drawing illustrating this last instance (fig. 50), I should estimate its length also at fifteen feet. Captain D'Abnour saw one of the foreflappers rising to the height of about six feet from the water and inclining itself at a considerable angle upon the body (106 A). The hindflappers are said to be smaller than the anterior (119), and about ten feet long (154).

As to the *breadth of the head*, some observers mention its diameter, and some its circumference, or they compare its thickness either with that of the neck, with that of the trunk, or with some well-known object; this is the reason that we meet with the following statements: it is rather broad (31), where the head was connected with the body (read neck) it was a little larger than the body (read neck) (34), the head was rather larger than the body (read neck) (48), much smaller than the body (69), narrow in proportion to the throat: evidently the animal had contracted its neck, so that this latter grew much thicker (69), about two feet in diameter (150), about three feet in circumference (69), at least three feet in circumference (29), about as thick as a ten gallon keg (92), about six feet thick (148).

The *neck* is somewhat smaller than the head (31), as is also stated in other accounts: smaller than the head (109), much thinner than the head (91), comparatively narrow (148), and may be two and a half feet in circumference (48), just behind the head sixteen inches thick (118), about the thickness of a man's waist (124), about two feet in diameter (149), or about four feet thick (148).

The *thickness of the animal* has commonly been compared with that of different objects, a circumstance which makes it difficult to fix the true diameter. Moreover it is in many instances difficult to make out whether the animal's neck, just behind the head, is meant by the observer, or the animal's chest or breast, which is the thickest part of the trunk. For the animal generally swims in such a way that a little part of its back rises above the surface of the water, completely hiding its thickest part and its flappers, so that it makes the impression to be a serpentine animal without any appendages, and of a uniform size. So the animal is said to be ten or twelve inches thick (147), about twelve inches (113), about fourteen inches (102), fifteen inches (19), as thick as a halfbarrel (39, 41, 44, 48, 63), as thick as a common firkin (63), about twenty two inches (17), as thick as a barrel (34, 41, 80), as thick as a man's body (46), as thick as a wine barrel (2, 85), as thick as a stout man (94), as thick as a barrel of two hogsheads (12), three feet (17), as thick as a sloop's boom (24), three to four feet in circumference (25), as thick as a full-grown ox (79), about two feet in diameter (92), inconsiderable (95), as thick as a large horse (109), he is the thickest just behind the head (103), several ells (115), as thick as our main mast (135), thirty feet from its head-end the body seemed about as thick as the ship's long-boat (126), it appeared about seven feet across the broadest part of the back (121), at the shoulder about fifteen to twenty feet (148), the shoulder was the thickest part of the body, about twenty feet (122).

The *tail-root* had, on one occasion, a diameter of four feet (146), but as it is generally hidden under water, it is only in a few instances that it was actually observed.

The *tail ends* in a point (fig. 19, fig. 20), and consequently is mostly said to resemble that of a serpent or snake. It is also said to be as pointed as a boat-hook (8), or very pointed (12).

Comparison of the dimensions. Supposing that the dimensions of the several portions of the animal are relatively nearly the same in individuals of different ages, we are able to draw up a table of comparative and relative dimensions. We learn from the officers of the *Daedalus* that the vertical diameter of the neck was about 1 1/3 feet. From the officers of the *Osborne* we have the following estimations of dimensions: horizontal diameter of the head about 6 feet, horizontal diameter of the neck about 4 feet. We know from several eye-witnesses that the neck is round, so that we may suppose that its vertical diameter is the same as its horizontal or transversal one. Consequently the transversal diameter of the neck of the *Daedalus* animal was 1 1/3 or 4/3 feet; and that of its head 6/3 = 2 feet. For a moment I will suppose that in these animals a head of about 2 feet broad has a length of about 3 feet, and this I may do, as the heads of the animals which I consider as allied to sea-serpents, have nearly these relative dimensions. In the same way I may put the length of the head of the *Osborne* individual at about 9 feet. The distance from the head to the foreflapper in the *Daedalus* animal was about twenty feet. We may consequently suppose that the same portion measured sixty feet in the individual seen by the officers of the *Osborne*. As to the question whether this portion is to be called the neck as I have done hitherto? I answer without hesitation *no*, this length also includes a portion of the animal's trunk, viz. the part from its shoulder to the point where the fore limb is free. In the animals which, in my opinion, are allied to the sea-serpent, the upper arm is, so to say, "imbedded" in the trunk's integument, is not free, as in man, and nearly immovable, and this portion is about one third of the whole length of the limb. Consequently we may conclude that, if the free part of the foreflapper is about fifteen feet, the portion of the trunk from the place where the fore limb in seated on the body to the shoulder is about seven feet and a half. Consequently the individual of the *Osborne* had a neck of about 53 feet. As the size of the individual of the *Daedalus* was about one third of that of the *Osborne*, its neck was about 17 1/2 feet long. For the same reason the foreflappers of the *Daedalus* individual were five feet in length. The distance from the foreflapper to the hind flapper in the *Daedalus* animal measured about 20 feet, consequently the *trunk* measured 22 1/2 feet, so that the distance from the foreflapper to the hindflapper of the *Osborne* animal must have been about 60 feet, and the length of its trunk about 67 feet. Summing up the lengths of the head, the neck, and the trunk, we have for the *Daedalus* animal 43 feet. This individual swam with its body in a straight line; "sixty feet at least were visible *à fleur d'eau"* are the words of Captain M'Quhae, substantiated by the reports of two of his officers. Yet it was obvious that this was not the whole length of the animal, and that a great length of tail was hidden under water. The animal was estimated to be from eighty to ninety feet in length. I have not a single reason to doubt this statement, and therefore conclude that the tail of the animal was about as long as the distance from the animal's nose to its hindflappers. But I will not be too bold and only give it a length of about forty feet. If this is within the bounds of truth, of which I don't doubt in the least, the length of the tail of the individual, seen by the officers of the *Osborne* measured about 120 feet. Captain Hope who had the opportunity to observe the four flappers together in a very favourable position, states that the foreflappers are larger than the hindflappers (119). I venture to estimate

Conclusions 375

the length of the last at about 2/3 of that of the foreflappers. So we may estimate the length of the hindflappers of the two individuals at 3 1/3 and 10 feet respectively. As to the breadth of the animal's trunk the officers of the *Osborne* state that it was from fifteen to twenty feet in their individual. We may safely suppose that the animal did not expose its greatest breadth, which must have been a little below the surface of the water, so that I don't hesitate to fix the greatest diameter at 20 or 21 feet. The body gradually diminishes towards the tail, and this in its turn towards its end, which, as we have observed, is pointed.

The reason why I have deduced my different relative proportions only from the reports of the officers of the *Daedalus* and of the *Osborne*, is that they had a very favourable opportunity to estimate them. The former saw the animal swimming with its body in a straight line, and with its neck quite stretched, not contracted, showing the greater part of its length, and swimming in such a way that it was seen just from aside, so that the different *lengths* of the portions of the body could easily be estimated. And the latter saw the animal just from behind, so that the different *breadths* of the animal could be seen; moreover the dimensions of the foreflappers were visible.

I have ventured to draw up the following table of the animal's proportions for ten individuals, differring in age or sex.

Length of head.	$3/4$	1	2	3	4	5	6	7	8	9
Length of neck.	4	6	$11^2/3$	$17^1/2$	$23^1/2$	$29^1/2$	$35^1/3$	$41^1/6$	47	53
Length of trunk.	$4^7/12$	$7^1/2$	15	$22^1/2$	$29^2/3$	$37^1/6$	$44^2/3$	$52^1/2$	$59^1/2$	67
Length of tail.	$8^2/3$	$13^1/3$	$26^2/3$	40	$53^1/3$	$66^2/3$	80	$93^1/3$	$106^2/3$	120
Total length.	18	$27^2/3$	$55^1/3$	83	$110^2/3$	$138^1/3$	166	$193^2/3$	$221^1/3$	249
From occiput to foreflappers.	$4^1/3$	$6^2/3$	$13^1/3$	20	$26^2/3$	$33^1/3$	40	$46^2/3$	$53^1/3$	60
Breadth of head.	$5/12$	$2/3$	$1^1/3$	2	$2^2/3$	$3^1/3$	4	$4^2/3$	$5^1/3$	6
Breadth of neck.	$3/12$	$4/9$	$8/9$	$1^1/3$	$1^2/3$	$2^1/6$	$2^2/3$	$3^1/9$	$3^1/2$	4
Breadth of trunk.	$1^1/3$	$2^1/3$	$4^2/3$	7	$9^1/3$	$11^2/3$	14	$16^1/3$	$18^2/3$	21
Length of foreflapper.	1	$1^2/3$	$3^1/3$	5	$6^2/3$	$8^1/3$	10	$11^2/3$	$13^1/3$	15
Length of hindflapper.	$1/9$	$1^1/6$	$2^1/3$	$3^1/2$	$4^1/2$	$5^1/2$	$6^2/3$	$7^5/6$	9	10

I am far from asserting that these dimensions will prove to be correct, if ever an individual falls into the hands of men, but I am sure that they are approximately correct.

Perhaps you will in no case admit the possibility of the existence of an animal of 250 feet! Well, I leave it to you to fix yourself the utmost possible length of our Sea-Serpent!

b. Form.

The name we give to an unknown object will naturally depend on the impression it makes on us at first sight. To some the animal was like a log of wood or a floating tree; comparisons which will be spoken of below. It is called an animal of the fish kind (60), or a most remarkable fish (118), or a very large fish (29), and to be eel-shaped (33), or to resemble a large eel (118, 152). Some persons say it appeared to be of a uniform size (34), and others that it gradually tapers towards the two extremes (41), and appeared round (43). One of the eye-witnesses says: I do not undertake to say he was of the snake or eel kind, though this was the general impression on my family, the spectators and myself (63). Generally it is compared with a snake (5, 17, 18, 25, 26, 37, 41, 44, 60, 80, 118, 135, 152) or serpent (26, 36, 39, 41, 42, 43, 44, 48, 60, 80, 103, 118, 121, 147, 157). Curious is the statement of one that it was an enormous sea-serpent, without, however, having ever heard of such an animal (132)! Remarkable is the opinion of an officer of the *Daedalus:* it was, he says, rather of a lizard than of a serpentine character, as its movement was steady and uniform, as if propelled by fins, not by any undulatory power (118). Remarkable too is Pontoppidan's comparison of an animal which he himself, believing that sea-serpents have no fins, or paws, or flappers, did not mention in his paragraph about the subject, viz. with a crocodile (14). Captain Hope who had an opportunity to observe the animal from above, described it as a large marine animal with the head and general figure of the alligator, except that the neck was much longer, and that instead of legs the creature had four flappers somewhat like those of turtles, the anterior pair being larger than the posterior (119). In my opinion the comparison of Lieutenant Haynes, of the *Osborne,* who saw the fore part of the animal from behind, deserves all our attention; he says: the animal resembled a huge seal, the resemblance being strongest about the back of the head (148, fig. 45).

The *shape of the head* has also been described in different ways. There is the statement that it is of a form somewhat oval (31); here it evidently was seen in rather an oblique direction; also that it was as round as a flour-barrel (158, evidently seen in front), and bullet-shaped (148, seen from behind, fig. 45). The head is also said to appear like a triangular rock (74), or like a nun buoy (131), or like a boat keel uppermost, and the reader has only to look at our fig. 31, to conceive how these comparisons arose. In another instance the observer declared it to have nearly the shape of a ten-gallon cask (102), which is nearly the same as "of a form somewhat oval". Major Senior asserts that the shape of the head was not unlike pictures of the dragon he has often seen (149); the explanation of this curious comparison I have given in treating of his report. The head, says somebody, resembled the end of a log (150), and: the thick bluff head had but little resemblance to a snake's (150); but he saw the animal in late evening twilight. But most eye-witnesses declare it to resemble that of a snake (29, 60, 97, 101, 118, 121), or serpent (29, 48, 61, 63, 74), or something that of a rattle snake (39); and evidently seen in a somewhat oblique direction, it is said to be shaped much like that of a sea-turtle (38). I can only explain these different comparisons by supposing that to some extent the head really resembles these various head shapes, being flattened above and somewhat blunt at its end. Though the officers of the *Daedalus*, too, compared it with that of a snake, their drawing (fig. 30) shows the head of a mammal. The proportions of the length and height, the outlines of the jaws, the extension of the mouth-split, the situation of the nostril and the eye, the flattened appearance of the forehead and nose, the bluntness of the snout and the presence of the two cushions on the crown of the head (the external visible masticatory muscles) are true mammalian characters. It therefore is not wonderful also to find such a head compared with that of a bull-dog (152A), that of a walrus (129), that of a seal (8, 29, 148), and that of a sea-lion (36). When the animal held its head at nearly right angles with its neck, which has often been the case, and opened its nostrils as wide as possible (and the nostrils are exceedingly large), such a head, with its flattened nose and forehead, and with its somewhat protruding eyes, resembled that of a horse (9, 63, 124). We observe that the head is compared with *seven* different head-shapes, *five* of which are mammalian. It is obvious that the observers compared it with the heads of those animals which involuntarily and at once occurred to them. To which of these types are we to direct our attention? Which of these types will the sea-serpent's head resemble most? I say, that of the sea-lion. And why? Because the animal, with the head of which that of the sea-serpent was compared, was not present at the time, except in Mr. Kriukof's case. He was daily surrounded by sea-lions; the image of the sea-lion's head was as firmly impressed on his memory as that of a dog on his master's; and I greatly doubt whether the other observers were acquainted with sea-lions. These animals, especially the species of the Northern Pacific, are only of late years to be seen in the zoological gardens, and it remains to be found out whether the most recent eye-witnesses of the sea-serpent ever saw a sea-lion, and if so, whether the features of the animal had been impressed on their memory so as to recognize the same shape in the head of another animal. Moreover the head of a sea-lion, especially that of *Zalophus californianus* has some resemblance to a snake's.

The *neck* being round is said to resemble "something of a serpent's (74), or of a common snake's (97, 101), and tapering small from the head to the body (121). It is obvious that this observer used the expression "tapering" in a sense contrary to the usual one, for he had a fair opportunity to see the animal's head, long neck and upper part of the trunk with the two foreflappers, and he goes on with the words: and it appeared to measure about seven feet across the broadest part of the back.

The *trunk* must be broadest before and smallest behind, as may be inferred from the following statements: its shoulders are considerably broader than the head (31), from the shoulders it tapered towards the tail (31, 39, 91, 150), the breadth diminished remarkably towards the tail (92), from the shoulder (estimated to be about twenty feet) diminishing towards the tail to about twenty four inches (122), evidently the end of the latter was hidden under water. Moreover, the body is said to be round (102, 115, 117), even as a snake's (92), and on one occasion, when seen from behind, is said to be developed in form like that of a gigantic turtle (148, fig. 45), which we need not say, was the result of the upper part of the back being only visible. Remarkable is the use of the term "shoulders", for even if the flappers of the animal were never actually observed, we are now obliged to conclude that the animal was possessed of fore-limbs. Equally remarkable is the statement: "there is a distinct difference in thickness between the body and the tail; the trunk is not gradually growing smaller, where the tail begins, but at once and very distinctly" (8, 12, 146); for such an animal has rumps, and consequently also thighs and hind-limbs.

The *tail* itself is cylindrical (146), like that of a snake (101),and tapering to its end (8, 12, 146, 150, fig. 19). Twice the animal's head and tail were plainly visible above the surface (135, 162), the trunk being wholly hidden under the surface of the water; it was called a snake; the shape of the tail was not mentioned; evidently the tail was pointed, else it would have been described as resembling that of a fish or of a whale; evidently it was also tapering to its end, else it would have been described as a cord or whiplike. The same was the case in n°. 152 A; the observer firmly believed he saw an enormous serpent.

Position and shape of flappers. Hans Egede said that the animal had two flappers on the fore-part of the body (5), but the drawing of Mr. Bing, his brother missionary (fig. 19), is not accurate, as the animal's neck is drawn too small, the head too large, and the flappers themselves are badly represented. It seems, however, that the indented edge of the foreflappers did not escape the eyes of Mr. Bing. Mr. Bakewell asserts that the flappers are described to resemble those of turtles; most probably the foreflappers are meant here, as these are occasionally seen above the surface, which is hardly ever the case with the hindflappers. In an animal which was estimated at from 80 to 90 feet in length, one of the fore-flappers was occasionally visible at about twenty feet in the rear of the head, consequently at about one fourth of the whole length (118). Captain Hope states that the flappers were somewhat like those of turtles, the anterior pair being larger than the posterior (110). According to the figures 36, 45 and 50 on the right, the foreflappers resemble those of a sea-lion. In the figures 36 and 45 the hindmost edge is drawn indented. In the animal of the *Daedalus*, which was from 80 to 90 feet in length, one of the hindflappers was occasionally visible at about forty feet in the rear of the head, consequently at about the centre of the whole length (118). Of course they were invisible to Egede and Bing, as the middle part of the animal's body was hidden under water (fig. 19).

The *fore-head* is described as high and broad and flat (29, 41, 44, 60, 69, 118, 157, fig. 30), or depressed (56) and once Mr. Senior thought to observe in it, together with the eyebrow, a bull dog appearance (149).

The *snout or muzzle* is called long and sharp (5, fig. 19), sharp (115, 120), tapering to a point (48), rather pointed (91), pointed (118), though the accompanying figure (fig. 30) contradicts this, pointed like that of a porpoise (122), an elongated termination (148), not pointed but bluntly round (92), not pointed but seemed rather blunt (94), a blunt and quadrangular beak as cows and horses have, evidently with the nostrils opened as wide as possible, rather blunt (48), apparently blunt (102), bluff (150), obtuse (56), the head, estimated at eight or six feet long, consequently at five or four feet broad, tapered to the size of a horse's (34), the snout being somewhat similar in form to that of a seal (148).

The *upperjaw* projects considerably (118); we may safely read projects.

Under the jaw there was a quantity of loose skin, like a pouch (126). This it seems is occasionally the case, and it is not impossible as it even occurs in allied animals.

The *nostrils* are seldom mentioned. It is evident that the animal is able to close them; they are, however, delineated (fig. 19, fig. 24, fig. 36), or indicated with a crescentic mark (fig. 30), and mentioned to have been distinctly visible (118), and described as large. It is also evident that when the animal opens them as wide as possible, the beak appears quadrangular, as is the mouth of cows and horses. This comparison agrees with the description of the nose sides or flaps which are here said to be "nearly semicircular flaps or valves overarching the nostrils, which were in front" (143).

Of the *whiskers* Pontoppidan already tells us that on the sides of the nostrils there are a few stiff hairs or bristles, as other animals have, with a good nose. These whiskers are mentioned afterwards only once: "on the nose there are thick hairs, as on a seal's, two or three quarters of an ell long" (103). Were these whiskers not seen by them who compare the head with that of a seal (8, 29) with that of a walrus (129), or with that of a sea-lion (36)? I believe they were, and that, through inadvertency, they are not mentioned in the reports.

The *mouth* is transverse (56) and large (9, 56); it is rarely mentioned, but once stated to have been distinctly visible (118); once it was estimated at fifteen inches (56) (I may ask: large, long, or when opened?), and once we find the firm assertion that when open it looked like that of a serpent! (41).

The *eyes* were not always seen; it may be that the distance was too large, or that the animal kept them closed (115, 128, 130, 137, 146). They are mentioned as to have been only visible in 31, 80, 101, 118, 126, 152, 158; but sometimes we get a short description. They are round (92, fig. 30), about the size of an ox's (48), about 3 1/3 inches in diameter (102), about 5 inches in diameter (92), large (91, 122), large as a plate (32, 103), disproportionately large (36), broad, very large (92), relatively large (112). We observe that the size of the eyes, when opened as wide as possible, has struck the observers; they must be disproportionately large. But if we wish to know the relative largeness, we have only to consult n°. 92 and 102, where the eyes are estimated at 3 1/2 and 5 inches. On both occasions the observers estimated the head to be as long as a ten gallon cask, and about of the same thickness. As to the lustre of the eyes we read that: they are not glossy (103), generally, however, glossy (122), brilliant, flaming, sharp (44), very bright (48), and glittering (63, 92). It seems that the eyes, seen in their axis are dark (44, 103), or black (9, 103), and that, when seen in an oblique direction they seem to be blue or better tin-coloured, for they are said to resemble rather a pair of pewter plates. We also conclude that when seen in the axis and reflecting the daylight by their *tapetum lucidum* they glisten like those of a cat (91), or have a peculiar glimmer in their cavity (143), and this glimmer or glistening was said to be red (33), or reddish like a burning fire (5), or crimson (92). The eye is delineated in fig. 19, 24, 27, 28, 29, 30, 31, 36.—One of the eyewitnesses of no. 48 states that there is a small bunch on each side of his head, just above his eye; another too said: there appeared a bunch above the eyes (48). It is also said that the eyes are prominent, and stand out considerably from the surface, resembling in that respect the eyes of a toad (60). It is easy to understand that one thought such eyes similar to the horse's (56), and that another saw a bull-dog appearance in forehead and eye-brow (149). This heavy eye-brow is delineated too (fig. 19, 26). The situation of the eyes is over the jaws (56), and nearer to the mouth of the animal than to the back of the head (60, fig. 30).

Neither *ear-holes* nor *external ears* are mentioned. If external ears are present, they must be exceedingly minute; the absence, however, is very probable; at all events earholes must be present, but they are evidently very small, and capable of being closed, as in seals. Curious is the assertion "the ears seemed to be diaphanous" (143).

There is a slight hollow at the *top of the head* (60, fig. 30).

The *features* resemble those of an alligator (148), but made on others the impression as being those of a seal (29).

c. Skin.

Except in two cases (39, 157) when the animal was very near, scales are not mentioned, and the skin was apparently smooth (9, 10, 11, 12, 13, &c., &c., &c.); it is stated to be destitute of scales (149), altogether devoid of scales (148), smooth (13, 41, 43, 48, 56, 59, 60, 92, 103, 114, 115, 118, 146, fig. 27, 28, 29, 30, 31, 45), like a mirror, shining (114), shining strongly (117), with a very bright reflexion (46), looking similar to an eel's (59). But an animal which has whiskers on its upperlips, *must have a hairy skin*. Remarkable is therefore the assertion: the skin appeared rather to resemble in sleekness that of a seal (148), and still more: that it is as woolly as a seal's (8). Such a hairy skin becomes smooth as a mirror and shines strongly, when it is wet, as may be seen in seals, sea-lions, and sea-bears.

2. Internal Or Anatomical Characters.

It is not astonishing that we don't know much of its anatomical characters, as it never had the honour to be dissected by the able hand and keen scalpel of an anatomist. Yet it is clear that if the animal opens its mouth, there is an opportunity to learn something about its teeth, tongue, etc. Generally it keeps its mouth shut, once only this is stated (126), as if the observer watched an opportunity to see it opening its mouth. Though we have several accounts mentioning the animal opening its mouth (39, 41, 48, 65, 81, 109, 118, 144, 149), *teeth* are not always seen, either because the distance was too great, or because the position was not favourable. Teeth are delineated (fig. 19); they are mentioned in 65, 81, 109, 118, described as formidable in 109, and as jagged in 118.

Of the animal's *tongue* we have the following observations: "There rose from his head or the most forward part of him, a prong or spear about twelve inches in height, and six inches in circumference at the bottom, and running to a small point. I thought it not the tongue, as I saw the prong before I saw the head, but it might have been" (43, distance forty rods, with a spyglass); "I was struck with an appearance in the front part of the head like a single horn, about nine inches to a foot in length, and of the form of a marlinespike. There were a great many people collected by this time, many of whom had before seen the same object and the same appearance" (44); "he threw out his tongue about two feet in length, the end of it appeared to me to resemble a fisherman's harpoon" (48); "he raised his tongue several times perpendicularly, or nearly so, and let it fall again" (48); "he threw out his tongue a number of times, extended about two feet from his jaws, the end of it resembled a harpoon" (48); "he threw his tongue backwards several times over his head, and let it fall again" (48); "the colour of his tongue was a light brown" (48).

Conclusions 381

To the descriptions of the teeth and tongue no great value can be attached, as such organs need close examination. The length of the tongue is, anatomically spoken, not an impossibility, as it is known that animals with a long neck generally have a long tongue.

3. Colours, Individual Variations

Just as in some species of the order of Pinnipeds, there seem to exist indeed some individual variations with regard to the colour of the sea-serpent.

Just as in the dark specimens of the Pinnipeds, the colour of the sea-serpent becomes lighter in drying; i.e. the real colour of the animal comes to light. Properly we should say: their colour is light, but, when wet, it becomes a dark one. It is evident that the real colour of the sea-serpent, being dried by the sunshine, is grey (9, 61, 64), a light ash-colour (25), grey and yellow (147), pale yellowish (146), or yellow (71).

Just as in Pinnipeds, the colour of a wet individual appears much lighter when it is very close to us, than when we see it at some distance. Three times the colour is called grey (65, 66), though not a single fact is mentioned, from which it may be made out, whether the animal was very near or far off. The colour of an individual which was so close that it could be struck with a handspike was greyish (72), that of one a few yards distant, light fawn coloured (122), at about thirty feet distance the colour seemed to be a very dark grey (102), still farther a greyish brown (79).

Though some persons call the colour only dark, or brown, or black, it is noteworthy that those who describe it more minutely, agree that the backpart of the head, the neck, the trunk and the tail are dark, and that the under part of the head and the neck is light coloured. With regard to the colour, the animal is evidently longitudinally divided into a dark one above and a light one beneath.

The dark colour of the upper part seems to vary a little, as may be seen from the following appellations: dark (41, 48, 51, 63, 67, 80, 85, 103, 115, 131, 152 A, 154), very dark (42, 48), somewhat dark (95), dark dull (130), evidently a chocolate brown, or mahogany brown, or chestnut brown, for it was compared with a red snake (36), chocolate colour (44), dark chocolate colour (48), colour of a pilot fish (151), old mahogany brown (92), dirty brown (121), brown (43, 81, 92, 144), deep brown (34), dark brown (39, 44, 46, 56, 69, 97, 115, 117, 118, 135), blackish brown (91), approaching to black (63), nearly black (41, 95, 97) almost black (48), blackish (65, 94, 117), black (34, 42, 60, 85, 114, 120, 126, 138, 149, 150, 152, 155), as black as coal-tar (152). The tints of the figures also evidently represent a dark colour (figg. 28, 29, 30, 41, 45, 46). By some witnesses the colour of the head is observed to be darker than that of the body; we may safely read for "body" the "neck". Once the colour of the shoulders is reported to be much darker than the rest of the body (122).

On this dark upperpart spots, stripes, streaks etc. of a lighter hue are observed more than once: the colour was that of a conger eel, consequently brown with lighter streaks (144), spotted, and with light flames, or maculated, with distinctly visible light spots like a turtle or a lackered table, apparently shaded with light colours (41), streaked with white in irregular streaks (97), on an under ground of fawn colour there were large brown spots behind the shoulders (122), maculated with large white spots (130), covered with several white spots (131), brown with black spots (162). See also figg. 37 and 38.

In some individuals there is a black ring round the eye (29), and the region of the mouth is also black, so that they resemble those horses which we call moorish heads or blackfaces (9).

The sides of the underjaw seem to be very light coloured: white (34, 41, 126, figg. 28, 29, 30), as is also the throat: whitish (117, figg. 28, 29, 30) yellow (25), muddy white (56), yellowish white (118), brownish white (118), light coloured (126), white (69, 144), "the underpart of its head appeared nearly white" (41), "several feet of its belly" (read throat) "which were visible appeared nearly white" (41); very remarkable is the supposition of Mr. Matthew Gaffney: "I suppose and do believe that the whole of his belly was nearly white" (41), this really seems to be the case, for we read in 106A that the tail is longitudinally divided into two sections, white and black, and in n°. 144 that the whole animal was longitudinally divided into two sections, white and black. Of course in both cases the black side was the back-side, as was very well supposed by Captain Drevar in n°. 144.

I am of course unable to decide in how far the problematic dark stripe, curved downwards, on each side behind the underjaw, and as long as the head, delineated in figg. 28 and 29, will ever be found to come up to reality.

The representation of the colours in fig. 31 is very bad, as the animal's back is drawn lighter than the underpart, and I believe that such alternating broad bands of a light and dark colour don't exist in reality, but are here the result of drawing with a pencil.

4. Sexual Differences, Mane.

It is unquestionable that some individuals have a mane, and that others have not.

The mane seems to begin near the occiput, and to extend over the whole length of neck and trunk, being thickest near the head, and diminishing gradually to the tail where it evidently passes imperceptibly into the common hair-coating. The mane is said to have been visible on its head (135); at the back of the head (figg. 17, 24, n°. 107), which no doubt means just behind the occiput. Further: on the neck (9, 11, 12, 101, 103, fig. 31), from the back of the head a mane commenced (91), just behind the head the mane was thickest and got thinner further backwards (91), close behind the head a mane commences along the neck (92), the mane stretched rather far hindwards (92), the head was provided with a mane hanging down (152A); evidently the mane extends from the head over the whole length of the neck and the trunk (18? fig. 28, fig. 29). The mane near the head is long (9, 152 A), tolerably long (92), two feet long, and all along the neck and back: not very long (91), that it is of some length, we must suppose, for it is said to wash about to and fro in the water (91, 118, 120), and to spread to left and to right floating on the water (92), when the animal swims. The colour of the mane seems to be white (9) when dried up by the sunshine, but else it has the same colour as the rest of the body (102), brown (92, 152A). The mane resembles that of a horse (91, 92, 103, 118) or rather seaweed (118, 130).

Probably a mane was present in n°. 51, and 74; the back from afar, was irregular, uneven, and deeply indented; irregular and had a rugged appearance; see also fig. 36.

Twice it is stated that there was no mane (26, 115, see also fig. 19 and 27), but we have so many reports which don't mention the mane, and which surely would have mentioned it, if it had been present, that we are obliged to believe that those individuals had no mane. In other instances the distance was too great to observe a mane, even if the animal had been provided with one.

I am sure that here we have one of the differences between males and females. But, as I also firmly believe that there is a difference in size between males and females, I should not be surprised that, if these animals were better known to zoologists, the males would, in general, prove to surpass the females twice in size and four or six times in weight. In my opinion large individuals are, therefore, males, and must have a mane, or at one time have had one. The probability exists that they lose the greater part of their mane at a certain age, or that they were moulting when they were seen; which would account for the fact that in some large individuals no mane was observed.

I have ventured to draw the outlines of the animal from the descriptions. Fig. 72 represents it as seen from aside, with the divisions of the colours, and fig. 73 as seen on the back with the whiskers and the extension of the mane in the males.

5. Physiological Characters.
a. Nutritory functions.

1. *Eating, Food.*—Its eating cuttles, lobsters and all kind of sea-crabs, may be true. With the greatest certainty it may be said to feed on fish. We have found the following notices which decide this: "He often disappeared and was gone five or ten minutes under water; evidently he was diving or fishing for his food. He remained in nearly the same situation and thus employed for two hours. All kind of fish abound in the cove where the animal was seen" (35). "It sometimes darted under water with the greatest velocity, as if seizing prey" (69), which in this instance surely was fish. "Large shoals of small fish were rushing landwards in great commotion, leaping from the water, crowding on each other, and showing all the symptoms of flight from the pursuit of some wicked enemy" (133), and suddenly a sea-serpent appeared. "There was an unusual abundance of fish close in shore" (150), a sea-serpent soon made its appearance.

Not only does the animal prey on fish, but, by way of change, also on sea-mammals. When on Behring's Isle Mr. Kriukof tells us that "the sea-lions were so terrified at the sight of the monster, that some rushed into the water, and others hid themselves on the shore. The sea often throws up pieces of the flesh, which, according to the Aleutians is that of this serpent" (36). Evidently such pieces of flesh are washed aland only when a sea-serpent had made its appearance, otherwise there would be no reason to ascribe such pieces of flesh to sea-serpents. Sea-reptiles don't exist in those regions; it is highly improbable that the pieces of flesh were of sea-birds; they are not of fishes, as in that case they would not have been called *flesh*, consequently they are of sea-mammals. Of what kind of sea-mammals these pieces of flesh were, is not the question now, but I am sure that the sea-lions would not be so terrified, if they did not know the sea-serpent to be a terrible enemy.

There is moreover no doubt, that sea-serpents sometimes prey on the smaller kind of whales, as dolphins, porpoises, grampuses, &c. It sometimes appears suddenly amidst a shoal of these animals: "It was surrounded by porpoises and grampuses" (56); "There was an immense shoal of grampuses, which appeared in

384   The Great Sea-Serpent

FIG. 72.—SEA-SERPENT, SIDE VIEW, DRAWN FROM THE DESCRIPTIONS.

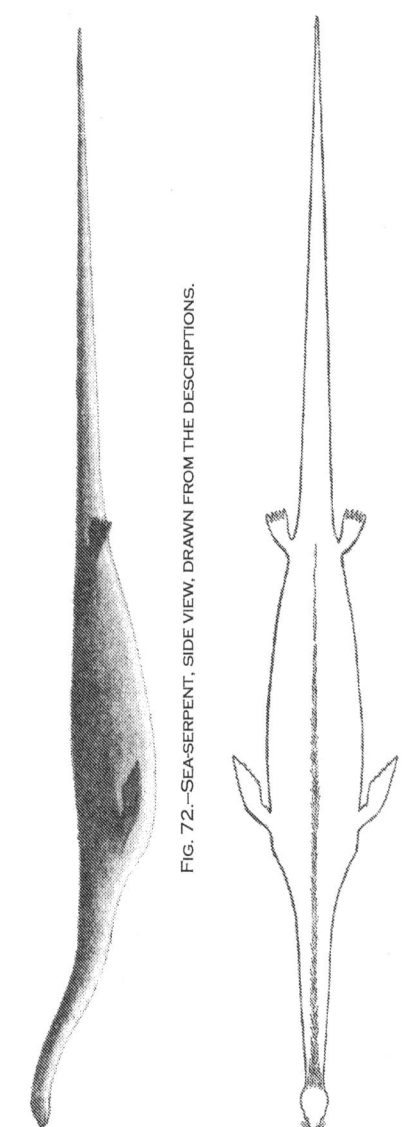

FIG. 73.—SEA-SERPENT, BACK VIEW, OUTLINES, DRAWN FROM THE DESCRIPTIONS.

an unusual state of excitement", no doubt because they were pursued by a sea-serpent (97); "an immense shoal of porpoises rushed by the ship as if pursued" (124), and gracefully a long neck, moving like that of a swan rose from the depths. Our suppositions in this respect are confirmed by the reports of Captain S. West, who saw the sea-serpent "engaged with a whale" (54), and of Captain Davison, stating that a sea-serpent seized a whale on the belly (read pectoral fin) (151, fig. 49).

The manner of darting on its prey is well described in n°. 149 and 152. I am convinced that the individuals in n°. 154 and 106 A were diving for food in a playful manner, with their body and part of their tail floating on the surface.

2. *Breathing.* Nobody will doubt that sea-serpents respire by gills as fish do; they move or swim, as is stated in numerous reports, with the head constantly above water, or when holding it nearly on the surface, it is evident that their nostrils are always just above the surface. When diving or fishing for food the average time that they remain under water is about eight minutes (63). It is probable that they may remain under it for half an hour or still longer. When having remained so long under water, and appearing on the surface, the animal suddenly exhales with such a force that "we at first imagined it to be a whale spouting" (83), and "every time he put his head out of water, he made a noise similar to that of steam escaping from the boiler of a steamboat" (101). The same noise is usually heard when a whale "spouts" (See H. Lee, *Sea Fables Explained*, 1883, London), see also fig. 36. But also when the animal is swimming or lying still on the surface with its head on the level of the water, occasionally exhaling when its nostrils are not quite above water, it "spouts water from it not unlike the blowing of a whale" (74); "near one extremity we saw what looked like foam or froth as though it was spouting water" (114). The breath of the animal is occasionally also seen condensed by the cold, forming little curling clouds, "it blew like a whale", said Egede (5, fig. 19), "it squirted from its mouth a stream of foamy stuff, resembling long shavings from a pine plank" (158). In general, however, the animal swims with its head some feet above the surface of the water, so that it is very natural that "there was an entire absence of blowing or spouting" (148).

3. *Excretion.* In one report we read that the animal left a greasy trail behind him (156). It is very probable that such a large sea-animal, provided as it is with rather a thick layer of bacon under its skin, secretes a quantity of liquid fat, large enough to leave "a greasy trail"; this will certainly happen when it is severely wounded.

Without any doubt it is true that it may "emit a very strong odour" (61).

b. Functions of the senses.

1. *Feeling.*—Of course but little can be noticed about the animal's feeling. Pontoppidan tells us that it has whiskers "like other animals which have a good nose." How far the Bishop believed that those whiskers had anything to do with the animal's sense of smell, I cannot tell. But certainly they have not. Well developed whiskers are rarely found but in animals which catch their prey in a stealthy way, such as cats, dogs, viverrides, mustelides, and numerous allied animals, and in animals which live in holes, as mice, rats, &c. It is known that all these animals can go through holes, crevices, fissures, slits or clefts which are large enough to admit their whiskers. Whiskers are organs of feeling. Consequently seals, sea-

lions, sea-bears, &c., and also sea-serpents will on numerous occasions find their whiskers of great use for the purpose of feeling with them.

Further it must not astonish us that sea-serpents are usually observed in fine weather when there is no wind. They seem to dislike wind, and therefore, if having no special purpose in view, they disappear as soon as the wind begins to blow (3, 92, 94); they even seem to be very sensible of the least wind.

Warmth on the contrary seems to he very welcome to them, as they are often seen on hot days, and even basking in the sun (114, 137).

2. *Taste.* The taste of the animal is, of course, only to be known by the food it takes.

3. *Smell.* There is no doubt that, guided by their smell they prey on fish, but it is clear that we shall never know any more particulars about it. Only it is stated, and it seems to be true, that they cannot bear the smell of castoreum and asa foetida, and that Norwegian seamen and fishermen up to the days of Rathke (1840) would never forget to bring one of these drugs with them, to drive them away. (Pontoppidan).

As far as I know, zoologists accept three reasons why some animals emit some strong odour; viz. to drive away their enemies, or to recognize one another, either in the neighbourhood or from afar, or to flatter and to attract the other sex. With which purpose sea-serpents emit a strong odour, this surely will be very difficult to decide, but in all probability they smell it themselves.

4. *Hearing.* The observations about the animal's hearing are, as may be expected, but very few. That an animal hears, can only be asserted when it gives unmistakable signs that it has heard, for instance a sudden turning of its head towards the origin of sound, or the running away from it. So we have the statements that the sea-serpent "was not pleased with the noise of our oars" (69); "the fishermen advise to be very quiet when a sea-serpent approaches and to avoid rowing, because the least noise attracks it still more"; "on both days it seemed to keep about us, and as we were always rowing then, we were inclined to think it might perhaps be attracted by the measured sound of the oars" (137, 138); "on my coo-ee the fish started off seawards out of sight and under winter" (150).

5. *Sight.* The numerous statements that a sea-serpent swims with its head some feet above the surface of the water prove that it looks straight before it. Further we have found it several times mentioned that it followed a boat, and finally the assertion that it raised its head and neck several feet above the water, evidently to take a survey towards the ship passing or to take a view of objects, or to look about for prey (31, 36, 60, 63, 74, 80, 93, 121, 128, 131, 145, 149, 152 A).

c. Functions of the muscular system.

1. *Relative mobility of organs.* We have already mentioned that the eyes, like the nostrils and the mouth, may be shut or opened wide. Yet they do not seem to be very movable (103).

The head may be held at right angles with the neck (70, fig. 24). The animal can bend its neck in several directions, moving it like that of a swan (121, 151, fig. 49), consequently bent dorso-ventrally in the form of a stretched S. When only the forepart of the neck, curved in such a way, is visible above water, the observers naturally say that it is curved (97), or bent in a semicircle (115). It can also turn its head a little sideways (60, 63, 93). The swimming in vertical undulations is surely a proof of dorso-ventral flexibility. It has the power to hold its body in a straight line, quite stiff, even in swimming. Also it has the power to bend its neck, trunk and tail dorso-ventrally into numerous "bunches", unless it is not the whole mass of its body, but only the layer of muscles, bacon and its skin, which it is able to bend in such a manner, for it is observed lying perfectly still, showing, however, numerous bunches (34, 42, 61, 64, 67, 69, 106 A, 154). In this condition it may even swim (60, 63). These bunches according to its body-length, may be of the size of a barrel (34), or from six to seven feet from each other, and from three to four feet high (154, fig. 50). On some occasions it gave the impression of a creature crooking up its back to sun itself (137), for there was no appearance of undulation; when the lumps sunk, other lumps did not rise in the intervals between them (137). Twice it is observed only with its head and its tail above water, the body slightly under (135, 162), and once casting itself backwards, and in doing so, its tail rose high above the water (5) so that the animal was bent dorsally in the form of an U or horse-shoe (fig. 19).

Its lateral flexibility is also astonishing. In turning it bends its body quite in the form of a horse-shoe, the head nearly touching its tail end (39, 41, 44); in turning twice immediately after each other or in playing, its body is bent in the form of the letter S (63, fig. 37, fig. 38). Also it may play in circles (39). Once, seized by a spermwhale, evidently in its trunk, it wound itself laterally round the head and upperjaw of its attacker (144). Its tail is said to lash the water (151? 158), and to wind itself up, and to rest for a moment on a part of the trunk (106 A). In short it is as limber and active as an eel (44).

Provided, as sea-lions are, with rather a thick layer of bacon under its skin, the animal, when it bends its body in the form of a horse-shoe, either laterally or dorsally, naturally shows in the concave side of the curve, wrinkles or folds (5) in its skin. When its head is held nearly at right angles with the neck, the skin under the chin is contracted into folds, which led to the description that the animal had some "gills" (read "gill-splits", 56). When its neck is a little contracted, it may happen that three folds of the skin encircle the neck, which when held so for some time, and exposed to the sun, dry on their highest part, and when stretched again, will show "three yellow collars" (71). It may also be that "at about six feet from the jaws there is a protuberance on its back like a small watercask" (126), or that "a kind of scroll, or tuft of loose skin, encircles the neck about two feet from the head" (131).

The flappers may he lifted up so high that they are occasionally visible above the surface (106 A, 118, 137, 154, fig. 50); when the animal is swimming with extreme rapidity, they may be raised still higher, so that they are almost entirely above the surface (129, 148, fig. 36, fig. 45), but then they are not directed hindwards, but forwards, "they were turned to the contrary way" (129, fig. 36, fig. 50). The flappers move alternately: "the movements of the flappers were those of a turtle", "the monster paddled itself along after the fashion of a turtle" (148), and have "a semirevolving motion" (148). When the animal swims with vertical undulations, it may press the flappers close against the body, so that seen from above, it is as if the flappers were wanting (82).

2. *Motions.* Hitherto we have considered the animal by itself, let us now see how it moves in the water.

The first sign of the presence of a sea-serpent may, of course, be very different. Generally, when the animal was met with it was already swimming on the surface;

sometimes it lay still, and it appeared to be a wreck or a small rock, but on approaching gradually changed into a living animal; and sometimes, though rarely, it appeared on the surface not far from the vessels. It is a proof that it may remain a tolerably long time under water before it comes to the surface to breathe. This may happen in two ways; viz. 1. After it has swam a long time just below the surface, it will gradually raise its head above it, and 2. When it has swum for some time very deep below the surface, it will rise perpendicularly upwards. Instances of the *first* manner of coming to the surface will be found in the following passages: "the first sign of the sea-serpent coming up was a rushing in the water ahead of the ship; at first we imagined it to be a whale spouting" (83), "attention was first directed to it by the broken action of the water" (126). Apparently this happened also in the animal of Captain Tremearne (129). In the *other* manner of coming to the surface, going upwards with great speed, a large portion of the animal is shown to the spectators: "it raised its head high above the surface (1, 31, 36), even so high that the foreflappers became visible (5, 121); "arising out of the depths of Ocean, stretches to the skies its enormous neck, masthead high"; "it raised itself slowly and gracefully from the deep" (124), "it suddenly stood quite perpendicular out of the water to the height of sixty feet" (145); "a head and neck rose out of the water to a height of about twenty or thirty feet (149, 151, 152, see also fig. 19, fig. 46, fig. 48, fig. 49). Once it struck a vessel in coming to the surface (122) so that it may be supposed that the animal had its eyes shut.

Generally it swims with vertical undulations (1, 2, 9, 10, 11, 12, 18, 23, 28, 29, 30, 31, 39, 41, 42, 43, 44, 48, 51, 60, 63, 65, 66, 67, 70, 81, 82, 83, 85, 91, 92, 94, 95, 101, 102, 103, 113, 114, 115, 117, 119, 126, 128, 137, 138, 139, 150, 155, 157, see also the following figures 24, 26, 27, 32, 33, 34, 35, 39, 47, 51). The undulations may be large or small, so that their number differs, but also the animal's higher or lower position in the water is cause, that their number may greatly vary. Of course it is not always easy to account for a small number of coils. This number is mentioned to be two or three (102), three (113), three to four (138), three to five (117), four or more (139), seven (137, 157), not more than seven (137), seven or eight (9), not more than eight (41), at least ten (85), ten or twelve (44, 60), thirteen to fifteen (63), fifteen to twenty three (63), fourteen (69), several (83), twenty five (2). In our illustrations we find four (fig. 40, fig. 47, fig. 51), six (fig. 26), seven (fig. 24 fig. 39), eight (fig. 35), eleven (fig. 27, fig. 34) and twenty (fig. 33).

The motion of the animal is said to be *wrongly* serpentine (29, 91, 103, 119, 157), like that of a snake (101, 115, 155), like that of an eel (117), and *rightly* vermicular (82), like that of a caterpillar (41), like that of a leech (94).

The coils are said to resemble or to be as large as ten-gallon kegs (41), half-barrels (60), flour barrels (60), large kegs (117), those of a dromedary (83), about three feet long (117).

The space between the coils, for there is always a space visible between them, is sometimes large, at other times small; it was a space of one fathom (9), of seven feet (69), or of three feet (60).

The whole animal swimming with vertical undulations, and seen from afar, resembles a string of tuns or hogsheads, a large shoal of fish (read porpoises) with a seal at one end of it (29), a string of empty barrels tied together (60), a string of casks tied together (60), a string of large casks, gently bubbing up and down (114), a long chain of rocks (106A), a long chain of enormous rings (106 A), a number of

Conclusions 389

barrels linked together (106 A), eight seals in a row (137), a flock of wild ducks swimming (157).

The height of the coils above water was, according to the animal's lower or higher position in the water, or according to its bulk, about six inches (41), eight or ten inches (39), at least three feet (114), only a few feet (106A); we also find the notices: "apparently about one third of the upperpart of its body was above water" (93), "it partly raised itself above the surface of the water" (94).

As is to be expected, the bunches decrease in size towards the tail (69, 102); of coarse this will always be the case.

It seems that sometimes the undulations are limited only to the trunk of the animal: "I saw no bunches towards I thought the end of the tail, and I believe there were none; from where I judged his navel might be, to the end of his tail there were no bunches visible" (44); "the first bunch appeared ten or twelve feet from his head" (69); "about thirty feet behind the head appeared the first coil" (81).

The reader will remember (see *Relative mobility of organs*) that the animal may crook up its back, or the layer of bacon of its back, when lying perfectly still. It seems evident that it also is able to swim with its flappers, whilst its back is in such a condition: "the bunches appeared to be fixed" (60); "his bunches appeared to be not altogether uniform in size, and as he moved along some appeared to be depressed and others brought above the surface, though I could not perceive any motion in them" (63); "the protuberances were not from his motion, as they were the same whether in slow or in rapid movement" (69). See also n°. 137.

I am convinced that the animal, swimming with vertical undulations, usually presses its flappers to its body. Once it was seen from above (82) and it seemed to be eel-shaped, and the flappers must have been invisible, at least they are not mentioned; it swam with vertical undulations.

But there are reasons to believe that the animal, swimming with vertical undulations, at a moderate rate, also uses its flappers. Once it was seen from above, moving with vertical undulations, and its flappers are tolerably well described (119). And when we read: "the motion of his body was rising and falling, the head moderately vibrating from side to side" (48), "the motion of his head was sideways and quite moderate, and the motion of his body was up and down" (48), "his motion was partly vertical, partly horizontal" (69), "serpentine movements, some up and down, some to the side" (91), we must conclude that the animal swimming with vertical undulations may indeed also use its flappers. If only the foreflapper and the hind one of the right side were used, the animal would turn to the left, if, on the contrary, it used its two left flappers, it would turn to the right; consequently when the right foreflapper (leaving for a moment the hindflappers out of consideration) is moved backwards with a strong action, the head must move a little to the left, and it will move to the right, when the left foreflapper is propelled backwards.

The instances in which the animal swims with its body in a straight line, propelling itself only with its flappers, are few in comparison with its swimming with vertical undulations (3, 18, 34, 38, 56, 59, 83, 93, 104, 115, 118, 120, 129, 130, 132,138,143, 145, 146, 147, 150, 160, see also figg. 28, 29, 31, 36, 45). The animal in this position resembled some drift of sea-weed (143), a mast of a vessel floating (83), an enormous log of timber floating (83), a trunk of a large tree floating (104), an unwrought spar (18), a long spar (150), a log of wood (150), an immense tree floating (157).

A change in its mode of swimming is sometimes also witnessed, it may be that it first swam with vertical undulations, and then with its body in a straight line, or vice versa (3, 83, 115).

In swimming the end of the tail only (118, 122, 146), or nearly the whole tail (31, 34, 38, 60, 63, 69, 74, 80, 81, 85, 93, 102, 114, 115, 121, 148, 150) is concealed under water and invisible. The flappers are always below the surface of the water and invisible (31, 34, 80, 85, 122, 138, 146, 150), save the above-mentioned four times (118, 129, 137, 148). The head may be held just at the surface of the water (31, 39, 44, 66, 74, 91, 137, 146, 148, figg. 32, 33, 37, 38), so that it sometimes is recorded as not having been visible (41, 113, 114), or may be, and this is generally the case, held above water (31, 44, 51, 63, 83, 91, 97, 128, figg. 24, 26, 27, 28, 29, 51). The height above water is said to be but little (94), some feet (70), well above water (150), several feet (155), high (32), considerable (102), quite erect in the air (95), six inches (48, 63), eight inches (44), one foot (38, 41, 42, 92, 137, 138), two feet (9, 39, 63, 80, 138), three feet (63), four feet (17, 19, 29, 60, 118), five feet (19, 29, 60), six feet (60, 74, 97), seven feet (60, 101, 142), eight feet (101), ten or twelve feet (131).

The head may, of course, sometimes be gradually laid down (63), or gradually raised higher (51), is generally held in an acute angle (94), which is of course the case when it is only a few feet above the surface, and the angle becomes the less acute the more the head is elevated; but sometimes the neck is curved (97) in the form of a semicircle (115). The head may be held constantly above water as long as the animal was visible (29, 31, 92, 94, 118), or raised and lowered at intervals (128, 129, 148).

Sometimes, evidently when darting on some prey, the animal raises its whole neck quite stiff in the air: "head and neck stood upright like a mast" (56), "the whole neck raised above water like a snake preparing to dart on his prey" (115), "the animal protruded its head above water to the length of about thirty feet at an angle of sixty degree to the horizon" (126), "a large spar sticking out of the water one end, and some thirty feet above the level of the sea" (132), "it resembled the lower mast of some wrecked vessel, passing rapidly" (132), "darting rapidly out of the water and splashing in again, head and neck to a height of about twenty or thirty feet out of the water" (149, fig. 46), "head and neck reared about thirty feet out of water" (151), "a neck rose out of the water, about twenty feet, moving with great speed" (152), "at first it was taken to be an immense tree floating, but this illusion was soon dispelled as the neck was thrown twenty feet in the air" (160).

When swimming the whole animal is not always above water, but may occasionally dip under without any noise, or disappear with a distinctly audible splash (31, 39, 41, 44, 60, 63, 69, 74, 114, 117, 126, 132, 137, 139, 149, 151, 152, 157).

The speed is said to be: faster than we could row (9), rapid (31, 97, 114, 117, 134, 137), an incredible velocity, like an arrow, moderate (29), the greatest rapidity (29), a great rapidity (34, 138), slow (39, 115, 120, 131, 137), much more rapid than whales or any other fish (48), very rapid (63, 69, 132), nearly still (69), very slow (83), very swiftly (94), a great swiftness (101), that of a light boat rowed by four active men (117), very quick (123), at a great rate (137), at a rapid pace (149), a great speed (152), a great velocity (157)—or it was estimated at—two miles an hour (83, 120), three miles an hour (39), four miles (60), ten miles (146), ten to twelve miles (42, 138), twelve to fourteen miles (48), fifteen miles (41, 118, 149), fifteen or twenty miles (35), twenty miles (44, 156), twenty four miles (38), twenty to thirty miles (41), thirty miles (122, 155), thirty-six to forty-two miles (51), sixty miles (43, 50).

The animal may swim for a considerable time with the same speed, steadily and uniformly (48, 118, 134, 138, 146), or decreasing, or increasing it (29, 51, 60, 69).

Of course the animal swimming rapidly propels the water before it, so that the water curls up before its throat (51, 93, 118), or even foams (44, 63, 85, 95, 115, fig. 26), and when it swiftly darts forwards for prey and elevates its flappers above water, the motion of its flappers causes distinctly visible splashes (137, 149, 152, fig. 46, of course in n°. 129 and 148 the movements of the flappers must also have caused a severe splashing, though this is neither mentioned nor delineated, figg. 36, 45). Also when it drops its neck like a log of wood into the water, an enormous splash or sprey on both sides was visible (149, 152).

In the open sea the animal generally swims "as straightforward as you could draw a line" (39, 41, 114, 134), "not deviating in the slightest degree from its course, which it held on apparently on some determined purpose" (118), seldom it is recorded as "taking a turn" (114, 122, 128), but when in a harbour it may move "in several directions" (41), as if "playing" (39, 63, 69, 130), "in circles" (39), or "bringing the body into a letter S" (63, 130). The mode of turning is so characteristic and unique that I feel obliged to repeat all that I have found about it:—"he turned short and quick and the first part of the curve that he made in turning resembled the link of a chain, but when his head came parallel with his tail, his head and tail appeared near together" (39),—"his motion when he turned was quick; the first part of the curve that he made in turning was of the form of a staple, and as he approached towards his tail he came near his body with his head, and then ran parallel with his tail, and his head and tail then appeared near together" (41),—"in changing his course he brought his head to where his tail was, or in fact to the extreme hinderpart visible; raising himself as he turned six or eight inches out of water" (41),—"he turned quick and short and the first part of the curve that he makes in turning is in the form of a staple, but his head seems to approach rapidly towards his body, his head and tail moving in opposite directions, and when his head and tail came parallel they appear almost to touch each other" (41),—"when he changed his course he diminished his velocity but little; the two extremes that were visible appeared rapidly moving in opposite directions, and when they came parallel, they appeared not more than a yard apart" (41),—"he turned very short; the form of the curve when he turned resembled a staple; his head seemed to approach towards his body for some feet, then his head and tail appeared moving rapidly, in opposite directions, and when his head and tail were on parallel lines they appeared not more than two or three yards apart" (44),—"he turned slowly, and took up considerable room in doing it" (69),—"it turned with considerable noise" (117).

When the animal swims, either with vertical undulations, or with its body in a straight line, holding, however, its head just at water-level, so that the nostrils are only above the surface to breathe, it generally shows nearly its whole length, only the very end of its tail being under water. In such a condition it must swim very easily, for the water carries its total weight, so that it is actually null, and the animal in swimming has only to surmount the friction and the resistance of the water made against an object in motion. But as soon as the head is lifted above the surface, the weight of it must immediately be carried by the body. It is therefore not astonishing if an observer states: "its progressive motion under water was rapid; when the head was above water, its motion was not near so quick" (31), "when immersed in the water his speed was greater" (41). It is very natural too, that when the head is held above water, and when consequently the body must carry the weight of the head, the body sinks a little deeper into the water: "his head was now more elevated above the water, and his body more depressed below" (51), and that when the animal has raised its whole neck quite erect in the air, the body has sunk so deep that it is: "not visible at all" (149), and that "the disturbance on the surface was too slight to attract notice" (149). Therefore figg. 33, 34, 35, 37, 38, 46, 48 and 49, are tolerably well delineated. Fig. 33 shows us the animal swimming with vertical undulations, holding its head on the level of the water, and having nearly its whole length visible on the surface. In fig. 34 the head is held a little above the surface, and the end of the tail is already below it. Fig. 35 shows the head still more elevated while of the tail nothing more is visible. Figg. 37 and 38 represent the animal floating on the surface, showing the ridge of its whole back. In figg. 46, 48 and 49 the animal's neck is elevated as high as possible, but its body is of course too deep to be seen.

A few lines above we have spoken of the increased speed of the animal swimming under water. The question arises how was this to be seen; and the answer is given by the eye-witnesses themselves: "I saw it coming rapidly under water" (31), "when moving under water you could often trace him by the motion of the water on the surface, and from this circumstance I conclude he did not swim deep" (41), "we could trace his course under water" (69), "swimming below the surface so that merely a stripe indicated the rapid course" (117), "in swimming under the surface the animal swims not deeply, for on the surface one can trace its course" (126), "and moved away just under the surface of the water, for we could trace its course by the waves it raised on the still sea" (137).

This, however, is not always the case. The animal can swim so deep that its course is not betrayed on the surface. Once "it swum directly under a boat" in which two men were (41), and once "it passed below the boat at the depth of eight or ten feet, swimming slowly with a vermicular motion" (82), which shows us at the same time that it swims under water with vertical undulations. There is, of course, reason to believe that it may also occasionally swim with its body in a straight line; and Captain Hope saw it at still greater depths swimming evidently with its flappers and with vertical undulations (119).

So we have gradually approached to the way in which the animal disappears from the surface of the vaste ocean. In some instances it is only said that "it disappeared" (36), "it all at once vanished" (74), "it all at once disappeared" (74), "it suddenly disappeared" (132, 143, 155), evidently withdrawing itself beneath the surface of the water deep enough to avoid a rippling of it. In other instances the *way how* it disappeared is more circumstantially described: "it sank" (49, 60, 69, 117, 137), "it sunk gradually into the water" (63), "it sunk quietly beneath the surface" (134), "it sunk rather abruptly" (137), "it sunk apparently down" (39), "he did not turn down like a fish, but appeared to settle down like a rock" (41), "he apparently sunk directly down like a rock" (41); this "sinking like a rock" is of course effectuated by a sudden upward movement of all the flappers together. But the animal may also plunge violently under water (31), or go down with a tremendous splash (157), or when it is swimming with its neck high elevated above the surface, it dives like a duck head foremost (124, 151), and finally, when it has apparently remained a long time under water in great depths, and suddenly comes to the surface with so much force that its head, long neck, and a part of its trunk with its formidable foreflappers become visible, it throws itself backwards, and in doing so, raises its enormous tail high above the surface of the water (5), and disappearing under the waves, the last part which is visible of it, is the end of the tail (fig. 20). Generally, however, it happens that the swimming animal grows gradually smaller and smaller to the eyes of the observers, and at last disappears in the distance to be seen no more.

3. *Voice*.—In none of the reports gathered in this volume there is a single notice about the animal's voice. It is probable that the individual gripped by the spermwhale (144) uttered a sound which, however, was not heard amidst the tremendous noise, made by the two animals fighting.

d. Generation, Growth.

I am sure that nobody will believe any longer, as was the case in 1817, that sea-serpents are oviparous. Animals with a hairy skin, safe the *Monotrymata*, are viviparous, consequently sea-serpents are viviparous.

Though Pontoppidan believes that sea-serpents "seek the other sex most probably in July and August", and that "July and August are its paring time", I am satisfied that March and April must be taken as their months of amours, and that July and August are the months of whelping.

A new born pup most probably has a length of about twenty feet (14).

It seems that the months during which two sea-serpents were seen together are July and August, probably also September (23, 27, 66, 72). It would seem, therefore, that a male remains in the neighbourhood of his companion during her pregnancy and probably also during the first month or during the first two months of the new-born young.

It seems also that the females are much smaller than the males, as the pups are comparatively very small, and as twice one of the two which were seen together is described smaller than the other (23, 66).

We have already met with two instances in which the head of the individual is delineated or described as having a hollow at its top (60, fig. 30). I am satisfied that these were two males not yet full-grown, showing the two cushions of their enormously developed masticatory muscles, which were not yet closed in the centre of the top of the head, and whose skulls therefore, could not show the occipital and medial crests.

6. Psychical Characters.
a. Not taking notice of objects.

There are instances that the animal is reported as taking no notice at all of men, vessels or other objects (29, 34, 48, 82, 83).

b. Taking notice of objects.

At other instances, however, the animal was thought to notice objects (43), or is said to have turned its head two or three times slowly round towards and from the vessel, as if taking a view of some object on board (60), or that it slowly turned its head towards the observers (93), and numerous are the reports that it lifted itself high above the surface apparently to take a survey towards the vessel, or to take a view of objects (31, 36, 60, 63, 74, 80, 93, 121, 128, 131, 145, 149, 152 A).

c. Curiosity, probably mixed with suspicion.

The many instances that sea-serpents are said to have followed a boat (31, 36, 103, 110, 117, 158) or to have taken a survey towards vessels, sufficiently prove that they are curious beings, and that their curiosity as in so many animals, is generally mixed with some suspicion, which of course is again a proof that the animal is constantly prepared for selfpreservation. One of the most striking proofs of this is to be read in n°. 92: the individual swam towards a boat, passed within a few feet or some fathoms, and swam away, to repeat the same movement two times.

d. Suspicion.

That some of the eye-witnesses got the impression that it is sometimes really suspicious may be seen from the following lines: "he appeared to avoid the boat wherein I was" (39), "he seemed suspicious of the boat" (69), "they chased the animal fruitless for seven hours" (59), "Captain George Little made many attempts of pursuing and killing it, but without any result, as the serpent ever kept a distance of a quarter of a mile" (19), "on both days it seemed to keep about us, and as we were always rowing then, we were inclined to think it might perhaps be attracted by the measured sound of the oars." (137, 138).

e. Harmlessness.

The animal is evidently a quite harmless creature. Though very close to several boats, it offered them no molestation (32). "After the shot of Matthew Gaffney "it turned towards him immediately, sank down, went directly under his boat, and made its appearance one hundred yards from where it sank and continued playing as before" (41), "he appeared to us to be a harmless animal" (63), "it was harmless" (69). A proof of perfect harmlessness may be found in n°. 92: it approached a fisherman in his boat to within six feet and offered him no molestation. See also n°. 94 and 112.

f. Timidity.

Pontoppidan already concluded that these animals are really timid ones, "for when it follows a boat, the fishermen throw any object, for instance a scoop, at it, and then the animal generally plunges into the deep", and Mr. Prince also says "he appeared to us to be a timid animal" (63).

g. Fearlessness.

It were perhaps better if I used here the expression: "Involuntary consciousness of the harmlessness of vessels, boats, and men", in which, however, it was often mistaken! "It did not appear to avoid anything" (41), "it appeared to be amusing itself, though there were several boats not far from it" (41); after the shot of Matthew Gaffney "it did not appear more shy (41); once it lay extended on the surface, the night was falling, and a boat rowed by four men, passed just before its snout at an oar's length, and yet it remained lying quite still (43), "it did not appear to be at all disturbed by the vessel" (48, 80, 93, 112, 118); it may swim or come to the surface very close to boats, and swim parallel with them (72, 109, 112, 121, 157).

h. Fear.

A stronger expression of suspicion is evidently to be seen in the animal's sinking and being seen no more at the approach of a vessel (49).

i. Fright.

I think that in the following we see true expressions of fright. When Lorenz von Ferry fired at it, the animal plunged down under water and was seen no more (9); some strangers fired at it and it suddenly disappeared (90); it gracefully rose once from the deep, but seeing a ship, it immediately disappeared (124); it once raised its head out of the water within twenty yards of a ship, when it suddenly disappeared, but here its curiosity got hold of its fright, and after half a minute it made its appearance again in the same manner (131).

j. Fury.

The animal does not always plunge down after a shot, and is then seen no more: Matthew Gaffney fired at it, when it was thirty feet from him. The animal turned towards him immediately after the shot, sank down, went directly under his boat and made its appearance at about one hundred yards from where it sunk. It continued playing as before, and did not appear more shy (41); once when it was fired at, it turned and pursued the boat to the shore and then disappeared (110); a boatmen struck it with a boathook, upon which it immediately gave him chase (112); when Lund fired at it, it stretched its long neck quite erect in the air, like a snake preparing to dart on its prey, and darted towards Lund, who reached the shore in time (115). I am convinced that the animal, when fired at and hit, in most instances grows suddenly furious and darts on the enemy, but it seems that its fury is soon dispelled by the emotion of fear, suspicion, timidity, etc. Hitherto I have not found one single proof that it ever attacked a man, with the result of having hurt him, though it had more than once a favourable opportunity of doing so.

k. Toughness.

It is evident that the animal is a tough one; it is not easy to kill it. A single rifle-ball seems to be insufficient, and I think the only manner to kill it is by explosive balls or by harpoons loaden with nitro-glycerine, which will at once destroy a considerable part of its brain and skull, or body.

l. Playsomeness.

Like the seals and sea-lions in our Zoological Gardens, sea-serpents have often been seen amusing themselves for hours when in a harbour, gracefully gliding in circles, as has been stated above. Twice an individual just as in seals, showed its head and tail quite above the surface, the body slightly under (135, 162), stretching itself comfortably; at other times crooking up its back to sun itself (114, 137).

m. Sensibility of fine weather.

Evidently the animals feel comfortable *in fine weather* and when there is *no wind*. Repeatedly we have found the statement that they disappear as soon as the wind begins to blow. But as they are air-breathing animals, they are obliged to come every now and again to the surface, and it is, therefore, not wonderful that there are reports which, though in a slight degree, contradict the other statements. But upon the whole it is clear that in such circumstances the animal will only raise their nostrils for a moment above the surface of the water in order to breathe, and this is clearly the reason why in many instances they are never high enough and long enough above the surface to be observed by men.

When the animal appeared, the *weather* is reported to have been calm (2, 3, 5, 25, 29, 61, 64, 79, 103, 128, 130, 137, 144, 157), quite calm (35), good (60), clear (34, 60, 63, 83, 114, 128, 132, 152, 154, 162), very clear (60), fine (44, 79, 128, 129, 144, 146, 152), brisk (114), sunshiny (137, 149, 157), warm and sunshiny (138), hot (150, 157), very hot (64), excessively sultry (61), cloudy (131), dark and cloudy (118).

The *surface of the sea* is described as smooth (34, 41, 126, 146), quite smooth (80), very smooth (29), perfectly smooth (44, 137, 148), extremely smooth (63), smooth as a mirror (92, 95), as smooth as a glass (150), as smooth as the surface of a pond (114), calm (2, 60), quite calm (115), almost calm (60), perfectly calm (83, 119), exceptionally calm (148), moderate (144). But there may be also some sea on (120), or a sharp sea on (122), or the surface may be only little moved by waves (154), or occasionally disturbed by slight flaws of wind, "catpaws" (128), or there may be a long ocean swell (118), or a strong ebb tribe (51).

In the reports we read that there was no *wind* (48), not a breath of wind (150), not a breath of air (114, 137), a very little wind (29), a light wind (34, 126, 132), a light air of wind (60), a fresh wind (118, 129), a variable wind (132), a moderate wind (144), a gale of wind (124), a light breeze (80, 130), a brisk breeze (51), a fresh breeze (104, 120), or there were strong breezes (122, 131).

7. Enemies.

Undoubtedly sea-serpents have some enemies of which we are and probably will remain ignorant. But spermwhales and men are certainly their most terrible foes, the former on account of their enormous beak with formidable teeth (144), the latter on account of their nets (14), boathooks (112), harpoons (59, 121), and rifles (9, 19, 41, 69, 90, 110, 115, 129, 130).

8. Repose, Sleep, Death.

I believe that repose and sleep are the same for the animal, and that like a seal, it is always on the look out, shutting the eyes for only a few seconds. I say, I believe so, for I cannot deduce it from one of the reports. Once it is said that it lay motionless, without bunches, holding its head above water, and that the eyes were visible (80); another time it lay perfectly still, spouting like a whale; consequently the nostrils were just below the surface, or just at water level, so that the water was sprayed by every exhalation; it had a rugged appearance, consequently it was most probably a male with a mane (74). The other instances in which the animal was evidently resting are the following: it lay almost motionless in the sea; probably in a straight line, for undulations or bunches are not mentioned (17). It was in the evening between eight and nine o'clock; it lay extended on the surface of the water, it appeared straight, exhibiting no protuberances, "we were within two oars' length of him, when we first discovered him and were rowing directly for him. We immediately rowed from him, and at first concluded to pass by his tail, but fearing we might strike him with the boat, concluded to pass around his head, which we did, by altering our course. He remained in the same position, till we lost sight of him. We approached so near to him, that I believe I could have reached him with my oar" (43). It lay perfectly still extended on the water, probably with its body in a straight line, for no protuberances are mentioned; neither its head nor its tail were visible; yet I believe that its nostrils were above water level, and so it remained for half an hour (46). Very seldom it seems to avail itself of an opportunity to support itself on a sand bank. I have found but one case in which it is, however, stated that the bank had about four feet water upon it. "It lay dormant on the rocks, partly on the rocks, partly in the water," resembling from afar a large log of wood. "It lay stretched out, partly over the white sandy beach, which had four or five feet water upon it, and lay partly over the channel" (45).

Till now it seems that no individual has ever been killed by the rifle balls of men. It is probable that the individual attacked by the sperm-whale (144) was finally killed by it, but it is also probable that it escaped. Yet I believe that sperm-whales may occasionally wound sea-serpents to death.

Generally, however, I believe that these animals die a natural death.

Dead sea-serpents are more likely to sink than to float, as the enormous neck and tail are most probably not provided with a comparatively thick layer of bacon, and are, therefore, too heavy for the comparatively small quantity of air in the animal's lungs, and for the layer of bacon of the animal's trunk. Yet it may occasionally occur that sea-serpents dying near some shore, may be stranded by the waves. Pontoppidan reports that a dead sea-serpent stranded on the cliffs near Amond in Nordfjord and that its carrion caused a dreadful smell (6), and that another stranded near the isle of Karmen (7), and that the stranding of dead sea-serpents took place in more localities (7). Such carrions must be a dainty to all kinds of mews, which sometimes even follow living individuals (69). The fear of the Norwegians of sea-serpents, even of such carrions, is great enough to keep them at a considerable distance. It may be true "that some time ago a part of a skeleton of a sea-serpent was present in the Museum of Natural History at Bergen". It is possible that the fate of this part of a skeleton was the same as that of so many meteoric stones (see my Preface), or as that of the two eggs of *Platypus* or *Ornithorhynchus*, which reached the Manchester Museum in the year 1829, and remained there for some years, till they were condemned to the rubbish hill (*Nature*, 11 Dec. 1884, p. 133), and it was not before September 1884 that zoologists knew that *Ornithorhynchus* and *Echidna* are really oviparous, and that the Manchester Museum was once in the possession of two eggs!!

9. Geographical Distribution.

The Rev. Abraham Cummings, after having mentioned that the animal swims with vertical undulations, wrote in August 1803: "this renders it highly probable that he never moves on land to any considerable distance, and that the water is his proper element" (29).

I wish to express here my firm conviction that these animals never come ashore, nor even on the ice, but always remain in the water. It is true that we have one observation that an individual rested upon a sandy beach, which, however, at that time had about four feet water upon it. But we have other observations that individuals which, following a boat, come into shallow water, immediately and apparently with some difficulty took a turn and went away (31, 115).

It seems that in Norway it has happened a few times that these animals, which are in the habit of frequenting the fjords, swam even up the mouths or the lower parts of rivers, consequently swam in fresh water, which probably gave rise to the fable of these animals being born on land, remain there till they are too large to hide themselves, and then swim down to the sea, where they can move much more easily. Their swimming in fresh water is once recorded, viz. in the Hudson-mouth, New Jersey, U. S. A. (158).

Moreover they are sea-animals, and according to their air-breathing condition, live on the surface, though they may sometimes seek great depths (119).

I have already shown that these animals like *sunshiny* and *hot* weather. They don't like wind, and consequently we may conclude that they are averse of cold weather and of cold water. Therefore they are seen near Norway especially in July and August, which led Pontoppidan to suggest that they "perpetually live in the depths of the sea, except in July and August". The Bishop seems not to have hit upon the idea that the sea-serpents could be migratory animals.

The sea-serpents, it is true, may remain for a long time in a place where they enjoy all that they can possibly wish to have, i. e. room enough, bright weather and plenty of food. They may stay a few days in the same fjord (3, 4, 96) or in the same place or harbour (31 and 32, 34 and 35, 37, 38, 39, 40, 41, 42, 43, 44, 45, 46, 47, 48 and 49, 50 and 51, &c., &c.). But then, it may be that the fish is flown for the enemy, or that the season proceeds, the sea-serpents look for an other provender place, or swim to a warmer part of the ocean, i. e. *they migrate*.

Conclusions 399

And so we come to their *horizontal geographical distribution*. We may at once assert that they are cosmopolites though we have not a single report of an appearance at a higher degree than 46° S. latitude, i. e. they have not been met with in the Antarctic Ocean.

Up to this time the animals have appeared 1. In the *Arctic Ocean*, and 2. In the *Atlantic Ocean*.

   a. All along the coasts of Norway from North Cape up to the boundary of Norway and Sweden, east of Christiania fjord (l, 3, 4, 6, 7, 8, 9, 10, 11, 12, 13, 14, 57, 58, 61, 64, 65, 66, 67, 68, 72, 79, 85, 86, 87, 88, 89, 90, 91, 92, 94, 95, 96, 102, 103, 107, 108, 109, 110, 111, 111 A, 112, 113, 115, 117, 125, 157). Of the whole coast of Norway that of the northern provinces (washed by the Arctic Ocean) seems to be frequented more than that of the southern. It seems that they appear along these coasts almost every year.
   b. Along the coasts of Sweden, from the boundary of Norway and Sweden, east of Christiania fjord, to the southmost point of Sweden, Falsterbo. I have but one report (2), and the locality of the appearance of the animal I have *supposed* to have been in the Sund near Malmö.
   c. In the Baltic or Swedish Sea. According to Olaus Magnus it is also recorded from this sea, but I think that this happens no more.
   d. North of Scotland: between Iceland and the Faroe Isles (124), between the Faroe Isles and the Hebrides (56, 153, 154), and near Dunvossness, one of the Shetland Isles (78).
   e. On the eastern coast of Scotland (141, 142, 143).
   f. Along the western coasts of Scotland, Wales and England (31, 32, 82, 137, 138, 140, 155, 156).
   g. A hundred miles west of Brest, France, (152).
   h. In the Gulf of Biscay (74).
   i. West of Portugal (120).
   j. In the Mediterranean (148).
   k. North-east of the Azores (25).
   l. South of the Azores and west of the Canaries, 29° N., 34° W., (128).
   m. From the Canaries to Cape Verde (135).
   n. In a line from Cape Verde to the Cape of Good Hope and a little further south (93, 114, 118, 129, 130, 131, 132, 152A), not along the coast, except three appearances in Table Bay (114, 130, 152 A).
   o. In Davis Straits, 64° N., (5).
   p. Along the east coast of North America from Newfoundland to Florida (15, 16, 17, 18, 19, 20, 21, 22, 23, 24, 26, 27, 28, 29, 30, 34, 35, 37, 38, 39, 40, 41, 42, 43, 44, 45, 46, 47, 48, 49, 50, 51, 52, 53, 54, 55, 59, 60, 62, 63, 69, 70, 71, 73, 75, 76, 77, 81, 83, 84, 97, 98, 99, 100, 101, 105, 106, 106 B, 107 A, 121, 133, 134, 158, 159, 160, 162). So these coasts seem to be frequented almost every year. In Mr. Traill's paper on the subject (*Proc. Roy. Soc. Edinb.* 1854, Vol. 3,) we read: "I shall not here discuss the notices we have, from time to time, received of late years of a great sea-serpent seen by mariners in crossing the Atlantic to America". I am convinced that these meetings took always place not far from the American coast. Our n°. 161 is also one of these "notices received of a sea-serpent seen by a mariner in crossing the Atlantic *from* America".

    q. In the Gulf of Mexico (106 A.)
    r. East of Cape San Roque (144, 145).
    s. East of La Plata river mouth (80).
    t. In the South Atlantic (104).
  3. In the *Indian Ocean.*
    a. In the Gulf of Aden (149).
    b. Probably between 40° lat. and 20° lat. S., and between 50° and 70° long. E (123).
    c. In lat.. 2° N., long. 90° E. (147).
    d. In the Malacca Straits (146).
    e. Near the coast of Australia (136).
    f. In Geographe Bay (150).
  4. In the *Pacific Ocean.*
    a. South of Australia (122).
    b. Near Cape Satano, the southmost point of the Isle of Kiu Siu (Japan) (151).
    c. Near Behring Isle (36). The Aleutians declare that they have often seen this animal (36).
    d. In the Gulf of California (119).

That so many appearances took place in the Atlantic and so few in the Indian Ocean and in the Pacific only results from the Atlantic being the great highway of nations.

Along the coasts of Norway they appear only "at certain times" (2) i. e. evidently "in the dog days" (92), viz. from the 23th. of July to the 23th. of August, and when we consult those reports which mention the dates of the appearances we observe that they really appear along the Norwegian coasts in July (61, 92, 115) and August (9, 64, 68, 117, 157), but that after the dog days they swim further south: from the 24th. of August to the 9th. of September one or more individuals appeared in Christiania fjord (85, 86, 87, 88, 89), and in the month of October (?) an individual was observed near Ibbestad, in the neighbourhood of Christiansand (111 A). The occurrences between the Faroe Isles and the Hebrides took place in the last days of May (153, 154) and in July (56), those on the east coast of Scotland in the middle of November (141, 142, 143), those on the western coasts of Scotland, Wales and England: in June in the neighbourhood of Coll and Eigg (31, 32), in the last days of August in the neighbourhood of Loch-Hourn (137, 138, 139, 140), in the beginning of September near Orme's Heads, Wales, (155), and in the middle of October in Bristol Channel (156). The occurrence a hundred miles west of Brest, France, took place on the 5th. of August (152), that west of Portugal on the 31st. of December (120), that in the Mediterranean on the 2d. of June (148), that northeast of the Azores on the 1st. of August (25), that south of the Azores and west of the Canaries on the 30th. of March (128), that between the Canaries and Cape Verde on the 16th. of May (135), and those between Cape Verde and Cape of Good Hope and southwest of the latter: on January 26 (132), February 16 (130), July 8 (129), in the end of July (93), in the summer (114), on August 6 (118), on November 12 (152 A), and on December 12 (131).

Egede saw an individual in Davis' Straits in July (5); the sea-serpents frequent the coast of North America from Newfoundland to Florida in February (121), March or April (101), May (19, 97, 161), June (34, 35, 53, 54, 60, 83, 84, 106B?, 162), July (29, 55, 75?, 81?, 98, 99, 100?), August (37, 38, 39, 40, 41, 42, 43, 44, 45,

46, 47, 48, 49, 59, 62, 63, 69, 73, 105?, 133, 134, 158, 159, 160), September (70, 71, 77, 106?), and October (50, 51). It occurred in the Gulf of Mexico in April (106 A), was east of Cape San Roque in July (144, 145), and visited the South Atlantic east of Uruguay in January (80).

January was the month in which it appeared in the Gulf of Aden (149), September in about lat. 15° S. and 60° E. (123), May in about lat. 2° N. and long 91° E. (147), September in the Malacca Straits (146), and March in Geographe Bay (150).

In May it was observed south of Australia (122), and in April south of Kiu Siu, Japan (151).

A few lines above I have already expressed my firm conviction that they are migratory and don't like cold water. If this be true, they will be *generally* observed (and I purposely draw the reader's attention to the expression "generally", for animals are not bound by *laws* of nature), in the northern hemisphere when summer is there, and they will *generally* appear in the southern hemisphere when summer visits those parts of our globe. To follow this *rule* they must be able to migrate from north to south, and vice versa. Consequently the Atlantic and the Pacific are the only two oceans in which we shall observe that *generally* this rule is followed, for in the Indian Ocean the animals are checked in their course towards the north by the continent of Asia.

We are therefore obliged to take no account of the appearances which occurred in the Indian Ocean. And as we have *only two* appearances observed in the Pacific, of which the dates are mentioned, we are also obliged to pass over those in the Pacific too.

Let us now see where the animals were met with in the different months.

January.
South of St. Helena.   19° S. (132).
East of Uruguay.   34 1/2° S. (80).

February.
East coast of North America.   31° N. (121).
Table Bay.   34° S. (130)

March.
East coast of North America.   42° N. (101).
South of the Azores.   29° N. (128}.

April.
East coast of North America.   42° N. (101).
Gulf of Mexico.   24° N. (106 A).

May.
Near Butt of Lewis.   58 1/2° N. (153, 154).
East coast of North America.   44° N. (19).
East coast of North America.   43° N. (97).
East coast of North America.   40° N. (161).
Between Canaries and Cape Verde.   22° N. (135).

June.

Coast of Norway.	64° N. (103).
West coast of Scotland.	57° N. (31, 32).
East coast of North America.	45° N. (83).
East coast of North America.	42° N. (34, 35, 60, 84, 106 B).
East coast of North America.	41° N. (53, 54, 162).
Mediterranean.	38° N. (148).
East coast of North America.	37° N. (52).

July.

Coast of Norway.	65° N. (61).
Coast of Norway.	64° N. (103).
Davis' Straits.	64° N. (5).
Coast of Norway.	63° N. (92, 115).
Between the Far-Oer and the Hebrides.	60° N. (56).
East coast of North America.	44° N. (29, 55).
East coast of North America.	42° N. (98, 99).
East of Cape San Roque.	5° S. (144, 145).
West of Cape of Good Hope.	35° S. (129).
South West of Cape of Good Hope.	38° S. (93).

August.

Coast of Norway.	70° N. (68).
Coast of Norway.	66 1/2° N. (157).
Coast of Norway.	66° N. (64).
Coast of Norway.	63° N. (9).
Coast of Norway.	60° N. (117).
Coast of Norway.	59° N. (85, 86).
West coast of Scotland.	57° N. (137, 138, 139, 140).
100 miles west of Brest.	48° N. (152)
North east of the Azores.	42° N. (25).
East Coast of North America.	42° N. (37, 38, 39, 40, 41, 42, 43, 44, 45, 46, 47, 48, 49, 59, 62, 63, 69, 73, 133, 134).
East coast of North America.	41° N. (158, 159, 160).
Between St. Helena & Cape of G. H.	24° S. (118).

September.

Coast of Norway.	59° N. (87, 88, 89).
North of Wales.	53 1/2° N. (155).
East coast of North America.	42° N. (71).
East coast of North America.	41° N. (77).
South west of Cape of Good Hope.	38° S. (126).

October.

Near Ibbestad, Christiansand.	58° N. (111 A).
Bristol Channel.	51° N. (156).
East coast of North America.	41° N. (50, 51).

Conclusions 403

                November.
East of Scotland.   58° N. (141, 142, 143).
Near Monillepoint.   34° S. (152A).

                December.
West of Portugal.   41° N. (120)
North-east of St. Helena.   15° S. (131).

What conclusions may now be drawn from these facts?

1. That these animals seldom appear in the North Sea, between Great Britain, France, Belgium, the Netherlands and Denmark (141, 142, 143); that they don't frequent the Baltic Ocean since two centuries; that they seldom appear in the so-called Skagerrak (85, 86, 87, 88, 89, 111A); rarely show themselves in the Gulf of Mexico (106 A) or in the Mediterranean (148); but that they moreover inhabit the whole of the Atlantic Ocean.

2. That, when they remove their quarters, they seem to swim *as much as possible* in the so-called warm ocean-currents. The number of appearances, it is true, is very small, but surveying the foregoing list of appearances in the different months I am inclined to think that these animals in their migration from north to south really swim *against* the current, while, on the contrary, in their migration from south to north they move with the current. Only a very few times they were met with in the so-called cold ocean-currents.

3. We observe that in the month of August some individuals reached the highest northern latitude, i. e. 70 degrees, and that a series of appearances took place from 70° N. to 41° N. latitude,—that in the month of September they seem not to appear beyond 59° N. latitude; and so on;—so that we may conclude that in the beginning or in the middle of August they have reached their most northern point and begin to migrate towards the south, as in December we read of no appearances beyond 41° N. latitude, and in January of no one beyond 19° S. latitude. And further we conclude that they seem to leave the southern hemisphere to migrate again towards the north already in January, for in February they generally have already reached the northern latitudes, in March still higher, and so on.

4. We observe that in one month not all the appearances took place in the same latitude, consequently in one and the same month they are scattered over a vast portion of the ocean.

5. When the migration from north to south begins, which of course must be influenced by the early or late setting in of autumn, it seems that not only the individuals which have proceeded to the most northern coasts of Norway, but also some other individuals begin their migration towards the south. I think that we must find in this fact the explanation that even in July appearances took place at from 5° to 38° southern latitude, and that on August 6 an individual was seen at lat. 24° S. swimming *towards the S. W.* Though I have no appearances in the South Atlantic in the month of October, I am convinced that the greater part of the individuals are there during this month, as well as in November, December and January.—The reason that there are so few reports from these regions is of course that in comparison with the North Atlantic, a far smaller number of vessels visits the South Atlantic.

The two appearances which happened in the Pacific, and of which the dates are mentioned, are:

	April.	
South of Japan		31° N. (151)
	May.	
South of Australia		43° S. (122)

And those of the Indian Ocean:

	January.	
Gulf of Aden		12° N. (149)
	March.	
Geographe Bay		33° S. (150)
	May.	
Indian Ocean		2° N. (147)
	September.	
Straits of Malacca		3° N. (146)
Indian Ocean		15° S.? (123)

Suppose that some individuals in the Atlantic migrate towards the south beyond the latitude of the Cape of Good Hope and get much farther than 20° eastern latitude, they will come into the Indian Ocean. I think that when these individuals returning to the north, find themselves checked by the continent of Asia, they will swim in any direction, and that perhaps most of them will find back the outlet round the Cape of Good Hope or south of Australia, so that in such cases individuals will be met with in the South Atlantic, or in the South Pacific, at times that one would not expect to find any.

10. Nomenclature.

Gesner and Pontoppidan believed that there were at least two species of the same genus. Aldrovandus, however, doubted of this, and thought that there was only one species. Dr. Hamilton was evidently of the same opinion. Rafinesque Schmaltz at last believed that there were several species.

In his *Dissertation on Water-Snakes, Sea-Snakes and Sea-Serpents*, (Nov. 1819) he gives his different species different names. Of the Massachusett's Sea-Serpent (his n°. 1) he says:

"It is evidently a real sea-snake, belonging probably to the genus *Pelamis*, and I propose to call it *Pelamis megophias*. It might, however, be a peculiar genus; in that case the name of *Megophias monstrosus* might have been appropriated to it".

Of Captain Brown's sea-serpent (his n°. 2) he writes: "It had eight gills under the neck; which decidedly evinces that it is not a snake, but a new genus of fish! I shall call this new genus *Octipos* (meaning eight gills beneath). And its scientific name will be *Octipos bicolor*" (see n°. 56).

Mr. W. Lee's sea-serpent according to Rafinesque Schmaltz (n°. 4 of his "Additions") "appears to be the largest on record, and might well be called *Pelamis monstrosus*; but if there are other species of equal size, it must be called *Pelamis chloronotis* (see n°. 30).

The author of the present volume proposed in Nov. 1881 to give it the name of *Zeuglodon plesiosauroides* (see our Chapter on Various Explanations).

It is one of the laws of Nomenclature that the oldest name of a species or genus has the priority, no matter whether the author wrote it right or wrong, and whether the author placed his species, or genus, in a genus, or family, or group, other than zoologists would do at present.

Consequently the oldest specific name of the sea-serpent is *megophias*, and this specific name must be kept. Rafinesque placed his species in the genus *Pelamis*. This genus, however, was established by Daudin, in 1802, for some real sea-snakes, and with some other genera it forms the family of *Hydrophidae* Sws. It must, therefore, be rejected.

Rafinesque himself doubting of the identity of the Great Sea-Serpent with the common small sea-snakes, proposes in that case the name of *Megophias monstrosus*. Here we have the oldest *generic* name for these animals, viz. *Megophias*. In my opinion, the only name to be given to the sea-serpent is that of

Megophias megophias (Raf.) Oud.

I know that such a double name will offend the eyes and ears of some zoologists. But it will not do to give a wrong name simply to please some zoologists; and it is here the question: by what name must these animals be called according to the law of nomenclature, and then I say:

Megophias megophias (Raf.) Oud.

and its synonyms are:

Pelamis megophias, Raf., Nov., 1819, (n°. 1),
Megophias monstrosus, Raf., Nov., 1819, (n°. 1),
Octipos bicolor, Raf., Nov. , 1819, (n°. 2),
Pelamis monstrosus, Raf., Nov., 1819, (Add. n°. 4),
Pelamis chloronotis, Raf., Nov., 1819, (Add. n°. 4),
Zeuglodon plesiosauroides, Oud., Nov., 1881.

The name of *Halsydrus Pontoppidani*, proposed by Mr. Patric Neill, for the "great sea-snake cast ashore on the isle of Stronsa" (Phil. Mag. Vol. 33, p. 90, Jan., 1809) can of course not be accepted as the scientific name of the sea-serpent, although it is older than *Megophias megophias* (Raf.) Oud. (See our Chapter on Would-be Sea-Serpents.)

Nor can there be any question to consider the name of *Hydrarchos Sillimanni*, proposed by Dr. Koch for his so-called fossil sea-serpent, as a synonym of *Megophias megophias* (Raf.) Oud. (See our Chapter on Hoaxes).

C. Conclusions

1. Comparison With Allied Animals.

It will be quite superfluous to tell my readers to which order of animals I think that this *Megophias megophias* belongs. It runs like a red thread through my whole volume, that I firmly believe that it belongs to the Order of *Pinnipedia*.

More than once I have already shown the relation to this Order, but probably not often enough to convince some headstrong scepticals, or even those who believe in the existence of sea-serpents, but think that they belong to other orders of the Animal Kingdom.

I will first show my readers some drawings and sketches of sea-lions and of a sea-bear.

Fig. 74 represents a sea-lion of the Brighton Aquarium. I think it is a *Zalophus californianus* (Less.) Allen. We observe that it has a rather pointed, rather blunt snout, with whiskers; that the eyes protrude like those of a toad, that there is a little bunch a little above and behind the eye, that its neck is long in comparison with that of common seals, that in this position the neck is narrower than the head, and the shoulders are visible, that the flappers resemble somewhat those of turtles, that the body is round and slender, and the skin smooth and glittering in the sun, though, in fact, it is hairy and not shining when it is dry.

Fig. 75 shows the same species in another position. The neck is not extended as much as possible, and so the head seems to be as large as the neck; the forehead and nose form nearly a straight line; in the bunch above the eye protruding from the surface we clearly see the heavy eye-brow; the head is held at nearly right angles with the neck, so that the latter gets wrinkles on the throat, which resemble four gills (read gillsplits), or pouches of loose skin. Compare for a moment the left foreflapper with the flappers of a sea-serpent, drawn in figg. 36, 45, and 50. The skin is smooth and shining, though when dry it is hairy and dull.

Fig. 76 is a drawing of *Eumetopias Stelleri* (Lesson) Peters, also a sea-lion. This genus is characterized by its considerably vaulted fore head (*eu* = well developed, *metopion* = forehead). The skin shows numerous folds or wrinkles, on the throat a fold again forms a distinctly visible "gill".—The form of the foreflappers resemble those of a turtle. The neck is in comparison with that of seals much longer and as it is not extended as much as possible, it is thicker than the head. The skin is smooth, being wet.

Fig. 77 represents the same species. Here the animal swims with vertical undulations.

Fig. 78 represents the same species with its neck totally contracted so that several wrinkles encircle it, resembling "kinds of scrolls, or tufts of loose skin", and it seems as if the animal has no neck at all.

Fig. 79 shows us the same species standing nearly upright in the water, with its neck contracted, so that it looks as having no neck, or a neck much larger than the head; the head seen in front is as round as a barrel; the skin is wrinkled. The individual looks at us, as if it would take a view of us.

Fig. 80 is the same individual in the same position but seen from aside. The head is now much longer, the snout neither too pointed, nor too blunt; the head is held at nearly right angles with the neck, forming a "gill" (read gillsplit) by wrinkling the skin on the throat.

Conclusions 407

Fig. 74.–*Zalophus californianus* (Less.) Allen?–Drawn by W. P.
from a living specimen in the Brighton Aquarium.–
From the *Illustrated London News* of Jan. 6. 1877.

Fig. 75.–*Zalophus californianus* (Less.) Allen.–?
–Drawn by W. P. from a living specimen in the Brighton Aquarium.–
From the *Illustrated London News* of Jan. 6. 1877.

Fig. 76.—*Eumetopias Stelleri* (Lesson) Peters.—
Drawn by the animal-painter G. Mützel from a living specimen
in the Zoological Gardens of Berlin.—
From the *Illustrirte Zeitung* of Jan. 27, 1877.

Fig. 77.—*Eumetopias Stelleri* (Lesson) Peters.—
Sketched by the animal-painter G. Mützel, from a living specimen
in the Zoological Gardens of Berlin.—
From the *Illustrirte Zeitung* of Jan. 27, 1877.

Conclusions 409

Fig. 78.–*Eumetopias Stelleri* (Lesson) Peters.– Sketched from a living specimen by the animal-painter G. Mützel in the Zoological Gardens of Berlin.– From the *Illustrirte Zeitung* of Jan. 27, 1877.

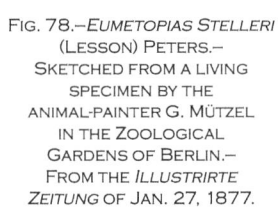

Fig. 79.–*Eumetopias Stelleri* (Lesson) Peters.– Sketched by the animal-painter G. Mützel from a living specimen in the Zoological Gardens of Berlin.–From the *Illustrirte Zeitung* of Jan. 27, 1877.

Fig. 80.–*Eumetopias Stelleri* (Lesson) Peters.– Sketched by the animal-painter G. Mützel from a living specimen in the Zoological Gardens of Berlin.–From the *Illustrirte Zeitung* of Jan. 27, 1877.

FIG. 81.–*OTARIA JUBATA* (FORSTER) DESM.–
FROM THE "LIST OF THE VERTEBRATED ANIMALS NOW OR LATELY LIVING
IN THE GARDENS OF THE ZOOLOGICAL SOCIETY OF LONDON, 1877."

FIG. 82.–*CALLORHINUS URSINUS* (LINNÉ) GRAY.–FROM BREHM'S "THIERLEBEN".

Fig. 81 is a drawing of *Otaria jubata*, quite dry. The head is held at nearly right angles with the neck forming two "gills". The snout is rather blunt, apparently quadrangular in front. The nostrils are at the end of the snout and wide open, "nearly semicircular valves overarching" them. The eyes are wide open and disproportionately large. The neck in comparison with that of seals is long. The skin is hairy, the hairs of the neck are much longer. This mane begins at the occiput. The form of the flappers is like that of a turtle's. Compare the form of the foreflappers with that of figg. 36, 45 and 50. The body is round and slender.

Fig. 82 represents a sea-bear, *Callorhinus ursinus*, quite dry. The little hairy bunch which is visible in the forepart of the back, is the shoulder of the other side. The hairs of the back-line are longer than the others, forming a mane extending all over the neck and back. The reader will see that I have represented this animal with only four toes on both the foreflappers and hindflappers; this is because I give a facsimile of the figure occurring in Brehm's "Thierleben".

It is not the place here to give a monograph of Pinnipeds, but to compare the different known characters of the sea-serpents with those of the other of Pinnipeds, and therefore I am obliged to take the same order I have followed above.

Dimensions. At first sight it will be doubted if such an enormous animal can be a pinniped; It is so immensely large in comparison with the known species of this order! Suppose for a moment that whale-bone whales, spermwhales and finwhales were not yet known, and that one of these animals was caught; what would be our astonishment! Suppose that pythons and boas were not yet discovered, and somebody showed us a skin of a python of 26 feet long, I think that the first thought would be "you are a handy fellow, but you will not cheat me with your story!" I will add here some other striking comparisons.

The largest known now living cartilaginous fishes are of 36 (*Selache maxima*) and of 42 feet (*Carcharodon Rondeletii*); but a fossil species of the latter genus reached a length of 81 feet (*Carcharodon megalodon*), and earlier Northern truthful and accurate writers even mention 100 feet as occasional dimension of the *Selache maxima*, an animal eagerly pursued by the Norwegians for the oil of its liver.

We, who in our latitudes look already with amazement on a salmon of 5 feet length, must be perplexed when seeing for the first time an osseous fish of 10 (*Thynnus thynnus*), of 15 (*Arapaima gigas*), or of 20 feet (*Regalecus Banksii*).

The largest known living Amphibium is 4 feet long (*Cryptobranchus*), and caused great astonishment, when it was discovered, but fossil *Amphibia* have been found larger than 15 feet (*Mastodonsaurus*).

The largest actually measured living Reptile has a length of 30 feet (*Crocodilus*), but some fossilized reptiles show a length of 38 feet (*Hadrosaurus, Ichthyosaurus*), 45 feet (*Elasmosaurus*), 58 feet (*Rhamphosuchus*), 70 feet (*Brontosaurus*), nay even of 100 (*Liodon*) and of 115 feet (*Atlantosaurus*), and probably many kinds of Reptiles are still longer, the skeletons of which have been dug up only partially!

Whale-bone-whales of 88 feet, spermwhales of 90 feet, and finwhales of 120 feet are occasionally mentioned to have been measured in the foregoing century, but at present such dimensions are not more recorded, because these animals have been so incessantly persecuted for ages!

Well, let us stop here, and say that there are many wonders still hidden in the sea, and that there will be always a chance that of every species of animals individuals will be discovered, still larger than the largest specimen ever measured. If of all Pinnipeds the sea-elephants were hitherto the largest known, this is no more the case: they are surpassed by sea-serpents. If of all known living and fossil animals the *Atlantosaurus* and the *Balaenoptera* were hitherto the largest known, this is no more the case: they are surpassed by the *Megophias*.

Of all Pinnipeds the family of the *Auriculata* (Eared Seals) has the longest necks. In this particular they are surpassed by sea-serpents.

None of the hitherto known living Pinnipeds has such an enormous tail as the sea-serpent, but the fossil *Basilosaurus*, an animal more or less allied to the earless seals, has an enormous tail. Of the singular appearance of a family of which some members have immensely long tails, and others are almost wholly without, we have more instances in the animal kingdom. Of the Monkeys the family of the *Simiidae* have no tails, whilst the other families have generally long tails. Amongst the tailed monkeys we find in one *genus* species with very long tails, as the *Macacus cynamolgos* (the Macaque Monkey), and others with very short tails, as the *Macacas maurus* (Moor Macaque). This difference in the length of the tail is present *in all orders* of the *Quadrupedia*.

Form.—The shape of *Megophias megophias* is exactly that of *Zalophus californianus*, with a longer neck, and with a tail as long as trunk, neck, and head together. The shape of the head too, in my opinion, more resembles that of *Zalophus californianus* than that of any other Pinniped. The shape of the neck, the trunk, and the flappers is exactly that of the same portions of the *Auriculata*, especially in *Zalophus californianus*, viz: all are slender: "The body is rather slender, and the head is narrow, long, and pointed, and with this slenderness of form is coordinated a corresponding litheness of movement". (Allen, *History of North American Pinnipeds*, p. 276). It may be that the hindflappers have a form hitherto unknown in Pinnipeds, as we have of the hindflappers neither a description nor any tolerable illustration. The forehead being flat, very much resembles that of *Zalophus californianus*. The snout or muzzle too, is of all Pinnipeds most resembling that of *Zalophus californianus*.

All Pinnipeds have whiskers. In some species they are large, as in *Callorhinus ursinus*, the sea-bear, in other comparatively small, as in *Monachus tropicalis* Gray, and in the males of the genus *Macrorhinus*, and even very small in the *Trichecidae*.

The eyes of *Megophias megophias* seem to be comparatively larger than those in other species of Pinnipeds, though *Otaria jubata* and *Phoca foetida* are known to have comparatively large eyes. I have nowhere found any remark about the colour of the eye, with regard to its *tapetum lucidum,* and till now I have had no opportunity to convince myself of the *tapetum* of *Zalophus* or *Eumetopias* being red. But is it not remarkable that Mr. H. W. Elliot too asserts of *Eumetopias Stelleri:* "it has a really leonine appearance and bearing, greatly enhanced by the rich, golden-rufous of its coat, ferocity of expression, and *bull-dog-like muzzle and cast of eye*"? (Allen, *Hist. N. Am. Pinn.* p. 258).

Skin.—As in all Pinnipeds the skin is hairy, most probably the hairs are quite stiff and not woolly like fur.

Colours, Individual Variations.—We have only to read different descriptions of seals, sea-lions, and sea-bears, to observe that every species varies much as to its colour, but that in some there is a wide range of individual variations. Only in a few species the under part is darker than the upper part, but generally the upper part is much darker than the under part, and with regard to their colours the animals are so to say longitudinally divided into two sections, dark above, lighter beneath. Their being variegated with spots or streaks occurs in many species, less in sea-lions and sea-bears, more in seals, but is the most striking in the Hooded Seal (*Cystophora cristata*, (Erxl.) Nilss.). If we closely examine this species, the question arises: is not the lighter colour the groundcolour, and are not the dark spots and streaks and circles secondary appearances? And I think that this question must be answered in the affirmative. Remarkable is also the black colour of the region of the mouth and round the eye in some individuals of sea-serpents. This singularity occurs also in some specimens of other Pinnipeds. Of *Eumetopias Stelleri* "the end of the nose.... is naked and.... dull blue black" (Allen, *Hist. N. Am. Pinn.* p. 234, 235); of *Zalophus californianus* we read: "A third is.... blackish around the eyes and nostrils" (Allen, *Hist. N. Am. Pinn.* p. 277). In a foetal specimen: "nose and face, to and around the eyes" are "black" (Ibid., p. 278); and Nilsson's black variety of the Ringed Seal (*Phoca foetida* Fabr.) has "nose and eye-rings uniform black" (Ibid. p. 602).

Sexual differences, Mane.—The males of some species of Pinnipeds have a mane, i. e. the hairs of the neck are longer than on the rest of the body. Of *Eumetopias Stelleri* "the hair is longest on the anterior upper portion of the body, where on the neck and shoulders it attains a length of 40 mm.; it decreases in length posteriorly, and toward the tail has a length of only 15 mm." (Allen, *Hist. N. Am. Pinn.* p. 234). Of the hairs of *Callorhinus ursinus* we read: "It is longest on the top of the head, especially in the males, which have a well marked crest. The hair is much longer on the anterior half of the body than on the posterior half, it being longest on the hinder part of the neck, where in the males it is very coarse. On the crown the hair has a length of 42 mm.; on the. hinder part of the neck it reaches a length of 50 to 60 mm. From this point posteriorly it gradually shortens, and near the tail has a length of only 20 mm. The males have much longer hair than the females, in which it is much longer than in *Eumetopias Stelleri*." (Allen, *Hist. N. Am. Pinn.* p. 315).

The difference in size of males and females is also a peculiar character of some species of Pinnipeds, as may be seen from the following tables:

NAME	VERY OLD MALE.	VERY OLD FEMALE	RATIO.
Zalophus californianus	8½ ft.	6¾ ft	100 : 81
Eumetopias Stelleri	13 »	9 »	100 : 69
Macrorhinus leoninus	25 »	15 »	100 : 60
Macrorhinus angustirostris	22 »	13 »	100 : 59
Callorhinus ursinus	8 »	4 »	100 : 50

In *Callorhinus ursinus* the female, as we observe, attains only half the length of a male. The weight of a fullgrown female being less than one sixth that of a full-grown male.

The losing of hair when the animals grow very old, is very striking in both *Odobaenus rosmarus* and in *Odobaenus obesus*.

Food.—The food of all Pinnipeds consists of mussels, and other mollusks, especially, however, of all kinds of fish, but that they are not averse to cetacean flesh, may be proved by the following fact: Mr. Brown says of *Odobaenus rosmarus*: "I have only to add that whenever it was killed near where a whale's carcass had been let adrift, its stomach was unvariably found crammed full of the krang or flesh of that *Cetacean*" (Allen, *Hist. N. Am. Pinn.* p. 135). *Eumetopias Stelleri* occasionally eats birds (Ibid. p. 274).

Breathing.—Even in seals and sea-lions it may be occasionally observed that they "blow like a whale"; I myself saw it more than once, when the animals lay with their nose at water level, or when they appeared on the surface after having remained under water for a long time. It is sufficiently known that the average time these animals remain under water is eight or ten minutes, but they have also been observed lying quite still on the bottom for more than three hours. I read in Mr. Allen's work (p. 180) that also walruses "blow not unlike a whale".

Excretion.—The emitting a very strong odour is also known in Pinnipeds. Krascheninikow says of *Callorhinus ursinus*: "Such as are old, or have no mistresses, live apart; and the first that our people found upon *Behring's* Island were such old ones, and all males, extremely fat and stinking" (Allen, p. 342). Of *Eumetopias Stelleri* Choris reports: "L'odeur qu'ils répandent est insupportable. Ces animaux étaient alors dans le temps du rut" (Allen, p. 254), and of *Phoca foetida* Kumlien asserts:

"It is only the adult males (called *Tigak*, = Stinker, by the Eskimo) that emit the horribly disagreeable, all-permeating, ever-penetrating odor that has suggested its specific name. It is so strong that one can smell an Eskimo some distance when he has been partaking of the flesh; they say it is more nourishing than the flesh of the females, and that a person can endure great fatigue after eating it. If one of these Tigak comes in contact with any other Seal meat it will become so tainted as to be repulsive to an educated palate; even the atluk of the Tigak can be detected by its odor." (Allen, p. 624).

Respecting the foetid odour emitted by this species, Dr. Rink observes as follows:

"It derives its scientific name from the nauseous smell peculiar to certain older individuals, especially those captured in the interior ice-fjords, which are also on an average perhaps twice as large as those generally occurring off the outer shores. When brought into a hut, and cut up on its floor, such a seal emits a smell resembling something between that of assafoetida and onions, almost insupportable to strangers. This peculiarity is not noticeable in the younger specimens or those of a smaller size, such as are generally caught, and at all events the smell does not detract from the utility of the flesh over the whole of Greenland".—*Danish Greenland, its People and its Products* p. 123 (Allen, *Hist. N. Am. Pinn.* p. 624).

Feeling.—Also in seals and sea-lions in our Zoological Gardens we may often observe that they dislike wind, and hold only the top of their nose above water, that they shut their eyes, and like to bask in the sun.

Smell, Hearing, Sight.—It is also known of Pinnipeds that their smell is very good and their hearing very sharp, but that their sight is quite limited. This must not surprise us. Their eyes are adapted to see under water, but such eyes don't see so well in the air. Yet I have observed that seals distinguish their keeper from other persons at a distance of twenty or thirty yards.

Relative mobility of organs.—Every one who has ever witnessed the graceful movements of seals and sea-lions, especially those of *Zalophus californianus* will admit that these animals, like sea-serpents, are "as limber and active as an eel". There is not one movement made by the sea-serpent, which cannot be made in perfectly the same way by sea-lions, especially by *Zalophus californianus*, save the movement of the tail.

Motion.—The same may be observed in comparing the motions of sea-serpents with those of *Zalophus californianus*. They too may appear on the surface, exposing head, neck, and so much of the forepart of the trunk, as to show their flappers; nay, they may like all kinds of whales, jump clear out of the water. When swimming slowly, they may occasionally swim with vertical undulations, they usually, however, propel themselves by means of their flappers, holding their body in a straight line; and sometimes horizontal undulations are distinctly visible; in darting on some prey they swim not only with their flappers, but undulate their body both horizontally and vertically at intervals. Of course generally only one or two, seldom three undulations are to be counted.

I don't know if sea-lions have ever been seen swimming with *fixed bunches*, or folds. When at rest their skin may enormously wrinkle, like that of walruses, and as is shown in our fig. 78.

In swimming the sea-lion usually holds its head above water, and may occasionally raise its long neck as high as possible to take a view of a boat or another object.

Owing to the form and size of its flappers the speed of the sea-lion is really astonishing; it is much less in seals.

Though in a less degree, than in sea-serpents, the water curls up before its chest, or better throat, in swimming; foam is occasionally observed, and waves are seen in the form of a V, a wake is of course formed, and a rushing may be heard at times.

That seals swim so low under the surface of the water, that the course of the animal can be traced only by the rippling surface, I have myself witnessed, but I do not know if sea-lions, especially, if *Zalophus californianus*, are in the habit of swimming in this way.

The manner of disappearing of the sea-serpent is exactly the same as that of other Pinnipeds. They may turn down with a severe splash, or sink gradually below the surface, or even, by a sudden upward motion of their flappers, "sink down like a rock".

As to the *voice* of other Pinnipeds it is different in the different species, but as we have not a single statement of the voice of sea-serpents, comparison is out of the question here.

Generation.—The rutting time and the time of whelping differ in different species, but on an average the month of March and April may be fixed upon as the paring time, and July and August as those in which the females bring forth the young ones.

In some species the males are much larger than the females, and the new born young ones, like the young sea-serpents are in exact proportion to the old males, as may be seen from the following table.

NAME.	VERY OLD MALE.	NEW BORN YOUNG ONE.	RATIO.
Zalophus californianus	$8^1/_3$ ft.	$2^1/_3$ ft.	$1/_3$—$1/_4$
Macrorhinus angustirostris	22 »	4 »	$1/_5$—$1/_6$
Eumetopias Stelleri	13 »	2 »	$1/_6$—$1/_7$
Callorhinus ursinus	8 »	10 in.	$1/_8$—$1/_9$

Taking notice of objects.—It is well enough known that seals will sometimes keep near a vessel, turning their head towards it; or will play round the vessel, disappearing on one side, reappearing on the other, as if playing hide and seek; from this it may be concluded they are in no dread of the vessel, but are curious, and suspicious of the living objects on it. I don't know whether sea-lions and sea-bears behave in the same way, but I know that walruses do.

Curiosity and Suspicion are known characters in all kinds of Pinnipeds, and it is noteworthy that they are most striking in walruses and seals.

Harmlessness and Timidity.—There is hardly any Pinniped which is not harmless and timid.

Fearlessness is a common trait in walruses and sea-elephants. One may come very near them. On the other hand scores of them, especially of the former, will sometimes follow a boat, roaring and crying and uttering the most horrible sounds, which may be expressions of their curiosity, suspicion, and fury, but it may also be a way they have of driving away their enemy.

Fear on the contrary, though less noticeable in walruses, is a prominent trait in seals, sea-lions and sea-bears. When men approach them they fly away as fast as possible, and in their hurry to reach the water crawl over each other, and roar, and cry, and lament in a most horrible way.

Fright.—It is superfluous to touch upon this subject in Pinnipeds; every one knows the effects and consequences of a shot at these timid animals.

Fury.—As in sea-serpents, most Pinnipeds, but especially sea-lions, sea-bears and walruses only get furious when wounded, or when neared while they are protecting their offspring.

Toughness.—I know of no observations about this character in seals, sea-lions, sea-bears, and sea-elephants, but I believe that they are not tough; one heavy blow with a thick cudgel on the nose killing them instantly, but the toughness of walruses is known well enough; these animals are not an easy prey; they may be struck with axes on their cranium and hit by several rifle balls in their brain, and yet not die; they die a hard death.

Playsomeness is a well known character of all Pinnipeds; it may of course be less observable in the bulky and unwieldy walruses.

Remark.—It is time that the volume comes to an end, and therefore I have made my comparison as short as possible. I have only to advise those who wish to know more about the agreement of sea-serpents with Pinnipeds, to read Allen's often quoted work *"History of North-American Pinnipeds"*, and his *"On Eared Seals"*, (*Bull. Mus. Comp. Zool. Harvard College.* Cambr. Mass. Vol. II, n°. 1.), and Brehm's *Thierleben.*

There is one great difference between all the known Pinnipeds on one side, and sea-serpents on the other. The former are gregarious or social animals, only living in colonies or great herds, whilst *Megophias megophias* is a solitary being. This remarkable difference can be only accounted for by the two facts 1. That this species is a cosmopolitan, and 2. That these animals become extinct and that there exist at present only a very few individuals.

I don't know if I have convinced my readers of the existence of sea-serpents, and if so, if they are convinced that these animals are closely related to Pinnipeds. But I am obliged to proceed on my way, and consider the rank which sea-serpents occupy in the system of Nature.

2. Its Rank in the System of Nature.

Zoologists admit as a fact that Pinnipeds originate in true land-animals. We are convinced that these land-animals were long-tailed Viverrine animals. The tail must have been longer than one half of the total length. This is no impossibility, as we have still living forms, the tail of which is as long as half of the total length of the animal, e. g. *Herpestes Widdringtonii.* The dentition must have been the typical carnivorous one: i 3/3, c 1/1, m 7/7; or there were more molars, perhaps 8/8, as a genus of wild dogs, *Otocyon*, has 8 molars on each side of each jaw; its dentition is i 3/3, c 1/1, m 8/8. (The *Cynoidea*, or dog-like animals are also considered as having their origin in Viverrine animals.)

Some of the descendants of these long-tailed Viverrine animals had gradually got such characters, that zoologists would term them long-tailed Musteline animals. They may be called *long-tailed ancestors of weasels and stoats*, for our common weasel (*Putorius vulgaris* L.) and our common stoat (*Putorius ermineus* L.) are still living descendants of them, though the tail has become very short, most probably because they have accustomed themselves to live in holes. The long tail has shown itself to be an inconvenient organ for this new manner of living, and therefore has gradually become shorter.

Some of these *long-tailed ancestors of weasels and stoats* took to another manner of living, compelled thereto by certain circumstances. They viz. took to eating fresh water fish. Gradually this grew to be a habit; they learned to swim, which happened by vertical undulations, they paddled with the feet, and used the tail as a rudder. This group may be called *long-tailed ancestors of polecats and minks*, for our common polecat (*Putorius putorius* L.) and the Russian minks (*Putorius lutreolus* L.) are still living descendants of them, though the tail has become short, because they have accustomed themselves to live in holes. The long tail has shown itself to be an inconvenient organ for such a manner of living, and therefore has gradually become shorter, not so short, however, as in weasels and stoats. Zoologists place the polecats and minks in the same genus as the weasels and stoats. The minks live especially in the neighbourhood of rivers and brooks, often go into the water and swim exceedingly well. Besides on poultry and rats, they feed on frogs, crabs, cray-fish, and all kinds of fish.

Some of these *long-tailed ancestors of polecats and minks* got so used to the water, that it finally became their proper element, and they came ashore only to rest from swimming, to bask themselves in the sun, or to find another brook or river. They began to feed on fish, crayfish, and frogs, and only when driven by hunger they fed on rats and poultry. It is evident that those individuals which by nature were best adapted to their new element, must gradually have survived their less privileged brethren, and so we may admit that a form gradually arose, which swam very easily with vertical undulations, using the tail as a rudder and as propelling organ. Also of great advantage must have been more sharply pointed teeth, and more jagged molars, smaller ears, a more woolly skin, and toes on the hind limbs, which were capable of expansion and more or less provided with a web. This group may be called *long-tailed ancestors of otters,* for all the known species of otters (*Lutra*) are still living descendants of them, though the tail has become shorter, shorter than one third of the total length of the animal, because they too like to live in holes. The face greatly resembles that of the polecat and mink, but the upper lips are thicker and the whiskers are longer and stronger.

The change was not only great enough for zoologists to create for this group a new genus: *Lutra* Storr, but even to establish for it a new subfamily *Lutrina* Gray.

These *long-tailed ancestors of otters* were again survived by their congeners which were still better adapted to the new medium, so that from them another group gradually arose, which had broader webs on the hind feet. This group may be called *long-tailed ancestors of fin-tailed otters,* for the fin-tailed otter (*Lutra Sanbachii* Gray) is a still living descendant of them. The tail of this animal is shorter than that of its ancestors, longer, however, than that of the otters (*Lutra*), surpassing one third of the animal's total length. Moreover it is somewhat flattened and shows on its hindmost half lateral fin-like dilatations. The change was great enough for zoologists to place the animal into a new genus: *Pteronura* Gray. Its ancestors, however, were not provided with these lateral fin-like dilatations on the tail.

Some of these *long-tailed ancestors of thin-tailed otter* which in their migration had reached the sea-shore, probably by following the course of rivers, began to accustom themselves to eat sea-fish, and ended by feeding on them exclusively. The sea-water became their home, and their resting places and nests were found on the strand, and among sea-weed; they seldom came ashore to sleep or to sun themselves. Besides on sea-fish, they fed on crabs, lobsters, mussels, and some sea-weed. They left off eating poultry, frogs, and rats. The long tail was of great profit, as they used it as a rudder and as propelling organ in swimming with vertical undulations. Of course those individuals which were the best adapted to this new manner of living, survived the less privileged by nature, and so a group gradually arose which had a sharper dentition, and smaller ears; the skin was also changed to the must valuable fur, the toes of the hind-legs had become more webbed, and with such legs the animals could swim more easily; those of the fore-limbs had sharper nails, and with such nails the animals could more easily crawl upon the rocks; the eyes were larger, and with such eyes the owners could see better in great and dark depths, and in the sea-water near the shore, which is commonly troubled; the whiskers were longer and stronger, consequently the upper-lips, in which these whiskers were planted and which contained numerous and thick sensorial nerves, were very thick, and with such whiskers the animals could exceedingly well touch and feel when searching for their food between stones and sea-weed, and in the sandy bottom. The face resembled but little more that of the otters and fin-tailed otters, and the large eyes and shorter ears gave it a slight resemblance to seals. This group may be called *long-tailed ancestors of sea-otters,* for our sea-otters (*Lutra lutris* L.) are still living descendants of them. But as these animals have accustomed themselves to live more among sea-weed, ice, and rocks than their direct ancestors, the long tail must have been inconvenient, so that individuals with a shorter tail must have survived the others, and finally a species arose with a tolerably short tail: our sea-otter. To make up for this loss of tail, the hind-feet had become more webbed, and were gradually stretched more backwards, and, modified in this way, they were valuable swimming organs. The change was great enough for zoologists to create a new genus for this animal, which is called *Enhydra* Cuv.

Some of the *long-tailed ancestors of sea otters* took to a still more aquatic, or better pelagic life, migrated more towards the north, accustomed themselves to the icy regions, to swim greater distances and to remain longer under water. The consequences of this change in the manner of living were that all little adapted to this new life became extinct, and that all which were better privileged survived them, so that at last a group of animals arose of which we may safely admit that they had the following characters: The head and fore-feet resembled still more those of seals, the hind-legs were still more able swimming organs, and less fit for terrestrial locomotion, they were smaller than the fore-legs, because they were not always used in swimming, as the best manner of swimming must have been by means of vertical undulations; the long tail surpassed half of the total length, and served as a rudder and as propelling organ; the ears were still smaller, the dentition was still a normal carnivorous one (i 3/3, c 1/1, m 7/7), especially the molars were sharp and pointed, and on the skull were found peculiar modifications which are so distinctly visible on that of Pinnipeds. The animals must have resembled our common seals, having, however, small external ears, and a tail, surpassing one half of the total length. It is difficult to believe that these animals, which I will call *Propinnipedia*, moved on land; probably they came from time to time aland or on the ice to rest with the fore-part of the body on it, leaving, however, most certainly the long tail in the water. These *Propinnipedia* gave origin to two groups of animals, which are marked below with A and B.

A.—This group, by their having lived almost constantly far from land, and having come only very seldom near the shore to rest, supporting themselves on the chest or breast, clinging with the nails of the fore-legs to the beach, rock, or ice, changed in such a way, that zoologists can hardly reckon them any longer among Pinnipeds, but generally consider them as a link between Pinnipeds and Whales. Professor D'Arcy W. Thompson (*Studies from the Museum of Zoology in University College*, Dundee, Vol. I, N°. 9, 1890) rejects any affinity of this group to Whales. I should like to go still farther and pretend that it has just as much claim to the title of Pinnipeds, as seals, sea-elephants, sea-bears, sea-lions, and sea-serpents. The skull was somewhat lengthened in front; the brain-case diminished in size; the deciduous dentition probably cut the gum; the permanent dentition was the typical heterodont carnivorous one (i 3/3, c 1/1, m 7/7); the nostrils were placed on the tip of the nose, as in seals, but directed upwards; the fore-limbs were perfectly those of seals, and provided with nails; but the rest of the body must have *resembled* that of a slender and elongated dolphin, or whale, with an enormous *pointed* tail. The most successful manner of swimming for these animals was by means of vertical undulations, which, as the forepart of the body (head and trunk) was somewhat bulky, and therefore somewhat inflexible, were strongest in the tail-part of the animal; consequently the hind-legs, used less and less, disappeared, if not quite, at least for the greater part. The animals were still hairy, though the hairs were most probably thinly scattered; the whiskers remained on the lips. The head was relatively large, not with regard to the animal's total length, but to the trunk, and therefore the neck was very short. Externally the neck must not have been plainly visible. The animals could not move the head as easily as seals and sea-lions do, and therefore it was of great advantage that the nostrils were directed upwards. The vertebrae have the type of those of the Pinnipeds.—Such animals are now extinct, but their fossil remains are found and called *Basilosaurus* by Harlan in 1824 (afterwards Owen gave them the name of *Zeuglodon*, 1839).

B.—This second group is called *Pinnipedia* by Illiger in 1811, and Allen gives of it the following characters:

"Limbs pinniform, or modified into swimming organs, and enclosed to or beyond the elbows and knees within the common integument. Digits of the manus decreasing in length and size from the first to the fifth; of those of the pes, the first and fifth largest and longest, the three middle ones shorter and subequal. Pelvis with the iliac portion very short, and the anterior border much everted; ischia barely meeting by a short symphysis (never anchylosed) and in the female usually widely separated. Skull generally greatly compressed interorbitally; facial portion usually short, rather broad, and the brain-case abruptly expanded. Lachrymal bone imperforate and joined to the maxillary, enclosed wholly within the orbit. Palatines usually separated by a vacuity, often of considerable size, from the frontals. Tympanic bones separated also by a vacuity from the exoccipitals. Dentition simple, generally unspecialized, the molars all similar in structure. Deciduous dentition rudimentary, never truly functional, and generally not persistent beyond the foetal stage of the animal. Permanent incisors usually 6/4 or 4/4, sometimes 4/2 (*Cystophora* and *Macrorhinus*) or even 2/2 (*Odobaenus*); canines 2/2; molars 5/5, 6/5, or 5/3."

And we may add: Tail either very long: about as long as one half of the animal's total length, or very short: almost disappearing between the hind-legs.

Already very early the Pinnipeds divided themselves into two different branches, marked below with I and II.

I.—The members of this branch changed their manner of living. They very often crawled on land, ice, and rocks; the long tail was a very unconvenient organ in their new manner of living, consequently all the individuals with a somewhat shorter tail than their congeners' were better adapted to the new manner of living and survived them, so that at last a group of animals arose of which the tail has become very short, almost disappearing between the hind-legs, and to make up for this loss the hind-legs grew much larger than the fore-legs, were turned hindwards, gradually grew incapable of being turned forwards, and of no use in terrestrial locomotion. This branch is called *Inauriculata* by Péron in 1816 (afterwards called *Phocidae* by Gray in 1825, and *Reptigrada* by Elliot Coues, invited thereto by Allen in 1880). The characters are described by Allen as follows:

"Hind-legs not capable of being turned forward, and not serviceable for terrestrial locomotion. Neck short. Skull with the mastoid processes swollen, but not salient, and without distinct alisphenoid canals. Anterior limbs smaller than the posterior, the first digit little, if any, longer than the next succeeding ones, all armed with strong claws, which are terminal. Hind feet capable of moderate expansion, short; digits (usually) all armed with strong claws, and without terminal cartilaginous flaps. Femur with no trace of the trochanter minor. Without external ears. Postorbital processes wanting, or very small. Incisors variable (6/4, 4/4, or 4/2). Deciduous dentition not persistent beyond foetal life."

The group includes all true seals and sea-elephants.

II.—This branch is called *Gressigrada* by Elliot Coues in 1880, who was thereto invited by Allen, though this skilled zoologist was then unaware of the existence of the sea-serpent, or at least must have doubted its belonging to this branch. I have not a single reason to give another name to it; I purposely keep the name of *Gressigrada*, to avoid the increase of synonyms. The early forms of the *Gressigrada* must have had hind-legs which were smaller than the fore-legs, and a tail, which was as long as the head, neck and trunk together. They had also small external ears, and a somewhat lengthened neck. Further characters are: "Hind-legs capable of being turned forward and used in terrestrial locomotion. Neck lengthened (especially in section b). Skull with the mastoid processes large and salient (especially in the males), and with distinct alisphenoid canals. Anterior feet either nearly as large as the posterior, or much larger, their digits rapidly decreasing in length from the first to the fifth, with distinct claws, and with a broad cartilaginous border extending beyond the digits." (They are called flappers.) "Hind-feet susceptible of great expansion, the three middle digits only with claws, and all the digits terminating in long, narrow, cartilaginous flaps g united basally." (The hind-feet may also safely be called flappers.) "Femur with the trochanter minor well developed".—Already at a very early date the branch of the *Gressigrada* divided itself into two sections, which are marked below with a and b.—

a.—The members of this section changed their manner of living. They very often crawled on ice, land, and rocks; the long tail was a very inconvenient organ in their new manner of living, consequently all the individuals with a somewhat shorter tail than their congeners' were better equipped, and survived the others, so that at last a group of animals arose of which the tail has become very short, scarcely, if at all, visible, being enclosed within the tegument of the body, and to make up for this loss, the hindflappers grew much larger than the fore-flappers. The further characters for this group are: "Without external ears. Form thick and heavy. Anterior portion of the skull greatly swollen, giving support to the enormously developed canines, which form long, protruding tusks. Incisors of deciduous (foetal) dentition 6/6; of permanent dentition 2/0. No postorbital processes, and the surface of the mastoid processes continuous with the auditory bullae."—This section is called *Trichecidae* by Gray in 1821 (afterwards it was named *Trichechidae* by Gray in 1825, *Broca* by Latreille in 1825, *Campodontia* by Brookes in 1828, *Trichecina* by Gray in 1837, *Trichechoidea* by Giebel in 1847, *Trichechina* by Gray in 1850, *Rosmaridae* by Gill in 1866, *Roemaroidea* by Gill in 1872, and *Odobaenidae* by Allen in 1880!!!). The section contains only the walruses.

b.—The early forms of this section must have had hind-flappers which were smaller than the fore-flappers, and a tail which was as long as the head, neck and trunk together. The animals were very slender and elongated in form, the neck being *somewhat more elongated;* external ears, though small, were still present. Further characters are: "Anterior portion of the skull not unusually swollen, and the canines not highly specialized." They came very seldom aland, and when doing so, they must have only supported themselves on their breast and on their fore-flappers, leaving the long tail always in the water. They swam with vertical undulations, using also sometimes the flappers.—For this section I choose the name of *Tenuia*, or Animals which are slender.—Very early the section of the *Tenuia* divided itself into two smaller divisions which are marked below with 1 and 2.—

1.—The members of this division changed their manner of living. They very often crawled on ice, land and rocks; the tail was a very inconvenient organ in their new manner of living, consequently all the individuals with a somewhat shorter tail than their congeners', were better equipped and survived the others, so that at last a group of animals arose of which the tail has become very short, almost disappearing between the hind-legs which on the contrary to make up for this loss of tail, gradually became larger, so as to become even larger than the anterior feet. The further characters of this group are: "With small external ears. Incisors of deciduous dentition 6/4, only the outer on either side cutting the gum; of permanent dentition 6/4, the two central pairs of the upper with a transverse groove. Postorbital processes strongly developed. Surface of the mastoid processes not continuous with the auditory bullae."—This division was called *Auriculata* by Péron in 1816, (afterwards also called *Otariina* by Gray in 1825, *Otariadae* by Brookes in

1828, *Arctocephalina* by Gray in 1837, and *Otariidae* by Gill in 1866) containing the sea-bears and sea-lions.

2.—The members of this division did not accustom themselves to live in the midst of ice and rocks, consequently they retained the long tail, and small hind-legs. As the animals retained also their slenderness and extraordinary litheness, a long neck with a relatively small head must have been of great use to them, and consequently those individuals which had a longer neck than the others survived their less privileged congeners, so that at last a group arose with a very long neck and a comparatively small head. It seems that the external ears disappeared. They never came aland or on ice-floes. They even abandoned the cold regions and currents of the ocean, better liking the warmer parts. Their ordinary mode of swimming is with vertical undulations. Seldom do they swim with the body in a straight line, by means of their flappers. This little division for which I propose the name of *Longicaudata*, or Long-tailed Animals, consists only of one genus: *Megophias* Raf., including only one species *Megophias megophias* (Raf.) Oud., the sea-serpent.

I purposely have not mentioned the genera *Squalodon* and Stenodon, and the group of *Plagiuri* (Art., 1735; *Physeteres*, Klein, 1741; *Cetacea*, Briss, 1756; *Cete*, Linn, 1758), as the recent cetologists still differ in opinions as to their relation to *Basilosaurus* and the *Pinnipedia*.

I think the following phylogenetic table will in a more practical manner show the rank which in my opinion sea-serpents occupy in the System of Nature.

To many of my readers the above sketch of the rank of the sea-serpent in the System of Nature will no doubt seem to be too bold. They will say that the affinity of the sea-serpent to sea-lions and sea-bears (to the *Auriculata*) is expressed here too dicisively, that, scientifically spoken, the sea-serpent is not yet known, that at best its existence is only beyond a doubt, and that when a specimen fell into the hands of men, it might be shown that the close affinity to the *Auriculata* was only apparent, and that in reality the relation is more remote. I confess that there is much to say in favour of this reasoning, but *at all events the sea-serpent is a true Pinniped*. It has four flappers, a hairy skin, and strong whiskers. Its head *resembles* that of a sea-lion, its long neck *resembles* that of a sea-lion, its trunk and its foreflappers resemble those of a sea-lion. But these *resemblances* may be explained as resulting from convergency. When viewed in this way it seems to be more careful to consider the origin of the sea-serpent in the following manner.

The ancestors of *Pinnipedia* and *Basilosaurus*, which I have called *Propinnipedia*, had most probably hind-legs which were smaller than the fore-legs, and most certainly a tail which was nearly as long as the head, neck and trunk together. They had small external ears. Their most successful manner of swimming must have been by means of vertical undulations. It is difficult to believe that the *Propinnipedia* moved on land; probably they came only from time to time aland, or on the ice, to rest, leaving, however, most probably the long tail in the water. These *Propinnipedia* divided themselves into two branches.

All the members of the *first* branch got a tendency to bulkiness. The head grew longer and larger, consequently the neck grew shorter; the jaws grew longer, consequently the teeth began to stand widely apart; in consequence of the little mobility of the head the nostrils, placed at the top of the nose, became turned

Conclusions

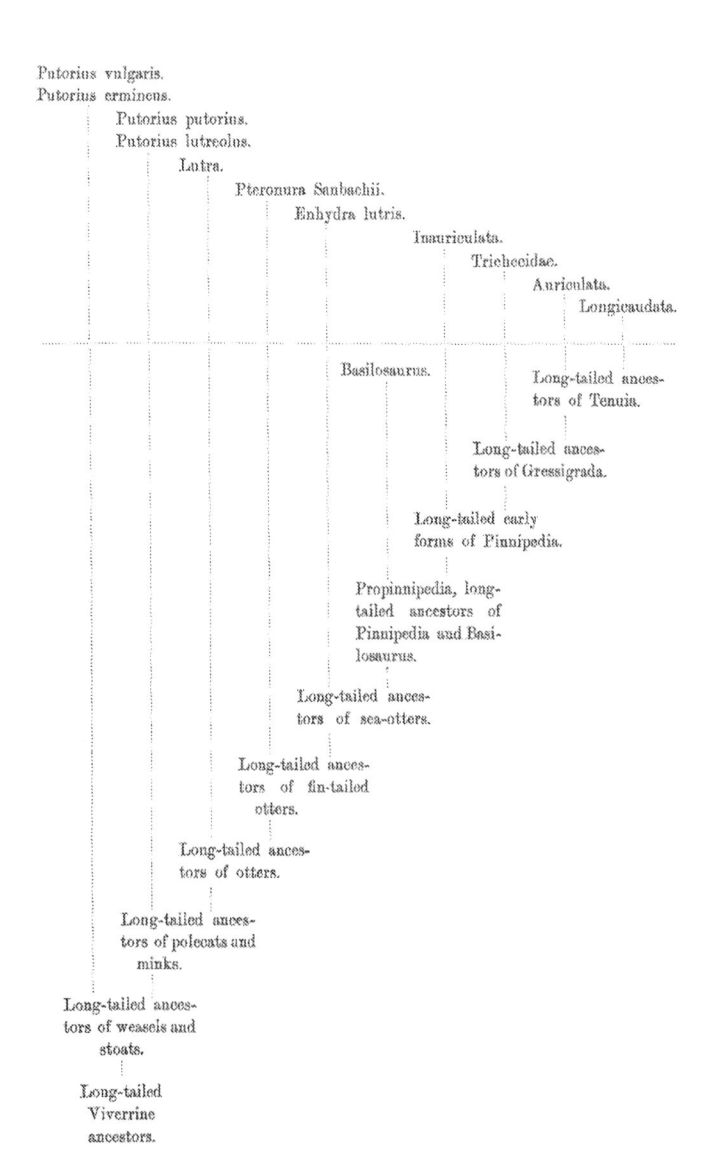

Putorius vulgaris.
Putorius ermineus.
   Putorius putorius.
   Putorius lutreolus.
    Lutra.
       Pteronura Sanbachii.
        Enhydra lutris.
           Inauriculata.
            Trichecidae.
             Auriculata.
               Longicaudata.

       Basilosaurus.
            Long-tailed ancestors of Tenuia.
          Long-tailed ancestors of Gressigrada.
         Long-tailed early forms of Pinnipedia.
        Propinnipedia, long-tailed ancestors of Pinnipedia and Basilosaurus.
       Long-tailed ancestors of sea-otters.
      Long-tailed ancestors of fin-tailed otters.
     Long-tailed ancestors of otters.
    Long-tailed ancestors of polecats and minks.
   Long-tailed ancestors of weasels and stoats.
  Long-tailed Viverrine ancestors.

upwards, or probably got their seat a little more towards the top of the head; and in proportion as the animal got a thick layer of bacon, the hairs became thinly scattered. Probably it is here better to say: in proportion as the animal lost its hairs, it got a thick layer of bacon. The warm-blooded mammals are possessed of the hair, because hair was to them what feathers are to a bird. The air enclosed between the hairs and the feathers is a worse conductor of temperature than the hairs or feathers themselves. As soon as the manner of living has changed so much that air could no longer come between the hairs, the hairs themselves lost their reason of existence, hence a thick layer of bacon gradually replaced them. Probably this is a better way to explain the presence of bacon and the absence of hair, than to say that the hair disappeared because the animals obtained a layer of bacon, and could therefore dispense with them, or that the layer of bacon checked the development of hairs.—In short we may admit that the animals, of which we treat at present, were thinly scattered with hairs. The whiskers in all probability were still present, and even well developed. This branch has wholly become extinct. The fossil remains were called *Basilosaurus*.

All the members of the *second* branch did not show a tendency to bulkiness, they retained the relatively small head and well developed neck, the head consequently could very well move on the trunk. These are the *Pinnipedia*.

Already very early they divided themselves into two sections.

All the members of the *first* section accustomed themselves to crawl more on land, ice, and rocks, and as the long tail must have been an inconvenient organ in this new manner of living, all the individuals which had a smaller number of caudal vertebrae survived their congeners; consequently a form at last originated with a very short tail: our well known order of Pinnipeds for which I now propose the name of *Brevicaudata*.

All the members however, of the second section accustomed themselves more to the sea, and therefore all the members which were best adopted for this manner of living successively survived their less privileged congeners, and finally the sea-serpents remained; animals which are so excellently adapted to an aquatic life and rapid movement, that their tendency to become extinct can only be explained by the singular phenomenon that colossal animals bring forth very few young ones, only two, or only one, at a time, and only after very long intervals. For these animals I already proposed above the name of *Longicaudata*. They form with the *Brevicaudata* the order of *Pinnipedia*.

If this view is better, (and who will tell us this with any certainty?) the phylogenetic table should be altered as follows:

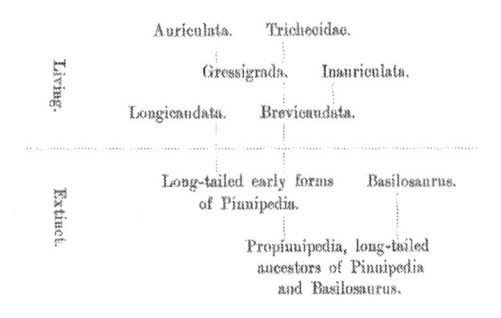

	Auriculata.	Trichecidae.	
Living.		Gressigrada.	Inauriculata.
	Longicaudata.	Brevicaudata.	
Extinct.		Long-tailed early forms of Pinnipedia.	Basilosaurus.
		Propinnipedia, long-tailed ancestors of Pinnipedia and Basilosaurus.	

In the first table I have tried to show two things.

Firstly:—With a horizontal dotted line I have separated the still living animals or groups from those who have become extinct; the former are placed above, the latter beneath the dotted line.

And Secondly:—With the different lengths of the vertical dotted lines I have tried to show the different relative lengths of time-periods wanted by the different species or groups to be formed, so to speak, from that species or group which in this table is placed exactly beneath it, and with which it is united by a dotted line.

It is clear that the evolution must have happened, geologically spoken, with extreme rapidity there, where the animals were entirely changing their manner of living, be it from a terrestrial one into an aquatic one, or otherwise; and that the evolution happened less rapid, or even, geologically spoken, very slowly, where the animals remained terrestrial or aquatic beings, and only changed their manner of living in so far, that they became troglodytes or semi-troglodytes, or became from carnivorous only piscivorous or semi-carni-semi-piscivorous. I believe that by this hypothesis the problem is solved why remains of *Basilosaurus* are already found in Eocene layers together with remains of Viverrine ancestors of *Carnivora*, *Pinnipedia* and *Basilosaurus*, whilst those of true *Pinnipedia*, *Lutrina* and *Mustelina* appear for the first time during the Miocene period, and whilst remains of true *Viverra*'s (the genus) do not seem to have made their appearance before the Pliocene period.

Appendix.

Since the book was written, I have corresponded with Prof. Dr. M. Forster Heddle, of St. Andrews, Mr. J. A. Harvie Brown, of Dunipace (Larbert), Misses Kate and Forbes J. Macrae, both of Heathmount (Inverness), Mr. Gilbert Bogle, of Newcastle-on-Tyne, Prof. R. Collett, of Christiania, and Mr. R. P. Greg, of Coles (Buntingford). The five first-named corresponded with me as eye-witnesses, and kindly sent me their statements, written immediately after the appearances they had witnessed; Prof. Collett courteously presented me with a copy of his dissertation *Lidt om Soe-Ormen eller Soe-Slangen;* Mr. Greg who since many years has been collecting with great zeal accounts and reports concerning the matter, had the rare liberality to send me his whole collection to make use of. To all these ladies and gentlemen I feel here called upon to tender my warmest thanks.

Space does not allow me to give a verbal reprint of the various hoaxes, would-be sea-serpents, reports, and principal contents of papers, nor to treat of them separately. This I leave for an eventual second edition. But all the appearances which I have placed under the *Reports and Papers* are explicable by reference to the *Megophias*. With the initials "R. P. G." I have marked those statements, accounts, etc., which I got from Mr. R. P. Greg.

Literature.

Besides the newspapers, dissertations, and books, mentioned in the subsequent parts, the following are additions to my first chapter:
* 1707.—F. Leguat. Voyage et aventures en deux isles désertes des Indes Orientales.
* 18...—Het Nederlandsch Magazijn.
* 1874, February.—The Cape Monthly Magazine
* 1870.— The Shipping Gazette, London.
* 1875.— The Daily Telegraph.
  1879, September 25?—The Royston Crow.—(R. P. G.).
* 189...— Bassett, Sea-phantoms; or legends and superstitions of the sea and sailors in all lands and all times. Chicago.

Hoaxes.

The account of captain L. Bijl, of 1858, July 9, (see p. 96) must be a hoax, for 1. 27° 27' N. lat. and 14° 51' E. long. is a point in the middle of North-Africa, and 2. even if E. long. were a misprint instead of W. long., it is impossible that a barque should travel over such a distance as from 27° 27 N. lat. and 14° 51 W. long. to 37° 55 S. lat. and 42° 9' E. long. *in nine days!*

A tale in the *Standard* of 1879, March 27, of a dead sea-serpent found floating near Monegan (Manhegin?) Island near Portland, Me.—(R. P. G.).

Collision of the Norwegian barque *Columbia* from London to Quebec, with a huge floating creature on the 4th. September, 1879; the ship sunk.—*Manchester Guardian* of 1879, Sept. 25.—(R P. G.).

A sea-serpent of 55 feet in length, light pink coloured. "Several times it opened its mouth, disclosing fangs about 4in. in length".—It was on 5th. August 1885, in lat. 29° 35' N. and long 34° 50' W.—(R P. G.).

A sea-serpent caught off Newfoundland, October 11, 1886, and stuffed.— *Manchester Evening Mail* 1887, September; *Evening Mercury* of St. Johns, N. F., 1887, September 12; *The Marine Industrial News*.—The monster was from head to tail "a fraud", or "a Yankee humbug".—Letter from Mr. G. Fitz Gerald, of St. Johns, and from Prof. G. V. Morse, of Portland, Me., to Mr. R. P. Greg.—(R. P. G.).

The London Globe of Aug. 15, 1887, mentions a fight between a sea-serpent and a whale, witnessed near Fort Papham in moonlight, some three weeks back, etc.—(R. P. G.).

A stranded sea-serpent.—*Boston Courier* 1887, November.—Cape May, N. Jers.— Hoax? or would-be sea-serpent? (*Regalecus?*)—(R. P. G.)

The sea-serpent is distinctly seen in Georgetown Harbour, on the 20th. of August, 1888, sleeping on the surface, &c.—*Chambers' Journal*, 1888, Nov. 24.— (R. P. G.).

"Exciting chases after boats' crews."—A splendid hoax.—St. Johns' (N. F.) *Evening Telegram* of Aug. 25, 1888.—(R. P. G.)

The Bishop of Adelaide or a certain Mr. Bishop of that town has found a sea-serpent lying dead on the shore.—*The Times* of Nov. 11, 1891.—(R. P. G.)—Mr. G. Bogle wrote to the Bishop, who promptly answered it was entirely untrue.—(G. B.)

Conclusions 427

"Narrow escape of a boats' crew."—*The North British Daily Mail* of September 1892.—(Forwarded to me by Prof. Heddle.)

Would-be Sea-Serpents.

1880 August.—The sea-serpent of Captain Hanna, of Pemaquid, Me.—Bulletin of the U. S. Fish Commission, Vol. III, N°. 26, p. 407.—Without any doubt a fish, but very problematic.— *Naturen*, 1884, N°. 2.—(Forwarded to me by Prof. Collett.)
1880 August 11.—Between Yokohama and San Francisco, lat. 48.37. long. 180.—Captain Thos. U. Brocklehurst, of Henbury Hall, Macclesfield, Cheshire, saw on board the *Oceanic* a snake-like fish, 40 feet long, about 18 inches in the whole length thick.—Letter from Mr. Thos. U. Brocklehurst to Mr. R. P. Greg.—Without any doubt an eel-shaped fish.—(R. P. G.)
1883, July or August.—A newspaper of this month mentions the capture of a genuine sea-serpent in the Java Sea.—*Hydrophis*.—(R.P.G.)
1883, October 8.—In the Red Sea, lat. 23° N., long. 37° E., on board the ss. *Madura*.—Witness Mr. A. Eisses, of Groningen.—*Nieuwe Groninger Courant* of August 16, 1892.—The neck had the thickness of the upper arm of a man.—Appearance perfectly the same as that witnessed by Mr. G. Verschuur (see p. 99).
1886 or 1887.—The sea-snake-like bird, reported by Count Joachim Pfeil, the German African explorer—a little snake-like neck rising out of the water, which when fired at, rose into the air, proving to be a bird—is of course a kind of *Plotus*, and most probably *Plotus levaillantii* Temm.—A Hertford newspaper of 1887.—(R. P. G.)
1888?—In Mrs. Caddy's book *To Siam and Malasia in the Duke of Sutherland's Yacht* is a description of a sea-serpent she witnessed near Bangkok "which rose slowly out of the water in two large luminous curves, like two arches of a low bridge".—?—(R. P. G.)
1889, August.—*Standard* of 1889, August 15.—A monstrous fish was seen floundering in shallow water on the Bancals Rocks, not far from the Island of St. Honorat, near Cannes, and had a beak like a parrot.—Most probably therefore it was a calamary.—(R. P. G.)

Reports and Papers.

Without date.—A sea-monster at Maringonish in the Gulf of St. Lawrence, judged to be a hundred feet in length, seen by two intelligent observers within 200 yards of the shore.—Description too short.—Doubtful.—(R. P. G.)
1570, July. —A monstrous fish seen in Loch Fyne (Fine), having great eyes, and at times standing above the water as high as the mast of a ship.—*Diurnal and Remarkable occurrents in Scotland,* 1513—1575, Maitland Club, Scotland, 1833.—(R.P. G.)
1639.—A vague report of a certain Josselin, but most probably based on truth.—Cape Ann.—*Atlantic Monthly* of June, 1884.—(R. P. G.)
1779.—"In an Eastern Harbour" (which?)—Eye-witness E. Preble, midshipman in the *Protector*, and several other officers and crew.—*Atlantic Monthly* of June, 1884.—(R. P. G.)
1817, August 14. (N°. 41, see p. 169).—Another confirmation of this appearance will be found in the *Gloucester Telegraph* of that year. Here it is also mentioned

that in the Rogers family there is preserved a picture by "Jack" Beach, or better a copy of this picture by Joseph H. Davis, representing the sea-serpent in the harbour of Gloucester on this day.—*Atlantic Monthly* of June, 1884.—(R. P. G.)—This is of course the drawing, spoken of on p. 173 of the present volume. Here I may note that Pontoppidan also speaks of a picture in the collection of Jacob Severin, representing the animal as it appeared to Egede.

1818, August 13 and 14.—Partly about Nahant, and partly near Gloucester.—Multitudes of spectators.—*Atlantic Monthly* of June, 1884.—(R. P. G.)

1819, August 19.—This seems to be the exact date of the appearance witnessed by Mr. Samuel Cabot. Mr. Prince and others saw it "a few days previously".—*Atlantic Monthly* of June, 1884.—(R. P. G.)

1820, August 10.—Off Swampscott.—Andrew Reinolds, Jonathan B. Lewis, Benjamin King, Mr. Joseph Ingalls.—*Atlantic Monthly* of June, 1884.—(R. P. G.)

1823, July 12.—The animal was seen moving into the harbor (Lynn Harbour?) from Nahant.—Mr. Francis Johnson (in April 7, 1884, still alive).—*Atlantic Monthly* of June, 1884.—(R. P. G.)

1826.—"In 1826 it again appeared off Nahant, as is recorded very briefly in the *Lynn Miror*".—*Atlantic Monthly* of June, 1884.—See also n°. 84, p. 236; it might have been the same individual.—(R. P. G,)

1838? (N°. 104, see p. 253).—Captain Beechy made his voyage to the Pacific in the *Blossom* in the years 1825, 26, 27 and 28. It is therefore probable that he saw the sea-serpent in one of these years, but also possible that he was commander of the *Blossom* before 1825 or later than 1828.

1841, July 14.—A monster with a straight black head, 10 feet out of the water, spouting "a column of water in the air", but "it was not a whale".— Gulf of Mexico.—Stephen's *Central America*, 1842, Vol. II, p. 464.—Description too short.—Doubtful.—(R. P. G.).

1849.—Seen (where?) by Mr. Marston, of Swampsott.—*Atlantic Monthly* of June, 1884. —(R. P. G.).

1854, spring.—A gigantic serpent, first called by the look-out man as "the biggest log ever seen", afterwards rearing its snake like head as high as the funnel of the steamer out of the water, and plunging down.—Eye witnesses: Captain Peat, of the *Wm. Scalrook*, and Captain Rollins, of the *Isabel*.—Before the mouth of Savannah River, Georg. and S. Car.—Miss Murray, *United States, Canada and Cuba*, 1855, Putnam & Co., New York, p. 235.—(R. P. G.).

1872.—Prof. Schlegel in his *De Dierentuin van het Koninklijk Zoölogisch Genootschap Natura Artis Magistra te Amsterdam*, Vol. III, p. 45, points out that as early as 1837 he *proved (nota bene)* the impossibility of the existence of such a more than gigantic animal.

1872, August 20 and 21. (N°. 137 and 138, see p. 322).—The following is the account which the Rev. J. Macrae sent to the *Inverness Courier*, August 1872, prefaced by the Editors of this paper:

"A gentleman on whose intelligent observation and accuracy we have perfect reliance, sends the following account of a strange animal now to be seen about the West-Coast of Invernessshire and which, if not the veritable or traditional sea-serpent, must be the object so often represented under that appellation".

"On Tuesday last, 20th. August, I went on a trip to Loch Hourn in my small sailing boat. I was accompanied by my friend, the Rev. Mr. T. of Kent, my two daughters, my grandson, and a servant lad. While we were proceeding along the sound of Sleat it fell calm, and we were rowing the boat, when we observed behind us a row of dark masses, which we took at the first glance for a shoal of porpoises; but a second look showed that these masses formed one and the same creature, for it moved slowly across our wake, about two hundred yards off, and disappeared. Soon afterwards what seemed to be its head reappeared, followed by the bumps, or undulations of its body, which rose in succession till we counted 8 of them. It approached now within about 100 yards, or less, and with the help of binoculars we could see it pretty distinctly. We did not see its eyes, nor observe any scales: but two of the party believed that they saw what they took to be a small fin moving above the water. It then slowly sunk, and moved away just under the surface of the water, for we could trace its course till it rose again, by the large waves it raised above it, to the distance of a mile and upwards".

"We had no means of measuring its size with any accuracy, but taking the distance from the centre of one bump or undulation of its body to that of another at 6ft. (it could not be less) the length of the portion visible above the water, would be about 50 feet, and there may have been 20 or 30ft. more of its length which we did not see".

"Its head seemed blunt, and looked about 18in. in diameter, and the bumps were rather larger than the head. When in rapid motion the bumps disappeared, and only the head and neck could be seen, partly above the surface of the water. It continued to rush about in the same manner as long as we remained within sight of the place, but did not again come so near us that day".

"On the afternoon of the next day, August 21, as we were returning home we encountered our strange acquaintance again within the entrance of Loch Hourn, and saw him careering swiftly along the surface of the water, which was now slightly rippled with a light air of wind. It passed once abeam of us, at a distance of about 150 yards, with its head half out of the water, and we distinctly heard the whizzing noise it made as it rushed through the water. There were no organs of locomotion to be seen, and its progress was equable and smooth, like that of a log towed rapidly. Neither its appearance nor mode of progression had any resemblance to those of any known cetacean, shark, or fish of any kind. In case any of your readers should imagine that I, as well as the subject of my report am a mere myth, you will please to give my name to this communication, and I believe that among a pretty wide circle of persons who know me there is none who consider me capable of stating as true what I do not believe to be so; or so little acquainted with the sea, as not to know a whale, a porpoise, a shark, or a herring barrel, when I see them. I am Sir, your obedient servant"

"Glenelg Mame".
"J. Macrae .

Miss Kate Macrae's narrative, written on the spot, runs as follows:
"In the yacht 'Leda', 20th. and 21th. August 1872.—We were becalmed in the sound of Sleat about 3 miles from Glenelg, the day was intensely hot, the lads were rowing slowly. I was facing the stern, when I saw about a half mile behind, a dark object suddenly emerge, about the size of a small cask. I exclaimed, and called the attention of the others to it; immediately a second, third, fourth, fifth, thing appeared like this". (Here Miss Macrae has drawn six bunches exactly resembling those drawn by her father, see fig. 39). "We thought at first it was the back of a cormorant, but were undeceived by seeing the animal swim swiftly just under

the surface of the water towards a rowing boat of country people which was nearer it than we were, the people evidently astonished ceased rowing, and the creature disappeared quietly without the least agitation of the water. Our boys then resumed their oars, which they had dropped to gaze, and next we saw the animal coming swiftly towards us, from the direction of the boat; it raised the water before it, and left a wake on the calm sea behind it, like what a small steam launch would. As our rowers paused again, it turned to the outer side of our yacht, and disappeared, but I noticed that something like a rounded paddle, the breadth of two hands worked to and fro raising the water in a clear dome as it went down; the colour of it a dark brown, and shape like this". (Here Miss Macrae has drawn a thick curved line in the form of a horse-shoe, the opening turned downwards). "In a few minutes afterwards, the row of lumps appeared again about a mile behind, and this time a triangular fin stuck up from about the 4th. lump, and apparently 10ft. the size of our jib, and the animal moved slowly along on the surface".

"Next evening as we were slipping gently along near the mouth of Loch Hourn on the N. side, my nephew called out, that he saw the sea-serpent again. Swimming across from Skye, by the time I caught sight of it, it was far away, but showed more lumps, I counted 12, there were two sloops trying to get up into the Loch, and the crews were in their boats towing them, the animal looked 4 times as long as one of these vessels, it was swimming leisurely, and plainly pursued those vessels; then making a sweep across the mouth of the Loch came towards us, and passed not far outside the boat. I distinctly heard its rush through the water, just under the surface; the first waves it made, were unbroken, but some way from the head the water was broken, and foaming".

"Later, at 9 P. M. just as we neared Glenelg sailing and rowing, and with a good deal of ripple on the sea, we saw it coming straight astern, then it turned away northward and passed out of sight through Kyle Rhea".

"Kate Macrae."

Miss Forbes J. Macrae wrote to me under date of July 22, 1892:

"I fancy I have had a closer view of the sea-serpent than most people. About an hour before we were becalmed and saw it rise in its length astern of us, we had been slipping down in our boat along the coast, by the help of a strong tide and a very light wind. Looking at what I could see of the water under the edge of the mainsail of our small cutter yacht, I noticed at about an oar's length from the boat a dark brown shining creature lying on the water, or rather a part of a creature for there was neither head nor tail nor fin visible, it seemed about six feet in length and the highest part of it was about a foot out of the water. None of the others were looking that way, so I was the only one who saw it. I asked my father if porpoises were in the habit of basking on the top of the water. He said he was not aware of their being in the habit of doing so, and we thought no more of it; till the next appearance of the animal made us think that it must have been one of its ridges I had seen as we sailed just close to it,'.

The following is the statement of Mr. Gilbert Bogle in the *Newcastle Weekly Chronicle* of 1877, December 31:

"As considerable attention has lately been drawn in your columns to the sea-serpent, both mythological and otherwise, perhaps the following description of the strange creature seen by me and others in 1872 will be of some interest. An account of this creature, attested by credible witnesses, appeared in the May number of the *Zoologist* in 1873:—

"On the 20th. of August, 1872, the Rev. J. Macrae of Glenelg, Rev. David Twopenny, Miss Forbes, and Miss Kate Macrae, a servant lad, and I left Glenelg Bay in Mr. Macrae's yacht Leda for a sail up Loch Hourn. The day was hot and calm, and, the yacht being a small one (seven tons), we had recourse to rowing in order to reach Sandaig, six miles distant, where we intended to dine. While still about a mile distant from Sandaig, one of the ladies called out that there was a shoal of porpoises playing astern, and on looking in that direction there appeared to me a number of dark objects, which at first sight seemed not unlike porpoises, making a considerable commotion on the surface of the sea, the only peculiarity being that they all followed each other in a line. As they rapidly approached, I then perceived that the black lumps which I at first thought porpoises could not be so, but were evidently parts of one and the same creature. This impression seemed to come over the minds of all at the same time, and every appearance of the creature afterwards clearly verified it".

"I was looking at it through a binocular (we had three on board), and when it came to within one hundred yards of the stern it dived below, the surface of the sea remained agitated at the spot where it had disappeared for some time afterwards. Just before it went down, as it came head on towards our stern, it raised a succession of waves. The first was unbroken, and through it I distinctly saw the colour of the creature, and what appeared to be a small fin on the back or neck, moving rapidly sideways, and two or three yards behind the head. Its colour was a dark slaty brown, somewhat similar to that of a porpoise."

"While we were all speculating about this strange creature, it suddenly appeared about a quarter of a mile off between us and Skye, going at a rapid rate along the calm surface of the sea, and leaving a large wake behind. It was only now that I had any idea of the creature's length. It kept cruising about on the surface after this for more than an hour, sometimes only four or five bumps or dark raised portions of its body appearing above the surface, about the size of herring barrels, at other times up to eight. I noticed that the less the speed the more bumps appeared, always commencing from the first in rotation, and that when going very fast only one or two appeared."

"After landing on Sandaig, where we had dinner, we started for Loch Hourn, the weather still being very calm and sultry, with hardly a cat's-paw on the water. We had barely entered the mouth of the loch when this creature again made its appearance, proceeding in the same manner as before along the surface of the sea, sometimes coming quite close. There was a large schooner yacht not far off, in tow of a noisy steam launch, which about this time probably frightened the animal, as it was not seen again that night."

"As evening fell, a breeze sprang up, and we reached Loch Hourn Head early next morning. After paying a visit to the Barrasdale oyster beds, we set sail for home in the afternoon, with a nice breeze on the quarter, but on reaching the mouth of the loch the wind died away again and we had to take to the sweeps. Just about the place where the animal was last seen, my attention was called by someone to a peculiar swirling of the water not far off, and I immediately noticed what was evidently the same creature swimming up to the yacht at a very rapid rate. When a short distance off it dived beneath the surface, quickly re-appearing off the starboard beam nearer than at any previous time, and going at such a great speed that I could distinctly hear the rushing sound of the breaking water. At this time there were no bumps to be seen, and I can only liken the appearance of our visitor to a log almost entirely submerged and dragged very rapidly through the sea, the water falling over each side of the head in a kind of cascade, while a series of broken waves formed immediately behind, gradually subsiding in the wake."

"It afterwards kept swimming about for a considerable time, and I had an opportunity of judging of its length so far as visible, compared with the hulls of two trading schooners of about 100 tons each some little distance from us. When apparently the same distance away as the traders, and going slowly, it appeared fully as long from the head to the eighth bump as the length of one of the schooners on waterline, which would be at least sixty feet; but how much of the animal remained under water I had no means of estimating. The head seemed to be square or blunt, but I did not see under it, and did not notice its eye or mouth. The bumps, or dark raised portions, appeared to me to be about eighteen inches above the water, and three or four feet long, with a distance of four or six feet between each bump. I could not say whether the bumps were the convolutions of a snake-like body or the raised portions of a large body underneath the water. I am inclined to think the latter, as the bumps always kept the same distance apart, and appeared to be protuberances on the back of, possibly, a lizard shaped reptile. That it caused a large displacement was evident from the waves and commotion raised when swimming at or near the surface, as I could distinctly trace its progress with the naked eye at a distance of from two to three miles."

"We lost sight of the creature after leaving the mouth of Loch Hourn, but just as night fell I noticed it going past at a rapid rate in the direction of Kyle Rhea, a narrow strait which separates Skye from the mainland. I afterwards heard that it was seen that same evening by fishermen and others passing through these narrows, and it struck them all at the time as being quite different from anything they had been accustomed to."

"The above is a bare statement of fact, and was written down by me immediately after getting ashore, while my recollection of the creature's appearance was perfectly fresh and vivid. Having cruised for many summers amongst the West Highland lochs, I am perfectly familiar with the appearance and habits of whales, seals, porpoises, &c., which can often be seen in great numbers. To these, the creature I have described bore no resemblance whatever."

"Gilbert Bogle, Newcastle.

From this gentleman I received three splendid pen-drawings, representing the animal witnessed by him on that occasion, but alas too late to be reproduced for this edition.

1872, August 22 and 23. (N°. 139 and 140, see p. 322).—On one of these days it seems also to have been seen by Lord Macdonald's steam yacht in Loch Hourn.— Eye-witnesses: Lord Macdonald, of Armadale, Skye, Rev. Mr. Mc. Neill, minister of Skye, Mrs. G. C. Lysons, of Painswick, Strand, and others.— (R. P. G.)

1873, March.—Mr. Basil Clochrane, Capt. R. N., of Windlesham House, Bagshot, Surrey, on board the *Orontes*, from the West Indies to England saw a sea-serpent.— Letter from eyewitness to Capt. Geo. Drevar (see p. 329).—(R. P. G.)

1875, July 8 and 13. (N°. 144 and 145, see p. 329).—The letter from Capt. Geo. Drevar to the Editor of *The Calcutta Gentleman*, 1876, February (?), contains no news about the two appearances.—(R. P. G.)

1875, July 17.—Off Plymouth, Cape Cod Bay.—Captain Garton of the ss. *Norman*, and several people on board the ss. *Roman*.—*Atlantic Monthly* of June, 1884.—(R. P. G).

1875, July 30.—On board the yacht *Princess*, between Nahant and Egg-Rock.— Mr. Francis W. Lawrence, Mrs. Lawrence, Rev. Arthur Lawrence, rector of St. Paul's Church, Stockbridge, Mass., Miss Mary Fosdick, Albion W. Reed, Robert O. Reed, Mr. J. Kelsoe and Mr. J. P. Thomas, both of Swampscott.—*Atlantic Monthly* of June, 1884.—(R. P. G.)

1876, September 11. (N°. 146, see p. 341).—An account in the *Times* of 1876, December 28, furnishes no news.—A rough drawing made by Mr. Anderson, and now in the possession of Robert Holt, of Liverpool, owner of the steamer, hardly agrees with the depositions, and cannot give the idea of a salamander, a newt, or a frog.—(R. P. G.)

1876.—Some Pitcairn islanders saw a sea-serpent near Norfolk Island.—Letter from one of the Pitcairn islanders to Mr. Palmer of Liverpool.—*Liverpool Mercury*, 24 February, 1877.—"Mr. John Adams and his boat's crew saw it near Norfolk-Islands".—Letter from Mr. Marcus Lowther, Capt. R. N. of Penge, London, S. E., to Capt. Geo. Drevar (see p. 329).—(R. P. G.)

1877, March.—Mr. R. A. Proctor, in his *"Strange Sea-Monsters" (Gentleman's Magazine)* says amongst other assertions: "naturalists have been far less disposed to be incredulous than the general public". If it were only true! Hitherto at least *zoologists* have not admitted even the possibility of the existence of a still unknown species, called "sea-serpent".—(R. P. G.)

1877, July 15.—About two miles off the mouth of Gloucester Harbour, Mass.— Mr. George S. Wasson and Mr. B. L. Fernald.—*Atlantic Monthly* of June, 1884.—(R. P. G.)

1878, summer.—Fjord near Aalesund.—*Naturen*, 1884, n°. 2.—(Forwarded to me by Prof. R. Collett).

1882, October 11.—Near Bude, Cornwall.—Eye-witnesses: Rev. E. Highton, Vicar of Bude, with several friends.—The *Times* of October 12, 1882.—(R. P. G.)

1883, August. 1.—The *Evening News* of this date communicates and gives partly a review of Mr. Lee's *Sea Monsters Unmasked*.—(R. P. G.).

1884, February.—Prof. R. Collett, of Christiania, wrote a paper in the Norwegian language headed *Something on the sea-serpent* (*Naturen*, 1884, n° 2).—The writer does not seem to be a believer in the existence of a sea-serpent. The arguments against its existence are 1. A sea-serpent of considerable dimensions would in the course of centuries not have failed to have been observed and caught. 2. In the depth of the Ocean there are undoubtedly creatures, which as yet are unknown, but all specimens caught, be they as abnormal as possible, are referred to existing well-known forms. 3. No known vertebrated animal, can, on account of its structure, move in vertical undulations.—Against these arguments I may say: 1. Before, 1861, and 1873 the krakens were *fables*, and yet they existed! Mr. Rafinesque Schmaltz &c., see p. 431, line 6 from below to p. 432, line 5 from above. 2. Do "naturalists" not constantly refer the sea-serpents to existing well-known forms? 3. Among Reptiles the *Plesiosaurians* had a long neck and this neck could certainly be bent vertically; among Birds the *swans* are able to bend the long neck vertically, and *all Mammals* can move in vertical undulations, especially the *Mustelina, Lutrina,* and *Pinnipedia;* and the horizontal position of the tail of the *Sirenia* and *Plagiuri* is a strong proof that their ancestors moved in vertical undulations.—Prof. Collett's private opinion is that the sea-serpents observed in the fjords of Norway, were mostly specimens of the basking shark. I, however, firmly believe that the Norwegian fishermen know the basking shark so well, that such an animal would never have been taken by them for a sea-serpent! They know these sharks and their habits far better, I should think, than Prof. Mitchill, Prof. Mantell, Prof. Melville, Mr. Buckland and Prof. Lütken all together. Moreover in none of their descriptions there is question of a backfin, or of backfins, which are the first visible parts of a basking shark!

1884, June.—*The Trail of the Sea-Serpent*, by Mr. J. G. Wood, in the *Atlantic Monthly*.—A very interesting paper, with historical notes and many new appearances, however, not without some zoological inaccuracies. He believes the sea-serpent to be an elongated whale, a *Basilosaurus* or an animal allied to it, and that the short neck of the *Basilosaurus* may be an error of the restorer *(nota bene!)*.—(R. P. G.).

1884, June 2.—The *Manchester Guardian* gives a review of Mr. J. G. Wood's paper, and as Mr. Wood comes to the conclusion that the animal must be an elongated whale, the *Manchester Guardian* ends (how insipid!): "Very like a whale".—(R. P. G.).

1885, October 4.—Near Umhlali (Umlazi?) in Morewood's Bay, South Africa.—(R. P. G.).

1886(?), summer.—Prof. Heddle informs me that a few summers ago, (and from one sentence of his letter I deduce that it was before 1887) a sea-serpent was seen in Loch Duich. "The description was very much what we are familiar with".

1886, August. (N° 158).—The description of the eyes as having a greenish hue struck me so, that I at first did not attach belief to the assertion, but now I know that this is not an impossibility, as I since observed that the *tapetum lucidum* of the eye of a dog may reflect the daylight as well in a reddish as in a greenish hue.

1887, July 30.—Prof. Heddle wrote to me on May 6th., 1892: "I would just say that having taken bearings on the land, in order to estimate—(of course roughly)—the *length*, and the *speed*, I set down the length at from 60 to 65 feet. There was a very low flat head like a large skate, say 4 1/2 feet—a gap not so great,—ten 'hummocks' increasing in bulk and altitude towards the central one, but not much—gaps not so great as the size of the hummocks, next a space, about equal to two hummocks, then three hummocks, the central one largest, the last small".

"The thing I saw appear three times—first time end on was a worthless observation, except that on this occasion the whole was *rushing* through the water. On the other two occasions there was hardly any forward motion at all. The whole disappeared at the same moment, and reappeared also at the same moment, about two seconds thereafter more than its own length in advance; so that there must have been either an exceedingly rapid rush under water—*or* a second animal. The disappearance and reappearance were both without the *least* splash; but at the moment of disappearance the second time *the foremost two of the last three hummocks coalesced into one*".

"During one of the appearances I got the focus of the binoculars so sharp that I distinctly saw water falling over towards me, between some of the hummocks and myself. There was no consecutive filling up of the interspaces whatever, or appearance of vacuities where the hummocks had but now been".

"There was certainly no *vertical* serpentine motion—and I could see no *lateral* one".

"My impression was that, setting aside the quiescent low head, I *did not see a solid substance at all,*—except when the tail hummocks momentarily appeared—

and that what I did see was water being thrown over laterally by the undulous lashings of a long back fin of a dark colour, which gave opacity".

"I cannot set the 'hummocks' down to *surge waves* of a rushing short fish; because I cannot so explain such surges being always the same both in *number* and in *place:* nor can I so explain the appearance of an apparently solid head— and an apparently continuous tail".

"The above is all from memory".

The following is the

"Relation regarding a *Phenomenon* seen by the crew and Owner and guests of the yacht Shiantelle on the W. coast of Scotland on 30th. July 1887 as told by J. A. Harvie Brown, and seen by him, and written in his Journals of that date".

"At 10" to 15" to 10 am. I was called quickly on deck by Cowell, and I went up from breakfast. "What is that"? said Cowell. After some time I saw between me and the shore to the E., which shore was about one mile distant, undulations upon almost calm water (The ship was moving at the rate of about half a knot an hour) being similar in appearance, and having the motions of the (described and supposed) Sea-Serpent. I counted with the binoculars twelve or perhaps thirteen humps at almost perfectly regular distances the one from the others. The first of these humps appeared to be moving rapidly through the water across the line of vision, and to be breaking and spraying water, and the other eleven or twelve (I had only time to count them once) maintained all their relative positions with one another and collectively with the first, *yet* did not appear in themselves to me to move, though slight ripples of water were visible, nearly throughout the whole length. The whole disappeared and reappeared at least four times to me, apparently simultaneously or almost so throughout its length. When last it was seen, it was moving on a course almost parallel with the shore, which shore runs N. E. or thereby. The distance from the ship at which time I first saw it, and from that time to its final disappearance was estimated by me at about half a mile by eye (but this may have been an over-estimate of distance)".

"John Campbell, seaman, and mate on board the yacht, standing at the helm, deposes in a seperate document—drawn up and written by R. L. Cowell, Steward, from his oral statement—which seperate statement, was at once closed, without being read by either Dr. Heddle or myself, and still remains so".

"R. L. Cowell, Steward, who was on deck at the same time as John Campbell (having laid and served our breakfast) deposes in similar manner in a seperate statement, also closed and not read by Dr. Heddle and myself".

"But John Campbell on being examined by us deposes on cross-examination that:—While we were at breakfast in the Saloon, he saw approaching from the direction of Corrie Chreachan a series of large undulations which passed "within 40 yards" then "within 30 yards" and again "within the length of the ship" (which is 56 feet) from the stern of the vessel, and travelling at a great pace; that he saw nothing above the surface of the water except broken water in front of the first or foremost undulation. That except this, he saw nothing but the perpendicular swellings (vertical swellings), as it were 'skins of water' pushed up from beneath, and a long track or wake of slightly disturbed water, left for a long distance behind. It was seen approaching from the direction of the Sound between Scarba and Jura, or Corrie Chreacan, and passed the stern of the vessel. It was therefore heading at the time nearly E. The Ship's head was lying about E. half N."

"R. L. Cowell saw it almost or quite simultaneously with John Campbell on its first appearance."

"N. B. The time between his calling me on deck and the time I first observed the appearance, I have described, I put down at *about half* a minute (as, before seeing it, after getting on deck, I asked one or two questions as to bearings, before I could get sight of it with my glasses). After my first look I called up Dr. Heddle. It was after calling up Dr. Heddle, that I made out the counting of the humps, and the other appearances described. I may have been 5 to 10 seconds between my being called up, and my reaching the deck, aft of the companion, and I then got the glasses and unscrewed them to focus, while I was asking the questions as to bearings. Roughly speaking, I calculate, that from the first appearance to Campbell and Cowell, till its final disappearance, it must have been, inclusive of disappearances and reappearances, about 15 minutes in sight or observation. When *they* saw it, it must have been travelling very rapidly; and not nearly *so* rapidly when we observed it at the greater distance. My estimate of distance when I saw it, *may* be an over-estimate put at half a mile."

"Before J. Campbell saw it he heard a heavy splash, and saw the marks of the same, near the vessel—about half an hour before he saw what he describes—but no importance is attached to this, as a heavy fish some time after the disappearance, was seen shortly after to splash near the vessel; and Pellocks were also seen in the vicinity. The Pellocks however did not splash but rolled in their usual way. Not for one moment can their motion be compared by any of us, with the other appearances observed." (Here Mr. Brown has drawn a bunch, then a gap, larger than the bunch, and then eleven smaller bunches, separated one from the other by a gap as large as the half of one of these smaller bunches, the whole drawing representing exactly the animal swimming with vertical undulations and seen at a considerable distance.)

"Without actually fixing the position of the ship we consulted the chart and as nearly as we could arrived at it by bearings. It will be seen that the deepest water runs from the E. extremity of Corrie Chreacan very much along the line which the object or objects seen, was seen to follow; and that where its appearance was last noted the soundings show a very rapid shoaling from 30 fathoms to 17 about the position of our ship, being in from 15 to 17 fathoms.—"

"I think it right to add to the above account as written down on the spot, that after the statements which were kept sealed for a long time after, were consulted and every consideration given to the whole tale and phenomenon personally I came to the conclusion, and feel very certain still, that it was simply a *Tide-rip* or *Tidal wave* coming from the direction of Corrievreachan between Scarba and Jura running Easterly and then N. Easterly along the smooth water where soundings showed the meeting of the shallow of the deep. I have questioned Light-house-keepers since who have the most continuous chances of observation, within often, calm seas, and they have assured me such a phenomenon is not at all rare or unusual 'under certain conditions of tides in certain localities'. Sailors have less chance to witness these phenomena perhaps than light-house-keepers, as they are seldom and long stationary at all states of tides."

Notwithstanding this conclusion of Mr. Brown, I feel persuaded that he, Prof. Heddle and others really saw the same appearance as did the Rev. J. Macrae and others (see n° 137 and 138). The long back fin of a dark colour, which gave opacity and threw water over laterally by its lashings, of course was one of the animal's fore-flappers.

1889, August 15.—A good little paper on the subject, and partly a plea for the existence of the creature is in the *Standard* of that date.—(R. P. G.)

1891, July 24.—East coast of North Island, New-Zealand.—*The Standard*, 1891, September 22.—(R. P. G.):—

"Mr. Alfred Ford Mathews, a surveyor, living at Gisborne, on the east coast of the North Island, wrote to the papers to the effect that while on board the *Manopouri*, another of the Union Company's steamers, on the voyage from Auckland to Gisborne, on Friday, July 24th., he and several others distinctly saw a sea-serpent resembling the one seen from the *Rotomahana* off Portland Island. This time it appeared north of the East Cape, which is some distance to the north of where it was seen by the *Rotomahana* a week later. The time, Mr. Mathews states, was between eight and nine in the morning. The 'monster' was also seen by the ship's officer in charge. It would from time to time lift its head and part of its body to a great height perpendicularly, and when in that position would turn its body round in a most peculiar manner, displaying a black back, white belly, and two armlet appendages of great length, which appeared to dangle about like a broken limb on a human being. It would then suddenly drop back into the water, scattering it in all directions. It had a flat head, and was about half a mile distant from the ship. The reason, Mr. Mathews added, that he had not mentioned the matter before was that people were likely to treat it with derision."

1891, August 1.—Off the East-coast of North Island, New Zealand, on board the *Rotomahana*, a steamer of the Union Steam-Shipping Company.—*Standard* of 22th. September, 1891; *Newcastle Evening Chronicle* of September 23, 1891.—(R. P. G. and Gilbert Bogle.)

"The Chief Officer, Mr. Alexander Lindsay Kerr, on being interviewed by a newspaper reporter said:—

"On Saturday morning last, August 1st., about 6.30 o'clock, we were off Portland Light, between Gisborne and Napier. I was on deck looking over the weather side, to see if I could see the land, when I saw the object, whatever it was, rise out of the water to the height of about 30ft. Its shape was for all the world like a huge conger eel, with the exception that it had two large fins that appeared to be about 10 feet long. The creature was not more than 100 yards away at the outside, and I should estimate its girth at between ten and twelve feet. I could not see its back as it was coming straight towards the steamer, but its belly and fins were pure white. The creature's head did not appear to be particularly definite, the neck running right up to the head the same as that of a large eel. It was broad daylight at the time, and the sun was shining clearly. When it went beneath the water it did not fall forward like a fish that is jumping, but drew itself back as if with a contortion. I only saw it the once which was the last time it rose. I looked out for it, thinking it might pass under the ship and reappear on the other side, but I did not see it again. Had the weather not been so rough the steamer might have gone alongside and ascertained its dimensions. One of the Quartermasters Peter Nelson, was watching the thing, and it so startled him that he took upon himself to rush on to the bridge and ask me if I had seen it, a thing a sea-man never does unless something very exceptional occurs. A landsman might do so, but a sea-man never, unless under exceptional circumstances, such as these. I have been to sea for twenty seven years, and have been engaged in nearly every known trade from whaling in Greenland to the slave trade, and have been in almost every part of the world, but I never saw any object at sea like the one that revetted my attention on

Saturday morning last. I have always been sceptical with regard to the sea-serpent stories, I have heard and read, and a smile has always come across my face at them, but I have been too long at sea, and have seen too many remarkable things, to deny positively that there was such a thing, had a landsman or a lady told me about the creature on Saturday, while I should have given them credit for being quite sincere, I should have taken no notice of it, as they are so apt to make mistakes at sea. I am too much accustomed at sea, however, to have made any mistake. When we got to Napier, I mentioned the circumstance there, when they pointed out that there had been a shock of earthquake shortly before the time we saw the creature, which may have been the cause of sending it to the surface. As to its length I could give no opinion, but as the creature rose some 30ft. out of the water I should imagine there were still two-thirds of it in the water, but that is only my supposition."

"Peter Nelson, the Quartermaster, referred to gave his story as follows:—

"It was about 6.30 on Saturday morning last, August 1st. It was a bright clear morning with the sun shining brightly. The weather, however, was rough, with a heavy sea. I had just come from the wheel at six o'clock, and was standing on the lee-side looking out, and all at once I saw this thing appear rising out of the water about 30ft. It went down again. It did not go forward like a fish jumping, but seemed to draw itself right back under water as if it contracted itself. It came up and went down again in the same way about four times. The first time I saw it was about a mile off the ship to leeward; the last time I saw it was about 100 yards from the ship. The time occupied in traveling the distance seemed to be about two minutes. It looked like a huge conger-eel or snake, except that it had two large fins. The fins seemed to be about 10ft. long, and were situated about 20ft. from the head. The tips of the fins were about touching the water. Where the fins joined the body the latter seemed to bulge out. I did not see the fins the first time it rose, but I saw them each time afterwards. The belly and the fins were pure white. I saw the back part. It was the colour of an eel. The head and neck were like those of an eel. It was nothing like a whale. Had it been at all like a whale I should have taken no notice of it, as it is such a common thing to see whales at sea. It was not more than one hundred yards away the last time I saw it. The thing was glistening in the sun. I could not see its eyes. Had the sun not been shining, or had it been night, I might have been able to see its eyes. Every time it went down there was a distinct splash that could be heard quite plainly. The time being so early in the morning and the sea being so rough, there were no people about except the watch on deck, who were aft scraping the decks. The Chief Officer was on the bridge. I spoke to him about it. He said he had seen it. I have often heard of a sea-serpent before, but never saw one, nor have I ever seen any one who had seen one, but have spoken to men who have seen other men who professed to have seen the creatures. I have always laughed at the sea-serpent story but never denied it. Call it what you like, but after my experience of Saturday morning I am decidedly of opinion that what I saw is a fish or creature that is never hardly seen. I never saw any thing like it before, although I have been at sea twenty five years and have seen a great many queer things." In reply to a question, Nelson said, "I am not a very frightened sort exactly, but I suppose I should have been frightened if it had come much closer."

I have reprinted here these three reports of two different appearances, because they so completely corroborate the hitherto so wonderful-seeming report of Egede (5), and figure of Bing (fig. 19). As to the remark of Prof. Hutton, of Canterbury

College (N. Zeal.) "that if the animal had great fins or flappers, as reported, they would no doubt be used for swimming, and it is improbable that the creature would wave them about in the air like wings", I only remark in my turn, that Prof. Hutton seems never to have observed the movements of seals, and sea-lions, for these animals really "wave the flappers about in the air like wings".

Last Word.

In Mr. Warburton's account (83) we read: —

"I immediately called to the passengers, who were all down below, but only five or six came up..... The remainder refused to come up, saying there had been too many hoaxes of that kind already."

Dr. Andrew Wilson mentions in his *Leisure Time Studies*, p. 101:—

"And so great in some minds is the fear of popular ridicule regarding this subject, that one ship-captain related that when a sea-serpent had been seen by his crew from the deck of the vessel, he remained below; since, to use his own words: "had I said I had seen the sea-serpent, I should have been considered to be a warranted liar all my life after"!"

And Captain Drevar wrote to the Editor of the *Graphic* (144):—

"My relatives wrote saying that they would have seen a hundred sea-serpents and never reported it, and a lady also wrote that she pitied any one that was related to any one who had seen the sea-serpent."

I hope that within a few years this fear of meeting with a sea-serpent will no more be heard of.

Should any one be induced by this publication to make an extract of it, to criticize it, to write a paper against it, or to publish new evidences, etc., etc., I kindly request him to send me a copy of his work, for it is impossible for me to get hold of all what hereafter may be written about the subject, or to consult each notice.

COSIMO

COSIMO is a specialty publisher of books and publications that inspire, inform, and engage readers. Our mission is to offer unique books to niche audiences around the world.

COSIMO BOOKS publishes books and publications for innovative authors, nonprofit organizations, and businesses. **COSIMO BOOKS** specializes in bringing books back into print, publishing new books quickly and effectively, and making these publications available to readers around the world.

COSIMO CLASSICS offers a collection of distinctive titles by the great authors and thinkers throughout the ages. At **COSIMO CLASSICS** timeless works find new life as affordable books, covering a variety of subjects including: Business, Economics, History, Personal Development, Philosophy, Religion & Spirituality, and much more!

COSIMO REPORTS publishes public reports that affect your world, from global trends to the economy, and from health to geopolitics.

FOR MORE INFORMATION CONTACT US AT
INFO@COSIMOBOOKS.COM

- ❋ if you are a book lover interested in our current catalog of books

- ❋ if you represent a bookstore, book club, or anyone else interested in special discounts for bulk purchases

- ❋ if you are an author who wants to get published

- ❋ if you represent an organization or business seeking to publish books and other publications for your members, donors, or customers.

COSIMO BOOKS ARE ALWAYS AVAILABLE AT ONLINE BOOKSTORES

VISIT COSIMOBOOKS.COM
BE INSPIRED, BE INFORMED

Lightning Source UK Ltd.
Milton Keynes UK
UKHW012139200319
339558UK00001B/8/P

9 781602 060128